INDEX OF

NORTH CAROLINA ANCESTORS

CONTRIBUTED BY

1003 OF THEIR DESCENDANTS

North Carolina Genealogical Society

Raleigh

1981

ISBN   0-936370-01-7

Printed in the United States of America
By McNaughton & Gunn
For The North Carolina Genealogical Society, Inc.
     P.O. Box 1492
     Raleigh, North Carolina 27602

CONTENTS

ABBREVIATIONS

NORTH CAROLINA COUNTIES

001	ALAMANCE	053	HYDE	105	WILSON
002	ALBEMARLE	054	IREDELL	106	YADKIN
003	ALEXANDER	055	JACKSON	107	YANCEY
004	ALLEGHANY	056	JOHNSTON		
005	ANSON	057	JONES		
006	ASHE	058	LEE		
007	AVERY	059	LENOIR		
008	BATH	060	LINCOLN		
009	BEAUFORT	061	MACON		
010	BERTIE	062	MADISON		
011	BLADEN	063	MARTIN		
012	BRUNSWICK	064	MCDOWELL		
013	BUNCOMBE	065	MECKLENBURG		
014	BURKE	066	MITCHELL		
015	BUTE	067	MONTGOMERY		
016	CABARRUS	068	MOORE		
017	CALDWELL	069	NASH		
018	CAMDEN	070	NEW HANOVER		
019	CARTERET	071	NORTHAMPTON		
020	CASWELL	072	ONSLOW		
021	CATAWBA	073	ORANGE		
022	CHATHAM	074	PAMLICO		
023	CHEROKEE	075	PASQUOTANK		
024	CHOWAN	076	PENDER		
025	CLAY	077	PERQUIMANS		
026	CLEVELAND	078	PERSON		
027	COLUMBUS	079	PITT		
028	CRAVEN	080	POLK		
029	CUMBERLAND	081	RANDOLPH		
030	CURRITUCK	082	RICHMOND		
031	DARE	083	ROBESON		
032	DAVIDSON	084	ROCKINGHAM		
033	DAVIE	085	ROWAN		
034	DOBBS	086	RUTHERFORD		
035	DUPLIN	087	SAMPSON		
036	DURHAM	088	SCOTLAND		
037	EDGECOMBE	089	STANLY		
038	FORSYTH	090	STOKES		
039	FRANKLIN	091	SWAIM		
040	GASTON	092	SURRY		
041	GATES	093	TRANSYLVANIA		
042	GLASGOW	094	TRYON		
043	GRAHAM	095	not assigned		
044	GRANVILLE	096	TYRRELL		
045	GREENE	097	UNION		
046	GUILFORD	098	VANCE		
047	HALIFAX	099	WAKE		
048	HARNETT	100	WARREN		
049	HAYWOOD	101	WASHINGTON		
050	HENDERSON	102	WATAUGA		
051	HERTFORD	103	WAYNE		
052	HOKE	104	WILKES		

TITLES

CPT	CAPTAIN
COL	COLONEL
DR	DOCTOR
ESQ	ESQUIRE
GEN	GENERAL
GOV	GOVERNOR
JDG	JUDGE
LT	LIEUTENANT
MAJ	MAJOR
REV	REVEREND
SGT	SERGEANT
SHF	SHERIFF

COUNTRIES

ATS	AT SEA
CUB	CUBA
ENG	ENGLAND
FRA	FRANCE
FWI	FRENCH WEST INDIES
GER	GERMANY (INCLUDING ALSACE)
GRB	GREAT BRITAIN
HOL	HOLLAND
HUN	HUNGARY
IRE	IRELAND
JAM	JAMAICA
MEX	MEXICO
SCO	SCOTLAND
SWE	SWEDEN
SWI	SWITZERLAND
WAL	WALES

U.S. STATES

AL	ALABAMA
AK	ALASKA
AR	ARKANSAS
AZ	ARIZONA
CA	CALIFORNIA
CO	COLORADO
CT	CONNECTICUT
DC	DISTRICT OF COLUMBIA
DE	DELAWARE
FL	FLORIDA
GA	GEORGIA
HI	HAWAII
IA	IOWA
ID	IDAHO
IL	ILLINOIS
IN	INDIANA
KS	KANSAS
KY	KENTUCKY
LA	LOUISIANA
MA	MASSACHUSETTS
MD	MARYLAND
ME	MAINE
MI	MICHIGAN
MN	MINNESOTA
MO	MISSOURI
MS	MISSISSIPPI
MT	MONTANA
NC	NORTH CAROLINA
ND	NORTH DAKOTA
NE	NEBRASKA
NH	NEW HAMPSHIRE
NJ	NEW JERSEY
NM	NEW MEXICO
NV	NEVADA
NY	NEW YORK
OH	OHIO
OK	OKLAHOMA
OR	OREGON
PA	PENNSYLVANIA
RI	RHODE ISLAND
SC	SOUTH CAROLINA
SD	SOUTH DAKOTA
TN	TENNESSEE
TX	TEXAS
UT	UTAH
VA	VIRGINIA
VT	VERMONT
WA	WASHINGTON
WI	WISCONSIN
WV	WEST VIRGINIA
WY	WYOMING

INTRODUCTION

The purpose of this book is to stimulate the exchange of genealogical information among researchers who are working on the same family lines so that investigation need not be repeated as each new descendant of an early North Carolinian begins the search for his or her ancestors.

The book consists of three indexes and a supplement. The indexes are based on a computerized compilation of information sent to the North Carolina Genealogical Society on printed "ancestor entry forms" supplied to prospective contributors during 1979 and 1980. The first index, which comprises the main body of the book, is the Ancestor Index. Ancestral names are listed in alphabetical order; a name submitted as Adam Johnson/Johnston, however, appears after William Johnson--a computer reads "Johnson/Johnston" as a different surname from "Johnson." In the extreme right-hand column of the Ancestor Index is a five-digit number. This is the computer code number assigned to each contributor. The same computer code was used for all ancestral names submitted by that contributor (e.g., the names of John Adams, William Adams, and Samuel Garland were submitted by contributor #01011. The number 01011 appears in the extreme right-hand column beside the names of each of these gentlemen, regardless of their place in the alphabetical Ancestor Index, and other Adamses and Garlands are followed by the computer codes for their respective contributors.) When more than one contributor submitted information about an ancestor, that ancestor was entered in duplicate so that the names of all contributors would be included in the compilation. By referring to the Contributor Index (see below), therefore, the reader can identify the sources for all of the ancestral information contained in the Ancestor Index.

Abbreviations in the Ancestor Index are in accordance with U.S. Post Office guidelines and the standards found in most English-language dictionaries. Because there are no standardized abbreviations for the names of North Carolina counties, these names have been translated into the numerical codes assigned to them by the North Carolina State Archives. Explanations of abbreviations and numerical county codes are on the page opposite this introduction; they also appear on the outside back cover of this volume for ready reference when using the book.

Although the Section 1 contains a good deal of biographical information, the birth, death, and marriage data is included solely to identify specific ancestors and distinguish them from others of the same name. The Society does not vouch for the accuracy of this information and advises researchers that lineage compilations should not be based on Index of North Carolina Ancestors without verification from other sources.

The second section of the book, the Spouse Index, is an alphabetical list of the husbands and wives whose names appear in the Ancestor Index. Each spouse's name is followed by the name of the pertinent ancestor. By turning to the ancestor's name in Section 1, the researcher may find additional information about the marriage. In some cases, particularly when a spouse's name is in doubt (indicated by a question mark in the Ancestor Index) or when a spouse enjoyed a double surname, such as La Flamme, the computer was unable to alphabetize the name properly. The computer was also unable to index the maiden names of women who married as widows. All of these "problem" names were indexed by hand and appear in a separate alphabet at the end of the master Spouse Index. The reader is advised to check both alphabetical series in this portion of the book.

The third section of the book consists of a two-part Contributor Index. The first part is an alphabetical list of contributors, together with each person's computer code number. The second part of this Index is a list of computer codes arranged in numerical order, together with the name and address of the contributor to whom that code number was assigned. When a reader identifies an ancestor of interest in Section 1, the name and address of the person who is working on that family line is located by referring to this section of the Contributor Index. The reader should write directly to the contributor to inquire about family relationships, collateral lines, or documentation of the facts concerning life events. The Society does not have this kind of information in its files and does not have sufficient staff to reply to inquiries. (It is considered polite in genealogical circles to enclose a stamped, self-addressed, legal size envelope in all requests for information by mail.)

At the State Archives and in the Secretary of State's Land Grant Office, the public records are filed, normally, under the name of the county as it was when a given event* occurred. Church and cemetery records, however, are found by looking in the county where the church or cemetery is now. To help the researcher locate records pertinent to a specific ancestor, a table of the North Carolina counties that gives formation dates, parent county or counties, and offspring county or counties has been included in Section 4, Supplement. The Supplement also includes an outline map of the current North Carolina counties to help identify adjacent counties.

The Society is indebted to Anne Correll, who edited the original ancestor entry forms and corresponded with contributors; to Helen F.M. Leary, who worked with the computer programmers and attended to the many details publication of a book entails; to Independent Data Processing, Inc., of Raleigh, who did the computer work; to the many members of the Society who so patiently proofread the printouts: Betty Camin, Michelle Francis, Weynette P. Haun, Margaret M. Hofmann, Hugh B. Johnston, Jr., Paul Kuhn, Jo White Linn, B. Ransom McBride, Eleanor Reeves, and Anna T. Sherman; and to the 1003 contributors without whose enthusiastic support this project would not have been possible.

---

*No public record of birth was kept in North Carolina until 1913; prior to that date, the researcher is more likely to find proof of the relationship between child and parent in the place where the parent died, not in the place where the child was born.

1

Ancestor Index

Name of Ancestor	Birth			Death		Lived	Marriage			Name(s) of Spouse(s)	Contributor Code No.
	Date	Place	NC County	Date Place	NC County	NC County	Date	Place	NC County		

A

Name of Ancestor	Date	Place	NC County	Date	Place	NC County	NC County	Date	Place	NC County	Name(s) of Spouse(s)	Contributor Code No.
ABBEY, WILLIAM CHESTER	1850	NY		1924	NC	076		1	1888	SC	ELIZABETH RALSTON DOZIER	20030
ABERNATHY, ALEX/ALEXANDER		NC	040	1894	NC	040		1			MATTIE MCCORKLE	60189
ABERNATHY, HENRY		NC	064	1908	NC	040		1			SALLIE CLANTON	60189
ABERNATHY, ISAAC LINDSAY	1923	NC	040					1	1944	TX	LELLA ARVILLA WAGNON	60189

ANCESTOR INDEX	BIRTH	PL	CO	DEATH	PL	CO	LIVD	MARRIED	PL	CO	SPOUSE NAME	CODE
ABERNATHY, JAMES F	1785	NC	060	1850	MO			1		060	FRANCES R ABERNATHY	20078
ABERNATHY, WILLIAM HENRY	1884	NC	040	1944	NC	040	065	1 1920	GA		TUPSY CO [SIC] HOLMES	60189
ABRAMS, JAMES ROBERT	1834	NC	053		GA			1			MARY JANE PATTY	60130
ABRAMS, JOHN				C1794	NC	?053						60130
ABRAMS, JOHN WASHINGTON	1830	NC	053		GA			1			MARY LITTLE ABERNATHY	60130
ACOCK, FRANCES		NC	?100	C1805				1 C1769	NC	?100	WILLIAM COURSEY	20415
ACOCK, JOHN		NC	?100		NC	?100						20415
ACREE, EDWARD		NC	?010	C1792	NC	010		1	NC	010	SARAH	20415
ACREE, JOHN R	1780	NC	010	1843	TN			1 1800	NC	010	MARY BROWN	20415
ADAMS, ABRAHAM	1767	VA		1846	IN		?085	1 C1790			KATHERINE SWARTZLANDER	60128
ADAMS, CHARLOTTE	C1821	NC	019					1 1838	NC	019	LEVI BELL	27537
ADAMS, CHESLEY MEREDITH	1813	NC		1859	TX			1 1846	TX		MARTHA E STEPHENS	27740
ADAMS, ELIZABETH/BETSEY ANN	1795	NC	085	1870	IN			1 1818			RESIN T SARGENT	60128
ADAMS, GREEN	C1793				TN		029					25158
ADAMS, JAMES				C1759	NC	009		1			MARY	19130
ADAMS, JEMIMA	1792	NC	085	1855	IN			1			DANIEL ADAMS	60128
ADAMS, JOHN	1720			1815	KY		104	1			LETTIE SIMPSON	01011
ADAMS, JOHN FRANKLIN	1799	NC	085	1876	OR			1 1820			REBECCA HINKLE	60128
ADAMS, NANCY ELENER	1801	NC	085	1877	IL			1 1820			STEPHEN NOLAND	60128
ADAMS, NIMROD	C1775			1824	NC	085		1			NANCY ETCHINSON	60313
ADAMS, NIMROD JR	1816	NC	085	1896	IN			1 1836	IN		SARAH JANE SPENCER	08023
ADAMS, NIMROD SR	C1775			1824	NC	085		1			NANCY ETCHISON	08023
ADAMS, RACHEL	1757	NC	073					1			JOHN MOON	60593
ADAMS, SARAH/SALLY E	1804	NC	?085	1888	IN			1 1823			JACOB LITTLE	60128
ADAMS, STEPHEN BEECHER	1807	NC		1874	IN		085	1 1830	IN		LYDIA ALLENDER	60313
ADAMS, WILLIAM				C1778	TN		104					01011
ADAMS, WILLIAM		NC						1			SARAH HUGHES	27740
ADAMS/ADDAMS, MARY/POLLY	C1740	VA		1833	GA		067	1 C1770	NC	005	JOHN W ROBERTSON/ROBINSON	60423
ADER, POLLY	1819	NC	?085	1892	NC	038		1			ANDREW BURK	60467
AGEE, ELIZABETH	C1770						086	1			MICAJAH KEGG/CAGE SMITH	08226
ALBEA, JOSEPH	C1772	MD		1832	NC	054		1			JANE BEALL	04050
ALBRIGHT, CATHERINE	1786	NC	073	1842	NC	073		1 1810	NC	073	JOHN R STOCKARD	27441
ALBRIGHT, HENRY	1759	PA		1840	NC	073		1	NC	073	MARY GIBBS	27441
ALBRIGHT, ISAAC	1797	NC	073					1 1818	NC	073	PHILOPENA RICH	16035
ALBRIGHT, JACOB		PA		1791	NC	073		1			SOPHIA CATHERINE WELDER	27441
ALBRIGHT, SARAH S	1825	NC	073	1879	AR			1 1843	TN		ROBERT W HANKINS	16035

2

ANCESTOR INDEX	BIRTH	PL	CO	DEATH	PL	CO	LIVD	MARRIED	PL	CO	SPOUSE NAME	CODE
ALDERSON, SIMON SR				C1712	NC	009	008	1			ELIZABETH	19130
ALEXANDER, ABIGAIL	1748			1817	NC	065		1	NC	065	FRANCIS BRADLEY	20095
ALEXANDER, ELIJAH	C1760	NC	?005	1850	TN		065	1 1783	NC	065	SARAH	20095
ALEXANDER, GEORGE	C1715	IRE		1780	NC	081		1			JANE RHEA ?	60306
ALEXANDER, JANE	1782	NC	081	1833	IN			1 C1799			ABRAHAM ELLIOTT	60306
ALEXANDER, JOHN	1777	NC	065					1 1804	NC		ELIZABETH TRAVIS	60470
ALEXANDER, RUTH	1769	NC	065	1853	IA			1 1789	NC	065	JOSEPH CLARK	20095
ALEXANDER, SAMUEL	1756	PA		1833	IN		081	1 C1780	NC	081	SARAH DENNIS	60306
ALEXANDER, WILLIAM	C1728	?MD		1805	NC	065		1 C1750			REBECCA	20095
ALFORD, KISER	C1813			C1890	NC	039		1 1841	NC	039	MARTHA M UPCHURCH	21115
ALGEE/ALGEA, ROBERT	1788	NC	065	1858	TN			1 1811	NC	065	JANE HAYES	60337
								2 C1824	TN		ELIZABETH STOCKARD	
ALLEN, ALEXANDER	C1782	NC	073	1835	NC	073		1			JANE SCOTT	60092
ALLEN, ANNE/ANNA	1797	NC	?065	C1860	TN			1 1813	NC	065	EDWARD HALL	60519
ALLEN, DRURY		NC	005	1823				1			NELLY ALLEN	60277
ALLEN, GEORGE				C1806	NC	073		1			ELIZABETH ANDERSON	60092
ALLEN, HENRY DAVIS	1782	NC		1873	AL			1 1804	TN		MARY/POLLY BARNES	15045
ALLEN, IRVIN	C1827	NC	?013	C1888	KY		107	1 1850	KY		LYDIA BARRETT	25242
								2	KY		ELIZABETH SANDLIN CLARK	
ALLEN, JOHN	1749	PA		1826	NC	073		1 C1779	NC	073	RACHEL STOUT	03270
ALLEN, JOSEPH	1783	NC	073	C1847	NC	081		1 1807	NC	081	MARTHA COX	03270
ALLEN, MARY	C1770	?NC		C1835	AL			1 C1794	TN		JOHN BIRDWELL	60177
ALLEN, NANCY EMILY	1768	NC	073	1847	AR			1 C1790	NC	073	ALEXANDER TROUSDALE	60404
ALLEN, SAMUEL	1815	NC	081	1873	NC	081		1 1836	NC	081	ELIZABETH LAWRENCE	03270
								2 1841	NC	081	EDITH HENSON	
ALLEN, SIMON ELWOOD	1844	NC	081	1924	NC	081		1 1866	IN		URSULA ANN MASTEN	03270
ALLEN, WILLIAM		NC	056	1789	VA			1			ANN	60277
ALLEN, YOUNG		NC	?056	1774	NC	?099		1			MARTHA	60277
								2			NANCY COLEMAN	
ALLIGOOD, MOSES	C1844	NC	009	C1883	NC	009		1 C1864	NC	009	ELLEN WOOLARD	24320
ALLISON, EPHRAM	C1837	NC	?013	1923	NC	093	050	1 C1856	NC	?050	JULIA ALLISON	60582
ALLISON, HUGH	1771	NC	092	1846	MO		104	1 1788			REBECCA HARTT SAUNDERS	60027
ALLISON, JOSEPH	C1750	NC	?044	1826	IN		073	1 C1774			JANE DONALDSON	60575
								2 1809	NC	073	BETSY MADDEN	
ALLISON, JOSEPH, GEN	1788	NC	073	1861	NC	073		1 1810	NC	073	MARTHA/PATSY WOODS	60575
ALLISON, JULIA	C1835	NC	?013				080	1 C1856	NC	?050	EPHRAM ALLISON	60582
ALLISON, SARAH ADDELINE	1857	NC	050	1948	NC	093		1 1880	NC	093	THOMAS BASERY SIMS/SYMS	60582
ALLISON, THOMAS WILLIAM	1795	NC	104	1864	MO			1 1816	KY		ROXANNA SNYDER	60027
								2 1856	MO		NANCY ORR	

ANCESTOR INDEX	BIRTH	PL	CO	DEATH	PL	CO	LIVD	MARRIED	PL	CO	SPOUSE NAME	CODE
ALLISON, WILLIAM	1742	?PA		1827	NC	054		1 C1764			AGNES/NANCY	27303
ALLISON, WILLIAM	C1738	?MD		1818	NC	104		1 C1760	?NC		LUCY/LUCINDA	60027
ALLRED, JOHN				C1757	NC	?073	081					02478
ALLRED, SOLOMON	1734	NC	081					1			MARY	02478
ALLRED, SOLOMON	C1762	NC	?073	C1839	TN		081					02478
ALLRED, WILLIAM	C1784	NC	081					1			RACHEL BROWN ?	02478
ALSTON, JAMES		NC	024	1761	NC	073	024	1 C1740	NC	028	CHRISTIAN LILLINGTON	60207
ALSTON, JOHN	C1673	ENG		1758	NC	024		1 C1701			MARY CLARK	17147
ALSTON, JOHN	1748	NC	028	1814	NC	073	099	1	NC			60207
ALSTON, JOHN JR, MAJOR	1768	NC	?056	C1810	TN		099	1 1797	NC	073	ELIZABETH KENNON	60207
ALSTON, JOSEPH JOHN	1712	NC	?024		NC	047		1			ELIZABETH CHANCY	17147
ALSTON, MARTHA/PATTIE		NC	?024	1814	NC	041		1			SAMUEL SUMNER	17147
AMICK/EMMICH, CATHERINE	C1810	NC		C1835	IN			1 1828	IN		DAVID CORTNER	60262
AMICK/EMMICH, PETER	1787	NC		1846	IN			1	?NC		MARGARET BLAKE	60262
AMIS, WILLIAM	C1727	VA		C1813	NC	044		1 C1750			MISS RALPH/ROLPHE	60425
AMOS, EASTER/HISHA	C1832	NC	090	1910	TN			1 1853	NC	090	WILLIAM H WOOD	60566
AMOS, FRANCIS	C1773	VA		1863	NC	090						60566
AMOS, GEORGE WASHINGTON	1797	NC		1857	NC	090		1 C1825			ELIZABETH/BETTY HENNIS	60566
AMOS, JOHN RUFUS		NC		1865	GA			1			N FRANCIS BUFFORD	60308
AMYETT, LEMUEL R	1808	NC	057	1851	MS			1 1836	NC	?057	MARY S RAMSEY	60254
AMYETT, PETER				1778	NC	028		1			MARY	60254
AMYETT, VINCENT				1790	NC	057		1			SUSANNA	60254
ANDERSON, CHARITY	C1725	PA						1 C1742	NC	073	THOMAS LAPSLIE	12015
ANDERSON, CORNELIUS	C1822	NC	?104	C1907	AR			1 1840	NC	104	ETTA M QUEEN	20007
ANDERSON, ELIZABETH	1802	NC	029	C1885	NC	029		1 1823	NC	029	ISAAC POPE	13052
ANDERSON, ELIZABETH	C1794	NC		1855	IN			1 C1816			JOHN CLARK	60223
ANDERSON, HENRY								1 C1800	NC	037	LOVEY STATON	05035
ANDERSON, ISAAC	1787	MD		1857	IN		046	1 C1810	NC	046	BARBARA DYER/DYAR	60223
ANDERSON, JAMES		NC		C1805	KY			1	NC		NANCY IRVIN	20415
ANDERSON, JESSE	C1785			C1835	NC	029						13052
ANDERSON, JESSE STATON	1812			1883	NC	099		1 1837	NC	099	MARY TODD	05035
								2 1857	NC	099	MARY ANN TUCKER	
								3	NC	099	MRS MARGARET (TUCKER) TODD	
ANDERSON, JOHN	C1703	IRE		1756	NC	073		1 C1724	PA		ANN MOORE	12015
ANDERSON, MARY	1777	NC		1864	KY			1 1799	KY		ROBERT COURSEY	20415
ANDERSON, NANCY	C1770			C1859	NC	?046		1 1786				60223

4

ANCESTOR INDEX	BIRTH	PL	CO	DEATH	PL	CO	LIVD	MARRIED	PL	CO	SPOUSE NAME	CODE
ANDERSON, REUBEN	C1795	NC	?046	C1840	IN			1 C1812	NC	046	ZIPPORAH DYER/DYAR	60223
ANDERSON, SAMUEL PETERSON	1848	NC	099	1912	NC	099		1 1873	NC	099	LAURA ELLA HOOD	05035
ANDERSON, SAMUEL TILDEN	1877	NC	099	1947	NC	069		1 1903	NC	056	JULIA BLANCHE RICHARDSON	05035
								2 1912	NC	069	MARY CECILIA ROWE	
ANDERSON, WILLIAM	C1727	PA		1786	NC	073		1	NC	073	JENNET MEBANE	12015
ANDREW, JULIA ANN				1878	NC	001		1 1846	NC	073	HEZEKIAH MAY	21080
ANDREW/ANDREWS, GEORGE WASHINGTON	1814	NC		1909	NC	090		1			AMANDA/MANDY MARTHA KNIGHT ?	60469
ANDREWS, ALFRED GRAY	1799	NC	063	C1880	MEX			1 1829	NC	063	WINIFRED HYMAN	20080
ANDREWS, EDMUND	C1725	NC		C1790	NC	079		1 C1764	NC		AGNESS WALLACE	20080
ANDREWS, WARREN				C1774	NC	096		1			SARAH	19130
ANDREWS, WARREN				1774	NC	096		1			SARAH	20080
ANDREWS, WARREN DANIEL	1765	NC	079	1833	NC	063		1 1790	NC		BARSHEBA GAINER	20080
ANGEL, J/JOHN WILLIAM	C1809	VA			AL		?107	1 C1840	?VA		MARY J BRAGG	60190
ANGEL, JAMES MADISON	1842	NC		1934	AL			1 1863	AL		SUSAN ARTIMISS MITCHELL	60190
ANGLE, BARBARA							002					60106
ANGLE, BENJAMIN							092					60106
ANGLE, BENJAMIN D							090					60106
ANGLE, CHARLES							092					60106
ANGLE, GEORGE							073					60106
ANGLE, JOHN							092					60106
ANGLE, LAURANCE							092					60106
ANGLE, LEDBETTER							092					60106
ANGLE, MILLIE	1779	NC					092	1 1795	GA		PASCHAL TRAYLOR	60106
								2 1823	GA		RESE WATKINS	
ANGLE, STEPHEN							092					60106
ANGLE, THOMAS	C1761	VA			GA		092	1 1802	GA		SUSANNAH MORRIS	60106
ANTHONY, PHILIP	C1721	GER		1796	NC	060		1	?PA		BARBARA	03015
APPLE, ADAM	C1728	GER		C1815	NC	046						27542
APPLE, DANIEL	C1761	PA		C1849	NC	046		1	NC		SPOON	27542
APPLE, JOHN	C1786	NC	046	C1864	NC	046		1	NC		MARY BARBARY WAGONER ?	27542
APPLE, PETER	1834	NC	046	1881	NC	046		1 1858	NC	046	ELIZABETH/BETTIE HUFFINES	27542
APPLEWHITE, ANDREW JACKSON	1859	NC	070	1913	NC	076		1 1886	NC	076	DRUSILLA FLOWERS KELLY	27537
APPLEWHITE, GEORGE WILLIAM	1857	NC	070	1907			076					27537
APPLEWHITE, JAMES HENRY	1848	NC	070	1912			076					27537
APPLEWHITE, SUSAN	1855	NC	070	1915			076	1			ARMISTEAD H BORDEAUX	27537
APPLEWHITE, WILLIAM GASTON	1851	NC	070	1912			076					27537
APPLEWHITE, WILLIAM HENRY	1825	?VA		1896	NC	076		1 1847	?VA		JANE/SUSAN MARSHALL	27537
ARD, DAVID	1784	?NC	?011	1857	AL			1 C1813			MARGARET	60373

ANCESTOR INDEX	BIRTH	PL	CO	DEATH	PL	CO	LIVD	MARRIED	PL	CO	SPOUSE NAME	CODE
ARMSTRONG, BARBARY	1806	NC		1847	NC	035	070	1 1823	NC	035	THOMAS DAVIS	17085
ARMSTRONG, EDWARD	1768			1827	NC	070	035	1 1791	NC	035	MARY SHEFFIELD	17085
ARMSTRONG, JAMES	1758	VA		1819	TN		092	1 1782	VA		NANCY LANIER	06005
ARMSTRONG, JAMES	1701	IRE		C1796	NC	073		1 1735	PA		MOLLIE BIRD ?	60151
ARMSTRONG, JOHN		NC			NC	059		1		NC	COGDILL	03065
ARMSTRONG, JOHN	C1815	NC		C1846	IN			1 C1835			NANCY BALL	08240
ARMSTRONG, JOHN		NC						1 1825	NC	035	HANNAH DAVIS	17085
ARMSTRONG, JOHN							070	1 C1767			BARBARA	17085
ARMSTRONG, JOHN				1806	NC	073		1			ANNA	27441
ARMSTRONG, JOSEPH	1764	NC	073	1846	NC	073		1 1786	NC	073	FRANCES TINNEN	27441
ARMSTRONG, PARTHENIA	1807	NC	073	1860	NC	001		1 1828	NC	073	JOHN W FAUCETT	27441
ARMSTRONG, WILLIAM	1722			1782	NC	092		1			CATHERINE	06005
ARMSTRONG, WILLIAM	1737	PA		1788	TN		073	1 1765	NC		MARY JANE LAPSLEY	60151
ARNETT, JESSE	1796	NC	090	1876	IN			1 1817	NC	090	MARGARET WILLIAMS	27429
ARNETT, VALENTINE							090	1 C1795	NC	090	SARAH	27429
ARNOLD, FERNIE	C1802	NC		1836	TN		028	1 1822			MARIAN GWINN	27602
ARNOLD, JAMES	C1765			1808	TN		028	1	?NC		DORCAS TAYLOR	27602
ARNOLD, JAMES ELMER	1928	NC	020					1 1946	NC	020	EDITH MARIE SMITH	60436
ARNOLD, JAMES WELDON FRANKLIN	1876	NC	020	1951	NC	020		1 1903	NC	078	MARY MAGDALENE/MAGGIE BOWES	60436
ARNOLD, JAMES/JIM WHITE	1814	NC	020	1899	NC	020		1 1840 / 2 1870	NC / NC	020 / 078	SARAH M RICE / EUPHRASIA ANGELINE BLALOCK	60436
ARNOLD, LUKE	1788			1853	NC	020		1 1810	NC	020	SUSANNAH PARKER STADLER	60436
ARNOLD, THOMAS	C1790	NC			IL			1 1812	NC	020	POLLEY SEWELL	27413
ARNOLD, WILLIAM	1759	VA		C1825	GA		090	1	?VA		ELIZABETH SHELTON	27356
ARNOLD/ARENDELL, BENJAMIN							044					25100
ARNOLD/ARENDELL, REDDICK	C1756	NC	044	C1835	SC							25100
ARNOLD/ARENDELL, RICHARD				1762	NC	044		1			ELLENOR	25100
ARRINGTON, ARTHUR		VA		1801	NC	069	037	1			MARY WEST ?	12125
ARRINGTON, ARTHUR JR				1795	NC	069		1 1758			MARY SANDEFUR	12125
ARRINGTON, ELBERT S.	1841	NC	049	1932	NC	049		1 / 2 1884	NC / NC	/ 055	ELIZABETH GILLILAND / CATHERINE BLANTON	40690
ARRINGTON, JOHN D.	1792	NC	069	1865	AL			1 1812			MARTHA JOHANNA WILLIAMS DRAKE	12125
ARRINGTON, RENA MAY	1907	NC	055	1967	WA			1 1939	WA		ROBERT/ROY FRANKLIN THOMPSON	40690
ARRINGTON, THOMAS	1794	NC		1881	NC	049		1 1816	TN		SEBITHA BELL	40690
ARRINGTON, THOMAS DEXTER	1879	NC	049	1946	NC	049		1 1900	NC	055	NANCY JANE HILL	40690
ARRINGTON, WILLIAM, GEN	1766	NC	037	1812	NC	069		1 C1789 / 2 1809	NC		ANNE JACKSON / MARY ANN WILLIAMS	12125
ARWINE/ERVIN, LOVIE CLEMENTINE	C1814	NC	?020	1883	TN			1 1843			DAVID BURNET WALKER	60234

ANCESTOR INDEX	BIRTH	PL	CO	DEATH	PL	CO	LIVD	MARRIED	PL	CO	SPOUSE NAME	CODE
ARWINE/ERVIN, RICHARD	C1765			1831	TN			1 1788	NC	020	NANCY LOVE	60234
ASHE, JOHN BAPTISTA	C1695	ENG		1734	NC	070		1 1719			ELIZABETH SWANN	27286
ASHE, MARY SYBIL	1850	NC	073	1927	CA			1 C1873	?CA		JOHN OWEN MILLER	27286
ASHE, RICHARD DAVIS	1793	NC	073	1821	NC	073		1 C1816			ANNA L MOORE	27286
ASHE, RICHARD JAMES	1821	NC	073	1899	CA			1 C1845	NC	073	MARY PHOEBE MITCHELL	27286
ASHE, SAMUEL, GOV	1725	NC		1813	NC	070		2 1769			MRS ELIZABETH (JONES) MERRICK	27286
ASHE, THOMAS JONES	1770			1795	NC	?073		1 1790			SOPHIA DAVIS	27286
ASHMORE, JAMES					?NC			1			ELIZABETH BALCH	60363
ASHWORTH, JOHN	1735	VA		1805	NC	013	094	1 C1762	NC	065	NANCY ANN WOOD	27318
ASHWORTH, MARY/POLLY	1773	NC	?085	1865	NC	?013	?014	1	NC	013	JOHN WILLIAMS	27318
ASKEW, ANNA	C1800	NC	051					1			JOSIAH HARRELL	27531
ASKEW, DAVID	C1745	?VA		1816	NC	010		1	NC	010	MILLICIENT OUTLAW	60337
ASKEW, SARAH ELIZABETH							028	1			GEORGE WASHINGTON CHARLTON	10010
ATCHISON/ETCHISON, EDMUND	C1757	VA		1845	NC	033		1 1779	NC	085	EDITH RICHARDSON	02065
ATKINS, JOSEPH	C1730	?NC		C1815	VA							60576
ATWOOD, JANE	1826	NC	092	1904	IL			1 1849	NC	006	JOHN JACKSON ROYAL	08130
								2 1867	KY		ALFRED MAC JACOBS	
ATWOOD, THOMAS	C1803	VA		C1899	NC	004	006	1 1825	NC	092	MARY/POLLY STEELMAN	08130
AUSTIN, ELIZABETH	1872	NC	107	1935	NC	013		1 1889	NC	062	SQUIRE JAMES PENLEY	17100
AUSTIN, GREEN	C1807	NC	?056	C1847	?FL			1 C1845	?FL		REBECCA WARD	27346
AUSTIN, JOHN	1774	NC	?056	1846	AL			1 1803	NC	056	SARAH YOUNGBLOOD	27346
AUSTIN, JOHN	C1720	VA		1806	NC	056		1			MARY	27346
AUSTIN, MARY	1840	NC	014	1928	MO			1 C1865			RIAL BARNETT	60258
AUSTIN, SAMUEL	C1822	NC						1	NC		MATILDA P	17100
AUSTIN, THOMAS F	C1854	NC	107					1 1869	NC		NANCY ARROWWOOD	17100
AWALT, BARBARA	C1795	NC	?016				014	1			MR TIPPS	25191
AWALT, CATHERINE	C1790	NC	?065				014	1			MR WEAVER	25191
AWALT, ELIZABETH	1799	NC	016	1866	IL		014	1 C1830	?TN		JOHN BEAN	25191
AWALT, EVE	C1790	NC	?065				014	1			JOHN PYLANT	25191
AWALT, GEORGE	1779	NC	?065		AR		014	1 1800	NC	?016	CATHERINE SPECK ?	25191
AWALT, JACOB	C1788	NC	?065	1866	TN		014					25191
AWALT, JOHN	C1787	NC	?065				014	1 C1815	?NC	?014	CATHERINE LIMBAUGH	25191
AWALT, MICHAEL	C1755	PA		1835	TN		065	1 1778	NC	?065	EVA SPECK	25191
AWALT, MICHAEL	C1785	NC	?065	1835	IN		014	1 1811	NC	014	SARAH TIPPS	25191
AWALT, MICHAEL	1785	NC		1835	IN			1 1811	NC	014	SARAH TIPPS	60455
AWALT, NANCY ANN	C1803	NC	?016	C1885	TN		014	1 C1827	?TN		SOLOMAN LIMBAUGH	25191
AWALT, POLLY		NC	?016				?014	1			JOHN BRIMAGE	25191
AWALT, SOPHIA	C1802	NC	?016				014	1 C1822	?TN		REUBEN WEBB	25191

ANCESTOR INDEX	BIRTH	PL	CO	DEATH	PL	CO	LIVD	MARRIED	PL	CO	SPOUSE NAME	CODE
AXUM, REDERICK BARTLEY	1879	NC	097	1968	AR			1 1883	AR		CUMIE ELIZABETH BETTS	60532
AXUM, SAMUEL	1808	NC		C1855	NC	005		1			ELIZABETH	60532
AXUM, WILLIAM THOMAS	1851	NC	005	1922	AR		097	1 C1869	NC	097	MARY FRANCES HELMS	60532
AYCOCK, BURRELL	C1783	NC	103					1 1808	LA		ANNA PAULINE GAUTREAUX	60539
AYCOCK, JOHN	C1735			C1802	NC	099						60507
AYCOCK, LUNSFORD	C1786	NC	100	C1855	MS			1 1813	NC	099	MRS MARY ANN (BROWN) BUTLER	60507
AYCOCK, NEWTON H	C1817	NC	099	C1863	MS			1 C1842	MS		NANCY ANN HAMILTON	60507
AYCOCK, SIMON	C1760	NC	034				103	1			ELIZABETH BENNETT	60539

B

ANCESTOR INDEX	BIRTH	PL	CO	DEATH	PL	CO	LIVD	MARRIED	PL	CO	SPOUSE NAME	CODE
BABER, MARY/POLLY	1784	VA		1853	MO			1 1807	NC	086	ADAM MARTIN	60460
BADGER, FELIX HARVEY	1803	NC	104		TN			1			MARY	60062
BADGER, JOHN H	1787	SC		1882	TN		104	1			NANCY BLEAKLEY	60062
BADGER, JOSHUA	C1755			C1833	KY		104	1 C1785	?SC		SABRA	60062
BADGER, LOUISANA	C1800	NC	104		GA			1 1821	KY		JOHN HALE	60062
BADGER, RACHEL	1795	SC		1871	GA		104					60062
BAGLEY, BENJAMIN	1785	NC	?022	1870	GA			1			RACHEL	60197
BAILEY, ROBERT ALONZA	1871	NC	063	1937	NC	063		1 1896	NC	063	MARY LOUISE BARNHILL	24240
BAILEY, WARNER GORDON				C1838	NC	063		1 C1828	NC	063	NANCY HARRISON	24240
BAILEY, WARNER GORDON JR	1836	NC	063	C1883	NC	063		1 C1858	NC	?063	MARY ANN GURGANUS	24240
BAILEY, WILLIAM	C1802	SC					026	1 C1836			PHOEBE BOYLES	60272
BAIRD, SAMUEL	1801	NC		1856	IL			1 1829	IL		FANNIE HARRIS	27631
BAIRD, WILLIAM SR		NC			IL			1	NC		JANE HOLLAND	27631
BAITY, JOHN MORGAN	1807	NC	085	1873	IN			1			RACHEL EASTEP	08023
BAITY, WILLIAM SR	C1775			1848	NC	033		1 1798	NC	085	ANNA HADDOX	08023
								2 1829	NC	085	MARY BINKLY	
BAKER, ABRAM/ABRAHAM, REV	C1748	NC	056	C1795	NC	?059						13264
BAKER, APSALY	1809	NC	079	1885	NC	045		1 C1840	NC	079	TUNNEL/TURNER MURPHREY	13264
BAKER, BANJAMIN	1799	NC		1880	IL			1	TN		MATILDA	25161
BAKER, ELIZABETH	1761						102	1			CASPAR CABLE	20350
BAKER, HENRY	1814			1896	NC	090		1			MARGARET M	27700
BAKER, HENRY		VA		1770	NC	024		1			CATHERINE BOOTH	60384
BAKER, HENRY, COL	C1670	NC	024	C1739	NC	024		1	VA		ANGELICA BRAY	19130
								2	NC	075	RUTH CHANCY	
BAKER, JAMES	1792	NC		1877	NC	039		1 C1825	NC		MARTHA	20007
BAKER, JESSE	C1774	NC	034	C1825	NC	079	059					13264

ANCESTOR INDEX	BIRTH	PL	CO	DEATH	PL	CO	LIVD	MARRIED	PL	CO	SPOUSE NAME	CODE
BAKER, JESSE	1774	NC		1864	IN							60450
BAKER, JOHN	C1720	?VA		C1775	NC	034	059					13264
BAKER, JOSEPH SR				1831	NC	073						17150
BAKER, MARGARET	1828	NC	039	C1868	AR		?099	1 1850	NC	039	WILEY NICHOLS	20007
BAKER, MARGARET	1855			1948	NC	090		1			JOHN EDGAR SLATE	27700
BAKER, MARTHA/MATTIE JANE	1874	SC		1951	CA		026	1 1889			MILTON WAKELAND COOPER	60267
BALCH, HEZEKIAH JAMES, REV	C1740	MD		C1776	NC	065		1	NC	065	MARTHA ANN MACCANDLESS/MCCONNELL	60565
BALDRIDGE, ALEXANDER	1717	IRE		1805	NC	060		1	PA		JANE RAMSEY	06005
BALDRIDGE, JOHN	1754	PA		1823	TN			1 1780	NC	085	ISABELLA LUCKEY	06005
BALDWIN, CHARLES	1787	NC	011	1848	NC	027		1 C1810	NC	011	AMELIA KELLY	60403
BALDWIN, DAVID	C1785	NC	011	1846	NC	027		1			JOANNAH SMITH	27562
BALDWIN, ELIZABETH CHRISTILLA	1833	NC	027	1907	NC	027		1 C1852	NC	?027	JOHN W OWEN	27562
BALDWIN, JESSE	1750			1825			082	1			ELIZABETH STRINGFELLOW	60590
BALDWIN, JOHN		NC	011	1791	NC	011						60403
BALDWIN, JOHN JR	1781	NC	046	C1825	IN			1 1803	NC	085	CHARLOTTY PAIN	27429
BALDWIN, JOHN SR	C1755						046	1 C1776	NC	046	JEMIMA	27429
BALDWIN, KELLY	1826	NC	027	C1865	?SC			1 1848	NC	027	MARY G HAYNES	60403
BALDWIN, STONEWALL JACKSON	1861	NC	027	1949	FL			1 1900	NC	027	ELIZABETH DRUSCILLA MEARES	60403
BALDWIN, WILLIAM	C1723	MD		1802	NC	085	073	1 C1745	MD		ELIZABETH	27429
BALDWIN, WILLIAM		NC	011	1801	NC	011		1			PENELOPE	60403
BALL, WILLIAM	1766			1844	NC	104	085	1 1788			SARAH CAMPBELL	08240
BALLARD, DEVEREUX	1756	VA		C1837	?SC		047					02478
BALLARD, ELIZABETH	1778	NC	046		IA			1 1800	TN		JOHN B HAWORTH	60378
BALLARD, JOHN FRANKLIN	1821	NC	060	1898	NC	060		1 C1845			SALLIE L MCMIN	07115
BALLARD, MARY ANN		NC		1847	TN							20245
BALLARD, SOLOMON M	1820	NC	067	1862	MS			1 1843	NC	067	MARY ELIZABETH DUMAS	60404
BALLARD, WILLIAM				C1774		047		1			ELIZABETH CLOPTON	02478
								2			ELIZABETH MORRIS	
BALLARD, WILLIAM	1715	VA		1775	NC	047		1			MRS ELIZABETH (CLOPTON) MORRIS	07078
BALLARD, WILLIAM SORRELL							047					02478
BANKS, CLARA ELIZABETH	1871	NC	062	1940	NC	013		1			WYATT GENTRY	25108
BANKS, CLAUDE	1888	NC	013	1963								25108
BANKS, DOUGLAS				1929	NC	064	013					25108
BANKS, EDWARD MILLON	1899			1973	NC	013						25108
BANKS, FRED	1893	NC	013									25108
BANKS, HENRY C	1839	NC		1918	NC	013	062	1 C1863	NC		LAURA ANDERS/ANDREWS	25108
BANKS, JOHN RILEY	1864	NC	013	1945		013		1			JANEY J ALLEN	25108
BANKS, LESTER	1892	NC	013									25108

ANCESTOR INDEX	BIRTH	PL	CO	DEATH	PL	CO	LIVD	MARRIED		PL	CO	SPOUSE NAME	CODE
BANKS, LORENZO INGHAM	1897	NC	013										25108
BANKS, NAT	1908	NC	013										25108
BANKS, POLLY/MARY ANNA	C1883	NC	013	1947	VA		062	1	1896	NC	013	JAMES JACKSON MASSEY	25108
BANKS, THOMAS	1709			1789	GA			1	1743			SARAH CHANDLER	13105
								2	1748	NC	044	BETTY WHITE	
								3	1786	NC	044	SUSANNAH HUNT	
BANKS, THURMAN OZZIE	1895			1932	NC	013							25108
BANKS, WILLIAM	1766	NC	044	1820				1				ANNIE HENDERSON	13105
BANKS, ZEKE	1885	NC	013										25108
BANNING, BENONI	1744	ENG		1827	NC		014	1	1769	MD		ANN FRAZIER	60291
BANNING, JEREMIAH	1789	NC			IL			1				ELIZABETH ANN BROOKS	60291
BANNISTER, BETHANY	1719			C1794	NC	030		1				THOMAS MIDYETT	25254
BARBEE, CHRISTOPHER		VA	065	1777	NC	099		1				MARGARET	14020
BARBEE, DELILAH	C1770	NC	073		NC	022		1	C1790	NC	073	SANFORD JENKINS	08200
BARBEE, GEORGE	1781		022		?TN			1	1802			ELIZABETH CHAPMAN	60595
BARBEE, GRAY	C1747		022					1				NANCY CAIN ?	60595
BARBEE, JOHN	C1770	NC	073	1818	NC	073		1	1790	NC	073	ESTER HERNDON	60377
BARBEE, JOSEPH		VA		1773	NC	022	073	1				MARY FEARN ?	08200
BARBEE, JOSEPH							073	1				MARY BOHANNAN ?	60595
BARBEE, REUBEN	1794	NC	073	C1860	?AL			1	1816	NC	099	GILLY/ABIGAIL DILLIARD	60377
BARBEE, ROSE	C1763	NC	073		NC	099		1	1780	NC	099	JAMES HARWARD	14020
BARBEE, SOLOMON G	1812		022					1	1833			NANCY TRICE	60595
BARBEE, WILLIS MONROE	1827	NC	073	1909	TX			1	1851	AL		OPHELIA PEASE	60377
								2	1882	TX		SARA JOHN WOOD	
BARCLAY, AMBURS	C1806	?VA					?020	1				ELIZABETH GEORGE NEWMAN	27599
BARCLAY, GEORGE WASHINGTON	1844	NC		1911	KY			1	1866	GA		MALINDA MISSOURI CARDEN	27599
BARCLIFT, SAMUEL	C1785	NC	?077	1848	TN			1	1812	NC	?075	MILLICENT COMMANDER	60310
BARCLIFT/BARTLETT, JOSHUA				C1755	NC	077		1				SARAH SNODEN	60544
								2				MARY BLAKE	
BARCLIFT/BARTLETT, MIRIAM	C1741	NC	077	C1787	NC	028		1	1759	NC	051	FRANCIS DELAMAR	60544
BARCLIFT/BARTLETT, WILLIAM				C1696	NC	024	077	1				ELIZABETH	60544
BARCLIFT/BARTLETT, WILLIAM				C1747	NC	077		1	1698			ANN DURANT	60544
BARDIN, CHARITY	1827	NC	103	1890	MS			1	1845	MS		GEORGE BROWN YOUNG	60018
BARDIN, JACOB	1705	NC	?008	1786	?NC	?103	056	1	1729			SARAH	60018
BARDIN, JAMES	1730	?NC	?028	1805			103	1				MARY	60018
BARDIN, WILLIAM	1771	NC	034	1837	NC	103		1	1807	NC	103	NANCY COOK	60018
BARKER, ALEXANDER	1791	NC	020	1878	TN			1	1820	TN		MARGARET DODSON	27375
BARKER, EDWARD R	1832	NC	006					2	1859	NC	006	CAROLINE MASSEY	60541
BARKER, EDWARD/NEDDIE	1795	VA			NC	006		1	C1815			REBECCA PENNINGTON	60541
								2	C1820	NC	006	MELVINA CHURCH	
								3				CATHERINE HOWELL	

ANCESTOR INDEX	BIRTH	PL	CO	DEATH	PL	CO	LIVD	MARRIED	PL	CO	SPOUSE NAME	CODE
BARKER, GEORGE	1759	VA		1841	TN		073	1 1783	NC	020	FRANKY KERR	27375
BARKER, GEORGE	C1730	?VA		C1788	NC	020	073	1			SUSANNA	27375
BARKER, GEORGE WASHINGTON	1868	NC	006	1933	NC	006		1 1899	NC	006	MAMIE JONES	60541
BARLOW, JOHN				1829	MS		083	1 C1791			LYDIA	24073
BARNARD, ASA							046	1			HULDAH	20333
BARNARD, CYRUS	1819	NC	046	1915	IN			1			MARY C PADDOCK	60386
BARNARD, MARY	1797	NC	046	1849	IN			1 1821	NC	046	JETHRO STARBUCK FOLGER	20333
BARNARD, TRISTRAM		NC						1 1818	NC	046	LYDIA GARDNER	60386
BARNES, DELAIAH/LILA	1839	NC	?049	C1905	TN		049	1 2	NC TN		JOSEPH BARNES ? ELI WEST	27533
BARNES, JACOB				C1764	NC	037		1			JULIAN WHITLEY	15045
BARNES, JAMES		NC	?024	1811	NC	041		1 2			 ELIZABETH SUMNER	17147
BARNES, JAMES	1812	NC	?049	C1906	TN		049	1	NC		MARY HUMPHREY ?	27533
BARNES, JOSEPH		?NC	?037	C1796	TN			1	?NC	?037	SELAH DELOACH	15045
BARNES, MARY/POLLY	1787	NC	037	1856	AL			1 1804	TN		HENRY DAVIS ALLEN	15045
BARNES, SARAH JANE	1858	NC		1917	MI			1 1884	TN		JAMES BUCHANAN WILHOIT	27533
BARNES, WILLIAM				C1773	NC	096		1 2			MARY ELIZABETH	17147
BARNES, WOODWARD	C1814	NC			TX			1 C1836 2 C1852	NC NC		 MARY L	60395
BARNES/BARNS, ALLEN	C1780	?NC		C1845	SC		?037	1 C1800	SC		AVA SINGLETON	27303
BARNETT, ANDREW JACKSON	1826			1909	TN		013	1			MARTHA COBURN/COGBURN	60077
BARNETT, JEFFERSON	C1862	TN					062	1 C1880	NC	062	MARGARET ROGERS	60077
BARNETT, MARY ELLEN	1846	NC	023	1931	MO			1 1870	TN		WILLIAM RUSSELL STACY	60077
BARNETT, SARA JANE	1830	NC	?028	1905	NC	031		1			STEPHEN CASEY	13120
BARNETT, STEPHEN		NC			NC			1			ESTER MIDGETT	13120
BARNETT, THOMAS		?VA		C1779	NC	044		1 1754	VA		SARA CROSHA GRAVES	03035
BARNETT/BARNETTE, ROBERT				1777	NC	020	?073	1			SARAH	60575
BARNHART, ESTHER	C1815	NC	016	C1852	NC	016		1 1833	NC	016	THOMAS ALLEN STILL	12210
BARNHART, JACOB	C1787	NC	?065	1849	TN			1 1809	NC	016	RHODA COX	60337
BARNHILL, ABRAM PEAL	1846	NC	063	1902	NC	063		1 C1866	NC	063	LUCRECY L JAMES	24240
BARNHILL, GIDEAN W	1822	NC	063	1847	MEX			1 C1840	NC	063	CYNTHIA PEAL	24240
BARNHILL, SAMUEL	C1765	?PA		C1835	NC	063		1 C1783				24240
BARNHILL, SAMUEL JR	C1788			1842	NC	063		1 C1815	NC	063	MARTHA HOPKINS ?	24240
BARRETT, JABIS	C1800							1 1823 2 1853	NC NC	078 078	MARY/POLLY SOUTHARD SUSAN JACOBS	60543
BARRETT, SAMUEL	C1838			C1863				1 C1856	NC	?013	LEAKEY BALL	27334
BARRETT, SAMUEL	1802	NC	068	1890	NC	068		1 1828	NC	068	ELIZABETH LEE GRAHAM	27758

ANCESTOR INDEX	BIRTH	PL	CO	DEATH	PL	CO	LIVD	MARRIED		PL	CO	SPOUSE NAME	CODE
BARRETT, SARAH A	C1830	NC	078	1863	NC	078		1	1848	NC	078	WILLIAM A OAKLEY	60543
BARRETT, WILLIAM					NC	068		1				PATIENCE	27758
BARRETT, WILLIAM	1754			1840	NC	068		1	C1783	NC	068	ANN SOWELL	27758
BARRETT, WILLIAM RILEY	C1832	NC	068	1906	NC	099		1	C1855			JANE C MUSE	27758
BARROW, SHEROD	1810	NC		1876	TN			1	C1825	NC		REBECCA	60584
BARROW, SHERROD	1810	NC			TN			1		NC		REBECCA	60457
BARRY, JAMES BUCKNER	1728	IRE		1788	NC	019		1	1756			MARY MAGDELON NOBLE	60408
BARRY, JAMES BUCKNER	1821	NC	072	1906	TX			1	1847	NC	072	SARA ANNAPOLIS MATTICKS	60408
BARRY, JOHN DECATUR	1833	NC	070	1867	NC	070		1		NC	070	FANNIE GREEN ?	60186
BARTLESON, RICHARD	1717	NJ		1787	NC	085		1	1746	?DE		JANE GROOMS	60011
BARTLESON, SUSANNAH		NC	?085	1822	MO			1	1804	KY		JOHN DEAN	60011
BARTLESON, ZACHARIAH				1806	KY		085	1				CATHERINE	60011
BASNIGHT, MARY/POLLY	1824	NC	030	1899	NC			1	1842	NC	096	EDWARD DANIEL MIDGETT	13120
BASS, ANDREW	1698	VA		1770	NC	028		1				ELIZABETH SMITH	21165
BASS, DOCTOR	1812	NC		1850	AR			1	1836	GA		ELIZA FRANCES PORTER	60545
BASS, RICHARD	1730	NC	028	1792	NC	103		1				SARAH MCKINNIE	21165
BASS, SARAH	1764	NC	028		NC	?056		1				JOSEPH BOON	21165
BATCHELOR/BACHELOR/BACHLOTT, BENNETT	1798	NC			GA			1 2 3	C1817 1827 1858	GA GA		WATTS ANN READY MARTHA TRAYWICK	27303
BATSON, THOMAS	C1765	IRE		1831	TN		047	1	1788	VA		ELIZABETH IVES	08065
BATTLE, ELISHA	1723	VA		1799	NC	037		1	1742	VA		ELIZABETH SUMNER	60123
BATTLE, JAMES PHILIPS	1829	NC	037	1865	NC	037		1	1858	NC	037	KATE ROUTH HORNE	60123
BATTLE, JETHRO	1756	NC	037	1813	NC	037		1		NC	047	MARTHA/PATTY LANE	60123
BATTLE, JOSEPH SUMNER, I	1791	NC	037	1847	NC	037		1 2	1826	NC NC	099 037	REBECCA DUNN MARY ANN HORN	60123
BATTLE, JOSEPH SUMNER, II	1860	NC	037	1918	SC			1	1893	SC		LEILA MOULTRIE CHAPMAN	60123
BATTS, ELIZABETH/BETSY		NC						1	C1855				08219
BATTS, FRANCIS NATHANIEL	1831	NC		1889	TN			1	1853	KY		MARY LOUISE BARD	02135
BATTS, GERALDUS	C1780	NC	?037		KY			1 2		NC		BETSY NANCY	02135
BATTS, ISAAC	1813	NC		1861	KY			1	1838	KY		CATHARINE ETHLANA TARPLEY	02135
BATTS, JOSEPH		NC			KY			1					02135
BAUCOM, ISHAM					KY			1	1798	NC	099	ALEY PENNEY	60562
BAUCOM, JOHN		NC	099	1800				1				RACHEL	60562
BAUCOM, JOHN		NC	099	C1840									60562
BAUCOM, NICHOLAS				1761	NC	056	028	1				SARAH	60562
BAUM, ABRAHAM	1742	NC	030	1833	NC	030		1 2				SARAH MRS MARY T	20335

ANCESTOR INDEX	BIRTH	PL	CO	DEATH	PL	CO	LIVD	MARRIED	PL	CO	SPOUSE NAME	CODE
BAUM, MAURICE				1784	NC	030		1			MARTHA	20335
BAUM, PETER				1812	NC	075		1			BRIDGET	20335
BAXLEY, BARNABAS	1781	NC		1863	IN		065	2	1817	IN	MARY TROUT	60246
BAZEMORE, JESSE	1835	NC	010	1891	TN			1			MRS CANDICE (TEMPLETON) PATRICK	60081
BAZEMORE, JESSE JR		NC	010	C1807	NC	010		1	1799	NC	010 PENELOPE BAZEMORE	60081
BAZEMORE, JESSE SR		NC	010	C1809	NC	010		1		NC	010 FRANCES	60081
BAZEMORE, JOHN				C1809	NC	010						60081
BAZEMORE, THOMAS	C1804	NC	010	C1848	TN							60081
BEACH, ALLEN	1816	VA		1877	NC	070		1		?VA	THERESA ALDERMAN ?	05070
BEACH, CATHERINE M	1850	VA		1889	NC	012		1	1867	NC	070 HENRY ARTHUR WESCOTT	05070
BEAL/BEALE, BENJAMIN JOSEPH	1875	NC	022	1932	VA			1			HALLIE	60172
								2	1897	NC	022 JULIA LACY TYSOR	
BEAL/BEALE, ELLEN ELAINE	1899	NC	022					1	1917	VA	THEODORE BRADLEY PURVIS	60172
BEALES/BEALS, THOMAS	C1718	MD			NC	046	085	1	1741	NC	SARAH ANTRIM	27429
BEALS/BALES, AARON	1790	TN		1847	IN		081	1	1811	TN	ALICE MANIFOLD	60120
BEALS/BALES, JOHN	1717	PA		1796	NC	046	085	1	C1738	MD	MARGARET HUNT	60120
BEALS/BALES, WILLIAM	C1745	VA		1814	NC	022	046	1	1769	NC	085 RAHCEL GREEN	60120
BEAM, JOHN TEETER	C1732	GER		C1807	NC	060		1	C1764	SWI	REBECCA RANYOLDS	60466
								2	1781	NC	060 ELIZABETH RUDOPH	
BEAM, NANCY ANN/ANNA	1773	NC	094	C1855	TN		026	1	1800	NC	060 JENKEY JENKINS	60466
BEAM, SUSAN AARON	1853	NC	040	1929	NC	065	026	1	1873	NC	040 ALBERT DIXON ESKRIDGE	05070
BEAMAN, IVY	1819	NC	045	1900	MS		037	1	1844	NC	037 THERESA ANN EASON	60535
BEAMAN, JEREMIAH	1757	VA		1836	NC	045	034	1	1786		RUTH BARROW	60535
BEAMAN, MILES	1788	NC	034	C1858	NC	045	034	1		NC	045 MARGARET BERGERON	60535
BEAMAN, THOMAS W	1830	NC		C1885	MO			1	1849	NC	092 REBECCA A LEWIS	03015
								2	1866	NC	106 CATHERINE S LEWIS	
BEARD, BYTHEN B	1826	NC	056					1	C1847	TN	ELIZABETH D MCCOMMON	60361
BEARD, COUNCIL JONES	1804	NC	056		TN			1	1823	NC	056 NANCY ROSE	60361
BEARD, NEILL	C1777	NC		1849	MS		011	1	C1798	NC	029 ELIZABETH CARVER	60571
BEARD, NEILL CARVER	C1805	NC	029	C1861	NC	029		1	1831	NC	029 MAHALA/MAHALY MARSH	60571
BEARD, WILLIAM B CARVER	1814	NC	029	1898	TX			1	1837	MS	MARY JANE MAY	60571
BEARD, WILLIAM ELVIN	1824	NC	056	1900	TN			1	1846	TN	ANN CATHERINE MCALEXANDER	60361
BEASLEY, ANN	1770							1	1790	NC	024 JAMES MING	13175
BEASLEY, EPHRAIM OXFORD	1826	NC	056	1916	NC	056		1	1845	NC	056 EDITH AVERY	14030
								2	C1857	NC	056 ELIZABETH	
								3			MRS MARILDA (COLLINS) BEASLEY	
BEASLEY, JOSHUA	1784	NC		1879	NC	056		1	1805	NC	099 JUDITH FERRELL	14030
								2	1869	NC	056 WINIFRED WEBB	
BEASLEY, MARY	C1792	NC	?104		IN			1			THOMAS TIREY	60348
BEASLEY, NANCY	C1805	NC		1841	GA			1	1829	NC	029 ZACHARIAH HAM	27404

ANCESTOR INDEX	BIRTH	PL	CO	DEATH	PL	CO	LIVD	MARRIED	PL	CO	SPOUSE NAME	CODE
BEASLEY, NANCY J	C1803	NC		1881	IL			1			SIMPSON L DORRIS	04155
BEASLEY, SARAH								1 1701	NC	002	THOMAS GRAY	14030
BEASLEY, SOLOMON	1772	NC			AL		028	1				27600
								2 1799	NC	028	CASSANDER ECLIN	
								3	NC			
								4	NC			
								5 1843	AL		CAROLINE HODGES ?	
BEASLEY, THOMAS				1795	NC	024		1			MARTHA	13175
BEASON/BEESON, RICHARD	1792			1844	NC	090		1 1819	NC	085	MARY ROBERTSON	13120
BEATTY, ABEL/MAC	1851	NC	060	1917	OK			1 1870	MO		SARAH J MCCLURE	17046
BEATTY, FRANKLIN R	C1819	NC	060	1861	AR			1 1839	NC	060	ROSA ELENOR FARWELL	17046
BEATTY, JOHN				C1774	NC	060		1			ELIZABETH	17046
BEATTY, THOMAS JR	C1780	NC	060	1831	NC	060		1 C1800			SARAH WHEELER	17046
BEATTY, THOMAS SR	C1732	?NC		C1787	NC	060	?065	1 C1764			MARGARET ALBERNATHY ?	17046
BECK, ISAIAH S JR	1803	NC	046	1896	GA			1 C1824	SC		RUTHY BARKER	60311
								2 C1829	GA		ELIZABETH TANNER	
BECK, ISAIAH S SR	1778	NC	046	1854	GA			1 C1801	NC		DORTHY/DORCAS BARKER	60311
								2 1804	NC	046	DORCAS YORK	
BECK, JAMES	1789	NC	?044				085	1 C1813			MARGARET CANNADY ?	60259
								2 1834	IN		MRS LYDIA (DITTEMORE) COTTER	
								3 1850	IN		MRS MARY (MORRISON) MAINS	
BECK, JEFFREY	1752	VA		1838	SC			1 1771	NC	046	MARY MCDANIEL	60311
BECK, JEFFREY JR	1752	VA		1838	SC		073	1 1771	NC	046	MARY MCDANIEL	60241
BECK, JEFFREY SR	C1726	?PA		C1779	NC	081	073	1 1744	PA		LYDIA PHILLIPS	60241
								2			SUSANNAH GIBBS ?	
BECK, JEFREY	C1722	?PA		1779	NC	081		1 1743	PA		LYDIA PHILIPS	60311
								2 C1760	?NC	?073	SHUSANNA	
BECK, JOHAN FREDERICK		GER		1800	NC	044		1			NANCY	60259
BECK, MICHAEL	C1763	NC	?044				085	1 C1787	CN	?044	ANNE	60259
BECK, SAMUEL	1796	NC	081	1876	GA			1 1812	SC		TABITHA LANGSTON	60241
BECK/BECKE, ANN		?VA			NC	?047	010	1 C1735	VA		DANIEL HIGHSMITH/HYSMITH	10010
BEDDINGFIELD, HENRY	C1787	?NC	?039		NC	039						25235
BEDDINGFIELD, MARTHA	1824	NC	039	1910	NC	039		1 1837	NC	039	WILLIAM WESLEY HILL	25235
BEDWELL, ROBERT T	1759	DE		1842	IN			1 1776	NC	085	ELLENDER BLACK	17075
BEDWELL, THOMAS	C1780	NC	085	C1845	IN			1 1799	KY		MARY HOLSTON	17075
BEESLEY, AUSTIN/ORSTON/GUSTON	1807	NC		1852	AL			1 1830	AL		ELIZABETH HAYS/HAYES	27600
								2 1840	AL		CECILIA/CALLIE ANN MOORE	
BEESON, HENRY HARRISON	1832	NC	046	1925	NC	081		1 1860	NC	046	OLIVE JANE BLAIR	02175
BEESON, ISAAC	1729	PA		1802	NC	046		1 C1749			PHOEBE STROUD	02175
BEESON, ISAAC	C1780	NC	046	1847	SC			1 1801	NC	046	LEVISA WILLIAMS	02175
BEESON, JOHN	1825			1904	NC	038		1 1847	NC	090	ELIZABETH HITCHCOCK	60456
BEESON, RICHARD	1684	PA		1777	NC	046		1 1706			CHARITY GRUBB	02175
BEESON, RICHARD	1755	VA		1781	NC	046		1 C1778	NC	046	MARY	02175

ANCESTOR INDEX	BIRTH	PL	CO	DEATH	PL	CO	LIVD	MARRIED	PL	CO	SPOUSE NAME	CODE
BEESON, RICHARD MARION	1807	NC	046	1835	NC	046		1 1830	NC	046	ASENATH GARDNER	02175
BELISLE, BERRY	C1790	?NC										27260
BELISLE, IRA	1815	NC	?047					1 1835	TN		LUCINDA SMITH	27260
BELISLE, LITTLEBERY	C1800	NC						1			MILLY BRADLEY ?	27260
BELL, ELIZABETH	C1780	NC	034	C1845	NC	103		1 C1805	NC	103	JESSE JONES	13264
BELL, HANNAH		VA		C1788	NC	022		1 C1742	VA		WILLIAM THOMPSON	60110
BELL, JAMES	C1732			C1793	NC	012		1			SARAH	13052
BELL, JOHN	C1710						070					13052
BELL, JOHN W	1819	NC		1876	TX			1 1843	TX		OLA SARAH MABRY	60236
BELL, JOSHUA				1793	NC	037		1 C1760	NC	037	PHEREBY NORFLEET	27441
BELL, MARGARET	C1787	NC	012					1 1804	NC	012	SAMUEL A STANALAND	13052
BELL, REASON WRIGHT	C1765	NC	037	1827	NC	037		1 C1820	NC	037	MARY BRITT	27441
BELL, ROBERT	1785	NC	?085	C1865	NC	013		1	NC	013	SARAH	03133
BELL, ROBERT JAHUE	1857	NC	023	1935	GA			1	GA		MATILDA LORENA CHASTAIN	03133
								2 1904	GA		LINDORA TERESA MCKIBBEN	
BELL, SAMUEL	C1755	NC	012	C1810	NC	012		1			LYDIA	13052
BELL, SEBITHA	1795	TN		C1875	NC	049		1 1816	TN		THOMAS ARRINGTON	40690
BELL, THOMAS	1748	VA		C1834	NC	013		1 1772	VA		JANE MONTGOMERY	03133
								2 1788	NC	?104	SARAH EVE	
								3	NC	013	JANE MOORE	
BELL, WILLIAM	C1745	NC	?037	1802	NC	103		1 C1765	NC		ELIZABETH	13264
BELL, WILLIAM		VA		1754	NC	037		1 1721			ANN JONES	27441
BELL, WILLIAM					TX			1	NC		CYNTHIA	60236
BELLENFANT/BALLANFANT, JOHN		FRA		C1800	NC	084		1 C1784	VA		LOUISA YEOMANS	60425
								2 C1797	NC	084	SALLY RAY ?	
BELVIN, ALMOND L	C1820	NC	?099					1 1845			CONSTANCE THOMPSON	25235
BELVIN, JETHRO	C1780	NC	?099			?099		1 1801			POLLY PARHAM	25235
BELVIN, MARY A	1848	NC	099	1929	NC	036		1 1868	NC	099	JAMES WASHINGTON NORWOOD	25235
BENFIELD, MILES/MILUS	C1825						054					27438
BENGE, THOMAS SR	1740				NC	104		1 1760			SUSANNAH LEWIS	60336
BENNET, CHARLES		NC										60010
BENNET, DUKE		NC										60010
BENNET, NEOMA	1814	NC		1888	TN			1			DAVID C JONES	60010
BENNET, SPIERS		NC										60010
BENNET, WALDROM		NC										60010
BENNET, WILLIAM		NC		C1828	TN			1			NANCY	60010
BENNETT, ELISHA	C1750	?VA		1835	NC	046		1 C1780	?VA		MARY COBLE	21167
BENNETT, ELIZABETH							103	1			SIMON AYCOCK	60539
BENNETT, LUCY CLARISSA	1817	NC		1872	IA			1 1834	IN		ABEL EDWARDS	60487

15

ANCESTOR INDEX	BIRTH	PL	CO	DEATH	PL	CO	LIVD	MARRIED	PL	CO	SPOUSE NAME	CODE
BENNETT, WILLIAM ABNER	1831	NC		1902	TX			1			MARTHA EMALINE SMITH	60368
BENOIT, RACHAEL VIOLANTE	1854	LA			NC	046		1			JAMES PRICE PICKETT	27467
BERRY, -EMPHY (SIC)	C1800	NC	?018		NC	?018	?030	1 C1820	NC		MARY/POLLY MERCER	02180
BERRY, FANNY BUSH	1858	NC	030	1928	NC	018		1 1884	NC	018	WILLIS B PUGH	02180
BERRY, JACOB				C1805	NC	016		1			MARGARETT	60260
BERRY, JAMES MERCER/MONROE	C1823	NC	?018	1887	NC	018	030	1 C1842		030	SARAH WALKER	02180
								2 1857	NC	030	DORCAS JARVIS	
								3 C1864	NC	018	LYDIA BURGESS	
BERRY, MATHIAS				C1830	NC	060		1			CATHARINE	60260
BERRY, MATHIAS	1796	NC	016	1868	IN			1 1827	NC	060	NANCY DOWNEY	60260
BERTRAM, ELIZABETH	C1806	NC		1857	IL			1 C1827	KY		DAVIS STOCKTON	60033
BEST, JOE HARVEY	1852	NC	053					1 1875	NC		MARY ADELINE CASEY	13120
BEST, JOHN	1827	NC		1868	NC	053		1			MRS MARY ANN (HAMILTON) PUGH	13120
BEST, JOHN/JACKIE	1802	NC		1884	NC	063		1 C1827	NC	063	SALLIE MANNING	24240
BEST, THOMAS	C1775	NC		1818	NC	037		1 C1800	NC	063	MARY/POLLY SHERROD	24240
BIGGS, DAVIS	1763	?NC		1845	MO			1 1781	NC	018	ANNA MORRIS	03020
BIGGS, JOHN	1727	ENG		1778	NC	018		1 1760	VA		REBECCA MCCUNE	03020
BILLITER, EDWARD				1795	NC	090	092					60158
BILLITER, ZEBIDEE				C1817	NC	090	092	1 C1783	NC	?092	ANNA	60158
BILLS, JOHN	1788	NC	085	C1824			092	1 1813	NC	085	SUSSANNA POWELL	60573
BINKLEY, DANIEL	1805			1871	NC	?106		1			CAMMELIA RHOADES	10010
BINNS, EDWIN SOLOMON, DR	1825	NC	039	1884	TX			1 1855	TX		SUSAN ADALINE BARNETT	08120
BINNS, JOSEPH	C1800	VA		C1870	MS		039	1			MARTHA	08120
BIRCHFIELD/BURCHFIELD, JEREMIAH	1780	NC	014	C1835	VA		107	1 1813	NC		REBECCA SHORT	60019
BIRD, CATHERINE	C1762	NC	035	1843	TN		060	1 1785	NC	060	DAVID COBB	60443
BIRD, JOHN	1754	NC	035	1843	AL			1			ELIZABETH	60443
BIRD, WILLIAM	C1758	NC	035									60443
BIRD/BURD/BYRD, SPENCER	C1790	NC		C1845	KY			1 1825	KY		SARAH STROW	20415
BISHOP, AARON	C1770						046	1			SARAH ?	60250
BISHOP, EDMUND	C1730						065	1			ANNY/ANNA	60250
BISHOP, JAMES					NC	073						08200
BISHOP, JOHN								1 C1790	NC	028	MRS SARAH COOPER	06080
BISHOP, JOHN	C1770						046					60250
BISHOP, MARGARET ALICE	1824	NC	073	1913	NC	036		1 1844	NC	073	NASH CHEEK	08200
BISHOP, MASON	C1770						010					60250
BISHOP, MOSES	C1770						010					60250
BISHOP, NATHAN	C1770						046					60250
BISHOP, ROBERT	C1760						046					60250

16

ANCESTOR INDEX	BIRTH	PL	CO	DEATH	PL	CO	LIVD	MARRIED	PL	CO	SPOUSE NAME	CODE
BISHOP, SARAH	C1762	NC	028	C1812	NC	028		1	NC	?028	GEORGE COOPER	06080
								2	NC	028	JOHN BISHOP	
								3 1802	NC	028	WILLIAM PHYSIOC	
BISHOP, WILLIAM GLOVER	C1730						065	1			LUCY	60250
BIZZELL, PATIENCE E	C1817	NC						1 C1835	NC		SELDON TRYON	60552
BLACK, CALVIN				C1876	NC	085		1			BETTY	60527
BLACK, CHARLES	C1823	NC		1862	VA			1 1847	NC	084	MARY GLENN	27542
BLACK, JAMES MADISON	C1870	NC	085	1957	KS		081	1 1893	IL		JANE ATKINSON	60527
BLACK, MARY LOUELLA	1874	NC	068	1929	NC	016		1 1890	NC	082	J O A HARVELL	19183
BLACK, W J	C1847	NC			NC		068	1			NANCY CORDELL	19183
BLACKMAN, MARY	1790	NC	068	1864	AL			1 C1808	NC	?068	DUNCAN NICHOLSON	60040
BLACKNALL, JOHN	C1765			1813	NC	044	100					25100
BLACKWELDER, MARGARET	1722			1803	NC	016		1 1745			MARTIN PHIFER SR	60593
BLACKWELL, JOHN	C1823	SC					086	1			NANCY MALISSA SCATES	60272
BLACKWOOD, JOHN	C1775			1844	NC	060		2			JANE	60215
BLAIR, COLBERT	C1730	PA		1805	NC	014		1			SARAH MORGAN	27553
BLAIR, COLBERT	C1775	NC	014	1846	IL			1			JANE MURRAY	27553
BLAIR, HUGH				1783	NC	092	?085	1 C1749	NC		MARY DAWSON	60393
BLAIR, JOHN	1799	NC		1871	IL			1 1817	KY		ELIZABETH ISAACK	27553
BLAIR, JOHN				1778	NC	046		1 C1762			JANE	60443
BLAIR, JONATHAN	1776	NC	046	1842	TX			1 C1799	KY		SARAH SLOSS	60443
BLAIR/BLEAR, COLBERT	C1730	PA		1805	NC	014		1 C1750			SARAH MORGAN	02175
BLAIR/BLEAR, ENOS	1750			1834	NC	081		1 1773			HANNAH MILLIKIN	02175
BLAIR/BLEAR, JAMES					NC	?085		1			MARY EOSENTRICE COLBERT	02175
BLAIR/BLEAR, JOHN	1800	NC	081	1859	NC	046		1 1819			ELIZABETH TOMLINSON	02175
BLAIR/BLEAR, OLIVE JANE	1829	NC	046	1906	NC	081		1 1860	NC	046	HENRY HARRISON BEESON	02175
BLAKELEY, FANNIE MILLER	1863	NC	040	1929	NC	086		1 1883	NC	040	ROBERT BROWN QUINN	05070
BLAKELY, AQUILLA	C1857	NC										60334
BLAKELY, ELI D	C1847	NC						1 C1866	NC			60334
BLAKELY, ELIZA I	C1840	NC										60334
BLAKELY, FRANCIS M	C1851	NC										60334
BLAKELY, GEORGE W	C1839	NC						1 C1866	NC			60334
BLAKELY, HENRY	C1863	NC										60334
BLAKELY, JOHN C	C1855	NC										60334
BLAKELY, LASKY P	C1857	NC										60334
BLAKELY, MALISSA	C1852	NC										60334
BLAKELY, MARGARET	C1854	NC										60334
BLAKELY, MARTHA E	C1846	NC										60334

ANCESTOR INDEX	BIRTH	PL	CO	DEATH	PL	CO	LIVD	MARRIED	PL	CO	SPOUSE NAME	CODE
BLAKELY, MARY ANN	1849	NC	092	1914	NC	106		1 1869	NC	106	JOHN HAMPTON TUCKER	60334
BLAKELY, TEMPLE	C1808	NC						1 C1835	NC		JANE STEWART	60334
BLAKELY, WILLIAM F	C1859	NC										60334
BLAKLEY, CHARLES	C1735			1818	TN		044	1 1765			MARGARET DAVIS	60327
BLALOCK, ALFRED	1815	NC	078	1888	NC	078		1 1843	NC	020	HARRIET HARRISON	60543
								2 1884	NC	078	MARY BROWN	
BLALOCK, CHARLES	1778	NC	029	1845	TX			1 1801	NC	?068	SARAH ANN BRAZIER	60437
BLALOCK, FRANKLIN PIERCE	1851	NC	078	1931	NC	020		1 1869	NC	078	MARY JANE OAKLEY	60543
								2 1906	NC	001	MARTHA JANE MOORE	
BLALOCK, JOHN	1762	VA		1846	NC	014	107	1 1797	NC	073	POLLY DORMAN	23040
BLALOCK, MILLINGTON SR	1741			1827	NC	078		1 C1766				60543
BLALOCK, RICHARD		?VA		1805	NC	029		1			RACHEL	60437
BLALOCK, ROBERT	1781	NC	020	C1855	NC	078		1 1808	NC	078	NANCY BLALOCK	60543
								2 C1814	NC		JUDITH PEARCE	
BLALOCK, WILLIAM		?VA			NC	029		1	NC	?029	LUCY WOMACK	60437
BLALOCK, WILLIAM DAVID	1870	NC	078	1951	NC	020		1 1897	NC	020	SARAH DELILAH STADLER	60543
BLALOCK, WILLIAM JESSE	1819	NC		1903	AL			1 1849	AL		MARY ELIZABETH BARRETT	60102
BLALOCK/BLAYLOCK, WILLIAM	C1802	NC		1882	AR			1			MARY WILSON	60119
BLANKENSHIP, JOHN TURNER	C1847	NC	?086		NC	?107		1 1868	NC	062	MARY CAROLINE BURLESON	60390
								2			KATE TIPTON	
BLEDSOE, WILLIAM DAWSON	C1832	NC	?073	1906	MS		?099	1	NC	036	MRS MARY ANN (MARTIN) SCOTT	60228
BLEVINS, WILLIAM	C1800	NC			TN		066	1 1820				05059
								2 1845			POLLY GOUGE	
BLOODWORTH, JOHN, MAJ	1730	ENG		1808	GA		070	1 1754	NC	070	TAMSIE AXSON	60535
BLOODWORTH, THOMAS	1773	NC		1836	GA		005	1 C1798			TAMSIE PROCTER	60311
BLOODWORTH, THOMAS, MAJ	1755	NC	070	1836	GA		028	1 1802	NC	070	TAMSA PROCTER	60535
BLOUNT, CHARLESWORTH	1721	NC	024	1784	NC	024		1 1744	NC	024	MARY CLAYTON	19230
BLOUNT, JACOB C	1817	NC	079									06050
BLUE, CATHERINE		NC	068	1889	NC	068		1 1858	NC	068	WILLIAM PITT CAMERON	22005
BLUE, DUNCAN	1734	SCO		1814	NC	068		1			MARGARET CAMPBELL	22005
BOATRIGHT, REBECCA	C1817	VA		C1890	KY		084	1 C1837			SAMUEL RICHARD FORD	60292
BOBBITT, JOHN	1678	VA		1736	NC	047		1 1703	VA		SARAH GREEN	02280
BOBBITT, JOHN RICHARD	1725	NC	024	1791	NC	100		1 1743	NC	010	AMY ALSTON	02280
BOBBITT, LEWIS	1703	VA		1769	NC	100		1 1726	VA		ELIZABETH MOORE	02280
BOBBITT, LEWIS JR	1742	VA		1818	NC	100		1 1733	NC	100	MARY PERSON	02280
BOBBITT, MILES	1731	VA		1794	NC	100		1 1761	NC	100	MARY POWELL	02280
BOBBITT, WILLIAM M	1738	NC		1825	NC	099		1 1759	NC	100	MARTHA TURNER	02280
BOGGAN, JAMES JR							005					60590
BOGGAN, JAMES SR							005					60590
BOGGAN, PATRICK							005					60590

ANCESTOR INDEX	BIRTH	PL	CO	DEATH	PL	CO	LIVD	MARRIED	PL	CO	SPOUSE NAME	CODE
BOGGAN, WILLIAM JR							005					60590
BOGGAN, WILLIAM SR							005					60590
BOGUE, ROBERT	C1703	NC	077	1788	NC	057		1 1738	NC	077	RACHEL PEARSON	60082
								2 1775	NC	077	MARIAM PEARSON	
BOHANNON, ABNER				1828	NC	022		1			ELIZABETH MINTER	27269
BOHANNON, DUNCAN, II	1704			1760	NC	073		1			SUSANNAH MAY	27269
BOHANNON, RICHARD				1805	NC	022		1			ELIZABETH	27269
BOLICK, CALVIN SAVANNAH	1849			1899	NC	065		1			RHODA CATHERINE CHESTER	60153
BOLICK, ROBERT THEODORE	1873			1927	NC	054	065	1			NANCY LUVATER KELLY	60153
BOLIN/BOWLING, SARAH	1815	NC		1895	IA			1 C1834			ISAAC DARTING	60471
BOLLINGER, GEORGE FREDERICK	1770	NC	094	1842	MO			1	NC	060	ELIZABETH HUNSUCKER	60349
BOLLINGER, MATTHIAS	1768				MO			1 1789	NC	060	PRISCILLA PETERSON	60349
BOLLINGER, SALOME/SALMA	1796	NC	060	1869	MO			1			JACOB LEWIS CONRAD	60349
BOND, JAMES		NC	024	1770	NC	024		1 C1754	NC	024		12040
BOND, LEWIS	1815	NC	010	1853	TN			1 1839	TN		MARTHA ELIZABETH HARE	60375
BOND, LEWIS BATE	1768	NC	010	1851	TN			1 1799	NC	010	HANNAH OLDHAM DAWSON	60375
BOND, RICHARD	C1685			1728	NC	024		1 C1705	VA			12040
								2 C1710	VA		SARAH	
BOND, RICHARD	C1708	VA		1795	NC	041	024	1 C1730	NC	024		12040
BOND, THOMAS	C1710			1767	NC	010						60337
BONNER, ABIGAIL	C1710	NC	009	C1790	KY		079	1 C1725	NC	009	CPT SIMON JONES	13264
								2 C1770	NC	?037	AQUILLA SUGG	
BONNER, THOMAS	C1690			C1765	NC	009	008	1			ABIGAIL DAW	19130
BONNER, THOMAS, SHF	1680	?VA		1765	NC	009		1 C1705	NC	009	ABIGAIL JONES	13264
BOOKER, JOHN				1799	NC	022						60028
BOOKER, PHERIBY/FERRABEE							099	1			WILLIS HICKS	60028
BOOKOUT, LEVI	C1785				NC	086		1			PROTHANIA PARKER	25100
BOON, JOSEPH GREEN	1805	NC	056	1871	TX			1 C1829	TN		HARRIETT N LATHAM	21165
BOON, JOSEPH, I	C1690	VA		1728	NC	024		1			ELIZABETH	21165
BOON, JOSEPH, II	C1707	NC	024	C1790	NC	056						21165
BOON, JOSEPH, III	1752	NC	056	1836	NC	056		1			SARAH BASS	21165
BOON, JOSEPH, IV	C1785	NC	056	C1812	NC	056		1 1803	NC	103	MARY G GREEN	21165
BOONE, BENJAMIN	1754	NC	085	1836	TN		054	1 1783	NC	085	MARY WILSON	27586
BOONE, CATHERINE	C1757	NC	085					1 1780	NC	085	MARK WHITAKER	27586
BOONE, ELIZABETH	1752	NC	085					1			WILLIAM WHITE	24153
BOONE, ELIZABETH	C1770	NC	085				033	1 1801	NC	085	SAMUEL LITTLE	27586
BOONE, HANNAH	1779	NC	085	1857	NC	033		1	NC	085	JAMES PENRY	27586
BOONE, JAMES					NC	071		1	NC	071	LUCY TYNER/TINER	12140
BOONE, JAMES MONROE	1788	NC	085	1856	AR		054	1			SOPHIA SMITH	27586

19

ANCESTOR INDEX	BIRTH	PL	CO	DEATH	PL	CO	LIVD	MARRIED	PL	CO	SPOUSE NAME	CODE
BOONE, JOHN	1727	PA		1803	NC	085		1 C1753	NC	085	REBECCA BRYAN	27586
BOONE, JOHN JR	C1781	NC	085		TN			1	NC	085	ELIZABETH LITTLE	27586
BOONE, JOHN WILSON	1786	NC	085				054	1			CENA WOOD	27586
BOONE, JUDITH DEANES	1859	NC	071	1937	FL		079	1 1882	NC	071	JOSEPH ALVIN DUPREE	12140
BOONE, MARY	C1760	NC	085					1			JOHN MCDANIEL	27586
BOONE, MARY/POLLY	1797	NC	085	1835	TN		054	1	TN		LEMUEL BROADWAY	27586
BOONE, NANCY		NC	085					1	NC	085	JACOB CLIFFORD	27586
BOONE, NOAH WEBSTER	1807	NC	054	1860				1			MINERVA JANE TRAMMELL	27586
BOONE, REBECCA		NC	085	1816	NC	085		1 1793	NC	085	JOHN FROST	27586
BOONE, REUBEN HOLMAN	1792	NC	085	1857			054	1			FINETTA REES/REESE	27586
BOONE, RHODA	1803	NC	054	1846	TN			1 1820	TN		ANTHONY WAYNE REAGOR	27586
BOONE, SAMUEL	1728	PA		C1809	KY		085	1 C1748	?PA		SARAH DAY	08130
BOONE, SAMUEL	1801	NC	054	1860	TN			1			CYNTHIA CARRIGER	27586
BOONE, SARAH		NC	085					1	NC	085	JOHN WILSON	27586
BOONE, SARAH	1783	NC	085	1867	TN		054	1			JOHN DONALDSON	27586
BOONE, SQUIRE	1696	ENG		1765	NC	085		1 1720	PA		MRS SARAH MORGAN	08130
BOONE, WILLIAM	1812	NC	071	1881	NC	071		1 1837	NC	051	JUDITH PERRY DEANES	12140
BOONE, WILLIAM/BILLY	1790	NC	085	1854	TN		054	1 1824	TN		SALLY/SALLIE HOWARD	27586
BOSLOCK, JOSHUA, DR	1792	SC		1859	GA		104	1 C1810	TN		MARTHA CAROLINE SLAUGHTER	60062
BOSS, HENRY					NC	085		1 C1790			MARY GOSS	25185
BOSS, PHILIP				C1807	NC	085		1 C1768	PA		ANNA SPEIDEL	25185
BOSS, PHILIP	1791	NC		1863	IN			1 1821	IN		MARY/POLLY WYMAN	25185
								2 1826	IN		MARY/POLLY FULK	
BOSTICK, ABSALOM, I	1738	VA		1803	NC	092	090	1 1762	VA		BETHENIA PERKINS	60519
BOSTICK, ABSALOM, II	1769	NC	085	1855	KY		090	1 1794	NC	092	NANCY DALTON	60519
								2 1822	NC	084	DOLLY WHITE	
BOSTICK, ABSALOM, III	1796	NC	?090	1841	NC	084	?092	1 1817	NC	090	SUSANNAH DALTON	60519
BOSTICK, JONATHAN SMITH	1819	NC	090	1887	TN			1 1840	NC	084	SARAH ANN SMITH	60519
BOSWELL, MATHEW JR	C1770	VA		1816	NC	090		1 C1795	VA		MARY	60300
BOVEY/POVEY, CONRAD					NC	065						27318
BOVEY/POVEY, MARY MAGDALAN	C1740			C1808	NC	014		1	?NC	?065	JACOB SETZER	27318
								2	NC		CONRAD MINGUS	
BOWEN, CHRISTINA CHANEY	1839			1885	NC	?090		1 1857	NC	038	CALVIN FREDERICK FULK	60467
BOWEN, CLIFTON	1701	NJ			NC	035	070	1			ELIZABETH HARRIS	60384
BOWEN, CLIFTON	1735	NJ		1806	GA		035	1			MARTHA	60384
BOWEN, THOMAS				C1828	NC	009		1			MARY ADAMS	19130
BOWERS, DAVID GILES?	C1783	NC	039	1856	TN		?099	1 C1801	NC	039	BETTY NICHOLSON COOK	60404
BOWERS, GILES	1716	VA		1796	NC	039		1			SARAH BEAL	06005

ANCESTOR INDEX	BIRTH	PL	CO	DEATH	PL	CO	LIVD	MARRIED	PL	CO	SPOUSE NAME	CODE
BOWERS, GILES SR	1715	?VA		1800	NC	039	044	1 C1740	NC	?037	SARAH	60404
BOWERS, MARY	C1780	NC	039		TN		020	1			JOHN GOODLOE	06005
BOWERS, PHILEMON	C1756	NC	044	1794	NC	039	044	1 1777	NC	044		60404
BOWLES/BOYLES, JOHN	C1755			C1825	GA			1 1781	NC	073	ELIZABETH BOYL	60507
BOWMAN, EDMOND	C1744	NJ		1794	NC	090		1 C1766	NJ		GRACE REYNOLDS	12125
BOWMAN, EDMOND	1795	NC	046	1842	NC	046		1 C1815	NC	046	CELIA PEEBLES	12125
BOWMAN, RICHARD	C1772	NJ		1843	NC	046		1 C1794	NC	046	ELIZABETH DEAN	12125
BOWMAN, WYATT FLETCHER	1820	NC	046	1882	NC	038		1 1846	NC	046	MARY ELIZA LINDSAY	12125
BOYCE, HARRISON	C1775	NC	071	C1845	NC	071		1			SARAH COTTEN	25141
BOYCE, HENRY TARPLEY	1826	NC	071	1897	NC	071		1 1849	NC	071	MARTHA ANN SYKES	25141
BOYCE, ISTALENA LEIGH	1872	NC	071	1962	NC	071		1 1895	NC	071	MILLS HENRY CONNER	25141
BOYCE, JACOB	1793	NC	024	1861	NC	?024		1			NANCY FOREHAND	27562
BOYCE, JUDITH ANN	1828	NC	024	1905	NC	?024		1			STEPHEN RICHARD GOODWIN	27562
BOYCE, SION	C1750	NC	071	1819	NC	071		1			SARAH	25141
BOYD, MARIA	1744	IRE		C1830	TN		065	1 1768	?NC	?005	WILLIAM RAMSEY	60164
BOYKIN, ALSEY	1808	NC	069	1884	NC	105		1 1827	NC	069	CHELLY FULGHUM	02343
BOYKIN, BENJAMIN	C1711	VA		1786	NC	103	037	1			DIANAH	02343
BOYKIN, BENJAMIN	C1710			C1785	NC	103		1			DIANAH	27554
BOYKIN, DRURY	C1743			1823	SC		069					27554
BOYKIN, EDWARD JR	C1676	ENG		1743	NC	071		1			JUDITH HILL	27554
BOYKIN, HARDY				1832	NC	069		1 C1758				02343
BOYKIN, HARDY JR	C1786	NC	069	1837	NC	069		1 C1806	NC	?069	MARY/POLLEY	02343
BOYKIN, MARY				C1774	NC	037		1			SAMUEL DELOACH	15045
BOYST, CHARLES HENRY	1862	NY		1947	NC	046		1 1893	NC	046	LIZZIE VANCE MONROE	60544
BOYST, FLORENCE ELIZABETH	1911	NC	046					1 1932	NC	046	FRANK MILLER CHEDESTER	60544
BOYST, J RAYMOND	1899	MO		1965	VA		046	1 1921	NC	046	REBECCA OGILVIE FORTSON	60544
BOYST, NELLIE SAFFORD	1880	NC		1932	NC	013	046	1 1903	NC	046	ROBERT GRIER FORTUNE	60544
BOYST, OSCAR ALBERT	1897	MO			WV		046	1 1921	WV		MYRTLE MAE FARLEY	60544
BOYST, WILLIAM MARSHALL	1894	MO		1978	NC	065	046	1 1923	GA		LOLLIE MAUDE HARRIS	60544
BRACEWELL/BRASWELL, MARY	C1765	NC	037	C1829	NC	037		1 C1789	NC	037	WILLIAM BRITT	27441
BRACEWELL/BRASWELL, RICHARD				1772	NC	037		1			ELIZABETH	27441
BRACEWELL/BRASWELL, ROBERT		VA		1736	NC	010		1			SARAH	27441
BRACEWELL/BRASWELL, SOLOMON SR		NC	037	1798	NC	037		1	NC	037	MARY DELOACH	27441
BRACKEN, ISAAC	C1745	DE					073	1 1769	DE		RACHEL STALCOP	60268
BRADFORD, JENNY	1753			1816	NC	010		1 1770	NC		JAMES FOLKS	60576
BRADFORD, THOMAS	C1785	NC		1861	TN			1			NANCY MCDOWELL	60438
BRADLEY, ANDREW JACKSON	C1822	NC	086	1891	TN			1			MARY ELVIRA TRENTHAM	27268

ANCESTOR INDEX	BIRTH	PL	CO	DEATH	PL	CO	LIVD	MARRIED		PL	CO	SPOUSE NAME	CODE
BRADLEY, ELIZABETH	1780	NC	065	1857	NC	065		1	1800	NC	065	ALEXANDER STINSON	20095
BRADLEY, FRANCIS	1743			1780	NC	065		1				ABIGAIL ALEXANDER	20095
BRADLEY, GEORGE WALTON	1764	NC	?015	1835	NC	086		1	1791	NC	086	SARAH GOODBREAD	60402
BRADLEY, GEORGE WALTON	C1764	NC	100	1835	NC	086		1	1791			SALLY GOODBREAD	60582
BRADLEY, JOHN				1778	NC	086		1					27268
								2				MARY LEDBETTER	
BRADLEY, JOHN SR	C1720	VA		1778	NC	094		1	C1760	VA		MARY LEDBETTER	60582
BRADLEY, SALLY/SARAH	1798	NC	086	1837	NC	013		1	1817	NC	013	ISAAC LEDBETTER	60582
BRADSHAW, BENJAMIN	C1750	?NC		1782	NC	035		1				MARY	12019
BRADSHAW, JAMES	C1738						028						12019
BRADSHAW, JOHN	C1710						056						12019
BRADY, JOHN TYSON	C1836	NC	068		TN								60538
BRAGG, MARY J	1821	VA			AL		?107	1	C1840	?VA		J/JOHN WILLIAM ANGEL	60190
BRANCH, ELIAS	C1788	NC	035	1853	GA			1	C1810	?SC		LUCY DE VAUGH	27756
BRANCH, WILLIAM	C1760	NC		C1830	GA			1	C1781	NC	035	HESTER	27756
BRANDON, GEORGE C	1792	NC		1844	IN		092	1	1815			QUINTILLA HUTCHINS	60322
BRANDON, JOHN	C1775	NC	?085	1830	TN			1	C1800			ANNA	27365
BRANDON, JOHN	1691	ENG		1756	NC	085		1				MRS ELIZABETH LOCKE	60593
BRANDON, MARY ELIZABETH	1730			1790	NC	085		1	1799	NC	104	BETSY JONES	60593
BRANN, JAMES	1789	NC		1863	TN			1		NC		MRS REBECCA (JONES) KNIGHT	60208
BRANN, JOHN	C1777	?VA			NC	?084	078	1	1800	NC	020	PATSEY FOSTER	60388
BRANN, VINCENT	C1805	?NC		1884	NC	084		1	C1842	NC	?078	TIMEY/TINNA BROOKS	60388
BRANN, VIRGINIA	1882	NC	084	1955	UT			1	1903	UT		WILLIAM ALBERT ADAMS	60388
BRANN, YANCEY M	1852	NC	084	1882	NC	084		1	1872	NC	?084	SOPHRONA CHRISMON	60388
								2	1882	NC	084	SARAH F MASSEY	
BRANTLEY, JOHN		?VA		C1781	NC	022	073	1				HANNAH	60485
BRANTLEY, PHILLIP	C1750	?NC		C1824	GA		100	1	C1777	NC	?022	NANCY ANN	60485
BRASHEARS/BRASSIEURS, ROBERT	1704	MD			NC	046		1				CHARITY DOWELL	04200
BRASSFIELD, JESSE	C1775	NC	099	C1820	NC	092		1	1797	NC	099	RACHEL SMITH	17075
								2	1804	NC	099	MARY REVIS	
BRASSFIELD, JOHN	1735	NC		1788	NC	099		1				ELIZABETH	17075
BRASSFIELD, JOHN EDWARD	C1700	ENG			NC			1		VA			17075
BRASSWELL, JANE	C1752			1832	NC			1	C1800	NC	?092	JOHN HUTCHINS	60322
BRAY, EDWARD	C1720	?VA		C1810	NC	092		1	C1759	?VA		SARAH MAYNER/MAYNARD	27420
BRAY, LITTLEBERRY							092						19040
BRAY, MARY				C1820			022	1	C1771			ISAAC CARTER	27420
BRAY, NICHOLAS ADAMS		CT		1816	NC	057	028	1	1785	NC	028	ELIZABETH WICKLIFFE	60519
BRAY, THOMAS HEADENGRAND	1805	NC	057	1891	GA			1	1829	GA		MARY ANN SMITH	60519
								2	1832	GA		MARTHA WILLIAM SMITH	
								3	1842	GA		MARTHA S ROSE	

22

ANCESTOR INDEX	BIRTH	PL	CO	DEATH	PL	CO	LIVD	MARRIED	PL	CO	SPOUSE NAME	CODE
BRAY, WILLIAM	C1778	NC	092	1861	OH			1 1801	NC	092	ELIZABETH DENNY	19040
BRAY, WILLIAM M	C1813	NC		C1889	AL							60373
BRAZIER, JAMES				1790	NC	029						60437
BREWER, ISIAH		NC						1	?NC			60442
BREWER, RUSSELL	1785	NC	?085	1858	TN			1 C1804	?NC		NANCY TOLIVER	60286
BREWER, WILLIAM	1793			1881	NC	068		1			ELIZABETH	19183
BREWER, WILLIAM	1819	NC			?IN			1 1844	NC	046	ELIZABETH J POE	60442
BREWER, WILLIAM J	C1806	NC		1837	TN			1 C1828	?TN		ABIGAIL PRICE	60286
BREWER/BRUER, AMBROS/AMBROSE	1753	VA		1855	TN		068	1	NC	029	OMA RICHARDSON	07018
BRIDGES, AUGUSTUS W	C1819	NC						1 1839	SC		AGNES DUNN SMITH	27554
BRIDGES, EPHRAIM	1810	NC	?086	C1857	MS			1 1830	NC	?086	SARAH B	60088
BRIDGES, HENDERSON DIAL	1812	NC	?086		MS			1 1835	NC	?086	DIDEMA	60088
BRIDGES, MOSES	1773			C1835	MS		086	1 1796			MARY BLACKBURN	01006
BRIDGES, SAMUEL	1799	NC	?086		MS			1 C1828			NANCY TATUM	01006
BRINKLEY, JAMES W	1812						?010	1 1843	NC	051	MRS PARTHENIA SESSUMS	27276
BRINKLEY, REDDING STARKE	C1809	NC		1892	GA		072	2 1852	GA		MRS SUSAN ANN (HARRIS) WATSON	60227
BRINKLEY, REDDING STARKE	1809	NC		1892	GA			1				60282
								2 1852	GA		MRS SUSAN ANN (HARRIS) WATSON	
BRINSON, MARGARET ELLEN	1860	NC	028	1936	NC	028		1 1875	NC	028	THOMAS ANN LAND	60030
BRINSON, SIMON SIKES	1805	NC	?028	C1798	NC	028		1			SARAH T BLAND	60030
BRISTOW, JOHN	1748	VA		1820	SC		044	1			SUSANNAH PARRISH	60384
BRITT, BENJAMIN	1800	NC	?103					1			MARTHA	20007
BRITT, HENRY SR				1830	NC	103						20007
BRITT, MARY	C1800	NC	037	1864	NC	047		1 1821	NC	037	REASON WRIGHT BELL	27441
								2 1830	NC	037	WILLIS BRADLEY	
BRITT, NANCY JANE	1835	NC	103	1900	AR		045	1 1856	NC	103	SIMON PETER WATERS	20007
BRITT, WILLIAM				1812	NC	037		1 C1789	NC	037	MARY BRACEWELL	27441
BRITTAIN, JAMES	C1699				NC		?073	1 C1726	VA		MARY WITTY	60366
BROCK, HULEY	C1826	NC			TX			1 C1860	?TN		JULIA	60239
BROGDON, MALACHI	1784	NC		1859	SC			1 C1805	SC		MARY TOBIAS	17005
BROGDON, MEREDITH	1754	NC	099	1844	GA			1			ELEANOR REDFERN	03041
BROOKS, AARON	C1794	NC	?086	1858	GA							60332
BROOKS, DAVID	C1786	NC	046					1 1810	NC	086	ELIZABETH SMART	02412
								2 C1815	NC	086		
BROOKS, ELIZABETH							060	1 1754	NC	005	JACOB HEYL	25087
BROOKS, ELOISE	1905	NC	009				011	1 1929	NC	009	ROBERT CALHOUN JORDAN	11145
BROOKS, HOWARD LUCAS	1875	NC	053	1958	NC	009		2 C1895	NC	009	MARY ELIZA WINDLEY	11145
BROOKS, ISAAC	1727	?EN		1825	NC	022	073	1	?VA		RUTH TERRELL	20007
								2			HANNAH HARPER	

ANCESTOR INDEX	BIRTH	PL	CO	DEATH	PL	CO	LIVD	MARRIED	PL	CO	SPOUSE NAME	CODE
BROOKS, JAMES JEREMIAH	C1839	NC	078	1898	NC	078		1 1883	NC	078	SALLIE ANNE COMPTON	60559
BROOKS, JEREMIAH	C1773	VA		1871	NC	078		1 1795	NC	020	ELIZABETH THOMAS	60559
BROOKS, JOAB SR	C1735	ENG		1775	NC	022	?073	1 C1760			KATHERINE DIMMAUX	19230
BROOKS, JOHN JR	C1785	NC	079	C1851	NC	?079		1 C1814	NC	079	SUSANNAH BLOUNT	06050
								2	NC	079	MARY KENNEDY	
BROOKS, JOHN, ESQ	1690	ENG		1767	NC	073	011	1	ENG		SUSAN	20007
BROOKS, LARKIN	C1790				NC		078	1 C1810			NANCY SMITH	60388
BROOKS, LOGAN	C1814	NC	078	C1880	NC	078		1 C1835	NC		MARY SUSAN PEARCE	60559
BROOKS, NANCY	1827	NC	086	1902	TX							60332
BROOKS, PRISCILLA	1725	VA			NC	081		1 1746	VA		JOHN LEWIS	60362
BROOKS, STEPHEN	1728			1797	NC	053		1			MARY FARROW	20335
BROOKS, SUSANNAH WARREN	1815	NC	022	1883	NC	022		1	NC		SHERWOOD WHITE	20007
BROOKS, TINEY/TIMEY/TINNA	C1812	NC		C1882	NC	084	078	1 C1842	?VA		VINCENT BRANN	60388
BROOKS, WILLIAM	1745	PA		1844	NC	086		1 C1784			NANCY	02412
BROOKS, WILLIAM N	1813			1860	NC	053		1			MAHETTABLE TUNNELL	20335
BROOKS, WILLIAM TERRELL	1767	NC	073	1824	NC	022		1 1792	NC	022	SUSANNAH WARREN	20007
BROWN, ALSEY	1787	NC		1871	IL			1 1809	NC	028	JOHN CASS MOYE	08053
BROWN, AMOS M	1815	NC		1876	NC	035		1			ANNIE JANE BATTS	08219
BROWN, ANDERSON G	1828	NC		1904	IL		046	1 C1856	IL		ELIZA J	60504
BROWN, ANDREW JACKSON	1783	NC	060	1863	MO			1 1803	NC	060	ISABELLA YOUNG	60200
								2 1815	NC	060	SARAH MILLER	
BROWN, BENJAMIN	C1807	NC		C1865	NC	102		1 C1834			NANCY TUGMAN	60557
BROWN, BRANSON/BRENSON/BRANT	1832	NC	081	1875	IL		046	1 1855	IL		ISABELLA JANE SHEPHARD	60504
BROWN, CATHERINE PERMELIA	1800	NC	085					1 1816	NC	085	ABRAHAM TEAGUE	13105
BROWN, CECIL C	1869	NC	099	1909	NC	099		1 1899	NC	099	CORA LESTER DILLARD	02450
BROWN, DANIEL	C1710			C1791	NC	081		1			GRACE THOMPSON	60485
BROWN, DOUGLAS REAMS	1954	NC	099									02450
BROWN, EMELINE DAVIS	1861	NC	011	1918	NC	027		1 C1878	NC	027	MILLARD FILMORE OWEN	27562
BROWN, FANNY		NC					046	1	IL		MR SPOON	60504
BROWN, FANNY, MRS	C1801	NC			IL		046	1 C1819	NC			60504
BROWN, FREDERICK		NC	?011	1779	SC			1 C1760			MISS BRITTAIN	60498
BROWN, HANNAH	C1835	NC			IL		046	1 C1854	IL		JAMES A HOUSER	60504
BROWN, HOWELL	1779	NC		C1870	NC	035		1			PENNEY	08219
BROWN, ISAAC	1796	NC		1878	IN			1			MRS MARY MENDENHALL	60386
BROWN, JACOB	1755	NC	073	1831	NC			1 1776	NC		MRS MARY ARMFIELD	60386
BROWN, JAMES	C1738	IRE		1788	TN		085	1 C1759	?VA		JANE GILLESPIE	19230
BROWN, JAMES	C1711	VA		C1770	NC	010						20415
BROWN, JAMES	1812	NC	011	1876	NC	011		1 C1839	NC	011	MARY JANE LOCK	27562

24

ANCESTOR INDEX	BIRTH	PL	CO	DEATH	PL	CO	LIVD	MARRIED	PL	CO	SPOUSE NAME	CODE
BROWN, JAMES	C1805	NC		C1874	MO		064	1 C1839	NC	?014	HAZY	60400
BROWN, JAMES JR	C1805	NC	099		NC	099		1 1824	NC	099	MARY GRADY	02450
BROWN, JAMES SR	C1751	MD			NC	099						02450
BROWN, JANE	C1837	NC	073					1			WILLIAM WOODS	60305
BROWN, JEREMIAH	1771	NC	005	1838	MO			1			MARY ANN BALLARD	20245
BROWN, JOEL	C1750	NC	?010	C1835	TN			1 C1722	NC	010	MARY SEAY	20415
BROWN, JOHN CHARLES	1847	NC	064	1905	MO			1 1877	MO		GRACE EMMELINE TURNBOUGH	60400
BROWN, MARY	1777	NC	010	1846	TN			1 1800	NC	010	JOHN R ACREE	20415
BROWN, MARY	C1785	NC	011	C1830	NC	011		1 1806	NC	011	ALEXANDER CALEZANCE MILLER	27286
BROWN, MILTON		NC					046					60504
BROWN, NANCY	1798	NC	081	1872	IL		085	1 1823	NC	081	GEORGE HENDRICKS	60323
BROWN, NANCY ANN	1788	NC		1847	IN			1 1806	NC	092	JOHN HOPPES	60454
BROWN, NANCY CLORINDA	1839	NC	006	1930	WA			1 1859	NC	102	WILLIAM HAYES	60557
BROWN, PETER		NC					046					60504
BROWN, RANCHER A	1833	NC		1909	IL		046	1 C1859	IL		LUCENIA MAX	60504
								2 C1866	IL		MARIAH	
								3 1878	IL		MARY FELTNER	
BROWN, REBECCA								1 1801	NC	099	DAVID HOLDER	60591
BROWN, REGINALD REAMS	1926	NC	099					1 1947	NC	099	EMMA JEAN JONES	02450
BROWN, ROBERT	C1819	NC	010		NC	010		1			SUSAN ANDREWS	60280
								2			PENACE EARLY	
								3				
								4			VIRGINIA PITTMAN	
BROWN, ROYAL REAMS	1906	NC	099	1947	NC	099		1 1925	SC		NORMA BLANCHE WESTER	02450
BROWN, SARAH	1820	NC		1872	IL		046	1	IL		SAMUEL LAYTON	60504
								2			WILLIAM SHEPHARD/SHEPHERD	
BROWN, THOMAS				1812	NC	028		1			AMEY	08053
BROWN, THOMAS SR	C1720			C1800	NC	011						27286
BROWN, THOMAS W	1812	NC	092	1872	MO			1 C1830			EASTER ALLRED	02478
								2 1860			MRS NANCY E (BLADES) HOOD BATSON	
BROWN, THOMAS, GEN	1744	NC	011	1814	NC	011		1 1780				27286
BROWN, THOMAS, I	C1675	VA		1718	NC	024		1 C1700	?NC		CHRISTIAN MAULE	20415
BROWN, WILLIAM					?TN		092					02478
BROWN, WILLIAM C	1817	NC	039	1896	NC	039	044	1 C1850	NC	039	MATILDA COGHILL PENDERGRASS	02435
BROWN, WILLIAM C	1832	NC	099	1891	NC	099		1 1854	NC	056	EMILY A JONES	02450
BROWN, WILLIAM GEORGE WASHINGTON	C1760	?NC					060	1	NC		ELIZABETH THOMPSON	60200
BROWN, ZIMRI	1801	NC		1851	IN			1 C1822	KY		JANE DOLLARHIDE	60271
BROWNLOW, JAMES	C1774	NC	022	C1817	TN			1	NC	022	MARY	60460
BROWNLOW, JOHN					NC	029		1	NC	029	SARAH COUNCIL	60460
								2 1770	NC	022	REBECCA EVANS	
BROWNLOW, JOHN	C1795	NC	022	C1774				1 C1815	TN		GRIGSBY	60460

ANCESTOR INDEX	BIRTH	PL	CO	DEATH	PL	CO	LIVD	MARRIED	PL	CO	SPOUSE NAME	CODE
BRUTON/BREWTON, DAVID	C1739	?VA		1816	SC			1 C1761	NC	005		60531
BRUTON/BREWTON, JAMES	C1763	NC	005	1816	?AL							60531
BRUTON/BREWTON, SAMUEL	C1763	NC	005									60531
BRYAN, ELIZABETH	1776	NC	085	1869	MO			1 C1796			OLIVER HAMPTON	08023
BRYAN, JAMES M	1809	NC	013	1890	NC	050		1			JANE CHILDERS	09030
BRYAN, MARY ANN	1804	NC	037	1880	GA			1 1825			JESSE JOLLEY	10120
BRYAN, MORGAN	1671			1763	NC	085		1 1719			MARTHA STRODE	08023
BRYAN, SAMUEL SR		PA		1798	NC	085		1			ELIZABETH MCMAHAN	08023
BRYAN/BRYANT, FREDERICK	C1750	?NC	?009	C1821	NC	079		1 1780			AMELIA PUGH	60414
BRYAN/BRYANT, FREDERICK JAMES HENRY PUGH	1838			C1920	NC	079		1	NC	079	HARRIET LOUISE BRYANT	60414
BRYAN/BRYANT, JAMES	C1808				NC	079		1	NC	079	PRISCILLA WHITEHURST	60414
BRYAN/BRYANT, WILLIAM	C1777	?NC	?079		NC	079		1 C1802	NC	079	MARY MANNING	60414
BRYAN/BRYANT, WILLIAM	C1720	?NC	?024		NC	?079		1			MARY BLOUNT	60414
BRYAN/BRYANT, WILLIAM	C1682	VA			?NC	?010		1			MARY	60414
BRYANT, JOHN THOMAS	1815	NC		1893	IA			1 1839	IN		ELIZABETH SANDY	60442
								2 1842	IN		MARGARET STIERWALT	
BRYANT, JOSEPH	C1775	NC	063		NC	047		1			MRS CATHERINE BRYANT	60594
BRYANT, THOMAS		NC	?092	1854	IN			1	NC			60442
BRYANT/BRIANT, ROLAND		NC					044	1			MARY ROSA HUNT	02355
BUCHANAN, ARTHUR	C1776	?NC	094	C1825	NC	014		1 C1805	?NC	014	TEMPERANCE VANCE	02470
BUCHANAN, CALVIN JOSEPH MINTER	C1825	NC	022	1864	MS			1 C1845	MS		RUTH M BATEMAN	60078
BUCHANAN, GEORGE W	1818	NC	014	1885	VA			1 C1845	VA		SARAH HAMILTON	02470
BUCHANAN, HENRY GRADY	1893	NC	044	1966	LA			1 1917	AR		LUCILLE MARSHALL	06065
BUCHANAN, JAMES				C1805	NC	014		1	?NC	094	ELIZABETH WILLIS	02470
BUCHANAN, JAMES	1765	NC		1858	NC	055		1			MARTHA BLACK	20220
BUCHANAN, JOHN RUFFIN	1830	NC	044	1915	NC	044		1 1852	NC	044	NANCY A PITTARD	06065
BUCHANAN, JOSEPH MINTER	C1802	NC	?022					1 1822	NC	022	MARTHA H H BUCHANAN	60078
BUCHANAN, JOSEPH SPEARS	C1783	NC	099	1853	MS			1	NC		CHARITY WILLIAMS	60078
BUCHANAN, MARTHA G	C1799	NC	?044	C1875	TN			1 1816	NC	044	THOMAS A MITCHELL	60337
BUCHANAN, MARTHA H H	C1804	NC		C1846	MS			1 1822	NC	022	JOSEPH MINTER BUCHANAN	60078
BUCHANAN, WILLIAM RUFFIN	1865	NC	044	1904	NC	044		1 1891	NC	044	VIRGINIA TUNSTALL	06065
BUCK, DANIEL HARGETT	C1855							1 1874	NC		VITIA CASSIE GARNER	27537
								2			FANNIE SABISTON	
BUFFALOE, ARTHUR					NC	?071						24139
BUFFALOE, HENRY	C1740	?NC	?010	1806	NC	099	?071	1 C1773	?NC		NANCY EMBRY	24139
BUFFALOE, JAMES TURNER	C1842	TN		1913	LA			1 C1875	NC		WINEFRED JANE BUFFALOE	27302
BUFFALOE, MATTHEW	C1739			1820			071	1 C1758			NANNY	27302

ANCESTOR INDEX	BIRTH	PL	CO	DEATH	PL	CO	LIVD	MARRIED		PL	CO	SPOUSE NAME	CODE
BUFFALOE, MATTHEW G	C1800	NC	?071					1	1839	TN		KEZIAH BROWN	27302
BUFFALOE, VERNON SIDNEY	C1876	NC	?099	1946	AR			1	1904	MS		MINNIE AGNES HARGROVE	27302
BUFFALOE, WILLIAM	C1760	NC		1858			071	1	C1799			WINEFRED VOLUNTINE	27302
BUFFKIN, BENJAMIN H	1757			1849	?SC		027	1				FATHEREE	24032
BUFFKIN, BETHEL	1806	SC		1881			027	1				MARY CROWSON	24032
BUFFKIN, ELENDER/ELEANOR	1837	NC	027	1906	NC	027		1	1859	?NC	027	JOSHUA SOLES	24032
BUFFORD, N FRANCIS		NC			GA			1				JOHN RUFUS AMOS	60308
BUIE, ANN	1814	NC	083				005	1				MR CUNNINGHAM	27697
BUIE, DANIEL	1797	NC	068				005	1				MARY LEMMONS	27697
BUIE, GILBERT		NC	083				005	1				NANCY	27697
								2				CATHERINE	
BUIE, JOHN		NC	083				005						27697
BUIE, JOHN ALEXANDER	1816	NC	083				005						27697
BUIE, NEILL		NC	083				005	1				DOROTHY MERCER	27697
BUIE, WILLIAM	1770	SCO			NC	068	005	1				MARGARET MCIVER	27697
BULL, AMBROSE	C1750	NC	028	1789	NC	028		1	1777	NC	028	ELIZABETH MORAN	60461
BULL, JACOB AARON	1810	VA		1894	AR		020	1	1867	AR		FRANCES ELIZABETH BURFORD	60532
BULL, ROBERT	C1788	NC	028		AR			1	1811	GA		SUSANNAH SULLIVAN	60461
BULL, WILLIAM C	C1785	NC		1835	AL		020	1	1805	VA		ANNA TURNER	60532
BULLARD, CATHARINE/KATY	C1785	VA		C1861	NC	?029		1	1803	NC	029	JOHN MORGAN	13090
BULLARD, JAMES				1832	NC	011	083	1		NC	011	SARAH PITTMAN	20333
BULLARD, JOHN					IL		083	1		NC	011		20333
BULLARD, JOHN WILLIAM	1795	NC	011	1869	IL			1				MARY WEST	20333
BULLARD, ROBERT				1897	AL			1		NC	011	KATIE MCLEAN	20333
								2				SUSAN MIZELL	
BULLEN, JACOB	1785	NC	?085	C1854	IN			1				ISABEL	60264
BULLOCK, ALLEN	C1760	?NC					044						60490
BULLOCK, FRANCIS	C1760	?NC			AL		044	1	1767	NC		RACHEL VESTAL	60490
BULLOCK, JOHN	1768	?NC		1850	TN		044	1		NC			60490
								2	1832	TN		EFFIE HUDDLESTON	
BULLOCK, RICHARD	C1695	VA		1766	NC	044		1				ANNE HENLEY	23015
BULLOCK, SARAH	1720	VA					044	1				JOHN SIMS	23015
BUNCH, ISHMAEL	C1740	NC	024	1830	IN		077						60574
BUNCH, SOLOMON	1787	NC			TN			1		NC		ANN	60457
BUNN, ELIZABETH	1809	NC	005	1880	AL			1				DAVID MORGAN	60042
BUNN, GREEN WALKER	1788	NC	099	1851	NC	039		1	1813			MARY/POLLY WRENN	04065
BUNN, JESSE	C1760			1816	NC	099		2	1813			LEVINIA WALKER	04065
BUNN, JOSIAH H	1833	NC	039	1910	NC	039		1	1859			MARY MAE LAFATER	04065
BUNYARD, JOHN	C1785	NC		C1835	IN			1				NANCY	25185

ANCESTOR INDEX	BIRTH	PL	CO	DEATH	PL	CO	LIVD	MARRIED	PL	CO	SPOUSE NAME	CODE
BURCH, CHARLES HILL	1861	NC	073	1927	NC	036		1 1903	NC	022	VELLA LEE HORTON	60110
BURCH, ELIJAH	1774	IRE		1847	NC	073		1 1813	NC	073	ELEANOR/NELLY MASON	60110
BURCH, WILLIAM HENRY	1816	NC	073	1889	NC	073		1 1856	NC	073	MARGARET BURROUGHS LONG	60110
BURCHAM, JOHN SR	C1738	VA		C1812	NC	092		1 1758	VA		ROSIANNA SWERINGEN	60022
BURCHAM, JOSEPH	1708	NJ		1775	NC	005		1 C1730	NC	070	REBECCA BORDON	60022
BURCHAM, LEVI	1774	VA		1854	VA			1 1794	NC	092	NANCY STONEMAN	60022
BURCHETT/BORCHETT, LAWSON	1817	NC	104		WV			1 C1845			ELIZABETH	60019
BURCHETT/BORCHETT, NANCY JANE	1846	NC	?104	1936	WV			1 1869	VA		ELI HAWKS	60019
BURFORD, PHILIP				1796	NC	100	?015					60532
BURFORD, PHILIP G G	1800	NC	100	1852	AR			1	TN		TABITHA TANKERSLY	60532
BURFORD, PHILIP TERRELL	1763	NC	?044	1834	TN		015	1 1781			RECECCA CLACK	60532
BURGESS, ABY	C1820	NC	018	1891	NC	018		1 1856	NC	018	PAUL PUGH/PEW	02180
BURGESS, HEZEKIAH/LONG'KIAH	C1802	NC	018					1 C1830	NC	018	LYDIA WRIGHT	02180
BURGESS, SIMEON	C1801	NC	018	1850	NC	018		1 C1830	NC	018	ELIZABETH TILLETT	02180
BURGIN/BURGAN, BENJAMIN/BEN	1743	WAL		1823	NC	014	085	1 1772	NC	085	LEAH MAN	23065
BURGIN/BURGAN, ELIZA	1817	NC	014	1909	NC	013	064	1 C1837	NC	014	LAMBERT CLINGMAN CLAYTON	23065
BURGIN/BURGAN, JOHN	1774	NC	085	1837	NC	014		1 C1797	NC	085	ELIZABETH/BETTY MAN	23065
BURK/BURKE, ANDREW	1816	NC	?085	1895	NC	038		1			POLLY ADER	60467
BURK/BURKE, EDWARD	1790			1872	NC	032		1			MARY	60467
BURKETT, FREDERICK	C1785	NC		C1845	WV							60560
BURNEY, ADAM	1765	NC	046	1849	AL			1			ELIZABETH CUNNINGHAM	60228
BURNEY, CHARLES		IRE		C1787	NC	046		1			MARY LACKEY	60228
BURNEY, SAMUEL	1763	NC	046	1849	AL			1			NANCY	60228
BURNS, AQUILLA	1738	VA		C1823	TN		085					06005
BURNS, BRICE	C1780	NC	104	1850	IN		?006	1 C1800	NC		LAVINIA	25087
BURNS, PHILIP	1759	NC	?085	1849	KY			1 C1786	NC	?014	CATHERINE	60062
								2 1814	KY		CATHERINE GILBERT	
BURNS/BURNES, JOHN A	C1740			C1805	NC	014	085	1 C1781	NC	085	ANNE WALKER	23065
BURNS/BURNES, SARAH	C1782	NC	014	C1865	NC	049		1 C1807	NC	014	JOHN LEATHERWOOD	23065
BURRIS, MARTIN	C1798	NC			IN			2 1837	OH		FRANCINA DENNY	04103
BURRIS, SOLOMON	1754	NC	?005	1845	NC	089		1 1783	NC	092	JUDITH TAYLOR	24165
BURROW, JOEL	C1778	VA		1825	AL		081	1 C1800	NC		ELIZABETH	60519
BURROW, PHILLIP	1774	?VA		1861	AR		046	1 1797	NC	073	MARGARET SHOFNER	60337
BURROW, WILLIAM	1808	AL		1863	MS		081	1 1835			SUSAN YORK	60519
BURT, HARDY	1798	NC	099	1844	MS			1			MARTHA LANE	07078
BURT, JOHN	C1750	VA		1820	NC	099		1			SUSAN	07078
BURT, LEROY	1803	NC	047	1869	TN			1 C1828			HESTER ANN	27546

ANCESTOR INDEX	BIRTH	PL	CO	DEATH	PL	CO	LIVD	MARRIED	PL	CO	SPOUSE NAME	CODE
BURTON, G WASHINGTON	C1811	VA		C1860	NC	090		1 1833	NC	090	MARY MANUEL	60494
BURTON, JAMES MADISON	1836	NC	090	C1900	VA			1 1858	VA		MUIRAM SHOWALTER	60494
BURTON, JOHN	1779	NC	046	1855	NC	046		1 C1812			CATHERINE STUART ?	08095
BURTON, NANCY KENAN	1759	NC		1854	AL			1	NC	035	WILLIAM FREDERICK	27356
BURTON, SAMUEL	C1782	NC	070	C1849	NC	070	?072	1 C1814	NC	070	ZILPHIA WHEELER	12210
BUTLER, JAMES AUGUSTUS	1863	NC	033	1908	NC	054		1 1897			NANNIE MARTIN	27475
BUTLER, JAMES AUGUSTUS	1907	NC	054					1 1932	NM		DORIS MATILDA COUMBE	27475
BUTLER, JOHN	C1726	VA		1787	SC		073	1			ANNE ARMSTRONG	17090
BUTLER, JOHN	C1821				NC	010		1			CAROLINE FAULK	60280
BUTLER, LUCIUS QUINTUS CINCIN NATIUS	1806	NC	054	1886	KY		033	1 2 1845			ELIZABETH ADELINE WHITLOCK AMELIA ELVIRA PRATHER	27475
BUTLER, MARCUS	C1846	NC	010		NC	010		1 1866			MARY CAROLINE BROWN	60280
BUTLER, WILLIAM	C1736	VA		1790	SC		073	1 C1759	NC	073	PHOEBE CHILDRESS	17090
BUTLER, WILLIAM	C1741			1790	SC		081	1			PHOEBE CHILDRESS	27475
BUTLER, WILLIAM	1770	NC	046	1883	NC	054	081	1 1799 2 1804	NC NC		ANNA GOODEN ELIZABETH BEAN	27475
BYERS, MILLY M	1811	NC		1862	NC	086		1 1827 2 1834	NC NC	086 086	NOAH SULLINS JACOB BROOKS	02412
BYRD, GEORGE W	1791	VA		1871	NC	107	064	2			ELIZABETH	60430
BYRD, GEORGE WASHINGTON/WASH	C1851	NC	107				064					60430
BYRD, JOEL		NC			GA							17025
BYRD, MALCOLM/MACK B/BERRY	1848	NC	107	1933	NC	107		1 1871	NC	107	ALLEY E DEYTON	60430
BYRD, MRS ELIZABETH	1810	NC		1901	NC	107		1			GEORGE W BYRD	60430
BYRD, NANCY CAROLINE	1835	NC		1894	TN		107	1 C1849	NC	107	WILLIAM ENSLEY MCCOURRY	60430
BYRD, ROBERT	1817	NC		1883	GA			1 1846	GA		MARY ANN BOWERS	17025
BYRD, RUTH	1850	NC	107	1929				1			THOMAS MCCOURRY	60430
BYRD, WILLIAM	C1801	NC		C1881	TN			1	TN		ELIZABETH SHOOPMAN	60390
BYRD/BIRD, EDWARD		NC	010	1802	NC	087		1			MARY KING	02550
BYRD/BIRD, JOHN				1716	NC	024		1 1697	NC	077	REBECCA SUTTON PETERSON	02550
BYRD/BIRD, JOHN		NC	?024	1761	NC	035	?010	1			CATHERINE KING	02550

C

CABLE, CASPER	1755			C1827			?104	1			ELIZABETH BAKER	20350
CABLE, JACOB	C1785	NC	?104				?102	1			NANCY BOLLINGER	20350
CABLE, MILEY PEMIE	1845	NC		1910	TX			1 C1864			JACOB A MABERY	60580
CAFFEY, LEVEN STOKES	1819	NC		1885	MO			1 1844	TN		CELIA PERRY	20385
CAFFEY, THOMAS	C1793	NC		1890	MO			1 1812	NC		SARAH STOKES	20385

ANCESTOR INDEX	BIRTH	PL	CO	DEATH	PL	CO	LIVD	MARRIED		PL	CO	SPOUSE NAME	CODE
CAGLE, LITTLETON YOUNG	1809	NC		1899	TN			1				KATIE ROSS	60044
CAIN, ANDREW	C1818	NC	046	C1867				1	1842			NANCY JANE FLIN	60398
CAIN, DANIEL	1789	NC		1862	KY			1	1808			TEMPERANCE/TEMPY VANNOY	02252
								2		KY		ELIZABETH HUSKE	
CAIN, JOHN	1760	NC			NC	?046		1	1802	NC	090	MARTHA KNIGHT	60261
CAIN, PETER	C1765	NC		C1814	KY			1				CATHERINE	02252
								2				CATHERINE	
CAIN, THOMAS		?DE		1838	NC	033		1				MARY	04050
CALDWELL, ALEXANDER	C1735	PA		1784	NC	046		1	C1770	PA		MARGARET	20085
CALDWELL, MARGARET		NC	046					1	1804	TN		JOHN M ROGERS	20085
CALDWELL, MARTHA		NC	046					1	1813	TN		PHILIP COLE	20085
CALDWELL, MARY		NC	046					1		TN		PETER NOE	20085
CALDWELL, RACHEL		NC	046										20085
CALDWELL, SAMUEL	1772	NC	046	1841	TN			1	C1798	TN		MARY ROGERS	20085
CALDWELL, THOMAS	1779	NC	046	1857	TN			1		TN		ELEANOR	20085
CALLAHAN, DAVID HARRIS	1856	NC	011	1910	NC	011		1				ANNIE DAVIS	60000
CALLAHAN, ISAAC	1780	IRE		1864	NC	011		1				JARRE TURNER	60000
CALLAWAY, JOSHUA	1757	?NC	?072	1816	GA		085	1	1778	NC	?005	ISABELLA GRAVES HENDERSON	60008
CALLEN, JOHN KERR	C1805	NC	?065	C1866	AL		?016	1				NANCY SERINA KENNEDY	60360
CALLEN, NANCY	C1807	NC	?065		AL			1				LAIRD KIRKPATRICK	60360
CALLICOATTE, SPENCER CLAYBORN	C1816	NC	?081	C1877	TX			1	1841	NC	081	SALINA SPENCER	06159
CAMERON, JOHN 'MERCHANT'	C1749	SCO		C1804	NC	068		1				MARGARET MONROE	22005
CAMERON, NEIL	1805	NC		1874	MO			1	1837	MO		MRS MERCY CARLISLE	60221
								2	1846	MO		FRANCES MATSON	
								3	1863	MO		MRS BERTHAMIA HANCOCK	
CAMERON, NEILL		NC	068		NC	068		1	1809	NC	068	MARY WORTHY	22005
CAMERON, NEILL BLUE	1859	NC	068	1940	NC	068		1	1881	NC	068	MARTHA ADELAIDE WADSWORTH	22005
CAMERON, ROSA JANETTE	1882	NC	068	1952	NC	068		1	1909	NC	068	GEORGE WASHINGTON GARNER	22005
CAMERON, WILLIAM PITT	1824	NC	068	1898	NC	068		1	1853	NC	068	FLORA BAKER	22005
								2	1858	NC	068	CATHERINE BLUE	
CAMPBELL, ARCHIBALD	C1760			1820	AL		073	1	1784	NC	073	REBECCA KIRK	08070
CAMPBELL, DUNCAN GREEN	1787	NC	073	1828	GA			1	1808	GA		MARY WILLIAMSON	08070
CAMPBELL, ELIZA JANE	1808	NC		1897	AL		011	1	1824			OWEN SWINDAL	27269
CAMPBELL, JAMES	C1750	VA		1814	NC	047		1	C1772			SUSANNAH MASON ?	25100
CAMPBELL, JAMES				1842			011	1	1786			KATHRINE LAMON	27269
CAMPBELL, JOHN					NC			1				MARY EDWARDS	08070
CAMPBELL, JOHN	1775	NC		1837	AL		047	1				DRUSILLA S	25100
CAMPBELL, LAUGHLIN				1791	NC	081							60194
CAMPBELL, MARGARET	C1752			1808	NC	022		1		NC		JAMES UNDERWOOD	60194

ANCESTOR INDEX	BIRTH	PL	CO	DEATH	PL	CO	LIVD	MARRIED	PL	CO	SPOUSE NAME	CODE
CAMPBELL, MARGARET ANN	1764			1816	NC	065		1 C1785	NC	065	MOSES NEELY	60518
CANNADY, WAGSTAFF				C1812	NC	099		1			BETHALEM	03035
CANNON, CATHERINE	C1774	NC	079	C1855	NC	079		1 C1800	NC	079	HARDEE JOHNSON	13264
CANNON, ELIJAH	C1804	NC	?014	C1865	AL			1 C1830	NC		ELIZABETH	60444
CANNON, LEWIS	C1745	NC	079	1818	NC	028		1 C1780	NC	?079	SARAH PUGH	13264
CANNON, WILLIAM F	1820	NC					064	1 1844	NC	006	ELIZABETH SHULL	03041
CANTERBURY, GIDEON							?092					25223
CANTERBURY, JEDATHEN		VA		C1785	NC	104	?092					25223
CANTERBURY, JONATHAN							?092					25223
CANTRELL, CHARLES	1753	NC	073									08190
CANTRELL, ELIJAH/ELI	1794	NC	084					1			MRS MARTHA CLEBURN	08190
CANTRELL, SAMUEL	C1813	NC			MO			1 C1843	?KY		MARGARET	17213
CARADINE, THOMAS	C1756			1820	SC		085					60167
CARAWAN, WILLIAM				1804	NC	053		1			AMY GREEN ?	20335
CARDWELL, THOMAS	C1747	VA		1800	NC	044		1 C1779	VA		MARY WILSON	17090
CARLETON/CARLTON, ELIZABETH	1701	IRE		C1788	NC	085		1 1722	PA		WILLIAM WHITAKER	23065
CARLILE, JAMES	1762	NC	037	1839	KY			1 C1779	KY		ELIZABETH CATES	60322
CARLOCK, MARGARET/PEGGY	C1784	NC		C1855	TN		016	1 1803	NC	016	BENJAMIN MASSEY	27560
								2 1815	TN		ABEL WILLIAMS	
								3 C1817	TN		ROBERT REED	
CARLTON, LYDIA	C1780	NC	?035		TN			1 1823	NC	?035	WILLIAM MATHIS	60083
CARLTON, THOMAS	C1760	PA			NC	?035						60083
CARMICHAEL, ARCHIBALD	C1753	SCO		C1827	NC	090	020	1 C1774			ELIZABETH NIX	17075
CARMICHAEL, DUNCAN	1754			1834	NC	090	020	1 1772	?VA		CHARITY WITT	17075
CARMICHAEL, DUNCAN/DUNKIN	1754			1834	NC	090	020	1			CHARITY WITT	03065
CARMICHAEL, JOHN HENRY	1789	IRE		C1874	CA			1 1819	NC	073	NANCY STALCUP	60017
CARMICHAEL, JOHN WESLEY	1820	NC	090	1877	IN			1 1840	IN		SUSANNAH CARMICHAEL	17075
CARMICHAEL, JOSEPH	1796	NC	020	1839	IN			1 1818	NC	090	ELIZABETH HOLDER	17075
CARMICHAEL, SOLOMON	1794	NC	020	1883	IN			1 1812	NC	090	SAYRE/SARAH/SALLY GRUBBS	17075
CARMICHAEL, SUSANNA	1821	NC	090	1906	IN			1 1840	IN		JOHN WESLEY CARMICHAEL	17075
CARPENTER WILLIAM R	1828	NC	104		NC	104		1 1858	NC	104	HENRIETTA SMITH	60001
CARPENTER, ELIZABETH	1781	NC		1861	SC			1 1801			JOHN WADSWORTH	27740
CARPENTER, MARY	1823	NC						1			JOHN W MAY	60358
CARR, WILLIAM	1814	NC	084	1875	IL			1 1839	NC		NANCY FOSSETT	60266
CARR/KERR, ESTHER	1797	NC	065					1 1819	NC	065	ELIHU J MCCRACKEN	14050
CARRIGAN, CALVIN	C1814	NC	?073					1			SARAH CRAWFORD	27775
CARROLL, ABSALOM	1762	NC	056	C1828	MS			1				60112
								2				
								3				
								4 C1800	SC		ELEANOR ROBINSON	

ANCESTOR INDEX	BIRTH	PL	CO	DEATH	PL	CO	LIVD	MARRIED	PL	CO	SPOUSE NAME	CODE
CARROLL, JESSE JR	1774	NC	035	1828	NC	087		1 1801	NC	087	MARGARET/PEGGY MERRITT	17080
CARROLL, JESSE SR	C1750	NC	044	1802	NC	087	039	1 1769	NC	087	MARY RACHEL GAVIN	17080
CARROLL, JOHN	1798	NC		C1875	GA			1 C1825	GA		CYNTHIA	60082
CARROLL, JOHN	C1720			1761	NC	056		1 C1740			STANDLEY	60112
CARROLL, LEWIS	1808	NC	087	1872	NC	087		1 1832	NC	087	CATHERINE ELIZA LAMB	17080
CARROLL, RACHEL	1826	NC	087	1932	NC	029	035	1 1855	NC	087	ISHAM ROYALL	17080
CARROLL, SARAH	1806	NC		1864	TN			1 C1821	TN		PHILIP LOW	60390
CARROLL, WILLIAM	C1720	VA		1781	NC	044	039	1 C1750	VA		ELIZABETH	17080
CARRUTHERS, JOHN	C1710	SCO		C1751	NC	028		1			CONTENT	07078
CARRUTHERS, SAMUEL MITCHELL	1789	NC	?009	1845	MS			1 1811	TN		NAOMI BROWN	07078
CARRUTHERS, WILLIAM	1736	NC	028	1811	NC	009		1 1773	NC	?009	SARAH HARVEY	07078
CARSON, PETER		NJ		C1815	SC			1 1786	NC	060	RACHAEL COX	60238
CARTER, ALEXANDER	1774	NC	035	1852	NC	028	103	1 1795	NC	035	SARAH HERRING	13264
								2 1803	NC	035	SUSANNA STEWART	
								3 1841	NC	028	MARY CASEY	
								4 C1849	NC	028	JENNET	
CARTER, AUGUSTUS HENRY	1820	NC	056									20450
CARTER, BIRBEN JACKSON	1819	NC	056									20450
CARTER, DANIEL BRYANT	1797	NC	035	1859	NC	035		1 C1813	NC	035	NANCY WARD	13264
CARTER, EDWARD	C1675	VA		1736	NC	070	010					13264
CARTER, EDWARD	C1710	NC	028	C1794	NC	059	070	1			ELIZABETH	13264
CARTER, EDWARD POLK	1849	NC	084	1900	KY			1 1864	TN		MARTHA JANE POTTER	27599
CARTER, ELISABETH	C1822	NC	092	1913	NC	104	106	1			JOHN T WOODRUFF	10010
CARTER, EMILY JANE	1823	NC	056	1907	MD			1 1842	NC	056	HENRY GERHARDT	20450
CARTER, G W	1818						084	1			S A	27599
CARTER, HARRIET COLSON	1831	NC	056					1 1851	NC	056	JOHN C F GERHARDT	20450
CARTER, HENRY	1811	NC	046	1877	IA		022	1 1835	IN		CELIA MORRIS	27420
CARTER, ISAAC	C1750			1802	NC	092		1 C1770			MARY BRAY	02357
CARTER, ISAAC	C1750	PA		1802	NC	092	022	1 C1771			MARY BRAY	27420
CARTER, JAMES MONROE	1829	NC	056	C1865	NC	056		1 1857	NC	056	JULIA ROBERTS	20450
CARTER, JOHN C	1872	NC	103	1931	NC	059		1			DORAH MEASLEY	07040
CARTER, JOSEPH	C1771			1841	NC	092		1			MARGARET HINSHAW	02357
CARTER, LOVE	C1819	NC	022	1908	MO			1 1839	NC	020	RILEY WILSON WILLIAMS	13006
CARTER, MARY ELEANOR	1834	NC	056					1 1855	NC	056	WILLIAM HARTSFIELD	20450
CARTER, MARY VIVIAN	1901	NC	059					1 1919	NC	103	BENNIE HENRY MOZINGO	07040
CARTER, RUTH	1792			1882	NC	106		1 1814	NC	092	BENJAMIN HINSHAW	02357
CARTER, SOLOMON	C1715	NC	028	1809	NC	035	070	1 C1760	NC	035	CONSTANTINA	13264
CARTER, SOLOMON	1787	NC	022	1833	IN		092	1 C1810			JANE REYNOLDS	27420

32

ANCESTOR INDEX	BIRTH	PL	CO	DEATH	PL	CO	LIVD	MARRIED	PL	CO	SPOUSE NAME	CODE
CARTER, WILLIAM	C1705	NC	028		NC	028						13264
CARTER, WILLIAM	1791	NC	056	1835	NC	056		1 1818	NC	056	APSOBETH OLIVER	20450
CARTER, WILLIAM BRYANT	1855	NC	057	1902	NC	057	035	1 C1880	NC	059	BARBARA EMMALINE HOWARD	13264
CARTER, ZENOS	1825	NC	035	1914	NC	057	059	1 C1848	NC	035	HEPHZIBAH JANE CAVANAUGH	13264
CARTWRIGHT, JOSEPH M JR	1773	NC	092					1 1799	KY		MARY WHITE	60152
CARTWRIGHT, JOSEPH SR		NC	?085	C1777	NC	104		1 1770	NC	085	EVE MILLER	60152
CARUTHERS, ROBERT	C1740	?NC		1811	TN		016	1		NC	MARGARET WHITE	60093
CARVER, ELIZABETH	C1780	NC						1 C1798	NC	029	NEILL BEARD	60571
CARVER, NANCY	1804	NC	078	C1879	NC	078		1 C1827			JOHN B OAKLEY	60543
CARVER, ROBERT				C1796	NC	011	029	1			ELIZABETH NEWBERRY	30571
CARVER, ROBERT				C1796	NC	?011	?029	1			ELIZABETH NEWBERRY	60571
CARWELL, ROY C	C1891	?PA					068	1 C1921	SC		ORADELL FEENEY	19183
								2 C1931			MINNIE ALMA	
CASEY, STEVEN	1818	NC	053	1891	NC			1			SARA JANE BARNETT	13120
CASH, HOWELL							020					60590
CASH, JAMES							044					60590
CASH, JOSEPH							044					60590
CASH, MARY FRANCIS		NC						1			MR CHEAIRS	60590
CASH, MOSES							020					60590
CASH, PETER							044					60590
CASH, WILLIAM							104					60590
CASPER, CANDICE	1957	CA						1 1978	NC	084	CHARLES SETLIFF	60417
CASPER, LONNIE ELDON	1934	NE						1 1959	NC	084	ROSEMARY NELSON	60417
CASPER, LONNIE ERNEST	1906	NE						1 1926	CO		MARY OPAL BOLLMAN	60417
								2 C1970	NC	084	NORMA NELSON	
CASSELL, JOHN AUTHOR/ARTHAR		NC			AR							60073
CASSTEVENS, THOMAS	1804	NC	?092	1852	IL			1 1826	TN		HESTER MASSY/MASSEY	60212
CATE, JOHN	C1753						?073					60501
CATE, SUSANNA	1807	NC	073	1884	TN			1 C1826	?TN		WILLIAM CATE	25199
CATE, THOMAS		NC		C1843	TN			1 1797	NC	073	ESTHER HASTINGS	25199
CATES, ADOLPHINE/DOLPHIN	C1827	NC						1			MARY	03120
CATES, CHARLES	C1785	?NC						1			CHARLOTTE	03120
CATES, CHARLES WILSON	C1822	NC						1			SARAH LYONS	03120
CATES, FELIX GRUNDE	1829	NC		1883				1			MELVINY ROBERTS	03120
CATES, LUELLEN	C1832	NC										03120
CATES, MELISSA	C1826	NC						1			STERLING CAPLE	03120
CATES, MINERVA J	1810	NC		1880				1			STEPHEN S BOOTH	03120
CATES, RICHARD GRANDE	1812	NC		1886				1			MARGUERITE WAINWRIGHT	03120

ANCESTOR INDEX	BIRTH	PL	CO	DEATH	PL	CO	LIVD	MARRIED	PL	CO	SPOUSE NAME	CODE
CATES, SUSAN	C1825	NC						1			MR MCMILLAN	03120
CATES, SYDNEY	C1822	NC						1			MARTHA FARROW	03120
CATHEY, ANDREW	1810	?NC		1858	MO			1			JANE ROSS	60101
CATHEY, GEORGE	C1714	IRE		C1789	NC	?014		1			JEAN	60101
CATHEY, GEORGE	1747	VA		1840	MO		?065	1	NC	?014	MARGARET CHAMBERLAIN	60101
CATHEY, GEORGE	C1787	NC		C1850	MO			1 1832	MO		ANNE MCFARLAND	60101
CATHEY, JAMES	C1684	IRE		1757	NC	085		1	IRE		ANN	60101
CATHEY, JOHN	C1750			C1824	IN		085	1			MARY LOCKE	60575
CATLETTE, LABON	1805	NC	044	1899	NC	039		1 1827	NC	044	EMILY RUDD	02435
								2 C1843	NC	044	DELACYE NAILING	
CATO, BENJAMIN	1777	NC										11100
CAUSEY, THOMAS	1797	NC	046	1865	NC	046		1 1819	NC	073	MARY WIMBLEY	05059
								2 1865	NC	046	EMILY JANE KIRKHAN	
CAUSEY, ZEBULON	C1750	?MD		1809	NC	046		1 C1770	DE		DIANA KIMMEY	21167
CAVE, JOHN	1795	VA		C1865	MO		092	1 1819	NC	092	JANE TOLBERT/TALBOTT	27348
CAVNESS, HENRY	1813	NC		C1855	TN			1	NC		CLOA	60457
CHAFFIN, CHARLES STANLEY	1845	NC	033	1914	KS			1 1869	IN		AMELIA FRANCIS ELLIS	60309
								2 1880	KS		HULDAH CLEMENTINE ALLMON	
								3 1908	KS		LIA A RAYROLDO	
CHAFFIN, JOHN ANDREW	1803	NC	085	1836	TX			1 1825	NC	085	EMILY GAITHER	60309
CHAFFIN, MARTIN ROWAN	C1829	NC	085	C1925	NC	033	036	1 1858	NC		MARY F MCCLENNON	60309
								2 1865	NC		EMMA FRANCIS BROCK	
CHAFFIN, NATHAN STANLEY	1819	NC	085					1			BAKER	60309
								2			ELVIRA GLASCOCK	
CHAFFIN, STANDLEY	C1783							1 1805	NC	085	ELLINDER BRYAN	60309
								2 1815	NC	085	SANEY OWINGS	
CHAFFIN, STANLEY	C1755	?VA		1824	NC	085		1 C1775				60309
								2 1802	NC	085	ELIZABETH OWEN	
								3 1812	NC	092	ELIZABETH MCGLAMERY	
CHAFFIN, WILLIAM OWEN	C1805	NC	085	1871	IN			1 1829	NC	085	TEMPIE/TEMPERANCE HENDRICKS	60309
								2 1834	NC		MEHITABLE WILSON	
								3 1842	NC	033	LYDIA V DAILEY	
CHAMBERS, ANNA	C1785	NC	?085					1 C1809	NC	?054	ROBERT W JOHNSON/JOHNSTON	60465
CHAMBERS, GEORGE	1816	NC	104		NC	104		1 C1840	NC	104	NANCY COLEMAN	08073
CHAMBERS, JAMES	1792	NC	104	C1870				1 C1815	NC		ELIZABETH	08073
CHAMBERS, SARAH MARINDA	1859	NC	104	1938	IN			1 C1882	NC	104	WILLIAM OAKLEY	08073
CHAMNESS, ANTHONY	1713	ENG		1777	NC	073	022	1 C1738	MD		SARAH COLE	27429
								2 1766	NC	073	RACHEL HAWORTH	
								3 1776	NC	022	MARGARET WILLIAMS	
CHANCE, BENJAMIN		PA			NC	034	103	1			RACHEL SHARPLESS	60009
CHANCE, JOHN	1781	NC	103	1874	GA		009	1 1811	NC	028	ZILPAH DOUGHTY	60009
CHANCE, OLDFIELD		MD					057	1	NC			60009
CHANCE, PHILEMON	1760	MD		1816	LA		034	1			LAVISA	60009
CHANCE, PLEASANT	1829	NC	056		IA			1 1845	IA		RUTH ANN FINCH	60009

ANCESTOR INDEX	BIRTH	PL	CO	DEATH	PL	CO	LIVD	MARRIED	PL	CO	SPOUSE NAME	CODE
CHANCE, PURNELL	C1769	DE		1850	IN		046	1			STARLING	60009
CHANCE, REDDEN	C1780	NC	103		IN			1	NC	103	SARAH	60009
CHANCE, SIMPSON	1761	NC		1838	GA			1 2			ELIZABETH REEVES MARGARET	60009
CHANCE, TILMAN		NC	046	1819	IN			1	1801	IN	NANCY HICKS	60009
CHANCE, VINCENT	1758	MD			GA		034	1			SARAH TAYLOR	60009
CHANCE, WILLIAM		MD		1767	NC	028	028	1		MD	ELIZABETH OLDFIELD	60009
CHANCY, EDMUND SR	C1642			C1680	NC	002						19130
CHANCY, JOHN SR	C1765	NC		1846	NC	027		1			SARAH	27562
CHANCY, SAMUEL	1798	NC		1862	NC	027		1	1821	NC	JULIA ANN JONES	27562
CHANCY, SARAH JANE	1826	NC	027	C1890	NC	027		1	C1847	NC	?027 JOHN CREECH	27562
CHANDLER, GEORGE W	1832	NC	020	1883	NC	020		1	1857	NC	020 ELIZABETH BOSWELL	17170
CHANDLER, JOSEPH JOHNSTON	1873	NC	020	1970	NC	020		1	1907	NC	020 CORA HELEN PINCHBACK	17170
CHANDLER, PLEASANT	1789			1857	NC	020		1 2	1816 1852	NC NC	020 MARTHA JEFFRIES 020 MRS JEMINA COBB	17170
CHAPMAN, NICHOLAS	1758	MD		1856	NC	014	085	1	1787	NC	086 SARAH MARY SEELY	25087
CHARLTON, GEORGE WASHINGTON	1856	NC					028	1			SARAH ELIZABETH ASKEW	10010
CHASTAIN, JOHN	C1743	VA		1803	SC		013	1	C1762	VA	MARY OBRYAN	60519
CHASTAIN, MARY ANN	1818	NC		1903	MO			1 2	C1840 C1860		JOHN BASSINGER REASON RUBISON	02478
CHASTIAN, ELIJAH	1776			1853	GA		049	1 2 3	C1794 1800 1819	NC SC GA	029 HANNAH ADAMS ANNA MIDDLETON CATHERINE CARSON	60519
CHASTIAN, MARY/POLLY	C1810	NC	049		?GA		055	1	C1829	NC	049 JOEL/JOSEPH SHELTON	60519
CHAUNCEY, EDMOND	1684	NC	075	1754	NC	075	002	1			SARAH KEILE	19075
CHAUNCEY, JOHN C	C1860	NC		1903	NC	009		1 2	1892 1897	NC NC	009 MARY M EBORN 009 FANNIE CUTHRELL	27573
CHEAIRS/CHEARS, MARY FRANCIS	1831	NC	?013		MS			1			ATLAS O JONES	60590
CHEAIRS/CHEARS, NATHANIEL							082					60590
CHEEK, JAMES	C1740	VA			NC	073	015					08200
CHEEK, JOHN	C1768	NC	015	1827	NC	073		1	1794	NC	073 SUSANNAH ESTRIDGE	08200
CHEEK, NASH	1823	NC	073	1904	NC	036		1	1844	NC	073 MARGARET ALICE BISHOP	08200
CHEEK, SUSAN MARGARET	1853	NC	073	1919	NC	022		1	1874	NC	073 ELBERT HERNDON	08200
CHERRY, ANNA				C1869	NC	037	079	1	1815	NC	037 LEMUEL THIGPEN	02195
CHERRY, MARCUS CICERO STEPHEN	1827	NC	079	1895	NC	079		1	1848	NC	?063 ARCENA VIRGINIA BEST	24240
CHERRY, RODERICK	1780	NC	079	1838	NC			1	1804	NC	079 JENNIE CHERRY	24240
CHERRY, SAMUEL	1736	NC	009	1815	NC	037		1	1756		MARY MOORE	24240
CHERRY, SAMUEL, II	1685	VA		1754	NC	009		1	C1730	?NC	GATSY ANN LLEWELYN	24240
CHESNUTT/CHESTNUTT, ALEXANDER	C1730	VA		C1795	NC	?087		1			SARAH MURPHY ?	02550
CHESNUTT/CHESTNUTT, CHARLES	C1760	NC	035	C1838	NC	087		1	C1797	NC	087 ELIZABETH PARKER	02550

ANCESTOR INDEX	BIRTH	PL	CO	DEATH	PL	CO	LIVD	MARRIED	PL	CO	SPOUSE NAME	CODE
CHESNUTT/CHESTNUTT, DAVID	C1734	VA		C1795	NC	087						02550
CHESNUTT/CHESTNUTT, JACOB				1805	NC	087		1			JANE/JENNY SCOTT	02550
CHESNUTT/CHESTNUTT, JOHN				1796	NC	087		1 C1778	NC	035	CHARITY PARKER	02550
CHESNUTT/CHESTNUTT, JOSHUA	C1730	VA		C1787	NC	087		1 C1750			MARTHA	02550
CHEVES/CHEEVES, JOHN	1732	VA		1809	NC	039	099	1	?NC	?015		60339
CHEVES/CHEEVES, SARAH/SALLY	1770	NC	015	C1855	TN		099	1			JOHN FIELDING CONDITT	60339
CHEVES/CHEEVES, THOMAS				1771	NC	099	039	1			MARY	60339
CHILDERS/CHILDRESS, NANCY	1769	NC	?085	1841	NC	013	032	1 1792	NC	085	JOSHUA WHITAKER	23065
CHILDRESS, PLEASANT		VA		1842	TN		020	1 1793	NC	100	SARAH BUSH	60207
CHILDRESS, THOMAS	1810	NC	020		TN			1 1832	NC	020	EMMA	60207
CHIPMAN, DEBORAH	1787	NC	046	1871	TX			1 1807	NC	046	MOSES WELBORN	17235
CHIPMAN, JOHN	1761	DE		1834	NC	046		1 C1784	NC	046	MARY/MOLLY HARRIS	17235
CHIPMAN, PEREZ JR	1729	DE		1801	NC	046		1 1751	DE		MARGARET MANLOVE	17235
CHRISMON, DAVID	C1832	NC	046	C1907	NC	046		1 1854	NC	046	FRANCES WATLINGTON	60388
CHRISMON, GEORGE	C1809						046					60388
CHRISMON, SOPHRONA	1854	NC	046	1882	NC	084		1 1872	NC	?084	YANCEY M BRANN	60388
CHRISTOPHER, JOHN	C1795	NC		C1839	?TN			1			ANN	60584
CHRISTOPHER, THOMAS	C1805	NC		C1833	?TN			1			ISABELLA RAY ?	60584
CHRISTOPHER, WILLIAM	C1802	NC		C1845	?TN							60584
CHURCH, BETSY								1 C1813	NC	?104	LEWIS TRIPLETT	60222
CLAMPITT, DINAH	C1778	?DE			NC			1 C1805	NC	090	AMOS BEESON	60378
CLAMPITT, EZEKIEL	1801	NC	090	1889	IN			1 1829	MC	090	RUTH WARREN	60378
CLAMPITT, GEORGE	1774	DE		C1835	NC	006		1 C1795	NC	?090	ANN	60378
CLAMPITT, HANNAH	1800	NC	090	1844	NC	032		1 1818	NC	090	SOLOMON WILLIARD	60378
CLAMPITT, JANE ELIZABETH	1796	NC	090		NC	?038	046	1 1817	NC	085	NOCHOLAS TALLEY	60378
CLAMPITT, JOHN	1799	NC	090	1841	IN			1 1822	NC	090	CATHERINE NICHOLSON	60378
CLAMPITT, MARY	1786	NC	090	C1820	NC			1 C1805	NC	090	ABSOLOM BEESON	60378
CLAMPITT, MATHIAS MASTEN	1790	NC	090	1837	AL			1 1815	NC	090	REBECCA NICHOLSON	60378
CLAMPITT, RICHARD	1748	DE		1820	NC	090		1 C1773	DE		DINAH PRATT	60378
								2 C1783	DE		ELIZABETH MASTEN	
CLAMPITT, RICHARD	1793	NC	090	C1885	IN			1 1818	NC	090	JEMIMA MATHEWS	60378
CLAMPITT, RICHARD C	1804	NC	090		IN			1 1826	NC	090	ISABELLA MATHEWS	60378
CLAMPITT, WILLIAM	1776	DE		1843	NC	090		1 C1798	NC	090	RUTH JOHNSON/JOHNSTON	60378
CLAMPITT, WILLIAM FRANKLIN	1813	NC	090	1887	MO			1 1837	IN		MARY ANN OSBORN	60378
CLANEY, GEORGE								1 1781	NC	073	REBECCA CLARK	60411
CLANEY, THOMAS	1781	NC	073					1			ANN	60411
CLANTON, ELLIS	1815	NC		C1903	MO			1 C1837	?TN			60289
								2 1846	MO		MARY L DURHAM	
								3 1871	MO		MRS ELIZABETH BROOM	

ANCESTOR INDEX	BIRTH	PL	CO	DEATH	PL	CO	LIVD	MARRIED	PL	CO	SPOUSE NAME	CODE
CLAPP, GEORGE VALENTINE	1702	GER		1773			?085	1			MARY ALBRIGHT	02540
CLARK, ALEXANDER								1 1808	NC	099	ELIZABETH ROBERTSON	60540
								2 1820	NC	099	CHARLOTTE CHAPPELL	
CLARK, ANTHONY	1739	IRE		1827	TN		060	1 1774	PA		MARY E OATES	60443
CLARK, ANTHONY JR	1790	NC	060	1865	TX			1 1813	NC	060	SARAH DUNLAP	60443
CLARK, BENJAMIN	C1826						014	1 C1852			PHETINA	07115
CLARK, GLADY ETHEL	1905	NC	028					1 1924	NC	009	WILLIAM HENRY PORTER	25171
								2 1952	NC	075	GORDON RANDALL STRASENBURGH	
CLARK, HENRY GASTON	1872	SC		1949	NC	088		1			ELLA QUICK	02357
CLARK, HENRY J, REV	C1765	NC						1			JANE	25242
CLARK, JAMES		NC	028	1806	NC	028		1	NC	028	DELIVERENCE CHAPMAN	25171
CLARK, JAMES	1820	NC	079	1877	NC	079		1	NC	079	WENIFORD LANCASTER	25171
CLARK, JAMES ALEXANDER	1802	NC	065	1875	IA			1 1826	TN		HARRIET REBECCA STINSON	20095
CLARK, JESSE OSBORNE	1883	NC	079	1957	NC	079		1 1904	NC	028	IDA MELISSA ANN GASKINS	25171
CLARK, JOHN S	1854	SC		1929	NC	088		1			MAGGIE GROOMS	02357
CLARK, JOSEPH	C1753	NC	065	1826	TN			1 1789	NC	065	RUTH ALEXANDER	20095
CLARK, LUCY C	1883	SC		1922	NC	088		1 1900			CALVIN RILEY REECE	02357
CLARK, WEEKS	1788	NC	079	1863	NC	079		1	NC	079	SUSAN SMITH	25171
CLARK, WEEKS H	1841	NC	079	1903	NC	079		1	NC	079	SUSAN GASKINS	25171
CLARK, WESLEY ELBER	C1812	NC		1895	MO			1			EMELINE HOLDER	60540
CLARK, WILLIAM				C1772	NC	065		1			MARY	20095
CLARK, WILLIAM		NC	028		NC	028		1			WINIFORD	25171
CLARK, WILLIAM DUNLAP	1814	NC	060	1887	TX			1 1838	TN		ELIZABETH R KELTON	60443
CLARK, WILLIAM THOMAS	1862	SC		1928	NC	088		1			SARAH ELIZABETH GROOMS	02357
CLARKE, JOHN				1850	NC	100		1			MARY LLOYD	25215
CLAYTON, GEORGE JR	1752	DE		C1815	NC	054	085	1 1784	NC	085	MARGARET/PEGGY THOMPSON	23065
CLAYTON, GEORGE SR	C1725	DE		1786	NC	054	085	1 C1745	DE		SARAH	23065
CLAYTON, LAMBERT CLINGMAN, COL	1806	NC	054	C1866	NC	013		1 C1836	NC	013	ELIZA BURGIN	23065
CLAYTON, THOMAS	1755	NC	028	1820	GA			1 1789	NC	028	SARAH/SARY DELAMAR	60544
CLAYTON, THOMAS	1790	NC	028	1834	GA			1 1813	GA		SUSAN HEATH BONNER	60544
CLAYTON, WILLIAM	C1773	NC			TN			1			NANCY	27682
CLAYTON, WILLIAM				C1781	NC	090		1			ELIZABETH	60321
CLEM, ADAM	C1765	?GA		C1819	AL		014	1 C1786	?GA		JEMIMA	13020
CLEM, MASON	C1792	NC	014		?AR			1			PHOEBE SEATON	13020
CLEM, WILLIAM	C1797	NC	014		?AL							13020
CLEM, WILLIAM		NC	?014		?GA							13020
CLEMENT, ALBERT WEST	1899	NC	099					1			LEAURIAH MAY LEE	27734

ANCESTOR INDEX	BIRTH	PL	CO	DEATH	PL	CO	LIVD	MARRIED	PL	CO	SPOUSE NAME	CODE
CLEMENT, SAMUEL	1770	NC	044					1 1788	NC	044	JUDITH KNIGHT	27734
CLEMENT, SIMON	C1734	VA			NC	044		1			SUSANNAH	27734
CLEMENT, THOMAS DUDLEY	C1845	NC	044					1			ELIZABETH BULLOCK	27734
CLEMENT, WILLIAM	1793	NC	044	1889	NC	044		1 1826			JANE DUDLEY GOOCH	27734
CLEMENT, WILLIAM WALLACE	1869	NC	044	1948	NC	046		1			MARY OTEALIA BEASLEY	27734
CLEMMER, DAVID	1811	NC	060	1907	MS		040	1 1834	NC	060	NANCY CANNON	60063
CLEMMER, LEWIS	1775	?PA			NC	040	060	1	NC	060	MARY/MOLLIE CLONINGER	60063
CLEMMER, VALENTINE		PA		C1780	NC	060		1			ELIZABETH T DETHROW	60063
CLEMSON, JOHN STARKEY	1808	NC	020	1887	MO			1 1834	MO		HANNAH RUTHERFORD	60026
CLEMSON, JONATHAN STARKEY	C1818	NC	020	1878	MO			1 C1846	?TN		LUMEGA FLOWER	60026
CLEMSON, MAGARA	C1802	NC	020	C1861	MO			1 1830	NC	020	JOSEPH DAMERON KNIGHT	60026
CLEMSON, WILLIAM	1774	PA	020	C1855	MO			1 1800	NC	020	MARY DELPS	60026
CLENDENON/GLENDENNING, ROSA/ROSIE	C1783	NC		C1880	TN			1 1805	TN		JOHN BRISBY	27686
CLEVELAND, BENJAMIN	1738	VA		1806	SC		104	1 1759	VA		MARY GRAVES	08070
CLEVELAND, JOHN	1760	VA			GA			1 1781	NC	104	MRS CATHERINE (SLOAN) MONTGOMERY	08070
CLEVELAND, MARY GRAVES	C1784			1858	GA		104	1 1800	NC	?092	ABEDNEGO FRANKLIN	08070
CLIFTON, BENJAMIN MINCE	1804	NC	047	1877	TN			1 1830 2 1853	TN TN		SALLY ORGAIN ROBERTS MRS MARY ANN WELLS	60576
CLIFTON, EDWIN	1764	VA		1826	TN			1 1794	NC	047	NANCY FOLKS	60576
CLIFTON, HENRY H	C1787	NC	096	C1850	?LA			1 C1812 2 C1826	NC TN	096	JANE CHERRY	60328
CLIFTON, JOHN	C1740	VA			NC	?096		1 C1760	VA			60328
CLIFTON, JOHN	C1765	VA			NC	?096		1 1786	NC	096	SARAH FARLOW	60328
CLIFTON, SAMUEL	1743	VA		1834	TN		047	1 1763	VA		SUSANNAH KERBY	60576
CLUBB, DANIEL	C1782	NC	060	1859	MO			1	NC	060	SALLY	60340
CLUBB, MOSES	C1816	NC	060	1880	MO			1 1844 2	MO		POLLY DANIEL SOPHIA	60340
COBB, AMBROSE	1729	NC	070	1797				1			SARAH	08190
COBB, AMBROSE		NC	?005					1 1783	NC	070	RACHAEL BLACK	08190
COBB, CLISBY		NJ		C1815	NC	?014	006					08190
COBB, DAVID	1756	VA		1827	AL		060	1 1785	NC	060	CATHERINE BIRD	60443
COBB, EASTER	1797	NC		1877	TX			1			THOMAS WILSON	60185
COBB, EATON	C1781			C1860	NC	037		1 1822	NC	037	MRS MARY (PARKER) THIGPEN	02195
COBB, ELLENER	C1812	NC						1 1841	NC	060	EZEKIEL SANFORD/STANFORD	60146
COBB, HARDY	C1811	NC						1 1832	NC	010	JERSEY CALE	60459
COBB, HENRY	1750	NC		1794	SC			1	NC		RACHEL WILSON	25129
COBB, HENRY JR	1782	NC	092	1853	SC			1	SC		ELLENDER PARIS	25129
COBB, JAMES JR	C1821	NC	?079					1 C1850	NC	079	MARY BELL	06050

ANCESTOR INDEX	BIRTH	PL	CO	DEATH	PL	CO	LIVD	MARRIED	PL	CO	SPOUSE NAME	CODE
COBB, JAMES M	1814	NC						1 1834	?NC		POLLY PETERS	08150
COBB, JOHN	C1838	NC	018		NC	?018						25167
COBB, MARTHA	1828	NC	037	1884	NC	037		1 1850	NC	037	JAMES THIGPEN	02195
COBB, MORRIS	1792			1854	MO		014	1 1813	NC		REBECCA GODFREY ?	08150
COBB, POLLY	1798	NC	060					1 1819	AL		RICHARD RISON	60443
COBB, SELINA/SALENA	1775	NJ		1859	NC	006	104	1 1793	NC	060	STERLING EDWARDS	08190
COBB, STEPHEN J	1817			1888	NC	083		1 1841			MARY BETHUNE	12144
COBBLE/CAUBLE/KABEL, ADAM	C1773	PA		C1860	IL			1 1803	NC	085	BETSEY CORL	60517
COBBLE/CAUBLE/KABEL, JOHN	1806	NC	085	1875	IL			1 1827	IL		ELIZABETH LYERLY	60517
								2 1834	IL		MALINDA LYERLY	
								3 1838	IL		DELILA LYERLY	
COBLE, ABNER	1809	NC		1889	KS			1			KATHERINE	60355
								2 1852			MARY JANE KIRK	
								3 1854	IA		JANE STOUGHTON	
COBLE, DAVID JR	1814	NC	067	1890	NC	089		1	NC	?067	PENNEY HOWARD	60288
								2	NC	089	ELIZABETH BARBEE	
								3	NC	089	MALINDA HINSON	
COBLE, DAVID SR	1774	?PA		1842	NC	089		1			MARTHA BRAY	60288
COBLE, GARB	1785	NC						1			BETSEY	60355
COBLE, ROSEY	1836	NC	?067		NC	?089		1	?NC	?089	WILLIAM VANHOY	60288
COCHRAN/COCKERHAM, JACOB JR	1783	NC	067	C1875	GA			1 1811	NC	067	PATSY POOL	60261
COCHRAN/COCKERHAM, JACOB SR	C1755	NC	005	C1835	GA			1 1775	NC	005	MARY ENGLISH	60261
COCKERHAM, CHARITY	C1800	?NC			?NC	?106						10010
COCKRUM, JAMES WALLACE	C1775						086	1 C1793			MRS ANN (SHEPPARD) BROWN	20229
COFFEY, ARCHELAUS	C1755	VA		C1783	NC	104		1 C1775	VA		ELEANOR WADE	60264
COFFEY, JAMES	C1728	VA		1786	NC	104		1 C1750	VA		ELIZABETH CLEVELAND	60264
COGDILL, FREDRICK	C1841				?MO		086					03065
COGDILL, JAMES	C1810	NC	?049		NC	?062		1			NELLIE WOODY	60321
COGDILL, SARAH							094					03065
COGDILL, WILLIAM JR	C1784	NC	060	C1865	NC	062	060	1	NC	?086	NANCY DAVIS	03065
COGDILL, WILLIAM SR	C1741			C1815	NC	013	094					03065
COGDILL, WILLIAM SR	C1755	NC			NC	?049						60321
COKER, BRUMBLY, REV	1753	NC	037	1818	NC	033		1 1782	NC	037	REBECCA GEORGE	02065
COKER, JAMES	C1714	VA		C1796	NC	037		1			MARY SPIER	02065
COKER, WILLIAM	1786	NC	085	1844	NC	033		1			SARAH MILLS	02065
COLE, ADOLPHUS ERVIN	C1824	NC	013	1863	TN			1 1848	GA		MRS MARANER (LYONS) LEATHERS	60146
COLE, ELIZABETH		NC	085	1870	TN			1 1800	NC	085	JOHN FEEZOR	60562
COLE, JOHN				C1806	NC	099	?056					12008
COLE, LOID/LOYD							099					12008
COLE, MATTHEW	C1780						013					60452

ANCESTOR INDEX	BIRTH	PL	CO	DEATH	PL	CO	LIVD	MARRIED	PL	CO	SPOUSE NAME	CODE
COLE, WILLIAM TEMPLE		IRE		1777	NC	085		1			SARAH JOLLEY	60562
COLE, WILLIAM TEMPLE, II				1809	NC	085		1			MARY	60562
COLE, ZACHARIAH	1797	NC	013	1865	AR			1				60452
								2			MARY ANN COOK	
COLEE, ABNER	1805	NC		1889	IN			1 C1828			SARAH	60006
								2 1871	IN		NANCY BOWMAN	
COLEE, HANNAH	1799	NC		1888	IN							60006
COLEMAN, BENJAMIN ANDREW	C1735	NC	?056	1813	NC	059	059	1 C1760			ELIZABETH GOODMAN	25168
COLEMAN, BENJAMIN STEPHEN	1775	NC		1815	GA			1 1800			ELIZABETH WOMACK	25168
COLEMAN, DAVID	1798	NC	016	1870	TN		061	1 1819	NC		SARAH LOVE	60345
COLEMAN, JOHN	C1796	NC	104					1 C1820	NC	104	SUZANNAH	08073
COLEMAN, JULIA	1798	NC		1866				1			BENNETT FERRELL	25168
COLEMAN, MARK	C1755			C1820	NC	049	016	1			MARGARET	60345
COLEMAN, NANCY	C1826	NC	104					1 C1846	NC	104	GEORGE CHAMBERS	08073
COLEMAN, NANCY	1800	NC		1888	GA			1 1817			MICKLEBERRY FERRELL	25168
COLEMAN, SARAH		NC										25168
COLEMAN, SHELLY		NC										25168
COLEMAN, WILLIAM BLOUNT	1792	NC		1847	NC	059		1			MARY CORNELL	25168
COLEY, FRANCIS	C1800	?NC		1874	VA			1 1824	VA		SARAH/SALLY VAUGHT	60090
COLLIER JONATHAN	C1795	NC			TX			1 1814	TN		CATHERINE STULTS	27322
COLLINS, ANDREW	1740	NC		1790	NC	099		1			MARTHA	20210
COLLINS, CREED	C1777	NC	099	C1857	TX			1			LYDIA	20210
COLLINS, ZACHARIAH	C1782			1838	KY		?056					60292
COLLY, NANCY	1767	NC		1858	GA			1	NC		LEWIS HALL	60164
COLTRAIN/COLTRANE, JACOB							081	1 C1790	NC	?081	JANE	27429
COLTRANE, JAMES	1798	NC	081	1874	NC	081		1 1823	NC	?081	ELIZABETH RICKS	08095
COLVARD, JESSIE	1800	NC		1879	TN			1			NANCY MERRIAM	60044
								2			SARAH A COOPER	
COLVERT/CALVERT, JAMES	1820	NC			AR			1			MARY A	60545
COLVERT/CALVERT, JOSEPH NORMAN	1779	VA		C1855	AR		057	1 C1800				60545
COLVERT/CALVERT, WILLIAM ISAAC	1810	NC		1882	AR			1 C1834			ELIZABETH WEEDON	60545
COMBS, CHARLES	1793	VA		1866	IN			1 1819	NC	092	ABIGAIL BRASSFIELD	17075
								2 1858	IN		MRS ANNA MCLAUGHLIN	
COMBS, JOHN	1759	?NC		1848	KY			1 1779	NC	104	BIDDY/MARGARET NANTZ	24153
COMBS, MASON	C1730	?VA		1785	NC	092						60297
COMBS, SYLVIA	C1775	?VA		1857	IO		092	1 C1805	TN		DANIEL PAINE	60297
COMMANDER, MILLICENT	C1793	NC	?075		?TN		?077	1 1812	NC	?075	SAMUEL BARCLIFT	60310
COMMONS, JOEL CLINTON	1791	NC	073	1870	TN			1 1818			SARAH GRAY	60096
CONDITT/CONDICT, JAMES BENNETT	C1803	MC	039	1879	AR			1			REBECCA VADEN	60339
								2			GEORGIA ANN WALL	
								3			MARGARET LUSTER	

ANCESTOR INDEX	BIRTH	PL	CO	DEATH	PL	CO	LIVD	MARRIED	PL	CO	SPOUSE NAME	CODE
CONDITT/CONDICT, JOHN FIELDING, II	1771	VA		C1855	TN		039	1		NC	?039 SARAH/SALLY CHEEVES	60339
CONLEE/CONLEY, DANIEL	C1771	NC		C1854	TN			1 1803	TN		MAHALA RANDOLPH	60109
CONLEY, HUGH	1792	NC		1875	NC	014		1		NC	HAZEY V FOX	20448
CONLEY, JAMES WESLEY	C1828	NC	014	C1892	NC	014		1		NC	MARY A	20448
CONNER, BURWELL	C1765				NC	071		1 1782			SUANNA FUTRELL	25141
CONNER, EDWARD	C1757	NC	035		SC			1 1807	NC	012	SARAH GRISSIT	60265
CONNER, ELIJAH WASHINGTON	1830	NC	071	1896	NC	071		1 1855			BARBARA POWELL	25141
CONNER, JOEL	1785	NC	071	1872	NC	071		1 1829			JUDITH STEPHENSON	25141
CONNER, MILLS HENRY	1868	NC	071	1928	NC	071		1 1895	NC		ISTALENA LEIGH BOYCE	25141
CONNOR, WILLIAM	1770			1856	NC	084		1 2			ISABELLE FRANCES	06015
CONRAD, JACOB LEWIS	1783	NC	060	1866	MO			1 C1812	NC	060	SALOME/SALMA BOLLINGER	60349
CONRAD, PETER	1782	NC	060	1843	MO			1 1810	NC	060	SARAH ABERNATHY	60349
CONRAD, RUDOLPH				1803	NC	060		1 C1776 2 C1780 3 1792	NC NC NC	060 060	CATROUT SCHUFORD ANNA MARIA SCHELL CHRISTINA STOCKINGER	60349
COOK, ABRAHAM				1793	NC	046		1 1756	NC	046	PHOEBE MILLS	60053
COOK, ABRAM/ABRAHAM	1721			C1800	NC	104	044	1 1781	NC	104	ELIZABETH CASS ?	60401
COOK, ADAM	C1750	?IR		1816	NC	006	014	1 C1770	NC	014		02295
COOK, DAVID	1814	NC	006	1850	NC	006	014	1 1838	NC	006	MARY M STANSBURY	02295
COOK, ELIAS G	C1819	NC		1884	AR			1 1840 2 1843 3 C1869	TN TN AR		CELIA JOHNSON SYBELLA DARBY MRS LORA GREEN	60046
COOK, JACOB		?NC	?103		?NC	?103						60018
COOK, MARGARET JANE	1839	NC	027	1913	NC	027		1 1857	NC	027	HENRY GREEN	24032
COOK, MARK		?VA		C1790	GA		047	1			RACHAEL WILSON	03155
COOK, MARY	1769	VA		C1850	KY		084	1 1784	NC	046	JAMES MCCUBBIN	25087
COOK, MARY ANN	C1810	NC	014	C1885	NC	066	107	1 C1830	NC	014	THOMAS M SPARKS	25087
COOK, MICHAEL SR	C1771	NC	014	C1845	NC	006	014	1 C1800 2 C1815	NC NC	014 006	CATHERINE ANN ELIZA	02295
COOK, NANCY	1779	NC	103	1830	NC	103		1 1807	NC	103	WILLIAM BARDIN	60018
COOK, RANSOM TURNER	1796	NC		1880	IL			1			ELIZABETH ANN DURHAM	60550
COOK, SHEMUEL	C1780	NC						1			NANCY ANN RUCKER	60083
COOK, YOUNG BRASWELL	1802			1869	NC	027		1 C1827			SARAH A	24032
COOK, ZADOCK	1769	NC	?047	1863	GA			1 C1789	GA		ELIZABETH COOK	03155
COOKE, NARCISSA ANN	1826	NC	044	1892	NC			1 1847	NC	044	KENNON HARPER WAINWRIGHT	25215
COOKE, RICHARD DONALDSON	1749			1811	NC	044		1 2			PRISCILLA BULLOCK ELIZABETH	25215
COOKE, RICHARD HENRY		NC	044					1 1809	NC	044	ELIZABETH BLACKNALL	25215

ANCESTOR INDEX	BIRTH	PL	CO	DEATH	PL	CO	LIVD	MARRIED	PL	CO	SPOUSE NAME	CODE
COOKE, RICHARD, DR				1785	NC	044						25215
COOPER, JERRY		NC	050					1		NC	050 MARTHA MAULDIN	60267
COOPER, LLOYD RANDOLPH	1890	NC		1971	GA			1 1911 2	LA		ANGIE MARIE LA FLAMME KATHLEEN THOMAS	60267
COOPER, MILTON WAKELAND		NC			NC			1 1889			MARTHA/MATTIE JANE BAKER	60267
COPELAND, CYNTHIA LUCILLE	1814	NC	?022	1899	KS			1 1835	TN		JOSIAH JONES	60016
COPELAND, JOHN	C1776	NC	?022	1873	MO			1 C1808	NC	?022	ZANA LASATER	60016
COPELAND, MASSEY M	1791	NC		1865	GA			1 C1810 2 1830 3 1831	?SC GA GA		ANN TREUTLEN MARY ANN JONES MRS AURY RHODES	60592
CORLEW, JOHN		?NC	?047	1762	NC	047		1			KEZIAH	25241
CORLEW, JOHN				C1761	NC	047	037	1			KEZIAH	60179
CORLEW, JOHN				C1785	NC	047						60179
CORLEW, PHILIP	1777	NC	047	1856	IL			1 1812	KY		ANNA KINCAID	25241
CORLEW, PHILIP	1777	NC		1856	IL			1 1812	KY		ANNA KINCAID	27553
CORLEW, PHILIP		NC	047	C1815	?KY							60179
CORLEW, PHILIP	1777	NC	047	1856	IL			1 1812	KY		ANNA KINCAID	60179
CORLEY/CAULEY/COLLEY, RICHARD							011					08165
CORLEY/CAULEY/COLLEY, ROBERT							011	1			SARAH	08165
CORLEY/CAULEY/COLLEY, VOLENTINE AUSTIN	C1770	NC	?022	1860	GA			1 C1790	SC		SARAH	08165
CORLEY/CAULEY/COLLEY, ZACHEUS	1762	NC	073	1849	AL			1 2 C1803	SC SC		ELIZABETH BURNETT	08165
CORRELL, DANIEL	C1800	NC		?NC			016	1 1822	NC	085	NELLY/ELLEN PENCE	03250
CORRELL, HEZEKIAH/KIAH ALEXANDER	1828	NC	?085	1899	NC	099		1 1851 2 1857	NC ?NC	085	ELLEN PARKS CAROLINE REBECCA RUSSELL	03250
CORTNER/COTNER, DAVID	1809	NC	046	1852	IN			1 1828 2 1836	IN IN		CATHERINE AMICK BARBARA WHITEMAN	60262
CORTNER/COTNER, GEORGE	1738	PA		1819	NC	046		1			MARIA CLAPP	60262
CORTNER/COTNER, JOHN MATTHEW	1782	NC	046	1852	IN			1 C1803	NC	?046	BARBARA LOW	60262
COSBY, ELIZABETH	1788	NC		1850	LA			1 1814	TN		JOSEPH MCADAMS	60497
COSBY, JAMES	C1760			1815			046	1 1787	NC	085	MARGARET MCBRIDE	60497
COSTIN/COSTON/COSTEN, JAMES	C1825						?072	1 C1850	NC	?035	CELIA R	25254
COTTON, JOHN				C1728	NC	010		1			MARTHA GODWIN	20210
COTTON, JOSEPH JR				C1795	NC	047						20210
COTTON, JOSEPH SR				C1772	NC	047						20210
COUCH, JOHN		?NC			KY		006	1			MARY/POLLY BOONE	60432
COUCH, MESHACH	1743			1824	NC	046		1 1773	?VA		MARY WELCH	60451
COULTER, DANIEL	1787	NC	060	1862	NC	021		1			NANCY ANN STILWELL	27441
COULTER, JOHANN MARTIN	C1728	GER		1808	NC	060		1 C1750			CATHERINE ROSANNA BOONE	27441
COULTER, PHILIP	1763	NC	065	1840	NC	060		1			CLARA WISE	27441

ANCESTOR INDEX	BIRTH	PL	CO	DEATH	PL	CO	LIVD	MARRIED	PL	CO	SPOUSE NAME	CODE
COUNCIL/COUNCILL, GEORGE WASHINGTON	1836	NC	029	1900	GA			1 1867	GA		MARTHA CAROLINE BARWICK	17220
COUNCIL/COUNCILL, MATTHEW		NC		1831	NC	083		1	NC		SALLIE WHEELER	17220
COUNCIL/COUNCILL, MICHAEL	1776	NC	083	1866	NC			1	NC		BARLOW	17220
COUNCIL/COUNCILL, SOLOMON BARLOW	1803	NC	083	1884	GA		029	1 1824	NC	029	ELIZABETH BLUE	17220
COURSEY, ROBERT	1774	NC	?100	1839	KY			1 1799	KY		MARY ANDERSON	20415
COURSEY, WILLIAM		NC	?100	C1805	KY			1	NC	?100	FRANCES ACOCK	20415
COVINGTON, URCILLA	1757			1848	NC	086		1 1773	NC	046	JOHN WALKER	05070
COVINGTON, WILLIAM					?GA		046	1 C1755			MORGAN	05070
COWARD, JONATHAN	1774	NC	?094	1853	NC	055		1			MARTHA HUDSON	20220
COWARD/COWART, NEEDHAM								1 C1774	NC	?034	PHEBE	06050
COWDEN, HUMPHREY NORRIS	1816	NC	054	1886	TN			1 1830	TN		EMELINE CLAYTON	60366
COX, AARON	C1780	NC	?090	C1860	TN			1			POLLY HILL	01054
COX, AARON								1 1787	NC	060	OLLY BAKER	60238
COX, ALEXANDER	C1815	?SC		1881	NC	012		1			ANN ELIZA FLOWERS	13052
COX, ALEXANDER	C1826	NC	030									25167
COX, ANDREW	1804	NC	068	C1880	AR							14020
COX, BENJAMIN	C1725	PA		1817	NC	081		1 1751	PA		MARTHA GARRETSON	03270
COX, BENJAMIN	C1752	?PA		1791	NC	081		1 1775	NC	046	REBECCA COX	03270
COX, CALEB	C1828	NC	030									25167
COX, CHARLES	1762	NC	073	1840	NC	081		1 1785	NC	081	AMY BARKER	03270
COX, CHARLES	1794	NC	081	1855	NC	081		1 1820	NC	081	HANNAH COX	03270
COX, DAVIS W	C1833	NC	?018									25167
COX, ELIJAH								1 1796	NC	060	JANE HUGGIN	60238
COX, ELISHA								1 1793	NC	060	MARGARET HOLLEN	60238
COX, ELIZABETH	1713	VA		1816	NC	092		1 C1731	?VA		STRANGEMAN HUTCHINS	60569
COX, HARMON	C1720	DE		1812	NC	081		1 1745	VA		JANE JOHN	03270
COX, HENRY	C1755			1835	NC	068		1			SARAH	14020
COX, ISAAC	C1723	PA		C1797	NC	081		1 1746	PA		OLIVE UNDERWOOD	03270
								2 1764	NC	073	MRS PHEBE (SCARLET) ALLEN	
COX, ISAAC	1786	NC		1855	IN			1				08190
								2			MRS SARAH (BOONE) WAGGONER	
								3			MARY	
COX, JACKSON C	C1829	NC	030		NC	018		1	NC	?018	MARY MATILDA COBB	25167
COX, JACOB	C1765	NC	073	C1838	NC	081		1 1791	NC	081	HANNAH MOFFITT	03270
COX, JOHN	1728	DE		1803	NC	081		1 1755	DE		MARY SCARLET	03270
COX, JOHN	C1685			C1760	?NC	?073		1 C1713	DE		MARY	03270
COX, JOHN				C1805	NC	060						60238
COX, JOHN EDWARD	1860	NC	018	1939	NC	075		1	NC	018	IDA CORA JONES	25167

ANCESTOR INDEX	BIRTH	PL	CO	DEATH	PL	CO	LIVD	MARRIED	PL	CO	SPOUSE NAME	CODE
COX, JOSHUA	1760	NC	073	1847	NC	081		1 C1781	NC	081	RACHEL DUSKIN	03270
COX, RACHAEL				C1825				1 1786	NC	060	PETER CARSON	60238
COX, RHODA	1790	NC	?065	'1853	TN			1 1809	NC	016	JACOB BARNHART	60337
COX, SOLOMON	C1730	DE		1812	OH		022	1 C1757	NC	073	RUTH COX	03270
COX, THOMAS	C1736	DE		1809	OH		081	1 1760	NC	073	SARAH DAVIS	03270
COX, THOMAS	C1735	PA		1771	NC	046		1 C1757	NC	073	MARTHA JENKINS	03270
COX, WILLIAM	C1807	NC	090	C1890	TN			1 C1829	TN		DELILAH CARROLL	01054
COX, WILLIAM	C1690			1767	NC	073		1 C1716	DE		CATHARINE KINKEY	03270
COX, WILLIAM	1761	NC	073	1845	NC	081		1 C1788	NC	081	RUTH COX	03270
COYLE, JESSIE		NC	081	1856	MO			1			JANE POWELL	60191
CRABTREE, ABRAM	C1800				NC	?073		1 1824			ISABELL BARTON	60131
CRABTREE, CHARLIE	1865	NC	073	1899	NC	073		1			VIRGINIA T STANLEY	60131
CRABTREE, PEARL TERRY	1892	NC	073					1 1910	OK		CHARLIE ROBERT MCCORNACK	60131
CRABTREE, WILLIAM	C1790	NC	?081	1857	IN			1 1812	KY		SARAH/SALLIE BENNET/BENNETT	60170
								2 1847	IN		MRS ELIZABETH (HUNT) BROWN	
CRABTREE, WILLIAM G	C1830	NC	073		NC	073		1 1852	NC	073	ELIZA MCCAULEY	60131
CRAFT, ARCHAELOUS	C1756	NC		C1840	KY			1 1785	NC	104	ELIZABETH ADAMS	25242
CRAFT, THOMAS	C1725	VA		1788	NC	044		1			ELIZABETH MORSE ?	25087
CRAIG, ISABEL	C1740	IRE			NC	073		1 C1760	NC	073	DAVID NELSON	02256
CRAIG, LUCY		NC	070		NC	?070		1 1819	NC	070	ELIJAH JEFFERSON PIVER	05070
CRAIGHEAD, ALEXANDER, REV	1706	IRE		1766	NC	065		1			AGNES BROWN	60166
								2			JANE/JEAN MARTIN	
CRAIGHEAD, ROBERT	1751	VA		1821	TN		065	1			HANNAH CLARK	60166
CRAIN, JESSE WILLIAM	1832	NC		1895	TX			2 1876	TX		MATILDA WALL/WALLS	60122
CRAIN/CRANE, AMBROSE		NC	?044				104					60581
CRAIN/CRANE, JOHN	1760	NC	?085	1836	TN			1	?NC		MILDRED WALTON	60581
CRAVEN, LYDIA C	1831	NC	081					1 1849	NC	081	MILLION REITZEL	08355
CRAVER, PHILIP		?VA		1820	NC	085						60531
CRAVER/GRABER/GREBER, ANDREW		GER		C1760	PA		085	1			GERTRAUT	03295
CRAVER/GRABER/GREBER, JOHN	C1794	NC	085	C1872	IL			1	NC	085	MARY TODD	03295
CRAVER/GRABER/GREBER, JOHN SR	1771	PA		1821	IL		085	1	NC	085	CATHERINE	03295
CRAVER/GRABER/GREBER, PHILLIP	C1745	GER		C1820	NC	085		1 1768			CATHERINE EBHECHT	03295
CRAVER/GRABER/GREBER, WILLIAM	1821	NC	085					1 1843	IN		SELINA WRIGHT	03295
CRAWFORD, DAVID M	1805	IRE		1885	NC	086		1 1835			MARY MCKINNEY	60139
								2 1852	NC	086	MARY E WALKER	
CREASMAN, COONROD	C1795	NC										27332
CREASMAN, RACHEL	C1816	NC						1 1839	MO		BENJAMIN KIDD	27332
CREASMAN/CHRISTMAN, ADAM	C1750	?PA		C1815	NC	060	085	1 C1775	?VA		REEL	23065

44

ANCESTOR INDEX	BIRTH	PL	CO	DEATH	PL	CO	LIVD	MARRIED	PL	CO	SPOUSE NAME	CODE
CREASMAN/CHRISTMAN, CATHERINE	1777	VA		1864	NC	013	085	1 1798	NC	060	JOSEPH STROUP	23065
CREASON/CRESON, HENRY	1820	NC	085		KY			1 1839	KY		ELIZABETH SMITH	03313
CREASON/CRESON, MICHAEL	1799	NC	085		KY			1 1819	NC	085	BARBARA PARKS	03313
CREASON/CRESON, NICHOLAS	C1752	?PA		1799	NC	085		1			SOPHIA BRUNER	03313
CREASON/CRESON, SAMUEL	1774	NC	085	1823	NC	085		1 1794	NC	085	SOPHIA BROWN	03313
CREDLE, DORCAS	1805			1870	NC	053	019	1 1822			JOHN WILLIS WILLIAMS	24210
CREDLE, FRANCIS	C1747				NC	?053						24210
CREDLE, JOHN	1777			1852	NC	053		1			PRISCILLA GIBBS	24210
CREECH, BENNETT	C1801	NC	056	C1871	NC	056		1 1825	NC	056	LYDIA WALL	03315
CREECH, JESSE	C1775	NC	056		NC	056		1 1798	NC	056	MARGARET WORLEY	03315
CREECH, JOHN	1819	NC	035	1904	NC	027		1 C1847	NC	027	SARAH JANE CHANCY	27562
CREECH, JOHN BUNYON	1832	NC	056	1905	NC	056		1 1862	NC	069	POLLY DRIVER	03315
CREECH, JOSHUA	C1775	NC		1848	NC	027		1			MARY JANE	27562
CREECH, JOSHUA SR	C1753	NC	034	C1835	NC	056		1	NC		SALLY STANFORD ?	03315
CREECH, JULIA COLUMBIA	1854	NC	027	1922	NC	027		1 1875	NC	027	DANIEL MORGAN HIGH	27562
CREECY, SARAH	C1760	NC	077		NC	?077		1 C1778	NC	?077	EDWARD WINGATE	27562
CREEKMORE, CALEB		?VA			?NC	?104		1 1794	VA		OLIVE KEETOR	60115
CREEKMORE, JOSEPH C	1840	NC	?104	1926	NC	065		1 1865	NC	104	SARAH J BROWN	60115
CREEKMORE, NICHOLAS		NC	?047		?NC	?104		1 1828	NC	092	ELIZABETH HINSHAW	60115
CRENSHAW, DAVID	1813	NC	065	1881	GA			1			JANE S	60293
CRESON/CRESSON, ABRAHAM	C1720			C1791	NC	092	085	1	?VA			08130
								2 1788	NC	092	MRS MARY LEWIS	
CRESON/CRESSON, JANE	C1762	NC	085	C1825	NC	092		1 C1778	NC	092	SAMUEL CUNNINGHAM	08130
								2 C1782	NC	092	CHARLES STEELMAN	
CRESON/CRISSON/CREASON/CRISHON, ABRAHAM				C1791	NC	092		1 1788	NC	092	MRS MARY LEWIS	21173
CREWS, GIDEON	C1745	?VA		1815	NC	044		1 C1769			JEMIMA WICKER ?	15098
CREWS, JAMES	1775	VA		1857	NC	038		1 1807	NC	090	POLLY FESSLER	13120
CREWS, JAMES, SR	C1750	VA		1831	NC	090		1			EMELIA	13120
CREWS, JOSEPH W	1782			1874	NC	038		1 1802	NC	090	ELIZABETH ROBINSON	60456
CREWS, MATTHEW		VA			NC			1			SUSAN RIVES ?	60456
CREWS, MILDRED	C1772	NC	044	1841	NC	090		1 1793	NC	044	JOHN HESTER	15098
CRIDER, GEORGE	1795	NC		1856	IN			1			CATHERINE	60553
								2 1832	IN		ELIZABETH/BETSY FLEETWOOD	
CRIM, FRANCIS	1799	NC	090	1876	IN			1 1816	NC	090	JOHN LINVILLE	15098
CRIM, JACOB		?VA		C1829	NC	090		1			MARY	15098
CRISP, SUSAN/SUCKEY		?NC						1 1828	NC	014	JOHN SETSER	27318
CRISP/CHRISP, HIRAM JR	1820	NC	017	C1890	NC	061		1 1844	NC	061	MIRA/MYRA DILLS	17135
CRISP/CHRISP, HIRAM SR	1795	NC						1 C1818				17135

ANCESTOR INDEX	BIRTH	PL	CO	DEATH	PL	CO	LIVD	MARRIED	PL	CO	SPOUSE NAME	CODE
CRISP/CHRISP, JENNIE	1881	NC	061	1956	MT			1 1905	OR		WILLIAM HULL	17135
								2 1908	WA		ARTHUR WIGFIELD	
CRISP/CHRISP, JOAB	1845	NC	061	1925	NC	061		1 1868	NC	061	EMILY ELIZABETH STANFIELD	17135
CRISP/CHRISP, WILLIAM MANSELL	C1715			C1783	NC	063		2			FRANCIS	17135
CRITTENDEN, HENRY		?VA		C1782	NC	071		1				60211
CROMARTIE, ALEXANDER	1772	NC	011	1839	NC	011		1 1799	NC	011	ELIZABETH DEVANE	12090
								2 C1824	NC	011	ELIZABETH KERR	
CROMARTIE, GEORGE	1804	NC	011	1892	NC	011		1	NC	011	MARY KELLY	12090
								2 1834	NC	011	MRS MARY JANE (HENDON) WHITE	
								3	NC	011	SARAH CLARK	
CROMARTIE, WILLIAM	1731	SCO		1807	NC	011		1			STEWART	12090
								2 1766	NC	011	RUHAMA DOANE	
CROMWELL, CINDERELLA	1800	NC	037	1891	NC	047		1 1820	NC	037	WILLIAM D PETTAWAY/PETWAY	27441
CROMWELL, ELISHA		NC	037	1821	NC	037		1 C1799	NC	037	ELIZABETH SUTHERLAND	27441
CROMWELL, THOMAS				1795	NC	037		1	NC	037	SELAH/CELIA	27441
CROSS, JOEL	C1770	NC	085	C1880	TN			1 1794	NC	085	SUSANNAH MOORE	60017
CROWDER, NANCY	1795	NC	060	1853	NC	026		1	NC	060	ARCHIBALD WILLIAMSON	05070
CROWELL, ELMINA R	C1820	NC		C1875	NC	?105	069	1 1836	NC	069	ALFORD/ALFRED THOMPSON/THOMSON	03250
CROWSON, JACOB							027	1 C1805			ELIZABETH HILL	24032
CROWSON, MARY	1808	SC			NC	027		1			BETHEL BUFFKIN	24032
CRUMP, ALEXANDER	C1812	NC	067	1886	TX		005	1 1837	NC	081	WINCY GOLDSTON	60421
CRUMP, JAMES F	C1843	NC	067	C1885	TX		005	1 1876	TX		JESSIE BRIGGS	60421
CRUMP, JOHN	C1750	VA			NC		067	1			MARY STEPHENS ?	60421
CRUMP, STEPHEN	C1788	NC	067	1857	NC	089	005	1 C1808	NC		SALLY EASLEY	60421
								2	NC		MRS DILLY (PARHAM) DUNN	
								3	NC		ELIZA ANN KENDALL	
CRUTCHFIELD, ELIZABETH	C1738	VA		C1808	NC	022		1 C1756	VA		WILLIAM MEACHAM	08200
CRUTCHFIELD, HENRY	C1715	?VA		1787	NC	022		1 C1737	?VA		MILLY	04195
CRUTCHFIELD, JAMES				C1790	NC	022						08200
CRUTCHFIELD, JOHN	C1775	NC	?015	1845	TN		?100					07095
CRUTCHFIELD, MARTHA/PATSY	1819	NC	022	1901	NC	022		1 1835	NC	022	MATTHIAS M JOHNSON	04195
CRUTCHFIELD, OLIVER M/MARTIN	C1797	NC	100	1869	KY			1 1818	TN		MARY/POLLY BURNETTE	07095
CRUTCHFIELD, RICHARD		?VA			?NC	?100	015	1			CATHERINE	07095
CRUTCHFIELD, SAMUEL				1795	NC	100	015	1			SARAH SHEARON	07095
CRUTCHFIELD, THOMAS	C1755	?VA		C1844	NC	022		1 C1810	NC	022	HANNAH PERRY	04195
CULBREATH, NEIL	C1755			1825	NC	087		1			MARTHA AUTREY	13052
CULBREATH, SABRA	C1780	NC	087	C1850				1			ALLEN HALL	13052
CULLEN, BRYAN	1680	NC			NC	?028						60519
CULLEN, FREDERICK P	1765	NC	?028	1846	GA		010	1 1791	NC	010	ELIZABETH WIMBERLY	60519
CULLEN, JONATHAN		NC	028	1757	NC	028		1	NC	028	TERMAH	60519
CULLEN, NATHAN	C1740	NC	?028	1785	NC	010		1	NC		CHRISTIAN LASSITER ?	60519

46

ANCESTOR INDEX	BIRTH	PL	CO	DEATH	PL	CO	LIVD	MARRIED	PL	CO	SPOUSE NAME	CODE
CUMMINGS/CUMMINS, GEORGE	C1742	NC	011	1808	NC	046	085	1 1759	NC	085	MRS SARAH COLLINS	60393
CUMMINGS/CUMMINS, GEORGE	1764	NC	085	C1830	TN		046	1 C1791	NC	?046	MARY MCQUISTON	60393
CUMMINS, REBECCA	1804	NC	?092	1869	MO			1 C1821	NC		NICHOLAS MORRIS	60325
CUNNINGHAM, CHRISTOPHER SR	C1720	VA		C1782	TN		?104	1 C1744			SUSSANNAH PATTON	60503
								2 C1751			MARY MUSGROVES	
CUNNINGHAM, HUGH				1824			085	1 1780			EALSE	60044
								2			MARY KENT	
CUNNINGHAM, HUMPHREY				C1805	NC	013	014	1 C1760	?NC	?085	RHODA SUMMERVILLE	04195
CUNNINGHAM, JAMES				C1790	NC	046						60228
CURRIE, EZEKIAL B	1763	NC	073	1851	NC	001	046	1 1800			ELIZABETH ALLEN ?	60092
CURRY, DUNCAN	1776	NC	?005	1852	GA		?011	1 1809	GA		JANE MICKLER	27532
CURRY, DUNCAN	1780	NC	?082	1849	GA			1 1810	GA		SARAH JANE SMITH	60396
CURTIS, JOHN JR	1760	VA		C1816	NC	099	056	1 1784	NC	099	MARY SHAW	60483
								2	NC	099	ELIZABETH	
CUTHBERTSON, RUTH								1 1852	NC	097	JOHN MCCOLLUM	60357
CUTHRELL, TEAGLE WALTER	1792			1841	NC	033		1 1823	VA		MRS MARTHA ANN (HERBERT) WHITBY	13120

D

ANCESTOR INDEX	BIRTH	PL	CO	DEATH	PL	CO	LIVD	MARRIED	PL	CO	SPOUSE NAME	CODE
DABBS, RICHARD	C1815	NC	005		TN			1			ELIZABETH EDWARDS	60242
DAIL, CORNELIA ADREN	1865	NC	024	1944	VA			1 1888	NC	?024	JOHN RICHARD WINGATE	27562
DAIL, WILLIAM ADISON	1845	NC	024	1886	NC	024		1 1865	NC	024	NANCY PENNY GOODWIN	27562
DAIL/DALE, WILLIAM RILEY SR	1795	NC		1877	TN			1 1817	TN		NANCY OVERTON	60321
DAILEY, BENJAMIN	C1760			C1815	NC	086		1 C1780	DE		ARZILLA CHRISTOPHER	02412
DAILEY, LYDIA V	1811	NC		C1873	IN			1 1842	NC	033	WILIAM OWEN CHAFFIN	60309
DALTON, DAVID	1740	VA		C1820	NC	090		1 1767	VA		SUSANNAH DAVIS	60519
								2			MRS ELEANORE (GOODE) MARTIN	
DALTON, NANCY	C1775	VA		C1820	NC	084		1 1794	NC	090	ABSALOM BOSTICK	60519
DALTON, SAMUEL	1699	?VA		1805	NC	090		1 C1735	?VA		ANNE DANDRIDGE REDD	60519
DALTON, SUSANNAH	1799	NC	?090	C1870	TN			1 1817	NC	090	ABSALOM BOSTICK	60519
DAMRON, MOSES	C1800	NC		C1840	MO			1 C1820				60327
DANIEL, CHARLOTTE	C1796	?NC	?044	C1880	GA			1 1810	NC	044	JOHN KNOTT	17070
DANIEL, ISAAC	C1805	NC			AL			1	NC		NANCY PARKER	60039
DANIEL/DANIELS, JOHN				1829	NC	030		1			MARY MATILDA BAUM	20335
DANSBY/DANSBE, DANIEL		?VA		C1749	NC	037	071	1			ELIZABETH	60178
DANSBY/DANSBE, ISOME	C1737	NC	037	C1787	SC							60178
DARDEN, CARR	C1760	VA		1825	TN		071	1 C1780	NC		SUSAN MARSHALL	60397
DARDEN, GEORGE, CAPT		?VA		1839	NC	?053	009	1			MARY ANN JESSUP ?	12140

ANCESTOR INDEX	BIRTH	PL	CO	DEATH	PL	CO	LIVD	MARRIED		PL	CO	SPOUSE NAME	CODE
DARDEN, JOHN				C1845	NC	071		1				MARY	60584
DARDEN, JULIA	C1790	NC		C1855	TN		071	1	C1800	TN		WILLIAM HENLY	60397
DARDEN, MELISSA ANN CARR	1829	NC	009	1907	NC	009		1	1847	NC	009	WILLIAM ZENAS MORTON	12140
DARDEN, MILLS	1799	NC		1857	TN		?071	1		NC		MARY	60584
								2	C1840	TN		TOMACIA	
DARNELL, BENJAMIN	1780	NC	104	1861	IL			1	1802	NC	104	FANNIE VIERS/VIARS	10154
								2	1849	IL		TEMPERANCE POTTER	
DARNELL, BENJAMIN JR	1820	NC	104	1877	IL			1	1843	IL		MRS SARAH A (NORDVIG) LARSON	10154
												HENDERSON	
DARNELL, JOHN	C1755			1780	SC		104	1				RACHEL	10154
DAVENPORT, ALFRED	C1811	NC		C1855	TN			1	C1834	TN		SARAH SWINGLE	60449
DAVENPORT, ELKANAH							101	1	1778	NC	096	RACHEL WYNN	02195
DAVENPORT, MARY	1779	NC	096	1858	NC	101		1	1799	NC	096	DEMPSEY SPRUILL	02195
DAVENPORT, WILLIAM BAKER	C1814	NC		1864	IA			1	1839	TN		MARY MAGDALEN SWINGLE	60449
								2	1854	IA		MRS MARY JANE (DYSON) MABIE	
DAVIDSON, ELIZABETH				C1835	NC	065		1	C1787	?NC		JAMES MCCRACKEN	14050
DAVIS, ANNIE WATTERS	C1820	NC	070	C1870	NC	022		1	C1840	NC	012	THOMAS CALIZANCE MILLER	27286
DAVIS, ARCHIBALD	1763	NC	044	1821	NC	039		1	1789	NC	039	ELIZABETH HILLIARD	60037
DAVIS, ARCHIBALD	1800	NC	039					1				LUCY MASSENBURG	60037
								2				CAROLINE C KEARNEY	
DAVIS, ARTHUR	C1819	NC		C1864			103	1				REBECCA AMANDA	60104
DAVIS, BAXTER JR	1773	VA		1839	KY		044	1	1801	NC	044	MARY EDMONDSON WEBB	60164
DAVIS, BAXTER/BAESTER	C1750	?VA		C1835	KY		011	1	C1770			P	27565
DAVIS, BENJAMIN	C1740				SC		069	1	C1760	NC	037		60498
DAVIS, CHARLES	1755				NC	090							60456
DAVIS, DAVID		?VA		1806	NC	092		1				ANNA	25127
DAVIS, DAVID	1756			C1806	NC	092		1				ANNA	60546
DAVIS, DENNIS HARRIS	1815	NC		1863	MS			1	C1844	MS		AULINE GARDNER	08185
								2	C1851	MS		SARAH GARDNER	
DAVIS, DOROTHY		PA			NC	070		1	1717	PA		EDWARD PEARSALL	17085
DAVIS, EVAN	1800	NC	092	1892	NC	092		1	1831	NC	092	HANNAH GARDNER	60546
DAVIS, FIELDER	C1804							1	1823	NC	090	ELIZABETH MERRITT	60456
DAVIS, FREDERICK SOBIESKI	1817	NC	070	1874	NC	022		1	1848	NC	070	ELIZABETH MOORE QUINCE	27286
DAVIS, GEORGE	1819	NC	092		IN			1	1841	IN		CHARLOTTY BALDWIN	27429
DAVIS, GEORGE	1762	?NC		1839	?TN			1	C1802	?NC		ANN EAKIN	60020
DAVIS, JAMES	C1780	?NC	?011	1854	KY			1	C1800	?NC	?011	SARAH	27565
DAVIS, JAMES	C1807	NC			?NC		005	1				ELITHA	60584
DAVIS, JEHU		ENG			NC	070		1				JANE ASSUP	27286
DAVIS, JEHU, III		NC	070		NC	070		1				JANE QUINCE	27286
DAVIS, JOB WORTH	1877	NC	038	1934	NC	038		1	1908	NC	038	DELLA SHORE	60546

ANCESTOR INDEX	BIRTH	PL	CO	DEATH	PL	CO	LIVD	MARRIED	PL	CO	SPOUSE NAME	CODE
DAVIS, JOHN	C1785	NC	?013	C1890	NC	062		1		NC	?013 NANCY	03065
DAVIS, JOHN	C1775	NC	?100	C1855	MS			1 1796	KY		MARY HAWKINS	25174
DAVIS, JOHN	1735	PA		C1785	NC	073	022	1 1759	NC	073	MARY CHAMNESS	27429
DAVIS, JOHN E	1850	NC	103		TX			1 1873	TX		EMMA C KELLAM	60104
DAVIS, JOSEPH	1785	NC	022		IN		?092	1 C1807	NC	?046	CATHERINE FARMER	27429
DAVIS, LEMUELL	1796			1871	NC	038		1 1819	NC	090	MARY MERRITT	60456
DAVIS, LEWIS	C1804	NC		C1865	TN			1			MARGARET HASTINGS	27699
DAVIS, LEWIS								1 1869	NC	038	LUCY A LONGWORTH	60467
DAVIS, MALINDA	1824	NC	013	C1873	NC	062		1 C1843		?013	ROBERT COGDILL	03065
DAVIS, MARTHA ELLEN	1870	NC	?038	1889	NC	038		1 1887	NC	038	WILLIAM LUTHER MORGAN	60467
DAVIS, MATTHEW	C1736	NC	047	C1786	TN			1			ELIZABETH	60201
DAVIS, NANCY	C1784	NC		C1865	NC	062	013	1	NC	?086	WILLIAM COGDILL	03065
DAVIS, NATHAN	C1797	NC		C1860	NC	081		1 C1827	NC	?081	REBECCA	27429
DAVIS, PETER				C1804	NC	100		1			MRS HANNAH (TURNER) DAVIS	60594
DAVIS, REECE WILLIAM	1790	NC	092		IL			2 1823 3 C1826	NC NC	092	PATSY CHILDERS MARTHA/PATSY HARRIS	25127
DAVIS, SHORE DAVID	1921	NC	038	1978	NC	038		1 1949	NC	038	MRS GAIL ADELINE (WILLIAMS) SMITHERMAN	60546
DAVIS, SYLVANUS DAVID	1832	NC	092	1896	NC	038		1 1861	NC	038	JANE TRANSOU	60546
DAVIS, THOMAS		NC	070		NC	070		1 1758			MARY MOORE	27286
DAVIS, THOMAS				1765	NC	047	037	1			HARTWELL HODGES	60037
DAVIS, THOMAS JUNIUS	1851	NC	022	1934	CA			1 1887	CA		SUSAN FRANCES MURPHY	27286
DAVIS, THOMAS JUNIUS	1782	NC	070	1865	NC	070		1 1810	NC	070	ELIZABETH MILDRED BROWN WATTERS	27286
DAVIS, W BAXTER SR		VA			NC	?044	044	1	VA		AMELIA HOPKINS	60164
DAVIS, WILLIAM	1763	NC	073	1833	OH		?022	1 1782	NC	?046	ANN MARSHILL	27429
DAVIS, WILLIAM PERRY	1827	NC	?092	1910	IL			1 1864	IL		MARGARET JANE DAGG	25127
DAVIS, WILY							038	1			CELIA	60467
DAVIS/DAVIES, MARY	C1760			1845	TN		092	1 1779	NC	085	HILLERY MASTERS	60171
DAWSON, HENRY		VA		C1800	NC		047	1			ELIZABETH EDWARDS	27600
DAWSON, MARTHA/PATSY/MATTIE	1774	?NC		1838	AL			1 C1800	?NC		JOHN HUSON/HUSTON	27600
DAWSON, NEWTON C	1811	NC		1872	NC	038		1 1833	NC	090	MARGENETH FULP	60148
DAWSON, WILLIAM	C1730			1797	NC	099		1			MARTHA	60507
DAY, BEHETHLAND	1798	NC	078	1874	TN							60283
DAY, PHILIP	1762	NC	073	1839	TN			1 1793	NC	078	MARY DOUGLAS	60283
DEAL, JOHN	1800	NC	045					1			SARAH BARNETT	60055
DEAL, WILLIAM	1774	NC						1 1793	NC	077	ANNA BUNCH	60055
DEAN, DANIEL	1784	NC	044	1868	NC	044		1 1807	NC	044	ELIZABETH CARNAL	03125
DEAN, MOSES C	1814	NC	044	1895	NC	044		1 1835	NC	044	LUCINDA R SHEARMAN	03125

ANCESTOR INDEX	BIRTH	PL	CO	DEATH	PL	CO	LIVD	MARRIED	PL	CO	SPOUSE NAME	CODE
DEAN, RICHARD	C1755			1830	NC	044		1		NC	044 FRANCIS SLAUGHTER	03125
DEAN, WILLIAM JASPER	1843	NC	044	1889	NC	044		1 1873	NC		044 ELIZABETH FRANCIS KNOTT	03125
DEANS, JOSEPH	C1853	NC	?010	C1904	NC	010		2 1895	NC		010 AMANDA E WHITE	25226
DEARMAN, GEORGE CHRISTOPHER	1845	NC	054	1925	NC	054		1 1865	NC		054 AMANDA CAROLINA RICHIE	60065
DEARMAN, HENRY	1766	GER		1841	NC	054		1 C1802	?NC		?054 MARGARET	60065
DEARMAN, HENRY W	1804	NC	054	1881	NC	054		1 1831	NC		054 NANCY M SUMMERS	60065
DEARMIN/DEARMON, JOHN BARNABAS	1804	NC	084	1848	IN			1 1825	NC		084 ELIZABETH GATES KELLAM	60281
DEATHERAGE, BIRD	1805	NC		1880	AR		?084	1 1824	TN		ELCIE MONS	60452
DEATON, SUSAN ELIZABETH	C1820	NC			TN			1	NC		MR BRADY	60538
								2 1853	TN		JAMES WALKER	
								3 1862	TN		WILLIAM BAKER	
DEBNAM, BARTHOLOMEW YATES	C1799			1873	NC	039	046	1 1826	NC		039 ELIZABETH S MACON	04065
								2 1840	NC		099 NARCISSA J HORTON	
DEBNAM, CATHERINE E								1 1837	NC		099 WILLIAM J HORTON	04065
DEBNAM, CHARLES FRANKLIN		NC	039		NC	099		1 1842	NC		099 MARTHA GREY HORTON	04065
DEBNAM, EDWARD				1860	NC	?099		1 1838	NC		056 NANCY J BULLS	04065
DEBNAM, JAMES A				1888	NC	?039		1 1840	NC		056 ADELINE WILLIAMS	04065
DEBNAM, PETER F								1 1821	NC		039 ALICE WADDAIL	04065
DEBNAM, ROBERT	1770			1823	NC	039		1			ANN FOSTER	04065
DEBNAM, THOMAS RICHARD		VA			NC	099		1 1834	NC		039 PRICALLA M MACON	04065
DEBNAM, WILLIAM RANDOLPH								1 1854	NC		039 SARAH F EAVES	04065
DEBOW, JANE	1750	NJ		1827	NC	020		1 1769	NC		ARCHIBALD MURPHEY	60043
DEBOW, SOLOMON	C1714	NJ		1783	NC	073		1	?NJ		HANNAH	60043
DEEN, DRURY	1785	NC		1858	AL			1	GA		MARY MASTIN ?	27600
								2 C1822	AL		LIDIA MCWILLIAMS	
DEES ELIAS	1816	ENG		1886	NC	029		1 1836	SC		MARY HAMILTON	60394
DEES, ELI MALACHI	1851	SC		1929	NC	040		1 1871	NC		029 CATHERINE ANN RATLEY	60394
DEES, SALLY	1892	NC	029	1946	NC	029		1 1909	NC		029 EDGAR CORNELIUS KOONCE	60394
DELAMAR/ DE LA MARE, FRANCIS	C1697	NC	002	C1741	NC	009		1			SUSANNAH	60544
DELAMAR/ DE LA MARE, FRANCIS	C1732	NC	009	C1799	NC	028		1 1759	NC		051 MIRIAM BARCLIFT	60544
								2 1788	NC		029 HASTY NELSON	
DELAMAR/DE LA MARE, FRANCIS		FR		1713	NC	075		1 1694			MRS SUSANNAH TRAVIS	60544
								2 C1703			MRS ANN (MAYO) POPE	
DELAMAR/DE LA MARE, SARY/SARAH	1765	NC	028	1818	GA			1 1784	NC		028 THOMAS CLAYTON	60544
DELLINGER, EPHRAIM	1810	NC	060	C1897				1 1830	NC		060 MRS ANNA ROBISON	07115
								2 C1867			MARY	
DELLINGER, JAMES MCDOWELL	C1868	NC		C1895	NC	060		1 1891	NC		060 MRS SUSANNA JANE (BEAL) PRICE	07115
DELOACH, MARG				C1795	NC	037		1	NC		037 SOLOMON BRACEWELL	27441
DELOACH, SAMUEL				C1764	NC	037		1			MARY BOYKIN	15045
DELOACH, SAMUEL				1764	NC	037		1			MARY BOYKIN	27441

ANCESTOR INDEX	BIRTH	PL	CO	DEATH	PL	CO	LIVD	MARRIED	PL	CO	SPOUSE NAME	CODE
DELOACH, SELAH		?NC	?037		TN			1	?NC	?037	JOSEPH BARNES	15045
DELP, MICHAEL								1 1782	NC	020	ELIZABETH STARKEY	60026
DENKINS/DINKINS, JOSHUA	1762	NC	079	1835	TN							04115
DENKINS/DINKINS, WILLIAM H	1800	NC	005	1842	TN							04115
DENNIS, JESSE	1799	NC	081	1860	WI			1 1823 2 1838 3 1857	NC IN IN	046	UNITY STANLEY MIRIAM BEESON MRS RACHEL (MOORMAN) HALL	60314
DENNIS, SARAH	C1758	PA					081	1 C1780	NC	081	SAMUEL ALEXANDER	60306
DENNIS, THOMAS	C1724	NJ		1803	NC	081		1 1757	PA		ELIZABETH WEBB	60306
DENNIS, WILLIAM	1769	NC	085	1847	IN			1 1790	NC		DELILAH HOBBS	60314
DENNIS, WILLIAM	1804	NC	081	1878	KS			1 1827	NC		REBECCA HODGIN	60314
DENNY, AZARIAH	1788	NC	092	1878	NC	092		1 1810	NC	092	ELIZABETH STONE	60529
DENNY, DAVID J	1861	NC	092	1948	NC	092		1 2	 NC	 092	REBECCAH ANN HANCOCK DELILAH LOUVENIA CANTER	60529
DENNY, ELIZABETH	C1784	NC	092	1869	OH			1 1801	NC	092	WILLIAM BRAY	19040
DENNY, FRANCINA	C1809	NC			IN			1 1837	OH		MARTIN BURRIS	04103
DENNY, SAMUEL	C1723	VA		C1800	OH		092	1 C1740			SOUTHARD	60529
DENNY, WILLIAM	C1750	VA		C1820	NC	092		1 C1771	VA		REBECCA HOOPER	60529
DENNY, JOEL		NC	092	1896	NC	092		1 1838	NC	092	NANCY BOAZ JONES	60529
DENSON, BENJAMIN		?VA		1781	NC	069	037	1 1747	VA		MARY WHITEHEAD	25117
DENSON, JOHN RIDDLE ?		NC	?069	C1815	?TN			1 C1800	NC	069	FRANCES E	25117
DENSON, JOSEPH		VA					103	1 1776	NC	?071	MARY WATKINS	25117
DENSON, JOSEPH	1795	NC	005	C1850	MS			1 1823	MS		ARAMINTA SMITH	60565
DENSON, MRS FRANCES E	1787	NC	?069	1846	IL			1 1817	IL		JOHN CAMPBELL WOOD	25117
DENSON, NATHANIEL/NATHAN		NC	005	C1838	MS			1			CHARITY COLSON	60565
DENSON, WILLIAM		VA					?005					60565
DEWEESE, ISAIAH	1764	DE		1844	NC	016		1 1788	NC	020	REBECCA BARNETT	60027
DEWEESE, JONATHAN	C1722	?DE		1777	NC	020		1 C1752	?DE		RACHEL MERCHANT ?	60027
DEWEESE, NANCY AVELINE	1842	NC	023	1923	MO			1 1859 2 1923	TN MO		JOHN TIPPETT FRANK DILLON	60253
DICK, THOMAS	C1765			1820	NC	046		1 1792	NC	046	JEAN ERWIN	12125
DICK, WILLIAM	C1745			1810	NC	046						12125
DICKENS, MASEN	1820	NC	069		NC	046		1 1840	NC	069	ANDERSON KING	60313
DICKINSON, JOHN JR	C1790	NC	019	C1865	NC	019		1 1811	NC	019	ANN NORRIS	06080
DICKSON, DOUGLAS	C1779	NC	104	C1860	NC	006		1 C1804	NC	006	JOANNA PENNINGTON	60187
DICKSON, HIRAM RAY	1824	NC	006	1898	MO			1 1844 2 1862			NANCY A SMITH TEMPERANCE LOUISE BRADSHAW FITZGERALD	60187
DICKSON, JAMES	1760	NC	035	1812	NC	035		1 1774 2 1797	NC NC	035 035	DOROTHY PEARSALL MRS SUSANNAH POWELL	15023
DICKSON, THOMAS	C1750	SCO		C1809	NC	006	104					60187

ANCESTOR INDEX	BIRTH	PL	CO	DEATH	PL	CO	LIVD	MARRIED	PL	CO	SPOUSE NAME	CODE
DICKSON, WILLIAM DOUGLAS	1804	NC	006	1880	MO			1 2 C1871			FRANCES CROSS DIANA	60187
DIETZ, ANNA MARIE	1796	NC	060	C1840	MO			1			SIEBERT SPENCER	11010
DIETZ, SOLOMON SR		PA		C1822	NC	060		2 1797	NC	060	ELIZABETH HUFFMAN	11010
DIGGS, BENJAMIN H	1798	NC	005	1871	TN							04115
DILLARD, CALVIN HENRY	C1800	NC	099		NC	099		1			POLLY BARBOUR	02450
DILLARD, CORA LESTER	1871	NC	099	1936	NC	099		1 1899	NC	099	CECIL C BROWN	02450
DILLARD, RUTH	C1800	NC	013		GA			1 C1820	NC	013	OBEDIAH DICKERSON	60261
DILLARD, WILLIAM H	1828	NC	099	1896	NC	099		1 1854	NC	099	ANALIZER SORRELL	02450
DILLON, DOLLIE JANE	1835	NC		1907	WA			1 1850	AR		HUBBARD PETTY	60155
DILLS, ANN		SC						1		NC	PETER DILLS	17135
DILLS, BARTLETT SR		NC	086		NC	049		1		NC	MISS/MRS HENSON	17135
DILLS, ELIZABETH (CROSKEY), MRS					NC			1 1719	SC		JOSEPH DILL	17135
DILLS, MYRA/MIRA	1824	NC	086	1886	NC	061		1 1844	NC	061	HIRAM CRISP	17135
DILLS, PETER		NC						1		NC	ANN DILLS	17135
DILLS, THOMAS	C1795	NC	086		NC	061		1		NC	ELIZABETH MARTIN	17135
DILLS, THOMAS		NC	086		NC	086		1		NC	ELIZABETH CUZZINE	17135
DIXON, BENAJAH	1786	NC	034	1834	NC	045		1 1807	NC	045	MARY HILL	13264
DIXON, CATHERINE	C1750	NC	056	1802	NC	072		1 C1775 2 1791	NC NC	057	SAMUEL FIELDS JEREMIAH WATSON	13264
DIXON, FREDERICK H	1765	NC	034	1828	NC	072		1		NC	CHRISTIAN	13264
DIXON, ISHAM	1792	NC	042	1863	NC	045		1 C1820 2 1838	NC NC	045 045	GATSEY FRANCES OLDS	13264
DIXON, JOHN HOLLIDAY, REV	1795	NC	042	1843	NC	045		1 2	NC NC	045 079	NANCY DARDEN PRISCILLA D BYNUM	13264
DIXON, LOGUSTINE	C1805	NC		C1860	AR			1			POLLY	60046
DIXON, MARY	C1769	NC	034		?NC	?045	045	1 C1790	NC	034	ABRAHAM DENNY	13264
DIXON, MURFREE	C1710	VA		C1810	NC	045		1 C1735	VA		MOURNING GARNER	13264
DIXON, OBEDIAH	1770	NC	034	1849	NC	045		1 C1795	NC	042	SALLY	13264
DIXON, SHADRACH	C1767	NC	034	C1845	NC	045		1 1788	NC	034		13264
DIXON, WASHINGTON	1806	NC	045	1856	NC	045		1 1828	NC	045	MARY ORMAND	13264
DIXON, WILLIAM H	C1796	NC			IA			1		NC	RACHEL	60450
DIXON, WILLIS	1763	NC	034	1843	NC	045		1 C1795 2 C1835	NC NC	042 045	SARAH HOLLIDAY MARY SUGG	13264
DIXON, WILLIS	C1820	NC	045	C1855	NC	045		1 1842	NC	079	MARY ANN BROWN	13264
DIXON, WINSOR	1802	NC	045	1858	NC	045		1 C1825 2 C1828	NC NC	059 079	SALLIE DUNN CLARA ALBRITTON	13264
DIXON/DICKSON, JANE	1848	NC	045	1935	FL			1 1869	NC	045	ELIJAH MCARTHUR	60224
DIXON/DICKSON, JANE	1848	NC	045	1935	FL			1 1869	NC	045	ELIJAH MCARTHUR	60224
DIXON/DICKSON, JOHN				1814	VA		104	1 C1794	NC	085	SUSANNAH LIPPS	60049

ANCESTOR INDEX	BIRTH	PL	CO	DEATH	PL	CO	LIVD	MARRIED	PL	CO	SPOUSE NAME	CODE
DIXON/DICKSON, JOHN OBADIAH	C1820						045					60224
DIXON/DICKSON, JOHN OBADIAH	C1820						045					60224
DIXON/DICKSON, WILLIAM H.	1795	NC	104	1875	MO		?006	1 1824	VA		ELIZABETH HEAD	60049
								2 1828	VA		MRS HANNAH (HENSLEY) LITTLE	
DOBBS, FORTUNE	C1727	IRE						1 C1750	NC		MARY ADAMS	27775
DOBBS, FORTUNE	1755	NC										27775
DOBBS, JOEL	1790	NC	?014	1842	MO			1 1815	TN		SALLY/SARAH MORGAN	60072
DOBBS, LODOWICK ADAMS	1759	NC						1 1782			SARAH ADAMS	27775
DOBBS, WILLIAM	1757	NC										27775
DOBSON, CRAWFORD	C1794	NC	090	1822	NC	090		1 1818	NC	090	FRANCES BARROW	60218
DOBSON, FRANKLIN	C1805	NC	090					1			VIOLET KING	60406
DOBSON, HENRY B BAKER	C1770	?NC	?092	C1828	?NC	?090	090	1 C1790	?NC		ELIZABETH	60218
DOBSON, HENRY B BAKER	1825	NC	090	1884	IL			1 1848	IL		NANCY MCMURTRY	60218
DOBSON, HENRY BAKER		NC	090				090					60406
DOBSON, WILLIAM	1796	NC	090	C1875	?IL			1 1823	NC	090	ELIZABETH LOWE	60218
DOBSON, WILLIAM CARLYLE	C1750			1822	NC	090		2 1793	NC	092	MARTHA NEELY	60218
DOBSON, WILLIAM CARLYLE	C1760	NC	085	C1815			090	1			MARTHA NEELY	60406
DOBSON, WILLIAM POLK		NC	085	1846			092	1 1802	NC	085	MARY/POLLY HUGHES	60406
DONALDSON, ALEXANDER				1800	NC	085		1			SARAH	07095
DONALDSON, ANN ADALINE	1803	NC	054	1868	TN			1			GEORGE S MALLORY	07095
								2			WILLIAM MORTIMORE STEVENSON	
								3			ADOLPHUS W ALEXANDER	
DONALDSON, JAMES	C1765	NC	?085	1842	TN		054	1			MRS ESTHER (NEILL) ALLISON	07095
DONALDSON, ROBERT							078	1			MARTHA WALKER	60050
DONALDSON, ROBERT	C1754				?TN		020	1 C1776	?NC		MARTHA WALKER	60494
DONALDSON, WILLIAM				1817	NC	054	085	1			ANN	07095
DONNELL, ELLIOTT				C1845	NC	084		1 C1830			CLARISSA MOORE	27375
DONNELL, JOHN ALBERT	C1832	NC	084	1868	AR			1 C1856	AR		ELIZABETH WOOLLEY	27375
DORMAN, ALLEN	1769	VA		1833	GA		037	1			MARY ELIZABETH MCNEELY	60285
								2			MARTHA	
DORMAN, MICHAEL							037					60285
DORMAN, MITCHELL				1785	NC	037		1			MARY	60285
DORMINY, JOHN B SR	1768	NC		1847	GA			1 C1796	GA		RACHEL BRADFORD	60498
DORRIS, JOHN							073	1			ANGEL MACE	04155
DORRIS, JOHN	C1775			1824	TN			1 1795	NC	073	PHEBE CULBERTSON	04155
DORSETT, JUDITH EMALINE	1846	NC			CO			1			MR SANFORD	60084
DORSETT, SOLOMON	1843	NC										60084
DORSETT, WILLIAM HEAD	1820	NC		1905	OK			1 1842	NC		MARY E PUNCH	60084
								2 1855	NC		CYNTHA CELINA PUNCH	
DORTCH, LEWIS		?NC		1818	NC	069		1			ANNE	25199

ANCESTOR INDEX	BIRTH	PL	CO	DEATH	PL	CO	LIVD	MARRIED	PL	CO	SPOUSE NAME	CODE
DORTCH, WILLIAM				C1778	NC	069		1			ANNE	25199
DOUGLAS, GEORGE	C1795	NC	?104		NC	006		1			ISABELL JOHNSON	60418
DOUGLAS/DOUGLASS, JOHN	C1730	NC	?010	C1805	TN			1 1765	NC	073	HANNAH DEBOW	60283
DOUGLAS/DOUGLASS, MARY	1772	NC	073	1839	TN							60283
DOUGLASS, ANGUS	1759	SCO		1819	NC	082						12019
DOUGLASS, DANIEL	C1735	SCO		1816	NC	082		1			EFFIE MCLEAN	12019
DOUGLASS, DANIEL	1762			1812	NC	083		1			CHRISTIAN	12019
DOUGLASS, DANIEL	1790	NC		1844	NC	083		1			CHRISTIAN MCLEOD ?	12019
DOUGLASS, DUNCAN C	C1795	NC	082									12019
DOUTHIT, EVAN	1769	NC	085	1849	TX			1 1791	SC		SARAH MCCULLOCH	02170
DOUTHIT, JOHN JR	1741	MD		1813	SC			1 1764	NC	085	ELINORE DAVIS	02170
DOWNEY, MARGARET				1833			046	1			WILLIAM RUSSELL	60032
DOYLE, SIMON	1768	VA		1843			020	1 1791	NC	020	ELIZABETH SARGENT	25229
DOYLE, SIMON W	1768	VA		1845	TN		020	1 1791	NC	020	ELIZABETH SARGENT	25229
DRAFFIN, JAMES	1740	IRE		C1778	NC	065		1			MARGARET	60233
DRAFFIN, JOSEPH	C1764	NC	065	1812				1			GRACE/GRACY	60233
DRAFFIN, MARY	1766	IRE					065					60233
DRAFFIN, WILLIAM SR ?	C1775	NC	065	C1811	SC			1			SARAH	60233
DRAKE, JAMES	1725	?VA		1790	VA		069	1			SOPHIA VALENTINE	12125
								2 1766			MRS HARTWELL (HODGES) DAVIS	
DRAKE, JOHN HODGES, DR	1767	NC	069	1859	AL			1 1794	NC	069	FRANCES WILLIAMS	12125
DRAKE, MARTHA JOHANNA WILLIAMS	1795	NC	069	1888	CA			1 1812	NC	069	JOHN D ARRINGTON	12125
DRAPER, CYNTHIA				C1858	NC	106		1			NORMAN SHAW	40690
DRIVER, JOHN E	1842	VA		1915	AR		099	1 1865	NC	099	AMANDA A GATTON	27594
DRIVER, JOHNATHAN/JIM		NC	?069	C1855	NC	?069		1	NC	?069	GINCY	03315
DRIVER, POLLY	1842	NC	?069	1908	NC	?069		1 1862	NC	069	JOHN BUNYON CREECH	03315
DUCKWORTH, JOHN	C1847	NC	?014					1				03213
								2 C1874			SAMANTHA-ELIZABETH JOHNSTON	
DUDLEY, ABNER	C1804	NC		C1865	IN		020	1 C1829	NC	020	ELIZABETH	60210
DUFF, ABRAM				1791	NC	046		1			MARY	60244
DUFF, JAMES								1 1773	NC	046	AGNES CARSON	60244
DUGGAN, JOHN SR				C1763	NC	096						19130
DUKE, EMILY C	1819	NC	051	1868	NC	051		1 1840	NC	051	JAMES N GREEN	27276
								2 1855	NC	051	WILLIAM A NICHOLS	
DUKE, EMILY C,	1819	NC		1868	NC			1 1840	NC		JAMES N GREEN	27531
DUKE, JAMES	C1815	NC	051		NC		010	1			GREEN	27276
DUKE, JAMES	1799	NC	073	1873	IN		092	1 1819	NC	092	CATHARINE REECE	60120
DUKE, JOHN	C1730	VA		1803	NC	073		1 C1750	?VA		LYDIA	60120

ANCESTOR INDEX	BIRTH	PL	CO	DEATH	PL	CO	LIVD	MARRIED	PL	CO	SPOUSE NAME	CODE
DUKE, ROBERT	C1775	NC	073	C1825	NC	073		1 1794	NC	073	ANN RHEW	60120
DUKE, WILLIAM	C1700	VA		1773	NC	073		1	VA		ELIZABETH	60120
DUKE/DUKES, ROBERT							071	1			ISABELLE VINSON	60331
DULANY/DULANEY, BENJAMIN	1748	NC	?072	1826	AL			1 1776	MD		RACHEL MURROW	60372
DULANY/DULANEY, BENJAMIN, REV	1784	NC	035	1852	AL			1 1814	SC		REBECCA HUTCHINSON	60372
DULANY/DULANEY, THOMAS, II	1689	IRE			NC	072		1 C1742	MD		ANN	60372
DULANY/DULANEY, THOMAS, III	1743	MD		1815	NC	072		1	NC	072	HELEN NEWTON	60372
DUNCAN, ANDERSON FULLER	1860	NC	022	1933	NC	013		1 1886	NC	?022	VIRGINIA ANN OVERTON	04195
DUNCAN, CHARLES	C1746	NC	085	1818	TN			1			LURANAH	60041
DUNCAN, DAVID SEYMORE	1832	NC	022	1891	NC	022		1 1854	NC	022	JANE ELIZABETH JOHNSON	04195
DUNCAN, ELIAS	C1750			C1830	?NC	027	012	1				27346
DUNCAN, ELIZABETH	1784	NC	022	1872	TN		022	1 1803	NC	022	WILLIAM EMERSON	05065
DUNCAN, JOHN	C1753			1810	NC	044		1 C1770	?NC	?044	CHLOE/CHLOAE	04195
DUNCAN, LEVIN	1810	NC	?027	1882	FL			1 C1831	?GA		SARAH FULLWOOD	27346
								2 C1851	?FL		MRS MARY BALL	
DUNCAN, MARSHALL	C1705	VA		1887	NC	092		1			ANN	60041
DUNCAN, MOSES	C1808						027	1			UNITY SIMS	24032
DUNCAN, MOSES	C1785	?NC	?012		?GA			1 C1809	NC	?027	CORBET	27346
DUNCAN, SEAMORE	C1774	NC	044	C1825	NC	044	073	1 C1795	NC	?073	PRISCILLA HICKS	04195
DUNCAN, UNITY	1841	NC	027	1924	NC	027		1 1867	NC	027	LABON FOWLER	24032
DUNCAN, WILLIAM	C1744	SCO		1835	TN		022	2 1779	NC	022	PATSY WEST	05065
DUNCAN, WILLIAM SEYMORE	1802	NC	073	1883	NC	022		1 1826	NC	022	ELIZABETH GRIFFIN JUSTICE	04195
DUNLAP, SARAH	1786			1868	TX			1 1813	NC	060	ANTHONY CLARK	60443
DUNN, JACOB					NC	037		1	NC	037		08185
DUNN, JOHN SR		VA			NC	037		1			ESTHER/EASTER	08185
DUNN, NANNA/NANNY					NC	037		1			DAVID SCARBOROUGH	08185
DUNSTON, EBENEZER	1827	NC	101	1888	NC	101		1 1859	NC	101	JULIA ELIZABETH ROWE	02195
								2 1885	NC	101	LENNIE EULALIA BLOUNT	
DUNSTON, JOHN	C1795	NC	?096	C1840				1 C1825	NC	101	HENRETTA SPRUILL	02195
DUPREE, JAMES		?VA			NC	071		1			MRS TABITHA (MORRIS) DUPREE	60594
DUPREE, LEWIS HENRY				1930	NC	099		1			ANNE FISH	60500
DUPREE, LEWIS, COL	1725	VA		1791	NC	012	011	1	VA		VANDALIA STARLING	13264
DUPREE, REBECCA	1766	NC	079	C1820	NC	045		1 C1783	NC	?079	MAJOR STEPHEN EASON	13264
DUPREE, STARLING, MAJ	C1740	?NC	?011		NC	079		1 C1765	?NC	?079	SUSAN	13264
DUPREE/DUPRE', JAMES	C1720	VA		C1780	NC	079		1 C1753	VA		MARY DONALDSON	12140
DUPREE/DUPRE', JOSEPH ALVIN	1847	NC	079	1901	NC	079		1 1882	NC	071	JUDITH DEANES BOONE	12140
DUPREE/DUPRE', THOMAS	1772	NC	079	1854	NC	079		1 C1792	NC	037	NANCY/ANN RENN	12140
DUPREE/DUPRE', THOMAS BIRD	1812	NC	079	1882	NC	079		1 1842	NC	079	PENINA MAY	12140
								2 1849	NC	079	SARAH W MAY	

ANCESTOR INDEX	BIRTH	PL	CO	DEATH	PL	CO	LIVD	MARRIED	PL	CO	SPOUSE NAME	CODE
DUPREE/DUPRE', THOMAS OHAGAN	1890	NC	079	1961	FL			1 1915	NC	050	ISABEL BOGART MORTON	12140
DURANT, GEORGE	1631			1693	NC	?024		1			ANNE HARWOOD	60318
DURANT, JOHN	1662	NC	002	1699	NC	077		1 1684			SARAH COOKE	19230
DURHAM, ELIZABETH ANN	1797	NC		1878	IL			1			RANSOM TURNER COOK	60550
DURHAM, ROBERT M	1803	NC	073		TN			1 1826	NC	073	SARAH/SALLY JONES	27322
DURHAM, WILLIAM GREEN	1827	NC	073	1901	TX			1 1852	TN		LOUISA YORK	27322
DYE, GILBERT	1803	NC		1853	MO			1 1821			PRISCILLA HARREL	27568
DYE, HENRY	1836	NC		1916	MO			1 1857			JOSEPHINE BUTRAM	27568
								2 1866			MARGARET LUCINDA PARNELL	

E

ANCESTOR INDEX	BIRTH	PL	CO	DEATH	PL	CO	LIVD	MARRIED	PL	CO	SPOUSE NAME	CODE
EARLE, ELEANOR KEE	1792	NC	086	1857	MS			1 1815	?SC		SILAS REAGAN WHITTEN	07078
EARLE, JOHN, COL	1737	VA		1804	NC	086		1 1757	VA		THOMASCINA PRINCE	07078
								2 1786			MRS REBECCA (BERRY) WOODS	
EARNEST, ANN	C1790	NC	104	C1860	NC	102		1 1811	NC	104	JOHN H STANSBURY	02295
EARNEST, HENRY	C1770	NC	?085	C1820	NC	104		1	NC			02295
EASON, ABNER	1820	NC	045	C1905	NC	045		1 C1851	NC	045	MARY	13264
EASON, ABNER	C1730	NC	?024	1794	NC	010		1 C1750	NC	?077	RACHEL DOCTON ?	60337
EASON, ISAAC	C1720	NC	?077	1787	NC	037	079					13264
EASON, JOHN	C1795	NC	042	C1845	NC	045		1 C1815	NC	?045	LOUISA	13264
EASON, MARTHA JANE	1855	NC	045	1898	NC	045		1 1876	NC	045	JAMES ROSS MAY	13264
EASON, STEPHEN	C1758	NC	037	C1818	NC	045		1 C1783	NC	?037	REBECCA DUPREE	13264
EASON, THEOPHILUS	C1790	NC	034	1845	NC	045		1 C1810	NC	045	ELIZABETH	13264
EASTARD, CATHERINE	C1780	VA		C1860	NC	006		1 C1800	NC	006	RICHARD PERRY	02295
EASTEP/ESTEP, MOSES	C1784	NC		C1860	AL			1 1803	NC	085	ELIZABETH JONES	08023
EASTEP/ESTEP, RACHEL	1810	NC	085	1873	IN			1			JOHN MORGAN BAITY	08023
EATMAN, ELISHA/ELITIA	C1807	NC	?069	1870	NC	105						03250
EATMAN, THEOPHILUS	C1770	NC		C1850	NC	069		1			BEDY/OBEDIENCE	03250
EATMAN, WOODSON	C1845	NC	?069	C1913	NC	099	105	1 C1864	?NC		ELMINA THOMPSON/THOMSON	03250
								2 1897	NC	099	BETTIE WHITE	
EBERHART, JACOB JR	1756	NC	085	1850	GA			1 1785			MATILDA SIMMONS	60367
								2 1820			ELIZABETH WYNN	
ECLIN, CASSANDER				C1803	NC			1 1799	NC		SOLOMON BEASLEY	27600
EDDINGS, JOHN HENRY	1882	SC		1955	NC	016	085	1 1903	SC		MARY LELIA IVEY	60065
EDGE, ALLEN	1796	NC	011	1869	NC	011		1			THEODOCIA/SOPHIA WEATHERSBY	13052
EDGE, AMANDA	1862	NC	011	1906	NC	029						13052
EDGE, JOHN JR	C1774			C1808	NC	011		1			DRUSILLA	13052

ANCESTOR INDEX	BIRTH	PL	CO	DEATH	PL	CO	LIVD	MARRIED	PL	CO	SPOUSE NAME	CODE
EDGE, JOHN SR	C1755			C1805	NC	011						13052
EDGE, JOHN WEATHERSBY	1836	NC	011	1921	NC	029		1 1859	NC		ELIZABETH A POPE	13052
EDMISSON, EMANUEL	1795	NC		1857	MO			1 1817	KY		NANCY JOHNSON	27348
EDMUNDSON, JESSE WRIGHT	1845	NC	103	1917	TX			1 1874	TX		ADA HYANTIAN LEONARD	07015
EDMUNDSON, WILLIAM BURWELL	1812	NC	?103	1867	NC	103		1 1837 2	NC		JULIA ANN PIPKIN MARY	07015
EDNEY, EDMOND	1795	NC		1832	TN			1 1786	TN		NANCY DAVIS	25158
EDNEY, NEWTON RENSHAR	C1737	NC	075	C1794	NC	018						25158
EDNEY, NEWTON RENSHAR JR	1763	NC		1835	TN			1 1786	NC		JANE SMITH	25158
EDNEY, PETE				C1752	NC	075						25158
EDNEY, ROBERT	C1710			C1758	NC	075						25158
EDWARDS, ABEL	1810	NC		1895	IA			1 1834	IN		LUCY CLARISSA BENNETT	60487
EDWARDS, ABIGAIL	C1806	NC			?IA			1	?IN		ALEXANDER LAMB	60487
EDWARDS, DAVID	1745	?VA		1782	NC	073		1			ELIZABETH MORRIS	08190
EDWARDS, DAVID	C1740	VA		1782	NC	073		1 C1762	NC	073	ELIZABETH MORRIS	60120
EDWARDS, EDMUND	C1815	NC	?013	C1866	?TN			1 C1840	NC		RUTH	60390
EDWARDS, FRANCIS COOK	1796	NC	?071	1822	TN			1 1822	NC	?071	SARAR CRAWFORD TYNER	12008
EDWARDS, ISAAC ?	C1788	NC			NC	045		1			CORNELIA ANNE	16030
EDWARDS, JANE ELIZABETH	1821	NC	045	1891	NC	045		1 1846	NC	045	HARDY ORMOND	16030
EDWARDS, JOHN				C1801	NC	073		1			MARY	08070
EDWARDS, JOHN	C1720	VA		1801	NC	073		1 C1738			MARY	08190
EDWARDS, JOHN	C1715	?VA		1801	NC	073		1			MARY PHILLIPS	60120
EDWARDS, JOHN SR	C1720			1796	NC	073		1			MARY	60418
EDWARDS, LUCINDA	C1815	NC	006					1			JACOB FOUTS/PHOUTS	08190
EDWARDS, LUCINDA	1815	NC	006					1 C1835	NC	006	JACOB FOUTS	60120
EDWARDS, MARCELLUS J	C1828	NC	045		NC	?099		1 2	NC	045	JULIA A DARDEN VIRGINIA	06050
EDWARDS, MARY							073	1 C1796			JOHN CAMPBELL	08070
EDWARDS, MARY/MOLLY	C1800	NC	?046		NC	032		1 1818	NC	046	JOHN CARROLL WREN/WRENN	24315
EDWARDS, NATHAN	1755	NC	010	1831	TN			1 1783	NC	010	JEMIMA IRIS COTTON	60283
EDWARDS, NATHANIEL				C1816	NC	071		1 1786 2	VA		MARY/POLLEY COOKE MARTHA	12008
EDWARDS, NEDDY	C1793	?NC	?104	1869	IN			1			SARAH JANE STACKHOUSE	60348
EDWARDS, REBECCA	C1811	NC						1 1833	AL		ISRAEL BROTHERS	02414
EDWARDS, RODERICK POWELL	C1835	NC	042				105	1 C1855			SALLIE A	06050
EDWARDS, SALINE				1860	NC	006		1			MISS/MRS EDWARDS	08190
EDWARDS, SARAH	1791	NC	010	1883	TN							60283
EDWARDS, SARAH POLLY ?	C1805	NC	006	C1865	IL			1			WILLIAM HENRY WOODY	08190

ANCESTOR INDEX	BIRTH	PL	CO	DEATH	PL	CO	LIVD	MARRIED	PL	CO	SPOUSE NAME	CODE
EDWARDS, STERLING	C1765	NC	073	C1818	NC	006	104	1 1792	NC		104 SALENA COBB	60120
EDWARDS, STERLING/STARLING	1772	NC	?073	C1818	NC	006	104	1 1793	NC		060 SELINA/SALINA COBB	08190
EDWARDS, SUSAN REBECCA	C1763	?NC					?013	1 C1783			WILLIAM STILES	60029
EDWARDS, THEOPHILUS	1765			1834	NC	045		1 1797	NC		042 ELIZABETH SHEPPARD	06050
EDWARDS, THOMAS	C1780	NC			NC		013	1		NC	MARY BRITTAIN	60366
EDWARDS, WILLIAM HENRY	1811	NC	006		IN							08190
EELBECK, DANIEL	C1720	VA					047	1		VA	ANN	12040
EELBECK, ELIZABETH, MRS	C1740	NC	037	1800	NC	047		1 C1760	NC		047 JOHN ELBANCK/EELBECK	12040
EELBECK, JOHN	C1720	VA		1764	NC	047	037	2 C1760	NC		047 ELIZABETH	12040
EELBECK, MARTHA ELIZABETH	1765	NC	047					1 C1782	NC		047 HANCE BOND	12040
								2 1797	NC		047 WILLIAM BURT	
EILAND/ISLAND, ABSALOM	C1750	?NC	?056	1814	GA			1 C1775	?SC		ANN/NANCY DANIEL	60112
EILAND/ISLAND, BRYANT	1806	GA		1878	MS			1 1828	AL		LYDIA WHATLEY	60112
EILAND/ISLAND, ENOCH	1782	NC		C1850	AL			1 C1805	GA		FRANCES ANNA TRAWICK	60112
EILAND/ISLAND, GEORGE	C1715	?NC	?030	C1750	NC	056	030	1 C1740	NC	?030		60112
EILAND/ISLAND, RICHARD	C1695	?VA		1735	NC	030		1 C1715			ELIZABETH	60112
ELEY, SAMUEL	C1736	VA		1771	NC	015		1 1759	VA		MARY HILLSMAN	08120
ELFE, THOMAS	C1784	SC		C1829			070	1 C1816	NC	?012	MARY JANE BLANEY	60117
ELFE, THOMAS BLANEY	1817	NC	070									60117
ELKINS, THOMAS	1783	NC		1854	GA			1 1808			ANN SIMPSON	60175
								2 1811	GA		SARAH POWERS	
								3 1830	GA		MRS MARIA P (TONDEE) PATTERSON	
ELLEDGE, BENJAMIN							104					60380
ELLEDGE, DANIEL							104					60380
ELLEDGE, ISAAC							104					60380
ELLEDGE, JACOB							104					60380
ELLEDGE, JOSEPH							104					60380
ELLEDGE, NANCY	C1788	NC			IL			1 1818	KY		NATHAN PHILIPS	60440
ELLEDGE, THOMAS							104					60380
ELLER, ADAM	1795	TN		1870	NC	013		1 C1817	NC		013 ELIZABETH/BETSEY	17187
ELLER, JACOB	C1754	?PA			?TN		013	1 C1773			MARY BIFFLE	17187
ELLER, JOSEPH	1792	TN		1863	NC	013		1 C1811	NC		013 SARAH KIRKLAND	17187
								2 C1848	NC		013 ELIZABETH CLORINDA HAMILTON	
ELLER, MICHAEL FRANKLIN/JOSEPH M	1835	NC	013	1906	ID			1 1867	MO		SUSAN ELIZABETH MCFERRAN	17187
ELLIOTT, ABRAHAM	1780	NC	081	1848	IN			1 C1799			JANE ALEXANDER	60306
ELLIOTT, ELIZABETH	1766	NC		1841	IN			1 1787	NC	?046	HUGH MAXWELL	60476
ELLIOTT, ISAAC					NC			1 1743	NC		077 ELISABETH MORGAN	60476
ELLIOTT, ISRAEL	1759	PA		C1815	IN		081	1			WILMET	60306
ELLIOTT, JACOB				C1790	NC	081		1			ELIZABETH	60306

ANCESTOR INDEX	BIRTH	PL	CO	DEATH	PL	CO	LIVD	MARRIED	PL	CO	SPOUSE NAME	CODE
ELLIOTT, JACOB	C1745	NC						1 C1761	NC		ELIZABETH	60476
ELLIS, CORNELIA DOCIA	1925	NC	099					1 1946	MD		WOODROW WILSON LEE	12075
ELLIS, HENRY GETER	1871	NC	044	1942	NC	073		1	NC	036	CORNELIA FRANCES RAGAN	12075
ELLIS, IRA	C1807	NC			IN			1 1830	NC	085	FRANCES STARR/STAR	60381
ELLIS, LONNIE WASHINGTON	1900	NC	073	1925	NC	036		1 1922	NC	099	ZELMA GEROY MILLS	12075
ELLIS, MARY	1762	VA		1849	KY		086	1 1783	NC	086	ALEXANDER DAVIDSON	60297
ELLIS, MOSES	1835	NC	044	1900				1	NC	044	MARY MANGUM	12075
ELLIS, RACHAEL	C1770	?VA		1842	IL		086	1 C1785	?NC		JOHN DAVIDSON	60297
ELLIS, SARAH	C1771	?VA		1820	MO		086	1 C1786	?NC		ALEXANDER DAVIDSON	60297
ELLISON, JAMES				C1818	NC	009		1 C1740			SARAH ALDERSON	19130
ELMORE, CICILIA	1777	NC			IL			1 1803	TN		JOHN HAWORTH	20333
ELMORE, THOMAS	1739	VA						1 1767	NC		ANN SANDERS	20333
EMERSON, ARCHIBALD	1806	NC	022	1882	TN			1 1826	TN			05065
EMERSON, JAMES				1786	NC	022	073	1 C1758			MARGARET/PEGGY	05065
EMERSON, WILLIAM	1780	NC	022	1862	TN			1 1803	NC	022	ELIZABETH DUNCAN	05065
ENGLAND, MARY E	1790	NC	029	1855	NC	?068		1 1818	NC	029	LT WILLIAM M JOHNSON	60147
ENGLISH, DAVID J	1858	NC	?107	1925	NC	066		1 C1880 2 C1910	NC NC	066 066	JANE SPARKS HARRIET	60315
ENGLISH, JACK DAVID	C1835	NC	?107					1 C1855	NC	?107	ELIZABETH OSBURN	60315
ENGLISH, JACK DAVID	1914	NC	066	1974	NC	066		1 1935 2 1956	NC NC	066 066	EDITH PITMAN BOBBIE JEAN HISE	60315
ENGLISH, JACK LEE	1943	NC	066									60315
ENGLISH, MILT	1893	NC	066	1964	NC	066		1 1913	NC	066	ZULA BUCHANAN	60315
EPHRAIM, HARRIS	1801	NC	085	1869	MO			1			ELIZABETH BLAIR POYNTER	08023
EPPES, RICHARD	C1776			1827	NC	047		1 1805	NC	047	HARRIETT DAVIS BOND	12040
EPPS, PHELOMA D	1837	NC	032	1907	AR			1 1847	AR		JOHN EDWARD HUGHES	07015
EPPS, PLEASANT	1789	NC						1	NC		ELIZABETH	07015
ERVIN/ERWIN, JOSEPH	C1729			C1793	NC	085		1			AGNES	60575
ERVIN/ERWIN, WILLIAM	C1772	NC	085	C1855	TN			1 1796	NC	085	MARY/POLLY CATHEY	60575
ERWIN, ALEXANDER	1750	PA		1830	NC	014		1 1770			SARAH ANN ROBINSON	60593
ERWIN, JAMES	1775	NC	085	1848				1 1808			MARGARET LOCKE PHIFER	60593
ERWIN/IRWIN, ALEXANDER	C1780	NC	014	C1812	NC	014		1 C1800				60533
ESKRIDGE, ALBERT DIXON	1850	NC	026	1895	NC	026		1 1873	NC	040	SUSAN AARON BEAM	05070
ESKRIDGE, JOHN GREEN	1803	NC	086	1891	NC	026		1 1837	NC	086	ELIZABETH H THOMPSON	05070
ESKRIDGE, RICHARD	1739	VA		1809	NC	020		1 1764	VA		ELIZABETH READ	05070
ESKRIDGE, RICHARD	1768	VA		1831	NC	086		1 1794	NC	?020	ELIZABETH REYNOLDS	05070
ESLICK/ESSLICK/EASLICK, FRANCIS MARION		NC			KY							60121
ESLICK/ESSLICK/EASLICK, ISAAC							044	1			TABITHA	60121

ANCESTOR INDEX	BIRTH	PL	CO	DEATH	PL	CO	LIVD	MARRIED	PL	CO	SPOUSE NAME	CODE
ESLINGER/ESSLINGER, ANDREW	1748	GER		1824	TN		046	1 C1775	NC	046	CHRISTIANA EVA	01040
ESLINGER/ESSLINGER, CHRISTIAN	1781	NC	046	1864	MO			1 C1800	TN		HANNAH	01040
ESTES, MARTHA O	1827	NC		C1900	AR			1 1845	TN		JAMES ALEXANDER WILKINS	05065
ESTRIDGE, SUSANNAH/SUSAN	1770			1872	NC	073		1 1794	NC	073	JOHN CHEEK	08200
ESTRIDGE, THOMAS							073					08200
ETCHISON, NANCY JANE ?	C1775			C1840	IN		085	1			NIMROD ADAMS	08023
ETHERIDGE, WILLIAM S	1774			1838	NC	030		1 2 1828			SARAH TILLETT MRS NANCY (FORBES) KELLAM	20335
EUBANKS, WILLIAM H	C1773	NC		1847	IL							60179
EUDY, CONRAD/COON	C1752				NC	067	005					24165
EVANS, MILLY CHRISTENE	1853	NC	106	1940	IN			1 1874	NC	106	THOMAS DAVID HUTCHENS	60120
EVANS, NICHOLAS	C1720			1773	NC	092						60120
EVANS, THOMAS	C1745	VA		1790	NC	090		2 1787	NC	092	ANNE POINDEXTER	60120
EVANS, THOMAS	1812	NC	092	1857	NC	106		1 1833	NC	092	SARAH SMITH	60120
EVANS, WILLIAM	1789	NC	090	C1855	NC	106	092	1 C1807	NC	092	REBECCA ANGELL	60120
EWELL, JAMES				1818	NC	079		1 C1790	NC	079	CHRISTIANA	02195
EWELL, JESSE M	C1798	NC	079	C1869	NC	063		1 C1820			ELIZA	02195
EXUM, WILLIAM	1784	NC		C1858	TN			1 C1805 2 1839	TN		ELIZA ALLEN	60188
EYTCHESON, HUGH RAY	C1790	NC		1845	IN			1 C1811	TN		SARAH C REDER	60271
EYTCHESON, WALTER		NC		1860	IN			1 2 C1832	NC ?IN		MARGARET/PEGGY	60271
EZELL, FANNIE	1831	NC		1906	TX			1			WILLIAM HENRY WARR	60317
EZELL, JOSIAH R	1801	NC										60317
EZELL, MIEL	C1765	VA		C1808	NC	047		1 1787	VA		PRISCILLA RIVES	25100
EZELL, WILKINSON	1840	NC										60317
EZELL, WILLIAM SR				1775	NC	070						25100

F

FADDIS/FADDES, ALEXANDER		NC	073					1	NC	073		13020
FADDIS/FADDES, JANE/JEANIE		NC	?073					1 1804	NC	073	WILLIAM HORN	13020
FADDIS/FADDES, JOHN							073	1	NC	073		13020
FAGGOT/FAGERT, JACOB	1721	GER		1800	NC	016		1			ANNA MARIA FISCHER/FISCHERN	06075
FAIR/FARE/FARR/FEHR, BARNABAS/ JOHANN BER		GER		1787	NC	090						15098
FAIRCHILD, CYRUS	1767	NJ		1853	NC	102		1	NC		SUSANNAH BRADLEY	27533
FAIRCHILD, EBENEZER	C1730	CT		C1805	NC	006		1 1750 2 1758	NJ		SALOME GABEL/GABLE MARY	27533

ANCESTOR INDEX	BIRTH	PL	CO	DEATH	PL	CO	LIVD	MARRIED	PL	CO	SPOUSE NAME	CODE
FAIRCHILD, LEVI	1826	NC	?006	C1890	TN			1 C1861	TN		ESTHER FREDDA DIDEN	27533
FAIRCHILD, LEWIS	1793	NC	?104	C1890	TN			1	NC		MELONA	27533
FAIRES, JOSEPH	1769	NC		C1845	NC	065		1			MARY	60460
FAIRES, ROBERT	1798	NC	065	1855	MO			1 1816	NC	065	SUSANNAH ORR	60460
FAISON, HENRY	1744	NC	071		NC	035		1 1773	NC		DIANA GRIFFIN	27356
FAISON, MARY	1777	NC			NC			1 1797	NC		COL THOMAS HICKS	27356
FARABOUGH, JAMES	C1790	NC	044	C1859	TN			1 1815	NC	044	DOROTHY COOPER	11070
FARABOUGH, THOMAS REDMOND	1822	NC	044	1911	TN			1 1846	TN		SARAH WARD	11070
FARABOUGH, WILLIAM THOMAS		NC	044		NC	?044		1 1831	NC	044	SUSAN BULLOCK	11070
FARLEY, DAVID	1745	NC		1830	OH			1			MRS MARY AIKEN	60309
FARLEY, SARAH	1779	NC		C1865	OH			1			ANDREW FARLEY	60309
FARLOW/FORLAW, SARAH	C1770	NC	096					1 1786	NC	096	JOHN CLIFTON	60328
FARMER, CATHERINE	C1788	NC	?073					1	NC	?092	JOSEPH DAVIS	27429
FARMER, ENOS	1780	NC	037									27335
FARMER, ISAAC	1802	NC	037									27335
FARMER, JOSEPH	1750	NC	037	1794	NC	037		1 1775	NC	037	ZELPHIA BARNES	27335
FARMER, SIMON		NC	037	1860	MS			2 1852	MS		SARAH H TRADEWELL	27335
FARMER, WILLIAM					OH		073	1			CATHERINE	27429
FARRAR, REBECCA	1804	NC	022	1841	NC	022		1	NC	022	AMBROSE E FOUSHEE	08200
FARRAR, THOMAS	C1780			1858	NC	022		1			ALSEY	08200
FARROW, ACENATH/ASENA	1826			C1875	NC	053	?030					24210
FARROW, JOSEPH	C1824			C1857	NC	?053	?030	1 1846	NC	053	CHARLOTTA ANN/ANNIE WILLIAMS	24210
FARROW, LOUISA DAVID	1840						030	1			JONATHAN SPIVEY HARRIS	24210
FARROW, LOUISA DAVID	1840						030	1			JONATHAN SPIVEY HARRIS	24210
FARROW, MAHATTABLE	1829	NC	?053				?030					24210
FARROW, NASA/NATHAN	C1792			C1875	NC	053	?030	1 C1820	NC	053	NANCY/NAOMI	24210
FARROW, NEBRINA	1832						053					24210
FARROW, RHODA	1822			1905	NC	053	?030	1	NC	?053	LEVI LEONADAS JARVIS	24210
FARROW, THOMAS	C1762			1815	NC	030	053	1			RHODA	24210
FAUCETT, JOHN				1864	NC	001						27441
FAUCETT, JOHN W	1807	NC	073	1870	NC	001		1 1828	NC	073	PARTHENIA ARMSTRONG	27441
FAUCETT/FAUSETT, DAVID	C1743	?NC	?044	1824	NC	073		1 C1764	?NC	?073	ELEANOR/ELLEN	05045
								2 1783	NC	073	ELIZABETH DAVIS	
FAUCETT/FAUSETT, RICHARD	C1769	NC	073	C1835	TN			1 1792	NC	073	MARY MCKEE	05045
FAULK, JAMES	1786	NC		1851	AL			1 C1804	?SC		RHODA SELLERS	60298
FAUSETT/FAUCETT, DAVID	C1745						073					08226
FAUSETT/FAUCETT, RICHARD	C1769	NC	073	C1835	TN			1 C1814			MARY MCKEE	08226

ANCESTOR INDEX	BIRTH	PL	CO	DEATH	PL	CO	LIVD	MARRIED	PL	CO	SPOUSE NAME	CODE
FEE JOHN	C1751	?VA		1834	OH			1 1779	NC	085	PARTHENIA KELLON	25097
FEEZOR, GEORGE		NC	085	1815	NC	085		1			MARY	60562
FEEZOR, JOHN	1781	NC	085	1858	TN			1 1800	NC	085	ELIZABETH COLE	60562
FEEZOR, NICHOLAS		?PA		1765	NC	085						60562
FELTON, ELISHA	C1755	NC	024	C1821	NC	051		1 C1775	NC			60483
FELTON, JOB		NC	024	1812	GA			1	NC	?024	ELISABETH	60359
FELTON, NOAH	C1725	NC	?024		NC	024	?041	1			HARREL	60359
FELTON, RICHARD III	1700	NC	?024	1776	NC	024		1	NC	024	ANN HARRELL	60359
FELTON, RICHARD JR		VA		C1740	NC	?024						60359
FELTON, RICHARD, III	C1700	NC		1776	NC	024		1			ANN HARRELL	60483
FELTON, THADDEUS WILLIAM	1817	NC	047	1877	AL			1 1837	AL		MARTHA BURCHET KING	60483
FELTON, WILLIAM	C1785	NC	051	1825	AL		047	1 1815			MARTHA ANN ELIZA	60483
FELTS, CARY	1756	VA		1840	TN			1 1790	NC	100	SARAH FOSTER	60088
FELTS, CHRISTOPHER	1795	NC	100					1 1822	TN		NANCY KIBLE	60088
FELTS, ELIZABETH/BETSY	1792	NC	100					1 1807	TN		JOHN HILL	60088
FELTS, ISAAC B	1834	NC	104	1900	NB			1 1861	MO		ELIZABETH T COLE	60256
FELTS, ISHAM B	1795	NC	104	1884	MO			1 1817	NC	104	SUSANNAH BROWN	60256
FELTS, LUCY FOSTER	1791	NC	100					1 C1802	NC	?100	LARVIS ALLEN	60088
FELTS, POLLY A	1802	NC	100					1 1819	TN		ARTHUR BLAND	60088
FELTS, SARAH/SALLIE A	1797	NC	100	C1843	TN			1 1812	TN		WILLIS L SHUMATE	60088
FELTS, WILLIAM	1767			1843	NC	104		1			SUSANNAH OLIVER	60256
FERGUSON, CLARISSA	1831	NC	104	1875	MO			1 1846	NC	104	LEWIS WATSON	60387
FERGUSON, CLARISSA W	1826	NC	099	1875	KY			1 1849	TN		ELISHA JAMES CRUTCHFIELD	07095
FERGUSON, GEORGE	C1760	?NC					081	1 C1791	NC	081	LYDIA HENDRICKS	60446
FERGUSON, JANE								1 C1789	NC	?104	THOMAS TRIPLETT	60222
FERGUSON, JESSE T	1805	NC	104					1 1830	NC	104	POLLY BROWN	60387
FERGUSON, RICHARD	C1766	VA		C1850	NC	104		1			VERLINDA TRIPLETT	60387
FERGUSON, RICHARD C	1791	NC		1869	TN		099	1 1814	NC	044	ELIZABETH BROGDON	07095
FERGUSON, SAMUEL	C1800	NC	081	1855	IL			1 C1822	NC	081	SARAH PIERCE	60446
FERRELL/FARRELL, ELIZABETH	C1758			1842	NC	099		1 1784	NC	099	JEREMIAH RHODES/ROHDS	03250
FERRIBO/FARABOUGH, JACOB					NC	?044		1			ABIZILLA	11070
								2			SUKE TIPPETT	
FESSLER, POLLY								1 1807	NC	090	JAMES CREWS	13120
FEWELL, BENJAMIN	1769	NC	084	1820	NC	084		1 1789	VA		ANN WALL	60169
FEWELL, JANE ANN	1821	NC	084	1898	MO			1 1842	MO		PHILEMON SUTHERLAND	60169
FEWELL, ZACHARIAH	1794	VA		1842	MO			1 1818	NC	084	SARAH ODINEAL	60169
FEWOX/FOX, EDITH							024	1			WILLIAM HARDY	60318

ANCESTOR INDEX	BIRTH	PL	CO	DEATH	PL	CO	LIVD	MARRIED	PL	CO	SPOUSE NAME	CODE
FEWOX/FOX, JAMES				1711			075	1			ANN	60318
FIELD, LYDIA	1763	NC		1852	IN			1			RICHARD LEWIS	60362
FIELD, WILLIAM				1805	NC	081		1			LYDIA	60362
FIELD, WILLIAM				1780	SC		081	1			LYDIA JULIAN	60362
FIELD/FIELDS, BENTON	C1824	NC	046		IN			1	1849	NC	046 MARTHA HARDIN	60596
FIELD/FIELDS, CHRISTOPHER	C1793	NC	046					1	1813	NC	046 ISABELLE HANNER	60596
FIELD/FIELDS, JEREMIAH	C1794	NC	046					1			ELEANOR SHERWOOD	60596
FIELD/FIELDS, JEREMIAH	C1790	NC	046					1	1815	NC	081 HARRIET FITCHETT	60596
FIELD/FIELDS, PETER	C1768	NC	?085	1816	NC			1	1788	NC	081 CHARLOTTE VICKREY	60596
FIELD/FIELDS, WILLIAM	C1730			C1780	NC	046		1 C1760			LYDIA JULIAN	60596
FIKE, NATHAN	C1740	NC	022					1			SUSAN FORSHEE	60139
FILGO, ANTHONY				C1777	NC	010		1			ANN CAKE	03250
FINCANNON, PETER	C1796	NC		C1880	NC			1			SALLIE HUNTLEY	03041
FINCANNON, WILLIAM	C1755			C1831	NC							03041
FINCH, EDWARD	C1755	?VA		C1824	NC	032						19115
FINCH, MARY/POLLY	C1780	VA		1839	IN			1 C1799	?NC		039 MARSHALL ROBARDS	19115
								2 1827	NC		032 THOMAS IVES	
FINLEY, MICHAEL	1768	NC	046	1843	IL			1 1792	NC		046 SINAH TAYLOR	60096
								2 C1803	KY		ELEANOR PAISLEY	
FISCUS, EVA MARIA	1762	NC	085	C1806	NC	090		1 C1781	NC		092 JACOB HILSABECK	60354
FISCUS, FREDERICK	C1707	GER		1772	NC	092		1 C1751	MD		EVA MARIA	60354
FISHEL, HENRY JR	1811	NC		C1886	IN		?090	1 1838	IN		TERESA ELIZA HOLLANBACK	08073
FISHEL, HENRY SR	C1775	PA			IN			1 C1796			BARBARA	08073
FISHER, ANGELET	C1760	NC	022	1833	MS			1 C1774			JOSEPH MAY	02540
FISHER, SAMUEL BURTON	1811	NC	070	1884	OR			1 1835	IN		JANE WHITTED	60121
								2 1838	IN		CALFERNA HICE	
FISHER/FISCHER, LOUIS/LEWIS/ LUDWIG		?VA		1827	NC	016	065	1			CHRISTIANA FRIESLAND/FREESLAND	06075
FITE, LEONARD	1760	NJ		1842	TN		060	1 C1781	NJ		MARGARETH CROSS	07027
FITE, LEONARD JR	1788	NC	060	1872	TN			1 C1810			ELIZABETH DUNCAN	07027
FLANAGAN, PHILIP	1805	?NC		C1850	VA			1 C1826			ELIZABETH	60090
FLEETWOOD, JUDITH	1759	NC	?010		KY			1 1777	NC		010 AARON FREEMAN	60412
FLEETWOOD, WILLIAM		NC	?010	1769	NC	010		1			ELIZABETH	60412
FLEMING, GEORGE				1849	NC	100		1 1801	NC		100 MRS BETSY (FLEMING) FLEMING	60594
FLEMING, JOHN MIDDLETON	1740	VA		1794	NC	092		1 1776	VA		JANE HORD	06005
FLEMING, MARTHA	1779	NC	092		TN			1	NC		092 MATTHEW JOUETT	06005
FLEMING, PETER				C1816	NC	100		1			MRS MARTHA FLEMING	60594
FLETCHER, NATHANIEL	C1820	NC	?049		MO			1	MO		MARGARET CHAMBERS	60035
FLOWERS, BENNET	C1796	NC		C1860	NC	012						13052

ANCESTOR INDEX	BIRTH	PL	CO	DEATH	PL	CO	LIVD	MARRIED	PL	CO	SPOUSE NAME	CODE
FLOWERS, ELIZABETH ANN/LILIAN	1823	NC	012	C1870	NC	012		1			ALEXANDER COX	13052
FLOWERS, HENRY	C1755			C1823	NC	012						13052
FLOYD, FRANCIS	1800	NC	085		IN			1	1823	IN	SUSANNAH MOTSINGER	60369
FLYNN/FLINN, ELIZABETH	1753	NC		1834	NC	090		1 C1773	NC	?085	ISAIAH GUYMON	01040
								2			MR HAUN	
FLYNN/FLINN, THOMAS	C1730			C1780			073	1 C1752	NC	?073	ELIZABETH LAUGHLIN	01040
FOARD/FORD, CHARLES DEEMS	1865	NC	054	1951	NC	021	070	1 1896	NC	070	FLORENCE HANBY	06090
FOARD/FORD, FRANCIS	C1753			1833	NC	078		1			SALLIE NORTH	06090
								2 1798	NC	020	MRS NANCY ANN (HAMLET) STEVENS	
FOARD/FORD, FREDERICK	1783	NC	085	1831	NC	085						06090
FOARD/FORD, HENRY				C1788	NC	065		1			REBECCA	06090
FOARD/FORD, JOHN	C1727			C1799	NC	065		1			CATHERINE ROBINET	06090
FOARD/FORD, JOHN HANBY	1901	NC	070	1977	NC	070	021	1 1943	NC	021	KATHRYN AUGUSTA SANDUSKY	06090
FOARD/FORD, JOHN HANBY JR	1944	NC	021				016	1 1969	NC	014	DONNA MARIE SUMMERS	06090
FOARD/FORD, JOHN HANBY, III	1977	NC	016									06090
FOARD/FORD, KATHRYN SUMMERS	1975	NC	016									06090
FOARD/FORD, OSBORNE GILES	1820	NC	085	1882	NC	021	054	1 1838	NC	085	LUCILE L ELLIS	06090
								2 1846	NC	085	ANN FOSTER COWAN	
								3 1854	NC	085	ELIZABETH ANN ALLISON	
FOARD/FORD, WYATTE	1757			1816	NC	085		1 1783	NC	085	ELIZABETH PEARSON	06090
FOGLEMAN, GEORGE	C1775	?NC	?073	1843	NC	073		1 C1797	?NC	?073	RACHEL SHADDY	05059
FOGLEMAN, ISRAEL	1812	NC	016	1867	IL			1 1838	IL		ELIZA JANE CORLEW	60179
FOGLEMAN, JOHAN MELCHIOR	1741	GER		1810	NC	016	065	1 C1787				60179
FOGLEMAN, MELCHIOR	1788	NC	065	1827	IL			1 1811	NC	016	ELIZABETH MEISENHEIMER	60179
FOLGER, JETHRO STARBUCK	1797	NC	046	1861	IN			1	?NC	?046	MARY BARNARD	20333
FOLGER, LATHAM		MA			IN		046	1 1777			MATILDA WORTH	20333
FOLK/FOLKS, JAMES	1750	?NC	?010	1782	NC	010		1 1770			JENNY BRADFORD	60576
FOLK/FOLKS, NANCY	1772			C1840	TN		047	1 1794	NC	047	EDWIN CLIFTON	60576
FOLK/FOLKS, WILLIAM							047					60576
FONTAINE, FRANCIS JR	1721	VA			?SC		?034	1	?NC	028	JASPER	27339
FONTAINE, FRANCIS, III	C1747	NC	028	?1781	?SC		034	1			JEMIMA JOHNSTON	27339
FONTAINE, JOHN		NC	028				?034	1			SUSANNAH	27339
FOOSHEE, ELIZABETH	1803	NC		1874	IL			1 1819	TN		JAMES BEAVERS	04080
								2 1859	IL		JACOB EMERICK	
FOOSHEE, JOHN A	1801	NC		1871	IL			1 1819	TN		MALINDA COOPER	04080
FOOTE, BRIDGET	1732	NC		1801	NC			1			SIMON HADLEY	60288
FORBES, SIMEON J	1822	?NC	?018	C1880	NC	018		1 C1844	?NC	?018	MARY MORRISETT	60346
FORBES, SIMEON LAWRENCE	1869	NC	018	1946	VA			1 C1900	VA		BESSIE ALMA NORSWORTHY	60346
FORD, ELI	1806	NC	020					1 1827	NC	020	ZEPORIAH STRADER	60258
FORD, GEORGE WASHINGTON	1810	NC						1			ANNIE	02414

ANCESTOR INDEX	BIRTH	PL	CO	DEATH	PL	CO	LIVD	MARRIED	PL	CO	SPOUSE NAME	CODE
FORD, HENRY	1805	NC						1			NANCY SAWYER	02414
FORD, JOHN H	C1818	VA					090	1 C1840			MARY C	60292
FORD, JOHN SHEPHERD	1802			1885	NC	086		1 1826	NC	086	SOPHIA CAMP	60139
FORD, JOSEPH					KY		014	1			RUTH PHILLIPS	02470
FORD, RICHARD	1798	NC						1			ISABELLA LOGAN	02414
FORD, SAMUEL RICHARD	C1815	VA		C1885	KY		084	1 C1837			REBECCA BOATRIGHT	60292
FORD, WILLIAM	1802	NC						1 1822			REBECCA TIPPETT	02414
FORREST/FORRESTER, ISAAC	C1750			C1797	NC	073		1 C1775				60507
FORREST/FORRESTER, WILLIAM	C1726			C1777	NC	073		1 C1749			LOUVENIA GRESHAM ?	60507
FORREST/FORRESTER, WILLIS N	C1785	NC	073	C1855				1 1812	GA		MARY/POLLY BOWLES/BOLES	60507
FORSYTH, EPPERSON	C1828	NC	044		TN			1 C1847	TN		ELIZABETH LOWRY	60509
FORSYTH, JAMES				1831	NC	044		1			FERIBA/PHERIBA	60509
FORSYTH, SIMPSON	C1826	NC	044		TN			1 1846	NC	044	CAHTERINE BLEDSOE	60509
FOSHEE, EDMUND	1832	NC		1865	GA			1 1848	AR		ELIZABETH HENDERSON	60132
FOSHEE, JOHN	1759			1842	NC	022						60132
FOSHEE, JOSEPH	1804	NC	022	C1875	AR			1			NANCY	60132
FOSSET, NANCY	1821	NC	090	1891	IL			1 1839			WILLIAM CARR	60266
FOSTER, PATSEY	C1780	?VA		C1845	NC	?084	046	1 1800	NC	020	JOHN BRAN	60388
FOUNTAIN, GRACE	C1714	MD		C1791	NC	028	009	1	MD		JOHN STILLEY	20415
FOUSHEE, AMBROSE E	C1795	NC	022	C1845	NC	022		1	NC	022	REBECCA FARRAR	08200
FOUSHEE, CORNELIA FRANCES	1826	NC	022	1887	NC	022		1 1847	NC	022	ISAAC NEWTON MANN	08200
FOUSHEE, JOSEPH	C1730	VA			NC	073						08200
FOUSHEE, JOSEPH	C1755	NC	073	1820	NC	022		1	NC	022	HAPPY STEWART	08200
FOUTS, ANDREW	1751	MD		1834	NC	081		1			RACHEL	60294
FOUTS, JACOB	C1700			C1765	NC	085		1			ANNA MAGDALENA	60294
FOUTS, MICHAEL	C1724	GER		1803	NC	081	085	1			CATHERINE VARNER	60294
FOUTS/PFAUTZ, DAVID/THEOBALD	C1718	GER		C1785	NC	081		1 1743	PA		CATHERINE SPENGEL	23065
FOUTS/PFAUTZ, HANNAH	1771	NC	046	1855	NC	013		1 1790	NC	081	JOHN GARREN	23065
FOUTS/PHOUTS, DAVID	C1745	MD		1821	OH		081	1 C1765	NC	081	ELIZABETH HUBER/HOOVER	60120
FOUTS/PHOUTS, DEWALD	1722	GER		1785	NC	081		1 1743	PA		CATRINA SPENGEL	60120
FOUTS/PHOUTS, JACOB	1806	NC	006					1 C1833	NC	006	LUCINDA EDWARDS	60120
FOUTS/PHOUTS, JOHN EDWARDS	1839	NC	006	1862	TN			1 1861	NC	104	MARTHA SHEPHERD	60120
FOUTS/PHOUTS, JOSEPH	C1779	NC	081	1856	NC	006		1 C1804	NC	006	SUSAN	60120
FOUTS/PHOUTS, JOSEPH WILSON	1862	NC	104	1913	NC	004	006	1 1883	NC	104	MARTHA MALINDA SHEPHERD	60120
FOUTS/PHOUTS, MINNIE ALICE	1886	NC	104	1967	IN			1 1905	NC	104	JAMES BASIL HAMM	60120
FOWLER, ABRAHAM	1794	NC	?087	C1855	FL		?027					60399
FOWLER, ALEXANDER	1820		027	1869	TX			1 1823	AL		MATILDA PATE	60399

ANCESTOR INDEX	BIRTH	PL	CO	DEATH	PL	CO	LIVD	MARRIED	PL	CO	SPOUSE NAME	CODE
FOWLER, DANIEL	1714			1793	NC	035		1 C1740			MARY ROLLINS	60399
FOWLER, DANIEL D	C1743			C1825	NC	027	087					60399
FOWLER, ELVIS	C1806	NC			IL			1 1825	NC	046	JUDA ROBINSON	25159
FOWLER, ELVIS		NC	?046		?IL							60549
FOWLER, EMILY JANE	1829	NC	046	1915	IN			1 1848	IN		LEWIS DEATON	25159
FOWLER, JOHN	1799	NC	046	1891	KS			1 1826	NC	046	MARY/MILLEY GLASS	60549
FOWLER, JOHN H	1825			1882	NC	090		1			MATILDA	27700
FOWLER, LABON	1832	NC	027	1927	NC	027		1 1867	NC	027	UNITY DUNCAN	24032
FOWLER, LUKE	C1788	NC	087	C1880	NC	027		1 C1810	?NC	?027	MARY	24032
FOWLER, MACK DANIEL/MCD	1872	NC	027	1951	NC	027		1 1896	NC	027	LUPHENIA SOLES	24032
								2 1919	?NC	?027	MRS IZZIE(FOWLER)FIPPS	
FOWLER, MARY ELIZABETH	1874	NC	090	1953	NC	090	032	1 1896	NC	090	JAMES SAMUEL SLATE	27700
FOWLER, RUFUS C	1845			1917	NC	090		1			OLIVIA BOLES	27700
FOX, DAVID	1791	NC	022	1856	NC	022		1			SARAH STALEY	24153
								2			ELEANOR	
FOX, GATSEY	C1794	NC		1866	IA			1	NC		BENJAMIN TUTTLE	60329
FOX, LOUIS TAYLOR	1838		022	1916	IN			1 1864	IN		PURLINA BLUNK	24153
								2 1871	IN		MRS SARAH ELIZABETH(HIGGINS)MOORE	
FOY, JAMES	C1737			1822	NC	072		1			ELIZABETH WARD	20030
								2			ELIZABETH WARD	
FRAIZER, JAMES				1817	NC	046		1 C1766			MARTHA MILLIKAN	08095
FRALEY, JESSE E	1817	NC	?054	1903	NC	?054		1 1839		?054	NANCY TURNER	25198
								2 1866		?054	MRS HARRIET ALVIN(HOWARD)GRIFFIN	
FRANCE, HENRY	C1736	?PA		1812	NC	090	085	1 C1757	VA		ELIZABETH JENNINGS	60404
FRANCKE, BARBARA	1730	NC	028	1825	NC	028		1 1753	NC	028	DANIEL SHINE	60057
FRANCKE, JOHN MARTIN	1682	GER		1744	NC	028		1 C1722	NC	028	CEVILLA MILLER	60057
FRANK, BARBARA	1761	NC		1826	NC	032	085	1 C1781	NC		JOHN CHARLES GRIMES	06005
FRANK, WILLIAM	1731	NC	028	1804	NC	085		1 1751	VA		BARBARA WALK	06005
FRANKLIN, ABEDNEGO/BEDNEY	1776	VA		1817				1 1800	NC	?092	MARY GRAVES CLEVELAND	08070
FRANKLIN, BERNARD	1731	VA		1828	NC	092		1 C1752	VA		MARY CLEVELAND	08070
								2 1807	NC	104	SUSANNAH FLETCHER	
FRANKLIN, NANCY ANNE		VA		C1818	KY		?104	1			MR CANTERBURY	25223
FRAZIER, ANN	C1780						?081					06158
FRAZIER, DAVID	C1754	?NC										06158
FRAZIER, ELIZABETH	C1774						?046					06158
FRAZIER, ELIZABETH	1808	NC	081					1 1825	NC	081	ABSOLOM DAVENPORT	06158
FRAZIER, ELIZABETH JANE	C1782	NC	081					1 1800	NC	081	JOHN RUSSELL	06158
FRAZIER, HARDY	C1825	NC	081					1 1847	NC	081	MARGARET HOLDER	06158
FRAZIER, JANE	1805	NC	081					1 1826	NC	081	TRAVIS DAVENPORT	06158

ANCESTOR INDEX	BIRTH	PL	CO	DEATH	PL	CO	LIVD	MARRIED		PL	CO	SPOUSE NAME	CODE
FRAZIER, JOHN	C1757	?NC						1				MARJORY STANLEY	06158
FRAZIER, JOSIAH	1803	NC	081					1	1830	NC	081	ELIZABETH FOUST	06158
FRAZIER, MARMADUKE	1823	NC	081					1	1847	NC	081	REBECCA CURTIS	06158
FRAZIER, MARTHA	C1773	NC	081	1861	NC	081		1	1812	NC	081	EDMOND HAYS	06158
FRAZIER, MARY/POLLY	C1790	NC	081					1	1813	NC	081	ENOCH SWOFFORD	06158
FRAZIER, NANCY	1813	NC	081					1	1830	NC	081	DANIEL FRAZIER	06158
FRAZIER, NANCY ANN	C1784	NC	081					1	1806	NC	081	THOMAS RUSSELL	06158
FRAZIER, RACHEL	C1777						?046	1				SOLOMAN REYNOLDS	06158
FRAZIER, REBECCA	1801	NC	081					1	1821	NC	081	JESSE PUGH	06158
FRAZIER, SALLY	C1821	NC	081					1	1848	NC	081	JESSE BURTON	06158
FRAZIER, THOMAS	C1752	?NC	?081										06158
FRAZIER, THOMAS	C1786	NC	081										06158
FRAZIER/FRAZER, SAMUEL	C1771	NC	081										06158
FREDERICK, PETER, CAPT	1722	NC	028	1763	NC	?035							27356
FREDERICK, WILLIAM	1750	NC	035	1830	NC	035		1		NC	035	NANCY KENAN BURTON	27356
FREEAR, RICHARD				1814	NC	071		1	1811	NC	039	EVALINA BELMONT WYNNE	25215
FREEMAN, AARON	1758	NC	010	1821	KY		034	1	1777	NC	010	JUDITH FLEETWOOD	60412
FREEMAN, ELISHA				1793	NC	072		1				BETTY	60562
FREEMAN, EMILY AUGUSTUS	1849	NC	009	1917	NC	009		1	1866	NC	009	THOMAS ROBBINS	27378
FREEMAN, JOHN	C1720	NC	024					1				ANN	60412
FREEMAN, JOHN				1785	NC	010		1				SARAH	60562
FREEMAN, JOHN AUGUSTUS	1819			1850	NC	009		1	1843	NC	009	MARY ELIZABETH SEELEY	27378
FREEMAN, KING		NC	010										60412
FREEMAN, NANCY	C1777	?NC						1	1797	NC	072	MATTHEW WISE	60562
								2				JOHN PROVOW	
FREEMAN, WILLIAM	C1690			C1736	NC	024							60412
FREESLAND/FRIESLAND, JOHN GEORGE DANIEL				C1802	NC	016	065	1				CARATHINE HAUS/HOUSE	06075
FRENCH, JANE	C1780	NC		C1832	AR			1		KY		JOHN DENTON	27699
FRICK/FRICKS/FRIX, JACOB	C1771						?085						60156
FRONABERGER, JOHN J	1798			1880	AR		060	1	1824	NC	060	ANNY BLACKWOOD	15005
FROST, EBENEZER B	C1795	NC	085	1836	AR			1	1816	NC	085	ELIZABETH GAITHER	60096
								2	1822	NC	085	NANCY WRIGHT CLARY	
FROST, THOMAS WRIGHT	1823	NC	092	1916	AR			1	1843	TN		POLLY BOONE	60096
FRUIT, JAMES	C1710			1800	NC	073		1				GIRZEL	17185
FRUIT, JOHN	C1735	WAL		1824	NC	081		1	C1754			SIBYL/SIBELLA/SYBIL	17185
								2	C1757			ELIZABETH PUGH	
FRY, GEORGE	C1761			1842	NC	021		1				CATHERINE ESLINGER	27441
FRY, JOHN	1784	NC	060	1856	NC	021		1	1808	NC	060	MARY MAGDALENE COULTER	27441

ANCESTOR INDEX	BIRTH	PL	CO	DEATH	PL	CO	LIVD	MARRIED	PL	CO	SPOUSE NAME	CODE
FRY, PHILIP	C1735	PA		C1820	NC	060		1 C1759	PA		SUSAN IKARD	27441
FRYER, JOHN A		NC		1839	TN			1			TABITHA AVERY	25229
FRYER/FRYAR, JEREMIAH	C1770	NC						1 C1800			REBECCA LOVELADY	60334
FULK, CALVIN FREDERICK	1836	NC	?090	1927	NC	038		1 1857	NC	038	CHRISTINA CHANEY BOWEN	60467
								2 1885	NC	038	LYDIA FULK	
FULK, FREDERICK	1790			1869	NC	038	090	1			CATHERINE MOSER ?	60467
FULKS, CHARLES		?PA		C1815	NC	060		1	?PA		BARBARA ANTHONY	03015
FULLBRIGHT, JOHN WILLIAM		GER		1808	NC	060		1 C1745	PA		CHRISTENAH HALSTEAD	60453
FULLER, DANIEL							086	1			MARY BABB	17240
FULLER, SARAH		?VA					081	1			THOMAS MILLSAPS	24073
FULP, GEORGE	C1718			1786	NC	092		1			MARY	06195
FULP, NANCY EMILY	1828			1884	NC	038		1 1845	NC	090	MARTIN WESTMORELAND	60456
FULP, THOMAS				C1886	NC	090						60456
FULP/FULPS, GEORGE	1778			1852	NC	038		1 1801	NC	090	JENNY WALKER	60148
FURR, HENRY				NC	085		065	1			RUSSENA	60234
FURR, LEONARD	1755			C1836	MS			1			ELIZABETH STUTTS ?	60234
FURR, PAUL	1786	NC	068	1867	GA			1 1815			SARAH GRIFFITH	60234
								2 1850			MAHALA DOBBINS	
FURR/FURRER, HENRY/HEINRICH	1731			1769	NC	065		1			RUSSENA	24165
FUSSELL, NANCY	C1800	NC		1874	TN			1 1815	TN		ALEXANDER WILSON	08040
								2 1843	TN		WILLIAM AMIS	
FUTRELL, JENKINS	C1809	NC	?071		TN			1			SARAH	27682

G

ANCESTOR INDEX	BIRTH	PL	CO	DEATH	PL	CO	LIVD	MARRIED	PL	CO	SPOUSE NAME	CODE
GAINER, JOSEPH	1818	NC	009	C1883	NC	079		1 C1840	NC	079	HARRIETT CHANCE	24240
GAINER, JOSEPH	C1725	NC	009	C1793	NC	079		1 C1750	NC		SUSANNAH	24240
GAINER, JOSEPH JR	C1764	NC	079	C1840	NC	?079	?009	1 C1789	NC		ELIZABETH MCKEEL	24240
GAINER, SAMUEL				C1752	NC	096	010	1			ANN	19130
GAINER, SAMUEL	C1700			1751	NC	096		1			ANN	24240
GAITHER, BENJAMIN		MD		1788	NC	085		1	MD		RACHEL JACOB	07017
GAITHER, GREENBERRY	1780	MD			NC			1 1814	NC	085	LURANAH VEACH	07017
GAITHER, JOHN	C1740	MD		C1840	NC	054	085	1	MD		ANNE JACOB	07017
GAITHER, JOHN MARTIN	1860	NC	054	1903	IL			1 1880	NC	054	EMILY ELIZABETH BAGGERLY	07017
GAITHER, LEANDER	1826	NC	054	1898	NC	054		1 1850	NC	054	MARY MARLIN	07017
								2	NC		JULIA RIVES	
GALLOWAY, HANNAH	1841	NC	093	1936	NC	093		1			CHRISTOPHER COLUMBUS WHITMIRE	60205
GALLOWAY, JOE BERRY	1821			1904	NC	093		1			MARTHA MELINDA HINES	60205

ANCESTOR INDEX	BIRTH	PL	CO	DEATH	PL	CO	LIVD	MARRIED	PL	CO	SPOUSE NAME	CODE
GALLOWAY, MARY ANN	1846	NC	093	1938	NC	093						60205
GAMBLE, KINCHEN	C1794	NC		C1880	AL			1 1820	AL		FANNY TRUSS	60116
GAMMILL, JAMES				1794	NC	090		1 C1766			MARGARET MILLER	60082
								2 C1791	NC	?090	LUCRETIA	
GAMMON, IVY		NC	047									60594
GAMMON, JAMES				1838	NC	047						60594
GAMMON, JOSHUA				1810	NC	047		1			SARAH	60594
GAMMON, NICHOLAS		NC	047		TN			1 1820	NC	047	MRS ASCENCION (MERRIT) BISHOP GAMMON	60594
GAMMON, RICHARD	C1796	NC	047	1858	NC	047		1 1829	NC	047	SARAH SILLS	60594
GAMMON, SAMUEL NICHOLAS	C1825	NC	047		?TN							60594
GAMMON, WILLIAM R	C1823	NC	047					1 1854	NC	047	MARTHA ANN GAMMON	60594
GARDNER, JAMES	1776	NC		1844				1 C1800			MARY	60488
GARDNER, JAMES MARION	1813	NC		1892	TX			1 C1842	GA		ELIZABETH JANE SKEEN	60488
								2			SARAH ELIZABETH ALLEN	
GARDNER, JANE E	1817	NC		1856	TX							60488
GARDNER, JESSE D	1809	VA		1882	NC	071		1 1835	NC	071	MARTHA MARTIN	60211
GARDNER, JOHN F	1810	NC										60488
GARDNER, MARY S	1806	NC		1876	TX							60488
GARDNER, RUTH A	1802	NC										60488
GARDNER, SOPHIA	1808			1817	NC							60488
GARDNER, WILLIAM	1810	NC	037	1884	NC	105	079	1 1828	NC	037	CINTHIA ELIZA BATTS	60051
								2 1871	NC	037	MRS SUSAN WOOTEN HARRIS	
GARDNER, WILLIAM	1803	NC		1880	TX							60488
GARDNER/GARNER, AULINE	C1825	NC	037	C1851	MS			1 C1844	MS		DENNIS H DAVIS	08185
GARDNER/GARNER, DAVID		NC					037	1 1823	NC	037	ELIZABETH ROBBINS	08185
GARDNER/GARNER, LOUVANNER	C1832	NC	037		?MS			1 1870	MS		QULLIA SUGG	08185
GARDNER/GARNER, SARAH/ADDIE	C1830	NC	037	C1868	MS			1 C1851	MS		DENNIS H DAVIS	08185
GARDNER/GARNER, SION WRIGHT	1794	NC		1853	MS		037	1 1823	NC	037	MARY W SCARBOROUGH	08185
GARLAND, SAMUEL	C1753			C1824	TN		047					01011
GARNER, ADDIE IRENE	1912	NC	068	1973	NC	068		1 1931	NC	046	WILLIAM HOWARD ULSH	22005
GARNER, BRADLEY					NC	?068		1			BARBARA	22005
GARNER, CHARLES							084	1			ELEANOR ANN STRAWMAT	60464
GARNER, DANIEL	C1777							1 1797	NC	086	CELIA HESLEP	60464
GARNER, GEORGE WASHINGTON	1888	NC	068	1969	NC	068		1 1909	NC	068	ROSA JANETTE CAMERON	22005
GARNER, JAMES				1760	NC	?073	084	1			MISS CHEVERAL	60451
GARNER, LAWSON	1798	NC	086					1			JANE LANGHAM	60464
GARNER, LEWIS	1793	NC	?068		NC	068		1			BETSY YOW	22005
GARNER, LEWIS OLIVER	1840	NC	068	1931	NC	068		1 C1858	NC	068	ELIZABETH MANESS	22005
								2 1880	NC	068	ARRENIA RITTER	

ANCESTOR INDEX	BIRTH	PL	CO	DEATH	PL	CO	LIVD	MARRIED	PL	CO	SPOUSE NAME	CODE
GARNER, SARAH	1818	NC						1 1837			WILLIAM GARNER	60505
GARNER, SHIVERAL	1758	NC	?073	1837	IN			1			ELIZABETH	60451
GARNER, WILLIAM	1817	NC						1 1837			SARAH	60505
GARREN/GARN, DAVID	1801	NC	081	1894	NC	013		1 1826	NC	013	MARGARET WHITAKER	23065
GARREN/GARN, JAMES	C1741	?PA		C1805	NC	081	?085	1 C1766	?PA			23065
GARREN/GARN, JOHN	1769	NC	?085	1843	NC	013	?085	1 1790	NC	081	HANNAH FOUTS	23065
GARREN/GARN, JOSEPH ROBERT	1838	NC	013	1923	NC	013		1 1859	NC	013	LEAH MALINDA CLAYTON	23065
GARREN/GARN, PETER	C1698	GER		?NC	?085		?070	1 C1725	PA			23065
GARRETT, JAMES WILLIAM	1820	NC	010	1875	TN							60283
GARRETT, JESSE		?NC	010	C1797	NC	010		1 1756	NC	010	RACHEL BLANCHARD	60283
GARRETT, TIMOTHY	1789	NC	010	C1865	TN			1			FRANCES	60283
GARRIS, AMY	1891	NC	059	1971	NC	103		1 1909	NC	059	PRESTON FRANKLIN GARRIS	07040
GARRIS, HOWELL	1847	NC	103	1915	NC	059		1			ELIZABETH	07040
GARRIS, JOHN WILLIAM	C1816	NC	103	1864	NC	103	059	1			SMITHY HAM	07040
GARRIS, PRESTON FRANKLIN	1877	NC	103	1936	NC	103	059	1 1909	NC	059	AMY GARRIS	07040
GARRIS, RANSOM JR	1850	NC	103	1922	NC	059		1 1878	NC	103	GEORGANNA VINSON	07040
GARRIS, RANSOM SR	C1820	NC	103	C1865	NC	103	059	1 C1845	NC	103	JULIA ANN CROOM	07040
GARRIS, WILLIAM M	1840	NC	103	1912	NC	103	059	1 1864	NC	103	MARTHA WARTERS	07040
GARRISS, JOHN		VA		1800	NC	071		1			ISABELLA	19130
GASH, JOSEPH DENNIS	1767	NC	?085	1805			013	1 C1787	NC	?014	DEMY/DENNA WOODFIN	60143
GASH, MARTIN ALLEY	C1730	ENG			NC	013		1 1766	NJ		ANN JOHNSON	60143
GASH, WILLIAM	1799	NC		1847	MO			1 1820	MO		STACEY ELIZABETH LONGMIRE	60143
GASKINS, ADAM	C1780	NC	028	1834	NC	028		1 1798	NC	028	ELIZABETH BLAND	25171
GASKINS, ALLEN	1823	NC	028		NC	028		1 1847	NC	028	SARAH JACKSON	25171
								2 1851	NC	028	MRS ANN MARIE EDWARDS	
GASKINS, FURNIFOLD		NC	028		NC	079		1	NC	079	SAPHRONIA VENTERS	25171
GASKINS, HARMON		NC	028	1827	NC	028		1	NC	028	ELIZABETH DURANT	25171
GASKINS, IDA MELISSA ANN	1888	NC	028	1931	NC	028		1 1904	NC	028	JESSE OSBORNE CLARK	25171
GASKINS, JOSEPH ALLEN	1855	NC	028	1929	NC	028		1	NC	028	MRS LAURA ANN(SMITH)AVERY	25171
								2	NC	028	CAROLINE SPRUILL	
								3	NC	028	JULIE IPOCK	
GASKINS, SILAS	1798	NC	028		NC	028		1 1821	NC	028	ELIZABETH ARTHUR	25171
								2 1837	NC	028	FANNIE H HOLTON	
GASKINS, SUSAN	1843	NC	079	1923	NC	079		1	NC	079	WEEKS H CLARK	25171
GASKINS, THOMAS		ENG		1791	NC	028		1			MRS ANN (BRIGHT) NELSON	25171
GASSAWAY, FRANCES	1790	NC		1862	GA			1 C1807			WILLIAM TAYLOR	60012
GATES, MICHAEL	1776	PA			IL		085	1	NC	085	CATHERINE GROVES	60269
GATLEN, SUSAN F	C1836	NC	?085					1 1854	NC	085	JAMES M MCCRACKEN	14050
								2 1867	NC	065	MATTHEW MOYLA/MOYLS	

ANCESTOR INDEX	BIRTH	PL	CO	DEATH	PL	CO	LIVD	MARRIED	PL	CO	SPOUSE NAME	CODE
GATLIN, GEORGIANNA VIRGINIA	1832	NC	037	1877	NC	028		1 1851	NC	037	LAMON SESSIONS DUNN	16030
GATLIN, THOMAS	C1805	NC		1838	NC	037		1 1829	NC	037	JULIA PENDER	16030
GAUNT/GUANT, WILLIAM	C1733	?NC		1809	SC		060	1 C1759			ANN/ANNA WOOD/WOODS	60507
GEDDIE/GEDDY/GADY, JAMES DANIEL	C1755	SCO			NC	029		1	NC	?029	CATHRIN ISABELLA MCPHAILL	60061
GEDDIE/GEDDY/GADY, JAMES DANIEL JR		NC	029	C1840	NC	029		1	NC	?029	JANET MAXWELL	60061
GEDDIE/GEDDY/GADY, JOHN	C1802	NC	029	C1866	AL			1	NC		NANCY	60061
GEDDIE/GEDDY/GADY, THOMAS	C1800	NC	029	C1858	AL			1 1826	AL		MARTHA J PHARES	60061
GEE, JOHN M	1801	NC	022	1870	TX			1 C1825			PHOEBE BREWER	27546
GENTRY/JENTRY, HEZEKIAH	C1736	VA		1824	SC		?046	1			CATARIN	08165
GEORGE, ELIAS		VA		C1771	NC	037		1			MARTHA	02065
GEORGE, WILLIAM		VA		1781	NC	037		1	NC	037	SELAH	02065
GEURIN, ISAAC W	C1784	NJ		C1856	AR		090					60332
GEURIN, NATHAN	C1765			C1819	NC	084						60332
GIBBONS, JOHN W	C1807	NC			AL			1			MARY HALL	60235
GIBBONS, STEPHEN	C1809	NC			AL			1			ELIZA SLOAN	60235
GIBBS, CASON		NC	053	C1828	NC	053		1 2 3			DINAH BARTEE NANCY LOCKHART PHEBA HARRIS	20335
GIBBS, HENRY				1777	NC	053		1			JANE SPENCER	20335
GIBBS, HENRY THE ELDER				1759	NC	053	029	1			ANNE	25254
GIBBS, JOSEPH JR		?NC	?053	1819	NC	053		1			ESTHER FARMER	25254
GIBBS, JOSEPH SR		?NC	?053	C1794	NC	053		1			MARY	25254
GIBBS, JOSEPH, SR				C1794	NC	053		1			MARY	20335
GIBSON, HANNAH	1764	?NC		C1840			090	1 1782	NC	092	SAMUEL JACKSON	60124
GIDEON/GIDDENS, EDWARD M	1787	NC	104	C1835	KY			1 C1810	NC		KATIE BUNTON	60454
GIDEON/GIDDENS, ELIZABETH	1798	NC	104	1867	MO			1 1815 2 C1839			SOLOMON DAVIS JDG JACOB PIKE	60454
GIDEON/GIDDENS, ELIZABETH	1818	NC			MO			1 C1836			WILLIAM CARPENTER	60454
GIDEON/GIDDENS, ISHAM G	1795	NC	104	1860	MO			1 C1820			NANCY MILLER	60454
GIDEON/GIDDENS, JAMES	1793	NC	104	C1848	AR			1 C1815	?GA		SUSAN	60454
GIDEON/GIDDENS, JAMES H	1813	NC	104	1881	TX			1 1832 2 C1870	TN		LUCINDA HAYS HENRIETTA	60454
GIDEON/GIDDENS, JAMES ISHAM	1749	IRE		1832	TN		014	1 1787	NC	104	MARTHA/PATTY MILLS	60454
GIDEON/GIDDENS, JOSHUA A	1816	NC		1873	TX			1 1839			MAHALA	60454
GIDEON/GIDDENS, SARAH/SALLY	1808	NC	104					1			HIRMA REED	60454
GIDEON/GIDDENS, WILLIAM	1791	NC	014	1868	MO		104	1 1813	NC	014	MATILDA WOODS	60454
GILBERT, ADELAIDE	1862	NC	068	1889				1 1882	NC	068	DR JOSIAH E CAVINESS	60037
GILBERT, BENJAMIN		NC	068					1			JANE CHEEK	60037
GILBERT, JAMES	1832	NC	068					1			MARY ELIZABETH ELLIS	60037

ANCESTOR INDEX	BIRTH	PL	CO	DEATH	PL	CO	LIVD	MARRIED	PL	CO	SPOUSE NAME	CODE
GILBERT, JOHN	C1795	NC			GA			1 C1822	NC		ELIZABETH RAY	27595
GILBERT, JOHN	C1784	NC		1891	TN			1 C1806	NC		SALLIE BOURLAND	60034
GILBERT, JOSEPH							073	1 1762			SIBERAH TYSON	60037
GILBERT, JOSEPH	1795	NC	068	1879				1			MARY/POLLY YOUNGER	60037
GILBERT, MARY	1828	NC		1871	GA			1 1846	GA		JEREMIAH M TAYLOR	27595
GILBERT, MARY	1734	MD		C1794	NC	092		1 C1756	MD		JOHN WELCH	60451
								2 1779	VA		JOHN BOOKER HOY	
GILBERT, WASHINGTON ALEXANDER	1814	NC		1894	MS			1 1842	AL		SARAH ELIZABETH OLIVER	60034
GILBREATH, ROBERT	1748	?NC	?046	1832	NC	046		1 1783	NC	046	ELIZABETH WALTON	05059
GILES, CHRISTOPHER DUNBAR	1826			1911	NC	014		1			DELPHIA JANE WINTERS	20448
GILES, CLEO A	C1911	NC	064				065	1 C1926			LEWIS O ROSS	19183
GILES, NOBLE ALEXANDER	C1808				NC	014		1			MARY	20448
GILES, WILLIAM SHERMAN	C1865	NC	064		NC	?064		1 1899	NC	064	EVA W SWANN	19183
GILL, CAROLINE	1846	NC	073	1924	NC	073		1 1878	NC	073	LEVI JONATHAN JOBE	02256
GILL, ELIZABETH	C1775			1867	NC	073		1 1802	NC	073	THOMAS SQUIRES SR	02256
GILL, INGRAM ALAN	1780	NC	054	1853	NC	054		1			MARY/POLLY TOMLIN/TOMLINSON	60118
GILL, JOSEPH	C1742	?VA		1820	NC	044		1 C1768	NC		ISABELLA OWEN	05045
								2 C1790			MARY	
GILL, ROBERT YOUNG	1909	NC	054	1967	NC	085		1 1928	SC		EVA ESTELLE MAYBERRY	60118
GILL, THOMAS	1769	NC	044	1839	TN			1 C1785	NC		NANCY	05045
								2 1816	TN		MRS ELIZABETH (JONES) COOPER	
								3 1820	TN		MRS SARAH (THOMPSON) DUKES	
GILL, THOMAS	1814	NC	054	1901	NC	054		1			MOLLIE/MARY TOMLIN/TOMLINSON	60118
GILL, THOMAS SR	C1780			C1853	NC	?073		1 1801	NC	073	MARY JONES	02256
GILL, THOMAS, II	1806	NC	?073		NC	?073		1 1826	NC	073	CATHERINE TATE	02256
GILL, WILLIAM	1750	VA		1797	NC	054		1 C1775	?VA		SUSANNAH YOUNG	60118
GILL, WILLIAM HENRY	1860	GA		1922	NC	054		1 1888	NC	054	MINNIE SUMMERS	60118
GILL, WILLIAM THOMAS	1929	NC	054					1 1952	VA		FAE CAROL GERARD	60118
GILLIAM, JAMES MASON	C1819	NC					073	1 1838	NC	073	SOPHIA MOORE	25159
GILLIAM, PRISCILLA	1766			1814	TN			1 1783	NC	044	JAMES HARRIS	60555
								2			WILLIAM HEARNE	
GILLIAM, ROBERT A	1843	NC	022	1909	TX			1			MARY WALL	25159
GILLILAND, ELIZABETH	1844	NC	013	C1884	NC	049		1	NC		ELBERT S ARRINGTON	40690
GILLILAND, JOHN	1815	NC		C1870	NC	013		1	NC		DICIA INGLE	40690
GILLILAND, JOHN	1774	VA		1873	IN		084	1 1797	NC	084	SUSANNAH HARRIS	60129
GILLILAND, JOHN BROOKINS	1812	NC	084	1898	IA			1 1832	IN		MARY SERRENA HERRON	60129
GILMORE, JOHN	C1808	NC		C1875	AL			1 C1830	AL		TEMPERANCE DEEN	27600
GINN, JESSE	C1796	NC	103	C1865	NC	103		1 C1820	NC	103	MILLY	13264
GINN, MARIMAN	C1825	NC	103	1903	NC	045		1 1850	NC	103	AVA	13264

ANCESTOR INDEX	BIRTH	PL	CO	DEATH	PL	CO	LIVD	MARRIED	PL	CO	SPOUSE NAME	CODE
GINN, MARY ANN	1854	NC	045	C1885	NC	045		1 C1874	NC	045	JESSE TAYLOR	13264
GIPSON, WILLIAM	1753	SC		1835	IN		084	1 1795	NC	046	NANCY ROARK	60385
GIST, BENJAMIN	C1725			C1810	TN		073	1 C1750	VA		MARY JARRATT	02470
GIST, THOMAS	1764	?NC	?073	1837	TN		073	1			ELIZABETH	02470
GIVENS, JOHN	1832	?NC		1862	NC	?097		1			ADALINE HAGINS	11100
GLASS, MARY/MILLEY	1810	NC	022	1885	KS			1 1826	NC	046	JOHN FOWLER	60549
GLASSCOCK, PETER JR	C1744	VA		C1815	NC	085		1 C1771	VA		ELIZABETH MADDEN	60225
GLASSCOCK, PETER SR	1714	VA		1783	NC	085		1 C1730	VA		JANE RECTOR	60225
								2 C1760	VA		MARY RECTOR	
GLENN, ABRAHAM	C1762	NC		1851	TN			1 C1793	NC		MARTHA/PATSY	12015
GLENN, JOHN	C1734	VA		C1808	NC	084		1 C1755			SARAH	12015
GLENN, MARY	C1825	NC	084		NC	084		1 1847	NC	084	CHARLES BLACK	27542
GLIMP, GEORGE				1829	TN			1 1799	NC	044	MILLY WHEELER	60029
GLOSSUP, WILLIAM		NC		C1863	?AL			1 C1853			ORA LITTRELL	60454
GLOVER, DARNEL	1774			1837	TN			1 1798	NC	100	ELIZABETH CANNON	60017
GLOVER, WILLIAM	C1760	MD			GA		104					60008
GODDARD, GEORGE SR				C1790	NC	063	096	1			PENELOPE	19130
GODFREY, ELIZA M							097	1			ANDREW JACKSON KING	11100
GODFREY, ELIZABETH							070	1 1729	PA		CHRISTOPHER OTTEY	60413
GODFREY, JOHN				1854	NC	097						11100
GODWIN, BARNABY		?VA					044	1			WILKINSON	60008
GODWIN, ELIZABETH	C1748	?VA		1812	GA		037	1 C1763			JOHN MILNER	60008
GODWIN, NEWETT WRIGHT	C1831	NC	?056	C1885	NC	?056		1 1851	NC	056	SARAH/SALLY BOWES/BARNES	03315
GODWIN, TOBIAS		NC	?056	C1845	NC	056		1	NC	?056	CHRISTIAN RICHARDSON	03315
GOFORTH, WILLIAM	C1775	NC		C1856	IL			1 C1806	?TN			60312
								2 C1818	?KY		MRS GERIAH (BARNES) MULLIS	
GOING, JOHN WILLIAM		NC						1 1837	MS		MARY CAROLINE SMITH	08165
GOMER, SARAH	1780			1863	NC			1 1799	NC	020	FLEMING THOMASSON	13120
GOOCH, DANIEL	1756				NC	044		1 1789			NANCY SNEAD	27734
GOOCH, JANE					NC	044		1 1826			WILLIAM CLEMENT	27734
GOOCH, JOSEPH	1732	VA		1790	NC	044		1			JANE DUDLEY	27734
GOODBREAD, MARY/POLLY	C1761	?NC	?086		KY			1 1782	NC	086	JESSE HENSON	06159
GOODBREAD, PHILLIP SR	1731	PA		1811	NC	086		1			CATHERINE	06159
GOODE, JOHN								1 1795	NC	086	JANE/JANIE HAWKINS	60349
GOODE, JOHN HAWKINS	1796	NC	086		KY			1	KY		SARAH/SALLY CLARK	60349
GOODLOE, JOHN	1768	VA		C1850	TN		020	1	NC	039	MARY BOWERS	06005
GOODNIGHT, HANS MICHAEL		GER		1781	KY		065	2 1762	?VA		MARY LANDERS	60085
GOODWIN, JOB	C1780	NC	?024					1			NANCY ARKILL	27562

ANCESTOR INDEX	BIRTH	PL	CO	DEATH	PL	CO	LIVD	MARRIED	PL	CO	SPOUSE NAME	CODE
GOODWIN, NANCY P	1848	NC	024	1930	VA			1 1865	NC	024	WILLIAM A DAIL	27562
GOODWIN, STEPHEN RICHARD	1820	NC	024					1			JUDITH ANN BOYCE	27562
GORDON, JOHN	1772	VA		1839	NC	090		1 C1790	NC	?092	BARZILLA MARTIN	01040
								2			MARY TUTTLE	
GORDON, SARAH	1791	NC	092	1872	UT			1 1809	NC	090	THOMAS GUYMON	01040
GORDON, THOMAS	1745	IRE		1803	NC	090		1 C1770	VA		SARAH WILSON	01040
GOSS, THOMAS JR	C1753	NC	044	C1833	GA			1 1775	NC	044	PATSY PUTNAM/PUTMAN	60278
GOSS, THOMAS SR	C1731	NC	010	1816	NC	044		1 C1752	NC	044	FRANCES SHERMAN	60278
GOSS, WILLIAM	C1675			C1746	NC	?044	037	1 1691	VA		ELIZABETH DIXON	60278
								2			MARY	
GOSSETT/GOSSET, ELIJAH	1800	NC	081	1889	IN			1 1822	NC	081	MARTHA HAYS	14020
GOSSETT/GOSSET, HENRY	C1755				NC	?081		1			SARAH NEWMAN	14020
GOSSETT/GOSSET, WILLIAM				C1799	NC	081		1			MARGARET	14020
GOTT, JONATHAN	C1745	NC		1843	KY							27348
GOTT, PETER	C1786	NC			MO			1 1805	KY		MARGARETTE CLEMMENTS	27348
GOTT, SUTTON	C1764	NC		C1850	KY			1			POLLY	27348
GRAHAM, BENJAMIN GIST	1839	SC		1901	NC	005		1 1863	NC	046	CAROLINA MCKNIGHT	07115
GRAHAM, EMMOR	1802	PA		1876	NC	065		1 1833	SC		TERESA EUSEBIA RICHARDS	07115
GRAHAM, JAMES	C1780	NC			?MS			1 C1800	NC		NANCY	60286
GRAHAM, JESSE	1804	NC		1887	TX			1 1827	?TN		MARTHA JANE FANNIN	60289
GRAHAM, JOHN	C1777	?NC		C1822	?AL		092	1 C1800	?NC		MARY	60289
GRAHAM, MARY, MRS	1781	NC		C1865	TX			1 C1800	?NC		JOHN GRAHAM	60289
GRAHAM, MILDEN	C1801	NC	029	C1855	NC	029		1			JOHNATHAN HAIR	13052
GRAHAM, ROBERT	C1765				NC	029		1			JOHNATHAN HAIR	13052
GRAHAM, WILLIAM B				1818	NC			1	NC		PEGGY HARRIS	60286
GRAHAM/GRIMES, JANE	1807	NC	092	1888	MO			1 C1827	?AL		ALVA ANDERSON LAMB/LAM	60297
GRAHAM/GRIMES, JOHN	C1777			C1830	AL		092	1 1798	NC	092	MARY PENNINGTON	60297
GRAHAM/GRIMES, JOHN		?VA			NC	092		1 1789	VA		MARY PENNINGTON	60300
GRANT, RACHEL	C1859	NC		1898	GA			1 C1877	NC	?023	JAMES SAMUEL MULLINS	08015
GRAVES, JOSEPH				1774	NC	092		1 1759			SARAH	08070
GRAVES, MARY				1800	SC		092	1 1759	VA		BENJAMIN CLEVELAND	08070
GRAVES, SARA CROSHA	1735	VA		1814	NC	044		1 1754	VA		THOMAS BARNETT	03035
GRAY, ALEXANDER	C1766	VA		C1812	?TN		014	1 C1790	VA		MARY	02470
GRAY, ELIZA ANNE	1847	NC	030					1 1875	NC	031	BENJAMIN TWIFORD	13120
GRAY, JAMES	1846	NC	104	1891	NC	104		1 ?1872	NC	104	AMELIAN ARNOLD	08095
GRAY, JAMES ALEXANDER	1846	NC	081	1918	NC	038		1 1869	NC	046	AURELIA BOWMAN	12125
GRAY, JOHN	1749	VA		1792	NC	081		1 1776	NC	081	JANNET GREER/GRIER	12125
GRAY, JOHN	1786	NC	?034	C1842	NC	059		1 C1807	NC	?045	EDITH MEWBORN	14030

ANCESTOR INDEX	BIRTH	PL	CO	DEATH	PL	CO	LIVD	MARRIED	PL	CO	SPOUSE NAME	CODE
GRAY, NANCY	1797	NC	075	1873	MO			1 1816	NC	075	SAMUEL C NASH	60414
GRAY, RANSOM	1777	?NC		1843	NC	065		1 1800	NC	016	NARCISSA ALEXANDER	60151
GRAY, RICHARD	C1798	NC	?030					1			ZILPHIA PAINE	13120
GRAY, RICHARD		NC	?099		KY							27291
GRAY, ROBERT	1814	NC	081	1881	NC	038		1 1841	NC	081	MARY MILLIS WILEY	12125
GRAY, SAMUEL	1778	NC	081	1856	NC	081		1 1801	NC	081	MARY SMITH	12125
GRAY, THOMAS				1801	NC	047		1			MARY	60594
GRAYBEAL, DAVID SMITH	1868	NC	006	1943	PA		066	1			MATTIE MORRIS	60439
								2	NC	066	IDA SLAGLE	
								3	NC	066	TEXAS SLAGLE	
GRAYBEAL, JOHN	1838	?NC		C1920	TN		006	1			TABITHA OSBORN	60439
GRAYSON, BENJAMIN	C1796	NC	?104					1 1817	NC		ELIZABETH THILBY	60156
GRAYSON, BENJAMIN	C1758						104					60156
GRAYSON, JAMES	C1786						104					60156
GRAYSON, JESSE	C1785						104					60156
GRAYSON, JOHN	C1771						104					60156
GRAYSON, JOSEPH	C1797	?NC	?104					1 1818	NC		DICY DYER	60156
GRAYSON, WILLIAM	C1779						104					60156
GREEN, FARNEFOLD	1674	VA		1714	NC	008		1			MRS HANNAH (KENT) SMITHWICK	60057
GREEN, GIDEON	1755			1799	NC	005		1			ELIZABETH ANDERSON/AUSTIN	60532
GREEN, HENRY	C1834	NC	011	1865	VA		027	1 1857	NC	027	MARGARET JANE COOK	24032
GREEN, JACOB	1780	NC	?005				067					60532
GREEN, JAMES	C1716	NC	028	1770	NC	034		1			MARY GRAY	21165
GREEN, JAMES N		NC		1847	NC	010		1 1840	NC		EMILY C DUKE	27531
GREEN, JAMES REDDICK	1845	NC	010	1913	NC	051		1 1870	NC	051	PRISCELLA E SESSOMS	27531
GREEN, JOHN	1802	NC	067	1882	AL			1 1828			BEDY TAYLOR WILLIAMS	14105
GREEN, JOHN	1802	NC	067	1882	LA			1 1828	AL		BEDY/OBEDIENCE TAYLOR WILLIAMS	60532
GREEN, JOSEPH	C1744	NC	?028	1803	NC	103		1			SARAH WHITFIELD	21165
								2			MRS HANNAH (GRAY) HAYWOOD	
GREEN, JOSEPH	C1800	NC	?086		?AL			1 C1830	NC	?086	MARGUETTE FRANKLIN	60025
GREEN, JOSEPH	C1783	NC		C1850	NC	?102		1 C1805	NC	?006	ELIZABETH SHEARER	60557
GREEN, JOSEPH HAMILTON	1824	NC		1865	LA			1 C1847	LA		ABAGAIL ELIZABETH COOK	14105
GREEN, JOSEPH P	1789	NC	100	C1860	GA			1 C1812			ELIZABETH JONES	60260
GREEN, JOSIAH		RI		C1850	NC	100						60260
GREEN, MARY C	1860	NC	027	1952	NC	027		1 1882	NC	027	SAMUEL COLUMBUS HAYES	24032
GREEN, MARY G	C1783	NC	103	1833	TN			1			JOSEPH BOON	21165
GREEN, SARAH/SALLY	C1808	NC	006	1862	NC	102		1 C1828	NC	?006	RANSOM HAYES	60557
GREEN, THOMAS CLINTON	1878	NC	051	1949	FL			1 1900	NC	051	SALLY J HOLLOMAN	27531
GREEN/GREENE, ESTHER		NC						1			MR HENSON	60373
								2			ABSALOM MATTHEWS	

ANCESTOR INDEX	BIRTH	PL	CO	DEATH	PL	CO	LIVD	MARRIED	PL	CO	SPOUSE NAME	CODE
GREEN/GREENE, GEORGE	C1760	?NC	?005				094	1 1784	NC	086	LUCY JONES	60373
GREEN/GREENE, JAMES	C1770	?NC	?094	1821	IL		094	1			SARAH HIX	60373
GREEN/GREENE, JAMES N	C1815	NC	051	1847	NC	051		1 1840	NC	051	EMILY C DUKE	27276
GREEN/GREENE, JAMES REDDICK	1845	NC	051	1913	NC	041		1 1870	NC	051	PRISCILLA A (SESSUMS) HOGGARD	27276
GREEN/GREENE, JARVIS	1750	NC	005	1782	KY		094	1 C1775	?NC		SARAH GRIGGS	60373
GREEN/GREENE, JOHN C	1788			C1855	NC	?051	?010	1 1807			ELIZABETH GRIGGS	27276
GREEN/GREENE, JOSEPH	C1740	NC	?051	C1805	NC	051	?010					27276
GREEN/GREENE, MOLLIE/MATTIE		NC						1	NC		MR RATTON	60373
GREEN/GREENE, NANCY	1760	NC	005	1834	IL		094	1 1787	NC		ROBERT ARMSTRONG	60373
GREEN/GREENE, WILLIAM	C1760	NC	051		NC	010		1 1794	NC	010	ANN LASSITER	27276
								2 1797	NC	010	PEGGY OUTLAW	
								3 1837	NC	010	CINITHA POWELL	
GREENWOOD, NANCY	1798			1880	NC	?106		1			JOEL REECE	60288
GREGG, HANNAH		NC					073	1			JOHN MORRIS	60070
GREGORY, JAMES	1783	NC	?014	1844	LA		?013	1			LIZZIE LEE	60180
GREGORY, JANE ELIZABETH	1822	NC	072	1904	GA			1 1843	FL		CALVIN ALEXANDER CURRY	60396
GREGORY, JASON	1781	NC	072	1838	FL			1	NC	072	AMITTEE WILDER	60396
GREGORY, JOB/JOBE	C1775	?NC	?075	C1835	NC	018		1			PEGGY ROBERTS	60307
								2			MARY HARRISON	
GREGORY, MARK R	1827	NC	018	1886	NC	018		1	NC	018	MRS MELLICENT (BROWN) JACKSON	60307
								2 1854	NC	018	MRS MARY (LAMB) BELL	
GREGORY, MARK ROBERTS	1866	NC	018	1950	VA		030	1 1889	NC	018	ADELAIDE UPTON	60307
GREGORY, MURIEL C	1897	NC	030					1 1926	VA		CHARLES H WILSON	60307
GRICE, DELILAH	1770	NC	?056	1825	KY			1 1789	NC	056	PETER WATKINS	60109
GRICE, JAMES P		?NC						1			NANCY C	10153
GRICE, JUNE C	C1820	NC	054									10153
GRICE, RUFUS HENRY	1860	NC	060	1918	NC	065		1			MARY EMMA ODELL	10153
GRIFFIN, HUGH	C1789	NC	073				043	1			SARAH CRANFORD	27775
GRIFFIN, JAMES THOMAS	1885			C1978	NC	010		1 1912			PATRICIA ELIZABETH MIZELL	24320
GRIFFIN, WILLIAM				1819	TN			1	?NC		MARGARET	24250
GRIFFIN, WILLIAM	C1800	NC	?073	C1845				1 1822	NC	073	MARY/POLLY FOWLER	25238
GRIFFIN/GRIFFIETH, WILLIAM		NC	028					1 C1779			RUTH WARD	20138
GRIFFIS/GRIFFITH, THOMAS	C1745	?VA		1808	TN		022	1 1770	?NC	071	ANN RAGLAND	07018
GRIFFITH, CALEB	1769	MA		1851	GA		079	1 1798	GA		JULIA ANN LITTLE	60234
GRIFFITH, DONALD	C1808	NC		C1859	TN			1 C1836	TN		ELIZABETH JANE DICKSON	07168
GRIFFITH, WILLIAM	C1790	NC		C1822				1			SARAH ANN	07168
GRIGG/GIRGGS, JOHN								1 1785	NC	099	MARY WOODWARD	60496
GRIGG/GRIGGS, BANNESTER		VA						1	NC	086	REBECCA RANDALL	60496

ANCESTOR INDEX	BIRTH	PL	CO	DEATH	PL	CO	LIVD	MARRIED	PL	CO	SPOUSE NAME	CODE
GRIGG/GRIGGS, JOEL								1 1817	NC	086	EUNICE PATTERSON	60496
GRIGG/GRIGGS, LEE							044					60496
GRIGG/GRIGGS, MINOS				1761	NC	044	085					60496
GRIGG/GRIGGS, RHODUM				1827	GA		044	1 1784	NC	100	MILLEY BAGLEY	60496
GRIGG/GRIGGS, ROBERT	1757	VA			TN		047					60496
GRIGGS, JOHN				1825	GA		039	1			MARY	60556
GRIGGS, RHODUM/RHODAM/RHODA							039	1			MILLY	60556
GRIMES, CHRISTINA	1794	NC	032	1858	IN			1 1811	NC	032	MATHIAS SAPPNEFIELD	06005
GRIMES, JANE	C1752				NC	081	022	1 C1770	NC	?073	GEORGE FRAZIER	06158
GRIMES, JOHN CAHRLES	1761	NC	085	1830	NC	032		1	NC	032	BARBARA FRANK	06005
GRIMES, NANCY	C1755							1 C1775	NC	022	ANTHORY RAINS	06158
GRIMES, RICHARD	C1730			1806	NC	081						06158
GRIMES, THOMAS	1738	VA		1797	NC	037		1 C1761			CHLOE LLEWELLYN	19130
GRIMES/GRYMES, ELIZABETH JOHNSON				1852	TN		020	1		073	REV WILLIAM MOORE	60595
GRIMES/GRYMES, LUDWELL							073	1 1756			MARY DAWSON	60595
GRINDSTAFF, HENRY	1789	NC	014	1870	NC	107		1 C1808	NC		CYNTHIA PENLAND	60155
GRINDSTAFF, ISAAC	C1754	NC		C1825	NC	014		1 1773	NC	014		60155
GRINDSTAFF, MICHAEL	1720			C1790	NC	014		1 C1740	?NC			60155
GRISHAM, AUSTIN	1771	NC	046	1853	IL		?022	1 C1793	?SC		FANNY POWERS	25241
GRISHAM, ELVIS	1801	NC	044		NC	044		1 1837	NC	044	MARY S PERKINSON	02435
GRISHAM, JAMES						046	022					25241
GRISSIT/GRESSET, SARAH					SC		012	1 1807	NC	012	EDWARD CONNER	60265
GROCE, LUCY	C1770	NC	005	1841	TN			1	NC		WELCOME USSERY	06005
GROVES, CATHARINE					IL			1	NC	085	MICHAEL GATES	60269
GRUBBS, JOHN	1799			1845	NC	090		1 1819	NC	090	SARAH KIRK	60456
GRUBBS, PATSY				?1854	NC	038						17075
GRUBBS, SAYRE/SARAH/SALLY	1797	NC	090	1841	IN			1 1812	NC	090	SOLOMON CARMICHAEL	17075
GRUBBS, THOMAS				1807	NC	090		1			PATSY	17075
GRUBBS, THOMAS				C1807	NC	090		1			PATSY	60456
GUDGER, JAMES MCREE	1818	NC	013	1887	NC	013		1 1839	NC	013	SARAH ANN MURRAY	04195
GUDGER, JOSEPH Y	1792	NC	013	1869	NC	013		1 1817	NC	?054	RACHEL ELIZABETH MCREE	04195
GUDGER, WILLIAM	1752	SCO		1833	NC	013	092	1 1775	MD		MARTHA/PATSY YOUNG	04195
GUERIN/GEURIN, DAVID CONGER	1776	NJ		C1858	TN		090	1			POLLY	60184
GUERIN/GEURIN, ISAAC WHITEHEAD	1784	NC		C1855	AR		090	1 2 1830	TN		ELIZABETH GINSEY RICHARDSON	60184
GUERIN/GEURIN, JOHN B	C1813	NC	?084	1883	AR		090					60184
GUERIN/GEURIN, NATHANIEL/NATHAN	1750	NJ		1819	NC	084	090	1 1775 2	NJ		ABIGAIL CONGER MARY/POLLY	60184

ANCESTOR INDEX	BIRTH	PL	CO	DEATH	PL	CO	LIVD	MARRIED	PL	CO	SPOUSE NAME	CODE
GUINN, JAMES MILES KILLIAN	1835	NC	061	1903	AL			1 1862	?AL		EMILY F BURTON	60359
								2 1869	AL		MRS MARY JANE(CULBERTSON)FOSTER	
GUINN, JAMES W	1804	TN		1866	TX			1 1830	NC	061	CATHERINE ANN DOBSON	60359
GULLEY, LAZARUS	1783	NC	056	1839	TN			1	?NC	?056	NANCY HENSLEY	27318
GULLEY, MEAD		NC	056	1803	NC	056		1	?NC	?056		27318
								2 1796	NC	056	SAVARA/AVIE ATKINSON	
GULLEY, ROBERT G							056					27318
GULLEY/GULLY, JOHN SR				C1793	NC	056	037	1			MARTHA	08090
GULLEY/GULLY, LEWIS	C1780	NC	056	C1850	TN		056	1 1807	NC	099	JANE ROWLAND	08090
GULLEY/GULLY, MEAD/MEED				C1803	NC	056		1 1796	NC	056	AVIE ATKINSON	08090
GULLEY/GULLY, ROBERT SR				C1814	NC	056		1 1798	NC	056	SALLY BRIDGERS	08090
GUNN, ALEXANDER	C1750			1830	NC	054		1				60215
								2 1791	NC	054	BEDDY OAKES GWYN	
GUNN, STARLING	1764	VA		1853	NC	020		1 1784			MARY ELIZABETH/POLLY HOOPER	60493
GUNN, SUSANNAH	1794	NC	020	1862	MO			1 1819	?NC		JAMES HENRY HARRIS	60493
GUNSTON, GEORGE				C1783	NC	092						27429
GUNSTON, JAMES	C1765	NC	?085	C1810	NC	092		1 C1790	NC	092	RACHEL WOOTON	27429
GUSTAVUS, MICHAEL		NC	005		GA							24073
GUTBRODT/GOODBREAD, JOHN	1753	NC		1808	NC	086		1 1779	NC	086	MRS MARY (LEDBETTER) BRADLEY	60402
GUTBRODT/GOODBREAD, JOSEPH	1750	PA		1844	MO		014	1 1777	NC	014	TOMASANN JOHNSON	60402
GUTBRODT/GOODBREAD, PHILLIP JR	1760	NC		1849	FL		086	1 1785	GA		CATHERINE SOUDER	60402
GUTBRODT/GOODBREAD, PHILLIPUS	1726	GER		1811	NC	086	073	1 1749	PA		CATHERINE	60402
GUYMON, ISAIAH	C1745	?VA		1819	NC	090		1 C1773	NC	092	ELIZABETH FLYNN	01040
GUYMON, ISAIAH	1753			1820	NC	090		1 1772	NC	?092	ELIZABETH FLYNN	60388
GUYMON, THOMAS	1787	NC	090	1855	UT			1 1809	NC	090	SARAH GORDON	01040
GUYMON, THOMAS	1787	NC	092	1855	UT			1 1809	NC	090	SARAH GORDON	60388
GWYN, JOHN	C1790	NC	084		KY			1			MARY BEARD	11070
GWYNN, HUGH				C1829	TN		084					02170
GWYNN, RANSOM	C1790	NC	?084					1			MARGARET	02170

H

HADDEN, SAMUEL	1730	NC		1831				1 C1770	NC			60586
								2 1794	KY			
HADDOX, ANNA	1773	NC	085	1827	NC	085		1 1798	NC	085	WILLIAM BAITY	08023
HADDOX, WILLIAM				1811	NC	085		1			ELIZABETH WARD	08023
HADLEY, HANNAH	1749	VA		1809	NC	022	073	1 1766	NC	073	JESSE JOHNSON/JOHNSTON	04195
HADLEY, JOSEPH	1787	NC	022	1857	IA			1 1808	NC	073	MARY HINSHAW	60558

ANCESTOR INDEX	BIRTH	PL	CO	DEATH	PL	CO	LIVD	MARRIED	PL	CO	SPOUSE NAME	CODE
HADLEY, JOSHUA	1703	IRE		C1760	NC	073		1 1725 2 1735	 DE		MARY ROWLAND PATIENCE BROWN	04195
HADLEY, JOSHUA	1703	IRE		1760	NC	073		2 1735	PA		PATIENCE BROWN	60120
HADLEY, JOSHUA	1743	DE		1816	NC	022		1 C1761	NC	073	RUTH LINDLEY	60558
HADLEY, MARGARET	1790	NC	092	C1838	NC	092		1 1807	NC	092	JESSE REECE	60120
HADLEY, MARY	1765	NC	029	1834	NC	029		1 1785	NC	029	WILLIAM ENGLAND	60147
HADLEY, SIMON JR	1766	NC	073	1831	NC	092	046	1 1786	NC	092	MARY SPENCER	60120
HADLEY, SIMON SR	1737	DE		1803	NC	092	073	1 1756	DE		BRIDGET FOOTE	60120
HADLEY, THOMAS	1728	DE		1781	NC	029		1 1750	PA		MARY THOMPSON	60147
HAILE/HAIL/HALE, JOHN								1	?NC		FRANCES/FANNY WEST	27303
HAINLINE/HANELINE, JOHN				1775	NC	085		1			CATHERINE	08010
HAINLINE/HANELINE, JOHN	1760	VA		C1834	KY		085					08010
HAINS/HANES, JONATHAN	C1750	PA		1833	NC	092		1 C1789	NC	092	FRANCIS/FANNIE GLASSOCK	60225
HAIR, JOHNATHAN	C1775			C1835	NC	029	?087	1			MILDEN GRAHAM	13052
HAIR, SARAH ANN	1831	NC	029				011	1 1849			GIDEON S JACKSON	13052
HAIRGROVE, STEPHEN MARION	1784	NC	046	1858	TX			1 1805	NC	046	NANCY MARY BROWN	60427
HAISLEY, EZEKIEL	1744			1828	IN		046	1			MARY BROWN	27429
HAISLEY, JESSE	1791	NC	092	1840	IN			1 1813	NC	092	RUTH KENDALL	27429
HALE, JOHN PURDUE	C1775			C1830			092	1 1797 2 1800	NC NC	046 046	SARAH MCGLAMERY/MCGLANMARIE MARGARET OLIPHANT	60237
HALE, OMARANNAH/MARANDA	1808	NC		1844	IN			1 1826	NC	090	JESSE VAUGHN	60237
HALEY, JOHN	C1793	NC						1			MATILDA	25185
HALEY/HAILEY, EDWARD T	1779	VA		1858	TN			1 2 1804	 NC		 SUSANNA PRATT	60025
HALL, AILA/MAHALA	C1825	?NC						1 1844	IL		ROBERT HALE/HAILS	60412
HALL, ANDERSON	1815	NC		1885	IL			1 1851	IL		ELIZA JANE BOURLAND	60412
HALL, CHARLES CHOAT	1848	NC	023	1932	GA			1 C1869 2 1881	NC NC	023 023	MARY JENKINS/DINKINS JOSEPHINE BATES	08015
HALL, EDWARD	1786	NC		C1865	TN		065	1 1813	NC	065	ANNE ALLEN	60519
HALL, ELIZA MORRIS	C1820	NC			IL			1 1847	IL		VOLENTINE MORRIS	60412
HALL, JAMES		IRE		1800	NC	054	085	1 1730	PA		PRUDENCE RODDY	60443
HALL, JANE	1734	PA			?NC	?054		1 2 C1778	NC NC	085 085	SAMUEL ROSEBOROUGH JAMES MCEWEN	60443
HALL, JOHN	1757	PA						1	NC	073	MARY PYLE	60349
HALL, JOHN A	C1803	SCO		?1880	NC	?023		1 1828	NC	086	ELIZA YOUNG	08015
HALL, JONATHAN	1787	NC		1864	IL		?099	1 C1810	NC		SARAH	60412
HALL, JONATHAN HENRY	1820	NC	?065	1899	AR			1 C1840 2 C1854	TN TN		CAROLINA PRISCILLA TODD MARY OWENS	60519
HALL, LEWIS	1756	NC	011	1821	GA			1 2	NC NC		 NANCY COLLY	60164
HALL, OLIVER	1789	VA		1847	NC	092		1 1818	VA		LUCY CARTER	60393

ANCESTOR INDEX	BIRTH	PL	CO	DEATH	PL	CO	LIVD	MARRIED	PL	CO	SPOUSE NAME	CODE
HALL, ROBERT	1783	NC	022					1 1812	KY		SARAH PYLE	60349
HALL, SAMUEL	1777	NC	022	1848	IL			1 C1820	NC	029	NANCY STEELE	27417
HALL, SARAH WATSON	1822	NC		C1864	IL			1 1842	IL		JOHN CURREY WATSON	60412
HALL, WILLIAM	C1818	NC		1895	IL			1 1854	IL		SARAH BISHOP	60412
HALL, WILLIAM BEDFORD	1870	NC	023	1914	GA			1 1890 2 1898	GA GA		MINDA L LANGLEY ADDIE MALINDA RUTHIE MULLINS	08015
HALL, WILLIAM NEUM	1835	NC	092	1887	NC	092		1 1859	NC	092	NANCY EMMALINE HAYMORE	60393
HALL, WILLIS	1812	NC		1864	IL			1 1839	IL		SERENA MURRAY	60412
HALTOM, CHARLIE	1777	NC	?005	C1855	NC	067		1	NC	067	RHODA ROSETTA HARRIS	60457
HALTOM, JOEL	C1807	NC	067	C1865				1 C1834	?GA		LUCINDA MORRIS	60319
HALTOM, PINKNEY	1813	NC	067	1888	TN			1 C1837	NC	067	HIXIE HARRIS	60457
HALTOM, SPENSER	C1730	NC	?005		NC	067		1			NANCY WEST	60457
HAM, WILLIAM	1819	NC						1	NC		ELIZA HAM	60486
HAM/HAMM, ENOCH	1814	VA		1899	VA		004	1 1836	NC	006	MALINDA TAYLOR	60120
HAM/HAMM, JAMES BASIL	1885	VA		1962	IN		004	1 1905	NC	004	MINNIE ALICE PHOUTS	60120
HAM/HAMM, JAMES FRED	1911	NC	004					1 1932	IN		MARTHA CHRISTENE STEWART	60120
HAM/HAMM, JOHN SR	1780	NC	046	1850	VA			1 C1800	VA		SARAH OSBORN	60120
HAM/HAMM, MARION BAZEL TAYLOR	1843	VA		1915	VA		004	1 1865	NC	004	REBECCA JANE FOWLKES	60120
HAM/HAMM, THOMAS	C1720			C1775	NC	046						60120
HAM/HAMM, WILLIAM SR				1799	SC		034	1			MARY PRUDENCE	27404
HAM/HAMM, WILLIAM SR	C1750			1812	VA		046					60120
HAM/HAMM, ZACHARIAH	C1800	NC		1883	GA			1 1829	NC	029	NANCY BEASLEY	27404
HAM/HAMM, ZACHARIAH	C1750			C1830	NC			1			CHRISTIAN WILLIAMS	27404
HAMBY, IVORY	1820	NC		C1890	TN			1 C1842	TN		SARAH BODKIN	27533
HAMILTON, GEORGE F	C1784	NC		1865	MS			1 C1809	TN		HANNAH FOSTER	60507
HAMILTON, JAMES F	1835	NC						1			NANCY CONGER	27593
HAMILTON, JOSEPH	C1763	NC	?073	C1839	TN							60461
HAMLET, ANN		NC	100				047					25156
HAMLET, HENRY		NC	067				082					25156
HAMLET, JESSE		NC	067					1 C1800			SALLY GATEWOOD	25156
HAMLET, JOHN	1757	VA		C1835	KY		067	1	NC	067		25156
HAMLET, NANCY					NC		047					25156
HAMLET, PETER		NC			NC		067					25156
HAMLET, RICHARD		NC	100									25156
HAMLETT/HAMBLET, AUGUSTEN							100					60576
HAMLETT/HAMBLET, JAMES	1795	NC	100	1887	TN			1 C1815 2 C1823 3 C1829	TN TN TN		ELLIOTT JANE CULTON ATKINS MARY JANE ATKINS	60576

ANCESTOR INDEX	BIRTH	PL	CO	DEATH	PL	CO	LIVD	MARRIED	PL	CO	SPOUSE NAME	CODE
HAMLETT/HAMBLET, RICHARD							100	1 C1770	?VA		ANN/NANCY CONNER	60576
HAMMOND, ARCHELAUS	1709	MA		C1773	NC	072		1 1729	MA		ELIZABETH WEEKS	01012
HAMMOND, CHARLES	C1747	MA			NC	011	072	2 1768	MA		ANNA STEWART	01012
HAMMOND, PAUL	C1769	MA		C1835	NC	?011	072	1 C1791	NC	?028	NANCY	01012
HAMPTON, AHAB							013	1 1791	VA		NANCY CHEATHAM	02252
HAMPTON, ANDREW				1805	NC	086	044	2			KATHRYN HYDER	08023
HAMPTON, EPHRAIM	C1740			1814	NC	085		1			LEMENDER HARRIS	08023
HAMPTON, MARTHA/PATSY	1815	NC	?104	1869	NC	102		1 C1834	NC	104	LUKE TRIPLETT	60222
HAMPTON, MARY/POLLY	C1791	NC		C1858	TN							60404
HAMPTON, MICAJAH							013	1			ANNE	02252
HAMPTON, OLIVER	1776	NC	085	1868	MO			1 C1796			ELIZABETH BRYAN	08023
HARDEN, JESSE	C1835	NC	083	1910	GA			1 C1872 2 C1906	?FL ?FL		MARTHA JENKINS COURTNEY ROGERS	60320
HARDEN, MARK				1795	NC	081		1			HANNAH HOLDER	19170
HARDEN, MARK JR	1789	?NC		1863	NC	081		1	NC	081	SARAH YORK	19170
HARDEN, RANALD	C1810				NC	?083		1 C1830	NC	083		60320
HARDEN, SUSANNAH	1774	VA		1846	NC	081		1 C1789	NC	081	ELI YORK	19170
HARDIN, RICHARD	C1780	?NC		1844	MS							60043
HARDIN, WILLIAM	1741	VA		1810	GA		?020	1 C1763			SARAH BLEDSOE	60043
HARDIN/HARDEN/HARDING, AMOS	1780	NC	?060	1840	TN			1 1798	TN		MARY GALLAHER	60565
HARDIN/HARDEN/HARDING, BENJAMIN	1780	NC	?060	1845	TX			1 1801	TN		MARTHA ANN/PATSY BARNETT	60565
HARDIN/HARDEN/HARDING, JOSEPH COL	C1734			1801	TN		065	1	NC	094	JANE/JEAN GIBSON	60565
HARDING, ELIZABETH	1778	VA		1840	NC	092		1 1793	NC	092	THOMAS WILLIAMS	60569
HARDING, WILLIAM	C1745	VA		1797	NC	092		1 1773	VA		OBEDIENCE HUTCHINS	60569
HARDISON, CARNAVELLA	1860	NC	063	1907	NC	009		1 1880	NC	063	WILLIAM ZENAS MORTON	12140
HARDISON, CHARLES	C1730	NC	063		NC	072		1 C1764				20415
HARDISON, GARBIEL	C1765	NC	072	1829	KY			1 C1799	NC		POLLY	20415
HARDISON, HANSEL	C1800	NC	009	C1844	NC	009		1 C1820			SENERSHA CARRAWAY	12140
HARDISON, JAMES	1759	NC	?096	1842	TN			1 C1788 2 C1808	?NC ?NC	?063 ?063	MARY ROBERSON MARY SMITHWICK	08040
HARDISON, JASPER	C1700	NC	?024	C1733	NC	?024	096	1			MARY/POLLY	12140
HARDISON, JASPER		NC		1733	NC			1			MARY	20415
HARDISON, JOSEPH	C1730	NC	096	C1788	NC	063		1			MARY	12140
HARDISON, WILLIAM	C1770			C1812	NC	009		1			ELIZABETH PERKINS	12140
HARDISON, WILLIAM JONATHAN	1828	NC	009	1908	NC	063		1 1855	NC	063	MARY ANN ELIZABETH ANDREWS	12140
HARDY, LEMUEL	C1698						010	1			ELIZABETH PARROTT	60318
HARDY, LEMUEL JR	1730	NC	010	1797	NC	034		1 1762			MARY SUTTON	60318
HARDY, WILLIAM							024	1			EDITH FEWOX	60318

ANCESTOR INDEX	BIRTH	PL	CO	DEATH	PL	CO	LIVD	MARRIED	PL	CO	SPOUSE NAME	CODE
HARGROVE, HIRAM HARDY	1783	NC	035	1853	LA			1 1808 2 1822 3 1834			WINNIFRED SIMS NANCY MARTIN GILBERT SARAH LEE	60553
HARGROVE, JOHN THOMAS		NC	047		TN							60275
HARGROVE, REUBEN	1757	NC	035					1			MORGAN	60553
HARKEY, DANIEL VALENTINE	C1824	NC						1 1844 IL 2 1849 IL			MARGARET ANN WELLER ELIZABETH WALCHER	27553
HARKEY, JESSE	C1822	NC	016				054	1 C1845 ?NC ?016 2 C1860 ?NC ?054			DOSEY ELIZA	60217
HARKEY, JOHN	C1788	NC		1864	IL			1			SARAH	27553
HARKEY, STOKES ALEXANDER	1854	NC	?016	1953	KY			1 C1878 KY			DORA	60217
HARMAN, ELIZABETH		NC	022					1			JAMES EVANS	60008
HARMAN, FANNIE	1765	NC	073					1			PHILEMON HARRINGTON	60008
HARMAN, HEZEKIAH	1763	NC	073					1			MRS PETTY DILLARD	60008
HARMAN, JOHN		NC	022					1 2	GA		WOMACK MRS ELIZ HARRIS	60008
HARMAN, KATIE		NC	022					1			JAMES LASSITER	60008
HARMAN, MARTHA/POLLY		NC	022					1			BARTHOLOMEW LIGHTFOOT	60008
HARMAN, MERRIMAN	1784	NC	022	1850	GA			1			NELLIE MAY	60008
HARMAN, REBEKAH		NC	022					1	GA		WILLIAM CLARK	60008
HARMAN, ZACHARIAH	1741			1808	NC		022	1 1763			REBEKAH PETTY	60008
HARMAN, ZACHARIAH	1789	NC	022	1846	GA			1 1808 SC			HARRIET SCOTT KING	60008
HARMAN/HARMON, ADAM		NC	085	C1847	NC	032		1			MARGARET CLODFELTER	60148
HARMON, J/JOHN W C	1829	?NC		1889	TN			1 1857 TN			NANCY JANE MILLS	27775
HARP, DIXON	1763	NC		1858	GA			1 ?1795 ?SC			CELIA EDMONDSON	03125
HARPER, ELIZABETH, MRS	C1785	?NC			GA							01035
HARPER, HUGHEY	C1765	?NC	?034	C1840	NC	045		1			ELINOR	03210
HARPER, JOHN	1756	PA		1834	KY		085	1 C1780 PA			BARBARA STRUBLE	23065
HARPER, JOSEPH	C1769	NC	?047				?039	1	NC	100	REBECCA HAZLEWOOD	60353
HARPER, LOTT	1782	PA		1866	NC	013	085	1 C1803 NC	085		MIRIAM WHITAKER	23065
HARPER, MARY ANN	C1806	NC	?100	1879	AR			1 1832 NC	039		ROBERT GARRETT GOODLOE	60353
HARPER, SAMUEL		?VA		1817	NC	100	015	2 1813 NC	100		PRISCILLA SANDIFER	60353
HARRELL, BARSHA EDNA	C1845	NC	051	C1893				1 1870 NC	051		KINDRED HOLLOMAN	27531
HARRELL, DAVID	1790	NC	?041		NC	037		1	NC	037	CHARLOTTE	60051
HARRELL, EDWARD				C1754	NC	010		1			ANN	19130
HARRELL, ELI	C1796	NC		C1855	AL			1 C1830			RACHEL	60542
HARRELL, JESSE	C1775	NC	?024	1848	GA		?041	1 C1794 NC			NANCY TURNER	60040
HARRELL, JOSIAH	C1797	NC	051					1			ANNA ASKEW	27531
HARRELL, MARTHA M	C1826	NC	?077	C1851	NC	077		1 1853 NC	077		LEVI WINGATE	27562

ANCESTOR INDEX	BIRTH	PL	CO	DEATH	PL	CO	LIVD	MARRIED	PL	CO	SPOUSE NAME	CODE
HARRELL, SETH	1809	NC	041	1890	TN			1 1836	TN		CYNTHIA LENORA ALGEE	60337
HARRELL, WILEY/WILLIE	1826	NC	037	C1895	NC	105	079	1 1850 2 1888	NC NC	037 105	WEALTHY FELTON MRS SALLY (EVANS) BAREFOOT	60051
HARRINGTON, CHARLES	C1720	VA		C1773	NC	022		1 C1746	NC	011	AGNES HILL	60176
HARRINGTON, HARDY	C1816	NC		C1859	TN			1 1840	TN		ELIZABETH STRAIN	60114
HARRINGTON, JOHN S	1816	NC	?083	1898	NC	048		1 1841			JANET MCLEAN	60176
HARRINGTON, SION	C1754			1828	NC	068		1 2			ELIZABETH WATTS ANN DALRYMPLE	60176
HARRINGTON, THOMAS				C1743			071	1			MARY	60171
HARRINGTON, THOMAS	1779	NC	022	1852	NC	048		1 1805 2 3			ANN STEPHEN KATIE BAKER LYDIA COLLIER	60176
HARRINGTON, THOMAS WATTS	1849			1921			048	1			ANNAH BROWN	60176
HARRIS, AARON	1809	NC	022	1851	MS			1 C1838	NC	022	ANGELETTE FISHER MAY	02540
HARRIS, ARTHUR	1758			1818	NC	067		1 2			FRANCES LEDBETTER CLARK	27328
HARRIS, BENJAMIN	1746	?NC		1816			022	1			MARY BOYKEN/BOYKIN	02540
HARRIS, BENJAMIN	1764	NC		C1850	IN			1	?NC		MARGARET INGLE	08265
HARRIS, BENJAMIN PROCTOR SR	1777	NC		1853	IL			1			MARGARET DENENT	27631
HARRIS, EZEKIEL	1743	NC		1810	OH			1			SARAH	20335
HARRIS, FRANCES E	1826	NC	020	1901	MO			1 1842	MO		WILLIAM HENRY LEE	60493
HARRIS, ISHAM SR	1741	NC	037	C1820	NC	044	047	1			MARTHA MABLE GREEN	60555
HARRIS, JAMES	1763	NC	085	1804	SC			1 1783	NC	044	PRISCILLA GILLIAM	60555
HARRIS, JAMES HENRY	1800	?NC		1872	MO		020	1 1819	?NC		SUSANNAH GUNN	60493
HARRIS, JAMES MAY	1842	NC	022	1925	MS			1 1869	MS		MARTHA ANN GRIFFIN	02540
HARRIS, JOHN	1769				NC	022		1 C1785	NC	022	SARAH HEADEN	02540
HARRIS, JOHN	1741	NC	037	1806	NC	067		1			PATIENCE TAYLOR	27328
HARRIS, JOHN	C1743	NC	037	1806	NC	067	044	1 C1769	NC	?015	PATIENCE TAYLOR	60404
HARRIS, LEMENDER	C1740						044	1			EPHRAIM HAMPTON	08023
HARRIS, LOVEY ANN	1862	NC	030	1903	NC	030		1 1880	NC	030	CHARLES H WILSON	60307
HARRIS, NATHAN	C1814	NC			NC	054		1			NANCY CAROLINE GROSS	60321
HARRIS, OBEDIAH	1741	?VA		1830	IN		?046	1 1761	VA		REBEKAH JOHNSON	08265
HARRIS, PLEASANT	1791	NC			IA			1 1811	IN		HANNAH MASSEY	08265
HARRIS, RACHEL CLARISSA	1857	NC		1901	NC	054		1			WILLIAM LARKIN WILES	60321
HARRIS, ROBERT				1786	NC	044		1			LEMENDER	08023
HARRIS, THOMAS DAVE	1841	NC	067	1914	TN			1 C1860			ANN ELIZA HALTOM	60457
HARRIS, THOMAS T				1775	NC	053		1			ELIZABETH	20335
HARRIS, VALENTINE	C1817			1880	NC	030		1			CAROLINE TRIPP	60307
HARRIS, WEST SR	1715	VA		1795	NC	067		1 C1740			MARY TURNER	60555
HARRIS/HARRISS, ICABOD	C1770	NC	079	1848	NC	079		1 C1797	NC		SARAH	24240

ANCESTOR INDEX	BIRTH	PL	CO	DEATH	PL	CO	LIVD	MARRIED	PL	CO	SPOUSE NAME	CODE
HARRIS/HARRISS, JOHN	C1760			1816	KY		044	1 1781	VA		MARTHA THOMAS	60195
HARRIS/HARRISS, MAJOR	C1730	NC	009	C1800				1 C1750			ANN	24240
HARRIS/HARRISS, TIMOTHY	C1660				NC	009						24240
HARRIS/HARRISS, WILLIAM	C1700	NC	008	C1775	NC	079		1 C1725			REBECCA	24240
HARRISON, ANDREW				1774	NC	073		1 1759			JANE DILLARD	60532
HARRISON, ANDREW	C1778	NC	020	C1838				1 1796	VA		MILDRED HOWELL READE	60532
HARRISON, CHARLES P	1797	VA		1820	NC	020		1 1820	NC	020	SUSAN BURTON PRICE	60532
HARRISON, EDMUND REID	1813	NC	020	1865	AR			1 1844	NC	020	ELIZA JANE HARRISON	60532
HARRISON, HARRIET	1820	?NC		1879	NC	078		1 1843	NC	020	ALFRED BLALOCK	60543
HARRISON, JAMES					NC	020		1			PENDERGRAST	60543
HARRISON, THOMAS	1748	VA		1799	NC	020	073	1 C1776	VA		MARY PENDLETON	60532
HART, ANDREW	1778						022	1			ABIGAIL	60301
HART, ELISHA B	C1817			1848	NC	069	099	1 1837	NC	039	SALLY HARRIS	25235
								2 1847	NC	069	NANCY W DEANS	
HART, HETH	C1750			1831	OH		022	1			ELIZABETH	60301
HART, JOEL	1782	NC	022									60301
HART, MARY	1787	NC	?079	1823	NC	045		1 1802	NC	045	JAMES ORMOND	16030
HART, ROBERT	1756	NC		1811	NC	045		1 C1782	NC	?079	HANNAH HOLLIDAY	16030
HART, SALLIE VANN	1881	NC	039	1955	IL			1 1911	NC	036	GROVER JACKSON NORWOOD	25235
HART, THOMAS	C1776						022					60301
HART, WILLIAM COLUMBUS	1840	NC	099	1885	NC	039		1 1866	NC	039	ANNIE BENNETT HILL	25235
HARTLINE, GEORGE	1732			C1797	NC	085		1			CHRISTIANA	60203
HARTLINE, HANNAH				C1825			085	1			PETER MILLER	60203
HARTMAN, PETER	1805	NC	085	1852	NC	085		1			SALLY HOFFMAN	60511
HARTNESS, ALEXANDER	1797	NC	054		NC	054		1			KEZIAH	60153
HARTNESS, CHARLES SHERIDAN	1899	NC	054					1 1928			LAURA BLANCHE ALEXANDER	60153
HARTNESS, HIRAM	1829	NC	054	1910	NC	054		1			MARTHA GIBSON	60153
HARTNESS, JAMES	1774				NC	054		1			SUSANNAH	60153
HARTNESS, JAMES	C1805	NC	054					1			BARBARY	60276
HARTNESS, JAMES ALEXANDER	1863	NC	054	1934	NC	054		1			JENNIE HENDERSON	60153
								2			ANNE SLOAN	
HARTNESS, JOSEPH MARION	1867	NC	023	1940	OK			1			CASSAN HARRIET WALKER	60276
								2			RACHEL	
HARTNESS, MARION	C1841	NC						1			MARY ANN JAMES	60276
HARTNESS, RICHARD ALEXANDER	1930	NC	054					1 1952			FRANCES CAROLE MOOSE	60153
HARTON, WILLIAM THOMAS	1850	NC	?099	1914	NC	070		1 1872	NC	073	IDA EMMA ROGERS	20030
HARVELL, J O A	1866			1899	NC		016	1 1890	NC	082	MARY LOUELLA BLACK	19183
HARVELL, LEROY COLON	C1891	?PA					068	1 1921	SC		ORADELL FEENEY	19183
								2 C1931			MINNIE ALMA	

ANCESTOR INDEX	BIRTH	PL	CO	DEATH	PL	CO	LIVD	MARRIED	PL	CO	SPOUSE NAME	CODE
HARVELL, WILLIAM	1818			C1894	NC		016	1 1845			MARTHA A	19183
HARVEY, ALDERSON ELLISON	1779			1837	NC	009		1 1808	NC	009	NANCY BARROW	02195
								2 1811	NC	009	CECILIA LANIER	
HARVEY, CHARLES	C1755	NC		1800	GA			1			FRANCES	60282
HARVEY, JAMES	C1770	NC	?081		AL			1 C1790				13175
HARVEY, JOHN				1805	NC	009		1			MARY	02195
HARVEY, JOHN DUNCAN	1794	NC	081	1843	TX			1 1815	NC	067	ELIZABETH SUGG	13175
HARVEY, NANCY		NC		C1841	?TN			1 1802	NC	092	ISHAM YOUNG	60159
HARVEY, SARAH	1753	NC	009		NC	009		1 1773	NC	009	WILLIAM CARRUTHERS	07078
HARVEY/HERVEY, THOMAS	C1740	FRA		C1805	NC	047		1			BETTY PRITCHETT	08065
								2			SARAH ANN	
HARVEY/HERVEY, WILLIAM				1803	NC	047		1 1788	NC	047	NANCY SULLIVANT	08065
HARWARD/HARWOOD/HARROD, GEORGE	1792	NC	099	1871	NC	068		1 1817	NC	099	ELIZABETH SUGG	14020
HARWARD/HARWOOD/HARROD, JAMES	1760	NC		1840	NC	099		1 1780	NC	099	ROSE BARBEE	14020
HARWARD/HARWOOD/HARROD, JOSEPH	C1686	VA		1769	NC	037		1	VA		SARAH	14020
HARWARD/HARWOOD/HARROD, RUFFIN	C1822	NC	099	C1880	AR		022	1 1841	NC	?068	HARRIET COX	14020
HARWARD/HARWOOD/HARROD, WILLIAM	C1735			C1804	NC	099		1			MARY	14020
HARWELL, LEMUEL	C1738	VA		1805	NC	054		1 C1765			LUCRETIA	60082
HARWELL, RANSOM	C1754	VA		1808	AL		?020	1			ANN	60082
HARWOOD, JOSEPH	1808	NC		1838	IN			1 1828	IN		NANCY ANN CHISMAN	27495
HASSELL, ASA	C1773	NC	096	C1858	TN							60283
HASSELL, JOHN		NC	096	1825	TN			1 C1767	?NC		ANN	60283
HASTINGS, HENRY	1784	NC	?073		TN			1			MARTHA	27699
HASTINGS, HENRY SR	C1728			1812	NC	073		1			ELIZABETH	27699
HASTINGS, JAMES SR	C1758			C1822	NC	073		1			HANNAH CRABTREE	27699
HASTY, WILLIAM		?VA		C1805	NC	103		1 C1787	NC	?103	JEMIMA HILL	01035
HASWELL, MARY ANN	1822	NC	044	1902	NC	039	044	1 1838	NC	044	JAMES RICHARDS	02435
HATLEY, MARGERAT/PEGGY	1807	NC	?067	1884	NC	089		1			JOSEPH/JOEY MORTON	24165
HATLEY, WILLIAM	C1800	NC	022	1847	IN			1 C1822	NC	022	MARTHA BOWERS/GILES	25161
HATTEN, FRANCIS	C1828	NC		1862	MO			1 1850	MO		JULIA ANN EASON	27332
HATTON, FRANCIS				C1828	NC	037	071	1			FRANCES GRIMES	19130
HAWKINS, BENJAMIN	C1770	?NC		C1805	?SC		086	1 C1790	?NC		SARAH CHAMBERS	60478
HAWKINS, EATON	C1750	VA		1812	SC		094	1 C1770			CATHERINE	60478
HAWKINS, JOSHUA	1725	VA		1803	SC		086	1 C1745	VA		SARAH COOK	60478
HAWKINS, MARY	C1780	NC	?065					1 C1805	NC		WILLIAM TUGMAN	60557
HAWORTH, ABSALOM	1805	NC	046	1863	MO			1 1828	NC	046	SARAH DAVIS	60274
								2 1845	MO		POLLY ALLISON	
								3 1848	MO		MARY STOVER	
HAWORTH, JOHN	1778						046	1 1803	TN		CICILIA ELMORE	20333

ANCESTOR INDEX	BIRTH	PL	CO	DEATH	PL	CO	LIVD	MARRIED	PL	CO	SPOUSE NAME	CODE
HAWORTH, JOHNATHAN	C1801	NC		C1870	KS			1			ELIZABETH	60160
HAWS, JACOB	C1766	NC	085	1813	KY			1 C1787	NC	014	HANNAH NEAL/NEIL	05045
HAWS, WILLIAM N	1789	NC	?014	1845	IL			1 1818	KY		ISABELLA WOMACK	05045
HAYES, DAVID	1720	?NC		1778	NC	065		1 1760	NC		JANE	60337
HAYES, MARTHA/MATTIE CAROLINE	1861	NC	102	1918	OR			1 1880	CO		WILLIAM D FRANKS	60472
								2 C1902	ID		GEORGE KENT	
HAYES, NANCY ELIZABETH	1868	NC	102	1958	WA			1 1887	WA		PRINCE DEXTER ATHEARN	60557
								2 C1892	CA		GEORGE WILLIAM GOODWIN	
								3 C1920	WA		P J PEDERSEN	
HAYES, RANSOM	C1806	NC	?104	1868	NC	102		1 C1828	NC	?006	SARAH/SALLY GREEN	60557
HAYES, SAMUEL COLUMBUS JR	1862	NC	027	1930	NC	027		1 1882	NC	027	MARY CATHERINE GREEN	24032
HAYES, SAMUEL COLUMBUS SR	C1823	SC			SC		027	1 C1851			ELIZABETH HUGGINS	24032
								2				
HAYES, WILLIAM	1837	NC	006	1908	WA			1 1859	NC	102	NANCY CLORINDA BROWN	60557
HAYGOOD, BENJAMIN	1758	NC	073	1841	GA			1 1777			MARY STEWART	60110
HAYGOOD, JAMES				1768	NC	073						60110
HAYGOOD, NANCY	1781	NC	073	1866	GA			1 1800			JOHN THOMPSON	60110
HAYMORE, DANIEL JR	1819	NC	092	1900	NC	092		1 1840	NC	092	MARTHA HALL	60393
HAYMORE, DANIEL SR	1778	VA		1850	NC	092		1 1799	VA		MARY/POLLY SCHOCKLEY/CHOCKLEY	60393
HAYMORE, FRANKLIN DEMARCUS	1849	NC	092	1931	NC	092		1 1869	NC	092	LUCINDA ADALINE TAYLOR	60393
HAYMORE, JOHN JR	C1749	?VA		1825	NC	092		1 C1775	VA		JENNEY	60393
HAYNES, ABRAHAM	1780	NC	087	1838	TN			1			SARAH TART	60029
HAYNES, BYTHEL	C1795	NC	?083	1842	NC	011	027	1 C1818	NC	027	ZILPHIA NICHOLS	27532
HAYNES, FRANCIS BYTHEL	C1734	NC	010	1770	NC	047		1 C1754	NC	?037	MRS ANN SMITH	27532
HAYNES, FRANCIS LAWRENCE	C1765	NC	?047	1821	NC	?027	083	1 C1788	NC	?011	BIGGS	27532
								2	NC	083	NANCY MASSEY	
HAYNES, JOHN JR	C1775	NC	087	1864	TN			1			MINERVA A	60029
HAYNES, JOHN SR	C1754	MD		C1824	NC	087	?032	1 C1774	NC	015		60029
								2 C1812			SUSANNAH CREEL	
HAYNES, KENNETH	1830	NC	027	1891	GA			1 1854	NC	027	CAROLINE BYRNE	27532
HAYNES, WILLIAM	1837	NC		1893	NC	105		1	NC		TEMPIE ANN MERCER	03315
HAYS, ELI	1799	NC		1878	IL			1 1823	IN		ELLEN HURLEY	60056
HEADEN, SARAH	1772			1825	NC	022		1 1785	NC	022	JOHN HARRIS	02540
HEARRELL, ELI	1776	NC		C1825	TN			1 C1802			SARAH DORRELL	60073
HEATER, CHARLES ROBERT	1868	WV		1946	NC	099		1			COLUMBIA LUCEIVIA CRISLIP	25141
HEATER, RUSSELL ORAN	1898	WV		1971	NC	099		1			JESSIE M CONNER	25141
HEATH, AMELIA/MILLY		?NC					046	1	?NC		WILLIAM THARP/THORP ?	04050
HEATH, CHARITY JANE	1853	NC	057	1913	NC	045		1 1868	NC	057	WILLIAM FRANKLIN JONES	13264
HEATH, JOHN	C1735	?MD		C1824	NC	090	046	1 C1764			SARAH	04050
HEATH, JOHN	C1776			C1865	NC	054	046	1 C1779	?VA		MISS/MRS THOMAS	04050
								2 1825	NC	085	HANNAH CAIN	

ANCESTOR INDEX	BIRTH	PL	CO	DEATH	PL	CO	LIVD	MARRIED	PL	CO	SPOUSE NAME	CODE
HEATH, JOHN	1800	NC	?057	C1875	NC	057		1 C1820	NC	057	LEVINA KILLEBREW	13264
HEATH, WILLIAM CURTIS, REV	C1820	NC	057	C1905	NC	057		1 C1840	NC	?057	MARY A COX	13264
HEATHAMN, ELIZABETH	C1776	NC		1865	IN			1 1799	NC	104	WILLIAM MCBRIDE	60370
HEATHMAN, JONATHAN	C1755	?NC	?085		?KY			1 C1775	?NC	?085	SARAH HULIN	60370
HELMS, ALLEN	1793	NC	065					1 C1816			ANNA RICH	60185
HELMS, ALLEN	1810	NC	005	C1885			089	1 C1840	NC		REBECCA ANN SMITH	60532
HELMS, ERNEST WILSON	1902	SC		1975	NC	065		1 2			ANNIE MEYERS ROSA HERRON	60205
HELMS, JOHN	1770	NC		C1855	NC	005		1			LAVINA/NINA GREEN	60532
HELMS, LONNIE OLIVER	1876	NC	097	1936	NC	065		1			MARTHA JANE BASS	60205
HELMS, MARY FRANCES	1853	NC	097	1926	AR			1 C1869	NC	097	WILLIAM THOMAS AXUM	60532
HELMS, MILUS	1820	NC	?065		GA			1 1843	GA		CORDELIA BROWN	60185
HELMS, TILLMAN JR	C1755	NC	005					1 C1780			ELIZABETH/MARY PRESSLEY	60185
HELMS, WILLIAM ALVERSON	1833	NC	005	1921	AR			1 1852	NC	097	ELIZABETH/BETSY ANN STEGALL	60532
HEMINGWAY/HEMENWAY, AMMA RIAH	1869	NC	029	1942	GA			1 1905	FL		ELIZA ADA ALLEN	60058
HEMINGWAY/HEMENWAY, ISAAC WILLIAM	1830	NC			NC	029		1 1853	NC	029	LOUISA MARIA/ELIZA DENNING	60058
HEMINGWAY/HEMENWAY, MICAJAH	1800	NC		C1837	NC	029		1 1821	NC	029	MARY WHITEHEAD	60058
HEMPHILL, JAMES		?IR		1786	NC	085		1 C1740	IRE		SUSANNAH	04195
HEMPHILL, ROSEANNAH	1777	NC	014	1852	NC	013		1 C1795	NC	?014	JOHN YOUNG	04195
HEMPHILL, THOMAS, CAPT	1746	?PA		1826	NC	014	085	1 1773	NC	085	MARY ANN MCKIE/MACKIE	04195
HENDERSON, CATHERINE	1805	NC		1890	GA			1 1822	GA		JACOB PAULK	27756
HENDERSON, DANIEL		NC	083	1825	GA			1	NC		SARAH/SALLIE MCBRIDE	27756
HENDERSON, DANIEL	1775	NC	011	1825	GA			1 1797	NC		SALLIE MCBRIDE	60498
HENDERSON, HIRAM	C1810	NC			MO			1			MARTHA	60160
HENDERSON, ISABELLA GRAVES	1763			1826	GA		085	1 1778	NC	?005	JOSHUA CALLAWAY	60008
HENDERSON, JOHN	1798	NC			GA			1 1820	GA		RHODA WHITLEY	27756
HENDERSON, JOSEPH	C1737	VA		1809	GA		005	2 C1770			ADELPHIA LEA	60008
HENDERSON, NARCISSA	C1790	NC	065	1857	TN			1	TN		JAMES L BALDRIDGE	06005
HENDERSON, RICHARD	1806	?NC		1883	AL			1 C1829	AL		CINDERELLA HUTTO	60373
HENDERSON, SAMUEL	C1780	NC		C1860	MO			1			RHODA	60160
HENDERSON, WILLIAM	C1770	VA		1853	NC	086						01035
HENDERSON, WILLIAM	1746			1822	TN		065					06005
HENDRICK, TIGNAL		NC	069					1 2			ELIZABETH SARAH	60174
HENDRICK, WILSON	1811	NC	069	1878	GA			1 1845	GA		CHERRY ELIZABETH MCCREA	60174
HENDRICKS, GEORGE	C1799	NC	081	1835	IL			1 1823	NC	081	NANCY BROWN	60323
HENDRICKS, LYDIA	C1775	NC	073	C1826	NC	081		1 C1791	NC	081	GEORGE FERGUSON	60446

ANCESTOR INDEX	BIRTH	PL	CO	DEATH	PL	CO	LIVD	MARRIED	PL	CO	SPOUSE NAME	CODE
HENDRICKS, SAMUEL	C1745	?PA		1824	NC	081		1 C1765			THEODATE	60446
HENDRICKS, WILLIAM	1795	NC	085	1868	OK			1 1816	GA		SUSANNAH/SOKINNEY	60554
HENDRIX, ABRAHAM		?MD					033	1			NANCIE/NANCY	60005
HENDRIX, SARAH	1787	NC										08165
HENDRIX, WILLIAM M	1816	NC		1899	GA			2			LUCINDA PATTERSON	08165
HENLY, WILLIAM	C1780	NC		C1831	TN			1 C1800	TN		JULIA DARDEN	60397
HENRY, ISAAC	1778	NC		1853	TN			1 1802			KATE SAILING/SALEN	27740
HENRY, JAMES		?VA			NC							27740
HENRY, WILLIAM	C1760	?NC		1840	GA			1			JANE RUSSELL	27382
HENSON, BARTLETT SR		VA		C1823	NC	014						60466
HENSON, EDMOND	C1768			C1796	SC		022	1			LOVICE/LUCY	60507
HENSON, JANE GOODBREAD	1783	NC	086	1874	KY			1			REV HENRY/HARRY DARNALL	06159
HENSON, JESSE	C1760	?VA		1843	KY			1 1782	NC	086	MARY/POLLY GOODBREAD	06159
HENSON, JESSIE H	1759	VA		1843	KY			1 1782	NC	014	MARY GOODBREAD	60402
HENSON, JOHN	1765	VA		1835	IL			1 1787	NC	014	JANE GOODBREAD	60402
HENSON, LAZARUS	C1786	NC		C1865	MS			1 C1807			CENY	60507
HENSON, NANCY	C1770	?NC		C1835	TN			1 C1785	NC		JAMES SIMPSON	60466
HENSON/HINSON, BARTLETT							014					03041
HENSON/HINSON, CALVIN					NC							08190
HENSON/HINSON, CALVIN COLUMBUS	1850			1937	NC	065		1 1884 2	NC		MARY MARGARITE MARKS ELIDA MARKS	08190
HENSON/HINSON, THOMAS							014					03041
HERDLEIN/HERTLEIN/HARTLINE, SAMUEL	C1801	NC	085	1830	IL			1 1820	IL		ELIZABETH HOLSHOUSER	60517
HERDLEIN/HERTLEIN/HARTLINE, JOHN GEORGE JR	1768	PA		1823	IL			1 1793	NC	085	MARIA ANN EARNHARDT/AARONHART	60517
HERDLEIN/HERTLEIN/HARTLINE, JOHN JORG/GEOR	1732	GER		1794	NC	085		1 1755	PA		MARIA CHRISTINA BOEHM	60517
HERMAN, GEORGE	1763	GER		1850	NC	021		1 1791	NC	060	ELIZABETH ESLINGER	27441
HERMAN, JOHANN WILLIAM	1736	GER		1813	NC	060		1 C1760			CATHERINE MOTZ	27441
HERMAN, JOHN DANIEL	1800	NC	060	1840	NC	060		1 1820	NC	060	MARY/POLLY KILLIAN	27441
HERNDON, AQUILLA	C1780	NC	073	1840	NC	073		1	NC	022	MARY MOORE	08200
HERNDON, BENJAMIN	C1748	VA		1823	NC	073		1 C1770	NC	073	LYDIA MASSEY	08200
HERNDON, CLAUDE NASH	1887	NC	022	1940	NC	046		1 1913	NC	036	ANNIE LEE MANN	08200
HERNDON, ELBERT	1843	NC	022	1924	NC	099		1 1874	NC	022	SUSAN MARGARET CHEEK	08200
HERNDON, MARY	1796			1855	NC	089	?037	1			MALICHI HARWARD/HARROD	24165
HERNDON, REUBEN	1807	NC	073	1855	NC	022		1 1833	NC	022	NANCY JENKINS	08200
HERNDON, RICHARD	C1708	VA			NC	073						08200
HERRING, BENJAMIN FRANKLIN	1846	NC	059					1			MRS MARY AGATHA (MCCARTY) LARKIN	60064

ANCESTOR INDEX	BIRTH	PL	CO	DEATH	PL	CO	LIVD	MARRIED	PL	CO	SPOUSE NAME	CODE
HERRING, HERON	C1770	NC		1817	GA			1 C1792	NC		ANN	20425
HERRINGTON, ISAAC	1754	?DE		1824	NC	018		1				23070
								2 C1805	?NC	018	AMELIA	
HERRINGTON, LUCY	1789	?NC	018	1881	IN			1 1809	NC	018	ELISHA PRICHARD	23070
HESLEP, ANDREW				C1781	NC	?086						60464
HESLEP, THOMAS	C1750	NC	?056									60464
HESTER, JOHN	C1770	?NC	?044	1813	NC	090		1 1793	NC	044	MILDRED CREWS	15098
HESTER, JOHN JR	1813	NC	090	1892	IN			1 1833	NC	090	MALINDA MCKILLIP/MCCALEB/MCCALEP	15098
								2 1850	IN		MRS EMELINE (LINVILLE) ZIKE	
HEWETT, JOSEPH	C1738			C1794	NC	012		1			HANNAH LEONARD	13052
HEWITT, SARAH	1826	NC	012	1885	NC		027	1			BENNETT PAGE	17025
								2	NC	027	PUGH FLOYD	
HEWITT, WILLIAM							012					17025
HEWITT, WILLIAM H JR	C1792				NC	012		1 1816	NC	012	ELIZABETH FISHER	17025
HIATT, AZARIAH	1770	NC	090	C1804	NC	090		1 1790	NC	090	MARY GRIGG	60393
HIATT, BENAJAH/BENNAJAH	1773	NC	046	1847	IN			1 1797	NC	046	ANNA ELIZABETH WHITE	60386
HIATT, GEORGE	C1698	ENG		1793	NC	046		1 C1724	PA		MARTHA WAKEFIELD	60386
HIATT, JOHN	1804	NC	046	1893	IN			1 1824	NC	046	REBECCA UNTHANK	60386
HIATT, MOSES	1791	NC	092	1857				1 1811			MARTHA/PATSEY DONELY	60393
HIATT, OTHNIEL	1804	NC	046	C1855	NC	046		1 1825	NC	046	POLLY PEGG	60219
HIATT, WILLIAM	1742	?VA		1814	NC	046		1 1769	NC	?073	CHARITY WILLIAMS	60386
HICKS, ABEL					NC	032						60407
HICKS, DANIEL					NC	032						60407
HICKS, GEORGE					NC	032						60407
HICKS, GEORGE A	C1792	NC		C1865	IA			1			ELIZABETH	60316
HICKS, ISHAM/ISOM	1801	NC	099					1			LUCINDA MIMS	60028
HICKS, JACOB					NC	032						60407
HICKS, MOSES				1810	NC	099		1			JEMIMAH	60028
HICKS, MRS ELIZABETH	C1795	NC		C1865	IA			1			GEORGE A	60316
HICKS, RICHARD N	C1796	NC						1 1816	TN		LUCINDA ELLIOTT	60321
HICKS, ROBERT					NC	024		1			ESTHER LUTEN	60407
HICKS, THOMAS	C1715	VA		1797	NC	035		2 C1740	?VA		ELIZABETH WILLIAMS	27356
HICKS, THOMAS	1776	NC	035	1817	NC	035		1 1796	NC	035	MARY FAISON	27356
HICKS, THOMAS					NC	024						60407
HICKS, WILLIAM	C1796	NC			TN			1			ELIZA	27531
HICKS/HIX, LEWIS DANIEL	1839	GER		1909	NC	046	092	1			JANE BROWN	10153
HIGDON, LEONARD	1754	NC	005	1837	NC	061		1 1791	NC	086	SUSANAH HARRIS	20220
HIGH, BUNBURY	C1811	NC	027	C1890	NC	027		1 1845	NC	027	CATHARINE HIGH	27562

ANCESTOR INDEX	BIRTH	PL	CO	DEATH	PL	CO	LIVD	MARRIED	PL	CO	SPOUSE NAME	CODE
HIGH, CATHARINE	C1818	NC	027	C1890	NC	027		1 1845	NC	027	BUNBURY HIGH	27562
HIGH, CLARA ANN	1768	NC	099	1838	MS			1 1787			CHARLES HARRIS	60196
HIGH, DANIEL MORGAN	1851	NC	027	1929	NC	027		1 1875	NC	027	JULIA COLUMBIA CREECH	27562
HIGH, ESAU	C1785	?VA		1830	NC	027						27562
HIGH, HENRY SEYMORE	1876	NC	027	1969	NC	027		1 1903	NC	027	MARY LIZ OWEN	27562
HIGH, JACOB	C1775	?VA		1842	NC	027						27562
HIGH, JOHN		VA		1777	NC	099		1			RUTH MARIN	60196
HIGH, OPAL ELIZABETH	1904	NC	027					1 1926	NC	083	GEORGE NEVILLE HARRELL	27562
HIGH, SAMUEL	1750	VA		1812	NC	099		1 C1767	NC	099	CLARA ANN JACKSON	60196
HIGHSMITH, DANIEL	C1710	?VA		C1771	NC	047	010	1 C1735			ANN BECK/BECKE	10010
HIGHSMITH, DANIEL	C1710	VA		C1772	NC	047		1 C1735	VA		ANN BECK	20425
HIGHSMITH, DANIEL	C1737	VA		C1807	NC	070		1	NC	?047	LUCRETIA	20425
HIGHSMITH, JAMES	C1760	NC	?047	C1830	GA			1	NC	?070	CHARITY	20425
HIGHTOWER, ALLEN L		NC	020	1889	TN			1	NC	020	JANE BURRIS	04053
HIGHTOWER, CHARNALD	C1760	VA		1829	MO		020	1 C1813	MO		EDA HALE	04053
HIGHTOWER, CHARNEL	C1760	VA		1793	NC	020		1			FRANCES	04053
HIGHTOWER, GREGORY		NC	020									04053
HIGHTOWER, JOSHUA		NC	020	1824	NC	020		1 1817	NC	020	JINCY WALL	04053
HIGHTOWER, ROBERT		NC	020									04053
HIGHTOWER, THOMAS	C1778	NC	020	1841				1 1803			POLLY/MARY THOMAS	04053
HIGSON, JOHN	1812	NC	053	1888	NC	009		1 1834	NC	053	ELENOR ATKINS	27573
								2 1845	NC		DORCAS WATSON	
								3 1851	NC		SARAH BENJAMIN HALL	
HIGSON, WILLOUGHBY	C1780	ENG		1826	NC	053		1			SALLY	27573
HILL, ANN	C1752	NC			AL			1	NC			60373
HILL, ANNIE BENNETT	1849	NC	039	1905	NC	039		1 1866	NC	039	WILLIAM COLUMBUS HART	25235
HILL, BRYANT	C1805	NC		1895	NC	049		1 1875	NC	049	MRS SUSAN MARIA (SHAW) NORMAN	40690
HILL, ELIZABETH				C1855	NC	027		1 C1805			JACOB CROWSON	24032
HILL, JANE				1849	NC	070		1 1820	NC	070	PARKER QUINCE	27286
HILL, LUCY	1760	NC		1825	GA			1 1775			DOZIER THORNTON	03125
HILL, MACAJAH				C1817	NC	027		1			MARY	24032
HILL, MARTHA	1814	NC	?065	1871	IN			1 C1835	IN		GEORGE WASHINGTON HINES	60426
HILL, MARY PENELOPE/PENNY	1713	NC		1786	NC	037	079	1 1729	NC	?077	JAMES THIGPEN IV	02195
HILL, NANCY	C1770	NC	?034	1847	NC	045		1 C1790	NC	034	AQUILLA SUGG	13264
HILL, NANCY JANE	1879	NC	049	1944	WA			1 1900	NC	055	THOMAS DEXTER	40690
HILL, NATHANIEL, DR		NC	070		NC	070		1			JANE DAVIS	27286
HILL, RHODA JANE	C1793	NC			GA			1 C1815	NC		DANIEL S MCCAY	60261
HILL, RICHARD	C1770	NC	034	C1830	NC	045		1 C1795	NC	042	ESTHER ALDRIDGE	13264

ANCESTOR INDEX	BIRTH	PL	CO	DEATH	PL	CO	LIVD	MARRIED	PL	CO	SPOUSE NAME	CODE
HILL, RICHMON A	C1775	NC										40690
HILL, ROBERT	C1682	VA		1765	NC	047	037	1 C1710	?NC		TABITHA	13264
HILL, ROBERT	C1712	NC	?024	1767	NC	?034	010	1 C1735	NC		HANNAH BRIGGS	13264
HILL, ROBERT	C1740	NC	?028	C1810	NC	045		1 C1765	NC	?034	MARTHA MURPHREY	13264
HILL, SUSANNAH, MRS	C1745	?VA		1819	NC	103		1			MR HILL	01035
HILL, WHIT M	C1790	NC	?065	1784	IN			1 1814	NC	065	MARY M SHARP	60426
HILL, WILLIAM	1737	MA		1783	NC	012		1 1757			MARGARET MOORE	27286
HILL, WILLIAM J	C1819	?NC						2 C1839			NICY UNICY ANN	60373
HILL, WILLIAM WESLEY	C1820	NC	?039	C1899	NC	039		1 1837	NC	039	MARTHA BEDDINGFIELD	25235
HILLIARD, RIGHTMAN/WRIGHTMAN	C1763	NC		1840	TN		099	1 1787	NC	099	ELIZABETH BROWN	60337
HILLIARD, WILLIAM	C1806	NC	099	1840	TN			1			ELIZABETH C SHELLEY	60010
HILLIARD, WRIGHTMAN/RIGHTMAN	C1762	NC	?073	1840	TN		?099	1 1787	NC		ELIZABETH BROWN	60010
HILLIS, JAMES	1782	NC		C1850	TN			1			MARY	60044
HILLIS, JOHN	1758	NC	085	1836	KY							60044
HILLIS, SAMUEL	1707			1782	NC	085		1			ANN LUCKIE	60044
HILLMAN/HILEMAN, GEORGE WASHINGTON	1813	NC	?045	1899	TX			1 1835 2 C1875	GA		EVALINA IVEY M ANNIE	60431
HILSABECK, FREDERICK	1730	GER		1799	NC	090	092	1 C1755			CATHERINA BERTSCHIN	60354
HILSABECK, FREDERICK	1785	NC	092	1857	IL		090	1 1810	GA		ELIZABETH THOMAS ANDERSON	60354
HILSABECK, HENRY	1772	NC		C1845	GA		090	1 1792	NC	092	ALSEY CHILDRESS	60354
HILSABECK, JACOB	1763	PA		1848	NC	090	092	1 C1781	NC	092	EVA MARIA FISCUS	60354
HILSMAN/HILLSMAN, BENNETT	C1711	VA		1784	NC	039		1			FRANCES HINDE	08120
HINNANT, JOHN SR				C1770	NC	056	010					25087
HINSHAW, ALMEDA	1819	NC	092	1898	NC	106		1 1838	NC	092	WILEY REECE	60120
HINSHAW, BENJAMIN	1782	NC	092	1866	IN		081	1 1807	NC	081	ANNIS BOWMAN	60386
HINSHAW, BENJAMIN JR	1795	NC	022	1860	NC	106	092	1 1814	NC	092	RUTH CARTER	60120
HINSHAW, BENJAMIN SR	C1749	PA		1842	NC	022	081	1 C1771	NC	073	ELIZABETH HINSHAW	60120
HINSHAW, CYRUS C	1823	NC	081	1900	IN			1 1843	IN		ELIZA J PITTS	60386
HINSHAW, JACOB	C1710	IRE		1796	NC	081		1 1735			REBECCA MACKIE	60115
HINSHAW, JACOB	1710	IRE		1796	NC	081		1 1735	IRE		REBECCA MACKIE	60120
HINSHAW, JOSEPH	C1750	PA		1833	NC	092		1 1788			RUTH MARSHALL	60115
HINSHAW, THOMAS		IRE			?NC			1 1708			MARY MARSHALL	60115
HINSON, JAMES	C1750	?VA			NC	?083	?103					27302
HINSON, JOSHUA	C1780	NC	?057	1866	NC	027	?103	1 2			 LUCY	27302
HINSON, LUCY	1808	NC	067	1885	NC	089		1 1827	NC	067	ALLEN BURRIS	24165
HINSON, WILLIAM	1810	NC	?083	1893	AL		027	1 1839	AL		MARTHA ANN PUGH	27302
HINTON, JOHN, COL				1784	NC	099	024	1	NC		GRIZELLE KIMBROUGH	27356

ANCESTOR INDEX	BIRTH	PL	CO	DEATH	PL	CO	LIVD	MARRIED	PL	CO	SPOUSE NAME	CODE
HINTON, JOSEPH				C1806	NC	022		1			PATTY	60176
HINTON, WILLIAM				C1761	NC	056		1			SOPHIA	60176
HINTON, WILLIAM LEWIS				C1837	NC	022		1			TEMPERANCE WILLIAMS	60176
HOARD/HORD, JOHN	C1705	NC	008	1753	NC	028						13264
HOARD/HORD, MARY	C1730	NC	?028	1797	NC	028		1 C1750	NC	028	JACOB JONES	13264
HOARD/HORD, PETER	C1680	?VA		C1730	NC	?028						13264
HOBBS, ELISAH	1744			1818	NC	081		1			FANNEY MCLAIN	60314
HOBBS, JOHN				1846	NC	073		1			CATHARINE CLAPP	21080
HOBGOOD/HOPGOOD, CHARLES	1817	NC		C1880	MS		005	1 C1837	NC		MARTHA LOWE	25158
HOBGOOD/HOPGOOD, THOPILAS	C1792	VA			MS		?005	1 C1817	NC		SARAH BIRMINGHAM	25158
HOCKETT/HOGGATT, PHILIP	C1687	SCO		1783	NC	046		1			MARY GLENDENNING	02175
HOCKETT/HOGGATT, WILLIAM	1727	PA		1772	NC	046		1 1760	NC	085	HANNAH BEALS	02175
HOCKETT/HOGGATT, WILLIAM	1763	NC	085	1843	NC	046		1 1791			HANNAH REYNOLDS	02175
HOCKETT/HOGGATT, WILLIAM	1799	NC	046	1880	NC	046		1 1821			HANNAH DAVIS	02175
HOCKETT/HOGGATT, WILLIAM BALES/ BEALS	1828	NC	046	1905	NC	046		1 1858 2 1861	NC	046	ELIZA JANE BRANSON SIBYL BRANSON	02175
HODGES, EDWIN GORHAM	1826	NC	009	1875	NC	009		1 1850	NC	?063	OLIVIA PARTHENIA EWELL	02195
HODGES, GENTRY COCKERHAM	1791	NC	?092	1870	IN			1 1814			CHARLOTTE REED	60523
HODGES, JOHN	1793	NC	009	1880	NC	009		1 C1814	NC	?063	SALLIE PERRY	02195
HODGIN, DANIEL WEBSTER	1847	NC	046	1910	IN			1 1882	IN		LYDIA ELVA WOOD	08265
HODGSON, GEORGE	1701	ENG		1764	NC	085		1 1729	DE		MARY THATCHER	08265
HODGSON, ROBERT	1738			1813	NC	046		1 1758 2 1794	NC	046	RACHEL MILLS RACHEL MILLS	08265
HODGSON/HODGIN/HODSON, GEORGE	C1790	NC						1			DELILAH RULE	60031
HODGSON/HODGIN/HODSON, RACHEL EMMALINE	1831	?NC		1905	MN			1 1850	NC	046	WILLIAM R REYNOLDS	60031
HODGSON/HODSON, DAVID	1765			1816	NC	046		1 1788	?NC	?046	ESTHER LAMB	08265
HODSON/HODGIN, SIMEON	1804	NC	?046	1869	NC	046		1			SARAH OTWELL	08265
HOGAN, DANIEL	1753	VA		1787	NC	073		1 1775	NC	073	SARAH LLOYD	08275
HOGAN, JOHN	C1750	VA		C1810	NC	073		1 C1772	NC	073	MARY LLOYD	08275
HOGAN, JOHN	1773	NC	073	1818	TN			1 1792	NC	073	MARTHA ANN KING	08275
HOGAN, MARGARET LLOYD	C1776	NC	073		TN			1 1794	NC	073	JOHN KIMBLE	08275
HOGAN, THOMAS	C1775	NC	073	C1852	KY			1 1795	NC	073	TABITHA/ABI STROUD	08275
HOGAN, WILLIAM		NC			KY			1 C1780	NC		SALLY FULLINGTON	60094
HOGG, JOHN				1795	NC	039		1			MARY	60516
HOGG, PINKETHMAN/PINKNEY	1776	?SC		1866	IL		085	1			SUSAN	60516
HOLBERT/HOBBERT, STEPHEN	C1775	NC			TN			1			GINNY	60321
HOLBROOK, GREENBERRY		NC	?016	1850	NC	085	054	1			SERENA	60477
HOLBROOK, JESSE C	1809	NC		1883	GA			1 C1829	SC		JANE ELROD	27756

ANCESTOR INDEX	BIRTH	PL	CO	DEATH	PL	CO	LIVD	MARRIED	PL	CO	SPOUSE NAME	CODE
HOLBROOK, JOHN		?VA		1804	GA		016					60477
HOLBROOK, JOHN FRANKLIN	1860	NC	060	1933	MI			1 1884	MI		ELIZABETH ELBA MOORE	60477
HOLBROOK, JOHN FRANKLIN	1840	NC	?054	C1862	NC	060	085	1 1859	NC	060	HAZELTINE JOHNSTON	60477
HOLBROOK, LARKIN		NC	092	1840	NC	006		1 C1808			SARAH	27756
HOLBROOK, VAICHEL	C1770			C1830	NC	016		1			CHARLOTTE	60477
HOLCOMBE, MAY					NC		013	1			MARY STAFFORD	20060
HOLDER, ALVIS WASHINGTON	1831	NC		1921	IN			1 1862	IN		LOUISA JANE ICE	60591
HOLDER, ANDERSON	C1834	NC	073									60591
HOLDER, CHARLES	C1775	?NC	?092	C1835	IN			1	NC		MARIA MARGRETHE KRAUSE	17075
HOLDER, DAVID	C1775	NC		C1851	NC	073		1 1801	NC	099	REBECCA BROWN	60591
								2 1831	NC	073	ELIZABETH HATCH	
								3 1850	NC	073	MATILDA SCOGGINS	
HOLDER, ELIZABETH	1797	NC	090	1867	IN			1 1818	NC	090	JOSEPH CARMICHAEL	17075
HOLDER, EMELINE	C1816	NC		C1900	MO			1			WESLEY ELBER CLARK	60540
HOLDER, MALINDA	C1842	NC	073									60591
HOLDER, WILLIAM								1 1811	NC	099	ELIZABETH JACKSON	60540
HOLDER, WILLIAM	C1832	NC	073					1 1851	NC	073	LUCY CLEMENT	60591
HOLDERFIELD, JOSEPH	C1772	NC	099	C1855	TN			1 1802	NC	099	NANCY GRANT	60441
HOLDERFIELD, WILLIAM KELLY	C1810	NC	099	C1890	AR			1 C1837	TN		HULDA LAXTON	60441
HOLLADAY, HENRY							073	1 1746	DE		MARY FAYLE/FAILE	60203
HOLLADAY, SARAH	1781	NC	022					1 1797	NC		AARON MARIS	60203
HOLLADAY, WILLIAM	1750	PA			IN		073	1			JANE ANDREW	60203
HOLLER, ANDREW							?060	1			POLLY BOLICK	60153
HOLLER, ANDREW JR							?060	1			LOVINA MILLER	60153
HOLLER, GILBERT	1842			1903	NC	054		1			MARTHA CAROLINE HUFFMAN	60153
HOLLER, LEWIS TATE	1871	NC	021	1947	NC	054	021	1			MARGARET LOUISE ISADORE CALDWELL	60153
HOLLIN, SARAH	C1808	NC			MO			1			FRANCES MARION WEATHINGTON	60416
HOLLINGSWORTH, VINCENT SR	1740	MD		1816	NC	006						25242
HOLLOMAN, ABNER	C1818	NC	051	C1882				1			SALLY HILL	27531
HOLLOMAN, KINDRED	C1844	NC	051	C1910				1 1870	NC	051	BARSHA EDNA HARRELL	27531
HOLLOMAN, SALLY J	C1881	NC		1907				1 1900	NC	051	THOMAS C GREENE	27531
HOLLOMAN, WRIGHT	C1773	NC		C1830	NC			1			SUSAN	27531
HOLMAN, DANIEL	C1750	?NC		1822	TN							04080
HOLMAN, THOMAS	C1785	NC		1827	IL			1 C1805			MARY/POLLY WARREN	04080
HOLMES, APSYLLAH	1770	NC		1854	GA			1 1790	GA		PITT MILNER	60008
HOLMES, JOHN		?VA		1803	GA		?047	1			CLOE BENTLEY	60008
HOLMES, JOHN				C1772	NC	085		1			GENNET WILSON	60461
HOLMES, RICHARD	C1760	NC	085	1818	AL			1 1781	NC	085	ELIZABETH MCGAUGHEY	60461

ANCESTOR INDEX	BIRTH	PL	CO	DEATH	PL	CO	LIVD	MARRIED	PL	CO	SPOUSE NAME	CODE
HOLT, GEORGE ANDERSON	C1770	NC		C1828		022		1 C1795	NC	022	PENELOPE JOHNSTON	20330
HOLT, GEORGE ANDERSON		?NC	?067	C1797	NC	022		1	?NC	?067	PENELOPE JOHNSTON	27543
HOLT, ISRAEL	1765	NC	073	1852	NC	001		1 C1787	NC	073	JANE	20135
HOLT, JACOB	C1737	VA		C1799	NC	073		1 C1760	NC	073		20135
HOLT, JACOB	1796	NC	073	1883	NC	001		1 1823	NC	073	MARY STEPNEY WILKINS	20135
HOLT, JOHN	1786	NC		1863	AR		104	1 C1816	NC	104	ELIZABETH POGUE	60243
HOLT, MICHAEL		GER		1767	NC	073		1	VA		ELIZABETH SCHEIBLE	20135
HOLT, RICHARD		?NC	?067	C1836	NC	022		1	?NC	?067	GEORGE	27543
HOLTZCLAW, HENRY	C1770	NC			IL		014	1 C1787	?NC		SARAH SHIRLEY	06159
HOMESLEY, JOSEPH	C1776	VA		C1825	?MO			1	?NC		BARBARA FULKS	03015
HONEA, TOBIAS	1776	NC	037	1841	AL							60462
HONEYCUTT, ELI B	1787			C1858	NC	089		1 C1808			LEAH STOUGH	07115
HONEYCUTT, JAMES MADISON	1832	NC	089	1904	NC	089		1 C1854			BEADIE A DRAKE	07115
HONEYCUTT, JOSEPH	C1780	NC	065					1			POLLY LOVE	60468
HOOKER, JAMES DIKERSON	1831			1893	NC	038	106	1			VIRGINIA PARKER	06195
HOOKER, WILLIAM	C1798						005	1			HARRIET	06195
HOOKS, WARREN	1802	NC	103	1876	TX			1			ELISABETH ROBERTS	25204
HOOKS, WILLIAM				C1819	NC	103		1			DORCAS BLAKE	25204
HOOKS, WILLIAM HENRY	1823	NC	103	1907	AR			1 1850	AR		ELIZABETH SCOTT	25204
HOOPER, JAMES WESLEY	1835	NC	060	C1914	GA		023	1 C1855			ELIZABETH	20105
HOOPER, JOHN	1783	GA		1871	NC	055		1			MARGARET LEDBETTER	60149
HOOPER, MARY ELIZABETH	1768	VA		1843	NC	020		1 1784			STARLING GUNN	60493
HOOPER, MARY TALITHA	1861	NC		1932	TX			1 1877	GA		JUNIUS HILLYER STANDRIDGE	60149
HOOPER, THOMAS JEFFERSON	1829	NC		1894	GA			1 1855			SOPHIA ANN WILSON	60149
HOOTEN, LITTLETON		?NC		C1844	SC							60090
HOPKINS, AMELIA		VA			NC	?044	044	1			W BAXTER DAVIS	60164
HOPPES, JOHN	1782	NC	092	1857	OH			1 1806	NC	092	NANCY ANN BROWN	60454
HORN, DAVID T F	1814	NC	073	1870	MO			1 1836	NC	073	CORNELIA JANE HOLLOWAY THOMAS	13020
HORN, MARY		NC	?085		NC	?092		1 C1780			ABRAHAM STOWE	04200
HORN, WILLIAM		?NC	?073		NC	?073		1 1804	NC	073	JEANY/JANE FADDIS	13020
HORN, WILLIAM JAMES	1838	NC	073	1874	MO			1 1871	MO		BURLETTA HARVEY	13020
HORTON, ABARHAM	C1722			1816	NC	092						27429
HORTON, CHARLES	C1784	NC	?039	1867	NC	099		1 1808	NC	099	MARY/POLLY BUNCH	04065
HORTON, CONSTANT WILLIAMS		NC	099	1845	NC	099		1			ANN HOUSE	04065
HORTON, DAVID	1728	NY		1785	NC	099		1 C1750			ANN	04065
HORTON, JAMES		NC	?085		OH		092	1 1778	NC	046	MARGARET BEALS	27429
HORTON, JAMES CHARLIE	1850	NC	022	1906	NC	022		1 1871	NC	022	NANCY JANE PARTIN	60110

ANCESTOR INDEX	BIRTH	PL	CO	DEATH	PL	CO	LIVD	MARRIED	PL	CO	SPOUSE NAME	CODE
HORTON, VELLA LEE	1877	NC	022	1944	NC	036		1 1903	NC	022	CHARLES HILL BURCH	60110
HORTON, WILLIAM	C1812	NC	?099	C1887	NC	022		1 1849	NC	073	ELLEN/ELLENDER TRICE	60110
HOSKINS, EDMUND	1774	NC	024	1845	MS			1 1802	NC	?024	ELIZABETH BLOUNT	19230
HOSKINS, JOHN	1699	PA		C1784	NC	046		1 C1750	PA		HANNAH ELLIS	60558
HOSKINS, MOSES	1763	PA		1839	IL		046	1 1784	NC	046	RUTH HODSON	60558
HOSKINS, MOSES	1790	NC	046	1848	IA			1 1810	OH		ELIZABETH HOGGATT	60558
HOSKINS, SAMUEL GRANVILLE	C1787	NC		1862	KS			1 C1808			FRANCES	60327
HOUGH, MARY	1754	NC	085				092	1 1772			ABRAHAM REECE	60288
HOUK, ADAM	1786	NC						1 C1808	VA		MARY A HALE	60567
HOUSE, BALISS	C1760	NC	010	1806	TN			1 1784	NC	010	PENELOPE BOND	60337
HOUSE, JOHN				1791	NC	037		1			MARY	60021
HOUSE, JOSEPH	1780	NC	037	1861	AR			1 1807	TN		ALCEY BEDWELL	60021
HOUSE/HAUS, ELIZABETH	C1820	NC	065		IL			1 1836	IL		FRIEND CRAIN	60581
HOUSE/HAUS, JOHN	C1770	?NC					065	1			CATHERINE/SARAH	60581
HOUSE/HAUS, MARX/MARK		GER					065					60581
HOUSTON, EDWARD	C1750	NC	035	C1825	NC	035		1 C1771	NC	?035	MARY MILLER	02145
HOUSTON, GEORGE	1819	NC	035	1889	GA			1 C1835	GA		ELIZABETH	02145
HOUSTON, HENRY	C1793	NC	035	C1841	GA			1 1816	NC	035	ELENDER JANE STOKES	02145
HOUSTON, WILLIAM, DR	C1710			C1794	NC	035		1 C1735	NC	?011	ANN JONES	02145
HOWARD, BENJAMIN	1742	MD		1823	NC	104		1 1762	MD		PRUDENCE SATER	60593
HOWARD, EDRIE BROWN	1906	NC	040				032	1 1926	NC	033	HOYLE K KOONTZ	11145
HOWARD, GEORGE	1770							1 1750			MATTHEW LOCKE	60593
HOWARD, JAMES	C1779	NC	?034	1835	NC	059		1 C1800	NC	?059	TREASY	13264
HOWARD, JESSE	1803	NC	059	C1910	NC	059		1 1839	NC	059	MARY W SMITH	13264
HOWARD, PENNEY	1810	NC	?067		NC	089		1	NC	089	DAVID COBLE	60288
HOWARD, SAMUEL	C1700	?NC		1761	NC	029		1 C1730	?NC		MARY	13264
HOWARD, THOMAS	C1730	?NC	?070		NC			1 C1765	NC	?029	RUTH	13264
HOWARD, VANBUREN ARVEY	1882	NC	060	1965	NC	040		1 1905	NC	?040	MAUDE LOUVANNIE BUMGARNER	11145
HOWELL, BENJAMIN				C1831	NC	103		1			AMERICA	03125
HOWELL, EDITH	C1760	?VA					037	1			EDMOND STUCKEY	27303
HOWELL, JOSIE		?VA			SC		?037	1 C1775	?NC		ADDISON SCARBOROUGH	27303
HOWELL, SARAH	C1857	NC	?107	C1930	WA		066	1 C1875	NC	?064	JESSE M SPARKS	25087
HOWELL, ZACHARIAH	C1811	VA						1 1829	NC		MARY	60322
HOWREN, WILLIAM	1791	NC	046	1868	IN			1 1810	NC	046	RACHEL WRIGHT	23070
HOWREN, WINSMORE	C1765	DE		C1835	NC	046		1	DE		SALLY	23070
HUBBARD, ALEY	1813	NC	006	1908	VA		?104	1 1837	NC	006	GEORGE WASHINGTON MILLER	02295
HUBBARD, RANDALL	C1780	?NC	?104	C1830	NC	006		1 C1800	NC	?006	POLLY SIZEMORE	02295

ANCESTOR INDEX	BIRTH	PL	CO	DEATH	PL	CO	LIVD	MARRIED	PL	CO	SPOUSE NAME	CODE
HUCKABEE, CHARLOTTE	1817	NC			TX			1 1853			WILLIAM WILSON	60185
HUCKABEE, JOHN	1785	NC	?068		MS			1			EVE MCGREGOR	60185
HUDGINS, ARTHUR VERNON	1882	NC	020	1957	NC	078		1 1907	NC	020	JANIE GERTRUDE MARSHALL	27596
HUDGINS, JAMES BOMAN/BOWMAN	1841	NC	078	1915	VA		020	1 1871	NC	078	MARTHA BANKS STANFIELD	27596
								2 1893	VA		HARRIET BROWN ENNIS	
HUDGINS, JOHN	1792			1843				1 1812	NC	078	MARY HARRIS	27596
HUDGINS, JOHN JOSIAH	1847	?NC	?078	1914	NC	078		1 1869			ELLA N ROYSTER	27596
HUDGINS, MARY ELIZABETH	1842	?NC	?078	1887				1 1865	?NC		JOHN L MOORE	27596
HUDGINS, NANCY REBECCA	1845	?NC	?078	1885				1 1873	?NC		CHARLES A BRIGHTWELL	27596
HUDGINS, THOMAS HENRY	1817	?NC	?078	1907	?NC	?022	?078	1 1839	NC	078	SARA/SARAH CARVER	27596
								2 1855	NC	078	MRS CATHERINE (GREGORY) RENN	
								3 1875			REBECCA L RIGGS	
HUDNELL, GEORGE WILSON	1852			1910	NC	009		1			MARY FOEMAN	24320
								2			CENDERELLA P GUTHRIE	
								3 1885			FLORENCE ELIZABETH DAVIS	
								4 1893			MARY ELLA DAVIS	
HUFF/HOUGH, DANEIL	C1720	NJ		1793	NC	090	092	1 1741	NJ		MARY WEHRLE	60120
HUFF/HOUGH, MARY	C1755	VA		C1825	NC	092		1 C1771	NC	092	ABRAHAM REECE	60120
HUFFINE, MARY	C1804	NC		1865	TN			1 C1820	NC		JACOB LINEBERRY	27758
HUFFINES, DANIEL				1822	NC	073		1			LUCRETIA	27542
HUFFINES, DAVID	C1780			C1831	NC	046		1			MARY	27542
HUFFINES, SOLOMON	C1820	NC			NC	046		1			SALLY CHRISTMON	27542
HUFFMAN, CATHERINE	C1780	NC	?060	C1815	NC	?006	?014	1 C1800	NC	?014	MICHAEL COOK	02295
HUFFMAN, CHARLOTTE		?VA			NC	?073		1	?VA		GRIFFITH THOMAS	13020
HUFFMAN, LAWSON	1805	NC	?046	C1880	IN			1 C1829	IN		MARY/POLLY RAWLINGS	19170
HUFFMAN, PETER JR	1777	NC	073	1821	TN			1 1799	NC	073	ELIZABETH TROXLER	27435
HUFFMAN, PETER SR	C1734	GER			NC	073						27435
HUGGINS, ELIZABETH	C1832	SC		C1870	NC	027		1 C1851			SAMUEL COLUMBUS HAYES	24032
HUGHES, DANIEL	C1768	NC		1850	KY							08240
HUGHES, JOHN FILLMORE	1865	NC						1			CORA BELLE YOUNGER	60553
HUGHES, LOUVICIA	C1820	NC		1883	GA			1 C1843			WILLIAM ROBERTSON	60308
HUGHES, THOMAS F	1799	NC		1877	TN			1 C1832	NC		REBECCA MARTIN	60345
HUGHES/HUSE, ANDREW	1755	PA		1843	SC		073	1			OBEDIENCE	11100
								2			NANCY MAULDIN	
HUGHEY, JAMES, SHF	1777	NC	?085				013	1			ELLEN	60473
HUGHEY, JOSEPH, SHF	C1770	NC	?085				013					60473
HUGHEY, SAMUEL	1802	NC	013	1811	NC	013		1			MARGARET YOUNG BRANK	60473
HUGHS, WILLIAM	1792	NC		1848	GA			1 C1812	?GA		MARTHA REBECCA CHILDS	60405
HUGHS, WILLIAM THOMAS	C1770	IRE		C1815	GA			1	?NC		ANN CHILDS	60405
HULLBROOKE, HARMONOUS				C1784	NC							60074

ANCESTOR INDEX	BIRTH	PL	CO	DEATH	PL	CO	LIVD	MARRIED	PL	CO	SPOUSE NAME	CODE
HUMPHREYS, JOHN		?NC		C1826	TN							27599
HUMPHREYS, JOHN HOWARD	C1772	NC			TN							27599
HUMPHRIES, WILLIAM	1794			1873	NC	026		1 C1820			ELIZABETH MCCRAW	60272
HUNSUCKER, ARCHIBALD MONROE	1842	NC	068	1918	MS			1 1866	LA		MARTHA JANE ARNOLD	60045
HUNSUCKER, MARGARET INEZ	1846	NC	068	1895	TX			1 1866	LA		JOHN A YOUNG	60045
HUNT, EBER		NC		C1837	IL			1			ANN	60056
HUNT, ELIZABETH								1 C1790	NC	085	JOHN TUSSEY	60027
HUNT, GERSHOM	C1723			1810	NC	085		1 1751			EUNICE FITZRANDOLPH	60027
								2			ELISABETH	
HUNT, THOMAS	C1735						046	1	PA		MARY ANN BEALS	60053
HUNTER, ABRAHAM	1769	NC		1853	GA			1 C1817			ANN	60230
HUNTER, BEN	C1770	VA					090	1 1791	NC	092	ANNE LONGINO	60255
HUNTER, DAVID				C1812	NC	063	096					60594
HUNTER, ISAAC				C1752	NC	024						01006
HUNTER, JAMES	C1733	PA		C1782	NC	046		1			MARY WALKER	01040
HUNTER, JAMES JR	C1769	NC	046	C1845	IL		081	2 C1799			MARGARET PHIPPS	01040
HUNTER, JANE	1809	NC	081	1892	UT			1 1833	IL		NICHOLS ROBERTSON	01040
HUNTER, REBECCA JANE BRUCE	1824	NC	046	1898	TX			1 1842	?TN		MAJ BLACKSTONE HARDEMAN	27311
HUNTER, SAMUEL, COL				1846	TX		046	1			REBECCA JANE BRUCE	27311
HUNTER, THOMAS		?VA		1803	NC	090	092	1	VA		RACHEL	60255
HUNTER, THOMAS	C1768	?VA		1805	NC	090	092	1 1790	NC	092	ELIZABETH ROBINSON	60255
HUNTINGTON, SARAH	1781	NC		C1869	AL			1 C1800			ELIAS PATRICK	60054
HURLEY, AMOS	C1750			1817	NC	022						27270
HURLEY, ELIJAH	C1780	NC	022	1820	TN			1			MARY	27270
HURST, WILLIAM WASHINGTON	C1785	NC		1852	AL			1 1810	GA		NANCY SCRUGGS	25145
HUSKEY, THOMAS	C1795	VA		C1855	NC	026		1 C1820	SC		SUSANNAH HUMPHRIES	02412
HUSON/HUSTON, JOHN	C1774	NC		1854	AL			1			POOLE	27600
								2	?NC		MARTHA/PATSY/MATTIE DAWSON	
HUSON/HUSTON, WILLIAM DAWSON	C1802	NC			AL			1	AL		ANNA BONDS	27600
								2 1871	AL		MARY J BEESLY	
HUTCHENS, JAMES	1822	NC	092	1886	NC	106		1 1850	NC	106	MARTHA YARBOROUGH	60120
HUTCHENS, JOHN	1738	VA		1825	NC	092		1 1757	VA		ALICE STANLEY	60120
HUTCHENS, JONATHAN	1762	VA		C1855	IN		092	1 1783	VA		ELIZABETH BEAVERS	60120
HUTCHENS, JOSEPH	1785	VA					106	1 1819	NC	092	SUSANNA MIKELS	60120
HUTCHENS, STRANGEMAN	1707	VA		1792	NC	092		1 1731	VA		ELIZABETH COX	60120
HUTCHENS, THOMAS DAVID	1854	NC	106	1931	IN			1 1874	NC	106	MILLY CHRISTENE EVANS	60120
HUTCHINS, STRANGEMAN	1707	VA		1792	NC	092		1 C1731	NC		ELIZABETH COX	60322
HYATT, ABEDNIGO BENJAMIN	1822	NC		1887	KS			1 1844	TN		LUCINDA TIPTON	60374
HYATT, EDWARD GAITHER	C1750			1817	NC	049		1 C1780	NC		HANNAH PARKER	60374

97

ANCESTOR INDEX	BIRTH	PL	CO	DEATH	PL	CO	LIVD	MARRIED	PL	CO	SPOUSE NAME	CODE
HYATT, SHADRICK	C1785	NC			NC	055		1			RHODA BRYSON	60374
HYDE, HEARTWELL	C1759			1836	NC		047	1			MARY REAVIS	25158
HYMAN, WINIFRED	C1802	NC	?063	C1880	MEX			1 1829	NC	063	ALFRED GRAY ANDREWS	20080

I

ANCESTOR INDEX	BIRTH	PL	CO	DEATH	PL	CO	LIVD	MARRIED	PL	CO	SPOUSE NAME	CODE
INGLE, DICIA	C1820	NC						1	NC		JOHN GILLILAND	40690
INGRAM, EDWIN	1751	VA		1833	NC	082		1 1771			NANCY ANNE MONTGOMERY	27328
INGRAM, JOHN		VA			NC	082	005	1			ELIZABETH KIRBY	27328
INGRAM, LEMUEL	1794	NC	005	1850	AL			2	NC		MATILDA WILKINS	60076
								3 1843	AL		REBECCA ALLEN	
IPOCK, JOHN PIERCE		?NC	?028					1			RACHEL STILLEY	10010
IPOCK, THOMAS BRYAN	1858	NC	028	1922	NC	103		1			ANNIE MINNIE CHARLTON	10010
IRVIN, NANCY		NC		C1805	KY			1 C1774	NC		JAMES ANDERSON	20415
IRWIN/IRVIN, ELIZABETH	1823	NC	046	1888	IN			1 1841	OH		PETER REINHEIMER	60493
IRWIN/IRVIN, GEORGE				1834	?OH		046	1			LYDIA	60493
IRWIN/IRVIN, JAMES	C1755						020					60493
ISAACS, PHOEBE	C1766	NC					006	1			ABRAHAM VANDERPOOL	60343
ISENHOWER/EISENHAUER, JOHN VALENTINE	1759	PA		1820	NC	060		1			SUSAN M NAFER	27441
ISENHOWER/EISENHAUER, JOSEPH	C1787			1847	NC	021		1			MARGARET/PEGGY HUNSUCKER	27441
ISENHOWER/EISENHAUER, ORPHA MAHALA	1827	NC	060	1914	NC	021		1 1844	NC	021	FRANKLIN HERMAN	27441
ISLEY, LEVI				1876	NC	001		1			ELIZABETH	02256
ISLEY, MARTIN	C1785			1859	NC	001		1			CATHERINE	02256
ISLEY, MARY CATHERINE	1829			1895	NC	?073		1 1848	NC		JAMES EMSLEY JOB	02256
ISRAEL, ANNIE BELL	1896	NC	013	1967	WA			1 1911	NC	013	WILLIAM GARFIELD PENLEY	17100
								2				
								3			IRA MCKINLEY	
ISRAEL, DAVID	C1850	NC	013					1 C1872	NC	013	JULIA C SLUDER	17100
ISRAEL, PLEASANT	C1814	NC	013	C1901	CN	013		1 1842	NC	013	SARAH E WOLFE	17100
ISRAEL, RALPH WEBB	1873	NC	013	1963	NC	013		1 1891	NC	013	HARRIET MELISSA PARHAM	17100
ISRAEL, SOLOMON	C1777	VA			NC			1 1797	NC	104	NANCY ALLOWAY-STRANGE	17100
IVES, ELIZABETH	1770	NC		1859	TN			1 1788	VA		THOMAS BATSON	08065
IVEY/IVIE, SUSAN REECE	1836	NC		1923	GA			1 1856	VA		JOHN WESLEY HALL	60173
IVY, TEMPIE	1821	NC		1875	MO			1 1842	KY		URIAS J ALLMON	60309
IVY/IVEY, HENRY				1794	NC	099		1			ANN	60562
IVY/IVEY, HENRY		NC		1859	KY			1 C1795	NC	099	AGNES PEOPLES/PEEBLES	60562

ANCESTOR INDEX	BIRTH	PL	CO	DEATH	PL	CO	LIVD	MARRIED	PL	CO	SPOUSE NAME	CODE

J

ANCESTOR INDEX	BIRTH	PL	CO	DEATH	PL	CO	LIVD	MARRIED	PL	CO	SPOUSE NAME	CODE
JACKSON, ALFRED	1803	NC	029	C1885	NC	029		1			ISABELLA MCRAE	13052
JACKSON, BENNETT		NC	087	C1847	NC	087		1			SARAH	27292
JACKSON, BIGGERS	C1785			1853	NC	029		1 1822	NC	029	MARY WHITLEY	13052
JACKSON, GIDEON S	1828	NC	029	1862	VA			1 1849	NC	029	SARAH ANN HAIR	13052
JACKSON, JAMES	C1755			1810	NC	029		1			NANCY	13052
JACKSON, JAMES	1785	NC	090	1853	IN			1			ELIZABETH HOOKER	60124
JACKSON, JESSE	C1775			1840	NC	029		1			EMILY	13052
JACKSON, JESSIE A	C1823	NC	047					1			ELISABETH/ISABELLA	10010
JACKSON, JOHN	C1745			1791	NC	029		1			JULIA ANN	13052
JACKSON, MARY CATHERINE	1823	NC	073	1864	IN			1 1839	IN		WASHINGTON MORRIS	60070
JACKSON, SAMUEL	1758	PA		1834	NC	090		1 1782	NC	092	HANNAH GIBSON	60124
JACKSON, TRAVIS	C1804	NC	087	1879	NC	087		1	NC	087	ELIZABETH MCLEOD	27292
JACOBS, HENRY		ENG			NC		024	1 1770	NC		SARA BROWN	17220
JACOBS, NANCY	1777	NC		1868	GA		029	1	NC		DUNCAN BLUE	17220
								2 1809	NC	029	DOUGALD MCMILLAN	
JAMES, CLIFTON	C1801	NC	?079	1849	NC	079		1			LYDIA MOORE	10010
JAMES, JAMES	C1824	NC	014	C1904	GA		?061	1 C1857	?NC	?014	SARAH/SALLY ANN FISHER	60190
JAMES, LEMUEL	C1730						079					10010
JAMES, MARY ANN	C1842	NC						1			MARION HARTNESS	60276
JAMES, THOMAS	C1716	?PA		1761	NC	070		1			MARY THOMAS ?	27356
JAMES, THOMAS		NC		1799	NC	070		1 1783	NC	099	MRS ELIZABETH (HINTON) RAND	27356
JARRELL, ABSALOM	1828	NC	081	1911	NC	081		1 1846	NC	081	NANCY YATES	08355
								2 1856	NC	081	ELIZA LOFLIN	
JARRELL, JOHN	C1787	?NC	?081	C1862	NC	?081		1	?NC	?081	RACHEL	08355
JARRELL, WILLIAM	1813	NC	081	1901	NC	081		1 1832	NC	081	CHARLOTTE BRISTOW	08355
JARVIS, CAROLINE	1848	NC		1915	VA		018	1 1867			JOHN UPTON	60307
JARVIS, CHARLES		NC	104					1 1811	NC	104	ELIZABETH BALL	25253
								2 1825	NC	104	SARAH HOWARD	
JARVIS, DORCAS	C1831	NC	030	1860	NC	030		1 1857	NC	030	JAMES M BERRY	02180
JARVIS, FOSTER, REV	C1795	NC	030	C1840	NC	030		1 C1818	NC	030	FANNIE GORDON	02180
JARVIS, JAMES	1789	NC	104		NC	104		1 1809	NC	104	LIDDIA MCBRIDE	25253
JARVIS, JOHN	1787	NC	104	C1858	NC	104		1 1811	NC	104	SALLY CHAMBERS	25253
JARVIS, JOHN, CAPT	C1760	NC	?030	1816	NC	030		1 C1781	NC	030	DORCAS ONEAL ?	02180
JARVIS, WILLIAM	1820	NC	104		NC	104		1 C1842	NC	054	LUCINDA KEMP	25253
JARVIS, WILLIAM J	1804			1860	NC	018		1			MARY	60307

ANCESTOR INDEX	BIRTH	PL	CO	DEATH	PL	CO	LIVD	MARRIED	PL	CO	SPOUSE NAME	CODE
JARVIS/GERVES, ELIZABETH	1775	NC	092	1837	TN			1 C1795	NC	092	JOHN WALKER	27686
JARVIS/GERVES, JOHN							?011	1			LUCY SAVAGE ?	27686
JASPER, CELIA	C1755	NC	?053	1831	NC	009		1			ARTHUR DAVIS	27378
JASPER, ISRAEL				C1785	NC	009		1			LURANA	27378
JASPER, SAMUEL				C1753	NC	053		1			ANN	27378
JEFFREYS, MARMADUKE NORFLEET	1786	NC	?039	1865	KY		071	1 1813	NC	039	HANNAH LOUISE HILL	01065
JELKS, DIXON/DICKSON	C1778	NC	069	1833	MS		047	1 C1799	NC	047	SARAH WALLICE/WALLACE	60419
JELKS, ELIZABETH		VA					069	1	NC		MR WIGGINS	60419
JELKS, ETHELDRED	C1720	?VA		1800	NC	069	037	1 C1740	VA		FILLIS/PHILLIS	60419
JELKS, ETHELDRED	C1769	NC	037	C1830	MS		069	1 C1790	NC		ELIZABETH/TAZZIE MERRITT	60419
JELKS, FILLITHA/TALLITHA		VA					069	1	?NC		MR UNDERWOOD	60419
JELKS, JANE/JENNY WILLIAMS	C1775	NC	037	C1844	MS		069	1 1806	GA		JOHN CRUTCHFIELD	60419
JELKS, ROBERT	C1773	NC	037		AL		069	1 C1795	NC		MARY/POLLY NICHOLSON	60419
JELKS, RUKINS	1770	NC	037	1820	MS		069	1 1791	?NC		CATHARINE/KATE ARICK/IRICK	60419
JELKS, SUSANNAH		VA					069	1	?NC		MOSES POWELL	60419
JELKS, WILLIAM	C1740	VA		C1786	NC		037	1 C1768	?NC		MARY WILLIAMS	60419
JELKS, WILLIAM	C1774	NC	037	1827	GA		069	1 C1796	NC	047	MARY WALLICE/WALLACE	60419
JENKINS, JENKEY	C1775	NC	?094	C1835	TN		086	1 1800	NC	060	NANCY ANN/ANNA BEAM	60466
JENKINS, NANCY	1808	NC	022	C1870	NC	022		1 1833	NC	022	REUBEN HERNDON	08200
JENKINS, ROBERT	C1740	?NC		1809	GA			1 C1760	NC	?085	MISS/MRS COMBS	60024
JENKINS, SANFORD	C1767	NC	044	1837	NC	022		1 C1790	NC	073	DELILAH BARBEE	08200
JENNINGS, JAMES	1757	VA		1837	NC	107	104	1 1781	NC	092	HANNAH MARTIN	27292
JENNINGS, JOHN THOMAS	1862	NC		1932	OR			1 1884 2 1898	MO MO		REBECCA MADISON GERTRUDE TIPPIT	60253
JOB, JAMES	1777			1829	NC	046		1 1797	NC	?046	ANN CORSBIE	02256
JOB, JONATHAN	1798	NC	?046	1877	NC	046		1 1825	NC	046	ESTHER WHITT	02256
JOBE, JAMES EMSLEY	1826	NC	046	1895	NC	046		1 1848	NC		MARY CATHERINE ISLEY	02256
JOBE, LUCY	1879	NC	046	1956	NC	001		1 1900	NC	046	JAMES WILLIAM SQUIRES	02256
JOHNSON, ALEXANDER				1844	NC	006		1 1790	NC	104	FRANKY/FRANKIE GAMBILL	60017
JOHNSON, ALLEN SR		NC	056		NC	056		1 1791 2 1814	NC NC	056 056	PEGGY WHITINGTON EDITH BARNES	03315
JOHNSON, AMOS		NC	?024	1848	NC	063		1	NC		ESTHER	27477
JOHNSON, CLARISSA JANE	1807	NC			IL		085	1 1825	IN		JESSE GREEN	60354
JOHNSON, ELIZA ANNE	1824	NC	029	1905	AL		068	1 1850	NC	068	AARON TYSON	60147
JOHNSON, GEORGE WASHINGTON	1851	NC	?056	1928	NC	056		1 1873	NC	056	JULIA A CROCKER	03315
JOHNSON, GIDEON	C1720	VA		1807	NC	044		1 2 C1748			GOODLOE NANCY URSULA ALLEN	60342
JOHNSON, HARDEE	C1770	NC	079	C1825	NC	079		1 C1795	NC	079	CATHARINE CANNON	13264
JOHNSON, HENRY	1738	IRE		1815	TN		010	1 1763	PA		RACHEL HOLMAN	60535

ANCESTOR INDEX	BIRTH	PL	CO	DEATH	PL	CO	LIVD	MARRIED	PL	CO	SPOUSE NAME	CODE
								2 C1748			NANCY URSULA ALLEN	
JOHNSON, HARDEE	C1770	NC	079	C1825	NC	079		1 C1795	NC	079	CATHARINE CANNON	13264
JOHNSON, HENRY	1738	IRE		1815	TN		010	1 1763	PA		RACHEL HOLMAN	60535
JOHNSON, ISSAC N	C1845	NC			TN			1			ELIZABETH HOWARD	60468
JOHNSON, JAMES	C1745	NC		C1817	NC	079		1 C1765	NC	079	MARY WOOTEN	13264
JOHNSON, JAMES H	C1815	NC	?056		NC	?056		1 1836	NC	056	HARRIET STEVENS	03315
JOHNSON, JOHN	1764	VA		1828	GA			1 C1787	NC	039	ANN EALY/ELEY	08120
								2 1823	GA		MRS JOICY (BOWDRE) FEARS	
JOHNSON, JOHN/JACK	1797	NC	?073	1860	NC	001		1 C1825	NC	?073	MRS ELIZABETH (FOGLEMAN) VESTAL	05059
JOHNSON, JOSHUA		?NC	?024	1795	NC	063						27477
JOHNSON, JOSIAH	C1775	NC	085	C1813	IN		085	1 C1796	NC	092	SARAH/SALLY WRIGHT	60354
JOHNSON, LEWIS JAMES	1826	NC	079	1910	NC	045		1 C1862	NC	045	SARAH ADELAIDE ROUSE	13264
JOHNSON, MARK		NC	056	C1829	NC	056		1	NC	056	SALLY	03315
JOHNSON, MARY ANN RANDOLPH	1870	NC	045	1933	NC	045		1 1886	NC	045	GANNON FRANKLIN GRAVES	13264
JOHNSON, REBEKAH	1742	VA		1801	NC			1 1761	VA		OBEDIAH HARRIS	08265
JOHNSON, ROBERT	1737	VA						1	NC	046	VIRGINIA CECILIA ELMORE	20333
JOHNSON, SAMUEL	1781	VA		1843	TN			1 C1800	NC	099	WINNEY/WINNIE NORTON	60017
JOHNSON, SIMON	1814	NC	?029	C1865	TX			1 C1834	NC	029	ELIZA CAMPBELL	60212
JOHNSON, WILLIAM	1749	VA		1830	TN		046	1 1773	NC	046	SARAH MCCLAREN	60342
JOHNSON, WILLIAM	1764	NC	010	1845	MS		010	1 1783	NC	010	DIANE ADAMS	60535
JOHNSON, WILLIAM A	1789	NC	046	1852	TN			2 C1812	?TN		MARY/POLLY GRIFFIN	60342
JOHNSON/JOHNSTON, ALFRED	1811	NC		1896	KY			1 1833	KY		WINNIFRED WRIGHT	02135
JOHNSON/JOHNSTON, ANGUS	C1790	NC		1861	TN			1			LUCY ISOM/ISHAM	60044
JOHNSON/JOHNSTON, HANNAH HADLEY	1788	NC	022	1835	NC	022						04195
JOHNSON/JOHNSTON, JACOB PROCTOR JR ?	1816	?NC		1902				1 1839	KY		NANCY WELLS	02135
JOHNSON/JOHNSTON, JACOB SR		NC		1845	KY			1	?NC		ELIZABETH WELLS	02135
JOHNSON/JOHNSTON, JAMES R	1810	NC	?054									60465
JOHNSON/JOHNSTON, JAMES RANDOLPH	1773			1836	GA			1	NC	081	SARAH NEEDHAM	10085
JOHNSON/JOHNSTON, JEMIMA	C1765			C1805	GA		028	1			FRANCES DE LA FONTAINE	24073
JOHNSON/JOHNSTON, JESSE	1746	PA		1831	NC	022		1 1766	NC	073	HANNAH HADLEY	04195
JOHNSON/JOHNSTON, JOHN	C1720				NC		073					04195
JOHNSON/JOHNSTON, JOHN	C1750			1810	NC	081	?046	1			JANE	10085
JOHNSON/JOHNSTON, JOHN	C1755			1830	NC	087		1			ELIZABETH	13052
JOHNSON/JOHNSTON, JOHN		VA		1802	GA			1	?NC		CATHERINE JOHNSON/JOHNSTON	60044
JOHNSON/JOHNSTON, MATTHEW	1803	NC	087	1881	NC	029		1			MARTHA HALL	13052
JOHNSON/JOHNSTON, MATTHIAS M	1816	NC	022	1882	NC	022		1 1835	NC	022	MARTHA/PATSY CRUTCHFIELD	04195
JOHNSON/JOHNSTON, ROBERT W		NC	?085					1 C1809	NC	?054	ANNA CHAMBERS	60465

ANCESTOR INDEX	BIRTH	PL	CO	DEATH	PL	CO	LIVD	MARRIED	PL	CO	SPOUSE NAME	CODE
JOHNSON/JOHNSTON, STEPHEN HOLLINGSWO	1838	NC	029	1911	NC	029		1 1866			CATHERINE MCKAY MCMILLAN	13052
JOHNSTON, BENJAMIN	C1715	NC	?024	1779	NC	072		1 C1740	NC	072	MARY	13264
JOHNSTON, HAZELTINE ANN	C1840	NC	060					1 1859 2 1865	NC NC	060 060	JOHN FRANKLIN HOLBROOK AARON BLAKE	60477
JOHNSTON, JOHN	1734	VA		1824	NC	039		1 2 1763 3			HOLLAND ELIZABETH CARR MRS MARTHA DENBY	08120
JOHNSTON, SARAH	C1780	NC	072	C1835	NC	035		1 C1801	NC	072	JAMES MARSHBURN	13264
JOHNSTON, THOMAS	C1670	NC	?024	1752	NC	072	024	1 C1710	NC	?010	ANN BASS	13264
JOHNSTON, WILLIAM M, LT	1790	NC	068	1871	AL			1 1818	NC	068	MARY E ENGLAND	60147
JOHNSTON/JOHNSON, ESAU	1800	NC	046	1888	WI			1 1826	IL		SALOMA/SALLY STARR	25126
JOHNSTON/JOHNSON, GIDEON	C1728	VA		C1807	NC	084		1 1748			URSULA ALLEN	60571
JOHNSTON/JOHNSON, GIDEON JR	1754	VA		1843	TN		084	1 1779	NC	046	MARY BAKER DEGRAFFENREID	60571
JOHNSTON/JOHNSON, HENRY JR	1779	SC		1851	WI		046	1 1799	NC	073	ELIZABETH STARR	25126
JOHNSTON/JOHNSON, HENRY SR							073	1			CATHERINE WHITESELL	25126
JOHNSTON/JOHNSON, LARKIN	C1764	NC		1852	VA			1 C1790	?VA		MARY/POLLY DAVIS	60344
JOLLEY, HENRY	1789	NC	?079	1850	UT			1 1806	NC	079	FRANCES MANNING	60388
JOLLEY, JESSE	1805	NC	?079	1897	GA		?063	1 1825			MARY ANN BRYAN	10120
JOLLEY, REUBEN MANNING	1808	NC	079	1849	IA			1 1829	?TN		SARAH PIPPEN	60388
JOLLIFF, JOSHUA G				1840	NC	077		1 1835	NC	024	MARY FELTON	24260
JONES, ALLEN B	1798	NC	047	C1852	NC	047		1			TABITHA HAWKINS	60594
JONES, ALSEY				C1838	?TN			1 1803	NC	071	HENRY MONGER	60159
JONES, AMBROSE	1767	NC	073	1806	MC	078		1			LUCY BAIRD	60500
JONES, AMBROSE	1718			1792	NC	044	020	1			CAHTERINE COLLINS	60500
JONES, ANDREW J	1820	NC		1856	IL			1 1843	IL		SARAHANN POWELL	04155
JONES, ATLAS O	1822	NC	013	1903	MS			1			MARY FRANCIS CHEAIRS	60590
JONES, BLOXUM	1793	NC	047					1 1817	NC	047	ESTHER BISHOP	60594
JONES, CAROLINE ELIZABETH	1849			1890	NC	081		1 1866	NC	003	WILLIAM FRANKLIN FRAZIER	06158
JONES, CECILIA/SISLEY	1814	NC						1 1832	IN		JESSE F SHELTON	20125
JONES, CHARLES PINCKNEY	1818	NC	046	1902	WA		009	1 1844	NC	029	SARAH ANN MCLAUCHLIN	60136
JONES, CHLOE	C1801	NC	?099	C1821	AL			1 1818	NC	099	WRIGHTMAN HILLIARD	60337
JONES, ELIZABETH	C1787			C1860	AL			1 1803	NC	085	MOSES EASTEP	08023
JONES, ELIZABETH	1827	NC	006	1877	NC	006		1 1851	NC	006	JAMES WELBORN SHEPHERD	60120
JONES, ESTHER HARRIET	1875	NC	013	1918	NC	093		1 1897	NC	013	RICHARD ISAAC EDBETTER	60582
JONES, GEORGE WILSON	C1824			1877	NC	003		1 C1842			ELIZABETH LITTLE	06158
JONES, HONOUR		NC	005		GA			1			RICHARD ODOM ?	60167
JONES, ISAAC	1797	?TN		1884	IL		046	1 1821	NC	046	MARGARET HOWELL	24243
JONES, JACOB	C1730			1787	NC	028		1 C1750	NC	?028	MARY HORD/HOARD	13264

ANCESTOR INDEX	BIRTH	PL	CO	DEATH	PL	CO	LIVD	MARRIED	PL	CO	SPOUSE NAME	CODE
JONES, JAMES	C1735	NC	009	C1795	NC	079		1 C1765	NC	079	RACHEL WATKINS	13264
JONES, JAMES	C1755	NC	028	1802	NC	057		1 C1780	NC	?057	SARAH	13264
JONES, JAMES	1794	NC	?092	1872	MO			1 1814	NC	092	ALICE H BILLS	60157
JONES, JAMES				1803	VA			1 C1768	NC	073	AMY HUMPHRIES	60500
JONES, JAMES		NC	047		NC	047		1			CELIA CORLEW	60594
JONES, JAMES ALEXANDER	1848	NC	103	1914	FL			1 1868	NC	035	S ANNIE W GARNER	01007
								2 1873	SC		SALLIE C NELSON	
JONES, JARVIS	C1760	NC	?075	C1830	NC	?046						60136
JONES, JESSE	C1775	NC	079	1847	NC	103		1 C1805	NC	103	ELIZABETH BELL	13264
JONES, JOHN	1772	VA		1865	NC	004	006	1 1798	NC	104	LEAH LONG	60120
JONES, JOHN E	C1853						?003					06158
JONES, JOHN SIDNEY	C1834	NC		C1895	NC	022		1 1858	NC	022	MARTHA HOLT	27543
JONES, JOHN SR	1746	NJ		1842	VA		006	1 C1770	VA		ANNIE NORMAN	60120
JONES, JOSHUA	1771	NC	015	1842	AL		100	1 1796	GA		SARAH A MORRIS ?	60519
JONES, LEONARD	1745	?MD		1839	AL		100	1			SARAH	60519
JONES, MARTHA	1810	NC	103	C1890	NC	045		1 1831	NC	103	HENRY TAYLOR	13264
JONES, MARTHA L	C1844							1 C1860	NC	003	JOHN MULLIS	06158
JONES, MARY	C1780				NC	?073		1 1801	NC	073	THOMAS GILL	02256
JONES, MARY MALVENA	1814	NC	?044		TN			1 1836	NC	039	JOHN R FULLER	60234
								2 1838	NC	044	WILLIE GRISHAM	
JONES, MARY/POLLY		?NC	?081	1838	IN			1 1817	NC	081	HARDEN YORK	19170
JONES, MARY/POLLY	1762	NC	028	1829	TN			1 1786	NC	026	FREDERICK TURNER	20080
JONES, NANCY K	1849							1 C1867	NC	003	ELISU WEAVER	06158
JONES, NATHAN							087					60590
JONES, NATHAN		?NC						1			DISEY BALDWIN	60590
JONES, NATHANIEL							099					60590
JONES, RANSOM	C1811	NC	013	C1880	NC	013		1 C1830	NC	013	MARY	60582
JONES, RICHARD	C1780			1862	NC	?001		1 1807	NC	073	ELIZABETH MARTIN	02256
JONES, RICHARD R	C1788	NC		1853	TX			1 C1818				60146
JONES, ROBERT C	1808	NC	047									60594
JONES, ROGER				1801	NC	028		1			SARAH	20080
JONES, SAMUEL	C1720	VA		1775	NC	085		1			SARAH	17240
JONES, SANDY CAMPBELL	C1867	NC	003									06158
JONES, SIMON, CPT	C1706	NC	009	1767	NC	079		1 C1725	NC	009	ABIGAIL BONNER	13264
JONES, SIMPSON	1805	?TN					046					24243
JONES, SOLOMON	1802	NC	013	1899	NC	050		1			MARY HAMILTON	09030
JONES, STEPHEN	C1773	NC	?085	C1885	NC	013		1 C1810	NC	013	JANE	60582
JONES, SUSAN	1814	NC	073	1899	NC	073		1 1839	NC	073	THOMAS SQUIRES	02256

ANCESTOR INDEX	BIRTH	PL	CO	DEATH	PL	CO	LIVD	MARRIED	PL	CO	SPOUSE NAME	CODE
JONES, THOMAS	C1835	NC			NC	022		1			MARTHA MANN	27543
JONES, THOMAS	1802	NC	006	1886	NC	004	006	1 1826	VA		JANE PHIPPS	60120
JONES, WALTER, REV	C1685			1728	NC	009		1 C1704	NC	?008	DOROTHY BODAT	13264
JONES, WILLIAM	1785	NC	057	1868	NC	057		1 C1820	NC	057	NANCY	13264
JONES, WILLIAM	C1825	NC	057	C1845	NC	057		1 C1845	NC	057	TEMPERANCE	13264
JONES, WILLIAM				C1797	NC	099	056	1 2			MARTHA	60483
JONES, WILLIAM	C1790	NC	100	1835	AL		100					60519
JONES, WILLIAM B	1796	NC	047									60594
JONES, WILLIAM FRANKLIN	1846	NC	057	1915	NC	045		1 1868	NC	057	CHARITY JANE HEATH	13264
JONES, WILLIAM GILBERT	C1846						?003					06158
JONES, WILLIAM H				1830	AL			2 1809	NC	044	ELIZABETH H BLACKNALL	25100
JONES, WILLIAM M	1849	NC	013	1930	NC	013		1 1869	NC	013	MARY ANN PRESSLEY	60582
JONES, WILLOUGHBY W	1800	NC	047									60594
JORDAN, BENJAMIN	1777	?NC		C1850	GA			1 C1804	GA		ELIZABETH	60090
JORDAN, DRURY JR	C1765	VA		1836	TN		071	1 1804	VA		SARAH/SALLY CATO	27602
JORDAN, JOHN ROBERT	1781			1844	NC	053		1 1808			NANCY MAYE	20335
JORDAN, ROBERT CALHOUN	1904	SC					011	1 1929	NC	009	ELOISE BROOKS	11145
JOUETT, MATTHEW, I	1722	VA		1779	NC	020		1	VA		SARAH	06005
JOUETT, MATTHEW, II	1775	NC	020	1830	TN			1	NC	092	MARTHA FLEMING	06005
JOYCE, JAMES P	1804			1876	KY		084	1 C1830 2	KY		LUCINDA HOPKINS MRS MATILDA JENKINS	60475
JOYCE, MARTIN VAN BUREN	1840	NC	084	1901	KY			1	KY		ANGELINA CONGER	60475
JOYNER, ABSOLEM	C1795	NC										60584
JOYNER, CORNELIUS	C1760	NC		C1845	?TN							60584
JOYNER, ELI	C1800	NC		C1865	TN			1			SARAH	60584
JOYNER, ELIZABETH	1797	NC		1873	TN			1			PERRY ODLE	60584
JOYNER, MACAJAH	1795	NC		1876	TN			1	?NC		MARTHA/PATSY	60584
JOYNER, SUSANNAH, MRS	1777			1842	NC	?051		1			NELSON JOYNER	60211
JOYNER, WILLIAM				1784	NC	069	?037					60584
JOYNER/JOINER, MATTHEW	1756			1832	NC	099	037	1			LYDA	20210
JUDD, AMOS	C1804	NC	104	1844	MO			1 1829	KY		LUCY CARTWRIGHT	60152
JUDD, NATHANIEL J JR	1779	NC	104	1852	MO			1 C1797	NC	104	DELPHIA SHEPHERD	60152
JUDD, NATHANIEL SR	C1755	?NC		C1825	NC	104		1			ELIZABETH OWENS	60152
JUDKINS, GRAY	C1770			1841	NC	009						02195
JUDKINS, ZACHARIAH G	C1800	NC	009	C1843	NC	009		1			HARRIETT	02195
JUSTICE, DAVID	1763	NC	073	1831	NC	022		1 1791	NC	022	SUSANNAH PYLES	04195
JUSTICE, ELI	C1795	NC	014	C1831	TN			1			MARY	60412

ANCESTOR INDEX	BIRTH	PL	CO	DEATH	PL	CO	LIVD	MARRIED	PL	CO	SPOUSE NAME	CODE
JUSTICE, ELIZABETH GRIFFIN	1799	NC	022	1863	NC	022		1 1826	NC	022	WILLIAM SEYMORE DUNCAN	04195
JUSTICE, JOHN				C1794	NC	022		1 C1760			ELIZABETH	04195
JUSTICE, JOHN	C1819	NC			TN							60412
JUSTICE, MARTIN	C1804	NC			TN			1			ISABELLA	60412
JUSTICE, REBECCA	1805	NC		1896	NC	055	049	1 1828	NC	049	JACOB SMITH	20220
JUSTUS, MOSES	1755	MD		1845	IL		065					60105

K

ANCESTOR INDEX	BIRTH	PL	CO	DEATH	PL	CO	LIVD	MARRIED	PL	CO	SPOUSE NAME	CODE
KEECH, WYRIOTT	1792				NC	009		1 1815	NC	009	PENELOPE BONNER HAMMOND	27573
KEEL, SAMUEL GRADY	1826	NC	009	1916	KY			1 1850 2 1866	KY KY		CYNTHIA RAY ANN ELIZABETH OWENS	02470
KEEL, WILLIAM KELLY	1823	NC	009	1877	VA			1 1847	VA		NANCY VANOVER	02470
KEELING, LEONARD	1795	NC	104	1852	IL			1 1835	IL		DEBORAH PERKINS	60421
KEEN, ZELLA	C1807	?NC		1868				1 C1820	?VA		LITTLETON WATSON	60304
KEGEL/CAGLE, GEORGE	C1745			C1825	NC	067		1			REBECCA	24165
KEITH, CORNELIUS	1743	VA		1820	SC		092	1			MARY LAFOON	27745
KELLAM, ELIZABETH GATES	1802	NC	084	1884	MN			1 1825	NC	084	JOHN BARNABAS DEARMIN	60281
KELLER, GEORGE N	C1830	NC	014	1864	VA			1 C1850			ELIZABETH TAYLOR	25098
KELLER, JAMES WILBURN	1819	NC		1903	NC	017		1 C1847			MARGARET EVELINE TURNER	25098
KELLER, JOHN WALTER	1876	NC	017	1962	NC	054		1 1895	NC	017	ALICE MATINA KELLER	25098
KELLER, MARTIN	C1750	PA		C1840	NC	014		1			ELIZABETH HARTEL	25098
KELLER, SOLOMON	1800	NC	014	1881	NC	017		2 1823	NC	014	SARAH WINKLER	25098
KELLER, W GRANVILLE	1852	NC	017		NC	017		1			ELIZA STAMEY	25098
KELLON PARTHENIA					OH			1 1779	NC		JOHN FEE	25097
KELLUM, NANCY	1780	VA		1851	TN		099	1 1801	NC	099	JONATHAN STEPHENSON	60337
KELLY, BURRELL/CHARLES ?	C1817	NC	041	C1880	NC	041		1 C1846	NC	041	DEBRA	25226
KELLY, CALEB	C1862	NC	041	C1926	NC	041		1 C1879	NC	041	MARY CAROLINE BUNCH	25226
KELTON, SAMUEL	C1791	NC	?085		TN			1 C1815	TN		ELIZABETH MANLEY	60443
KELTON, WILLIAM	1753			1813	TN		085	1	?NC	?085	ELIZABETH RAMSEY ?	60443
KEMP, BURRELL	C1760	?VA		1827	TN		044	1			NANCY	60195
KEMP, MURPHY	1800	NC		1879	IL			1 1821 2 1828 3 1848	TN TN IL		ANN ABIRD MARY/POLLY EMMA HOWELL MRS MARIAH JANE (LIEB) FUNK	17185
KEMP, MURPHY	1800	NC		1872	IL			1 1821 2 1828 3 1848	TN TN IL		ANN BAIRD MARY EMMA/POLLY HOWELL MRS MARIAH JANE (LIEB) FUNK	60195
KENDALL, JOHN	1762	PA		C1819	NC	081	046	1 C1781	NC	081	ANN	27429
KENDALL, JOHN	C1788	NC	?067		IA			1	NC	?067	ELIZABETH	60567

ANCESTOR INDEX	BIRTH	PL	CO	DEATH	PL	CO	LIVD	MARRIED	PL	CO	SPOUSE NAME	CODE
KENDALL, THOMAS		PA		1781	NC	046		1 1753	PA		MARGARET	27429
KENNEDAY, JOHN				1822			085	1			MARTHA	60567
KENNEDAY, RUBEN	1810	NC	085	1876	IL			1 C1828	NC	032	PRUDENCE WILBURN	60567
KENNEDY, DANIEL D	1812			1882	NC	032		1			BARBRA D	27700
KENNEDY, DAVID D	1856	NC	032	1934	NC	032		1			MARGARET LAMBETH	27700
KENNEDY, JULIUS HARRISON	1884	NC	032	1972	NC	032		1 1904	NC	032	NETTIE LUCINDA HUNT	27700
KENNEDY, MARCUS T C				1842	NC	065		1 1816	NC	065	PAMELA WISON	60108
								2			MARY HOUSTON	
KENT, HANNAH	1673	NC	077	C1711	NC	008		1 C1690			JOHN SMITHWICK	60057
								2 C1697			FARNEFOLD GREEN	
KENT, JOHN SR	C1715			1782	NC	085		1 C1740			MARY	23065
KENT, MIRIAM F	C1745			C1825	NC	085		1 1767	NC	085	PETER WHITAKER	23065
KERBY, EDMUND S	C1799	NC			TN			1 1832	NC	092	ELIZABETH C UPTEGROVE	27761
								2 C1848	TN		MARTHA A LEE ?	
KERNODLE, GEORGE	1784	NC	?046		NC			1	NC		SUSAN HUFFINES	27542
KERNODLE, GEORGE					NC			1			COBB	27542
KERR, ALEXANDER	1726	SCO		C1810	NC	020		1			MARY ELIZABETH RICE	27375
KERR, HUGH	C1780	?VA		C1855	TN			1 1802	NC	065	NANCY JANE BROWN	60366
KERSEY, ASHER	1807	NC	046	1902	IA			1 1829	IN		SUSANNAH MORGAN	60378
								2 1834	IN		EDITH SCHOOLEY	
								3 C1859	IA		SUSANNAH TALBERT	
KETCHUM, HUGH	1762	NC	073	1832	AL		104					60588
KETCHUM, JACOB				1778	NC	104						60513
KETCHUM, JONATHAN	C1780					006		1			SARAH	60513
KETNER, NATHANIEL	C1810			1879	NC	038		1			SARAH CONRAD ?	60467
KEY, CALVIN DOMAS	1828	NC	068	1899	TX			1 1854	AL		MARY ELIZABETH THOMAS	27476
KEY, ELEANOR	1833	NC	068	1932	NC	068		1			ISAAC WILLIAMSON	27476
KEY, JAMES							?068	1			SABEILLA BRITT	27476
KEY, MARTIN CRAWFORD	1830	NC	068		TX			1			MILLY M HAM	27476
KEY, PLEASANT TROY	1826	NC	068	1898	NC	082		1			MARY DUNLAP	27476
KEY, RILAND	1816	NC	068					1			TEMPERANCE KENNEDY	27476
KEY, SAMUEL	1840	NC	068	1871	TX							27476
KEY, THOMAS	1819	NC	068	C1865	TX			1			MARTHA HUSSEY	27476
KICKER, JARRELL	C1774	NC	100		GA			1 1793	NC	100	DELILA CAPPS	60438
								2	GA		TURNER	
KICKER, JOHN				C1795	NC	100	044	1			MARY	60438
KICKER, RICHARD							010					60438
KIGHT, EZEKIEL SR	1788	NC	?079	1841	IN			1 1809	KY		REBECCA MURPHY	27760
KILBY ANDREW FRANKLIN	1886	NC	104	1977	NC	104		1 1922	NC	104	BERNICE GRACE LOMAX	60001
KILBY JOHN	C1791	NC	104	C1850	NC	104		1	NC	104	NANCY A WALL ?	60001

ANCESTOR INDEX	BIRTH	PL	CO	DEATH	PL	CO	LIVD	MARRIED	PL	CO	SPOUSE NAME	CODE
KILBY JOHN JACKSON	1842	NC	104	1925	NC	104		1 C1866	NC	104	MARTHA JANE MCNEIL	60001
KILBY JOHN WESLEY	C1817	NC	104		NC	104		1 1839	NC	104	MARTHA WILCOXSON	60001
								2		NC	104 DELIAH BUMGARNER	
KILBY WILLIAM SR		VA		C1815	NC	104		1			FRANCES EDDINS	60001
KILGORE, ROBERT JR							073	1			WINNEY	03070
KILGORE, ROBERT SR							020					03070
KILGORE, THOMAS	C1715			1823	TN		073	1			LYDIA	60138
KILGORE, THOMAS JR					NC	?073	?020					03070
KILGORE, THOMAS JR	C1759	NC	073	C1857	AR		073	1 1786	NC	020	PHEBE LEA	60138
KILGORE, THOMAS SR	C1715			1823	TN		073	1			LYDIA	03070
KILLEBREW, HINCHEA	C1758			C1820	NC	057		1 C1780			MARY	13264
KILLEBREW, LEVINA	1799	NC	057	1882	NC	057		1 C1820	NC	057	JOHN HEATH	13264
KILLIAN, ANDREAS/ANDREW	C1702	GER		1788	NC	060		1			MARY	27441
KILLIAN, MARY/POLLY	1800	NC	060	1877	NC	021		1 1820	NC	060	JOHN DANIEL HERMAN	27441
KILLIAN, SAMUEL	C1762	NC	065	1813	NC	060		1 1784	NC	060	BARBARA HAGER	27441
KILLIAN/KILIAN, ANDREAS/ANDREW	1702	GER		1788	NC	060		2			MARY CLINE	60173
KILLIAN/KILIAN, DANIEL	C1758	NC	085	C1833				2 C1794			MARGARET WATTS	60173
KILLIAN/KILIAN, DANIEL WILKINSON	1834	NC	014	1895	TX			1 1861	NC	025	MARTHA ANN MCCLURE	60173
KILLIAN/KILIAN, GEORGE	1802	NC	014	1880	SC			1 1830	?NC		POLLY JOHNSON	60173
KILLION, GOODWIN	1790	NC	060	1860	TX			1 1808	NC	060	JANE SHARP	60497
KIMBALL, BARTHOLOMEW				C1794	NC	044		1			AGNES GILLIAM	60594
KIMBALL, MARY WOODMAN	1808	NH		1873	CA		010	1 1829	NH		SHERMAN DRIGGS	60069
								2 1838	TX		COL ELISHA RHODES	
KIMBRELL, HARRIS	C1778			1825	NC	067	085	1			DORCAS WOOD LEE	60507
KIMBRELL, JAMES T	C1817	NC		1882	MS		067	1 1834	SC			60507
								2 1843	GA		ELIZABETH E FORRESTER	
KIMBRO/KIMBROUGH, ELIJAH	1799	NC		1878	KY			1			MILDRED CROWDER	11070
KIMBRO/KIMBROUGH, ELIJAH GREEN	1829	NC		1910	KY			1		KY	MARTHA JANE CLARK	11070
KIMBRO/KIMBROUGH, THOMAS								1 1792	NC	020	ELIZABETH GRAVES	11070
KIMBROUGH, BUCKLEY/BERKELEY							?024					27356
KIMBROUGH, JEREMIAH	1778	NC	085	1850	OH			1 C1801	NC	?085	SARAH MENDENHALL	27429
KIMBROUGH/KIMBRO, JOHN	1745	NC	005	1799	GA			1			ANN LEGRAND	27280
KIME, HENRY	1759	NC	046	1833	IL			1 C1780	?PA		HANNAH RUDOLPH	60451
KIME, PHILIP	C1730	?PA		C1806	NC	046		1 C1753	NC		MRS PEGGY REITZEL	60451
KIMSEY/KIMZEY, BENJAMIN	C1725	SCO		1807	NC	014	013	1	SCO		AGNES LANE	60149
KIMSEY/KIMZEY, BENJAMIN	C1745	VA			NC	013		1	VA		MARGARET GREGG	60149
KIMSEY/KIMZEY, THOMAS M	1802	NC	013	1864	GA			1	NC		EMMILINE STOVER	60149
KING, ANDERSON	1820	NC	069		NC	046		1 1840	NC	069	MASON DICKENS	60313

ANCESTOR INDEX	BIRTH	PL	CO	DEATH	PL	CO	LIVD	MARRIED	PL	CO	SPOUSE NAME	CODE
KING, ANDERSON	C1795	NC					069	1 1818	NC	047	POLLY COLEY	60313
KING, ANDREW JACKSON							097	1			ELIZA M GODFREY	11100
KING, BENJAMIN	1777			1841	NC	050		1 C1799			REBECCA SHIPMAN	60366
KING, CALVIN K	1853	NC	046	1935	IN			1 1874	IN		EMILY POE	60313
KING, GILLY	C1816	NC	099	C1870	NC	099		1 1837	NC	099	JOHN JAMES KING	13264
KING, HARMON		?SC			NC	097	065					11100
KING, HARTWELL	1785	NC	099	1841	AL			1 1805	?NC		BURCHET CURTIS	60483
KING, HILLSMAN	C1780	NC	099	1867	NC	099		1 1811	NC	099	ALLEY MOORE	13264
KING, JAMES	1780	VA		1870	NC	078		1	NC	078	MARGARET ALEXSON	60500
KING, JAMES M	C1823	NC		C1875	?GA			1 1847 2 1863	GA GA		JENNET P/FANNIE HADEN MARY ANN TEMPLES	27346
KING, JOHN	C1735	?NC		1803	NC	099						13264
KING, JOHN JAMES	C1815	NC	099	C1865	?NC	?099		1 1837	NC	099	GILLY KING	13264
KING, JOHN W	1853	NC	099	1916	NC	099		1 1870	NC	099	SUSAN CATHERINE COOK	13264
KING, NATHANIEL		NC	?099		AR			1 C1823	NC	?099	ELIZABETH GREEN	27291
KING, RICHARD	1752	VA		1830	AL		099	1 2 1784			 EDITH JONES	60483
KING, RIGDON	C1770	NC	?028				?057	1 C1798	NC		MARY NEWCOMB	60082
KING, SOLOMON		VA		C1794	NC	041		1 2 C1752			AMY ABIGAIL LEE	01006
KING, VINCENT/VINSON	C1755	?NC		1836	NC	099		1 1784	NC	099	PEGGY BAYLA/BAILEY	13264
KING, WILLIAM	1805				NC	078		1 1830	NC	078	FRANCES C HOLLOWAY	60500
KIRK, ELI	1807	NC		1867				1 1827			MARY MELONEY/MALONEY	60548
KIRK, ELIJAH	1757	NC		1864	NC							60548
KIRK, JAMES		NC		1799	SC			1			SARAH	17240
KIRK, LEWIS				1808	NC	073	047	1			SARAH	08070
KIRK, REBECCA	1770	NC	046	1816				1 1784	NC	073	ARCHIBALD CAMPBELL	08070
KIRKPATRICK, LAIRD	C1798	NC	065	C1872	AL		016	1 1823 2 C1838	NC ?AL	?016	MARY SELLARS MCCURDY NANCY CALLEN	60360
KIRKSEY, CHRISTOPHER	C1734			1818	SC		022	1	?NC		PARTHENIA	60043
KIRKSEY, JEHU	1776	?NC		1846	AL		?022	1 1808	?SC		ELEANOR CROWE FOSTER	60043
KISER, ELIZA ALBERTHA	C1842	NC	026	1917	NC	086		1 1864	NC	086	THOMAS F PHILBECK	02412
KISER, PETER	C1808	NC	?060	C1878	NC	026		1 C1829	NC	?060	MALINDA	02412
KITTRELL, GEORGE		NC	044									02355
KITTRELL, JOHN	C1747	NC	010	C1800	NC	044		1 1772	NC	044	ELIZABETH SMITH	02355
KITTRELL, JOHN	C1776	NC	044	C1845	TN			1 1801	NC	044	ROSEY BRYANT/BRIANT	02355
KITTRELL, PLEASANT W	1783	NC	044	1854	TN			1 1812	NC	044	NANCY ATKINS	02355
KITTRELL, SAMUEL J	C1780	NC	044	C1850	TN			1 1805	NC		ELIZABETH A ATKINS	02355
KITTRELL, WILEY JR	C1774	NC	044									02355

ANCESTOR INDEX	BIRTH	PL	CO	DEATH	PL	CO	LIVD	MARRIED	PL	CO	SPOUSE NAME	CODE
KLAFTER, TIBOR/THEODORE	1921	HUN		1972	NC	065		1 1948	NY		HARRIETT ZEIF KLAFTER	60205
KNIGHT, ABLE	C1750	PA			NC	046	085	1	VA		RACHAEL	60214
KNIGHT, AMANDA/MANDY MARTHA?	C1819	VA			NC		090	1			GEORGE WASHINGTON ANDREW/ANDREWS	60469
KNIGHT, GEORGE WILLIAM	1844	VA		1920	NC	038	090	1 1868	NC	090	NANCY E JANE MARTIN	60469
KNIGHT, HULDAH ANN	1833	NC	020	1878	WA			1 1850	MO		HARBERT CORNELIUS RINGO	60026
KNIGHT, JOSEPH	C1772	NC		C1852	MO			1 1801	NC	020	JUDITH DAMERON	60026
KNIGHT, JOSEPH DAMERON	1811	NC	020	1901	WA			1 1830	NC	020	MAGARA CLEMSON/CLEMPSON	60026
								2 C1863	?MO		MRS NANCY (SINK) POWELL	
KNIGHT, JOSIAH TAYLOR	1846	VA		1922	NC	090		1 1866	NC	090	EMILY JANE BROWN	60469
KNIGHT, MIRTILLO/MERTILLA	1813	VA		1875	NC	090		1 1843	NC	090	NANCY TAYLOR	60469
KNIGHT, RACHAEL	1774	NC	046	1845	IN			1 1797	NC	046	JAMES MEREDITH	60214
KNIGHT, THOMAS	1742	VA			NC	046	085	1 1770	NC	085	ELIZABETH PITTS	60214
KNIGHT, WILLIAM WOODSON	C1805	NC	020	1860	MO			1 1836	NC	020	SUSAN PAYNE HARRISON	60026
KNOTT, CALEB	1795	NC	044	1855	NC	044		1 1823	NC	044	ELIZABETH TUCKER	03125
KNOTT, DAVID		?VA		1795	NC	044		1			CATHERINE	17070
KNOTT, ELIZABETH FRANCIS	1850	NC	044	1897	NC	044		1 1873	NC	044	WILLIAM JASPER DEAN	03125
KNOTT, HENRY E	C1828	NC			MO			1 1849	TN		CAMILLA MARTIN	25158
KNOTT, JAMES				1781	NC	044		1			MARY HOLIDAY	03125
KNOTT, JAMES	1762	NC	044	1820	NC	044		1 1784	NC	044	SALLIE BRASFIELD	03125
KNOTT, JAMES		?VA		C1782	NC	044		1			MARY	17070
KNOTT, JOHN	1740			1798	NC	044		1			MISS/MRS FORSYTH	03125
KNOTT, MILDRED ANN	1828	NC	044	1870	NC	044		1 1848	NC	044	FIELDING R KNOTT	03125
KNOTT, RISDON	1797	NC	044	1866	NC	044		1 1827	NC	044	MARY CURRIN	03125
KNOTT, SAMUEL WAITE	1855	NC	044	1933	NC	044		1 1879	NC	044	BETTIE F BUCHANAN	03125
KOONCE, ANGUS GARMAN				C1875			029	1 1839	NC	057	ANNIE FOSTER	60394
								2 1853			SARAH MITCHELL	
KOONCE, BERTHA	1910	NC	029					1 1935	FL	087	WESLEY S GUYNUP	60394
KOONCE, EDGAR CORNELIUS	C1887	NC	087	1965	FL			1 1909	NC	029	SALLY DEES	60394
KOONCE, GEORGE JR		NC	057	1809								60394
KOONCE, JOHN CICERO	1844	NC	029	1921	NC	029		1 1870	NC	029	SARAH MARGARET YOUNG	60394
								2			SUSAN HALL	
KOONTZ, CHARLES ALEXANDER	1864	NC	032	1951	NC	032		1			BESSIE LEIGH HEITMAN	11145
KOONTZ, HOYLE K	C1896	NC	032					1 1926	NC	033	EDRIE BROWN HOWARD	11145
KORNEGAY, ISAAC								1 1831	NC	035	MRS ESTHER (ALDRIDGE) WOOTEN	60230
KORNEGAY, JOHN B	1797	NC	035	1868	MS		?087	1 C1819				60474
								2 C1833	?AL		ANNIE	
								3 C1849	?AL		A A	
KORNEGAY, JOSEPH	C1774	?NC	?035	C1828	?NC	?035	?087	1 C1796			NANCY BECK	60474
KRAUSE, MARIA MARGARETHE	1775	NC	?092	C1855	IN		090	1			CHARLES HOLDER	17075
KRAUSE, WENDEL/WENDELL	1739	PA		1803	NC	092	006					17075

ANCESTOR INDEX	BIRTH	PL	CO	DEATH	PL	CO	LIVD	MARRIED	PL	CO	SPOUSE NAME	CODE
KUYKENDALL, ADAM	C1756	NC	005		AR		065	1			MARGARET HARDIN	60565
KUYKENDALL, MATHEW	1758	NC	005	1845	KY		065	1			JEAN HARDIN	60565
KUYKENDALL/KIRKENDALL, ABRAHAM	C1772	NC	?094	1870	GA			1 C1798	NC	013	ELIZABETH VANZANT	60582
KUYKENDALL/KIRKENDALL, ALFRED	1836	NC	013	C1867				1 1850	NC	050	KATHERINE COUCH/CAPPS	60582
KUYKENDALL/KIRKENDALL, JACOBUS/ JAMES	1721	NY		C1780	NC	086		1 C1751	NY		REBECCA/NANCY	60582
KUYKENDALL/KIRKENDALL, JOSEPH	1804	NC	013		NC	050		1 1823 2 1841	NC NC	013 050	RUTH GUICE SARAH CAPPS	60582
KUYKENDALL/KIRKENDALL, LOUISE NAOMIE	1860	NC	050	1941	NC	050		1 1880	NC	050	FERNANDO HAYNES NORMAN	60582

L

ANCESTOR INDEX	BIRTH	PL	CO	DEATH	PL	CO	LIVD	MARRIED	PL	CO	SPOUSE NAME	CODE
LACKEY, JOHN SAMUEL	1825	NC	060	1898	IA			1 1847			MRS ANNA C (BINGHAM) WILSON	12005
LACKEY, SAMUEL	1796	NC	060	1847	NC	026		1			SARAH CLINE	12005
LACY, PHILEMON		NC	073	1849	GA		022					12125
LACY/LACEY, LUCY	C1765	VA		C1852	MO		081	1 1781	NC	022	JOSEPH H MOUTRAY	60259
LACY/LACEY, PHILEMON	1725			1808	NC	?022		1			ANN/ANNE	60259
LADD, ELIZABETH	1762	VA		1841	IN			1 1781	NC	071	WILLIAM PATTERSON	60087
LADD, GERRARD	C1732	VA			?NC		071	1 C1759	VA		SARAH	60087
LAIRD, DAVID	C1790	VA		1837	IL		061	1 C1815	NC	?049	ANN TUMBLESON	60323
LAIRD, JOSEPH	1816	NC		1869	IL			1			ELIZA	60323
LAM/LAMB, ALVA ANDERSON	1806	NC	092	1856	MO			1 C1826	NC		JANE GRAHAM/GRIMES	60300
LAMAR, JAMES	1724	MD		C1787	GA		081	1	MD		VERLINDA OSBORN	12125
LAMAR, KEZIAH	1754	MD		1838	NC	081		1 1772	NC	081	ALEXANDER SMITH	12125
LAMB, ABNER	1786			1847	NC	018		1 1808			DINAH MCPHERSON	60307
LAMB, ESTHER				1857	NC	046		1 1788	?NC	?046	DAVID HODSON	08265
LAMB, LUKE	1734	?CT		1825	NC	018	030	1			BETSEY WILLIAMS	60307
LAMB, MARY	1826	NC	018	1905	NC	018		1 1847 2 1854	NC NC	018 018	JOSEPH BELL MARK R GREGORY	60307
LAMB, ROBERT												08265
LAMBERT, ABNER	1802	NC		1887	TN			1 C1822			RUTHA	27546
LAMBERT, ANDREW JACKSON ?	C1817			C1885	SC		027	1			PRUDENCE PIERCE	60528
LAMBERT, BENJAMIN	C1798			C1865	SC		027					60528
LAMBERT, THOMAS JR	1820	NC	056	1888	NC	089	049	1 1802	NC	099	NANCY PARTIN	24165
LAMBERT, THOMAS SR					NC	056		1			LOUISE LONG	24165
LAMKIN/LAMBKIN, GEORGE							094					60295
LAMKIN/LAMBKIN, SAMPSON							086					60295

ANCESTOR INDEX	BIRTH	PL	CO	DEATH	PL	CO	LIVD	MARRIED	PL	CO	SPOUSE NAME	CODE
LAMM, ELIAS W	C1825	NC	103	1891	NC	105		1 1853	NC	069	MARTHA JOHNSTON	02168
LAMM, SOLOMON	1824	NC	103	1891	NC	105		1			LOUISA TOMLINSON	02168
LAMM, STEPHEN	C1790	NC	103	1861	NC	105						02168
LAMM, WILEY WEDLE	C1863	NC	?105	1928	NC	056		1 1883 2 1910	NC NC	105 056	TEMPIE ANN E HAYNES KATIE BAILEY	03315
LAMM, WILLIE W	C1830	NC			NC			1 1855	NC	105	MRS CHRISTIAN (WILLIAMSON) HARRISON	03315
LAMM/LAMB, D/DOCK K	1876	NC	105	1910	NC	105		1 1897	NC	105	ANNIE WRIGHT EATMAN	03250
LAMM/LAMB, NATHAN	C1812	?NC			?NC	?105	069	1			LURANY/LANEY ROSE ?	03250
LAMM/LAMB, THOMAS RUFFIN	1840	NC	069	1915	NC	105	?103	1 1866 2	NC	105	NANCY ANN THORN/THORNE CATHERINE THORN/THORNE	03250
LANCASTER, LAURENCE		?VA		C1792	NC	100						60083
LANCASTER, SAMUEL		?NC			SC							60083
LANCASTER, WILLIAM		NC	?100		TN							60083
LAND, JAMES MADISON	1815			1871	NC	074		1			ANN ELIZABETH BAXTER	60030
LAND, JEREMIAH		VA		1836	NC	030		1 1793	VA		ELIZABETH SCURR	60030
LANE, BENJAMIN		?VA					037	1			ANN DREW	60244
LANE, ELIZABETH	C1720	MD			NC		028	1 C1740 2	MD		WILLIAM PROBART MR COLLIER ?	12040
LANE, JOSEPH JR	1710	?VA		1777	NC	047		1 1730			PATIENCE MCKINNE	07078
LANE, JOSEPH SR	1665	VA		1758	NC	037		1			JULIAN	07078
LANE, JOSEPH, III	C1730	NC			AL			1	NC		FEREBEE HUNTER	07078
LANE, MARTHA	1789	NC		1864	MS			1	NC		HARDY BURT	07078
LANE, SUSAN A	C1855	NC		1900	OK			1 1878	TX		EDMUND H DIDLAKE	60150
LANE, WILLIAM				1788	NC	047		1			ELIZABETH	60244
LANGFORD/LANGKFORD, BENJAMIN D	C1795	NC	100	1854	KY			2 1843	KY		MRS MARY ANN ELIZA CHERRY OTEY	20245
LANGLEY, JOHN	C1780	NC		1850	GA			1			MARY	03041
LANGLEY, THOMAS				1802	NC	020		1			MARY WILEY	03041
LANGSTON, FRANCES/POLLY	C1755	?NC		1820	SC			1 C1775			JOHN SINGLETON	27303
LANGSTON, LYDIA		?VA		C1791	NC	069		1 C1739			THOMAS WOODWARD/WOODARD SR	27303
LANIER, BENJAMIN	1786	NC		1854	FL			1 1805	GA		SARA PRIDGEN	60384
LANIER, BIRD THOMAS	1703	VA					035	1 1727	VA		MARY MADISON	60384
LANIER, CECELIA	1792	NC	009	1857	NC	009		1 1811	NC	009	ALDERSON ELLISON HARVEY	02195
LANIER, HOSEA G	C1815	?NC			NC			1 C1839	?NC		ANN/ANNIE RAINER/RAYNOR	08219
LANIER, JESSE	1757	NC	035	C1802	NC	035		1 1779	NC	035	SARAH WHALEY	13264
LANIER, JOHN	C1750	NC	096	C1794	NC	009		1 1775	NC	009	FANNY BARROW	02195
LANIER, LEMUEL	1707	VA		C1770	GA		035	1 1732	VA		HANNAH PETERS	13264
LANIER, LEMUEL	1729	VA		1770	NC	035	024	1 1752	NC		SARA HARDY	60384
LANIER, LEWIS	1753	NC		1792	GA			1	NC	035	MARGARET	60384

ANCESTOR INDEX	BIRTH	PL	CO	DEATH	PL	CO	LIVD	MARRIED	PL	CO	SPOUSE NAME	CODE
LANIER, REBECCA M	1825	NC	035		NC	035		1 1843	NC	035	ISAAC POWELL	13264
LANIER, THOMAS	1733	VA		1787	NC	035		1 C1754	NC	035	HERRING	13264
LANIER, THOMAS	1780	NC	035	C1855	NC	035		1 C1816	NC	035	THEANA HERRING	13264
LANNING, JOHN J	1814	NC	013	1879	GA			1			ANNA FINNEY	06085
LAPSLEY/LAPSLIE, THOMAS SR	1725			1781	NC	073		1	?PA		CHARITY ANDERSON	60151
LASLEY, IVY WESLEY	1836	NC	090	1920	NC	046		1 1856	NC	090	ELIZABETH TUTTLE	20448
								2 1889	NC		CALLIE HIGHFILL	
LASLEY, JOSEPH	1778	VA		1844	NC	090		1 1813	NC	090	NANCY GENTRY	20448
LASSITER, ELVA	C1800	NC	?041	C1865	GA			1 1824	NC	041	THOMAS P MORGAN	27346
LATTA, THOMAS B/BENTON	1782	NC	073	1848	KY			1 1803	NC	073	MARY ANN MOORE	07095
LAU/LOW, BARBARA	1785			1843	IN			1 C1802	NC	?046	JOHN MATTHEW CORTNER	60262
LAVENDER, WILLIAM	C1710				NC	028		1 C1730	NC	028	RACHEL ROMAN	12040
LAWRENCE, MARY		NC	?099				022	1 1819	NC	099	JACOB WOMBLE	27281
LAXTON, JAMES		?NC	?009	C1830	TN							60083
LAY, DAVID	C1735	ENG		C1815	?NC	020		1			SUSANNAH GIBSON ?	60561
LEA, PHEBE	C1755	NC	020		TN		?073	1 1786	NC	020	THOMAS KILGORE JR	60138
LEACH, DAVID	1801	NC	085	1878	IL			1 1822	NC	085	CATHERINE NAIL	27553
								2 C1838	IN			
								3 C1845	?IN		HANNAH STEELE	
LEACH, ZADOCK				C1845	NC	033		1 1794	NC	085	NANCY LOVELACE	27553
LEARY, CORNELIUS				1692	NC	077		1 1679	NC		MARY BENTLEY	60497
LEARY, ELIZABETH WORLEY		NC	096					1 1794	NC	096	HENRY SWANNER	60497
LEARY, JOSHUA		NC										60497
LEARY, RICHARD	1680	NC	077	1738	NC	096		1 1709	NC	077	SARAH LONG	60497
LEARY, THOMAS	1712	NC	077	C1780	NC	096		1	NC		ELIZABETH WORLEY	60497
LEATHERWOOD, ABEL JACKSON	1815	NC	049	1904		023		1 1840	TN		ELVIRA MCNABB	23065
LEATHERWOOD, EDWARD	C1750			C1809	NC	049	014	1 C1777	VA		SARAH/SALLY HUNT	23065
LEATHERWOOD, FELIX HARRISON	1841	NC	049	1912	NC	013	055	1 1871	TN		ANNE LAVINIA CARTER	23065
LEATHERWOOD, JOHN	1779	NC	014	1846	NC	049		1 C1807	NC	014	SARAH BURNS	23065
LEDBETTER, GEORGE, CAPT	C1740	VA			?SC		086	1 C1772	VA		ELIZABETH WALTON	12050
LEDBETTER, ISAAC	1796	NC	086	1837	NC	013		1 1817	NC	013	SALLY/SARAH BRADLEY	60582
LEDBETTER, RICHARD ISAAC	1877	NC	093	1939	SC			1 1897	NC	013	ESTHER HARRIET JONES	60582
LEDBETTER, RICHARD, III	C1738	NC	070	1841	GA			1 1768	NC	094	NANCY ANN JOHNSON	60582
LEDBETTER, SION/SIOMON B	1836	NC	013	1898	NC	093		1 1862	NC	093	MARGARET PINNER	60582
LEDFORD, JOHN		NC	?085		NC	032		1	?085		MARY	20350
LEDFORD, MARY	1797	NC	085					1	NC	?085	JOSEPH MYERS	20350
LEE, BATT				1834	NC	087		1			KEZIA HANDLEY	21115
LEE, BENONI	C1784	NC	?094	1840	IL			1 1804	KY		PATIENCE WALKER	14045
LEE, DAVID JR	1820	NC	051	1882	NC	010		1 C1851			NANCY VALENTINE	12068

ANCESTOR INDEX	BIRTH	PL	CO	DEATH	PL	CO	LIVD	MARRIED	PL	CO	SPOUSE NAME	CODE
LEE, DAVID SR	C1780	NC	051	1838				1			CATHERINE HUGHES	12068
LEE, ELIJAH	1793	NC	083	1876	MS			1 C1815 2 1830	NC MS		MARTHA ROWLAND/ROLLINS RACHEL RODGERS/ROGERS	60392
LEE, ELIZABETH	1791	MD		1857	MO		010	1 1807	NC	084	HENRY THOMPSON	60422
LEE, ISAAC ALFRED	1810	NC		1892	TX			1 2 1865	TX		VIANNIE MRS ELIZABETH T BOIL	60410
LEE, JACOB C SR	1801	NC		1878	TX			1 1833	MS		NANCEY BLAKELEY	60189
LEE, JAMES	1790	NC	103	1852	GA			1 C1820	GA		CINDERELLA SELLARS	60164
LEE, JAMES JR	C1725	NC	051	C1780								12068
LEE, JAMES SR	C1675			C1732	NC	010		1			SARAH	12068
LEE, JESSE	C1740	NC	010	1816	NC	083		1 C1755	NC		MIRIAM BAGGETT	60542
LEE, JESSE, JR	1740	NC	011	1831	NC	087		1 C1770	NC		SUSANNAH JOHNSON	60392
LEE, JESSE, SR		?VA		1816	NC	083		1			MIRIAM BAGGETT	60392
LEE, JOAB	1789			1858	NC	?056		1 1830			BETHENEA BLACKMAN	27734
LEE, JOEL	1820	NC	056					1			MELISSA LINDSEY	60095
LEE, JOHN	C1755	NC		1839	GA		103	1	NC			60164
LEE, JOHN	1678	VA		C1739	NC	010						60542
LEE, JOSEPH A	1830	NC			NC	?056	?103	1 2	NC NC		ELIZABETH DENNING ELIZABETH SINGLETON	27734
LEE, JOSEPH HENRY	1817	NC	060	1908	NC	040		1			SARAH CLANTON	60189
LEE, JOSHUA	C1700	VA		1774	NC	037		1 C1720			MARY	60542
LEE, JOSHUA	C1720	NC	008	C1800	NC	083		1 C1740	NC		MARY	60542
LEE, KEZIAH	C1765	NC	037	C1845	MS			1 C1800	NC	083	WILLIS LOE	60542
LEE, LAOMA	1878			1938	NC	087		1 1900			ANNIE ELIZABETH ATKINS	27734
LEE, LEMON HANDLEY	1810	NC	?087	1885	NC	087		1 1828	NC	087	LOVY JERNIGAN	21115
LEE, PATIENCE		NC			TN			1	NC	067	WILLIAM W POPLIN	60204
LEE, PLEASANT M	1825	NC			TX			1 1853	TX		JUSTINIA AUGUSTA NOLTE/NULTY	60547
LEE, RICHARD	C1776	NC	?094	C1835	IL							14045
LEE, SAMUEL		NC					083	1 2 3			SALLY LYNN BUNN SARAH SHAY PATRICIA OVERSTREET WEST	60189
LEE, STEPHEN	C1775	NC	011	C1835	MS			1 2	NC		MARY COX ? SARAH/SALLY	60392
LEE, WILLIAM BRITTON	1860	NC	010	1936	NC	010		1 1881	NC	010	MARY ELIZABETH HOBBS	12068
LEE, WILLIS	C1790						056	1			MARY LINDSEY	60095
LEE, WILLOUGHBY		MD		1824	NC	084	010	1			FANNY CRYER	60422
LEE, ZINA	C1787	NC		C1861	SC			1 C1804			THOMAS DAVIS	27554
LEEPER, ELISABETH							060	1 1792			ROBERT PATRICK	60161
LEGGETT, DAVID				1822	NC	063		1			PATIENCE	60497
LEGGETT, DEBE	C1800	NC						1			THOMAS SWANNER	60497

ANCESTOR INDEX	BIRTH	PL	CO	DEATH	PL	CO	LIVD	MARRIED	PL	CO	SPOUSE NAME	CODE
LEGGETT, ELIZABETH	C1798	NC		C1850	AL			1 C1820	NC		JESSE L SWANNER	60497
LEGGETT, JAMES SR				1785	NC	063		1			MARY	60497
LEGUIN/LEGWIN, LOTT M	1800	NC		1885	GA			1 1821	GA		MARY MCKEE	27366
LEGUIN/LEGWIN, MATTHEW	C1760	?VA		1798	NC	070		1 C1780			SARAH	27366
LEGUIN/LEGWIN, SAMUEL	C1782	?VA		C1845	GA			1	NC			27366
LEIGH, THOMAS				1822	NC	096		1 1794			ROSANAH SPRUILL	20335
LEIGH, WHITMILL W	1806	NC	077	1876	IL			1 1831	TN		DENIAH DODSON	06145
LEINBACH, JOHANNES JR	1712	GER		1766	NC	085		1 1735			ANNA CATHERINE RIEHM	10090
LEINBACH, JOSEPH	1769	NC	085	1841	NC			1			ANNE ELIZABETH HOLDER	10090
LEINBACH, LEWIS LUDWIG	1743	PA		1800	NC	090		1 1766	NC	085	ANNA BARBARA LAUER	10090
LEMAY, CORINNA PRISCILLA	1836	NC	099	1882	NC	099		1 1857	NC	099	JOSEPH DEMPSEY POWELL	05035
LEMAY, LOUIS	C1770	VA		1810	NC	044		1 1791	NC	044	LUCY PEACE	05035
LEMAY, THOMAS JEFFERSON	1802	NC	044	1863	NC	099	056	1 1828	NC	039	ELIZA ANN PRISCILLA SLEDGE	05035
LEMONS, JANE	1805	NC	060	1890	OR			1 1822	AR		MICHAEL RANDLEMAN	27657
LEMONS, JASON	1808	NC	?060	1892	MO			1 1835	IL		MARY RANDLEMAN	27657
LEMONS, MARIBAH	C1813	NC	?060	1887	MO			1 1832	IL		MARTIN CHRISTOPHER RANDLEMAN	27657
LENNON, DENNIS	C1742	NC	011	1805	NC	011		1			EXPERIENCE	12090
LENNON, JOHN	C1700	?VA		C1757	NC	011		1			ANN MOORE	12090
LEONARD, HENRY	C1740			C1772	NC	012	070	1			HANNAH	13052
LEONARD, JOHN	1739	IRE			NC	046		1			ABIGAIL MOODY	20333
LEONARD, JOSEPH	1765	PA		1853	NC	046		1 1787	NC	046	PHOEBE MACY	20333
LEROY, LEWIS	C1765	FWI		C1833	NC	009		1 C1797	NC	009	HELEN PALMER	12040
LEROY, MARY LOUISA	C1775	FWI		1818	NC	009	053	1 1802	NC	009	WILLIAM LANE LAVENDER	12040
LEWELLING/LLEWELLING, CHLOE		VA		1794	NC	037	063	1 C1761			THOMAS GRIMES	19130
LEWIN, JANE/JENNET	C1774	NC			KY		060	1 1791	NC	065	SOLOMON STANSBURY	60146
LEWIS, AARON L	C1815	NC		C1883	TN			1			AMA	60584
LEWIS, ASA	1792	VA		C1872	NC	106		1 1822	NC	092	BETSY SHINN	03015
LEWIS, GILTHA	C1782	NC			?TN							60584
LEWIS, GWEN	C1725			C1798	NC	073		1			ABRAHAM MASSEY	08200
LEWIS, JAMES	1779	?NC					104	1			SARAH COUCH	60432
LEWIS, JAMES GEORGE	1829	NC	047	1879	NC	009		1 1851	NC	037	CASSANDRA MARTIN JONES	27378
LEWIS, JANE	1796	NC	081	1863	CA			1 1820	IN		TILGHMAN WARFIELD CLARKE	60362
LEWIS, JANE MERIWETHER	1776	NC	044	1843	TN			1 1799	NC	044	SWEPSON SIMS	23015
LEWIS, JEREMIAH		?VA		C1795	NC	005	044	1			SARAH	27303
LEWIS, JESSE	1796	NC		1890	TN			1 1815	TN		MARY THOMPSON	60321
LEWIS, JOHN	1720	VA		1802	NC	081		1 1746	VA		PRISCILLA BROOKS	60362
LEWIS, JOSIAH	1728	NC	028	C1808	NC	011	070	1 1750	NC	070	ANN MULLINGTON	12090

ANCESTOR INDEX	BIRTH	PL	CO	DEATH	PL	CO	LIVD	MARRIED	PL	CO	SPOUSE NAME	CODE
LEWIS, LOTTIE	C1775	NC			?TN							60584
LEWIS, MARTHA ANN	1862	NC	009	1921	NC	009		1 1879	NC	009	JAMES HENRY HODGES	27378
								2 1885	NC	009	WILLIAM JAMES RHODES	
LEWIS, MATTHEW JR	C1812	NC		C1865	?TN			1			JOISA A	60584
LEWIS, MATTHEW SR	C1775	NC		C1845	TN		?099					60584
LEWIS, RICHARD				C1719	NC	024		1			ELIZABETH	12090
LEWIS, RICHARD	1759	NC	073	1827	IN		081	1 C1783			LYDIA FIELD	60362
LEWIS, ROBERT	C1738	VA		1780	NC	044		1 1760	VA		FRANCES LEWIS	23015
LEWIS, STARK	C1835	NC						1			M J	60584
LEWIS, WILLERFORD W	1818	NC						1	NC		SARAH LEWIS	60486
LEWIS, WILLIAM	1777	NC		1840	GA		104	1 C1802			ANN	03065
LEWIS, WILLIAM				C1731	NC	?009		1			MARY	12090
LEWIS, WILLIAM	C1740	NC	028	C1813	NC	?103		1	NC	028	MOURNING HERRING	27292
LEWIS, WILLIAM	C1775	VA			?TN			1 1794	NC	090	CHARITY CLAYTON	60321
LEWIS, WILLIAM	C1796	NC	104	1881	OR			1 1815	KY		HANNAH SNETHEN	60432
LEWIS, ZACHARIAH	C1776	NC	073	C1802	NC	073	082	1 1796		073	RACHEL BRACKEN	60268
LEWIS, ZEKE	C1805	NC										60584
LILLY, NATHANIEL JACKSON	C1809	NC		1886	LA			1 C1865	LA		LUCRETIA BARNHILL	27435
LIMBAUGH, AMELIA/MILLY	C1808	NC	?Y16				014	1 C1832	TN		ASA GRANT	25191
LIMBAUGH, CATHERINE	C1797	NC	?016				014	1 C1815	NC	014	JOHN AWALT	25191
LIMBAUGH, ELIZABETH/BETSY							014	1			CHARLES PENILINE	25191
LIMBAUGH, JOHN A	C1792	NC	?016	C1855	AL		014	1 1813	NC	014	SALLY HISE	25191
LIMBAUGH, LEAH		NC	?014	C1846	TN			1			MR BRANCH	25191
LIMBAUGH, LUCY ANN	C1810	NC	?014					1 C1833	TN		WILLIAM A MARSHALL	25191
LIMBAUGH, PETER	C1770	NC	?065	1846	TN		014	2 1845	TN		JUDITH C SMITH	25191
LIMBAUGH, PETER	1805	NC	?016	1850	TN		014	1 C1837	TN		POLLY TIPPS	25191
LIMBAUGH, POLLY/MARY	C1802	NC	?016				014	1 C1829	TN		PATRICK RAY	25191
LIMBAUGH, SARAH E/SALLY	1812	NC	?014	1903	TN			1 1838	TN		JOEL VANZANT	25191
LIMBAUGH, SOLOMAN	C1803	NC	?016	C1864	TN		014	1 1827	?TN		NANCY ANN AWALT	25191
LIMBAUGH, WILBURN	C1816	NC	?014					1 C1836	TN		CLAREDA ANN DIXON	25191
LINDER, CHARLOTTE	C1794			1870	TN		084	1 C1814			JOHN ORAND	60361
LINDER, NATHANIEL	C1750			C1796	NC	084		1			MARY	60361
LINDER, SALLY	C1795						084					60361
LINDLEY, ELEANOR/ELENDER	1750	PA		1783	NC	073		1 1769	NC	073	GEORGE MARIS	60203
LINDLEY, THOMAS	1706	IRE		1781	NC	073		1 1731	PA		RUTH HADLEY	60203
LINDLY/LINDLEY, JOHN	1747	PA		1790	SC			1 1768	NC	073	SARAH PYLE	27553
LINDLY/LINDLEY, SIMON	1769	NC	073	1827	IL			1 1789	SC		ANNA STANDLEY	27553

ANCESTOR INDEX	BIRTH	PL	CO	DEATH	PL	CO	LIVD	MARRIED	PL	CO	SPOUSE NAME	CODE
LINDSAY, ANDREW	1786	NC	046	1844	NC	046		1 1812	NC	046	ELIZABETH DICK	12125
LINDSAY, JOSEPH				1794	NC	100		1			RACHEL	60594
LINDSAY, ROBERT	C1740	?VA		1801	NC	046		2 1772	NC	046	ANN/NANCY MCGEE	12125
LINDSEY, ATHANATIOUS	1772	NC	073	1844	NC	073		1 1792	NC	073	SARAH LLOYD	12015
LINDSEY, CALEB	C1710	VA		1784	NC	022		1		VA	ROSANNAH/ROSE	12015
LINDSEY, CALEB	C1790						073	1			MARTHA BREWER	60095
LINDSEY, EDWARD	C1798	NC		1872	TN			1 C1820 2 1831	TN TN		RACHEL MURPHY LEVICY RUMBLEY	60097
LINDSEY, ELIZABETH	1819	NC	073	1878	TN			1 1841	NC	073	GEORGE JOHNSTON	12015
LINDSEY, JOHN SR	C1748	VA		1793	NC	073		1 C1765			MARY ROBERTSON	12015
LINDSEY, MARY	C1790						056	1			WILLIS LEE	60095
LINDSEY, MELISSA	1824	NC	073					1			JOEL LEE	60095
LINEBARGER, MICHAEL	1798							1 1819	NC	060	ANNE/ANNA PERKINS	25112
LINEBARGER/LEINBERGER, JOHN	1780	?PA		1847	IN		060	1 1799	NC	?060	MARY HOOTE	60125
LINEBERRY, DANIEL G	1801	NC	046	1893	NC	005	005	1			MARY JANE JAMES	19017
LINEBERRY, JACOB	C1800	NC		1857	TN			1 C1820	NC		MARY HUFFINE	27758
LINK, CATHERINE	C1785	NC	060	C1860	NC	066	014	1 1810	NC	060	ADAMS HOPPES	25087
LINK, JOHN	C1765	?PA		1816	MO		060	1			MRS MARGARET (FULBRIGHT) GRITES/ CRITES	60453
LINN, HUGH				1785	NC	085						12125
LINN, ROBERT				1801	NC	085		1 1794	NC	085	MARGARET LEONARD	12125
LINVILLE, DAVID	C1765	NC	085	1811	NC	090		1			DOROTHY FAIR/FARE/FARR/FEHR	15098
LINVILLE, EMELINE	1819	NC	090	1896	IN			1 1839 2 1850	IN IN		JOSEPH ZIKE JOHN HESTER	15098
LINVILLE, JOHN	1796	NC	090	1875	IN			1 1816	NC	090	FRANCIS CRIM	15098
LINVILLE, RICHARD	C1740	?VA		1821	NC	090						15098
LIPPS/LIPS, JOHN SR		NC	085				104	1			ELIZABETH	60049
LIPPS/LIPS, SUSANNAH	C1778	NC	085	1860	VA		104	1 C1794	NC	085	JOHN DIXON	60049
LIPS, DANIEL	C1802	NC	065	1888	IL			1		IL	CHARLOTTE	25161
LIPSCOMB, ARCHIBALD	1763	VA		1837	NC	078		1 C1781 2 1808	 NC	 078	 DOROTHY PALMER	17135
LIPSCOMB, ARTMESIA	1813	NC	078	1886	NC	061		1 1838	NC		WASHINGTON GREEN STANFIELD	17135
LIPSCOMB, THOMAS	1783	VA			NC	020		1 1807	NC	078	POLLY SARGENT	17135
LISTER, THOMAS JEFFERSON	1809			1874	NC	050		1			SARAH JOHNSON	60198
LISTER, THOMAS RITCHIE	1845	NC	050	1908	SC		?093	1			MARY ALICE CLAYTON	60198
LITCHFIELD, JOHN MILLER	1848	NC	053	1913	NC	009		1 1869	NC	103	SUSAN ELIZABETH THOMPSON	12140
LITCHFIELD, JOHN STOCKARD	1919	NC	009					1 1958	FL		YSOBEL MORTON DUPREE	12140
LITCHFIELD, JOHN WEST, REV	1815	NC	053					1 1837	NC	053	SOPHIA CARY WATSON	12140
LITCHFIELD, WILLIAM ANDERSON	1883	NC	009	1958	NC	009		1 1916	NC	009	GARNET KATHLEEN BONNER	12140

ANCESTOR INDEX	BIRTH	PL	CO	DEATH	PL	CO	LIVD	MARRIED	PL	CO	SPOUSE NAME	CODE
LITTLE, AARON L	1800	NC	016	1870				1 1825			MARY EMELINE POLK	07115
LITTLE, ABRAHAM	C1715	NC	?037	1789	NC	037		1 2			CELIA AMY LLEWELLYN ?	27280
LITTLE, ALLEN	1784	NC	?079	1853	GA		?037	1 1828	GA		MARGARET ELLEN MARSHALL	27280
LITTLE, FREDERICK		NC	?079	1802	GA		?037	1			NANCY	27280
LITTLE, ICHABOD HARRIS	1845	NC	079	1918	NC	063		1 1867	NC	079	DELSORA ELIZABETH GAINER	24240
LITTLE, JAMES HAMPTON	1842	NC	089	1912	NC	089		1 C1865			MARY JANE GREEN	07115
LITTLE, JAMES LABON	1835	NC		1918	NC	097		1 1857			ELIZABETH M GREEN	07115
LITTLE, LABON	C1803	NC						1 1830	NC		NANCY GREEN	07115
LITTLE, SAMUEL	1803			1874	NC	079		1 C1820	NC	079	REBECCA HARRIS	24240
LITTLE, WILLIAM	C1685	VA		1756	NC	009		1			MOURNING	27280
LITTLE, WILLIAM JOSEPH	1868	NC	079	1942	NC	063		1 1896	NC	037	AZELLA MAYO	24240
LITTLETON, JOHN ARNOLD	1807	NC		1877	TN		016	1			MARY/POLLY SCOTT	60093
LITTLETON, LEVY H	1822	NC	?016	1903	TX			1 1846	TN		MARY JANE DAY	60093
LITTLETON, THOMAS O		ENG					016					60093
LITTLETON, WILLIAM	1805	NC		1880	TN		016	1 1828	TN		SARAH SCOTT	60093
LITTRELL, ORA		NC			MO			1 C1853 2 1872	MO		WILLIAM GLOSSUP WILLIAM THOGMARTIN	60454
LIVERMAN, DIRECTOR	1800	NC		1877	TX			1 1823	NC	096	JAMES A SPRUIELL/SPRUILL	25251
LLOYD/LOYD, SARAH	C1776	NC	073	C1830	NC	073		1 1792	NC	073	ATHANATIOUS LINDSEY	12015
LLOYD/LOYD, STEPHEN	C1737	VA		1790	NC	073		1			MARTHA/POLLY MORRIS	12015
LLOYD/LOYD, THOMAS	C1715	VA		1792	NC	073		1	VA		TABITHA	12015
LOCK, MARY JANE	1821	NC	?011	1874	NC	011		1 C1839	NC	011	JAMES BROWN	27562
LOCK/LOCKE, JOHN		NC	047	1789	NC	047						10090
LOCK/LOCKE, JONATHAN		NC	047	1811	GA			1			MARY	10090
LOCK/LOCKE, SUSANAH	1805	NC		1877	IA			1 1825	TN		WILLIAM CATE	60501
LOCKE, JOHN	1759	?NC		1835				1			ELLENDER LIGHT	25127
LOCKE, MATTHEW	1730	ENG		1801	NC	085		1 1750			MARY ELIZABETH BRANDON	60593
LOCKYER, CHARLES JOHN	1830	ENG		1904	NC	009		1 1857	NC	009	MARY JANE KEECH	27573
LOE, DANIEL	C1768	?NC										60542
LOE, DAVID	C1745	?NC						1 C1770			ELIZA SIMS	60542
LOE, JOHN	C1765	NC	011	C1825	MS							60542
LOE, WILLIS	C1770	NC	011	1829	MS			1 C1800	NC	083	KEZIAH LEE	60542
LOGUE, ANN	C1720				?NC		?073	1			THOMAS THOMPSON ?	02470
LOGUE, EPHRAIM	C1730			C1780	?NC		?020	1			MARY	02470
LOGUE, JOHN	C1700			C1770	?NC	?073		2			MRS JANNET SCOTT	02470
LOGUE, JOHN		NC	?073	1793	TN			1			ELINOR	27268
LOGUE, MARGARET	C1720				?NC		?073	1			LAWRENCE THOMPSON ?	02470

ANCESTOR INDEX	BIRTH	PL	CO	DEATH	PL	CO	LIVD	MARRIED	PL	CO	SPOUSE NAME	CODE
LOLLAR, HUGH GAUNT	C1787	NC	014	C1872	MS			1 C1807 2 C1827	AL		CATHERINE	60507
LOLLAR, JACOB	C1750			C1841	AL		060	1 C1785	NC		ELIZABETH/BETTY GAUNT	60507
LOMAX ELIJAH	1812	NC	085		NC	104		1 C1846	NC	085	MRS NANCY (SETTLE) NORMAN	60001
LOMAX PINKNEY ASBURY	1851	NC	104	1929	NC	104		1 1886	NC	104	SARAH ELIZABETH CARPENTER	60001
LONDON, HENRY	C1767	VA		1850	NC	026		1 1802			MARY ELAM	25100
LONG, CHARLES	C1805	NC	073	C1863	NC	073		1 1825	NC	073	ELIZABETH SELF	60110
LONG, CONRAD		GER		1797	NC	073		1 C1759			CATHERINE MACRHINE	27441
LONG, JACOB	1765	NC	073	1849	NC	073		1 C1789	NC	073	CATHERINE SHEPHERD	27441
LONG, JACOB	1807	NC	073	1894	NC	001		1 1833	NC	073	JANE STEWART STOCKARD	27441
LONG, MARGARET BURROUGHS	1829	NC	073	1876	NC	073		1 1856	NC	073	WILLIAM HENRY BURCH	60110
LONGWORTH, LUCY A								1 1869	NC	038	LEWIS DAVIS	60467
LOPER/LOOPER, JOSHUA		?NC	?070	1806	GA			1			MARY	60175
LOPP/LAPP/LOOP, ANDREW	C1780	NC	085	C1835	?TN			1 C1799	NC	085	EASTER	25133
LOPP/LAPP/LOOP, JOHN HENRY SR	C1800	NC	085	1888	MO			1 C1820 2 C1830 3 C1835	?TN ?TN ?MO		MISS/MRS BLAKEMORE EDITH ZEBULIN ADA ELMORE	25133
LOPP/LAPP/LOOP, JOHN JR, COL	C1738			1801	NC	085		1			ELIZABETH	25133
LOPP/LAPP/LOOP, JOHN SR	C1700			1781	NC	085						25133
LORANCE/LOWRANCE, ELI	1814	NC		1888	KS			2 1847	IN		MRS SARAH (MOTSINGER) SPURGEON	06070
LORANCE/LOWRANCE, PETER	1790	NC		C1855	IN			1	?NC		ELIZABETH	06070
LOUDERMILK, HENRY	C1785	NC	014	C1840	GA			1 1821 2 1838	NC GA	014	MARGARET/PEGGY TAYLOR SALLY BUTTS	25178
LOUDERMILK, JACOB				C1805	NC	014		1			ELIZABETH	25178
LOUDERMILK, SOLOMON	C1790	NC	014	C1862	GA			1 2 1831	NC GA	014	MARY QUEST MELINDA PENCE	25178
LOUDERMILK, WILLIAM CANNON		NC	014		GA			1 1829	NC	014	SUSANAH BRADFORD	25178
LOVE, JAMES JR					NC	?090						60525
LOVE, JAMES SR				1800	NC	090						60525
LOVE, JOHN CROOK	C1783	?VA		1827	NC	090		1 1803	NC	090	FLORA CAMPBELL	60525
LOVE, JOHN JR	1797	NC	081	1868	IN			1 1817 2 1850	NC IN	081	NANCY WALL MRS HARRIET (SCOTT) PITTS	60127
LOVE, JOHN SR				1819	NC	081		1			BETHIER	60127
LOVELACE, ELIZABETH	1805	NC	?054	1880	NC	?054		1	?054		ALVIN HOWARD	25198
LOWE, EMILY	1845	NC	081	1919	NC	081		1			JOHN R HOBSON	10153
LOWE, WILLIAM PENDER	C1864	NC	081	1938	NC	065		1			LAURA TEMPIE HICKS	10153
LOWERY, JOHN	1749	NC		1841				1			HANNAH VANCE	25127
LOWRANCE, ALEXANDER EVELAN	1797	NC	060	1850	NC	003		1 C1819			RUEY COLE	60098
LOWRANCE, BOBBY LEE	1887	NC	003		VA							60098
LOWRANCE, EMMA ESTELLE	1894	NC	003									60098

ANCESTOR INDEX	BIRTH	PL	CO	DEATH	PL	CO	LIVD	MARRIED	PL	CO	SPOUSE NAME	CODE
LOWRANCE, ISAAC HAMPTON	1873	NC	003	1950	VA			1 1901			LEONA IRENE STEELE	60098
LOWRANCE, JACOB	1759	NC	085	1855	NC	085		1 1783	NC	085	REBECCA BEARD	60366
LOWRANCE, JONES HENDERSON	1849	NC	003	1928	NC	003		1 C1870			LOUISA MAYBERRY	60098
LOWRANCE, LAURA ANNIE	1883	NC	003	1910								60098
LOWRANCE, LUCINDA JANE	1871	NC	102	1958	NC	003		1 1893			WILL GWALTNEY	60098
LOWRANCE, MARTHA IDUMA	1880	NC	003	1957	NC	033		1 1903			MILTON HAMMER	60098
LOWRANCE, MILAS S	1821	NC	?104	C1911	NC	003		1 C1846			LOUISA M BARKLEY	60098
LOWRANCE, MINNIE BELL	1889	NC	003	1958	NC	021		1 1909			LEE O DRUM	60098
LOWRANCE, NANCY ELIZABETH	1878	NC	003	1880	NC	003						60098
LOWRANCE, ROMULUS EDWARD	1892	NC	003	1969	NC	054		1 1922			EDNA CAUDILL	60098
								2 1938	NC	054	SARAH JOHNSON	
LOWRANCE, WALTER GASTON	1875	NC	003	1882	NC	003						60098
LOWRANCE, WILLIAM ABNER	1885	NC	003	1955	NC	065		1			BERTHA THOMPSON	60098
								2			EASSIE SIGMON	
LUCKEY, ISABELLA	1761	PA			TN		060	1 1780	NC	085	CPT JOHN BALDRIDGE	06005
LUCKEY, JAMES		PA		C1799	NC	060		1			SARAH	06005
LUTEN/LUTON, HENDERSON				C1740	NC	024						01006
LUTEN/LUTON, JAMES	C1730	NC	?024	C1766	NC	024		1 1750	NC	024	MARY PUGH	01006
								2 1754	NC	024	MARY KING	
LUTEN/LUTON, KING	1792	NC	024	1860	TN			1 1813	TN		CAROLINE WALTON	01006
LUTEN/LUTON, KING	1763	NC	024	1837	TN			1 1784	MD		PROVIDENCE BAKER	01006
								2 1793	NC	024	MARY BAINS	
								3 1795	NC	024	ANN HOSKINS	
LUTEN/LUTON, THOMAS, MAJ		?VA		C1731	NC	024		1 C1680			MARY	01006
LUTHER, CALVIN	1820	?NC										60014
LUTHER, JAMES M	C1828	NC						1			LUCINDA WHITE	60014
LUTHER, WILLIAM	C1795	NC			NC							60014
LYDA, ANDREW	C1740	HOL		C1815	NC	013	086	1 C1760			MISS/MRS DAVIS	25149
								2 C1785			SARAH MACKEY	
LYDA, MARY	C1770	NC		C1840	TN		013	1 C1788	NC	086	BOAZ/BOOZE STILL	25149
LYDAY/LYDA, ABRAHAM	1775	NC	094	1852	NC			1 C1808	NC	013	ATHELENDA WEISS	60582
								2 C1821	NC	013	REBECCA SIMPSON	
LYDAY/LYDA, ANDREW	C1750	NC		1816	NC	013		1 C1770	NC	094	MARY	60582
LYDAY/LYDA, REBECCA	1836	NC	013		NC	093		1 1858	NC	050	JAMES WASLEY NORMAN	60582
								2 1865	NC	093	CHARLES CAMPFIELD	
								3 1868	NC	093	JOSEPH T BANKS	
LYERLY/LAYRLE/LIERLY, HENRY	1786	NC	085	1857	IL			1 1806	NC	085	MARY FITE	60517
LYERLY/LAYRLE/LIERLY, JOHANN CHRISTOPH	1710	GER		1786	NC	085		1	GER		ELIZABETH CHRISTINA	60517
								2			ANNA MARIA CATHERINA	
LYERLY/LAYRLE/LIERLY, ZACHARIUS/ ZAMAH/ZACH	1755	VA		1847	IL		065	1			CATHERINE VAN POOLE	60517
								2			CATHERINE MISENHEIMER	
								3			HARKEY	
								4 1823	IL		MRS SALLIE (PENROD) SNYDER	

ANCESTOR INDEX	BIRTH	PL	CO	DEATH	PL	CO	LIVD	MARRIED	PL	CO	SPOUSE NAME	CODE
LYLES, MRS JUDITH	C1785	NC		C1835	?TN			1	KY		B LYLES	60551
								2 C1810	TN		RALPH ROGERS	
LYNCH, HUGH	C1755	?VA		1822	NC	084						04050

M

ANCESTOR INDEX	BIRTH	PL	CO	DEATH	PL	CO	LIVD	MARRIED	PL	CO	SPOUSE NAME	CODE
MABERY, JACOB A	1842	NC	089	1918	TX			1 C1864			MILEY PEMIE CABLE	60580
MACE, GEORGE W	1825			1899	NC	050		1			MIRA WRIGHT ?	09030
MACE, HARVEY ALEXANDER	1836	NC	014	C1907	MO			1 1856	NC	107	MALINDA VANCE	23040
MACE, JAMES F	1848	NC	050	1909	NC	050		1 1866	NC	050	AMANDA BRYANT	09030
MACE, JONAS	C1770	NC	037	1835	NC	107		1 1805	NC	054	ELIZABETH NEWSOME	23040
MACE, JOSIAH	1808	NC			NC	107		1 C1827	NC		NAOMI CREASON/CRISSON	23040
MACE, WILLIAM		?VA		1760	NC	079	009	1 C1725			ANN HUMPHREY ?	25087
MACE, WILLIAM, I		VA		1761	NC	?079		1			ANN	23040
MACE, WILLIAM, II				1781	NC	037		1 C1750	NC	037	KISSIAH SUGG	23040
MACILMURRAY, JOHN							065					12019
MACILMURRAY, WILLIAM							065					12019
MACKEY, WILLIAM	C1781	NC	096	C1818	NC	063	101	1 C1809	NC	063	CLARA MORIAH BIGGS	27378
MACKIE, BENJAMIN	1824	NC	092	1880	NC	106		1 1847	NC		TENNESSEE REECE	60288
MACKIE, JOHN	1760			1822	NC	092		1	NC	092	NAOMI MOFFIT	60288
MACKIE, ROBERT	1794	NC	092	1847	NC	092		1 1817	NC	092	ANNA MARTIN	60288
MACKIE/MACKEY/MACKAY, JESSE		NC		1877	NC	106		1 1862	NC	106	PHYSA R WILLIAMS	60569
MACKIE/MACKEY/MACKAY, JOHN		IRE		1822	NC	092	?081	1			NAOMI MOFFITT	60569
MACKIE/MACKEY/MACKAY, JOHN HENRY	1862	NC	106	1949	NC	106		1 1880	NC	106	NANCY ELIZABETH SIZEMORE	60569
MACKIE/MACKEY/MACKAY, ROBERT	1794	NC	092	1872	NC	106		1 1817	NC	092	ANN MARTIN	60569
MACKIE/MACKEY/MACKAY, WILLIAM LUTHER	1883	NC	106	1973	NC	106		1 1915	NC	106	EULA ALCY WILLIAMS	60569
MAGNESS, BENJAMIN	1755	VA		1828	NC	086		1 1775			ELIZABETH MAUNEY	05070
								2 1809	NC	086	NANCY WALKER	
MAGNESS, MARY ANN	1787	NC	086	1862	NC	026		1			JOHN WASHBURN	05070
MAGNESS, PERRY GREEN	1722	ENG		1799	NC	060		1 C1747			SARAH HAMRICK	05070
								2			MARY	
MAINER/MANER/MAYNER, JOHN	1665	?VA		1729	NC	010		1	?VA		ELIZABETH	04135
MAINER/MANER/MAYNER, WILLIAM	C1700			C1782	SC		072	1 C1724	NC	?028	SARAH KEELE	04135
MALLARD, GEORGE		NC	028	1798	NC	035		1			COMFORT WOODSTOCK	04135
MALLISON, CHRISTOPHER A	C1780			1827	NC	009		1 C1795			MARY THOMAS HOOTEN	13175
MALLISON, HENRY HOOTEN	C1800	NC	053	C1848	NC	009		1 C1830	NC	009	ANN CARROW	13175
MALLISON, JAMES CLARK	1843	NC	009	1908	TX			1 1881			CARRIE INEZ ROWE	13175
MALLISON, JOHN M	C1710	NC	053	C1770				1			ELLONER	13175

ANCESTOR INDEX	BIRTH	PL	CO	DEATH	PL	CO	LIVD	MARRIED	PL	CO	SPOUSE NAME	CODE
MALLISON, WILLIAM W	1740	NC	053	C1811	NC	053		1				13175
								2			SARAH REED	
MAN/MANN, ELIZABETH	C1775	NC	085		NC	064	014	1 C1795	NC	014	JOHN BURGIN	23065
MAN/MANN, JOHN	C1729			C1757	NC	085		1 C1753				23065
MAN/MANN, JOHN	1749			C1825	NC	014		1 C1771	NC	085		23065
MAN/MANN, LEAH	C1754	?NC	?085		NC	014		1 1772	NC	085	BENJAMIN BURGIN	23065
MAN/MANN, ROBERT	C1721			C1757	NC	085		1 C1750			ELIZABETH	23065
MANGUM, ARTHUR	C1790	NC						1			PENNY	60201
MANGUM, MARY	1840	NC	044	1900	NC	036		1	NC	044	MOSES ELLIS	12075
MANN, ABSOLOM					NC	047						19227
MANN, ANNIE LEE	1890	NC	022	1966	NC	038	046	1 1913	NC	036	CLAUDE NASH HERNDON	08200
MANN, BURKHEAD NEWTON	1855	NC	022	1915	NC	036		1 1887	NC	022	MIRIAM GIBSON TUCKER	08200
MANN, ISAAC NEWTON	1826	NC	022	1904	NC	022		1 1846	NC	022	CORNELIA FRANCES FOUSHEE	08200
MANN, JESS/JESSE GREENE		NC						1 1842	NC	022	ELIZABETH PERRY	60537
MANN, JOSEPH ADOLPHUS	1849	NC						1 C1874			MARGARET WHITT	60537
MANN, ROLAND	C1765	VA		C1818	NC	022	092	1	NC		BARBARA HOLSTEIN ?	08200
MANN, THOMAS	C1740	VA		C1797	NC	022	092	1	VA			08200
MANN, WESLEY	1793	NC	022	1862	NC	022		1 1818	NC	022	DICEA EASTINGS WEST	08200
MANN, ZACHARIAH	1817	?NC		1905	NC	022		1	NC		CELINA WOODELL	27543
								2	NC		MARTHA PATTERSON	
MANNING, ASHLEY	1821	NC	079	1890	NC	079		1	NC	079	CHARLOTTE MATTHEWS	60414
MANNING, JOHN LAWRENCE GRAHAM	1846	NC	079	1921	NC	079		1 1870	NC	079	MRS MARGARET (BRYANT) BULLOCK	60414
								2 1886	NC	079	MARGARET ANN MORNING TAYLOR	
MANNING, JOHN OSCAR	1886	NC	079	1961	NC	079		1 1909	NC	079	MINNIE MANNING	60414
MANNING, MICAJAH	1864	NC	079	1934	NC	079		1	NC	079	FRANCES LOUISE BRYANT	60414
MANNING, MICAJAH	C1785				NC	079		1 C1805	NC	079	MARGARET WHITEHURST	60414
MANNING, WILLIAM	1810	NC	079	1861	NC	079		1 1844	NC	079	ELIZABETH MATTHEWS	60414
MARCOM/MARKHAM, BASLEY GRAVES	1817	NC	099	1856	KY			1 1838			HANNAH SEWELL	27593
MARCOM/MARKHAM, JOHN							073	1 C1750	VA			27593
MARCOM/MARKHAM, SAMUEL	C1755	VA					099	2 1803	NC	099	AVE YOUNG	27593
MARCOM/MARKHAM, SAMUEL JR	C1785	NC						1			NANCY	27593
MARCUS, SOLOMON D	C1777	NC	014	1841	TN			1 1802	NC	014	MARY F JAMES	04085
MARET/MERIT/MERRITT, BENJAMIN	C1760	VA		C1805	SC		073	1	NC	073	JUDITH HARBIN	27756
MARET/MERIT/MERRITT, BENJAMIN JR	C1790	NC	073		SC			1 C1815			LUCY KEESE	27756
MARIS, AARON	1774	NC	073	1843	IN			1 1797	NC	073	SARAH HOLIDAY/HOLADAY	60203
MARIS, GEORGE	1744	PA		1782	NC	073		1 1769	NC	073	ELEANOR LINDLEY	60203
MARKS, MARY MARGARITE	1863	NC		1920				1 1884	NC		CALVIN COLUMBUS HENSON/HINSON	08190
MARKS, THOMAS H	1835	NC		1918				1	NC		MARY HELEN BAILEY	08190

ANCESTOR INDEX	BIRTH	PL	CO	DEATH	PL	CO	LIVD	MARRIED	PL	CO	SPOUSE NAME	CODE
MARLOW/MARLER/MARLEY, NATHANIEL	C1777			1824	SC		012	1			MARTHA	13052
MARLOW/MARLER/MARLEY, WILLIAM P	C1807	SC		C1865	NC	012		1			REBECCA	13052
MARSH, LACY ALONZO NORWOOD	1878	NC	092	1954	OK			1 1909	OK		MARY ELLEN FOX	60052
MARSH, THOMAS DUNNAGAN	1811	NC	092	1881	VA			1 1831	NC	092	PRUDENCE CATHERINE GARNER SMITH	60052
MARSH, WILLIAM		NC	092	C1840	NC	092		1 C1805	NC	092	HANNAH DUNNAGAN	60052
MARSH, WILLIAM	1836	NC	092	1893	OK			1 1855	VA		ELLEN HICKS	60052
								2 1867	VA		SUSAN VIRGINIA TARTER	
MARSHALL, DAVID				1784	NC	047						27280
MARSHALL, JOHN F	C1786	NC	100	C1867	NC	003		1			RITTER	27406
MARSHALL, ROBERT NELSON	C1827	NC	?054	1865	VA		003	1 C1851	NC	003	DORINDA CHILDERS	27406
MARSHALL, STEPHEN	1767	NC	047	1831	GA			1	NC	047	ELIZABETH BURT	27280
MARSHALL, THEOPHILUS	1810	NC	?054	1902	NC	003		1			CLARISSA	27406
MARSHALL, THOMAS	1780			1861	NC	038		1 1802	NC	090	MILLY WAGGONER	60456
MARSHBURN/MASHBURN, BENJAMIN	C1742	NC	072	1824	NC	072		1 C1765	NC	072	HANNAH COX	13264
MARSHBURN/MASHBURN, DANIEL	C1720	NC	?024	1783	NC	072		1 C1750	NC	010	ELIZABETH RHODES	13264
MARSHBURN/MASHBURN, EDWARD	C1698	VA		1777	NC	072		1 C1715	?NC		MARY ANN	13264
MARSHBURN/MASHBURN, EDWARD	C1730	NC	010	1783	NC	072		1 C1750	NC	?010	ELIZABETH	13264
MARSHBURN/MASHBURN, JACOB JAMES	1851	NC	035	1913	NC	079	045	1 C1875	NC	028	ANN JULIA POWELL	13264
MARSHBURN/MASHBURN, JAMES	C1770	NC	070	1840	NC	035		1 C1801	NC	072	SARAH JOHNSTON	13264
MARSHBURN/MASHBURN, JAMES MADISON	C1820	NC	072	C1887	NC	028		1 C1845	NC	072	LOUISA POWELL	13264
MARSHBURN/MASHBURN, JETHRO	C1704	VA		C1752	NC	072	010	1 C1725	?NC		SUSANNA	13264
MARSHBURN/MASHBURN, JOSEPH	C1767	NC	072	1816	NC	072		1 C1790	NC	072	PENELOPE LEE	13264
MARSHBURN/MASHBURN, MATTHEW	C1703	VA		C1760	NC	071	010	1 C1725	?NC		SARAH	13264
MARSHILL, WILLIAM	1724	IRE		1803	NC	073		1 1746	DE		REBECCAH DIXON	27429
MARTIN, ADAM	1784	VA		1851	MO		086	1 1807	NC	086	MARY/POLLY BABER	60460
MARTIN, ANDREW				C1800	NC	092		1			MARGARET	27292
MARTIN, ANN/ANNA	1799	NC		1864	NC	106	092	1 1817	NC	092	ROBERT MACKIE	60569
MARTIN, ANNA	1799	NC	092	1864	NC	106		1 1817	NC	092	ROBERT MACKIE	60288
MARTIN, ELIZABETH	C1785	?NC	?073	C1865	NC	?001		1 1807	NC	073	RICHARD JONES	02256
MARTIN, EMILINE	C1830	NC	?029	C1861	NC	029		1 1851	NC	029	JAMES HENDERSON MATTHEWS	13090
MARTIN, GEORGE	1718	ENG			NC	?092		1			SARAH DIXON	60288
MARTIN, HENRY	C1740			1815	NC	073		1			SARAH	02256
MARTIN, JOEL SR	C1666	VA		C1716	NC	009		1 C1691	NC	002	ELIZABETH ALDERSON	19130
MARTIN, JOHN	1756			1836	NC	092		1 1783			MARGARET HADLEY	60288
MARTIN, JOHN	C1715	?NC	?010	C1759	NC	044		1 C1735	?NC	010	RACHEL HAWKINS ?	60404
MARTIN, JOHN HENRY	1845			1927	NC	106		1 1870	NC		MARY MALINDA HUNT	27475
MARTIN, JOHN R	C1810	NC						1			RACHEL ROSS	25115

ANCESTOR INDEX	BIRTH	PL	CO	DEATH	PL	CO	LIVD	MARRIED	PL	CO	SPOUSE NAME	CODE
MARTIN, LEWIS	1757			1834	MO		086	1			MARY	60460
MARTIN, NANNIE	1876	MO		1908	NC	054	106	1 1897	NC		JAMES AUGUSTUS BUTLER	27475
MARTIN, RUTH	1802	NC		1890	NC	106	092	1	NC	092	JESSE WILLIAMS	60569
MARTIN, SAMUEL	C1783	NC			NC	106		1 C1811	NC		ELIZABETH PLEDGE SCOTT	27475
MARTIN, SUSAN JANE								1 C1853	NC	?038	JAMES MADISON TESH	60428
MARTIN, THOMAS SCOTT	1813	NC	092	1878	NC	106		1 1844	NC		ANNE CLINGMAN POINDEXTER	27475
MARTIN, VALENTINE		?VA			NC		092	1			ELIZABETH DALTON	27475
MASK, JOHN JR	1729	VA		1813	NC	082	?029	1 1754	NC	?029	DRUSILLA RAIFORD	60404
MASON, BENJAMIN	1786	NC	?053	C1860	NC	053		1			MARY/POLLY JARVIS	24210
MASON, DAVID JARVIS	1830	NC	?053	C1900	NC	053		1			LUVENIA E BRIDGEMAN	24210
MASON, JAMES				C1820	NC	030		1			ZILPHA BAUM	20335
MASON, JOHN JR	C1710			C1752	NC	053		1 C1734			CATHERINE	24210
MASON, JOHN SR	C1665			1741	NC	053		1			MARY	24210
MASON, JOSHUA	1745	NC	053	C1811	NC	019		1			NANCY	24210
								2 C1795			ELIZABETH	
MASON, MARY ANN	1869	NC	?053	1954	NC	053		1 1888	NC	053	GEORGE HODGES WILLIAMS	24210
MASON, ROGER	C1690			C1756	NC	053		1			MARY	24210
MASON, ROGER JR				C1752	NC	053		1 1743	NC	053	SARAH JARVICE	24210
MASON, SAMUEL WARRINGTON	1837	NC						1			MARY CAROLINE MIDGETT	13120
MASSENGILL, HENRY	1758	NC		1837	TN		071	1			PENELOPE COBB	60306
MASSEY, ABRAHAM				1798	NC	073		1			GWEN LEWIS	08200
MASSEY, ABRAHAM	C1750	MD		C1787	NC	060	085	1 1774	NC	085	RACHEL SHERRILL	27560
MASSEY, BENJAMIN	C1780	NC	085	1814	TN		060	1 1803	NC	016	MARGARET/PEGGY CARLOCK	27560
MASSEY, GEORGE NEWTON	1879	NC	013	1953	KY		062	1			NETTIE JOHNSON	25108
MASSEY, JAMES JACKSON	1880			1907	KY		013	1 1896	NC	013	POLLY/MARY ANNA BANKS	25108
MASSEY, JOHN		NC	013				062					25108
MASSEY, LOUIS C	1878	NC	013	1904	CO		062					25108
MASSEY, LYDIA		?NC	?073	C1815	NC	073		1 C1770	NC	073	BENJAMIN HERNDON	08200
MASSEY, NICHOLAS	C1730	MD		C1801	NC	054	085	1 C1750	MD		HENRIETTA	27560
MASSEY, THOMAS		NC	013				062					25108
MASSEY, WILL		NC	013				062					25108
MASSEY/MASSY, BETSEY/ELIZABETH					NC	099		1 1800	NC	099	MOSES TODD	03250
MASTEN, JOHN	1761			1829	NC	090		1			ELIZABETH STANLEY	13120
MATHEWS, MARGARET MCCLAIN	1791	NC		1879	IN		085	1 1811	NC	054	SAMUEL THOMAS	60202
MATHIS, CARLTON	1801	NC	035	1888	TN			1 1823	NC	?035	MARY/POLLY SHELLEY	60083
MATHIS, JACOB ?	C1766	NC	?035		NC	?035						60083
MATHIS, SHADRACK	C1782	NC		C1870	SC			1 C1810	SC		MARGARET RODGERS	27554
MATHIS, WILLIAM					TN			1 C1796	NC	?035	LYDIA CARLTON	60083

ANCESTOR INDEX	BIRTH	PL	CO	DEATH	PL	CO	LIVD	MARRIED	PL	CO	SPOUSE NAME	CODE
MATHIS/MATHEWS, SHADRACK	C1783	NC		C1865	SC			1 C1810	SC		MARGARET RODGERS/ROGERS	60287
MATTHEWS, ALSA/ALSEY	C1790	NC	?029					1 C1809	NC	?029	CHARITY PENNY ?	13090
MATTHEWS, DAVID				C1847	NC	029		1			SARAH	13090
MATTHEWS, JACOB		NC	?037		NC	?029		1 1777	NC	?029	PHOEBE SMITH	13090
MATTHEWS, JAMES	1739	IRE		1825	TN			1 1766	NC	044	MARY DOAK	60425
MATTHEWS, JAMES HENDERSON	1820			1907	NC	048		1 1851	NC	029	MRS EMILINE (SUGGS?) MARTIN	13090
								2 C1834	NC	?029	ARABIA CATES	
								3 C1873	NC	029	MRS MARY (MCLEOD?) CAMPBELL	
MATTHEWS, JAMES MADISON	C1771	NC	046					1 1811	NC	046	DELILAH JOHNSON	60004
MATTHEWS, JOHN	1768	NC	044	1839	TN			1 1794	NC	065	MARGARET MCKIBBEN	60425
								2	TN		AGNES SCOTT	
MATTHEWS, JOSEPH	C1750	?VA			NC	?029		1			ANN	13090
MATTHEWS, WILLIAM							046	1			MARTHA	60004
MATTHEWS, WILLIAM	C1785	?NC	?079		NC	079		1	?NC	?079	MARY TAYLOR	60414
MAULDIN, BENJAMIN	C1755	MD			SC		073	1			ELIZABETH SYMMES	60008
MAULDIN, HENRY		?MD					057					60008
MAULE, CHRISTIAN				C1719	NC	?024		1 C1700	?NC		THOMAS BROWN	20415
MAUZY, FANNIE HEATON	1854	VA		1933	VA			1 1876	NC	022	LEONIDAS ALONZO TYSOR	60172
MAUZY, GEORGE	1799	VA		1883	NC	022		1 1823	VA		MARY FARQUHAR	60172
								2 1852	MD		MARY ELLEN YOUNG	
MAXWELL, ALEXANDER	1823	NC	029	1868	NC	029		1 1847	NC	029	SUSAN MCDANIEL/MCDONALD	17080
MAXWELL, DANIEL	1788	NC	087	1832	NC	029		1 1808	NC	029	MARGARET CATHERINE GEDDIE	17080
MAXWELL, HUGH	1762	NC		1838	IN			1 1787	NC	?046	ELIZABETH ELLIOTT	60476
MAXWELL, JOHN	1796	NC		1875	TN							13095
MAXWELL, JOHN	C1715	IRE		1762	NC	?056		1 C1745	NC		ELIZABETH MCCLENDON	60476
MAXWELL, MURDOCK MCKINNON	1850	NC	029	1912	NC	029		1 1878	NC	087	ROBERTA PRISCILLA ROYALL	17080
MAXWELL, STACY GILLIAM	1881	NC	029	1946	NC	029		1 1911	VA		FRANCES ELIZABETH MARSDEN	17080
MAXWELL, THOMAS	1765	NC	?035	1827	NC	029		1 C1780	NC	029	MARY MCPHAIL	17080
MAXWELL, THOMAS		SCO		C1827	NC	029	?087	1	?NC	?029	MARY MCPHAILL	60061
MAXWELL, WILLIAM	C1735	NC	070	C1784	NC	?035	070	1 C1760	NC		ELIZABETH/BETSY CAMPBELL/CROOM ?	17080
MAXWELL, WILLIAM	1794	NC	?022	1855	IA			1 1817	IN		CHARITY WRIGHT	60476
MAXWELL, WILLIAM ESQ	C1700	IRE		1739	NC	010	070	1 C1723	IRE			17080
MAY, ANGELETTE FISHER	1819	NC	022	1890	MS			1 C1839	NC	022	AARON HARRIS	02540
MAY, HARDEE	C1790	NC	079	C1850	NC	079		1 C1825	NC	079	GATTICE	13264
MAY, JAMES		NC	045	C1840	NC	079		1 C1815	NC	045	SUSANNA	12140
MAY, JAMES ROSS	1855	NC	045	1931	NC	045		1 1876	NC	045	MARTHA JANE EASON	13264
MAY, JAMES, CAPT	C1765	NC	079	C1825	NC	079		1 C1800	NC	?079	FANNY COBB	13264
MAY, JOHN	C1700	SCO		1764	NC	079		1 C1735	NC	?009	MARY STAFFORD	13264
MAY, JOHN	C1740	NC	?009	C1804	NC	079						13264

ANCESTOR INDEX	BIRTH	PL	CO	DEATH	PL	CO	LIVD	MARRIED	PL	CO	SPOUSE NAME	CODE
MAY, JOHN	1757			1844	NC	084		1 1779	VA		ELIZABETH HUNTER	60571
MAY, JOHN VINCENT	1776	NC	022	1853	MS			1 C1810	NC	022	ELIZABETH BAILEY RICHARDSON	02540
MAY, JOHN W	1823	NC						1			MARY CARPENTER	60358
MAY, JOSEPH	1750	NC		1805	NC	022		1 C1774			ANGELET FISHER	02540
MAY, JOSEPH								1 1818	NC	073	BARBARA HUFFMAN/HOFFMAN	21080
MAY, MARY JANE	1824	NC	084	1914	TX			1 1837	MS		WILLIAM B CARVER BEARD	60571
MAY, PENINA	1818	NC	045	1847	NC	079		1 1842	NC	045	THOMAS BIRD DUPREE	12140
MAY, ROBERT BOOKER	1787	NC	084	1855				1 2 1819	NC NC	084 084	BETSY WILSON TABITHA ALLEN JOHNSON/JOHNSTON	60571
MAY, WILLIAM L	1829	NC	079	1902	NC	045		1 C1853	NC	045	ESTHER SUSAN JONES ?	13264
MAYABB, JOHN D	C1820	NC	090	1889	MO			1 C1845	VA		ELIZA JANE FLINCHAM	60341
MAYES, MARTHA ELLEN	1850	NC	073	1923	NC	073						60130
MAYES, SAMUEL		NC	073					1			SALLIE PRITCH	60130
MAYNER/MAYNARD, SARAH		VA		1803	NC	092	022	1 C1759	VA		EDWARD BRAY	27420
MAYO, FREDERICK WILLIAMS	1804	NC		1852	TN			1 1828	NC	037	MANISIA GAINER MENETTA ANDREWS SHERROD	16035
MAYO, JESSE	1792	NC	?037	C1869	GA			1 C1815	GA		RACHAEL	20080
MAYO, JOHN	1759	NC	077	1842	GA			1 C1784	NC		ORPHA ELLIOTT	20080
MAYO, JOHN	1848	NC	037	1926	NC	079		1 1872	NC	037	SALLIE LOUISA CHERRY	24240
MAYO, LYDIA GREY	1749			1818	NC	037	079	1 1765	NC	037	JAMES THIGPEN	02195
MAYO, REUBEN	1806			1877	NC	037		1 C1832	NC		LUCINDA BEST	24240
MCADAMS, JOSEPH	C1757	PA		1840	IL		073	1 1788	NC	073		27531
MCADAMS, JOSEPH	1761	NC	073	1823	TN			1 1782	NC	073	MARGARET WHITSETT	60497
MCADAMS, JOSEPH	1790	NC	073	1866	TX			1 1814 2 C1853 3 C1860	TN TX TX		ELIZABETH COSBY RACHEL STRICKLAND NANCY MCGRAW	60497
MCALLISTER, JOHN	C1715			1768	NC	073		1 2			ROSANNAH WILLSON	02470
MCALLISTER, SARAH	C1748			1831	NC	073		1 C1768	?NC	?073	JOSEPH THOMPSON	02470
MCALPINE, ARCHIBALD BROWN	1815	NC	082	1867	TX			1 1842	AL		ELIZABETH JANE EDWARDS	60177
MCALPINE, JOHN	C1777	SCO		1827	NC	082	029	1 C1807	NC	083	SUSANNA PARELLA ANDERSON	60177
MCALPINE, MALCOLM	C1755	SCO		C1825	NC	083	029	1 C1775	SCO		MARY SMITH	60177
MCARTHUR, ELIJAH LEONARD	1848	NC		1921			045	1 1869	NC	?105	JANE DIXON	60224
MCARTHUR, ELISHA	C1830	NC					045	2 C1859	NC	045	PRISCILLA	60224
MCARTHUR, NANNIE RAY	1874	NC		1961	FL			1 1885	FL		JAMES H PEAVY	60224
MCBEE, THOMAS B	C1818	SC		C1875	NC	066	064	1 C1842	GA		MILLIE ADELAIDE BRYANT	25087
MCBRIDE, HANNAH	1810	NC		1863	IN			1 1835	IN		DANIEL PAFFORD	60261
MCBRIDE, JAMES				1808	NC	104		1			SARAH	60370
MCBRIDE, JOHN	C1769	IRE		1830	TN		?046	1 C1787	VA		ELIZABETH	60323
MCBRIDE, MARGARET	C1770	NC		1841	TN		046	1 1787	NC	085	JAMES COSBY	60497

ANCESTOR INDEX	BIRTH	PL	CO	DEATH	PL	CO	LIVD	MARRIED	PL	CO	SPOUSE NAME	CODE
MCBRIDE, PATRICK HENRY	1793	NC		1849	IL			1 1815	TN		MARTHA GOULEY	60323
								2 1849	IL		MRS MARY ANN HAYS	
MCBRIDE, ROBERTS	C1812	NC	104	1855	IN			1 1834	IN		MARY/POLLY BELL	60370
MCBRIDE, RUTH	1811	NC	104	1883	IN			1 C1833			WILLIAM ROUSSEAU	60370
MCBRIDE, SARAH	1804	NC	?104	1885	IN			1 1826	NC	104	WILLIAM WALKER	60370
MCBRIDE, WILLIAM	C1777	NC		C1855	IN			1 1799	NC	104	ELIZABETH HEATHMAN	60370
MCBRIDE, WILLIAM	1803	NC	104	1901	IN			1 1832	IN		REBECCA ROGERS	60370
MCCALL, CHARLES	1732	PA		1814	GA		065	1 1755	SC		CELET/CELETA WILLIAMS	60477
MCCALL, FRANCIS	1710	IRE		1794	NC	065		1 C1731	PA		MARY	60477
MCCALL, JEAN		NC	065		NC	065		1			CPT ROBERT PORTER	60477
MCCARTY, DANIEL		?NC	?044	1782	NC	060		1			AGNESS	60074
MCCARTY, ELIZABETH		?NC						1 1817	NC	060	SOLOMON PARKER	27413
MCCLAMMY, ELEANOR	C1725	?NC	070		NC	070		1 C1745	NC	070	ROBERT NIXON	27356
MCCLAREN, DANIEL	C1713	SCO			NC	084						60342
MCCLEARY, ELEANOR	1784	NC	065	1847	IL			1 1804	NC	065	ROBERT MONTGOMERY	25040
MCCLEARY, ROBERT	1736	PA		1791	NC	065		1	NC	065	ABIGAIL MCDOWELL	25040
MCCLEES, SAMUEL	1817			1859	NC	096		1			SARAH MANN	20335
MCCLELAN, WILLIAM	C1750	?VA		1824	GA		073	1 1781			FRANCINA VEASEY	60371
MCCLENDON, DENNIS	C1680	SCO		C1725	NC	010		1 C1700			MARGARET EARLY	60476
MCCLENDON, ELIZABETH				1762	NC			1 C1743	NC		JOHN MAXWELL	60476
MCCLURE, HENRY SAMUEL	C1835				NC	006		1 1855	NC	006	LEAH HOWELL	60541
MCCLURE, MARTHA ANN	1840	NC		1877	NC			1 1861	NC	025	DANIEL WILKINSON KILLIAN	60173
MCCLURE, MERI ETTA	C1858	NC			TN			1			TRAIN SULLINS	60541
								2			LINVILLE PRICE	
MCCOLLUM, ANDREW MALCOLM	C1812	NC		1863	AR			1 C1835	AL		REBECCA S	20210
MCCOLLUM, DANIEL	C1780	IRE		1825	NC	?065		1			MARGARET	60357
MCCOLLUM, DANIEL WESLEY	1813	NC	?065				?097	1		?065	JANE	60357
MCCOLLUM, JAMES N	1840	NC	?065				097					60357
MCCOLLUM, JOHN								1 1852	NC	097	RUTH CUTHBERTSON	60357
MCCOLLUM, JOHN W	1838	NC	?065				097					60357
MCCOLLUM, MARGARET A	1849	NC	097									60357
MCCOLLUM, MOSES A	1846	NC	097	1908	GA			1			ARRA PERNICE HAYS	60357
MCCOLLUM, ROBERT E	1842	NC	097									60357
MCCOLLUM, SARAH E	1845	NC	097									60357
MCCOLLUM, WILLIAM ISAAC	C1760							1 1796	NC	099	MARTHE THWEATT ROGERS	27375
MCCORKLE, AGNES/NANCY	1760	NC	085	1822	NC	054		1 1790	NC	085	ROBERT RAMSAY	20450
MCCORKLE, ALEXANDER	1722	SCO		1800	NC	054	085	1 C1745	PA		AGNES/NANCY MONTGOMERY	20450
								2 1791	NC	085	MRS REBECCA BRANDON	

ANCESTOR INDEX	BIRTH	PL	CO	DEATH	PL	CO	LIVD	MARRIED	PL	CO	SPOUSE NAME	CODE
MCCORKLE, ALEXANDER	C1752			1833	TN		085	1 C1775	NC	?085	CATHARINE MORRISON	20450
MCCORKLE, ELIZABETH	C1753			1829	NC	054	085	1 1774	NC	085	JAMES BARR	20450
								2 C1795	NC	?054	ANDREW KILPATRICK	
MCCORKLE, JAMES	1768	NC	085	1840	IN			1 C1791	NC	?054	ELIZABETH HALL	20450
								2 1796	NC	?054	ELIZABETH HALL	
								3 1821	OH		MRS ELIZABETH JOHNSON	
MCCORKLE, JOHN	C1749	PA		1800	NC	085		1 1774	NC	085	CATHARINE BARR	20450
MCCORKLE, JOSEPH	C1753			1828	OH		085	1 1775	NC	085	MARGARET SNODDY	20450
MCCORKLE, MARTHA	C1748	PA					085	1 1765	NC	085	WILLIAM ARCHIBALD	20450
MCCORKLE, ROBERT	1764	NC	085	1828	TN			1 1788	NC	085	ELIZABETH BLYTHE	20450
								2 C1795	NC	054	MARGARET MORRISON	
MCCORKLE, SAMUEL EUSEBIUS	1746	PA		1811	NC	085		1 1776	NC	085	MARGARET GILLESPIE	20450
MCCORKLE, WILLIAM	C1758	NC	?085	C1817	TN		085	1 C1780	NC	?085	MARGARET BLYTHE	20450
								2 1794	TN		MRS MARTHA (KING) PURVIANCE	
								3 1800	TN		JANE GRAHAM	
MCCOURRY, CHARLES CLAYTON	1859	NC	107	1940	TN							60430
MCCOURRY, ELIZABETH JANE	1856	NC	107									60430
MCCOURRY, HARIET P	1867	NC	107		MA							60430
MCCOURRY, JANE, MRS	C1810	NC		C1890	NC		107	1 C1825	NC		ZEPHANIAH MCCOURRY	60430
MCCOURRY, MARCUS NELSON	1853	NC	107									60430
MCCOURRY, MARGARET ALICE	1864	NC	107	1947	TN		107	1 1889	TN		NORRIS AMBROSE TUCKER	60430
MCCOURRY, MARTIN HALEN	1869	NC	107	1923	TN			1			MISS/MRS LAWSON	60430
								2			RENA HARTMAN	
MCCOURRY, MARY C	1860	NC	107									60430
MCCOURRY, TILMAN H	1862	NC	107	1908	AL							60430
MCCOURRY, WILLIAM ENSLEY	1828	NC	?013	1893	TN		107	1 C1849	NC		NANCY CAROLINE BYRD	60430
MCCOURRY, ZEPHANIAH	C1803	NC		C1885	NC		107	1 C1825	NC		JANE	60430
MCCRACKEN, ALEXANDER	C1725			1795	NC	073		1 1750	DE		ABIGAIL FAIL/FAYLE	20135
MCCRACKEN, ANN	C1754			1828	NC	065		1			JOHN MCLURE/MCCLURE	14050
MCCRACKEN, ANN	1794	NC	065					1 1838	NC	065	EDWARD L STEPHENS	14050
MCCRACKEN, BARBARA M	C1828	NC	065					1 1852	NC	065	JAMES F CALDWELL	14050
MCCRACKEN, ELEANOR	C1752						065	1	?NC	?065	JOHN BOHANNON/BUCHANAN ?	14050
MCCRACKEN, ELEANOR	1795	NC	065		?NC	?065						14050
MCCRACKEN, ELIHU J	1796	NC	065	1853	NC	065		1 1819	NC	065	ESTHER CARR/KERR	14050
MCCRACKEN, ELIZABETH	1788	NC	065	1829	NC	065		1 1809	NC	065	JAMES SAMPLE ALEXANDER	14050
MCCRACKEN, ESTHER	1792	NC	065					1 1822	NC	065	JAMES CLENNY	14050
MCCRACKEN, HUGH				C1755	NC	085	005	1			MARY	14050
MCCRACKEN, HUGH				C1760	NC	005		1 C1748			SARAH	14050
MCCRACKEN, HUGH	C1757	NC	005									14050
MCCRACKEN, HUGH	1771	NC	065	1843	KY							14050
MCCRACKEN, JAMES	C1750			1802	NC	065		1 C1770	?NC		JEAN/JANE	14050
								2 C1787	?NC		ELIZABETH DAVIDSON	

ANCESTOR INDEX	BIRTH	PL	CO	DEATH	PL	CO	LIVD	MARRIED	PL	CO	SPOUSE NAME	CODE
MCCRACKEN, JAMES	1778	NC	065	1829	IL			1 1804	KY		NANCY HOUCHINS	14050
MCCRACKEN, JAMES M	C1820	NC	065					1 1854	NC	085	SUSAN F GATLEN	14050
MCCRACKEN, JANE	1776	NC	065		?KY			1	?KY		JOSEPH SHIPLEY	14050
MCCRACKEN, JANE ELIZABETH	1826	NC	065	1916	GA			1 1860	NC	065	WILLIAM E EWING	14050
MCCRACKEN, JEAN/JANE, MRS	C1753			1786	NC	065		1 C1770	?NC		JAMES MCCRACKEN	14050
MCCRACKEN, JOHN	1828	NC	073	1896	NC	073		1 1858	NC	001	ELIZA ANGELINE HOLT	20135
MCCRACKEN, JOHN		SCO		C1810	NC	?085		1 C1768	PA		JEAN/REBECCA LYTLE	27301
MCCRACKEN, JULIA W	1854	NC	065					1 1876	NC	065	WILLIAM T SELLERS/SELLARS	14050
MCCRACKEN, MARGARET	1790	NC	065	1857	NC	065		1 1810	NC	065	AZARIAH ALEXANDER	14050
MCCRACKEN, MARTHA LOUISA	C1838	NC	065					1 1859	NC	065	JAMES PAGE	14050
MCCRACKEN, MARY	1773	NC	065		KY			1 1790	NC	065	ROBERT SHIPLEY	14050
MCCRACKEN, MARY ANN	C1822	NC	065		?NC	?064		1 1845	NC	065	WILLIAM MCKELVEY	14050
MCCRACKEN, MARY, MRS								2 C1756	NC	?056	HENRY JONES	14050
MCCRACKEN, ROBERT CARR?	C1824	NC	065	1892	NC	065		1 1845	NC	065	JANE D MCKELVEY	14050
								2 1850	NC	065	MARTHA A ROSS	
MCCRACKEN, ROBERT ED	1869	NC	065		?SC			1 1900	GA		CLARA S KING	14050
MCCRACKEN, ROBERT H	1857	NC	085	1935	NC	065	107	1 1882	NC	026	LULA CATHERINE MOORE	14050
MCCRACKEN, RUTH	1782	NC	065	1840	?IL			1 1805	KY		DANIEL DOUGLAS/DOUGLASS	14050
MCCRACKEN, SARAH	1775	NC	065	1856	KY			1 1802	KY		DAVID STICE	14050
MCCRACKEN, SARAH, MRS				1785	NC	065		2 C1762	NC	?065	JOHN HANNA/HANNAH	14050
								3 C1771	NC	?065	EDWARD MCMURRY/MCMURRAY	
MCCRACKEN, THOAMS	1794	NC	073	1892	NC	073		1 C1825	NC	073	CATHERINE TINNIN	20135
MCCRACKEN, THOMAS	1780	NC	065									14050
MCCRACKEN, THOMAS	1752	NC	073	1835	NC	073		1 C1777	NC	073	PRISCILLA HOLLOWAY	20135
MCCRACKEN, WILLIAM	C1756	?NC	?005				065					14050
MCCRACKEN, WILLIAM DAVIDSON	1798	NC	065	1872	GA			1 1825	GA		OLIVIA HEYDEN	14050
MCCRACKEN, WILLIAM DAVIDSON	1830	NC	065	1863	DE		?003	1 1858	NC	065	MRS MARY REBECCA (RUSS) RILEY	14050
MCCRACKEN, WILLIAM DAVIDSON MCKNETT	1859	NC	065	1923	NC	065	064	1 1882	NC	065	FANNY JANE CHRISTENBURY	14050
MCCRARY, ADOLPHUS	C1821	NC	050		NC	?050		1			JULIE ANN JONES	09030
MCCRARY, BOYD					NC	050		1			CHARITY MERRILL	09030
MCCRARY, JAMES	1735	PA		1820	KY		085	1 1765	PA		ISABELLA GIFFIN	60415
MCCRARY, JOHN	1771	NC	085	1857	IA			1 1795	NC	054	RUTH WASSON	60415
MCCRORY, MARTHA EMILY	1835	NC		1909	TN			1 1866	TN		JOHN LEVI PERRY	17129
MCCULLAH, ELIZABETH KENNEDY	1785	NC		1868	IA			1 1810	TN		SAMUEL EVANS	60004
MCCULLAH, JOSEPH	C1748			1822	TN		085	1			ELEANOR	60004
MCCULLOCH, MARGARET	1735			1792	NC	035		1			GEORGE MILLER	02145
MCCURDY, DARIUS	1815	NC	085	C1870	MS			1 C1835	?AL		ELIZABETH JONES	60286

ANCESTOR INDEX	BIRTH	PL	CO	DEATH	PL	CO	LIVD	MARRIED	PL	CO	SPOUSE NAME	CODE
MCCURDY, THOMAS	C1750			1821	KY		?073	1			MARY	08065
MCDANIEL, DORCAS	C1793	NC	046	C1858	IL			1 C1805	NC	046	DANIEL SMITH	27392
MCDANIEL, JAMES				C1760	NC	?028		1			MARGARET	27346
MCDANIEL, JOHN				1817	NC	057						27346
MCDANIEL, SILAS		NC	?057	C1845	FL			1 C1810	NC	?057	MARY	27346
MCDANIEL/MCDONALD, DANIEL	C1690			1734	NC	010		1 C1716			SARAH	17080
MCDANIEL/MCDONALD, JAMES	C1717	NC	024	1759	NC	028	010	1 C1730	NC	010	MARGARET BRYAN ?	17080
MCDANIEL/MCDONALD, JAMES I	C1735	NC	?028	1779	NC	011	010	1 C1760	NC	?011	AGNES GRAY ?	17080
MCDANIEL/MCDONALD, SUSAN	1826	NC	029	1909	NC	029		1 1847	NC	029	ALEXANDER MAXWELL	17080
MCDANIEL/MCDONALD, WILLIAM GRAY JR	1796	NC	029	1863	NC	087		1 C1820	NC	011	THAMER FORT ?	17080
MCDANIEL/MCDONALD, WILLIAM GRAY SR	C1765	NC	011	C1800	NC	029	011	1 C1790	NC	029	DICEY THAMES ?	17080
MCDONALD, ALLEN	1797	NC		1861	MS			1 1823	AL		KEZIAH WHITSETT	60179
MCDONALD, ARCHIBOLD	C1796	NC		C1865	AL			1 C1830	GA		HARRIET	60177
MCDONALD/MCDANIEL, ARCHIBALD	C1740	SCO		C1830	NC	011						60568
MCDONALD/MCDANIEL, REDDING	C1824	NC	011	C1895	NC	029		1 C1850	NC		PENELOPE SIMMONS	60568
MCDONALD/MCDANIEL, SMITH	C1795			C1870	NC	029	011	1			CHARLOTTE HALL	60568
MCDORMAN, JOHN	C1777				OH			1 1799	NC	046	JUDY BUNCH	60370
MCDOUGALD, NANCY	C1790	NC	029	1870	KS		014	1 1811	NC	029	WARREN MASSEY	60441
MCDOWELL, ABIGAIL	1740	PA		1805	NC	065		1	NC	065	ROBERT MCCLEARY	25040
MCDOWELL, LUCINDA	C1817	NC	?049		GA			1 1836	NC	061	WILLIAM WATSON	60261
MCEACHIN, ALEXANDER	1790	SCO		1881	MS		?082					27335
MCEACHIN, MALCOLM	1827	NC		1904	MS			1 1856 2 1874 3	MS MS AR		MARTHA PIPKIN MAGGIE COOK JOSEPHINE PATTERSON	27335
MCELROY, ARCHIBALD	1719	MD		1760	NC	056		1			CATHERINE SIMPSON ?	60507
MCELROY, ARCHIBALD JR	C1738	NC	028	1760	NC			1 C1759			SARAH	27270
MCELROY, ARCHIBALD SR	1719	MD		1760	NC	056		1			CATHERINE	27270
MCELROY, AVINGTON	C1836	NC	?028	C1797	GA			1 1770	NC	056	SARAH DAWSON	60507
MCELROY, ISAAC	1777	NC	056	1830	TN			1 C1780			SARAH FLOYD	60507
MCELROY, JAMES		NC	084		TN			1 1808 2	NC	084	MARY SMALL REBECCA STOKES	60010
MCELROY, MARTHA A E	1837	NC		1879	TN			1 1856	TN		WILLIAM DANIEL HILLIARD	60010
MCELROY, MICAJAH	1760	NC	099	1734	TN			1 C1781	NC	099		27270
MCELROY, WILLIAM		NC	084									60010
MCFALLS, ARTHUR	1752	VA		C1843	NC	107	014	1 1814	NC	014	EMZEY HOLLIFIELD	25087
MCFARLAND, ELEANOR R	1768	NC		1837	MO			1 1795 2 1810	NC KY		HOSEA GREEN TAPLEY STEPHEN CLEAVER	03020
MCFARLAND, ROBERT	C1731	?VA		1780	NC	020		1 1754	NC		MARGARET	03020

ANCESTOR INDEX	BIRTH	PL	CO	DEATH	PL	CO	LIVD	MARRIED	PL	CO	SPOUSE NAME	CODE
MCFARLIN, BENJAMIN				C1823	TN		046	1 1774	NC	046	ELIZABETH NELSON	60443
MCFARLIN, BENJAMIN JR	C1795	NC	084	1829	TN			1 1818	TN		MRS ELIZABETH (LAUGHLIN) BERRY	60443
MCGAUGHY/MCGAHA, JAMES	C1790	NC	086				061	1			SARAH	60091
MCGAUGHY/MCGAHA, JESSE	1804	NC	065	1898	NC	093		1			CANDACE HIGHTOWER	60091
MCGAUGHY/MCGAHA, JOHN	C1824	NC	049	C1897	GA		061	1 1847	NC	061	CAROLINE PATTON	60091
MCGAUGHY/MCGAHA, JOSEPH	C1790	NC	014					1			MISS/MRS HOGSED/HOGSHEAD	60091
MCGAUGHY/MCGAHA, LENO	C1798	NC	086									60091
MCGEE, DRUARY	C1825				NC	017		1 1850	TN		MARGARET SELINA CARLTON	25253
MCGEE, HOLLAND	1813			1899	NC	104		1 1831	NC	104	NANCY WRIGHT	25253
MCGEE, JESSE	C1775	NC	?022	1836	SC			1 C1790	NC	?022	TALITHA KITCHEN/KINCHEN	25129
								2 C1820	SC		NANCY LANDRUM	
MCGEE, JOHN				1773	NC	046	073					12125
MCGEE, NANCY	C1754	NC	073	1832	NC	046		1 1772	NC	046	ROBERT LINDSAY	12125
MCGEE, RALPH	C1800	NC	104					1 1822	NC	104	LUCINDA LIVINGSTON	25253
MCGEE, WILLIS	1793	NC	?022	1861	SC			1 1815	SC		MARY LIDDELL	25129
MCGEE/MCGHEE, JACOB LEROY	1802	NC	054	1870	MO			1 1823	SC		NANCY TEAGUE	08150
MCGILL, JOHN	1764			1819	NC	060		1			REBECCA MCKENNY	27593
MCGILL, REBECCA	1810	NC	060	1868	AR		?040	1 1830	NC	060	CHARLES H OATES	27593
MCGILL, WILLIAM		IRE			PA		060	1			ELIZABETH BELL	27593
MCGINN, JAMES	C1740				NC	065		1			ELIZABETH	27380
MCGINN, JAMES HARRIS	C1803	NC	065					1			LUCENDA	27380
MCGINN, THOMAS	C1767			1839	NC	065		1 1795	NC	065	ANN MCKINLEY	27380
								2 1800	NC	065	MARY TODD	
MCGINN, THOMAS H	C1842	NC	065					1			SARAH SELENE LOVELACE	27380
MCGLAUGHLIN, ABSOLEM	C1790	NC		1877	TN			1			R	60584
MCGREGOR, EVE	1797	NC	?029	1857	TX			1			JOHN HUCKABEE	60185
MCGREGOR, HECTOR		NC	?068									60185
MCHUGH/MCCUE, SAMUEL ROEBUCK	C1805	NC		C1885	SC			1 1828			SUSAN KEMP	60023
MCKAY, DANIEL MONROE		NC	085	C1849	NC	054		1 1807	NC	054	MRS CHRISTIAN (MCINTOSH) MCLEOD	60592
MCKAY, ZILPHA C	1836	NC	054	1906	MS		064	1 1856	NC	064	WILLIAM WHITE	60592
MCKEE, ALEXANDER	C1743			C1835	TN		073	1 C1770			MARY BEAN	08226
MCKEE, MARY	1774	NC	073					1 1792			RICHARD FAUSETT	08226
MCKEITHAN, DOUGALD	C1786	NC	068	1847	GA			1 C1805	NC		NANCY WADSWORTH	60040
MCKEITHAN, MARY CAROLINE/POLLY	C1824	?NC		C1885	GA			1 1842	GA		ADDISON BARNETT BROWN	60040
MCKEITHAN, NEILL	C1752	SCO		1835	NC	068		1 1785	NC	068	LOVEDY MCLAUGHLIN	60040
MCKINNE, BARNABY SR		VA		1756	NC	047	037	1 1720	VA		MARY EXUM	07078
MCKINNE, PATIENCE	1715	VA			NC			1 1730	NC		JOSEPH LANE	07078
MCKINNEY, ANN AMANDA	1834	NC		1916	TX			1 1853	MS		WILLIAM DAVID JARRATT	27773

ANCESTOR INDEX	BIRTH	PL	CO	DEATH	PL	CO	LIVD	MARRIED	PL	CO	SPOUSE NAME	CODE
MCKINNEY, CHARLES	C1770			C1857	NC	064	107	1 1813	NC	014	ELIZABETH LOWERY	05059
MCKINNEY, CHESTERFIELD		NC		C1848				1 C1832			LUCINDA MEEK	27773
MCKINNEY, MARTHA/PATSEY	C1777	?NC			GA			1 1790	NC	104	BENJAMIN PARR	17070
MCKINNEY, SAMUEL	C1800	NC			NC	066	017	1 C1820	?NC	014	MARGARET	05059
MCKNIGHT, MOSES	1791	NC	054	1849	TN			1 C1815	TN		ERIXENE MCEWEN ROSEBOROUGH	60443
MCKNIGHT, WILLIAM	1752	NC	005	1831	TN			1 1777	NC	085	ISABEL WADDELL	60443
MCLAUCHLIN, ARCHIBALD	C1791	SCO		1869	NC	029		1	NC		SARAH ANN	60136
MCLAUCHLIN, SARAH ANN	C1821	NC	029	1875	CA			1 1844	NC	029	REV CHARLES PINCKNEY JONES	60136
MCLEAN, ARCHIBALD	C1835	NC	083					1 C1851	NC	083	REBECCA PAUL	60224
MCLEAN, ISAAC	1837	NC	083	1908	NC	083		1 1885	NC	083	MARGARET LEGET	60224
MCLEAN, JOHN	C1807	NC	083	1863	NC	083		1 1836	NC	083	FLORA MCLEAN	60224
MCLEAN, JOSEPH N	1852	NC	083	1930	FL			1 1879	NC	083	MARY MCLEAN	60224
MCMAHAN, ELIZABETH				C1800			085	1			SAMUEL BRYAN	08023
MCMENAMY, JOHN				1800	NC	020						60575
MCMENAMY, WILLIAM	1760	NC	073	1835	NC	020		1 C1807			JEAN BARENTT	60575
MCMILLAN, CATHERINE MCKAY	1840	NC	011	1916	NC	029		1 1866			STEPHEN H JOHNSON	13052
MCMILLAN, GILBERT	1722	SCO		1772	NC	?011		1 C1747	SCO		CHRISTIAN MCBRYDE	27566
MCMILLAN, JOHN	1760	NC	020	1840	GA		090					60012
MCMILLAN, NEIL	1797	NC	083	C1865	NC	011	083	1 1816	NC	083	CATHERINE CAMPBELL	13052
MCMILLAN, RONALD	1780	SCO		1838	NC	027		1			MARY	12144
MCMILLAN, WILLIAM HENRY	1810	NC	029	1901	GA			1 1834 2 1837	NC FL	029	CATHERINE JEAN CAMPBELL MRS MARY CAROLINE (MULLER) BLUE	17220
MCMINN, JOHN A	C1774	NC	?094	C1808	NC	013		1	NC	013	ELIZABETH	60078
MCMINN, JOHN M	1803	NC	013	C1867	NC	050		1	NC	013	FRANCES SANDERS	60078
MCMINN, MARGARET CORA	C1838	NC	050	C1868	AR			1 1853	NC	050	WILLIAM WESLIE WOLFE	60078
MCMINN, ROBERT	C1745			C1797	NC	086		1			JANE	60078
MCNAIR, JOHN	1735	SCO			NC	082		1 1772			CATHRINE BUIE MCFARLAND	27697
MCNAIR, MALCOLM P	1804	NC	?082	1879	SC			1 1833	NC	082	EFFIE MCLAURIN	12019
MCNAIR, MALCOM, REV	1776	NC	082	1822	NC	082						27697
MCNAIR, MURPHY C		NC	082									27697
MCNAIR, NEILL	1796	NC	?082	1861	SC			1			MARY CRAWFORD	12019
MCNAIR, SARAH ANN	1773	NC	005		MS		083	1 C1794	NC	082	PETER WILKINSON	27697
MCNEAL, ARCHIBALD				1774	NC	065	011	1 C1760	NC	?065	MARTHA SPRATT/SPROT	19230
MCNEELEY, JAMES	C1783	NC	?020	1835	NC	020		1 1804	NC	020	MARY/POLLY YATES	60083
MCNEELEY, JOHN		?PA			NC	?020						60083
MCNEILL, ARCHABALD	1818	NC	068	1880	NC	068		1	?NC	?068	WINCY JANE BREWER	19183
MCNEILL, DANIEL	C1770	SCO			?NC	?068		1 C1815 2	NC ?NC	068 ?068	RACHEL SMITH PRATELY BRITT	19183

ANCESTOR INDEX	BIRTH	PL	CO	DEATH	PL	CO	LIVD	MARRIED	PL	CO	SPOUSE NAME	CODE
MCNEILL, HECTOR	C1750	SCO			NC	068		1	SCO		SALLY	19183
MCNEILL, JOHN		SCO		C1826	AL		082	1 1801	NC	082	NANCY MARTIN	27549
MCNEILL, JOHN C	C1816	NC	082	1875	AL			1 1841	AL		MARY A HAMILTON	27549
MCNEW, JAMES M	C1806	?NC		1869	NC	062						60479
MCNEW, WILLIAM RILEY	1837	NC	013	1915	TN			1 1866	NC	?062	HARRIET J ODELL	60479
MCPEAK, GEORGE WASHINGTON	C1801	?NC			TN			1			ELIZABETH SAUNDERS/SANDERS	60383
MCPEAK, PATTON A	C1816	?NC			TN			1	?NC		POLLY	60383
MCPHAILL, JOHN	C1770	SCO		1852	AR		083	1			BARBERY MALLOY	60516
MCPHERSON, DEMPSEY				1825	NC	018		1			CHARITY	60307
MCPHERSON, DINAH	1789	NC	018	1855	NC	018		1 1808	NC	018	ABNER LAMB	60307
MCPHERSON, JONATHAN		NC		1815	LA			1	NC		HANNAH	60086
MCQUEEN, MALCOLM	1786	NC	?011	1863	MS		?083	1 C1805				60179
MCQUEEN, MARGARET				1785	NC	011		1			PHILIP MCRAE	13105
MCQUISTON, MARY	1775	NC	046					1 C1791	NC	046	GEORGE CUMMINGS/CUMMINS	60393
MCQUISTON, MOSES	C1747	PA		1800	NC	046		1			ELIZABETH BLAIR	60393
MCQUISTON, ROBERT		IRE		1759	NC	085		1			JEAN RUTH	60393
MCRAE, CATHERINE	C1763			1837			005	1 1781			JOHN MCRAE	13105
MCRAE, CHRISTOPHER	1782	NC	011	1855	AR		083	1 1815			JANET MCRAE	13105
MCRAE, DUNCAN L	1816	NC	085	1863	AR			1 1851	AR		MARY ANN CHIPMAN	13105
MCRAE, JANET	1783	NC	005	1857	AR			1 1815			CHRISTOPHER MCRAE	13105
MCRAE, JOHN	1760			1840			005	1 1781			CATHERINE MCRAE	13105
MCRAE, PHILIP		SCO		1785	NC	011		1			MARGARET MCQUEEN	13105
MCREA, MARY ANN	1811			1859	GA			1 1826	NC	005	FREDERIC WARREN	27313
MCREE, ABRAHAM CRUSER	1786	NC	065	1879	NC	016		1			CATHERINE DAVIDSON	27406
MCREE, ANDREW	1756	NC	005	1801	NC	065		1 1791	NC	065	MARTHA ELLIOTT	27406
MCREE, DAVID	C1749	NC	011	C1805	NC	054						27406
MCREE, HUGH				C1803	NC	016		1			ANN	27406
MCREE, JAMES	1752	NC	005	1840	NC	013		1 1777	NJ		RACHEL CRUSER	27406
MCREE, JAMES POLK	1788	NC		1873	TN			1 1810	NC	065	MARIA BREVARD	27406
MCREE, JAMES, REV	1752	NC	005	1840	NC	013	065	1 1777	NJ		RACHEL CRUSER	04195
MCREE, JOHN		NC	065	C1802	SC			1			MARY	27406
MCREE, JOHN W	C1741	NC	011	1795	NC	065		1			RUTH ALEXANDER	27406
MCREE, MARY	C1751	NC	005		NC	065						27406
MCREE, RICHARD	C1737	NC	011	1830	GA							27406
MCREE, ROBERT				C1793	NC	011		1			MARTHA	27406
								2			JANE	
MCREE, ROBERT	C1702			1775	NC	065						27406

ANCESTOR INDEX	BIRTH	PL	CO	DEATH	PL	CO	LIVD	MARRIED	PL	CO	SPOUSE NAME	CODE
MCREE, ROBERT C	C1740	NC	011	1795	NC	065		1			MARGARET POLK	27406
MCREE, SAMUEL				C1798	NC	011		1			MARY WOMACK	27406
MCREE, SAMUEL	C1706			C1764			035	1	NC	?065	ELIZABETH POWELL	27406
MCREE, WILLIAM	1713	IRE		1789	NC	065	054	1 C1735	IRE		DINAH	04195
MCREE, WILLIAM	1766	NC	065	1845	TN			2 C1797	NC	065	JANE CRAIGHEAD	27406
MCREE, WILLIAM	C1675			C1751	NC	035						27406
MCREE, WILLIAM ELLIOTT	1784	NC	065	1860	TX			1			SARAH HOUSTON	27406
MCSWAIN, CATHERINE	C1763	NC		C1832	NC			1 C1782	NC		WILLIAM WADSWORTH	27740
MCSWAIN, MARTHA	C1760	NC						1 C1782	NC		JAMES HUDSON	27740
MCSWEEN, DONALD MURDOCH	C1725	SCO			NC	068		1			NANCY MCIVER	60040
MCSWEEN, SARAH	C1748	SCO		1822	NC	068		1 C1785	NC		JOHN WILLIAM WADSWORTH	60040
MEACHAM, ELIZABETH	1758	VA		1829	NC	022		1 1777	NC	022	IGNATIUS WEST	08200
MEACHAM, WILLIAM	C1730	VA		1808	NC	022		1			ELIZABETH	08200
MEARES, BETHEL		NC	011		NC	011		1	NC		ELIZABETH ANN COUNCIL	60403
MEARES, ELIZABETH DRUSCILLA	1874	NC	011	1917	FL			1 1900	NC	027	STONEWALL JACKSON BALDWIN	60403
MEARES, WILLIAM JAMES	1828	NC	011	1907	NC	011		1 1858	NC	011	DRUSILLA JANE PATE	60403
MEDFORD, GEORGE	C1790	NC	063	C1865	MS			1 1808	GA		SALLY BURGESS	60041
								2 C1845	MS		SUSAN	
MEDFORD, HENRY				1773	NC	047	063	1			ELIZABETH	60041
MEDFORD, HENRY FLETCHER				1773	NC	047						27548
MEDFORD, ISHAM	C1780	NC	063	C1848	TX			1 C1808	?SC		SARAH HOPKINS	60041
								2 1822	AL		RODA CRAWFORD	
								3 1846	TX		MRS REBECCA FINLEY	
MEDFORD, JAMES	C1757	NC	063	C1831	NC	063						60041
MEDFORD, JOHATHAN	C1786	NC	063		TX			1			SARA	27548
MEDFORD, JOHN		NC	047		?MS		063					27548
MEDLIN, BARTLETTE	C1810	NC	?039	1875	NC	039		1			RHODA	21115
MEDLIN, WILLIAM				C1840	NC	039						21115
MEEK, LUCINDA	1808	NC			MS			1			CHESTERFIELD MCKINNEY	27773
MEEKINS, JEREMIAH	1782	NC						1			MRS REBECKER (MIDGETT) SPARROW	13120
MEEKINS, ROGER							?030	1			MARGARET	13120
MEEKINS, WILLIAM				1772	NC	030		1			ELIZABETH	13120
MEEKS, JOHN	1792	NC		1863	TX			1			SARAH	60289
MEEKS, NACY	C1765	?VA		C1842	MS			1 C1790	NC		FRANCES HOLT	60289
MEGGS, JOHN		VA						1	NC	005	POLLY GORDON	60526
MEGGS, STEPHEN	1792	NC	005	1867	AL			1 1814	SC		LUCINDA ADELINE JOHNSON	60526
MEISENHEIMER, JOHAN JACOB	1720	GER		1801	NC	016		1 1746	PA		MARGARETHA REITER	60179
MEISENHEIMER, PETER	1755	PA		1835	IL			1	NC	065	MARY MAGDALENE KLEIN	60179
MELTON, ELIHUE	1798	NC		1885	AL			1			SARAH SIMMONS RICHARDS	60240

ANCESTOR INDEX	BIRTH	PL	CO	DEATH	PL	CO	LIVD	MARRIED	PL	CO	SPOUSE NAME	CODE
MELTON, MICHAEL HENDRICK	1792	NC	005	1851	MS			1 C1815	TN		RACHEL COCKRUM	20229
MELTON, MOURNING	1805	NC	069		TN			1			WILLIAM PAFFORD	60080
MENDENHALL, STEPHEN	C1750				NC	081	085	1 C1769	NC	085	ELIZABETH	27429
MERCER, COY JR		NC	075	1834	NC	018		1			DINAH	02180
MERCER, JACOB	1755	NC	030	1837	GA			2			JAEL GREEN	60240
MERCER, MARY/POLLY	C1800	NC	018					1 C1820	NC		-EMPHY (SIC) BERRY	02180
MEREDITH, JAMES	1747	VA		1823	NC	046	092	1 1769	VA		MARY CREWS	60214
MEREDITH, JAMES JR	1775	VA		1865	IN		092	1 1797	NC	046	RACHAEL KNIGHT	60214
MEREDITH, JESSE/JESSY	C1752	NC	010	1834	AL		010					27728
MEREDITH, LOUZINA	1815	NC	046	C1875	IN			1 1841	IN		ZENAS M SHRYER	60214
MERIDITH, DAVID				1782	VA		010	1			JANE	27728
MERRITT, JAMES	1747	NC	037	1837	TN			1 1768	?VA		MARY SCUTCHINS	07078
MERRITT, OBEDIAH	C1807	NC						1 C1844	TN		MILDRED SHEPHERD	60311
MERRITT, THOMAS				1758	NC	037	044	1			MARY	07078
MERRITT, THOMAS	1770	NC	037	1857	TN		099	1 1799	VA		REBECCA APPLEWHITE	07078
MESSER, COUNSEL B	C1804	NC		C1876	MS			1			SARAH	60199
METCALF/METCALFE, PAULINE	1816	NC	013	C1871	KY			1			PLEASANT HENSLEY	25242
MIDDLETON, JAMES, CAPT	1736	NC	072	1805	NC	035		1 C1765	NC	070	MARY ANN NIXON	27356
MIDDLETON, JOHN	C1680	?VA		1744	NC	072		1	?VA			27356
								2 C1725	?VA		SARAH	
MIDDLETON, ROBERT	1783	NC	035	1839	NC	035		1 1808	NC	035	ALICE JAMES	27356
								2 1821	NC	035	JEMINA HEYWARD WHITFIELD	
MIDDLETON, THOMAS JAMES	1818	NC	035	1895	AL			1 1840	AL		MARY ANN FREDERICK	27356
								2 1875	TX		MRS AMANDA (WILEY) SIMONTON	
MIDGETT, JOHN	1783			1838	NC	096		1 1806			LOIS SPRUILL	20335
MIDGETT, LEWIS	1782	NC	096	1851	NC	096		1			POLLY MANN	20335
								2 1819			MRS CHARLOTTE (PLEDGER) COMBS	
MIDGETT, SAMUEL, III	1755	NC	030	1832	NC			1 1804	NC		MRS SALLY (SPENSER) DANIEL	13120
MILAM, ADAM		?VA		1789	NC	100		1	VA			60518
MILAM, ROWLAND	C1760	VA		1828	TN			1 1785	NC	100	LIDDIA JACKSON	60518
MILAM, SARAH/SALLIE					NC	078		1 1801	NC	078	ROBERT/BOB SOUTHARD	60543
MILAM, SOLOMON	C1795	NC	100	C1849	AR			1 C1820	TN		ELIZABETH SMITH	60518
MILES, ABRAHAM/ABRAM				1804	GA		020	1			ELIZABETH TALBERT	25100
MILES, AQUILLA	C1749	NC	?044	1837	SC		073	1 1771	SC		HENRIETTA GIROUD	27673
MILES, THOMAS				1766	NC	073		2 1761	MD		MRS HANNAH MCCOMAS	25100
MILLER, ALEXANDER CALEZANCE	C1780	FR		1831	NC	011		1 1806	NC	011	MARY BROWN	27286
MILLER, ANDREW	C1767			1826	MO			1	NC	?060	JANE WILSON	60200
MILLER, ANGELINE	1811	NC		1889	AR			1 C1829	?AL		HARDIN GEORGE	60046
MILLER, CHRISTIAN	C1768	GER		1854	IL		092	1 C1790	?NC	?092	ARIAMINTA WHITEHEAD	60165

134

ANCESTOR INDEX	BIRTH	PL	CO	DEATH	PL	CO	LIVD	MARRIED	PL	CO	SPOUSE NAME	CODE
MILLER, ELI STALEY	1835	NC	081	1895	KS		046	1 1854			ANNA M WALKER	60480
MILLER, JAMES	1774	NC	028	1829	?NC	?057		1 1804	NC	057	SARAH WILLIAMS SHINE	60057
MILLER, JAMES SHINE	1807	NC	057	1881	GA			1 1829	NC	057	ELIZABETH OLIVER	60057
MILLER, JANE		NC	?065	C1840	TN			1 1822	NC	065	WILLIAM O SMITH	60431
MILLER, JOHN	1811	NC	?006	1882	IN			1 1830			SUSANNAH TIREY	60348
								2 C1873			HELEN SUTTON	
MILLER, JOHN	C1816	NC	081					1			SARAH STALEY	60480
MILLER, JOHN CAUBLE/COBLE	1820	NC	085	1902	MO			1 1846	TN		AMERICA ANN EZELL	60481
MILLER, JOHN KIMSEY	1826	NC	049	1908	TX			1 1846	NC	061	ARRENA TABOR	27488
MILLER, JOHN OWEN	C1842	NC	070	C1918	CA			1 C1873	?CA		MARY SYBIL ASHE	27286
MILLER, JONATHAN		NC		1847	TN			1	NC	090	FRY	60046
MILLER, JOSEPH	1794	NC		1892	NC	061						27488
MILLER, OLIVER	C1780	?NC										27595
MILLER, SARAH	C1795	NC		1860	MO			1 1815	NC	060	ANDREW JACKSON BROWN	60200
MILLER, THOMAS CALIZANCE	1812	NC	011	1865	NC	070		1 C1840	NC	012	ANNIE WATTERS DAVIS	27286
MILLER/MUELLER, ABRAHAM	1799	NC	085	1840	IL			1 1823	IL		NANCY MURRAY	60203
MILLER/MUELLER, PETER		NC	085	C1824	IL			1			HANNAH HARTLINE	60203
MILLER/MUELLER, WENDLE	C1729	GER		C1804	NC	085		1				60203
								2			CHRISTINA	
MILLIGAN, ISAAC	C1810	NC	?083		GA							17070
MILLIKAN, MAHLON	1829	NC	081		IN			1 1850	NC	081	NANCY DAVIS	27429
MILLIKAN, SAMUEL JR	1780	NC	081		NC	081		1 1817	NC	081	MARTHA COLTRAIN	27429
MILLIKAN, SAMUEL SR	1742	PA			NC	081	046	1 1767	NC	046	ANN BALDWIN	27429
MILLIKAN, WILLIAM	C1720	IRE			NC	046		1 C1740	PA		JANE WHITE	27429
MILLIS, EDWARD	1741			1817	NC	046		1			RACHEL HIGNITS ?	12125
MILLIS, JAMES	1764			1849	NC	046		1 1785	NC	046	MARY JACKSON	12125
MILLIS, MARY ELIZABETH	1858	NC	046	1938	NC	038		1			JAMES DODSON	60467
								2 1884	NC	038	WILLIAM THOMAS FULK	
MILLIS, WILLIAM THOMAS		NC	?046				038	1 1853	NC	046	MARY ELIZABETH WHEELER	60467
MILLS, EVERETT		?NC	?047									10010
MILLS, JOEL	C1803	NC	?014					1 1827	TN		POLLY CLOUD	60536
MILLS, MARTHA/PATTY				1834	TN		014	1 1787	NC	104	JAMES ISHAM GIDEON/GIDDENS	60454
MILLS, NATHAN	C1794	NC						1			SEALY MORGAN ?	12075
								2	NC	099	CANDACE WILSON	
MILLS, PRISCILLA	C1780	NC						1			MATTHEW/JOHN? RUST	60083
MILLS, RACHEL	C1740			1791	NC	046		1			ROBERT HODGSON	08265
MILLS, RACHEL	1758			1811	NC	046		1 1794	NC	046	ROBERT HODGSON	08265
MILLS, RACHEL	1783	NC	046					1 1813	?TN		PETER SIMMONS	25112
MILLS, WILLIAM		?NC			?TN			1 1802	NC	104	SALLEY STRUTTON	60536

ANCESTOR INDEX	BIRTH	PL	CO	DEATH	PL	CO	LIVD	MARRIED	PL	CO	SPOUSE NAME	CODE
MILLS, WILLIAM HENRY	1849	NC	099		NC	099		1		NC	?022 CORINNA THEDOCIA JACKSON POPE	12075
MILLS, ZELMA GEROY	1902	NC	099					1 1922	NC	099	LONNIE WASHINGTON ELLIS	12075
MILLSAPS, BENJAMIN KEENER	1865	NC	023	1936	OK			1 1886	NC	091	ELIZA JANE BURNS	27568
MIMS/MIMMS, DAVID				C1820	NC	022		1 1766	NC		ELIZABETH CULLEN	60028
MING, JAMES								1 1790	NC	024	ANN BEASLEY	13175
MING, JOSEPH				C1751	NC	024		1			RACHEL WARD	13175
MING, SAMUEL GREGORY								1 1815	NC	024	ELIZABETH BARTIE	13175
MING, THOMAS				C1798	NC	024		1			DELILAH	13175
MINTON, THOMAS	1812	NC	?010	1864	MO			1		KY	SARAH ANN SEAY	60094
MITCHELL, ELISHA, PROF	1793	CT		1857	NC	107	073	1 1819	CT		MARIA SYBIL NORTH	27286
MITCHELL, JAMES	C1707	VA		C1779	NC	044		1 C1730	VA		AMY ANN	03035
MITCHELL, JAMES? ROBERT		NC	?044	C1847	AL			1 1821			NANCY	60088
MITCHELL, JESSE ALPHUS	1829	NC	099	1895	LA			1 1850	AL		ELIZABETH EILAND	60112
MITCHELL, JOHN MITCHELL	C1790	NC	099	C1840	NC	099		1 C1808	NC	099		60112
MITCHELL, MARY PHEBE	1822	NC	073	1903	CA			1 C1845	NC	073	RICHARD JAMES ASHE	27286
MITCHELL, REUBEN	C1795	NC	?099					1			MARY	27555
MITCHELL, THOMAS A	C1797	NC	?044	1834	TN			1 1816	NC	044	MARTHA G BUCHANAN	60337
MITCHELL, WILLIAM		?NC	?099		NC	099		1 1845	NC	099	MALINDA BOYKIN	27543
MIZE, OBEDIAH	1781	NC	044	1859	AL			1 1802			SARAH FRAISER/FRASER	60371
MOCK, PHILIP	1824	NC	?032	1894	NC	038		1 1845	NC	090	MARY NEWSOME	13120
MOFFIT, NAOMI	1764	?NC		1840	NC	092		1		NC	092 JOHN MACKIE	60288
MOFFIT, NAOMI	1764			1840	NC	092		1		NC	092 JOHN MACKIE	60288
MOFFITT, CHARLES	C1750				NC	081		1 1772	NC	046	MARY COX	03270
MOFFITT, CHARLES	1801	NC	081	1881	NC	081		1 1826	NC	081	ELEANOR LAWRENCE	03270
MOFFITT, HUGH	1774	NC	046	1838	NC	081		1 1798	NC	081	HANNAH COX	03270
								2 C1814	NC	081	MARGARET NEEDHAM	
MOFFITT, NAOMI		NC		1840	NC	092		1		NC	JOHN MACKIE	60569
MOFFITT, WILLIAM	C1740			C1797	NC	081		1 C1763	NC	073	MARY DAVIS	03270
MOLER, HENRY SR	1780	NC	092	1855	IN			1 C1805	VA		SARAH REBECCA TOTTEN	60303
MOLER, JOHN	C1806	NC		C1861	?IN			1 1827	OH		SARAH WHEELBARGER	60303
MOLER, VALENTINE	C1750	GER		C1815	NC	054	092	1 C1775	GER			60303
MONTGOMERY, ELIZABETH							065	1 C1766	NC	065	WILLIAM HUSTON	25040
MONTGOMERY, JAMES	C1745	PA		1793	NC	065		1 1770	PA		ANN WOODS	25040
MONTGOMERY, JANE	C1788	NC		C1865	TN		014	1 C1804	NC		JOHN NELSON	07087
MONTGOMERY, JANE					NC	049		1			JOHN NELSON	60209
MONTGOMERY, JOHN	C1750			C1825	TN		049	1 C1775			SARAH MOORE	07087
MONTGOMERY, JOHN	C1710	IRE		C1778	NC	065		1 C1735			MARTHA MONTGOMERY	25040

ANCESTOR INDEX	BIRTH	PL	CO	DEATH	PL	CO	LIVD	MARRIED	PL	CO	SPOUSE NAME	CODE
MONTGOMERY, JOHN					NC	049		1			SARAH	60209
MONTGOMERY, JOHN	1767	IRE			?TN		013	1 C1788	NC	?014	MISS/MRS MOORE	60404
MONTGOMERY, JOSEPH		PA			KY		065	1 C1796	NC			25040
MONTGOMERY, ROBERT	1775	NC	065	1863	AL			1 1804	NC	065	ELEANOR MCCLEARY	25040
MONTGOMERY, WILLIAM	C1796	NC	013	1853	CA		049	1 C1816	NC	049	NANCY BALLEW	60404
MOON, EDOM	1782	NC		1879	GA			1			OBEDIENCE EDDINGS	60382
MOON, JAMES	1745	NC					022	1			ELIZABETH BRADLEY ?	60382
MOON, JESSE	1776	NC										60382
MOON, JOHN	1774	NC										60382
MOON, JOHN	1755	NC		C1795	NC	081		1 1780	NC		SARY	60382
MOON, JOHN	1717	PA					022	1			MARY FARMER ?	60382
MOON, JOHN	1752	VA		1813	NC	022		1			RACHEL ADAMS	60593
MOON, JOSEPH	1750	NC		1832	OH		081	1 1772	NC		ANN BROWN ?	60382
MOON, RACHEL								1 1758	NC	046	HENRY THORNBURGH	08265
MOON, RACHEL	C1762	NC		C1811	?TN			1 C1778			MARMADUKE BOOKOUT ?	60382
MOON, SIMON					NC	?046	085	1			LOWRY HUMPHREYS	08265
MOON, SIMON	1784	NC	022	1835				1 1807	NC		HANNAH STOUT	60593
MOON, THOMAS	1779	NC										60382
MOON, THOMAS	1742	NC		C1807	GA		022	1 1769	NC	?073	LEUCRECHER	60382
MOON, WILLIAM		NC						1 1813	NC	022	SUSANNAH HANCOCK	60382
MOORE, ABRAHAM	1805	NC	078	1862	NC	078		1 C1826	?NC	?078	ELIZABETH/BETSY BLALOCK	60543
MOORE, ANNA L	C1795	NC	073	C1880	CA			1 C1816			RICHARD DAVIS	27286
MOORE, BENJAMIN		?NC		C1837	NC	079		2 C1826			MARTHE/PATSY BOWERS	10010
MOORE, BURRELL	C1780			C1845	NC	037	079	2 1826	NC	037	RODA HEDGEPETH	60051
MOORE, CALVIN	1831	NC	037	1863	WV		105	1 1854	NC	037	EMMA ELIZA GARDNER	60051
MOORE, ELIZABETH	1782		020		TN		073	1 1807		020	FRANCIS DURRETT	60595
MOORE, ETNA	1850	NC	039	1915	NC	044		1 1874	NC	039	JOSEPH PURGERSON	02435
MOORE, GEORGE	1715	SC		1778	NC	070		1 1739			MARY ASHE	27286
MOORE, HENRY				C1840	NC	084						27375
MOORE, JACOB	1793	NC										15023
MOORE, JAMES		NC		1802	TN		073	1			MARY ANN IVEY	07095
MOORE, JAMES	1753	NC	073	1805	TN			1			CATHERINE ROBINSON	07095
MOORE, JAMES	1824	NC	092	1865	VA			1 1847	NC	092	ANNA BARBARY WALKER	14045
MOORE, JAMES	1761	NC	070					1			MISS/MRS LLOYD	27286
MOORE, JAMES H	C1810	NC		1847	IN			1 1840	IN		LUCRETIA BUTLER	60435
MOORE, JESSE	1781	NC		1874	IA			1 C1803			AMELIA/EMELIA STONE	60445
MOORE, JOHN	C1765			1843	NC	022		1			PHIRIBY	08200

ANCESTOR INDEX	BIRTH	PL	CO	DEATH	PL	CO	LIVD	MARRIED	PL	CO	SPOUSE NAME	CODE
MOORE, JOHN	1757	NC	079	1840	GA			1 1781	NC		MARY KELLERS	15023
MOORE, JOHN L	C1776	NC		C1853	MS			1 C1796			MARTHA/PATSY WHIDDEN ?	60507
MOORE, LEMUEL	C1812	NC		1884	WA			1 C1839	?IN			60435
								2 C1850	IN		MRS LUCRETIA (BUTLER) MOORE	
MOORE, MARTHA/POLLY							099	1 1785	NC	099	NEEDHAM FREEMAN	11100
MOORE, MARY	C1785	NC	022	1842	NC	073		1	NC	022	AQUILLA HERNDON	08200
MOORE, MARY ANN	1782	NC	073	1858	KY			1 1803	NC	073	THOMAS B LATTA	07095
MOORE, MIRIAM	1798	NC	060	1867	AR			1 1812	NC	060	JOHN NOLEN	60046
MOORE, MOREN	1786	NC		1872	GA			1 1808	GA		ELIZABETH SNOW	15023
								2 1809	GA		ANNY WAITES	
								3 1822	GA		ABIGAIL GRAVITT	
								4 1846	GA		ELIZABETH DOSTER	
MOORE, NATHANIEL	C1730	?VA		1808	NC	103	079	1	NC	071	FRANCES/FRANKY GILLIAM	60051
MOORE, ROGER	C1694	SC		1759	NC	070		1			MARY RAYNER	27286
MOORE, SARAH	C1758	NC		C1862	TN		049	1 C1775	NC		JOHN MONTGOMERY	07087
MOORE, SHADRICK JONES	1814	NC	056	1894	AR			1 C1838			TACY JONES	60181
MOORE, SOPHIA	C1819	NC			IN		022	1 1838	NC	073	JAMES MASON GILLIAM	25159
								2			JACK NORWOOD	
MOORE, THOMAS	C1750						?077	1			ROSANNA FOWLER	60445
MOORE, WILLIAM	C1780	VA		1853	NC	092		1			MARY	14045
MOORE, WILLIAM	1764			1849	NC	073		1 1791			MARTHA COLE	17150
MOORE, WILLIAM				?NC	?078			1			ELLIE COBB	60543
MOORE, WILLIAM, REV							073	1			ELIZABETH JOHNSON GRIMES/GRYMES	60595
MOORE/MOOR/MORE, JAMES	1824	NC	092	1865	VA			1 1847	NC	092	ANNA BARBARY WALKER	12065
MOORE/MOOR/MORE, WILLIAM	C1780	VA		1853	NC	092		1 C1800			MARY	12065
MOORMAN, ANDREW	1689	VA		C1770	NC	005		1	?VA		SARAH CLARK	60152
								2	?NC	?005	ANN DIGGS	
MOORMAN, JOHN	1769	NC	005	1842	NC	099		1 C1794	?NC	?082	SARAH THOMAS	60152
MOORMAN, JOHN THOMAS	1812	NC	082	1869	NC	082		1 1840	NC	082	ANNA ELIZA DAVIS	60152
MOORMAN, SARAH ELLEN	1852	NC	082	1933	TX			1 1873	TX		CICERO R HARPER	60152
MOORMAN, THOMAS		VA		1782	NC	082		1	?VA		SARAH CLARK	60458
MOOSE, DENNIS WILLIAM	1909	NC	054					1			EUNICE ELEANOR BOLICK	60153
MOOSE, ROBERT VERNON	1943	NC	054					1			ANITA LOUISE BUTLER	60153
MOOSE, THOMAS BOGLE	1830	NC	054	1918	NC	054		1			MARGARET MCQUARY	60153
MOOSE, WALTER LOVETT	1874	NC	054	1940	NC	054		1			NELLIE MAY HOLLER	60153
MORGAN, AARON	1840	NC	067	1929	KY			1 C1862	?TN			27257
MORGAN, CHARLES SR	C1755	?NC	?073	C1830	NC	?067	?022	1 C1785	?NC			27257
MORGAN, CHARLES/CHARLEY	C1788	NC	?022	C1865	NC	067	?022	1 C1810	NC	067	DELILAH	27257
MORGAN, DAVID C	1806	NC	005	1888	AL			1			ELIZABETH BUNN	60042
MORGAN, ELIZABETH	1825			1896	NC	013		1 1842	NC	013	THOMAS ALBERT STARNES	20380

ANCESTOR INDEX	BIRTH	PL	CO	DEATH	PL	CO	LIVD	MARRIED	PL	CO	SPOUSE NAME	CODE
MORGAN, ENOS	1765	NC		C1835	MO			1			NANCY ABERNATHY ?	60493
MORGAN, HARDY	C1775	?NC	?022	C1845	NC	067	?069	1 C1800	NC	067	ELIZABETH	27257
MORGAN, HENRY	C1812	NC	067	1902	TX			1 C1845	NC	067	ELIZABETH DENNIS	27257
MORGAN, ISAAC	C1775	NC		1848	IN		085	1 C1796			SUSAN FOUTS	60294
MORGAN, JAMES		NC	046					1			MARY DAVIS	03295
MORGAN, JAMES	1760	NC	005	1851	MS		065	1 1806	KY		NAOMI	60063
MORGAN, JAMES SR	C1750			C1805	NC	?085		1			MARY/MOLLIE DAVIS	60294
MORGAN, JESSE	1785	NC	086	1858	NC	013		1 1809	NC	086	POLLY GRANT	20380
MORGAN, JOHN				C1825	NC	029		1 1803	NC	029	KATY BULLARD	13090
MORGAN, JOHN	C1806	NC	067	C1885	KY			1 C1830	NC	067	PHOEBE	27257
MORGAN, JOHN	C1763	NC	?073	1844	MS		072	1 1799	VA		ELIZABETH SMITH ?	60063
MORGAN, JOHN L							038	1			MARY A	60467
MORGAN, JOSEPH	C1827	NC	067	C1894	KY			1 C1845	TN		SARAH JOHNSON	27257
MORGAN, MARTHA/BETSY	1768	?NC			IN			1 1789			WILLIAM WRIGHT	03295
MORGAN, PERMINTER	1755	VA		1824	NC	086	046	1 1775	NC	086	GRACIE JONES	20380
MORGAN, SELIA/CELIA CAMELINE	C1843	NC	067		KY			1 1875	KY		ALEXANDER GRIFFIN GRUGGETT	27257
MORGAN, SPENCER	1797	NC	?067		TN			1 C1822	NC	067	ELIZABETH TOLBERT	27257
MORGAN, THOMAS	C1797	NC	?041	C1858	GA			1 1824	NC	041	ELVA LASSITER	27346
MORGAN, WILLIAM LUTHER	1865	NC	038	1954	NC	036		1 1887	NC	038	MARTHA ELLEN DAVIS	60467
MORGAN, WILLIS	1811	NC	067	1862	GA			1 1836	NC	067	BETHANY BAILEY DELAMOUTHE	27257
MORRIS, ANNA	1753	NC	?018	1845	MO			1 1781	NC	018	DAVIS BIGGS	03020
MORRIS, ELIJAH	1791	NC		C1863	TX			1			SARAH	27740
MORRIS, ELIZABETH	1747			1827	IN		073	1			DAVID EDWARDS	08190
								2	NC	073	RICHARD WILLIAMS	
MORRIS, ELIZABETH								1 1831	NC	092	SAMUEL TRULOVE	60325
MORRIS, JESSE	C1729				NC	018						03020
MORRIS, JESSE	1805	NC			MO			1			NANCY	60325
MORRIS, JOHN		NC						1			HANNAH GREGG	60070
MORRIS, LUCINDA	C1807	NC		C1880	?IA			1 C1834	?GA		JOEL HALTOM	60319
MORRIS, MILLY								1 1828	NC	092	LABEN SMITH	60325
MORRIS, NICHOLAS	1803	NC	092	1869	MO			1	?NC		REBECCA CUMMINS	60325
MORRIS, WASHINGTON	1819	NC	073	1914	IN			1 1839	IN		MARY CATHERINE JACKSON	60070
								2 1864	IN		MRS ELVIRA F HAM	
MORRIS, WILLIAM JR	C1798	NC		1845	MO			1 1817	NC	092	CATHERINE BOSS	60325
								2 1830	NC	092	LUCINDY TRULOVE	
MORRIS, WILLIAM SR	C1770			C1825	NC	?092						60325
MORRISON, JOSIAH	1788	NC	?054	1868	TN			1 1807	TN		NANCY WELLS	60576
MORRISON, MALCOM	1772	SCO		1854	AL			1	NC		ELIZABETH	60061
MORRISON, THOMAS	C1750					?054						60576

ANCESTOR INDEX	BIRTH	PL	CO	DEATH	PL	CO	LIVD	MARRIED	PL	CO	SPOUSE NAME	CODE
MORRISON, WILLIAM	C1750						?014					60576
MORROW, DANIEL		NC		1846	KY		086	2 C1809	NC	086	MRS SARAH DAVIS	60475
MORROW, JAMES	1773	NC		1856	NC			1 1796	NC	086	ELIZABETH SUTTLE	27568
MORROW, LORENZA DOW	1822	NC	086	1907	NC	086		1	?VA		ROSA LISTER	27568
MORTON, EZEKIEL				1834	NC	067		1			ELIZABETH BRUMBALOW	24165
MORTON, ISABEL BOGART	1894	NC	062					1 1915	NC	050	THOMAS OHAGAN DUPREE	12140
MORTON, OLIVER	1763	MA		1848	GA		101	1 C1788	NC	096	SARAH EVERETT/EVRITT	60572
MORTON, THOMAS				1815	MS			1 1799	NC	078	ELIZABETH DONALDSON	60050
MORTON, WILLIAM ZENAS	1857	NC	009	1900	NC	062		1 1880	NC	062	CARNAVELLA HARDISON	12140
MORTON, WILLIAM ZENAS	1825	NC	009	1897	NC	009		1 1847	NC	009	MELISSA ANN CARR DARDEN	12140
MORTON, WINSLOW BRADFORD, CAPT	1798	ME		1837	CUB		009	1			ANN MARIE CHRIST	12140
MOSELEY, THOMAS	C1743	VA		C1790	NC	034		1			ELIZABETH	03210
MOSELEY, TULLY	1808	NC	059	1860	NC	059		1 1829	NC	?045	HOLLON HARPER	03210
MOSELEY, TULLY	C1765	?NC	?034	C1820	NC	059		1 C1789	NC	?028	SUSANNA JONES	03210
MOSELEY, WYLIE THOMAS	1830	NC	059	1897	NC	059		1 1850	NC	059	MARY ANN HARDEE	03210
								2 1872	NC	059	MARTHA ELEANOR HARPER	
MOSELEY/MOSLEY, REDDICK	C1767	?NC		1852	SC		083	1 C1796	?NC		NANCY	60287
MOSER, ADAM		GER		C1763	NC	073						60264
MOSER, DANIEL	C1800	NC		1886	MO			1 1821	NC	090	REBECCA MOSER	60192
MOSER, FRANKLIN		PA			NC	073	046					60192
MOSER, HENRY		PA			NC	060						60192
MOSER, JOHN		PA			NC	032						60192
MOSER, JOHN	1771	NC	046	1820	IN			1			MARY	60264
MOSER, JOSEPH	C1805	NC	081	1873	OR			1 1825	IN		ISABELLA DUNAGIN	60264
MOSER, LEONARD				1782	NC	092		1			SARA	60192
MOSER, PETER				1821	NC	090		1			MARGARET	60192
MOSER, TOBIAS	C1748	PA		1835	IN		081	1			NANCY MEYERS	60264
MOTSINGER, FELIX	1727	GER		1791	NC	085		2	NC	085	MRS ELIZABETH LONG	06070
MOTSINGER, GEORGE	1790	NC	085	1866	MO			1			POLLY GREEN	06070
								2 1826	IN		MRS MARY HOGGATT	
MOTSINGER, JACOB	C1761	NC	085	C1825	IN			1	?NC	?085	HANNAH	06070
MOUNGER/MONGER, HENRY	1781	NC		C1852	TN		100					60168
MOUNGER/MONGER, JETHRO W	1800	NC					100	1 1822	TN		ELIZABETH GALLIHER	60168
MOUNGER/MONGER, JOSEPH	1796	VA					100	1			ELIZABETH	60168
MOUNGER/MONGER, PETER	1775	NC					100					60168
MOUNGER/MONGER, SPELL	1778	NC					100	1 1799			RHODY COGWELL	60168
MOUNGER/MONGER, TABITHA				C1795	NC	100	100					60168
MOUNGER/MONGER, WILLIAMSON	1779	NC		1847	TN		100	1			SARAH GARDENHIRE	60168

ANCESTOR INDEX	BIRTH	PL	CO	DEATH	PL	CO	LIVD	MARRIED	PL	CO	SPOUSE NAME	CODE
MOUSER, ABRAHAM	1702				NC	060						60132
MOUSER, GEORGE	C1772	NC	060	1824	MO			1 1794			MARY SMITH/SCHMIDT	60132
MOUSER, JACOB FREDERICK	1743			1799	NC	060						60132
MOUTRAY, JAMES				1819	IN		022					60259
MOUTRAY, JOSEPH H	1760	VA		1846	MO			1 1781	NC	022	LUCY LACY/LACEY	60259
MOUTRAY, MARTHA/PATSEY	C1801	NC	022		MO			1 C1820	MO		DAVID GREENLEE	60259
MOYE, GEORGE WASHINGTON	1812	NC	028	1896	?IN			1 1839	IN		SEREPTA GRADDY	08053
MOYE, JOHN CASS	1783	NC	?028	1875	IL			1 1809	NC	028	ALSEY BROWN	08053
MOYERS, ASA/ASHER	1785	NC						1			NANCY	60044
MOZINGO, BENNIE HENRY	1899	NC	103	1933	NC	059		1 1919	NC	103	MARY VIVIAN CARTER	07040
MOZINGO, RUFUS JR	1867	NC	103	1936	NC	103		1			PAULINE ELLIS	07040
MOZINGO, RUFUS SR	1830	NC	103	1917	NC	103	059	1			GEORGIA WARD	07040
MULLEN, WILLIAM PETERSON	C1780	NC	051	1833	MS			1 1798	TN		MARY ELEANOR BECTON	60483
MULLEN, WILLIAM SCOTT	C1750	VA		C1806	TN		051	1 C1775	?VA		MARY BRITT/BRETT	60483
MULLINS, ABNER	C1810	NC	013	C1870	MO			1 1843	MO		CHANEY HALL	02252
MULLINS, ABNER SR							013	1 1789	VA		JEDIDAH JANE HAMPTON	02252
MULLINS, ALFRED B	1815	NC						1			JANE SEVACY	02252
MULLINS, DAVID	1790	NC		1866	MO			1 C1809	NC		REBECCA ANN ROBISON	02252
MULLINS, JACK							?023	1 C1856			MARY A L	08015
MULLINS, JAMES SAMUEL	C1857	NC		1900	GA			1 C1887	?NC	?023	RACHEL GRANT	08015
								2 1899	GA		NANCY RUTHA RATCLIFF	
MULLINS, MCCAMEY/M R	1817	NC		C1860	?OR			1	MO		CATHERINE MULLINS	02252
MULLINS, SARAH	1814	NC	013	1887	MO			1 1832	MO		JOHNATHAN WOLF	02252
MULLINS, WILEY MATTHEW	1787	NC		1851	IA			2			PRUDENCE ROBINSON ?	60338
MULLIS, JOHN	C1770	?NC		C1815	?KY			1 C1790	?TN		GERIAH BARNES	60312
MURKERSON, JOHN	C1770			C1829	GA		?029					27346
MURPHEY, ARCHIBALD	1742	PA		1817	NC	020		1 1769	NC		JANE DEBOW	60043
MURPHEY, ARCHIBALD DEBOW	1777	NC	020	1832	NC	020		1 1801	NC	073	JANE ARMISTEAD SCOTT	60043
MURPHEY, JAMES	C1812	NC						1 C1830	IN		NANCY	60471
MURPHEY, VICTOR MOREAU	1805	NC	020	1862	MS			1 1841	MS		LEAH MALONE	60043
MURPHREY/MURPHY, BENNETT JOHN	C1775	NC	028	C1825	NC	045		1 C1800	NC	045	MARGARET BEST	13264
MURPHREY/MURPHY, ELIZABETH	C1737	VA		C1800	NC	045		1 1755	NC	?056	JOHN SUGG	13264
MURPHREY/MURPHY, JOHN	1747	VA		C1817	NC	045	028	1 C1770	NC	?034	MARY ALDRIDGE	13264
MURPHREY/MURPHY, JOHN, CAPT	C1700	VA		1776	NC	034	028	1 C1730	VA		ELIZABETH HARRISON	13264
MURPHREY/MURPHY, MARTHA	C1750	NC	?056	C1825	NC	045		1 C1765	NC	034	ROBERT HILL	13264
MURPHREY/MURPHY, TUNNEL/TURNER	1813	NC	045	1894	NC	045		1 C1840	NC	079	APSALY BAKER	13264
MURPHY, JAMES	1805	VA		1864	TN		065	1 1830	NC	065	MARY E HIPP	60251
MURPHY, RACHEL	1803	NC		1830	TN			1 C1820	TN		EDWARD LINDSEY	60097

ANCESTOR INDEX	BIRTH	PL	CO	DEATH	PL	CO	LIVD	MARRIED	PL	CO	SPOUSE NAME	CODE
MURPHY/MURPHREY, BENNETT WILLIAM	1798	NC	042	1864	NC	045		1 C1825	NC	045	MARY JANE ALDRIDGE	13264
MURPHY/MURPHREY, DIXON	C1817	NC	045		?NC			1 C1845	NC	045	GIDEON ANN	13264
MURPHY/MURPHREY, EZEKIEL	1817	NC	045		NC	059		1 C1840	NC	045	LANEY HILL	13264
MURPHY/MURPHREY, GUILFORD	C1775	NC	028	1849	NC	028		1 1801	NC	028	ELIZABETH COX	13264
MURPHY/MURPHREY, JETHRO	C1759	NC	034	C1810	NC	045		1 C1790	NC	034	PENELOPE EVERETT	13264
MURPHY/MURPHREY, JOSIAH T HERDON	1827	NC	045	1873	NC	103		1 C1845	NC	045	ALCINDA A FRIZZLE	13264
MURPHY/MURPHREY, MICHAEL	1735	VA			NC		045	1 C1760	NC	034		13264
								2 1778	NC	035	MARY PARKER	
MURPHY/MURPHREY, OLIVER	1828	NC	045	1902	NC	045		1 C1855	NC	045	MARY JANE HARPER	13264
								2 C1864	NC	045	MARY ELIZABETH DIXON	
MURPHY/MURPHREY, WILLIAM	C1740	?NC		1794	NC	029	028	1 C1770	NC	009	LUCRETIA READING ?	13264
MURPHY/MURPHREY, WILLIAM SPENCER	C1780	NC	028		NC	079		1 C1815	NC	028	SUSANNA ROACH	13264
MURPHY/MURPHREY, WILLIS	1795	NC	042	1840	TX			1 C1820	NC	045		13264
								2 C1825	GA		PRISCILLA RENFROW ?	
MURPHY/MURPHREY, WILLIS EVERETT	1796	NC	042	C1860	NC	045		1 C1825	NC	045	AVA C ALDRIDGE	13264
MUSE, JAMES H	C1802	NC	068		NC	068		1			PATIENCE	27758
MUSE, JANE C	C1829	NC	068		NC	068		1			WILLIAM RILEY BARRETT	27758
MYATT, JAMES WILLIAM	1834			1913	NC	099		1			SPICY HONEYCUTT	60500
MYATT, NINROD	1887	NC	099	1964	NC	099		1 1911			IDA ELIZABETH DUPREE	60500
MYERS, CHRISTIAN	C1730						085	1			CATHEINRE MARGARET	20350
MYERS, JOHN	1822	NC	?060	1862	VA		016	1 1851	NC	016	MARY MATILDA GARMAN	12210
MYERS, JOSEPH	1797	NC	085					1 C1820	NC	085	MARY/MOLLY LEDFORD	20350
MYERS, NANCY	1821	NC	085					1			JOHN SUMMERS	20350
MYERS, PETER	C1753			C1822	NC	032						20350
MYRICK, MARGARET	1837	NC	068	1906	NC	068		1			WILLIAM DEDBERRY RITTER	22005

N

ANCESTOR INDEX	BIRTH	PL	CO	DEATH	PL	CO	LIVD	MARRIED	PL	CO	SPOUSE NAME	CODE
NATION, CHRISTOPHER	C1722	NJ		1801	NC	081	085	1			ELIZABETH	23070
NATION, JOHN	1698			1774	NC	046	085	1 C1720	NJ		BETHIAH ROBINS	23070
NATION, JOSEPH	C1750	VA		1804	TN		046	1 1770	NC	085	JERETER VICKREY	23070
NATION/NATIONS, JOHN	C1696	?VA		1772	NC	046		1			BITHIAH ROBINS	08120
NATION/NATIONS, JOSEPH	C1762			C1840	MS		046	1			ELEANOR ROBINS	08120
NEAGLE, ADLEY	C1805	NC	054	C1863	KY			1 1827	KY		MARGARET LAKE	60127
								2 1853	KY		HARRIET W OWENS	
NEAGLE, LOYD	C1775			C1845	KY		054	1			ELIZABETH	60127
NEAL, AARON	C1770	NC	044	1818	IL		039	1			NANCY JORDON	02065

ANCESTOR INDEX	BIRTH	PL	CO	DEATH	PL	CO	LIVD	MARRIED	PL	CO	SPOUSE NAME	CODE
NEAL, JAMES SAMUEL	1866	NC	?038	1948	SC			1 1892	NC	038	MARY LULA LASLEY	20448
								2 1900	NC		ELLEN ELIZABETH LASLEY	
NEAL, JEREMIAH		VA		1795	NC	039	044	1		NC	MARY	02065
NEAL, MOSES	C1765	NC	044	C1824	NC	039	100	1 1785	NC	100	BETSY/ELIZABETH GILL	02065
NEAL, THOMAS	C1840	NC	?090					1			ANN FULTON	20448
NEAL, YOUNGER				1784	NC	022		1 C1770			SARAH	19075
NEATHERY, HANNAH								1 1791	NC	046	JOHN MCGEE	27268
NEATHERY, JOHN	C1786	NC	?014		?TN			1 C1812	NC	?014	MARY WALKER	27268
NEATHERY, ROBERT				1805	NC	014	104	2 C1801			MARGARET POWELL ?	27268
NEATHERY, SARAH	1803	NC	014		?KY			1 1823	KY		WILLIAM EASLEY	27268
NEATHERY, THOMAS				1800	NC	014	104	1			SARAH SCOTT	27268
NEEDHAM, ALFRED	1807	NC	?075	1893	TX			1 1827	TN		MARY/POLLY DYER	60324
NEEDHAM, JOHN	C1745	NC	075	C1835	TN			1	NC	?075	REBECCA POOL	60324
								2 1780	NC	075	ANNA LETITIA/TISHA JENNINGS	
								3	?NC		MARY	
NEELY, MARY	1762	?NC	?044	1830	TN			1 C1782	NC	044	MATHEW PRYOR	60506
NEELY, MARY/POLLY	1785	NC	065	C1833	NC	065		1 1830	NC	065	JOHN TAYLOR	60518
NEELY, MOSES	1761	NC	005	1837	NC	065		1			MARGARET CAMPBELL	60518
NEELY, THOMAS		IRE			NC	065		1	NC	065	HANNAH STARR	60518
NEELY, WILLIAM				1782	NC	044		1			ELINOR	60506
NELSON, DAVID	C1720			C1795	NC	073		1 C1760	NC	073	ISABEL CRAIG	02256
NELSON, ELIZABETH					TN			1 1774	NC	046	BENJAMIN MCFARLIN	60443
NELSON, JOHN	C1765			1822	NC	073		1 1789	NC	073	JENET TATE	02256
NELSON, JOHN	1784	VA		1844	TN		014	1 C1804	NC		JANE MONTGOMERY	07087
NELSON, JOHN		NC	049	1844	TN			1			JANE MONTGOMERY	60209
NELSON, JONAS JR	1792	NC	071		NC	037		1	NC		FANNIE CRISP	27477
NELSON, JONAS SR	C1760			C1825	NC	037		1			MARY ODUM	27477
NELSON, JOSEPH	1831	NC	028	1903	NC	028		1 1874	NC	100	MARTHA SARAH WILLIAMS	60030
NELSON, JOSEPHUS, COL				C1830	NC	028		1 1830	NC	028	ESTHER E NELSON	60030
NELSON, MARGARET	1763	NC	?073	1824	NC	073		1 1785	NC	073	JAMES TATE	02256
NELSON, MARY/PEGGIE	1815	NC	073	1860	NC	073		1 C1834	NC	073	JOHN M PAUL	02256
NELSON, RACHEL	C1775	NC	?028	C1855	AL			1 1794	NC	028	WILLIAM WILLIAMS	60015
NELSON, THOMAS TIEGE?				C1790	NC	028						60030
NELSON, WILLIAM B	C1822	NC					?059	1	NC		NANCY	01007
NESBITT, THOMAS	C1775			C1859	NC	064		1			MANN	12050
NESMITH, THOMAS		PA			AL			1 C1770	NC	065	JENNET ROBESON	60260
NESMITH, WILLIAM		SC			AL			1 1795	NC	060	JEAN CRAIG	60260
NEVIN/NIVEN, ELIZA	1826	NC		1901	AL			1	?GA		WILLIAM L RAMSEY	27311

ANCESTOR INDEX	BIRTH	PL	CO	DEATH	PL	CO	LIVD	MARRIED	PL	CO	SPOUSE NAME	CODE
NEVIN/NIVEN, WILLIAM	1794	NC		C1850	AL							27311
NEWBERRY, JONATHAN				1838	NC	082		1			MARTHA CARTER	27328
NEWBERRY, WILLIAM				1789	NC	082						27328
NEWBERRY/NEWBURY, JOSEPH CADE/ CALVIN	C1804	NC		1862	TX			1	1826	GA	SUSAN ANDREWS	25195
NEWBERY/NEWBERRY, JAMES, REV	1799	NC	005	1853	SC			1			MARY LARGE	60265
NEWBOLD, LEVY	C1755	NC	072	1802	NC	072		1			SARAH	60562
NEWBOLD, PHOEBE		NC	072		IL			1		NC 072	HARNEY WISE	60562
								2	1839	IL	BENJAMIN HOWERTON	
NEWBOLD, PURNELL	C1725	MD		C1790	NC	072		1			POLLY	60562
NEWSOM, JOEL	C1708	VA		C1751	NC	071	010	1 C1735	?NC	?010	REBECCA DICKINSON	25087
NEWSOM, JOHN	C1740	?NC	?071	1790	NC	056		1 C1765	NC	056	PATIENCE HINNANT	25087
NEWSOME, HENRY	1817	NC	037	1862	NC	037		1	1849	NC 037	MRS NANCY (JOHNSON) COTTEN NEWSOME	60594
NEWSOME, MARY	1820	NC		1902	NC	038		1	1845	NC 090	PHILIP MOCK	13120
NEWSOME, WILLIAM		NC			NC	?051		1	1830	NC 071	REBECCA MARTIN	60211
NEWTON, EBENEZER	C1730			C1812	NC	086		1 C1751			ELIZABETH BUCHANAN	60461
NEWTON, NICHOLAS				1795	NC	068		1			MELONY MELTON	60395
NICHOLS, ANNIE AUGUSTUS	1852	NC	?099	1931	AR			1	1873	NC 099	GEORGE HENRY WHITE	20007
NICHOLS, WILEY	1826	NC	099	C1868	AR		?056	1	1850	NC 038	MARGARET BAKER	20007
NICHOLSON, ALEXANDER L	C1810	NC			AR			1	1844	GA	MRS MARTHA (MURDOCK) JEAN	60103
NICHOLSON, ARCHIBALD	1813	NC	068	1864	GA			1	1841	GA	MARY ELIZABETH HALL	60040
NICHOLSON, ATKINS	C1775			C1838	TN		039	1			ELIZABETH KNOTT	08040
NICHOLSON, DANIEL	1809	NC	068									60040
NICHOLSON, DUNCAN	C1777	SCO		1861	AL			1 C1808	NC	?068	MARY BLACKMAN	60040
NICHOLSON, DUNCAN LAFAYETTE	1817	NC	068	1860	AL			1 C1849	GA		MARY A NELMS	60040
NICHOLSON, ELIZABETH	1811	NC	068		?TX			1	1834	GA	ISAAC W JACKSON	60040
NICHOLSON, ISAAC W	1793	NC	030	1861	MS			1	1822	AL	MARTHA JEFFERSON GOODE	60384
NICHOLSON, JOHN	1815	NC	068									60040
NICHOLSON, JOSIAH	C1758	NC	030	1833	AL			1			ELIZABETH	60384
NICHOLSON, NANCY	1821	NC	068	1887	GA			1	1845	GA	JESSE HOWELL	60040
NICHOLSON, WILLIAM	1819	NC	068									60040
NITE, JOHN EDWARD	1805	NC		1849	TX			1			LUCY STEPP	60491
NIX, JOHN	1756	NJ			KY		086					60146
NIX, WILLIAM	1794	NC	060	1874	KY		086	1 C1812	KY		REBECCA STANSBURY	60146
NIXON, ROBERT	C1723	NC	?028	1799	NC	070		1	NC	070	ELEANOR MCCLAMMY	27356
NIXON, THOMAS		NC	070		NC	070						27356
NOBLE/NOBLES, JOHN		?NC		C1774	NC	079		1			ELIZABETH WARD	10010
NOLAND, PATIENCE, MRS	C1770	NC	065	C1822	TN			1 C1788	NC		PASKENS NOLIN/NOLAND	14019

ANCESTOR INDEX	BIRTH	PL	CO	DEATH	PL	CO	LIVD	MARRIED	PL	CO	SPOUSE NAME	CODE
NOLEN, JOHN	C1785	NC	060	C1837	NC	060		1 1812	NC	060	MIRIAM MOORE	60046
NOLIN, DANIEL	C1808	NC		1855	IL			1 C1833	TN		LUCINDA JOPLIN	14019
NOLIN, JAMES D	C1810	NC		1842	TN			1 C1831	TN		ARABELLA	14019
NOLIN, MARY, MRS	C1790	?NC		1851	TN			1 C1808	?NC		DAVID NOWLIN/NOLIN	14019
NOLIN, PASKENS	C1765	?NC	065	C1809	NC	065		1 C1788	?NC		PATIENCE	14019
NORFLEET, MARMADUKE	C1700	NC	077	1774	NC	?071	?010	1			ELIZA GORDON	01065
								2			JUDITH RHOADES	
NORFLEET, PHEREBY				C1798	NC	037		1 1765	NC	037	JOSHUA BELL	27441
NORFLEET, THOMAS	C1695	VA		C1749	NC	037		1			RUTH BLUNT	27441
NORMAN, DAVID C	1806	NC	092	1893	NC	092		1 1833	NC	092	MILLY	60546
NORMAN, ELLIS	1844	NC	092	1918	NC	106		1	NC	106	TEMPLE POINDEXTER	60546
								2 1870	NC	106	SUSAN ALSEY POINDEXTER	
NORMAN, FERNANDO HAYNES	1858			1922	NC	050		1 1880	NC	050	LOUISE NAOMIE KUYKENDALL	60582
NORMAN, JAMES WASLEY	C1838							1 1858	NC	050	REBECCA LYDAY	60582
NORMAN, LEECY	1866	NC	106	1976	NC	038		1 1905	NC	106	JULIUS RUFUS WILLIAMS	60546
NORMAN, ROBERT	1777	NC		1855	TN		073	1 1816	TN		MARTHA/PATSY COFFEE	27682
NORMAN, WILLIAM	C1750	VA		1827	GA		073	1	NC		NELLIE SHEPPARD	27682
NORMAN, WILLIAM	C1770	NC	092		NC	106		1			SARAH	60546
NORRIS, ANN	C1795	NC	019		NC	019		1 1811	NC	019	JOHN DICKINSION	06080
NORRIS, MATHEW		NC		C1825	NC	019		1 1793	NC	019	FRANCES FJREMAN	06080
								2 1810	NC	019	ELIZABETH REES	
NORWOOD, GROVER JACKSON SR	1886	NC	036	1935	IL			1 1911	NC	036	SALLIE VANN HART	25235
NORWOOD, JAMES WASHINGTON	1836	NC	099	1911	NC	036		1 1868	NC	099	MARY A BELVIN	25235
NORWOOD, JOHN WALL	1727	NC	010	1802	NC	039		1 1755			MRS LYDIA(HOCKNEY)LEDBETTER	25235
								2 1765			MRS LEAH CRAWLEY(LENOIR)WHITAKER	
NORWOOD, JOHN, CAPT	1759	NC		1822	NC	099		1 1782	NC	039	CLARY FERRELL	25235
NORWOOD, LETHAN	1799	NC	039	1847	NC	039		1 1829	NC	039	ELIZA BAKER	25235
NOWELL, JOHN		?NC		C1794	NC	056		1			MARA	03250
NOWELL, WILLIS W	1806	NC	099	1890	NC	099		1 1825	NC	099	ELIZABETH RHODES	03250
								2 1886	NC	099	MARY HINTON	
NOWLIN/NOLIN, DAVID	C1790	NC		1825	TN			1 C1808	NC		MARY	14019
NUTT, DAVID D		NC			NC	?020		1 1816	NC	020	AGNES JACKSON	60228

O

ANCESTOR INDEX	BIRTH	PL	CO	DEATH	PL	CO	LIVD	MARRIED	PL	CO	SPOUSE NAME	CODE
OAKLEY, CHARLIE CLEVELAND	1884	NC	078	1948	NC	078		1 1906	NC	078	CORA ALDINE FOX	60420
OAKLEY, JOHN B	1803	NC	?078	1864	NC	078		1 C1827	NC	?078	NANCY CARVER	60420
OAKLEY, JOHN B	1803	?NC	?078	1864	NC	078		1 C1827	?NC	?078	NANCY CARVER	60543

ANCESTOR INDEX	BIRTH	PL	CO	DEATH	PL	CO	LIVD	MARRIED	PL	CO	SPOUSE NAME	CODE
OAKLEY, LEVA LOUDEMA	1893	NC	104			·		1 1909	VA		HIRAM ALEXANDER HASH	08073
OAKLEY, MARY JANE	1849	NC	078	1904	NC	020		1 1869	NC	078	FRANKLIN PIERCE BLALOCK	60543
OAKLEY, MOSES LOWSON	1832	NC	078	1904	NC	078		1 1848	NC	078	ELIZABETH/BETTIE PAINTER	60420
OAKLEY, WILLIAM	1861	NC	104	1936	IN			1 C1882	NC	104	SARAH MARINDA CHAMBERS	08073
OAKLEY, WILLIAM	C1828	NC		?VA								08073
OAKLEY, WILLIAM A	1829	NC	078	1862	VA			1 C1848	NC		SARAH A BARRETT	60543
OAKLEY, WILLIE EVERETTE	1912	NC	078					1 1932	NC	078	CECILE WILKINS	60420
OAKLEY, ZACHARIAH/ZACH	1850	NC	078	1932	NC	078		1 1871	NC	078	MARY LEAH CLAYTON	60420
OATES, MARY E	1749	PA		1797	NC	060		1 1774	PA		ANTHONY CLARK	60443
OATES/OATS, CHARLES H	C1810	NC	060					1 1830	NC	060	REBECCA MCGILL	27593
OATES/OATS, JAMES				1703	NC	077		1	NC	077	ELIZABETH WYATT	27593
OATES/OATS, JOHN	1697	NC	077	1776	PA			1 C1732			FRANCES/FANNY REID	27593
OATES/OATS, JOHN	1775	PA		1849	NC	040		1 1799	NC	085	MARY BRALEY/BRALY	27593
OATES/OATS, MARY JANE	1833	NC	060	1873	AR			1 C1852			WILLIAM FOWLER	27593
OATES/OATS, WILLIAM	1734	ATS		1818	NC	060		1 1765			JEAN SLOAN	27593
ODELL, HARRIET JANE	1847	NC	013	1930	TN			1 1866	NC	?062	WILLIAM RILEY MCNEW	60479
ODELL, JOHN MARION	C1821	?TN		1873	NC	?062		1			NANCY	60479
ODOM, RICHARD				1797	NC	005		1			HONOUR JONES	60167
ODUM/ODHAM, HENRY								1 C1855	NC	?072	MARY MORTON	01012
ODUM/ODHAM, SALLIE	C1862	NC	?072	1929	NC	072		1 1877	NC	072	WILLIAM BURNS SMITH	01012
OGBURN, JAMES E		VA			NC	038		1 1831	NC	046	SARAH H TATUM	13120
OLDES, GIDEON	1811	NC		1884	TN		?073	1			MARY	60512
								2 1857	TN		SARAH A COWELL	
								3 1861	TN		RACHEL A COWELL	
OLDHAM, EPHRIAM	1815	NC	022	C1880	TX			1 1840	NC	022	JANE NEAL	60045
								2 C1846	NC	?068	SARAH A	
OLDHAM, GREEN	1843	NC	?022	1862	MD			1 C1861	AL			60045
OLDHAM, MARY FRANCES	1845	NC	?022		?TX			1 C1872	LA		MR BONNER	60045
OLDHAM, NANCY	1841	NC	?022					1 1866	LA		JOSEPH DEMPSEY	60045
OLDHAM, ROBERT D	1847	NC	?022	C1850								60045
OLDHAM, SARAH A, MRS	1825	NC	?068	C1900	TX			1 C1846	NC	?068	EPHRIAM OLDHAM	60045
OLIPHANT, MARY	1826	NC		1909	IN			1 1849	IN		JULIUS LOUIS COLEE	60006
OLIPHANT, WILLIAM		NC						1				60006
								2 1825	NC	046	MARY WYRICK	
OLIPHANT, WILLIAM	C1827	NC		IN				1			ELIZABETH BURNEY ?	60006
OLIVE, ABEL	C1755	NC	056	1809	TN		099	1 1783	NC	022	BETTIE WILLIS	60025
OLIVE, JAMES	1713	ENG		1804	NC	099	056	1 C1745	NC		ELIZABETH BURT	60025
OLIVE, JOHNSON					NC	099						27745
OLIVE, WILLIAM	C1790	NC	099	C1875	AR		022	1 1816	TN		MARTHA M?	60025

ANCESTOR INDEX	BIRTH	PL	CO	DEATH	PL	CO	LIVD	MARRIED	PL	CO	SPOUSE NAME	CODE
OLIVER, ALFRED LUNESFORD	1785	NC	020	C1837	MO			1 1803	TN		MILLY BOYD	60096
OLIVER, APSOBETH	1797	NC	056	1866	NC	056		1 1818	NC	056	WILLIAM CARTER	20450
OLIVER, DOUGLAS	1753	VA		1843	TN			1 1783	NC	020	MILDRED CARNELLE/KERNALL	60096
								2 1793	VA		CATHERINE DURRETT	
OLIVER, ELIZABETH	C1800	NC	056	C1855	?NC	?056		1 1823	NC	056	REDDEN RAIFORD	20450
OLIVER, HENRY	C1750			C1804	NC	056	103	1			LUCRETIA PEARCE	03125
OLIVER, LEVI	C1793	NC	?056	1869	NC	056	103	1 1820	NC	056	BATHSEBA RAIFORD	20450
OLIVER, MCKINNEY	C1794	NC	?056	C1872	NC	056	103	1 1821	NC	056	CHARLOTTE RAIFORD	20450
OLIVER, MCKINNIE	C1795	NC	056	1872	NC	056		1 1821	NC	056	CHARLOTTE RAIFORD	03125
OLIVER, NEEDHAM	C1770	NC	056	1846	NC	056		1 C1775	NC	?103	MARY WISE	03125
OLIVER, NEEDHAM	C1770	NC	?056	1846	NC	056	103	1 C1790	NC	?103	MARY WISE	20450
OLIVER, WILLIAM	1791	NC		1854	GA			1 1814	GA		MARY VENABLE/VENERABLE	60175
ORAND/ORRAN, JOHN		NC	084	1854	TN			1 C1814			CHARLOTTE LINDER	60361
ORAND/ORRAN, JOSEPH							084	1 C1816			RACHEL MILLER	60361
ORAND/ORRAN, MARY							084	1			MR MOORE	60361
ORAND/ORRAN, POLLIE							084					60361
ORMOND, HARDY	1819	NC	045	1871	NC	045		1 1846	NC	045	JANE ELIZABETH EDWARDS	16030
ORMOND, JAMES	1778	NC	079	1829	NC	045		1 1802	NC	045	MARY HART	16030
ORMOND, JAMES CLAY	1849	NC	045	1917	NC	074		1 C1875	NC	074	MARY ELIZABETH CAHO	16030
								2 1881	NC	074	JULIA VIRGINIA DUNN	
ORMOND, WILLIAM JR	1738	NC	009	1815	NC	045		1 1762	NC	079	ANNIE WATKINS	16030
ORMOND, WILLIAM SR	1696	ENG		1739	NC	009		1 1735	NC	009	ANN DARDEN	16030
ORMOND, WILLIAM THOMAS	1889	NC	074	1977	VA			1 1919	VA		HATTIE ESTELLE GALE	16030
ORMSBY, THOMAS H	C1812	NC	?070	C1863	?TN		?028	1 1840	MS		JANE BEARD	03328
								2 1849	TN		LUCY J FRANKLIN	
ORR, CHARLES		SCO		1788	NC	065						60460
ORR, JAMES	1743	NC	011	1829	NC	065		1 1770	NC	065	SARAH MCCONNELL	60460
								2 1785	NC	065	JANE LEMOND	
ORR, SUSANNAH	1793	NC	065	1857	MO			1 1816	NC	065	ROBERT FAIRES	60460
ORR, WILLIAM	C1761	NC	005	1821	TN			1 C1786	TN		CATY WALKER	60366
ORRELL, ADOLPHUS LAFAYETTE	1838	NC	046					1 1865	NC	029	MARGARET HILL BANKS	60326
ORRELL, DANIEL	C1760	MD		1831	NC	085		1	MD		NANCY	60326
ORRELL, DANIEL BLACK	1767	MD		1871	NC	032		1			MARY HUTCHINSON	60326
								2			MAHALA GARISON	
ORRELL, JAMES BRUCE	1875	NC	085	1937	FL			1 1897	SC		NELLIE OGILVIE SMITH	60326
ORRELL, LORENZO DOW	1811	NC	046	1868				1 1836	NC	046	ELIZA SPENCE	60326
OSBORNE, ALFRED	1834	NC	006					1			ANN?	60513
OSBORNE, ELIAS	C1778	NC	?085				006	1			MRS SALLY SIZEMORE	60513
OSBORNE, JAMES	1820	NC	006					1			RACHEL BLEVINS OSBORNE	60513
OTTEY, ANN, MRS		PA		1753	NC	070		1			JOHN OTTEY	60413

ANCESTOR INDEX	BIRTH	PL	CO	DEATH	PL	CO	LIVD	MARRIED	PL	CO	SPOUSE NAME	CODE
OTWELL, SARAH					NC	046		1			SIMEON HODSON/HODGIN	08265
OTWELL, SHADRACK					NC	046		1			ROSANNAH	08265
OUTLAND, NANCY		VA					022	1 1793	VA		THOMAS WOMBLE	27281
OUTLAW, ALEXANDER, COL	1738	NC	010	1826	AL		045	1 C1766	NC	035	PENELOPE SMITH	60034
OUTLAW, EDWARD	C1727	NC	024	1808	NC	010		1 C1756	NC	010	MARY	60337
OUTLAW, ELIZABETH	1767	NC	035	1821	AL		045	1 1780	VA		JUDGE DAVID CAMPBELL	60034
OUTLAW, RALPH	C1688	VA		C1760	NC	024		1 C1714	VA		ANN	19130
OVERSTREET, HENRY	1809	NC		1892	MS			1 C1836	?MS		NANCY H CARTER	25174
OVERSTREET, WILLIAM J	1813	NC		1892	MS			1 C1835	?MS		NANCY C HOUSTON	25174
OVERTON, ASA	C1769	?NC	?010					1			PATSEY TART	10010
OVERTON, DAVID	C1765	NC		1836	TN		?068	1	NC		LEVINA	60226
OVERTON, HENRY/JAMES HENRY		NC	051					1 C1862	NC	051	ZILLA ANN PARKER	04195
OVERTON, MOSES	1808	NC		1883	IN		?068	1 C1830	TN			60226
								2 1835	TN		SUSANNA FLETCHER	
OVERTON, VIRGINIA ANN	1864	NC	051	1952	NC	065	013	1 1886	NC		ANDERSON FULLER DUNCAN	04195
OVERTON, WILLIS	C1790	NC					079	1			KITTY PEELE	10010
								2			PINEY PEELE	
OWEN, ELIZABETH	C1799	NC	?090				092	1 1821	NC	092	DAVID MOCK	60255
								2 C1842	IN		WILLIAM GOODWIN	
OWEN, HEZEKIAH	1784	NC	085	1832	NC	032		1 1805	NC	085	ELIZABETH WISEMAN	25161
OWEN, JAMES	1784	NC	011	1865	NC	011	070	1	NC	?029	ELIZA MUMFORD	60186
OWEN, JOHN	C1742	?NC		C1835	NC	087	044	1 C1760			ANNA HAYES	27562
OWEN, JOHN	1790	NC	087	1859	NC	087		1 1815	NC	?087	SARAH BLAKE	27562
OWEN, JOHN	1787	NC	010	1841	NC	022	070	1 1813	NC	070	LUCY ANN BROWN	60186
OWEN, JOHN HUNTER	C1785	NC		1834	IN		092	1 1816	IN		SUSANNA ELROD	60255
OWEN, JOHN W	1823	NC	087	1866	NC	027		1 C1852	NC	?027	ELIZABETH CHRISTILLA BALDWIN	27562
OWEN, JOSIAH	1795	NC	090	1883	IA		092	1 1820	NC	092	POLLY PHILLIPS	60255
OWEN, MARY LIZ	1878	NC	027	1953	NC	027		1 1903	NC	027	HENRY SEYMORE HIGH	27562
OWEN, MILLARD FILMORE	1855	NC	027	1904	NC	027		1 1876	NC	027	EMELINE DAVIS BROWN	27562
OWEN, THOMAS	C1770	NC	044	C1830	NC	087		1 C1790			SARAH PARKER	27562
OWEN, THOMAS	1735	PA		1803	NC	011		1	NC	011	MARY GRADY	60186
								2	NC	?029	ELEANOR PORTERFIELD	
OWEN, THOMAS	C1760	ENG		1801	NC	090	?092	1 C1785	NC		MARGARET HUNTER	60255
OWNBEY, JAMES	1761	VA		1850	NC	086		1 1785	NC	086	JOANNA SIMS	20380
OWNBEY, JOHN	1735	ENG		1824	NC	086		1 C1760			NANCY PORTER	20380
OWNBEY, ROBERT LEE	1818	NC	086	1907	NC	013		1 1840	NC	013	MIRIAM HARPER	20380
OWNBEY, SIMS	1796	NC	086	1874	NC	013		1 1815	NC	086	RACHEL HODGE	20380
OWNBEY, SIMS	1841	NC	013	1922	NC	013		1 C1868	NC	013	GRACE CAROLINE STARNES	20380

P

ANCESTOR INDEX	BIRTH	PL	CO	DEATH	PL	CO	LIVD	MARRIED	PL	CO	SPOUSE NAME	CODE
PACE, DAVID	C1782	NC	099	1859	NC	099		1 1810	NC	099	KITTY WALL	17005
PACE, JAMES SR	C1745	NC	?037	1815	NC	099		2 1800	NC	099	LEVINA FOWLER	17005
PAFFORD, DANIEL	1813	NC		1893	IN			1 1835 2 3	IN IN IN		HANNAH MCBRIDE SALLY ROYER ELIZA STONE	60261
PAFFORD, JAMES	1765	ENG			NC	069						60080
PAFFORD, WILLIAM	1800	NC	069		TN			1			MOURNING MELTON	60080
PAGE, BENNETT	C1828	NC		1865	NY			1			SARAH HEWITT	17025
PAGE, DANIEL BENNETT	1863	NC	012	1942	AL			1 1885			ELIZABETH DORA REGISTER	17025
PAINE, JAMES	1776	NC	073	1840	TN			1 2 1817 3 1838	TN TN		MARY ALEXANDER WILLIAMS MRS ELIZABETH (BROWN) HANCOCK MRS RUTH (BARHAM) ABERNATHY	07027
PAINE, JAMES, COL	C1715			1783	NC	020		1			MARY HARDIN ?	07027
PAINE, ROBERT	1748	NC	044	1808	NC	078		1 1772 2 1790			ELIZABETH MILLER MRS AGGATHA (MARR) PERKINS	07027
PAINE, ROBERT	1799	NC	078	1882	MS			1 1824 2 1837 3 1839	TN TN AL		SUSANNAH BECK AMANDA SHAW MARY ELIZA MILLWATER	07027
PAINE, ROBERT, CPT	1748	NC	?044	1808	NC	078		1 1772	NC	073	ELIZABETH MILLER	60518
PAINE, SOLOMON	1787	NC	020					1	TN		POLLY TURNER	60518
PALMER, EDMUND		NJ		C1820	NC	085		1	NJ		MARTHA HANNAH BOWLBY	02065
PALMER, FRANCIS		PA		C1801	NC	085		1 1742	NJ		ELEANOR HOLLINGSHEAD	02065
PALMER, GEORGE	1807				NC	017		1	NC	014	LUCINDA WATSON	25253
PALMER, MCHAMEY	1829	NC	014									25253
PALMER, WILLIAM	1791	NC		1882	NC	017		1 1821	NC	014	MARY FOX	25253
PALMER/PARMER, JAMES BENJAMIN	C1799	NC		C1874	MS			1 2 C1829	AL		LOVEY WISE NANCY ANN JONES	60201
PARCEL/PERCEL, SARAH		ENG			NC		092	1			WILLIAM WOODY	08190
PARHAM, ASA MARTIN	1793	NC	044	C1885	NC	044		1 1824	NC	044	DELIA REAMS REAVIS	13264
PARHAM, ELIZA	1854	NC	044	C1910	NC	099		1 1860	NC	044	JOSEPH J WILSON	13264
PARHAM, HARRIET MELISSA	1876	NC	013	1946	NC	013		1 1891	NC	013	RALPH WEBB ISRAEL	17100
PARHAM, JOHN M	C1847	NC	013					1	NC		MRS MARTHA (INGLE) FRISBEE/ FRISBY	17100
PARHAM, LEWIS	C1755	VA		1816	NC	044		1 C1780	NC	044	LUCY REAVIS	13264
PARHAM, PHILLIP	C1823	NC						1	NC	013	ELIZABETH	17100
PARIS, HENRY	1750	NC	?072	1847	SC			1	NC	072	TALITHA MORGAN	25129
PARKER, ABIGAIL		NC						1 1828			THOMAS OZMENT	08145
PARKER, ADALINE	1826	NC	046					1			DR DAVID E CARTER	08145
PARKER, DR JOHN	1788	NC	046	1843	NC	046		1			CATHERINE PARSONS	08145

ANCESTOR INDEX	BIRTH	PL	CO	DEATH	PL	CO	LIVD	MARRIED	PL	CO	SPOUSE NAME	CODE
PARKER, ELISHA	C1789	NC		C1866	TN			1 1818	TN		MARTHA PATSEY JAMES	60334
PARKER, NANCY	1815	NC			AL			1	NC		ISAAC DANIEL	60039
PARKER, PLEASANT L	C1802	SC		1833	NC	082		1 1825	NC	056	EDITH LEE	27292
PARKER, ROBERT		NC			KS			1			BETSY HIGGINS	08145
PARKER, RUTH		NC		1877	IN			1	NC		BENJAMIN ROBBINS	08145
PARKER, SOLOMON	C1786	NC		C1860	IL			1 1817	NC	060	ELIZABETH MCCARTY	27413
PARKER, STEPHEN				1848	NC	046						08145
PARKER, VIRGINIA	C1843	NC	?005				106	1			JAMES DIKERSON HOOKER	06195
PARKS, ELTHA C A		NC		1856	?GA			1 1839	?NC	?092	MARY M WRIGHT	60113
PARKS, HARRIETT	1822	NC	103	1910	NC	045	059	1 1840	NC	103	ABNER ROUSE	13264
PARKS, LEVY	1806	NC		1865	IA			1			SUSAN SIMPSON ?	20095
PARKS, LITTLEBERRY	C1795	VA		1840	NC	103		1 C1820	NC	103	NANCY EDWARDS	13264
PARKS, MAJOR	C1755	VA		1842	NC	103		1 C1785	VA		MARY SMITH	13264
PARKS/PARKES, JOHN								1	NC			08090
PARNELL, HUBBARD	1859	NC	085	1938	IL			1 1882	IL		SARIELDA LANCASTER	27553
PARNELL, WILLIAM	C1822	NC						1			ROSANNA/ROSETTA	27553
PARRISH, BARNEY EDWARD	1810	NC	070	1883	NC	070	044	1				02435
								2 1875	NC	044	CYNTHIA GRISSOM	
PARRISH, DAVID	C1780	NC	?016	1843	IN		?022	1			PENELOPE/NELLY/ELEANOR	08240
PARRISH, FRANK	1854	NC	?099	1917	NC	056		1 1873	NC	099	MARGARET PARRISH	03315
PARRISH, GILBERT		NC			NC			1	NC			03315
PARRISH, ISAAC	C1774	NC		C1855	AL			1			SELENA	25145
PARRISH, JOE		NC			NC			1	NC			03315
PARRISH, MARGARET	1857	NC	?099	1939	NC	056		1 1873	NC	099	FRANK PARRISH	03315
PARRISH, RUFUS	1849	NC		1924	NC	048		1	NC	?048	LOUISE HODGE	03315
								2	NC	?048	FLORENCE COATS	
								3	NC	?048	SALLY HUNNYCUTT	
PARSONS, ELI	1810	NC			GA							08145
PARSONS, GEORGE	1799	NC			MO							08145
PARSONS, JANE	1805	NC			MO			1			MR ELLIOTT	08145
PARSONS, JESSE				1828	MO			1 1794	NC	105	ELIZABETH LAY	60561
PARSONS, JOHN/JACK	1802	NC		1857	VA			1 C1825			REBECCA PENNINGTON	60321
PARSONS, JOSEPH	1797	NC			MO							08145
PARSONS, MALINDA	1807	NC			MO							08145
PARSONS, RUTH	1795	NC			MO			1	NC		MR STEWART	08145
PARSONS, WILLIAM	1802	NC			MO							08145
PARTIN, NANCY	1818	NC	099	1900	NC	089	049	1 1842			THOMAS LAMBERT	24165
PATE, BENJAMIN					NC	027	099	1			DRUSILLA JOHNSTONE	21175
PATE, DRUSILLA JANE	1837	NC	011	1932	NC	027		1			WILLIAM JAMES MEARES	60403

ANCESTOR INDEX	BIRTH	PL	CO	DEATH	PL	CO	LIVD	MARRIED	PL	CO	SPOUSE NAME	CODE
PATE, EDWIN JOHNSON	1808	NC	011	1862	NC	027		1	NC		CATHERINE ANN CAMPBELL	60403
PATE, EDWIN JOHNSTONE	1808	NC		1862	NC	027		1 1826			CATHERINE ANN CAMPBELL	21175
PATRICK, JOHN	C1720	IRE					?060					60161
PATRICK, ROBERT	C1765	NC	?065	1835	KY			1 1792			ELISABETH LEEPER	60161
PATRICK, ROBERT	C1700	IRE		1776	NC	?094						60161
PATRICK, WILLIAM	C1720	IRE					?060					60161
PATTERSON, ELIJAH	1779	NC		1856	TN			1 1797	NC			60025
PATTERSON, GILBERT	C1720			1796	NC	022	011	1			SARAH	60519
PATTERSON, ISAAC	1797	NC			TN			1			ELIZABETH	60025
PATTERSON, JOHN	1796				NC	026	086	1			BARBARA WHITTIER	25100
PATTERSON, MARK	1785	NC	022	1862	TN			1 C1808	NC	022	DICEY RIDDLE	60519
PATTERSON, RACHEL	1800	NC	071	1870	OH			1 1817	OH		JOHN PLUMMER	60087
PATTERSON, SAMUEL	1820	NC	086	C1853	NC	026		1 C1844			EMELINE LONDON	25100
PATTERSON, WILLIAM	1734	VA		1812	OH		071	1 C1759	VA		KEZIAH	60087
PATTERSON, WILLIAM	1762	VA		1833	OH			1 1781	NC	071	ELIZABETH LADD	60087
PATTON, AARON	C1761	?NC	?094	1826	NC	013	?086	1 C1884	SC		MARY? MAGDALINE CUNNINGHAM	04195
PATTON, GEORGE	1786	NC	013	1840	NC	013		1 C1812	NC	013	NANCY PATTON	04195
PATTON, JOHN	C1720	IRE			NC	085						04195
PATTON, ROBERT	1742	IRE		1832	TN		013	1 C1755	NC	085	REBECCA	04195
PAUL, JOHN SR	1762			1851	NC	073		1 1795	NC	073	MARGARET PRATT	02256
PAUL, JOHN/JACK M	1805	NC	?073	1878	NC	073		1 C1834	NC	073	MARY NELSON	02256
								2 1863	NC	073	MARTHA CRAIG	
PAUL, SUSAN FRANCES	1847	NC	073	1920	NC	073		1 1867	NC	073	JAMES JONES SQUIRES	02256
PAYNE, FRANCIS FLEMMING	1787	?NC	?020	1856	VA			1 1807	NC	020	JOHN NOBLE	12100
PAYNE, WILLIAM	1800	NC		1870	IN			1 1838	NC		ELIZABETH BRANDON	60322
PAYNE, WILLIAM?							020					12100
PEARCE, GADSWELL, JR		NC					067	1 1810	GA		BETSY BLANKENSHIP	60391
PEARCE, GADSWELL, SR	C1755				?GA		067	1 C1774				60391
PEARCE, GEORGE WASHINGTON	C1850	NC	072									27374
PEARCE, JAMES	C1790	?NC		C1856	NC	072						27374
PEARCE, JAMES WILLIAM	C1875	NC	072	1946	NC	072		1 1921	NC	072	MRS LIZZIE CATHERINE (DAVIS) MARSHBURN	27374
PEARCE, JOHN GORDON	C1795	NC	067	1885	AL			1 1816	GA		MARGARET RUSSELL	60391
								2 1854	AL		MARY ANN WARREN	
PEARCE, JUDITH/JUDY	C1794	NC	078	C1859	NC	078		1 C1814			ROBERT BLALOCK	60543
PEARCE, OBADIAH	1763			C1850	NC	078		1 1794	NC	078	SALLIE/TULEY MOORE	60543
PEARCE, SION		NC					067	1 1806			ELIZABETH JONES	60391
PEARCE, WILEY	C1785	NC		C1835	GA		067	1 1804	GA		SUSANNAH JEFFERSON ?	60391
PEARCE, WILLIAM A	C1820	NC	?072	C1863	NC	072						27374

ANCESTOR INDEX	BIRTH	PL	CO	DEATH	PL	CO	LIVD	MARRIED	PL	CO	SPOUSE NAME	CODE
PEARSALL, EDWARD	1780	NC	035	1836	NC	035		1 1806	NC		ANNE GUY	17085
PEARSALL, JEREMIAH	1759	NC	070	1825	AL		035	1 2			HANNAH JOHNSTON PATIENCE MOULTON	17085
PEARSALL, JOHN	C1788	NC	035	1828	NC	085	103	1			ELIZABETH JAMES	17085
PEARSALL, JOHN DICKSON	1816	NC	035	1863	VA			1 1835			MARY WHITFIELD	17085
PEARSALL, SUSAN E		NC	035		AL			1 1829	NC		JAMES MADISON LARKINS	17085
PEARSALL, WILLIAM DICKSON	C1829	NC	035				103	1			MARY ANNE OUTLAW	17085
PEARSON, JOHN MICHAEL	C1852	NC	014	1908	NC	065		1 C1874			MARTHA A CLARK	07115
PEARSON, MICHAEL	C1820						014	1			MATILDA	07115
PEAVY, LITTLETON		NC			GA			1			MIMS	07168
PEAVY/PAVEY, DIAL							073					60295
PEAVY/PAVEY, JOSEPH							073					60295
PEEBLES, CELIA	1789			1829	NC	046		1 1806 2 C1815	NC NC	046 046	WILLIAM OGBURN EDMOND BOWMAN	12125
PEEBLES, DRURY	1757	VA		1820	NC	046		1 1784	VA		LUCY SAUNDERS	12125
PEEBLES, JEHU JR	C1734	VA		1813	NC	046		2 C1760	VA		CATY SMITH	12125
PEEBLES/PEOPLES, AGNES	C1774	NC	099	1859	KY			1 C1795	NC	099	HENRY IVY	60562
PEEBLES/PEOPLES, ELISHA				1795	NC	099		1			TEMPERANCE HILL	60562
PEEBLES/PEOPLES, JOHN S		VA		1790	NC	099		1			AGNES	60562
PEELE, PINEY	C1801	?NC	?063		NC	?079		1			WILLIS OVERTON	10010
PEELER, JOHN	1811	NC	085					1			NANCY	60511
PEGG, POLLY/MARY	C1807						046	1 1825	NC	046	OTHNIEL HIATT	60219
PELHAM, URIAH	C1760	NC	005		?AL							27356
PELHAM, WILLIAM	C1700			C1765	NC	005						27356
PELHAM, WILLIAM	C1725				SC		005					27356
PENCE, NELLY/ELLEN	1804	NC	?016		?NC			1 1822	NC	085	DANIEL CORRELL	03250
PENDERGRAFT/PENDERGRASS, JOB	C1753			1831	NC	014	073	1 C1775 2 1789	NC NC		NANCY EDWARDS MARY REEL	17090
PENDERGRAFT/PENDERGRASS, WILLIAM		VA		C1800	NC	073		1 C1748	VA		MARTHA	17090
PENLEY/PENLY, GARFIELD WILLIAM	1919	NC	013					1 1941	WA		CECELIA HEFFNER	17100
PENLEY/PENLY, ROBERT VANCE	1850	NC	107	C1933	NC	013		1	NC		SARA/SARAH ANN RICE	17100
PENLEY/PENLY, SQUIRE JAMES	1871	NC	062	1956	NC	013		1 1889	NC	062	ELIZABETH AUSTIN	17100
PENLEY/PENLY, WILLIAM	C1805	NC	014	C1875	NC	013		1 C1835	NC		MATILDA MILLER	17100
PENLEY/PENLY, WILLIAM GARFIELD	1891	NC	013	1919	NC	013		1 1911	NC	013	ANNIE BELL ISRAEL	17100
PENN, JOHN RICHARD?	C1789	NC	?085	C1873	AR			1 C1810	?TN		CATHERINE	60351
PENNELL, ELIAS	C1808	NC	014		NC	003		1 2 1878	NC	003	POLLY WALKER H MORIAH/JOLLY REED	25253
PENNELL, SUSAN	C1841	NC	014		NC	003		1 1858 2 C1870	NC NC	003 003	LARKIN BARLOW WILLIAM PENNELL	25253
PENNEY, ALEY	C1777	NC	099		KY			1 1798	NC	099	ISHAM BAUCOM	60562

ANCESTOR INDEX	BIRTH	PL	CO	DEATH	PL	CO	LIVD	MARRIED	PL	CO	SPOUSE NAME	CODE
PENNEY, CHARITY	C1790							1 C1809	NC	029	ALSA/ALSEY MATTHEWS	13090
PENNEY, EDWARD	C1730	VA		1782	NC	099	056	1			ELIZABETH	60562
PENNEY, EMMALINE	1814	NC						1			WILLIAM COOPER	02540
PENNEY, PENUEL/PENNIWELL	C1755			1806	NC	099		1			MARTHA	60562
PENNEY/PENNY, HENRY	C1754	NC	?005	1841	OH			1 1779			HANNAH BROWN	21095
								2 1831	OH		MRS MARY(THOMPSON)GIVENS	
PENNEY/PENNY, JOHN							?005	1 1752	SC		MARY ANN FINLEY	21095
PENNINGTON, ELIZABETH	C1800	NC	?006		NC	006		1 C1820	NC	?006	WELLS BLEVINS	02295
PENNY, ALEXANDER		NC			NC	?099	?056	1	NC	056	FERBY JOHNSON	60489
PENNY, EZEKIEL	1814	NC	099	1901	AL		044	1 1835	NC	044	CATHERINE WINSTON	60489
PENNY, JOB	1823	NC	099	1904	AL		044	1 1845	NC	044	LYDIA GRISSOM	60489
PENNY, JOSEPH	1822	NC	099	1875	TX		044	1 1841	NC	044	HELDA JACKSON	60489
PENNY, RILEY	C1795	NC	?099		NC	099		1	NC		JANE CARTER	60489
PENNY, SIDDA	1820	NC	099	1900	AL		044	1	NC	?044	THOMAS COLEY	60489
PENNY, SUSAN	1816	NC	099	1879	AL			1 1839	NC	099	CLEMON SMITH	60489
PEOPLES, HUGH	1748			1799	NC	022		1 1768			ABIGAIL	19075
PERDUE, NANCY W	1822	NC		1910	KY			1 1842	KY		JAMES BROWN MOSS	25229
PERDUE/PURDUE, NANCY	1823	NC		1910	KY			1 1842			JAMES BROWN MOSS	25229
PERISHO/PARISHO, ELLENER/ ELLENDER	1673	NC	077					1 1689	NC	077	WILLIAM BOGUE	60330
PERISHO/PARISHO, JAMES				1678	NC	077		1 C1672			HANNAH PHELPS	60330
PERISHO/PARISHO, JAMES	1676	NC	077					1 1696	NC	077	MARY MORGAN	60330
PERKERSON, DEMPSEY	1778	NC		1875	GA			1			NANCY WARD	60522
PERKERSON, JOEL	C1755	VA					044	2 1816	GA		SARAH BROWN	60522
PERKINS, AAROD	1769	CT		1827	VA		006	1			POLLY PENNINGTON	60079
PERKINS, ELIZABETH/BETSEY	C1759	VA			NC	014	060	1			JACOB SHERRILL	60339
PERKINS, GORDON	1773	CT		1851	VA		006	1			JOANNAH STAMPER	60079
PERKINS, JABEZ	1766	CT		1836	KY		006	1			NANCY ANNE	60079
PERKINS, JARED	1766	CT		1851	VA		006	1			PHEBE RUSSELL	60079
PERKINS, JOHN				C1790	NC	020						27375
PERKINS, JOHN	1733			1804	NC	060		1			CATHERINE LOWRANCE	60339
PERKINS, JOHNSON F	1815	NC	006	1884	NC	006		1 1844	NC	006	CATHERINE JOHNSON	60079
PERKINS, JOSEPH	C1738	CT		1832				1			MOORE	60079
								2			LOIS SPERRY	
PERKINS, LUCY	1776			1848			006	1 1796			JOSEPH YOUNG	60079
PERKINS, STEPHEN	1774	?CT		1844	VA		006	1			RUTH HITCHCOCK	60079
PERKINS, SUSANNAH							020	1 C1750	VA		GEORGE BARKER	27375
PERKINS, TIMOTHY	C1736	CT		1834	NC	006		1 C1764	?CT		MIRIAM SPERRY	60079
								2			FRANCES STURGILL	
PERKINS, TIMOTHY JR	1771	CT		1851	NC	006		1 1795	VA		TOBITHA ANDERSON	60079

ANCESTOR INDEX	BIRTH	PL	CO	DEATH	PL	CO	LIVD	MARRIED	PL	CO	SPOUSE NAME	CODE
PERRY, ABNER		NC	?010									60284
PERRY, GEORGE L	1825	NC	039	1902	TX			1 1853	TX		MARY ANN BEASON	60408
PERRY, HIMERICK/HYMERICK	C1780			C1857	NC	010		1 1809	NC	024	MARY LACKEY	60284
PERRY, ISRAEL				1779	NC	077		1			PRICILLA	01006
PERRY, JOHN	C1832	NC	?010									60284
PERRY, JOHN F	C1763			1861				1 1804	NC	?039	NANCY HINTON KITCHENS	60408
PERRY, JOHN LEVI	C1816	NC		1889	TN			1			NANCY M	17129
								2 1866	TN		MARTHA EMILY MCCRORY	
PERRY, JOSIAH	1741	NC	077	1821	NC	010		1 C1761			MISS FREEMAN	01006
								2			AMILLICENT FREEMAN	
PERRY, MARTIN VAN BUREN		NC	?024									60284
PERRY, NANCY	1824			1903	NC	069		1 1836	NC	069	NATHAN WRIGHT BATCHELOR	24250
PERRY, NOAH				C1824	NC	063		1			MILLIE	02195
PERRY, RICHARD	C1780	NC	?104	C1830	NC	006	?104	1 C1800	NC	?104	CATHERINE EASTRING/EASTARD ?	02295
PERRY, SALLIE	1799			1880	NC	009		1 C1814	NC	?063	JOHN HODGES	02195
PERRY, SIMON		?024										60284
PERRY, SOLOMON	C1740			C1800	NC	?006	?104	1 C1760	NC	?085		02295
PERRY, SOLOMON	1805	NC	?104	1891	NC	006	104	1 C1827	NC	006	ELIZABETH HAM	02295
								2 1863	NC	006	TOBITHA/BITHY HAM	
PERRY, ZACHARIAH		NC	?010									60284
PETERSON, JOHN C	C1759	NC	035	C1843	GA			1			ELIZABETH	60320
PETTAWAY/PETWAY, MARGARET S	1829	NC	037	1879	NC	047		1 1848	NC	037	DAVID BARNES BELL	27441
PETTAWAY/PETWAY, MICAJAH	C1757	CN	037	1849	NC	037		1 1775	NC	037	AMY SUGG	27441
								2 1828	NC	037	ELIZABETH SKINNER	
PETTAWAY/PETWAY, WILLIAM D	C1800	NC	037	1858	NC	037		1 C1820	NC	037	CINDERELLA CROMWELL	27441
PETTIGREW, GREEN JORDAN	1837	NC	073	1906	TX			1 1857	TN		MARY ELIZABETH DAMERON	60324
								2 C1881	TX			
								3 1882	TX		CLARA YOUNG	
PETTIGREW, THOMAS	C1795	NC	?073	1884	TN			1 1825	NC	073	CELIA TATE	60324
PETTY, JAMES R	1786	NC	022	1862	NC	?022		1 C1808	NC	022	MARY BINGHAM	60162
PETTY, JOHN	C1779	NC						1			MARY/POLLY	60155
PETTY, JOHN	1756	NC	073	1837	NC	022		1			MARY	60162
PETTY, REBEKAH	C1745	NC	073	1830	GA		022	1 1763	NC		ZACHARIAH HARMAN	60008
PETTY, STEPHEN DECATUR	1816	NC	022	1868				1 1843	AL		NANCY SIBLEY	60162
PEW/PUGH, RILEY	C1780	NC	?085					1			EDNA MOTSINGER	25185
PHARIS/FAIRIS/FARRISH, ISAAC	C1770			C1830	AL		029	1			MARY COLBREATH	60061
PHIFER, MARTIN JR	1756	NC	065	1837	NC	016		1 1778			ELIZABETH LOCKE	60593
PHIFER, MARTIN SR	1720	SWI		1791	NC	065		1 1745			MARGARET BLACKWELDER	60593
PHILIPS, NATHAN	C1788	NC		1852	IL			1 1818	KY		NANCY ELLEDGE	60440
PHILLIPS, BENJAMIN A	1833	NC		1903	NC	106		1 1871	NC	092	DICY A HURT	60520
PHILLIPS, ELIZABETH A	1834	NC		1901	NC	106		1 C1855	NC	106	WASHINGTON NEWSOM	60520

ANCESTOR INDEX	BIRTH	PL	CO	DEATH	PL	CO	LIVD	MARRIED	PL	CO	SPOUSE NAME	CODE
PHILLIPS, ENOCH	1830	NC		1901	NC	097		1 1849	NC	097	MARY M POOLE	27306
								2 1897	NC	097	MRS MAGGIE (BRANTLEY) BROOKS	
PHILLIPS, ISAAC	C1794	NC	?013	C1865	TN			1	?NC		NANCY BUNCH ?	60390
PHILLIPS, JEREMIAH	C1745			1805	NC	022		1			ANN	19075
								2			ANN	
PHILLIPS, JOHN T	1831	NC		1885	NC	106		1 1860	NC	106	ELIZA JANE SPILLMAN	60520
PHILLIPS, JOHN THOMAS	1862	NC	079	1903	NC	079		1 1880			LILLIE LEE WARREN	17140
PHILLIPS, LEWIS HENRY	1809	NC	?056	1867	NC	056	103	1 1833	NC	056	EMMALINE BOND	25254
PHILLIPS, MILDRED C	1828	NC		1892	NC	106		1 1853	NC	106	ALVIS PILCHER	60520
PHILLIPS, POLLY	1797	?NC	?092	1872	IA		090	1 1820	NC	092	JOSIAH OWEN	60255
PHILLIPS, SOLOMON	C1828	NC		C1870	NC	106		1 C1847	NC	092	FRANCES	60520
PHILLIPS, THOMAS	C1823	NC	079	C1880	NC	079		1 1849			MARY BEST	17140
PHILLIPS, THOMAS				C1847	NC	079		1			ELIZABETH	17140
PHILPOT, THOMAS	C1764	NC						1 C1796	NC		NANCY	01054
PHIPPS, BENJAMIN	1762	NC	?073	1838	VA			1 1782	VA		JANE HASH	60120
PHIPPS, DANIEL	C1720	?PA			NC	046						60120
PHIPPS, JANE	C1808	VA		C1857	NC	006		1 1826	VA		THOMAS JONES	60120
PHIPPS, JOHN	1791	VA		1849	VA		006	1 C1807	VA		RUTH HOWELL	60120
PHIPPS, JOSEPH	C1742	?VA		1828	NC	046		2			MARY	01040
PHIPPS, MARGARET	C1780	NC	046	C1845	IL			1 C1799	NC		JAMES HUNTER	01040
PHYSIOC, JOHN	C1708	?MD		C1765	NC	028		1 C1728	?MD		SUSANNA	06080
PHYSIOC, PETER	C1730			C1802	NC	028		1			ABIGAIL?	06080
								2 1794	NC	019	MRS DIANA BRINN HARRIS PARKER	
PHYSIOC, WILLIAM	C1775	NC	028	1838	NC	028		1 1802	NC	028	MRS SARAH COOPER BISHOP	06080
								2 1813	NC	028	REBECCA ELLIS	
PICKARD, ELISHA	C1775			1835	NC	073		1 1796	NC	073	SUSANNA O'DANIELS	17150
PICKARD, HENRY				1790	NC	022		1			ELIZABETH	17150
PICKARD, JOHN	C1730			1812	NC	073		1			PEGGY	17150
PICKETT, CECIL DOUGLAS	1899	NC	046	1962	TX			1 1933	LA		LUCILLE G RANDOLPH	27467
PICKETT, ELIZA	1809	NC	073	1891	NC	073		1 1828	NC	073	SOLOMON THOMPSON	60429
PICKETT, JAMES PRICE	1846	VA		1926	NC	046		1			RACHAEL VIOLANTE BENOIT	27467
PICKETT, WILLIAM				1824	NC	073		1			ELIZABETH	60429
PICKLE, JACOB	1779	NC			GA			1			SALLY	60216
PIERCE, JANE	1800	NC		1880	IN		?104	1 1833	TN		JACOB VAN HUSS	06005
PIERCE, JOHN	C1765	?NC		C1845	IN		081	1 C1785			CLARA	60446
PIERCE, SAMUEL BERRY	C1785	NC	?099	C1870	MO			1 C1803			WINNY	27555
PIERCE, SARAH	C1796	?NC		1861	IL			1 C1822	NC	081	SAMUEL FERGUSON	60446
PINKERTON, DAVID				1771	NC	073		1			MARY GLASS	12065
								2			MRS MARGARET TRICKEY	
PINKERTON, DAVID		NC	073	1782	NC	073		1	NC	073	ANNIE SPARKS	12065

155

ANCESTOR INDEX	BIRTH	PL	CO	DEATH	PL	CO	LIVD	MARRIED	PL	CO	SPOUSE NAME	CODE
PINKERTON, DAVID	1766	NC	073	1842	IN		013	1 C1798	NC	085	MARGARET PINKERTON	12065
PINKERTON, DAVID	1805	NC	013	1888	OR			1 1828	KY		MARY TURTLE/TUTTLE	12065
PINKERTON, DAVID				C1771	NC	073		2			MRS MARGARET TRICKEY	60264
PINKERTON, DAVID	1776	NC	073	1842	IN			1			MARGARET PINKERTON	60264
PINKERTON, DAVID	1805	NC	013	1888	OR			1 1828	KY		MARY TURTLE	60264
PINKERTON, MARGARET	1779	NC	073	1863	IN		013	1 C1798	NC	085	DAVID PINKERTON	12065
PINKERTON, WILLIAM		NC	073	C1805	NC	085		1	NC	073	SARAH EASLEY	12065
PINNELL, ELIZABETH							100					17165
PINNELL, JOHN				C1813	NC	039	044	1			MRS REBECCA MURPHY	17165
PINNELL, JOSHUA							044					17165
PINNELL, LEVY							039					17165
PINNELL, NICHOLAS							?044					17165
PINNELL, RIAL	C1778	NC	044	C1851	NC	039						17165
PINNELL, RICHARD				C1773			044					17165
PIPKIN, JULIA ANN	1820	NC		1855	NC	103		1 1837	NC		WILLIAM BURWELL EDMUNDSON	07015
PIPPIN, JOHN	C1751			1838	NC	039		1 C1776	NC	?015	REBECCA	60388
PIPPIN, LOFTUS	1786	NC	039	1843	IL			1			MARRY HALL	60388
PIPPIN, SARAH REBECCA	1812	NC	039	1889	UT			1 1829	?TN		REUBEN MANNING JOLLEY	60388
PIRKLE, RICHARD C A	C1848	NC		C1888	KY			1 1869			MOLLIE BOREN	60135
								2 1877	KY		SARAH ELMINA BUTT	
PITTARD, JOHN M	C1750	NC		C1820	NC	044		1			FRANKY	06065
PITTARD, NANCY A	1832	NC	044	1913	NC	044		1 1852	NC	044	JOHN RUFFIN BUCHANAN	06065
PITTARD, THOMAS M	1778	?NC		1865	?NC			1 C1813			POLLY NORMAN	06065
PITTS, CADWALLADER	1787	NC		1855				1 1809	NC		ELIZABETH STANLEY	60386
								2 1844	NC		MARY	
PIVER, ELIJAH JEFFERSON	1819	NC		1889	NC	012		1 1838	NC	070	LUCY CRAIG	05070
								2 1867	NC	012	SARAH NEWTON	
PIVER, GEORGE HOLLAND	1856	NC	070	1917	NC	012		1 1886	NC	012	MINNIE OLA KING WESCOTT	05070
PIVER, PETER		NC	019		NC	019		1 1814	NC	019	REBECCA ROGERS	05070
PLANCET, SALLY	C1792	?NC	?090					1	?NC	?090	CHRISTIAN SHOUSE	25027
PLEASANTS, JOSEPH G	C1795	NC	039		NC	099		1 1819	NC	039	RUTH TIMBERLAKE	25215
PLEASANTS, ROBERT	1782	VA		1845	NC	039		1			NANCY DUKE ?	25215
								2 1810	NC	039	ELIZABETH FLETCHER	
PLEASANTS, ROBERT F	C1806	NC	039	1889	NC	073		1 1830	NC	073	ANN HANCOCK	25215
PLEASANTS, THOMAS WYNNE	1798	NC	039	1864	NC	044		1 1830	NC	100	DICEY STEWART	25215
PLEASANTS, WILLIAM	1763	VA		C1811	NC	039		1			ELVIRA WYNNE ?	25215
PLEASANTS, WILLIAM DANIEL	1796	NC	039					1 1818	NC	099	CLARY MORRIS	25215
PLOTT, GEORGE	1811	NC		1889	AR			1 1843	NC	016	MARGARET WILKERSON	27402
PLUMBLEE/PLUMLEY, JOHN M	1790	SC		1861	NC	050	013	1 1814	NC	013	MARY DUGAN MURRAY	17170

ANCESTOR INDEX	BIRTH	PL	CO	DEATH	PL	CO	LIVD	MARRIED	PL	CO	SPOUSE NAME	CODE
PLUMBLEE/PLUMLEY, JOHN OATIS	1876	NC	050	1937	SC		050	1 1898	SC		ANNIE LATNA BALLENGER	17170
								2 1931	SC		MRS SARA FRANCES (WALL) COLLINS	
PLUMBLEE/PLUMLEY, WILLIAM	C1768	?VA		C1830	?SC		014	1 C1789	NC	?014	HESTER O'NEAL	17170
PLUMBLEE/PLUMLEY, WILLIAM P	1829	NC	013	1901	SC		050	1 1873	NC	050	ROXANNA JANE GULLICK	17170
PLUMMER, JEREMIAH	1775	NC	?011	C1885	GA			1	?NC		MARY	27594
POE, DAVID MILTON JR	1800	NC	046		IN			1 1821	NC	046	ELIZABETH PASCHAL	60313
POE, DAVID MILTON SR	1832	NC	046					1 1850	NC	046	ABIGAIL WILSON	60313
POE, JOHN	C1790	NC		1857	AL			1			SARAH THREET	60240
POGUE, ELIZABETH	1800	NC		1868	AR		104	1 C1816	NC	104	JOHN HOLT	60243
POINDEXTER, ANN CLINGMAN	1821	NC	?092	1906	NC	106		1 1844	NC		THOMAS SCOTT MARTIN	27475
POINDEXTER, FRANCIS	1764	NC		1800	NC	092		1			MRS JANE (PETILLO) LANIER	27475
POINDEXTER, FRANCIS ANDY/ ANDERSON	1795	NC		1885	NC		?092	1 1820			ROSANNAH FERRIER	27475
POINDEXTER, THOMAS	C1733	ENG		1807			092	1 1760			ELIZABETH PLEDGE	27475
POLK, CHARLES WILLIAM	C1784	NC	065					1 1806	NC	016	CATHERINE STERNS	60089
POLK, EZEKIEL	1747	PA		1824	TN		094	1 C1769	NC	065	MARY/MARIA WILSON	19230
								2 C1792			POLLY CAMPBELL	
								3 C1812			MRS SOPHIA (NEELY) LEONARD	
POLK, WILLIAM	1806	NC	065	1864	MO			1 C1829			MARY SHARP	60296
POLK, WILLIAM WESLEY		NC	065									60296
POLLARD, GEORGE							063					27378
POLLARD, THOMAS	1844	LA		1894	NC	009	101	1 1870	NC	101	PERMELIA F MASON	27378
POLLARD, THOMAS B				C1848	LA		063	1 1823	NC	063	AMELIA MACKEY	27378
PONDER, JOHN	C1791	?NC						1			WINNIE HOLCOMBE	20060
PONDER, JOSEPH	C1795	?NC		1876	KY		013	1			CATHERINE HOLCOMBE	20060
PONDER, RANSOM P	1809			1899	NC	080		2 1857	NC	080	MARGARET ELIZABETH SPLAWN	60198
PONDER, ROBERT	C1785	SC		C1855	NC	107	013	1			ELIZABETH HOLCOMBE	20060
POOL, MOSES	1781	NC		C1857	GA			1	NC		SARA	60163
POOL, PATSY	C1795	NC			GA			1 1811	NC	067	JACOB COCHRAN	60261
POOLE, GEORGE LOUIS	1905	NC	078	1968	NC	036		1 1928	VA		ERMA FLYNN	60500
POOLE, GEORGE WASHINGTON	1828			1910	NC	078		1 1866	NC	078	SUSAN M WILKERSON	60500
POOLE, LUDOLPHUS GRAVES	1876	NC	078	1945	NC	036		1			CORA VICTORIA SANFORD	60500
POOLE, MARY M	1824	NC		1896	NC	097		1 1849	NC	097	ENOCH PHILLIPS	27306
POOLE, SETH PETTY					NC	044						60500
POOLE, YOUNG PETTY					NC	044						60500
POPE, CORINNA THEDOCIA JACKSON	1861	NC	?022	1959	NC	058		1			WILLIAM HENRY MILLS	12075
POPE, ISAAC	C1805			C1841	NC	029		1 1823	NC	029	ELIZABETH ANDERSON	13052
POPE, WILLIAM LEONDOUS, REV	1820	NC	?022	1902	NC	099		1	NC	?099	SARAH LURENDIA BOWLIN	12075
POPLIN, CATHERINE	1809	NC	067					1			WILLIAM BLACKBURN	60204

ANCESTOR INDEX	BIRTH	PL	CO	DEATH	PL	CO	LIVD	MARRIED		PL	CO	SPOUSE NAME	CODE
POPLIN, WILLIAM W	1789	NC	067	1880	TN			1		NC	067	PATIENCE LEE	60204
PORTER, MOODY				1822	NC	037	047	1	1786	NC	047	PATSEY GODWIN	60384
PORTERFIELD, DENNIS	C1760	NC	029	1781	SC								60186
POTTER, GEORGE WASHINGTON	1813	NC	012	1865	IN			1	1830	IN		MARY ANN CARRUTHERS	60484
								2	1846	IN		ELIZA MALLORY	
POTTER, ROBERT	1773	NC	012	1835	NC	012		1	1803	NC	012	REBECCA LONG	60484
POTTER, ROYAL	C1771	NC	?094		IL			1	1793			REBECCA REAVIS	60373
								2				POLLY COX	
POTTER, SAMUEL	1780	NC	012	1847	NC	070		1		NC	012	RACHEL JANE	60484
								2	1837	PA		MRS ELIZABETH EURE	
POTTS, HENRY				1775	NC	085	005	1				MARGARET	17195
POTTS, JAMES	1754	NC	085	1844	TN			1				CELIA GIVENS	17195
POTTS, JOHN							?038	1				ELIZABETH	60467
POTTS, MARGARET		NC	085					1				STEPHEN POTTS	17195
POTTS, MARY	1753	NC	085	1823				1	1771			PETER THOMPSON	17195
POTTS, SARAH		NC	085										17195
POTTS, WILLIAM	1763	NC	085	1828	KY			1	1787	NC	085	MARGARET PURVIANCE	17195
POTTS, WILLIAM GEORGE	1857	NC		1907	NC	038		1	1881	NC	038	NETTIE WOODS	60467
POWELL, ANN JULIA	1848	NC	035	C1885	NC	045	028	1	C1875	NC	?035	JACOB JAMES MARSHBURN	13264
POWELL, BRITTAIN	1740	VA		1838	NC	035	070	1	1784	?NC		MARY	13264
POWELL, CADER	C1715			C1785	NC	051		1				ANN	01006
POWELL, DEMPSEY	1747	NC	010	1832	TN			1				ELIZABETH PERRY	01006
								2	C1800			MRS TALITHA (COTTON) HOBDY	
POWELL, GEORGE	C1694	VA		1736	NC	010		1				ANN	01006
POWELL, ISAAC	1820	NC	035		NC	045		1	1843	NC	035	REBECCA M LANIER	13264
POWELL, JACOB		NC	035	C1855	NC	035		1		NC	035	MARY	13264
POWELL, JAMES	C1787	NC	014	C1865	KY		104	1	1818	KY		FRANCES SANDERS	60292
POWELL, JEMIMA	1803	NC	?079	1855	NC	045		1	C1822	NC	?045	BENJAMIN SHEPPARD EDWARDS	06050
POWELL, LOUISA	1827	NC	035	C1890	NC	028		1	C1845	NC	035	JAMES MADISON MARSHBURN	13264
POWELL, ORSBURN	1796	NC		1869	IL			1	1819	?NC		ELIZABETH BOATRIGHT	04155
POWELL, RODERICK J	C1771	NC	?079				045						06050
POWELL, THOMAS	C1790	NC	051	C1865	TN			1	1814	TN		POLLY BOWERS	01006
								2	1842	TN		MRS MARY MOORE	
POWERS, JOHN	1757	NC	?009	1832	GA			1	1788			LYDIA LOPER	60175
PRATT, MARGARET				1837	NC	073		1	1795	NC	073	JOHN PAUL	02256
PRESSLEY, JOHN ROBERT	1815			1900	NC	013		1	1846	TN		JANE ELIZABETH ROACH	60582
PRESSLEY, MARY ANN	1852	NC	013	1929	NC	013		1	1869	NC	013	WILLIAM M JONES	60582
PRICE, ELIJAH		MD		1794	NC	063		1				NANCY	27740
PRICE, ELIJAH, COL	1791	NC	063	1852	TX			1	1821	NC	037	TEMPERANCE THOMAS	27740

ANCESTOR INDEX	BIRTH	PL	CO	DEATH	PL	CO	LIVD	MARRIED	PL	CO	SPOUSE NAME	CODE
PRICE, EPHRAIM	1761	VA		1845	GA		071	1 1791	?VA		MARTHA WILLIAMS	60371
								2 1828	GA		MRS ELIZABETH SAYERS	
PRICE, MATTHEW	1764	VA		1842	TN		078	1 1786	NC	020	ELIZABETH ESKRIDGE	02470
PRICE, MERRIDTH/MARADAY	1770	VA		1817	NC	020		1 1795	VA		MARY/POLLY MCDANIEL	60532
PRICE, NANCY	1805	NC	046	1859	IA			1 1823	NC	046	WILLIAM SIMPSON	25144
PRICE, SUSAN BURTON	1805	NC	020	C1865	NC	020		1 1820	NC	020	CHARLES P HARRISON	60532
PRICHARD, DAVID	1751	NC	075	1815	NC	075		1 1770	NC	075	SARAH SOLLEY	23070
								2 1781	NC	075	MIRIAM JENNINGS	
PRICHARD, DAVID SR	C1630	?VA		1697	NC	075		1			SARAH	23070
PRICHARD, ELISHA	1790	NC	075	1873	IN			1 1809	NC	018	LUCY HERRINGTON	23070
PRICHARD, JAMES	1720	NC	075	C1800	NC	075		1				23070
								2 1772	NC	075	MARY JENNINGS ?	
								3 C1780	NC	075	RUTH CASSE	
PRICHARD, SAMUEL	C1680	?VA		C1730	NC	075		1	?NC	075		23070
PRIDGEN, LUKE		NC			GA		035	1 1783	NC	035	AMELIA BOWEN	60384
PRIDGEON, NATHANIEL W	1804	NC		C1888	GA			1 1824	GA		POLLY WILLOUGHBY	17070
								2	?AL		MARY ANN	
PROCTER, JOHN				1790	NC	005		1			LINNIE EDWARDS	60311
PROCTER, TAMSIE	1778			1868	GA		005	1 C1798			THOMAS BLOODWORTH	60311
PROCTOR/PROCTER, WILLIAM DODSON		NC			MO			1			MATILDA/RACHEL E	13006
PRUITT/PREWIT, JOSHUA	1753	VA		1842	SC		046	1	NC		MARY FOWLER ?	17220
PRUITT/PREWIT, WILLIAM	1790	NC		1855	SC			1 1814	SC		FRANCES TUCKER	17220
PRYOR, JOHN	C1701	VA		C1771	NC	073		1 C1728	VA		MARGARET GAINES	03020
PRYOR, LUCY	1740	NC		C1830	NC			1 C1760	NC	073	JOHN HOSEA TAPLEY	03020
								2 C1772	NC		JOHN WOMACK	
PRYOR, MATHEW	1759	NC	044	1830	TN		020	1 1782	NC		MARY NEELY	60506
PUCKETT, MARTHA/PATTY	1801	NC	092	1863	IN			1 1819	NC	092	LEWIS WOOTON	27429
PUCKETT, THOMAS JR	C1781	NC	046	C1828	IN		092	1 1800	NC	?092	MARY	27429
PUCKETT, THOMAS SR	C1750	VA		1805	NC	092	046	1 C1770	VA		MARY TAYLOR	27429
PUGH, FRANCIS		?VA			?NC	?010		1			PHEREBEE SAVAGE	60414
PUGH, HUGH, JR.	C1745	NC	009	C1800	NC	079		1 C1770	NC	079	ELIZABETH BRYAN	13264
PUGH, HUGH, SR	C1720	NC		1793	NC	079	028	1 C1743	NC	028	CANNON	13264
PUGH, JOHN	C1805	NC	081		?NC	?081		1 1827	NC	081	BETSY DELANY HAYS	08355
PUGH, MARY	1828	NC	081	1908	NC	081		1 1853	NC	081	ALSON G JENNINGS	08355
PUGH, SARAH	1760	NC	079	1799	NC	079		1 C1780	NC	079	LEWIS CANNON	13264
PUGH, THOMAS	1726	NC	?010	1806	NC	?010		1			MARY SCOTT	60414
PUGH/PEW, PAUL	C1810	NC	018	1862	NC	018		1 C1845	NC	018	BATHSHEBA BURFOOT	02180
								2 1856	NC	018	MRS ABY (BURGESS) NEEDHAM	
PUGH/PEW, WILLIS B	1861	NC	018	1924	NC	018		1 1884	NC	018	FANNY BUSH BERRY	02180
PUNCH/PUNTCH, CYNTHA CELINA	1832	NC		1920	AR			1 1855			WILLIAM HEAD DORSETT	60084
PUNCH/PUNTCH, MARY E	1823	NC		C1854	?MO			1 1842	NC		WILLIAM HEAD DORSETT	60084

ANCESTOR INDEX	BIRTH	PL	CO	DEATH	PL	CO	LIVD	MARRIED	PL	CO	SPOUSE NAME	CODE
PURCELL, JOHN				C1785	NC	029						27566
PURCELL, MALCOLM	C1740	?VA		C1775	NC	029		1 C1770	?NC		BEATRICE TORREY	27566
PUREFOY, SARAH/MARY		NC	?028		TN			1 C1769	NC	?028	MARTIN WHITFORD	20415
PUREFOY, THOMAS NICHOLAS	C1659	VA			NC	?028		1			JUDITH SEARLES	20415
PURGERSON, JOSEPH SR	1800	NC	039		NC	039		1 1831	NC	039	EUNICE ADCOCK	02435
PURVIANCE, JOHN	1743	IRE		1823	TN		054	1 1764	NC	085	MARY JANE WASSON	60342
PURVIANCE, JOHN SR	1712	IRE		C1762	NC	085		1			MARGARET MCKNIGHT	60342
PYLE, JOHN, DR	C1721	PA		1804	NC	022		1 1744	DE		SARAH BALDWIN	27417
PYLE, JOHN, DR	1723	PA		1804	NC	022		1 1744	DE		SARAH BALDWIN	27553
PYLE, JOHN, DR	1723	PA		1804	NC	022		1 1744	PA		SARAH BALDWIN	60349
PYLE, MARY	C1755	PA						1 C1775	NC	022	JOHN HALL	60349
PYLE, SAMUEL				1802	NC	?073						60349
PYLE, SARAH	C1789	NC	022		KY			1 1812	KY		ROBERT HALL	60349
PYLE, WILLIAM	C1755	PA						1	NC	073		60349
PYOR, MATHEW JR	1787	NC		1869	TN			1 C1808	TN		HENRIETTA WILLIAMS	60506
								2 C1837	?NC		MARY/POLLY WILLIAMS	
PYRON, WILLIAM	C1756	VA		1750	NC	005		1 C1785	NC		MARY POWELL	60144
PYRON, WILLIAM	1793	NC	065	1844	NC	065		1 1812	NC	085	NANCY CROWELL	60144
PYRON, WILLIAM MONTGOMERY	1821	NC		1897	AL		065	1 1841	NC	065	URRISA/EUNICE WILLIAMS	27269
								2 1869	AL		MARTHA JANE COGBURN	

Q

ANCESTOR INDEX	BIRTH	PL	CO	DEATH	PL	CO	LIVD	MARRIED	PL	CO	SPOUSE NAME	CODE
QUEEN, ETTA MITTIE	C1822	NC	?104	C1907	AR			1 1840	NC	104	CORNELIUS ANDERSON	20007
QUEEN, HAMPTON	C1796	NC	?086	1855	IA		?014	1 1820	IN		HANNAH WILLIAMS	18010
								2 1852	IA		MRS MARY ANN BECHBILL	
QUINCE, ELIZABETH MOORE	1828			1853	NC	022		1 1848	NC	070	FREDERICK SOBIESKI DAVIS	27286
QUINCE, PARKER	C1796			1867	NC	070		1 1820	NC	070	JANE HILL	27286
QUINCE, PARKER	1743	NC	070	1785	ENG		012	1			SUSANNAH HASSELL	27286
QUINCE, RICHARD		NC	012		NC	070		1			ELIZABETH MOORE	27286
QUINCE, RICHARD	1717	ENG		1778	NC	070		1			MARY	27286
QUINCY, WILLIAM ADAIR	1810	VA		1889	NC	098	100	1 1843	NC	100	MRS MARY (FLEMING) QUINCY	60594
QUINCY, WILLIAM ADAIR JR	1846	NC	100				010	1 1881	NC	100	MRS ADDIE (FINCH) QUINCY	60594
QUINN, ROBERT BROWN	1859	SC		1946	NC	086		1 1883	NC	040	FANNIE MILLER BLAKELEY	05070

R

ANCESTOR INDEX	BIRTH	PL	CO	DEATH	PL	CO	LIVD	MARRIED	PL	CO	SPOUSE NAME	CODE
RABUN, JANE	1766	NC	047	1855				1 1790			JOHN VEAZEY	27280

ANCESTOR INDEX	BIRTH	PL	CO	DEATH	PL	CO	LIVD	MARRIED	PL	CO	SPOUSE NAME	CODE
RABUN, MATTHEW	1744	NC	037	1819	GA		047	1			SARAH WARREN	27280
RAGAN, CORNELIA FRANCES	1877	NC	?044	1906	NC	073		1	NC		HENRY GETER ELLIS	12075
RAGAN, WILL		NC	044					1			MARTHA DUKE	12075
RAGLAND, CHARITY				C1819	KY			1 1807	NC	044	JOHN WILSON	06015
RAGLAND, EVAN				1778	NC	044		1			AMY	06015
RAGLAND, STEPHEN				C1746	NC	071		1			MARY	06015
RAGLAND, WILLIAM				1823	NC	044						06015
RAGLAND/RAGLIN, STEPHEN		WAL		C1746	NC	071		1	VA		MARY	07018
RAGLAND/RAGLIN, WILLIAM	C1717	VA		1789	NC	022		1 C1740			SARAH AVENT	07018
RAINWATER, ABRAHAM	1784	NC	092		KY			1	NC			60492
RAINWATER, JAMES	C1734	NC	010	C1805	NC	092		1	NC			60492
RAINWATER, JOHN	C1705	NC		1777	NC	092		1 C1734	NC		MARY FUSSELL	60492
RAINWATER, WILLIAM	C1775	NC		C1855	AL			1			LYDIA	60347
RALLS, JOHN HECTOR	1785	VA		1823	GA			1 1814	GA		NANCY ATKINSON	04200
								2 C1818	NC	?092	SALLIE/SARAH STOWE	
RALLS, MARY ADELINE	1819	NC	?092	1860	GA			1 1840	GA		GEN GEORGE SEABORN BLACK	04200
RAMSEY, JANE	1714	IRE		C1800	NC	060		1	PA		ALEXANDER BALDRIDGE	06005
RAMSEY, JOHN	C1720	IRE		1775	NC	065		1 C1738	IRE			60164
RAMSEY, JOHN G	1795	NC	057	1855	MS			1			CARON H	60254
RAMSEY, MICHAEL	C1815	NC		C1854	TN			1 1841	TN		BELINDA COMMONS	60096
RAMSEY, THOMAS				C1815	NC	070						27303
RAMSEY, WILLIAM M JR	1781	NC	065	1833	TN			1 1804	TN		MARY/POLLY OVERALL	60164
RAMSEY, WILLIAM SR	1742	PA		1824	TN		065	1 1768	NC	065	MARIA BOYD	60164
RANDLEMAN, AUGUSTINE F C	C1805	NC	090	C1836	NC	090		1 1826	NC	090	CYNTHIA BANNER	27657
RANDLEMAN, JACOB	1790	NC	085	1849	MO			1 C1812	IL		MARY HOLCOMB	27657
RANDLEMAN, JOHN	C1784	NC	?085	C1841	IL			1 1826	IL		SARAH HOOK	27657
RANDLEMAN, JOHN FREDERICK HERMAN	C1757	GER		C1814	NC	090		1 1779	NC	085	MARY WRIGHT	27657
RANDLEMAN, JOHN WRIGHT	C1786	NC	085	1839	IL			1 C1813	NC	090	ELIZABETH W REED	27657
RANDLEMAN, MARTIN CHRISTOPHER	1761	NC	085	C1841	AR			1 1783	NC	085	MARY MAGDALENA FUR/FURRER	27657
RANDLEMAN, WILLIAM F	1802	NC	090	1868	NC	090		1 1825	NC	090	MARTHA SHORE	27657
RANYOLDS, REBECCA		SWI		C1779	NC	060		1 C1764			JOHN TEETER BEAM	60466
RATLEDGE/RUTLEDGE, BENJAMIN	1802	NC	085	C1882	TN			1	TN		MARY/POLLY MASSEY	25143
RATLEDGE/RUTLEDGE, JAMES JR	C1789	NC	085	C1835	TN			1			MARTHA ROSE SADLER	25143
RATLEDGE/RUTLEDGE, JAMES SR	C1749			C1813	NC	085		1 1774			SARAH GILKIE	25143
RAY, ANGUS WILKERSON	1806	?NC	?083	C1875	GA			1	?NC	?083	JEANETTE CURRIE	60048
RAY, EFFIE M L	1848	NC	083					1 1876	GA		A A RIVERS	60048
RAY, ELIZABETH	C1798	NC		C1865	?GA			1 C1822	NC		JOHN GILBERT	27595

ANCESTOR INDEX	BIRTH	PL	CO	DEATH	PL	CO	LIVD	MARRIED	PL	CO	SPOUSE NAME	CODE
RAY, FLORIA	1837	NC	083					1 1855	GA		SEABORN J VEAL	60048
RAY, HARRIET J	1850	NC	083		?GA							60048
RAY, HECTOR A	1842	NC	083	1862	GA							60048
RAY, HUGH	C1792	NC		1845	IN			1 C1811	TN		SARAH C REDER	60271
RAY, J ISABELLA	1812	NC		1872	TN			1			MR CHRISTOPHER	60584
RAY, JANE A	1840	NC	083	1923	GA							60048
RAY, MARY C	1846	NC	083		?GA			1 1867	GA		HIRAM C SLOAN	60048
RAY, NEILL ANGUS	1851	NC	083	1936	GA			1 1873	GA		ANNIE E CARTER	60048
								2 1896	AL		MRS LONA MATTIE (TINSLEY) BLOUNT	
RAY, PRICILLA	1835	NC	083	C1900				1 1857	GA		CHARLES D BASS	60048
RAY/RHEA, CHARLES W	1872	NC	107	1959	OK		013	1 1911	NC	107	MYRTLE LOIS WILSON	60133
RAY/RHEA, HENRY	1810	NC	013	C1855	NC	107	013	1 C1833	NC	107	ELIZABETH WILSON	60133
RAY/RHEA, HIRAM	1813	NC	013	C1855	NC	107	013	1 1839	GA		MELISSA BENNETT	60133
RAY/RHEA, HIRAM NEWTON	1852	NC	107	1921	NC	107	013	1 1868	NC	107	RACHEL ELIZABETH MCPETERS	60133
RAY/RHEA, THOMAS SR	1755	VA		1843	NC	107	013	1			HENSLEY	60133
REA, MARGARET HOUSTON	1792	NC		1884	IN			1 1812	NC		MATTHEW HOUSTON PATTON	25112
REA, ROBERT RIGHT	1761	PA		1852	IN		013	1 1786			AGNES PATTON	25112
READ, ELIZABETH		VA		1835	NC	020		1 1764	VA		RICHARD ESKRIDGE	05070
REAGAN, JAMES		?NC	?084	1828	TN		046	1			MARY	07078
								2			NANCY COOK	
								3			REBECCAH	
REAGAN, MARY	1766	NC	046	1836	TN			1 1784	?NC		JOHN WHITTEN	07078
REAVES, TEMPY	C1789	NC			AL			1 1811	NC	099	KINDRED STRICKLAND	27332
RECTOR, A B	C1835	NC	?021				021	1			ELIZABETH SHOOK	25162
RECTOR, PETER, JR.	1793	NC	085	C1827	NC	085		1			MARY/MARTHA MCKINNICK	60350
REDFEARN/REDFERN, JAMES					NC	?073	056					25134
REDFEARN/REDFERN, MILBURY/ MILBERRY	C1789	NC	?005		TN			1			RICE S JOHNS	25134
REDFERN/REDFERN, JOHN	C1745	NC	?028	C1826	TN		056	1 C1768			MARY TOWNLEY	25134
REECE, ABRAHAM	C1747	PA		1822	NC	092		1			MARY HUFF	02357
REECE, BETTY JOYCE	1935	NC	088					1 1953	SC		GERALD SAMUEL BRASWELL	02357
REECE, CALVIN RILEY	1881	NC	106	1961	NC	088		1 1900	NC	088	LUCY CLARK	02357
REECE, CURRIE	1912	NC	088	1968	NC	088		1			LONE MAE COX	02357
REECE, EDWARD HOUSTON	1856	NC	106	1926	NC	088		1 1879	NC	106	JULIA WISHON	02357
REECE, JESSE	1784	NC	092	1865	NC	106		1 1807	NC	092	MARGARET HADLEY	02357
REECE, RUTH					NC	106		1 1859	NC	106	PLEASANT G WILLIAMS	60569
REECE, TENNESSEE	1830	NC		1892	NC			1 1847	NC		BENJAMIN MACKIE	60288
REECE, WILEY	1814	NC	092	1888	NC	106		1 1838	NC	092	ALMEDA HINSHAW	02357
REED, ANNE	C1790	?NC		C1842	KY			1 1811	KY		ISAAC WHITE	24153

ANCESTOR INDEX	BIRTH	PL	CO	DEATH	PL	CO	LIVD	MARRIED	PL	CO	SPOUSE NAME	CODE
REED, DAVID	C1770	NC		C1842	MS			1 C1790			ELIZABETH	60588
REED, ELIJAH	1809	NC		1880	MS			1 C1830	AL		JUSTINA KETCHUM	60588
REED/REID, ELDAD SR	C1720				NC	085		1 C1745	?NJ			23065
REED/REID, MARY	1748	NJ		1832	NC	032	085	1 1764	NC	085	JOSHUA WHITAKER	23065
REEDY, JOHN	C1751	NC	?005		NC	006		1			ANNA	60418
REEVES, SYLVIA		NC	?104		IN		006	1 C1806			ALLEN BURTON	60348
REEVES/REAVES, DRURY JR	1775	NC		1856	GA			1 C1809	SC		ELIZABETH BROWN	60498
REGISTER, DAVID	C1803	NC			NC	027		1			DORCAS GORE	17025
REGISTER, DAVID JAMES	1828	NC	027	1914	NC	027		1			NANCY EVANS	17025
REGISTER, ELIZABETH DORA	1860	NC	027	1957	AL			1 1885			DANIEL BENNETT PAGE	17025
REGISTER, JAMES					NC	027						17025
REID, MARY	C1840	?NC	?020	1894	NC	020		1 1871	NC	020	ROBERT DICKY STADLER	60543
REID, THOMAS	C1816			1886	NC	001		1 1841	NC	020	MARY/POLLY SMITH	60543
RENDLEMAN, BARBARA	C1781	NC	085	C1805	NC	085		1 1801	NC	085	MATHIAS BARRINGER	27657
RENDLEMAN, ELIZABETH	C1775	NC	085		NC	085		1 1794	NC	085	JOHN STIREWALT	27657
RENDLEMAN, HENRY	C1776	NC	085		NC	?085						27657
RENDLEMAN, JACOB	C1769	NC	085	1832	IL			1 1804	NC	085	ELIZABETH FULLENWIDER	27657
RENDLEMAN, JOHN JR	C1772	NC	085	C1813	NC	085		1 C1793	NC	085	CATHERINE REEL	27657
RENDLEMAN, JOHN/SAMUEL	C1743			C1778	NC	085		1 C1767	NC	085	MARGARET SNAP	27657
RENDLEMAN, MARGARET		NC	085					1 1805	NC	085	HENRY FISHER	27657
RENDLEMAN, MARTIN	C1780	NC	085	C1832	?NC			1 C1800	NC	085	EXPERIENCE HARRIS	27657
RENN/WREN/WRENN, NANCY/ANN	C1772	NC	037	C1842	NC	079		1 C1792 2	 VA		THOMAS DUPREE RENN/WREN/WRENN, WILLIAM	12140
RENN/WREN/WRENN, WILLIAM		VA		1792	NC	037		1			HINES	12140
RENNICK, NANCY	1798	NC	?085	1854	IN			1 1817	NC	085	HENRY RIDDLE	60099
RESPASS, MARY		VA		1782	NC	009		1 C1730	VA		HENRY SHAW	19130
RESPESS, EUGENE BREHON	1875	NC	100	1964	GA			1 1906	NC	048	PEARL CAVINESS	60037
RESPESS, JEREMIAH G	1800	NC	009	1858	NC	009		1			MARY CLEMENTS	60037
RESPESS, RICHARD		NC	009	1837				1			ELIZABETH ORMOND	60037
RESPESS, RICHARD W	1843	NC	009	1909				1 1865	NC	100	ELIZABETH HILLIARD DAVIS	60037
RESPESS, THOMAS					NC	009		1 2			ESTHER BURTON MARY E CARROWAY	60037
REX/RECKS, NATHANIEL	C1794	NC			TN		085	1 1827	NC	085	JANE RARY/RAIREY	60067
REX/RECKS, WILLIAM	C1829	NC	?085	1879	AR			1 1852 2 C1863	TN AR		NANCY RAY NANCY ANN CROSS	60067
REYNOLDS, ELIZABETH	1772			1856	NC	026		1 1794	NC	?020	RICHARD ESKRIDGE	05070
REYNOLDS, HAMILTON	C1745	?VA		1814	NC	086		1 C1767			SARAH	05070
REYNOLDS, JANE	1790			1833	IN		092	1 C1810			SOLOMON CARTER	27420
REYNOLDS, JOASH	C1790	ENG		C1845	?NC	046		1 C1808				60031

ANCESTOR INDEX	BIRTH	PL	CO	DEATH	PL	CO	LIVD	MARRIED	PL	CO	SPOUSE NAME	CODE
REYNOLDS, JOSIAH	1769	NC		1833	TN		056	1 C1806			SARAH EXUM	19075
REYNOLDS, JUSTUS/JUSTICE	C1755			1823	AL		092	1 C1772			MARY WRIGHT	60215
REYNOLDS, SOLOMON	C1811	NC		1894	IN			1 1837	IN		THIRZIA WRIGHT	60137
REYNOLDS, WILLIAM	1779	NC			IN			1	NC		AMY	60137
REYNOLDS, WILLIAM R	1827	VA		1905	MN		046	1 1850	NC	046	RACHEL EMMALINE HODGSON/HODGIN	60031
REYNOLDS/RENNULS, JONAS JR	1801	NC	092	1828	IN			1 1827	NC	092	MARY HANES/HAINES	60225
REYNOLDS/RENNULS, JONAS SR	1751	VA		1812	NC	092		1 1783	NC	092	MARY	60225
REYNOLDS/RUNNELS, HAMILTON HAMBLETON	C1745	?VA		1814	NC	086	020	1 C1765	?VA		SARAH	60286
REYNOLDS/RUNNELS, JESSE	1789	?VA		1850	TN		020	1 C1817	NC	086	FRANCES/FANNY WILLIS	60286
RHOADES, CAMMELIA	1814	?NC		1886	NC	106		1			DANIEL BINKLEY	10010
RHODES, ELISHA, COL		NC	010	C1850	NC	010		1 1838	TX		MRS MARY WOODMAN (KIMBALL) DRIGGS	60069
RHODES, ELIZABETH	C1827	NC						1			MR ALLEN	60584
RHODES, GEORGE WASHINGTON	1833						009	1 1859	NC	075	REBECCA CARTWRIGHT	27378
RHODES, JAMES T	C1817	NC						1			HELEN	60584
RHODES, JOHN	C1792	NC			?IN			1			RUTH	04103
RHODES, JOHN	C1815	NC			TN			1			LUCINDA	60584
RHODES, JOSEPH T	1803	NC	057		GA			1	NC		ELIZABETH	60227
RHODES, JOSEPH T	1803	NC	?057	C1880	GA			1	NC		ELIZABETH	60282
RHODES, MARY	C1777	NC			?TN							60584
RHODES, MCCOMAS	1799	NC		1867	KY			1 1818			MARY E COLE	60273
RHODES, MILES	C1798	NC			?IN			1			MARGARET	04103
RHODES, THOMAS	C1794	NC			?IN			1 1828 2 1842	IN IN		HANNAH FREEMAN MARY ELIZABETH FREEMAN	04103
RHODES, WILLIAM	C1812	NC		1861	TN			1			MARY I	60584
RHODES, WILLIAM G	C1813				NC	010		1 2			ELIZABETH SOPHIA PILAND	60280
RHODES, WILLIAM JAMES	1865	NC	028	1918	NC	009		1 1885	NC	009	MRS MARTHA ANN (LEWIS) HODGES	27378
RHODES/ROHDS, ELIZABETH	C1809	NC	099	1874	NC	099		1 1825	NC	099	WILLIS W NOWELL	03250
RHODES/ROHDS, JEREMIAH		?MD		1839	NC	099	069	1 1784	NC	099	ELIZABETH FERRELL	03250
RHYNE/REIN, JACOB		GER		1794	NC	060						25100
RHYNE/REIN, THOMAS	1742	NC	060	1837	NC	060		1			BARBARA WISE/WEISS	25100
RICH, ALFRED WEBB	1830	NC	?049	1900	TN		049	1			MARTHA ANN NICHOLS	20220
RICH, ANNA	1797	NC	065		GA			1			ALLEN HELMS	60185
RICH, DAVID		NC	065	1847	GA							60185
RICHARDS, JAMES	1795	NC	044		NC	?037		1 1838	NC	044	MARY ANN HASWELL	02435
RICHARDSON, THOMAS				1803	NC	022						60491
RICHARDSON, WILLIAM FISHER	1787	NC	022									60491

ANCESTOR INDEX	BIRTH	PL	CO	DEATH	PL	CO	LIVD	MARRIED	PL	CO	SPOUSE NAME	CODE
RICHMOND, JOHN				C1787	NC	020		2			RACHEL	19095
RICKARD, DELILA/DELILAH JANE	C1829	NC	?032	1894	NC	032		1 1849	NC	032	JOHN WREN/WRENN	24315
RICKS, BENJAMIN				1775	NC	037		1			PATIENCE HELTY	60587
RICKS, CHARITY	1770	NC	037	1863	TN		069	1 C1791	NC	069	LEMUEL WRIGHT	60587
RICKS, LEWIS	C1741			C1782	NC	037		1 C1768	NC	?037	NANCY ANN JOYNER	60587
RICKS, WILLIAM				1771	NC	037						60587
RIDDLE, DICEY	1787	NC	022	1875	TN			1 C1808	NC	022	MARK PATTERSON	60519
RIDDLE, JULIUS	C1720			C1756	NC	073		1 C1745	NC	?011	NANCY MINTER	60519
RIDDLE, THOMAS	C1752	NC	073	1829	NC	022		1 C1780	NC	022	FRANCIS	60519
RIGGINS, LITTLETON	C1774	?NC		1843	AL			1	?NC		MARY	60059
RILEY, JAMES W	1810	NC	073	1878	NC	073		1 2 C1837	NC	073	MARY ELIZABETH WILKINSON	60429
RING, LEWIS	C1804	NC		1885	TN			1 1823	TN		JANE/JENNIE HOGG	60516
RINTELMAN/RINGLEMAN, CHRISTOP/ CHRISTOPHE	C1718	GER		C1778	NC	085		1 C1740	?GE		ANN DORTHEA	27657
RINTELMAN/RINGLEMAN, ELIZABETH	C1755				NC			1 1774	NC	085	ADOLPH NUSSMAN	27657
RINTELMAN/RINGLEMAN, JOHAN FRIE-DERICH HER	C1757	GER		C1814	NC	090		1 1779	NC	085	MARY WRIGHT	27657
RINTELMAN/RINGLEMAN, JOHANNES	C1743	GER		C1809	NC	085		1 C1767	NC	085	MARGARET SNAP	27657
RINTELMAN/RINGLEMAN, MARTIN CHRISTOPHE	1761	NC	085	C1841	AR			1 1783	NC	085	MARY MAGDALENA FUR/FURRER	27657
RINTELMAN/RINGLEMAN, SOPHIA	C1748	GER			NC			1 1766	NC	085	MARTIN MILLER	27657
RINTELMAN/RINGLEMAN, STIVAN	C1745	GER			NC	?085						27657
RIPPY, EDWARD		IRE			NC	?073						25100
RIPPY, EDWARD	1764	NC	073	1858	SC			3			MARY ELMORE	25100
RIPPY, EDWARD ROSS	1828	NC	?073	1899	SC			1			AMANDA QUINN	25100
RIPPY, MASTON	1802	NC	073	1892	SC			1 1820			MARY/POLLY ARNOLD	25100
RITCH, DAVID	C1777	?NC	?065	1847	GA							60090
RITCH, EMANUEL	1814	NC	?065	1884	GA			1 1835			SARAH JANE GILMORE	60090
RITTER, ARRENIA	1860	NC	068	1957	NC	081		1 1880	NC	068	LEWIS OLIVER GARNER	22005
RITTER, GEORGE D	C1820	NC					068	1 1846	NC	081	MILLY JACKSON	60332
RITTER, WILLIAM DEDBERRY	1837	NC	068	1906	NC	068		1			MARGARET MYRICK	22005
RIVERS, JOEL	C1753			C1827	AL		100	1 C1773			RHODA HARWELL	25100
ROACH, JOSEPH	C1785						086					25100
ROAPER, JOHN				1797	NC	047	037	1			LUCY	25100
ROARK, BARNABUS/BARNEY				1811	?SC		?092					25242
ROBARDS, JOHN	1749	VA		C1812	?NC	?099		1 1772	VA		SARAH MARSHALL	19115
ROBARDS, MARSHALL	1774	VA		1824	NC	032		1 C1799	NC	?039	MARY/POLLY FINCH	19115
ROBARDS, WILLIAM PETTIS	1813	NC	039	1885	IN			1 1840	IN		HANEY EMELINE MCHAFFIE	19115

ANCESTOR INDEX	BIRTH	PL	CO	DEATH	PL	CO	LIVD	MARRIED	PL	CO	SPOUSE NAME	CODE
ROBASON/ROBERTSON, HENRY SR				C1794	NC	063	096	1 C1743			MARTHA	19130
ROBBINS, JOHN R	C1790			C1852	NC	009		1			ELIZABETH	27378
ROBBINS, SAMUEL MARION	1834	NC	012	1917	NC	012		1 1856	NC	012	ELIZA BRINKMAN	02195
								2 1891	NC	012	CAROLINA FISHER WILLIAMS	
ROBBINS, THOMAS	1840	NC	028	1888	NC	009		1 1866	NC	009	EMILY AUGUSTUS FREEMAN	27378
ROBBINS, THOMAS FREEMAN	1877	NC	009	1942	VA			1 1901	NC	009	HILDA FRANCES POLLARD	27378
ROBERSON, BENJAMIN HARVEY	1852	NC	063	1925	NC	063		1 C1873	NC	063	CHLOE FRANCES COBURN	24240
ROBERSON, HARVEY BAKER	1820	NC	063	1852	NC	063		1 C1841	NC	063	MARY EMELINE LEGGETT	24240
ROBERSON, HENRY	1785	NC	063	1872	NC	063		1 1814	NC	041	NANCY ANN BAKER	24240
ROBERSON, HENRY	C1710			1794	NC	063		1 C1743				24240
ROBERSON, HENRY JR	1747	NC	?096	1828	NC	063		1 1783	NC	096	SARAH COLLINS	24240
ROBERSON/ROBESON, GEORGE	C1775	VA		C1859	NC	107	086	1 C1800	?VA		SUSANNAH WOODY	60154
ROBERTS, CORNELIUS	C1809	NC						1 C1833	GA		D	15023
ROBERTS, ELISABETH	1806	NC	103	1894	TX			1 1822	NC	103	WARREN HOOKS	25204
ROBERTS, GEORGE	1753			1832	NC	099	078	1 C1772				60519
								2 1776	NC		MARY	
ROBERTS, HARDIN	C1782	NC										15023
ROBERTS, JAMES DAVID JR	1823	NC		1861	MO			1 C1843	NC		ELIZABETH BURNS	04155
ROBERTS, JAMES DAVID SR	1800	?NC						1			MARY FERRILL	04155
ROBERTS, JOHN	1775	?NC						1			KISSIAH DAVIS	04155
ROBERTS, JOHN	1773	NC	099	1840	TN		099	1			NANCY	60519
								2 1830	NC	099	MRS EUNICE (ROGERS) JONES	
ROBERTS, JOHN O	1792	NC		1862	TN			1			NANCY	60213
ROBERTS, NANCY	C1787	NC		C1875	KY			1 1809	KY		ABRAHAM SANDERS	60577
ROBERTS, SARAH UNITY		NC	?060		NC	040		1	NC	040	THOMAS FRANKLYN BLAKELEY	05070
ROBERTS, WILLIAM				C1784	NC	081	047	1			SARAH	14240
ROBERTS, WILLIAM				C1784	NC	081	047	1			SARAH	17240
ROBERTS, WILLIAM HENRY	1825	NC	044	1908	NC	044	099	1 C1870	NC	044	CANDICE ANN RICHARDS	02435
ROBERTSON, DRURY	1728	VA		1797	NC	005		1 1750			SARAH CLIFTON	60507
ROBERTSON, WILLIAM	C1815	NC		1865	GA			1 C1843			LOUVICIA HUGHES	60308
ROBERTSON/ROBINSON, JEFFREY	C1783	NC	067	1816								60423
ROBERTSON/ROBINSON, JOHN W	1787	NC		1879				1 1822	TN		MARY GILLIAM LAVENDER	60423
								2 1848	GA		MARTHA AUGELINE FAIN	
ROBERTSON/ROBINSON, MILLS	C1785	NC		1814								60423
ROBERTSON/ROBINSON, NATHAN	C1777	NC	005	1807			067					60423
ROBERTSON/ROBINSON, TYREE	C1738	VA		1815	TN			1 C1770	NC	005	MARY/POLLY ADAMS	60423
ROBERTSON/ROBINSON, TYREE JR	C1774	NC	005	1829								60423
ROBERTSON/ROBINSON/ROBERSON, ANNES/ANNI							037					60576
ROBERTSON/ROBINSON/ROBERSON, ARCHELAS							037					60576

ANCESTOR INDEX	BIRTH	PL	CO	DEATH	PL	CO	LIVD	MARRIED	PL	CO	SPOUSE NAME	CODE
ROBERTSON/ROBINSON/ROBERSON, ELISHA							071					60576
ROBERTSON/ROBINSON/ROBERSON, MARMADUKE							009					60576
ROBERTSON/ROBINSON/ROBERSON, WILLOBY							039					60576
ROBINSON, HANNIBAL CRITTENDEN	1859	NC	023	1937	OK			1			ICIE ANN STROUD	60526
ROBINSON, JAMES	C1785	NC			AL			1			ANN DICKSON	15023
ROBINSON, JOHN A	1818				NC	014		1 1837	NC	049	LUCINDA LEATHERWOOD	60526
ROBINSON, JUDA	C1806	NC			IL		046	1 1825	NC	046	ELVIS FOWLER	25159
ROBINSON, SARAH	1750	NC	?005		NC	014		1 1770			ALEXANDER ERWIN	60593
ROBINSON, THOMAS		NC						1			HEM	60526
RODDY, PRUDENCE					NC	?085		1 1730	PA		JAMES HALL	60443
RODES/RHODES, FRANCES	C1853	NC	?073					1 2 1876	NC	073	RODES/RHODES SIDNEY HERNDON	27281
RODES/RHODES, MARTHA ANICE	1870			1911	NC	036		1 1883	NC	036	JACOB DAWSON WILLIAMS	27281
RODGERS/ROGERS, WILLIAM HARVEY	1856	NC	085	1928	NC	016		1 1891	NC		NANCY LOUISE ATWELL	03041
ROGERS, BENJAMIN D JR	C1815	NC	?099				073	1 1841	NC	073	MARTHA I PATTERSON	20030
ROGERS, EUNICE/UNITY	1805	NC	099	1873	TN			1 1823 2 1830	NC NC	099 099	VINKLER JONES JOHN ROBERTS	60519
ROGERS, JOB				1772	NC	099		1			MARY	60519
ROGERS, JOHN	C1729			1799	NC	099						27375
ROGERS, JOHN	C1729			C1802	NC	099		1			MARTHA THWEAP/THWEATT	27375
ROGERS, JUBILEE V	1784	NC	099	1855	TN			1 C1804 2 C1813	NC NC	099 099	HARRIET DAVIS	60519
ROGERS, MARTHA	C1780	NC	099					1 1796	NC	099	WILLIAM ISAAC MCCOLLUM	27375
ROGERS, PELEG		NC	099	1816	NC	099		1	NC	099	ELIZABETH	60519
ROGERS, REBECCA JANE DUDLEY	1791	NC		1880	NC	012		1 1814 2 1828	NC NC	019 012	PETER PIVER THOMAS M THOMPSON	05070
ROGERS/RODGERS, BENJAMIN	C1738	?MA		C1778	NC	010		1 C1759	NC	?047	SARAH HIGHSMITH	27714
ROGERS/RODGERS, JAMES WILLIAM SR	1894	NC	068					1 1925	NC	068	NONNIE NORMAN	27714
ROGERS/RODGERS, REUBEN	1761	NC	010		NC	035		1 1790	NC	035	CHRISTIAN ALDERMAN	27714
ROGERS/RODGERS, WILLIAM	1853	NC	068	1918	NC	068		1 1879	NC	068	LAURA CROOK	27714
ROGERS/RODGERS, WILLIAM COOPER	1812	NC	035	1892				1 1833 2 1842	NC NC	035 035	ESTHER ALDERMAN JEMIMA ALDERMAN	27714
ROLLINS, ELIZABETH, MRS							081					60260
ROLLINS, JOHN	C1762	?NC		1848	GA			1 C1800	NC	081	FRANCES POHL	60260
ROLLINS, WILLIAMSON	C1807	NC	081	1848	GA							60260
ROLLINS/ROLLINGS, CHARLES	C1753	?NC					079					10010
ROOK, JOHN	C1750	NC	071		TN							08065
ROOK/RUKE, STEPHEN	1775	MD		1855	NC	046		1 1798 2 C1830	NC NC	046 046	CHARLOTTE COUCH LOUISA	60451

ANCESTOR INDEX	BIRTH	PL	CO	DEATH	PL	CO	LIVD	MARRIED	PL	CO	SPOUSE NAME	CODE
ROSE, ABNER	C1763	NC	?085	1832	TN			1		NC	092 SALLY SUMMERS	60228
ROSE, ALEXANDER	C1738	SCO		1807	NC	078	020	1 1774	NC		020 EUNICE LEA	19177
ROSE, ALEXANDER		SCO			NC	078	?020	1 1774	VA		FRANCES LEA	19227
ROSE, ALEXANDER JR	1782	NC	020	1822	TN			1 1805	NC		020 MARY/POLLY VANHOOK	19177
ROSE, ALEXANDER JR		NC	078	1822	TN			1 1805	NC		078 MRS MARY/POLLY VANHOOK	19227
ROSE, BARZALAI/BAZIL SR				C1778	NC	092		1			SARAH	60228
ROSE, MEREDITH REDDICK	C1778			C1870	TN		069					25134
ROSE, MOREAU	1806	NC	078	1883	AR			1 1834	TN		NANCY MAY	19177
ROSE, WILLIAM R	1800	NC	069	1863	TN		069	1 1823	TN		ELIZABETH JOHNS	25134
ROSEBOROUGH, ERIXENE MCEWEN	1798	NC	054	1847	TN			1	TN		MOSES MCKNIGHT	60443
ROSEBOROUGH, JAMES					NC	085		1			MARGARET	60443
ROSEBOROUGH, SAMUEL				C1775	NC	085		1	NC		085 JANE HALL	60443
ROSEBOROUGH, SAMUEL	1773	NC	085	1853	TN			1 C1796	NC		054 ELIZABETH HALL	60443
ROSS, JAMES	1734			1829	NC	086		1			HANNAH	25100
ROSS, JAMES	1844	NC	026	1879	NC	026		1 1866			MARSILLA PARSADE PATTERSON	25100
ROSS, LANDRUM BEATTY	1869	NC	026	1891	NC	086		1 1891 2 1935			AMANDA OLA SHUFORD ENZA ELIZABETH SMART	25100
ROSS, LEWIS O	C1902	MA		1933	NC	065	021	1 C1926	?NC		?064 CLEO A GILES	19183
ROSS, MARGARET	1782	NC		1868	MO			1 C1800 2 1817	?TN IN		JAMES DUGGER ANDREW FERGUSON	60060
ROSS, MARTHA A	1831	NC		1903	GA			1 1850	NC		065 ROBERT MCCRACKEN	14050
ROSS, MOSES	1785			1878	NC	026		1			RACHEL BOOKOUT	25100
ROSS, OSBOURN	1823			1863	NC	103		1 1843			EASTER LETTIE BOOKOUT	25100
ROSS, RACHEL	C1810	NC						1			JOHN R MARTIN	25115
ROSS, WILLIAM	C1792	NC					079	1			REBECCA ROLLINS/ROLLINGS	10010
ROSSER, DAVID	1799	NC		C1867	?GA			1 1834 2 1850	GA GA		MARTHA COOK MARY MCDUFFIE	60279
ROUSE, ABNER	1820	NC	059		NC	045		1 1840	NC		?103 HARRIETT PARKS	13264
ROUSE, NOAH	1792	NC	059	C1865	NC	059		1 C1814	NC		059 NANCY	13264
ROUSE, SARAH ADELAIDE	1842	NC	045	1916	NC	045		1 C1862	NC		045 LEWIS JAMES JOHNSON	13264
ROUSSEAU, DAVID	1779	NC	104	1855	IN			1 1801	NC		092 NANCY SHORES	60370
ROUSSEAU, ELIZABETH								1 1803	NC		104 ABIRAM SHORES	60370
ROUSSEAU, ELIZABETH	C1820	NC	104									60370
ROUSSEAU, HILLAIRE	C1743			1829	NC	104		1 C1760 2 1802	VA NC		SARAH/POLLY ROGERS 104 BETTEY HERNDON	60370
ROUSSEAU, HILLAIRE	1802	NC	104	1890	AL			1 1827	TN		LUCRETIA JENNINGS	60370
ROUSSEAU, HIRAM	C1771			1853				1 1809	NC		104 SARAH MEREDITH MARTIN	60370
ROUSSEAU, JAMES HORACE	1812	NC	104	1883	MO			1 C1837			ELIZA PENCE	60370
ROUSSEAU, JOHN	1786	NC	104	1880	NC	104		1 1811	NC		104 SALLY GORDON	60370

ANCESTOR INDEX	BIRTH	PL	CO	DEATH	PL	CO	LIVD	MARRIED	PL	CO	SPOUSE NAME	CODE
ROUSSEAU, LUCY	C1775	NC	092					1 1791	NC	104	DAVID SHORES	60370
ROUSSEAU, MARY A	1813	NC	104	1899	NC	104		1 1834	NC	104	JAMES W TRANSOU	60370
ROUSSEAU, NANCY		NC	104	C1860	TN			1 1813	NC	104	JOSEPH HICKERSON	60370
ROUSSEAU, REUBEN	1804	NC	104	1874	IA			1 1825	NC	104	SARAH BAUGAS	60370
ROUSSEAU, ROBERT	C1818	NC	104	1855	IN			1 1842			ELIZABETH JOHNSON	60370
ROUSSEAU, SARAH								1 1801	NC	104	LEVI SHORES	60370
ROUSSEAU, SARAH	C1810	NC	104	C1855	IN			1 1825	NC	104	BENJAMIN F MARTIN	60370
ROUSSEAU, WILLIAM		NC	104	C1845	NC	104		1 1814	NC	104	SARAH WITHERSPOON	60370
ROUSSEAU, WILLIAM	1807	NC	104	1855	IN			1 C1833			RUTH MCBRIDE	60370
ROWE, JULIA ELIZABETH	1829	NC	101	1884	NC	101		1 1859	NC	101	EBENEZER DUNSTON	02195
ROWE, WILLIAM				C1850	NC	101	096	1 C1820	NC	101	JEMIMA NORMAN	02195
ROWLAND, JEREMIAH	1805	NC	067	1879	OR			1 C1823	NC	?067	NANCY CAGLE	17105
								2 C1829	?NC		LUCY BUTLER	
								3 1847			MRS MARY ANN (ANDERSON) SAPPINGTON	
ROWLAND, LOYD/LLOYD	1784	NC	?067	1858	TN			1 C1802	NC		MARY ANN	17105
ROWLAND/ROLAND, JANE		NC	099		TN			1 1807	NC	099	LEWIS GULLEY/GULLY	08090
ROWLAND/ROLAND, WILLIAM				C1795	NC	099		1 C1742	VA		MARY WOMACK	08090
ROYAL/RIAL/ROIL, JOHN JACKSON	1829	NC	?104	1865	AL			1 1849	NC	006	JANE ATWOOD	08130
ROYALL, ISHAM	1826	NC	087	1898	NC	087	035	1 1855	NC	087	RACHEL CARROL	17080
ROYALL, ISHAM	C1760	NC	087	1832	NC	087		1 C1790			ELIZABETH WHITNEY	17080
ROYALL, JOHN	1729	VA		C1790	NC	087		1 C1752	VA		SARAH?	17080
ROYALL, ROBERTA PRISCILLA	1858	NC	087	1944	NC	029	035	1 1878	NC	087	MURDOCK MCKINNON MAXWELL	17080
ROYALL, WHITNEY	1792	NC	087	1864	NC	087		1 C1820	NC	035	SARAH MARTIN	17080
RUBOTTOM, EZEKIEL	1770	NC	022	1857	NC	068	022	1			ELINOR BETTIS	60424
RUBOTTOM, THOMAS		WAL		1806	NC	068	022	1	DE		PHEBE DIXON	60424
RUCKER, NANCY ANN	C1780	NC						1			SHEMUEL COOK	60083
RUDD, ABSOLOM MANN		NC	047					1	NC			19227
RUDD, LEMUEL			047									19227
RUDD, NATHANIEL	1801	NC	047	C1880	AR			1 C1826	TN		NANCY CLARK	19227
RUDD, REBECCA	C1812	NC	047	C1890	AR		?020	1 C1830	TN		THOMAS H CLARK	19227
RUDD, WILLIAM SEYMOUR				C1823	NC	047	?020	1			MRS MANN	19227
RULE, DELILAH		NC			?NC			1			GEORGE HODGSON/HODGIN/HODSON	60031
RUPPE, DANIEL	1805	NC	092	1900	NC	026	092	1			ELIZABETH NEIGHBOURS	60272
RUPPE, HENRY	1796	NC	092	1882	?SC		092	1			ELIZABETH WILSON	60272
RUPPE, JACOB	1779				OH		092	1			MARGERY OLIVER	60272
RUPPE, JOHN	C1784	PA			GA		092	1			PHOEBE PILCHER	60272
RUPPE, MARTIN	1758	?PA			OH		092	1			MARY BARBARA MATHIAS	60272

ANCESTOR INDEX	BIRTH	PL	CO	DEATH	PL	CO	LIVD	MARRIED	PL	CO	SPOUSE NAME	CODE
RUPPE, MARTIN	C1794				OH		092	1			POLLY PILCHER	60272
RUPPE, POLLY	C1792						,092	1			WILLIAM WOOD	60272
RUSH, BENJAMIN					039	044	1				RACHEL	20350
RUSH, BENJAMIN JR	C1717			1801	NC			1			ALICE GRIGSBY	27269
RUSH, BENJAMIN THOMAS	1821	NC		1863			067	1			PATIENCE BALDWIN	27269
RUSH, MARTIN	1794	NC		1883	NC	067		1			SUSAN BELL	27269
RUSH, WILLIAM	1755	NC		1827	NC		067	1			ABIGAIL TERRELL	27269
RUSH, WILLIAM	1755	VA		1827	NC	067	015	1	1775	NC	015 ABIGAIL TERRELL	60404
RUSS, JOHN	1785	NC	012	1871	NC	082		1	1809	NC	012 RACHEL HILL	60389
								2	C1859	NC	082 SALEMMA HILL	
RUSS, MARY REBECCA	1830			1901	NC	040		1	1849	NC	065 JOHN RILEY	14050
								2	1858	NC	065 WILLIAM DAVIDSON MCCRACKEN	
RUSS, NATHANIEL JAMES	1859	NC	082	1928	SC			1		NC	082 MARTHA ANN SMITH	60389
RUSSELL, AARON	1761	NC		1845								25093
RUSSELL, AARON				C1815			067					60134
RUSSELL, CAROLINE REBECCA	1829	NC	?081	1894	NC	099	081	1	1857	?NC	HEZEKIAH ALEXANDER CORRELL	03250
RUSSELL, GEORGE WASHINGTON	1821	NC		1893	TN			1	C1849	TN	NANCY BROOKS	60457
RUSSELL, HIRAM	C1792	NC	090	1858	?MO			1	1816	KY	MILLE GRAHAM	60425
								2			MILTILDA RICHARDSON HARPER	
RUSSELL, JAMES B	C1829	NC	075	C1871	NC	031		1			MARTHA JANE FORBES	60459
RUSSELL, JAMES BOUSH E	1872	NC	031	1899	VA							60459
RUSSELL, JAMES WILSON MILLER	C1862	NC		1925	VA			1			ANNE VIRGINIA AYERS	60459
RUSSELL, JANE	1770	NC	073	C1855	GA			1			WILLIAM HENRY	27382
RUSSELL, JOHN STEWART	1838	NC	104	1926	TX			1			RHODA ESTES	25093
RUSSELL, LEVY	1792	NC	104	1883				1			HILEY ANDREWS	25093
RUSSELL, PINKNEY H	1816	NC		1891	TN			1	1845	NC	ELIZABETH F JONES	60134
RUSSELL, THOMAS	1793	NC			TN			1		NC		60457
RUSSELL, WILLIAM	C1788	NC		C1867	NC	?081	?067	1			REBECCA	03250
RUSSELL, WILLIAM JR				1810	NC	046		1			MARGARET DOWNEY	60032
RUSSELL, WILLIAM JULIAN	1864	NC	030	1951	NC	031		1	C1896	NC	010 RUTH MAUDE JOHNSON	60459
								2	1902	NC	010 MABEL CLARA JOHNSON	
RUSSELL, WILLIAM SR				1795	NC	046		1			MRS ELEANOR CROSS	60032
RUSSELL, ZEBEDEE	1805	NC		1886	NC	067	?081	1			PRUDENCE HOPKINS	60134
RUST, JOHN S	1801	NC		1881	TN			1	1823	NC	NANCY RUCKER COOK	60083
RUST, MATTHEW/JOHN ?	C1780	NC						1			PRISCILLA MILLS	60083
RUST/RUSS, JOHN SR				1819	NC	044		1			SARAH	60509
RUST/RUSS, MATTHEW				1806	NC	044		1	1791	NC	044 PRISCILLA MILLS	60509
RUST/RUSS, VINCENT		NC	044		TN			1	C1820	NC	?044 SUSAN STONE	60509
RUST/RUSS, VINCENT	C1772	NC	044					1	1797	NC	044 ANNA BRADFORD	60509

ANCESTOR INDEX	BIRTH	PL	CO	DEATH	PL	CO	LIVD	MARRIED	PL	CO	SPOUSE NAME	CODE
RUTLAND, JAMES REDDICK RAMEY		NC	010	1827	SC		071	1 1795	NC		JEMINA HORTON	60059
								2 C1800			DOROTHY SMITH	
RUTLEDGE, SAMUEL J	C1785	NC			TN			1			BETHIA R	60213
RUTLEDGE, THOMAS	C1729	?PA		1801	NC	035		1 C1763	NC	070	MRS CATHERINE (JAMES?) PEARSALL	17085
RYALS, THEOPHILUS	C1800	NC		C1853	MO			1 C1828			NANCY	60555
RYALS, WILL		NC	?048		NC	048		1	NC	?048	WILLIE JOHNSTON	03315

S

ANCESTOR INDEX	BIRTH	PL	CO	DEATH	PL	CO	LIVD	MARRIED	PL	CO	SPOUSE NAME	CODE
SAFLEY, JESSEE	1781	VA		1861	TN		?013	1 C1808	?NC	?013	PHATHA/FAITHA STILES	60029
SANDERS, AARON	1810	NC	046	1876	IN			1 1830	IN		SARAH EDMONSON	60401
								2 1849	IN		MRS NANCY CLEVENGER	
SANDERS, ABEDNEGO	1776	NC	046	1835	IN			1 1807	NC	104	AMY COOK	60401
SANDERS, ABRAHAM	C1789	NC		C1865	KY			1 1809	KY		NANCY ROBERTS	60577
SANDERS, ANNA	1743	VA		1815	TN			1 1767	NC	046	THOMAS ELMORE	20333
SANDERS, AXUM	1808	?NC	?005	1900	MS			1			ELIZABETH JANE LINDEY	27269
SANDERS, DANIEL S		NC	072	1854	NC	070		1 1825	NC	057	ELIZA FOSCUE	20030
SANDERS, HARDY	1807	?VA		1895	NC	068	?092	1			SALLY SMITH	19183
								2	?NC	?068	SARAH BREWER	
SANDERS, HENRIETTA	1801	NC	?072	1879	NC	?072		1			DAVID WARD SIMMONS	20030
SANDERS, ISHAM	1834	NC	068	1923	NC	068		1	NC	?068	MARY ANN MCNEILL	19183
SANDERS, JOHN	1758	VA		1792	NC	046		1 1780	NC	073	MILLEY MOORMAN	60458
SANDERS, WILLIAM GEORGE	1841	NC	?005	1911	MS			1			SUSAN RUSH	27269
								2 1880			FRANCES WHITE	
SANDERS/SAUNDERS, BENJAMIN	1746	VA		C1822	NC	022		1 1768	NC	029	LEAH SMITH	60575
SANDERS/SAUNDERS, THOMAS	C1779	NC	022	1848	TN			1 1797	NC	022	ELIZABETH ROOK	60575
SANDLIN, KENNEDA	1819	NC		1853	KY			1 1838			FANNIE MORRIS	27715
SANDLIN, LEWIS	C1776	NC		1854	KY			1			SARAH	25242
SANDLIN, LEWIS B	C1776	NC		1854				1			SARAH/SALLY	27715
SANDLIN, MARGARET	1799	NC						1 1817	KY		WILLIAM MORRIS	27715
SANER/SEHNERT, MARTIN	1797	NC			AR			1 1827	NC	085	MARGARET WELLMAN	02170
SANER/SEHNERT, PETER	1713	GER		1782	NC	092		1 1748	PA		MARIA GOEPHERT	02170
SANER/SEHNERT, PETER	1749	NY		1823	NC	?032		1 1780	NC	085	CATHERINE SCHAFER	02170
SANFORD, ELIZABETH	C1844	NC										60146
SANFORD, EZEKIEL	C1803	NC	081					1 C1826	NC			60146
								2 1841	NC	060	ELLENER COBB	
SANFORD, JAMES L	1830	NC	078	1890	NC	078		1 1853	NC	078	REBECCA KING	60500
SANFORD, JAMES T	1790	NC	044		NC	078		1 1822	NC	044	HANNAH AMIS	60500
SANFORD, JOSEPH	1842	NC	060	1928	TX			1 1867	TN		SARAH ALICE FINLEY	60146

ANCESTOR INDEX	BIRTH	PL	CO	DEATH	PL	CO	LIVD	MARRIED	PL	CO	SPOUSE NAME	CODE
SANFORD, ROBERT				1820	NC	044		1			ANN JONES	60500
SAPPENFIELD, MATHIAS, I	C1725	GER		1780			085	1			ANNA CATHERINA	06005
SAPPENFIELD, MATHIAS, II	C1770	NC	085					1	NC		ANNA SECHRIST	06005
SAPPENFIELD, MATHIAS, III	1790	NC		1873	IN		085	1 1811	NC	032	CHRISTINA GRIMES	06005
SARGENT, DEMPSEY	C1790	NC	?020		TN			1 1815 2	NC	020	A M BURTON CHARLOTTE COOK	60035
SARGENT, JAMES/DEMPSEY	C1765						020	1 1791	NC	020	RACHEL PHELPS	60035
SARGENT/SEARGENT/SARJENT, WILLIAM				1768	NC	073		1			SARAH LEA	17135
SARGENT/SEARGENT/SARJENT, DANIEL		NC	020	C1813	NC	078		1 1780	NC	020	DELPHY CARNEY	17135
SARGENT/SEARGENT/SARJENT, JOSEPH				C1780	NC	020		1			RUTH RANSOM	17135
SARGENT/SEARGENT/SARJENT, POLLY		NC	020		NC	020		1 1807	NC	078	THOMAS LIPSCOMB	17135
SAULS, DAVID		NC	056				022	1 1799	NC	099	LYDIA PENNEY	27543
SAULS, EDWIN M	1846	NC	103	C1912	NC	103		1 1867	NC	103	NANCY DAVIS	60577
SAULS, JAMES	1810	?NC		1892	NC	103	045	1 C1829	?NC	?045	SELVANY	60577
SAULS, NATHAN	1808	?NC		C1877	NC	045		1 C1829	?NC	?045	AMY MILLER ?	60577
SAUNDERS, AARON	C1822			C1885	NC	017		1 1845	NC	104	AVA O FOSTER	25253
SAUNDERS, WILLIAM	C1700	VA		C1760	NC	073	020	1 C1725	VA		FANNY ADAMS	60453
SAUNDERSON/SANDERSON, IVES				1836	NC	053		1			ELIZABETH	20335
SAUNDERSON/SANDERSON, RICHARD				1788	NC			1			ELIZABETH SPENCER	20335
SAWYER, ELISHA	1777			1853	NC	096		1 1799 2 1818			CATHERINE THORNTON KEZIAH DUNSTON	20335
SAWYER, MILES	C1808	NC	?018	C1848	NC	030		1 C1840	NC	?030	ZILPHIA HUTCHINS	03210
SAYLORS/SAILOR, LEONARD JR	1786	NC		1856	SC		060	1	SC		SARAH JOHNSON	17220
SAYLORS/SAILOR, LEONARD SR		NC		1811	SC		060	1	NC		MARY	17220
SCARBOROUGH, DAVID		VA		C1784	NC	037		1			NANNA DUNN	08185
SCARBOROUGH, ENOCH/ENOS	C1772			C1810	NC	037		1 C1800	NC	037	LUCYE/LOUVANNA FOREHAND	08185
SCARBOROUGH, MARY W	1802	NC	037	C1867	MS			1 1822	NC	037	SION WRIGHT GARDNER	08185
SCARBOROUGH/SCARBROUGH, JOHN SR	C1730						067	1 C1778	VA		ELIZABETH RACHEL JOHNSON ?	60151
SCHELHORN/SCHELLHORN/SCHOLLHORN, JOHN ADAM	C1740						090	1 C1782			MRS CATHARINA CREUTZFUSSER	60125
SCHELL, ANNA MARIA		PA			NC	060		1	NC	060	RUDOLPH CONRAD	60349
SCHOLES, ALLEN	1802	NC	014	1867	TN			1 2 3			MALINDA BROWNING MARY	60066
SCHOLES, JOSEPH					TN		014	1			DARICUS HUGHES	60066
SCHRAMM, NICHOLAS	C1725	GER		1793	NC	060	094	1 1749 2	PA		ANNA CATERINA KOENER MARGARET	25087
SCHWANNER/SWANNER, ASA	1832	NC	063	1899	AL		063	1 1852	AL		LURANEY BAREFOOT	60497
SCHWANNER/SWANNER, HENRY	1766	NC		C1855	NC	101	063	1 1794	NC	096	ELIZABETH WORLEY LEARY	60497

ANCESTOR INDEX	BIRTH	PL	CO	DEATH	PL	CO	LIVD	MARRIED	PL	CO	SPOUSE NAME	CODE
SCHWANNER/SWANNER, JESSE L	1798	NC		1867	AL		063	1	NC		ELIAZBETH LEGGETT	60497
SCHWANNER/SWANNER, MATHIAS TOBIAS				1743	NC	096	010	1			JEAN	60497
SCHWANNER/SWANNER, WILLIAM M				1777	NC	063	096	1			SARAH	60497
SCHYLER/SCHUYLER, JULIUS CONSTAN TINE WILLI	C1785	GER		1838	NC	090	092	1 1818	NC	046	NANCY RUSSELL	60032
SCOGGINS, WILLIAM FREEMAN	C1770	NC	060	1863	GA			1 1805	SC		PRISCILLA ALLEN	60012
SCOTT, JAMES		NC		C1832	TN			1			MARY/POLLY CARUTHERS	60093
SCOTT, JAMES	1798	NC	016	1872	MS			1	NC		MARY	60228
SCOTT, JOHN	1777	VA		1846	IN		092	1 1804	NC	092	RACHEL HORTON	27429
SCOTT, JOSHUA JEHU	C1787			1819	NC	099		1 1806	VA		HANNAH RIVERS	25100
SCOTT, NANCY	C1785	NC		C1875	AL			1 1810	NC	014	REUBEN TENNISON	27595
SCOTT, PHEBE	1758			1840	NC	090		1 1777	NC	092	MICHAEL FULP	06195
SCOTT, STEPHEN	1821	NC	?092	1889	IN		092	1 C1841	IN		MAHALA ARNETT	27429
SCRIBNER, WILLIAM	C1770	NC		C1853	MO							27531
SCULL/SKULL, EDWARD		VA		C1767	NC	051	010	1			CHRISTAIN	19130
SCURLOCK, JOSEPH	C1771	NC	022	C1835	TN			1 1800	NC	045	MRS MARTHA (GLASGOW) SHEPPARD	07187
SCURLOCK, MIAL		VA		1781	NC	022		1			SARAH HOWARD	07018
SCURLOCK, MIAL	C1720	VA		1781	NC	022		1 2 C1742			SARAH SARAH HOWARD ?	07187
SEABOLT, ELIZABETH							006	1 1798			JACOB CRUM	60586
SEAGRAVE, JACOB	C1763			1835	NC			1			ALINAIR	60578
SEAGRAVE, JOHN	C1738			1823	NC			1 2			SARAH PRIDDY PHEBE COOK	60578
SEAGRAVE, MOSES	C1833	NC		C1910				1			SUSAN CRABB	60578
SEAGRAVE, PHOEBE				C1810	NC		100					60578
SEAGRAVE, WILLIAM				C1844	NC		005					60578
SEAL/SEALS, WILLIAM		NC	068		GA			1			JUDITH POWELL	27280
SEARS, BISHOP H	C1805	NC						1 C1838	GA		MARGARET	15023
SEARS, SUSANNA	C1769	?GE		1855				1	NC		JOEL WHITE	60530
SEARS, VINCENT	C1790	NC		C1855	GA			1 C1827	GA		MARY	15023
SEARS, WYATT	C1788	NC						1 C1825	GA		F	15023
SEAY, JAMES		VA		C1773	NC	010						20415
SEAY, MARY	C1753	NC	?010		NC	010		1 C1772	NC	?010	JOEL BROWN	20415
SECREST, WILLIAM M	C1800	NC	065		NC	065		1 1820	NC	065	JANE WILEY	24243
SEELY, WARREN KELLY	1788	CT		1823	NC	009		1 1810	NC	009	JERUSHA DAVIS	27378
SEFIRD/SEFFERT, DANIEL	1798	NC	016				032	1			LYDIA DAYVAULT ?	06075
SELF, ADAM MOORE	1802	NC	?065	1865	TX			1			MAHALA KEYS	60107
SELF, GEORGE W	C1802			C1875	NC	013		1 C1833			SARAH J CROWDER	27334

ANCESTOR INDEX	BIRTH	PL	CO	DEATH	PL	CO	LIVD	MARRIED	PL	CO	SPOUSE NAME	CODE
SELF, MARY	1804	NC	?065		TX			1			WASHINGTON SMITH	60107
SELF, MELCHEZEDIC	C1777			1854	TX		?054	1 1801			CATHERINE MOORE	60107
SELF, SAMUEL	1777	VA		1850	TN			1 1797	NC	078	ELIZABETH DAVEY	17090
SELLARS, SAMUEL JR	C1775	NC	035	C1845	GA			1			MARY BISHOP	60164
SELLARS, SAMUEL SR	C1743	NC		1794	GA		035	1 1767	NC	035	ZILPHA SELLARS	60164
SELLARS, ZILPHA					GA			1 1767	NC	035	SAMUEL SELLARS	60164
SELLERS, JOHN	C1830	NC	012	1865	NY			1 C1855	NC	012	ELIZA	13052
SELLERS, KERENHAPPUCK	1816	NC	035	1890	MO			1 1834	TN		THOMAS ARRINGTON THOMPSON	60422
SELLERS, SAMUEL J	C1793	NC		C1880	NC	012		1			ANN	13052
SENTER, STEPHEN					NC	060		1 1779	NC	060	ANNE HOLLAND	11010
								2 1791	NC	060	WINEY MASSEY ?	
SESSOMS, NATHAN	C1810	NC			NC			1			PARTHENIA	27531
SESSOMS, PRISCELLA E	C1838	NC	051	1895	NC	051		1 1870	NC	051	JAMES REDDICK GREEN	27531
SESSUMS, NATHAN		?NC	?010	C1836	NC	037		1 1806	NC	010	PENELOPE PERRY	27477
SESSUMS, NATHAN HARRELL	C1817	NC		C1864	NC			1 1835	NC	?037	ELIZA KILLEBREW	27477
								2 C1857	NC	?037	MARTHA HARRIS	
SETSER/SETZER, ADAM	C1759	NC	060	1843	NC	017	014	1	NC	060	ELIZABETH ARNEY/HARMON	27318
SETSER/SETZER, JACOB	C1732	GER		C1780	NC	?060		1 C1754	NC	060	MARY MAGDALENE POVEY/BOVEY	27318
SETSER/SETZER, JOEL PATON	1839	NC	014	1923	TN			1 1867	TN		MARGET ISABEL DRAKE	27318
								2 1871	TN		LOUISA JANE BARNETT WHITE	
								3 1883	TN		MARGARET LOUVINA DRAKE	
SETSER/SETZER, JOHN, I	C1781	NC	?014	C1862	NC	017		1 C1802	NC	014		27318
								2 C1825	NC	104	SUSANNAH BRYANT	
SETSER/SETZER, JOHN, II	1808	NC	014		NC	?014		1 1828	NC	?014	SUSAN/SUCKEY CRISP	27318
SEWELL, JACOB	C1786	NC		1862	AR			1 C1820	TN		MARY TROUSDALE	60404
SEWELL, JAMES	1785	NC		C1865				1 1806			PHOEBE FAIRCHILD	27593
SEWELL, JOSEPH	1753	MD		1847	KY			1 1779	NC	104	MARY TOMPKINS	27593
SEWELL, POLLEY								1 1812	NC	020	THOMAS ARNOLD	27413
SHAMBURGER, PETER	1801	NC	068	1872	TX			1			ADALINE H BROWER	60427
SHAMEL/SCHEMEL, JOHN	1746			1813	NC	090		1 C1776				04080
								2 1799	NC	090	MRS HANNAH (MILLER) HOUSER	
SHAMEL/SCHEMEL, JOSEPH	1778	NC		1857	OH		090	1 C1810			ROSANNA DEMUTH	04080
SHANNON, WILLIAM	C1730	PA		1803	NC	046						12125
SHARP, MARY M	C1796	NC	?065	1870	IN			1 1814	NC	065	WHIT M HILL	60426
SHARP, SARAH	C1800	NC	084		?IN			1 C1821	?NC		HENRY JONES	60111
SHARP/SHARPE, MARINDA/RENDA	C1827	NC	?037	1859	NC	105		1			BERRY H THORN/THORNE	03250
								2 1851	NC	069	MARTIN R THORN/THORNE	
SHARPLESS, WILLIAM				1830	NC	070						60231
SHARPLESS, WILLIAM E	C1800	NC	070	1835	NC	070		1			RHODA CANNADAY	60231
SHAVER, EMBERY	C1828	NC	?092	1908	NC	104	?085					19017
SHAW, DANIEL				C1829	NC	029		1 C1783	NC		REBECCA BUIE	27740

ANCESTOR INDEX	BIRTH	PL	CO	DEATH	PL	CO	LIVD	MARRIED	PL	CO	SPOUSE NAME	CODE
SHAW, DAVID M	1777	NC		C1857	KY		099	1 1799	NC		CHARITY JANE	25134
SHAW, JOHN A	1848	NC						1 1871	NC	106	NANCY JANE WAGGONER	40690
								2 C1895	NC		MARTHA FENDER	
SHAW, JOSEPH B	1774	MD		1863	TN		073	1			MARTHA GOOCH	60251
SHAW, LEWIS D	1855	NC						1 1878	NC	106	MARY VICTORIA CHAPPELL	40690
SHAW, NORMAN				C1858	NC	106		1			CYNTHIA DRAPER	40690
SHAW, SUSAN MARIA	1846	NC		1918	WA			1 1860	NC	106	WILLIAM P NORMAN	40690
								2 1875	NC	049	BRYANT HILL	
SHEARER, ELIZABETH	C1792	?NC	?006	C1840	NC	006		1 C1810	NC	?006	JOSEPH GREEN	60557
SHEARER, ROBERT	C1765	?NC		1845	NC	006		1 C1790			SARAH	60557
SHEETS, ANDREW	C1774	NC	085	C1855	NC	006	104	1 C1794	NC	?104	MARY SHERRIER	02295
SHEETS, MARTIN	C1735	HOL		C1810	NC	085						02295
SHELBY, CALVIN	C1825	NC						1 C1845	?AL		EMILINE	60220
SHELBY, MOSES	C1795	NC			?AL			1 C1820	?NC		HARRIET	60220
SHELLEY, MARY/POLLY	1802	NC	?035	1882	TN			1 1823	NC	?035	CARLTON MATHIS	60083
SHELLEY, THOMAS/JACOB	C1780	NC	?035	1847	TN			1	NC	?035	KATE	60083
SHELSBERGER, JACOB	1805	NC		1871	NE			1 1830	IN		SUSANNAH SEMANS	60072
SHELTON, JESSE F	1804	NC						1 1832	IN		CECILIA/SISLEY JONES	20125
SHELTON, JOEL/JOSEPH	1807	SC					049	1 C1829	NC	049	MARY/POLLY CHASTAIN	60519
SHELTON, MARIE		NC						1	NC		ISAAC ROLLER	20125
SHELTON, RICHARD ELIJAH	1759	?VA		C1824	TN		099	1 1796	TN		TEMPERANCE STREET	60506
SHELTON, WILLIAM	1776	NC			NC	049	090	1 C1800	NC		LYDIA PARKER	60519
SHELTON, WILLIAM JASPER	1829	NC	049	1904	OK			1 1859	AL		LETTIE FOUST MORRIS	60519
SHEPHERD, ANNE	C1759	VA			NC	104		1 C1780			WILLIAM VIARS	10154
SHEPHERD, JAMES WELBORN	1827	NC	104	1899	NC	006		1 1851	NC	006	ELIZABETH JONES	60120
SHEPHERD, JOHN	C1730	VA		1810	NC	104		1			SARAH	10154
SHEPHERD, JOHN	1734	VA		1810	NC	104		1 C1755	VA		SARAH	60120
SHEPHERD, JOHN	C1760	VA		1812	NC	104		1 C1780	NC	104	PHEBE	60120
SHEPHERD, LARKIN	1794	NC	104	1849	NC	104		1 1817	NC	104	ALLY IRWIN	60120
SHEPHERD, MARTHA MALINDA	1864	NC	006	1906	NC	004		1 1883	NC	004	JOSEPH WILSON PHOUTS	60120
SHEPHERD/SHEPPARD, ELENDER PENELOPE	1783	NC	068	1870	TX			1 C1803	GA		JAMES FAULK	60298
SHERMER, THOMAS ALEXANDER	1854	NC	106	1915	NC	106		1			PHISA ANN HOOTS	60356
SHERRILL, ADAM, SR.	C1700	?PA		C1773	NC	094	085	1			ELIZABETH	60339
SHERRILL, ALEXANDER	1778	NC		1862	IL			1 1820	?TN		ELIZABETH RIDINGS	60105
SHERRILL, AMBROSE	C1783	VA		C1865	?IL		014	1 C1800	?NC		NANCY DAVENPORT	60285
SHERRILL, COLBERT	C1785	NC	060	C1830	NC	014	054	1			LYDIA CARLOCK/KERLOCK	60339
SHERRILL, ISABELLA	1803	NC	014	1888	WI			1 1831	IL		RICHARD HAZEL	60285
								2 1840	IL		OWEN 'SQUIRE' GUGERTY	

ANCESTOR INDEX	BIRTH	PL	CO	DEATH	PL	CO	LIVD	MARRIED	PL	CO	SPOUSE NAME	CODE
SHERRILL, JACOB	1739	?MD		1813	TN		060	1			HULDAH WILSON	60339
SHERRILL, JACOB L.	C1810	NC	014	C1875	AR		021	1 1844	AR		SUSAN L TATE	60339
SHERRILL, JACOB, JR.	C1759	NC	?005	C1830	NC	060	014	1			ELIZABETH/BETSEY PERKINS	60339
SHERRILL, JOHN		NC			IL							60510
SHERRILL, LETTICE	1784	VA		1857	AL		065	1 1806	AL		ISAAC NESMITH	60519
SHERRILL, URIAH	C1760						065	1 C1780			SALLY DUCKWORTH	60519
SHERRILL, WILLIAM	1750	NC		1829	NC	014	060	1 C1773	NC	085	ISABELLA LOWRANCE	60105
SHERRILL, WILLIAM							014					60339
SHERWOOD, DANIEL	1749	MD		1838	NC	046		1 1767	MD		FRANCES LINTHICUM	17105
SHIELDS, GEORGE W	C1810	NC	047									60594
SHIELDS, JOSEPH		NC	047									60594
SHIELDS, THOMAS				C1836	NC	047		1	NC	047	MRS CATHERINE (WHITEHEAD) SHIELDS	60594
SHINE, DANIEL	1690	IRE		C1741	NC	028		1 1715			ELIZABETH GREEN	60057
SHINE, DANIEL W	1729							1 1753	?NC		BARBARA FRANCK	60057
SHINE, JOHN	1759	NC						1 C1780	NC	057	CLARISSA WILLIAMS	60057
SHINE, SARAH W	1784	NC	057	1856				1 1804	NC	057	JAMES MILLER	60057
SHINN, ISAC ROSS	1812	NC		1897	TX			1 C1858	TX		SARAH/SALLIE THORNTON	60365
SHIRLEY, JOHN W	1785	NC		C1865	AR			1			SARAH	60448
SHIVERS, JESSE JR	1788	NC	079	1845	AL			1 1809	NC	079	NANCY BRIERLY	21165
SHIVERS, JESSE SR	1759			1819			?079	1			SALLY	21165
SHIVERS, JONAS SR	C1742	NC		1799	NC	079		1			SARAH	21165
SHIVES, DAVID WILSON	1821	NC	?085	1878	MO		099	1 1842	NC	033	SOPHIA WILHELM	60299
								2 1863	IL		MARY ANN GRIGG	
SHOAF, ALEXANDER LEWIS	1834	NC		1914	KS			1 1857	NC		SUSAN LOUISE CLAYTON	60210
SHOAF, HENRY	1807	NC		1883	NC	038	?032	1 C1830	NC		SARAH	60210
SHOEMAKER, CONRAD JR	C1775	?NC		C1844	IN		046	1 1788	?NC		JANE WITT	60100
SHOEMAKER, CONRAD SR	1737	GER		C1790	NC	046		1 C1761	PA		SUSANNAH YOUNGMAN	60100
SHOEMAKER, JESSE G	1809	NC	046	1888	IL			1 1834	NC	046	MARY ANN WILEY	60100
SHOEMAKER, JOHN	1793	NC	054				?104	1			PATSEY	04050
SHOEMAKER, TARLTON	1763	VA			TN		054					04050
SHOFNER, MARTIN	1758	GER		1838	TN		073	1 C1778	NC	?073	CATHARINE COOKE	60337
SHOOK, ELIZABETH	1837	NC		1922	NC	014	021	1			A B RECTOR	25162
SHORT, RICHARD		NC	100	1853	NC	100		1 1797	NC	100	MRS AGENES (RIGGAN) SHORT	60594
SHORT, WILLIAM	1766				VA		014	1			MARY/POLLY	60019
SHOUSE, CHRISTIAN	C1790	?NC	?090					1			SALLY PLANCET	25027
SHOUSE, HENRY	C1765							1	?NC	?090		25027
SHOUSE, HENRY SANDERS	1830	NC	090	1898	IN			1 1852	IN		MARY/POLLY HUBBELL	25027

ANCESTOR INDEX	BIRTH	PL	CO	DEATH	PL	CO	LIVD	MARRIED	PL	CO	SPOUSE NAME	CODE
SHUFORD/SCHEUFFERT, GEORGE	1689	GER		C1762	NC	005		1			GERTRUDE	25100
								2			RODY	
SHUFORD/SCHEUFFERT, JACOB RHYNE	1810	NC	060	1878	TX			1			MRS MELINDA JANE (WEBB) TOMS	25100
SHUFORD/SCHEUFFERT, JOHANNAS/ JOHN	1723	GER		1790	NC	060		1			SARAH	25100
								2			MARY CLAIR CONRAD	
SHUFORD/SCHEUFFERT, JOHN JACOB	1849	NC	013	1933	NC	026		1			MARGARET RIPPY	25100
								2			ELLA BRIDGES	
SHUFORD/SCHEUFFERT, JOHN MARTIN	1744	PA		1780	NC			1 1766			EVE CHRISTINA/CATHERINE WARLICK	25100
SHUFORD/SCHEUFFERT, MARTIN	1776	NC	094	1837	NC	060		1			ELIZABETH RHYNE	25100
SHULL, MARY	1814	NC	060	1900	NC	026		1 1840	NC	060	AARON BEAM	05070
SHULL, PHILLIP	1797	NC						1			PHOEBE WARD	03041
SHULL, SIMON	1767	NC	060	1813	NC	006	102	1 1790	NC		MARY SHEIFFLER ?	03041
SILANCE, JERRY THOMAS	C1881	NC	072	1951	NC	072		1 1907	NC	072	PAULINE WILLIAMS	27374
SILANCE, STEPHEN	C1850	NC	072	1914	NC	072		1			MARY ELLA KING	27374
								2 1884	NC	072	OLIVE KING	
SILANCE, WILLIAM	C1810	?NC	?072	1898	NC	072		1 1847	NC	072	ELIZABETH RITTER	27374
SILL/SILLS, ASWELL/OSWILL							070					60413
SILL/SILLS, JAMES							067					60413
SILL/SILLS, JESSE							086					60413
SILL/SILLS, PHILIP							067					60413
SILL/SILLS, PRISCILLA							070					60413
SILLS, FAITHY, MRS	C1785	NC	047		NC	047						60594
SILLS, HENRY E	1820	NC	047									60594
SILLS, ISHAM		NC	047		?TN							60594
SILLS, JOHN B	C1793			1858	NC	047		1			MRS CHARLOTTE (GRAY) SILLS	60594
SILLS, SOLOMON J	1816	NC	047									60594
SIMMONS, BELL	1786	NC	085	1844	MO		090	1 C1800			ELLEANDER HAWKINS	60508
SIMMONS, ELIZABETH/BETTIE	1873	NC	102	1918	OK			1 C1890	?NM		DAN GUNTER	60222
SIMMONS, JAMES	1794	?NC		C1854	TN			1	?NC		BARBARA MCGONIGLE	21173
SIMMONS, JESSE	1760	NC		C1836			090					60508
SIMMONS, JOHN	C1780	NC		1840	IN		046	1 1797	NC	046	ABIGAIL STARBUCK	60574
SIMMONS, KELLY	1808	NC	090	1882	MO			1 1834	MO		MALINDA SMITH	60508
SIMMONS, LACY/LACEY				C1789	NC	047						20210
SIMMONS, LETITIA	1818	NC	090	1883	MO			1 1836	MO		NERO ALEXANDER	60508
								2 1843	MO		WILLIAM GALE DEATHERAGE	
SIMMONS, NANCY		NC	090	1874				1			MATTHEW NELSON	60508
SIMMONS, NOAH	1812	NC	090	1879	TX			1 1837	MO		LUCY PEMBERTON VIVION	60508
SIMMONS, PETER	1790	NC	092	1835	IN			1 1813	?TN		RACHEL MILLS	25112
SIMMONS, SAMUEL	1802	NC	046	1882	OR			1 1821	IN		MAHALA AMY BUNCH	60574

ANCESTOR INDEX	BIRTH	PL	CO	DEATH	PL	CO	LIVD	MARRIED	PL	CO	SPOUSE NAME	CODE
SIMMONS, WILLIAM	1814	NC	090	1880	MO			1 1841	MO		CALPURNIA ALEXANDER	60508
SIMMONS, ZADOCK	C1765				GA		047	1			MRS SARAH (CLAYBOURN) COTTON	20210
SIMPSON, JAMES	1768	PA		1854	TN		?014					60466
SIMPSON, JOHN WESLEY	1824	NC	046	1912	?IA			1 1842	IN		MARY O'BRIANT	25144
								2 1855	IA		MARY POLLY WILLIAMS	
								3 1886	IA		MRS MARTHA V WICKHAM HAGEN	
SIMPSON, MARY/POLLY	1796	?NC		1879	TN			1	TN		HARMON LITTLE	60466
SIMPSON, NATHANIEL M	1829	NC	046		IA			1			SARAH ANN	25144
SIMPSON, ROBERT DRURY	1828	NC	046	1921	IA			1 1855	IN		MALINDA GRAHAM	25144
SIMPSON, THOMAS	1796	NC	084	1873	MO			1 1817	TN		NANCY MORELAND	27555
SIMPSON, WILLIAM	C1800	NC	046	C1862	IN			1 1823	NC	046	NANCY PRICE	25144
SIMS ERVIN HENDRICKS	1811	SC		1867	NC	097		1			SUSANNAH RIGGENS	06100
SIMS, AUSTIN	C1765	NC						1			NANCY FARMER	60056
SIMS, JOHN	C1712	VA		1769	NC	044		1 C1735	VA		SARAH BULLOCK	23015
SIMS, LEONARD HENLEY	C1739	?VA		1804	NC	044		1 1770	VA		SARAH SWEPSON	23015
SIMS, MANN	1759	NC	056	1823	GA			1 1786	GA		MARGARET MAGRUDER	60342
SIMS, SHERWOOD				1790	NC	100						60594
SIMS, SUSANNA	1801	NC	044	1851	TN			1 1816	TN		DANIEL T BARNES	23015
SIMS, SWEPSON	1775	NC	044	1850	TN			1 1799	NC	044	JANE MERIWETHER LEWIS	23015
SIMS, UNITY	C1811						027	1			MOSES DUNCAN	24032
SIMS, WILLIAM	C1715	VA		1814	GA		056	1 1740	VA		SUSANNAH BULLOCK	60342
SIMS/SIMMS, ELIZABETH	C1764	NC	099	C1848	GA			1 1780	NC	099	WILLIAM SUGG	14020
SIMS/SIMMS, JOEL		?NC	056	1801	GA		?099	1	NC		CHRISTIAN	14020
SIMS/SIMMS, WILLIAMS		?VA		1779	NC	099						14020
SIMS/SYMS, CHARLIE THOMAS	1892	NC	093	1971	OH			1 1921	SC		JUANITA NORMAN	60582
SIMS/SYMS, THOMAS BASERY	1857	NC	?050	1922	NC	093		1 1880	NC	093	SARAH ADDELINE ALLISON	60582
SINGLETARY, JOHN	C1755	NC	011	C1828	NC	011		1	NC	011	DEBORAH	60579
SINGLETARY, JOHN DUNHAM	C1804	NC	011	C1885	NC	011		1 C1824	NC	011	SARAH	60579
SINGLETARY, JONATHAN		NC	011	1865	NC	011		1	NC	011	SARAH ANNE HARRISON ?	12090
SINGLETARY, JOSHUA	C1810	NC	011	1840	NC	011		1 C1830			ANNA JANE LENNON	12090
SINGLETON, JOHN	C1753	?VA		C1800	SC		?022	1 C1775	?NC		FRANCES/POLLY LANGSTON	27303
SISK, FLOYD MELTON	1875	NC	054	1948	NC	016		1 1907	NC	054	LILLIE MAGNOLIA DEARMAN	60065
SISK, JAMES WESLY	1852	NC	054	1913	NC	054		1 1874	NC	054	MARY ADALINE CAMPBELL	60065
SISK, RUBEN LEROY	1910	NC	054	1975	NC	085		1 1929	SC		MARY BRITE EDDINGS	60065
SISSOM, JAMES				1844	TN			1	?NC		ANNA BYFORD	21173
SIZEMORE, LYDIA	C1775	NC	?092		NC	006		1 C1794	NC	?104	JAMES BLEVINS	02295
SIZEMORE, NANCY ELIZABETH	1861	NC	106	1946	NC	106		1 1880	NC	106	JOHN HENRY MACKIE	60569
SIZEMORE, NED		NC			NC	006	104					02295

ANCESTOR INDEX	BIRTH	PL	CO	DEATH	PL	CO	LIVD	MARRIED	PL	CO	SPOUSE NAME	CODE
SIZEMORE, WELLS	1795	NC	104		NC	006		1 C1820	NC	006	ELIZABETH PENNINGTON	02295
SKINNER, BENJAMIN JESSE	C1807	NC	045					1			CAROLINE STEVENS	17140
SKINNER, NATHANIEL	C1762			1837			059	1 1810			CHARLOTTE COLLINS	17140
SKINNER, WILLIAM HERRING JR	1861	NC	045	1933	NC	079		1 1887			LAURA ELIZABETH MOORE	17140
								2			LANIE ROUSE	
SKINNER, WILLIAM HERRING SR	1836	NC	045	1915	NC	079		1			ELVIRA WILSON	17140
SLAGLE, CHARLES		NC	107					1			POLLY RANDOLPH	60439
SLAGLE, FRANKLIN PIERCE	C1851	NC	?107	1911	NC	066		1			NAOMA YOUNG	60439
SLAGLE, TEXAS	1891	NC	066					1			DAVID SMITH GRAYBEAL	60439
SLEDGE, ALFRED A	1812	NC	100	1904			039	1 1845	NC	100	MARY BURGESS	04065
SLEDGE, JAMES	1752	VA		C1827	NC	100		1 1777	NC	015	REBECCA PERSON	04065
SLEDGE, STERLING	1805	NC		1868	AL			1 1829	TN		ELIZABETH SKILLINGTON	60516
SLEDGE, TURNER	C1778	NC	015	1819	NC	100		1 1809	NC	100	TOBITHA DAVIS	04065
SLOAN, ARCHIBALD							101					25204
SLOAN, JEANNE/JANE	1768						101	1 1797			ANDREW JACKSON	25204
SLOCUM, JOSIAS	C1720	NC	028	C1781	NC	024		1	NC		ELIZABETH HULLBROOKE	60074
SLUDER, FIDILEO	C1822	NC						1	NC		DILLIAD/GILLIAD RESTER ?	17100
											FRISBY	
SLUDER, JOHN SR	C1792	NC						1			POLLY/MARGARET	17100
SLUDER, JULIA C	C1850	NC	013					1 C1872	NC	013	DAVID R ISRAEL	17100
SMAW, HENRY				C1782	NC	009		1 C1730	VA		MARY RESPASS	19130
SMITH, ADAM	C1774				NC	090		1			EUNICE STARBUCK	06195
SMITH, ALFRED POOL	C1809	NC	056	C1860	TX		099	1 1829	NC	099	TELITHA WEATHERS	20210
SMITH, BENJAMIN	1819	NC	103		NC	?103		1 1853	NC		MARY OLIVER	03125
SMITH, BENJAMIN	C1768	NC	085	C1835	TN		032	2 1802	NC	085	ELIZABETH SIBELLA	20229
SMITH, BENJAMIN	C1800	NC										60468
SMITH, BURGESS	1808	NC	013	1856	GA			1 1828	GA		HARRIET WILLS JORDAN	60405
SMITH, BURNS B	C1827				NC	072		1 C1852	NC	019	MARY MIDYETT ?	01012
SMITH, CATHERINE	1808	NC	046		OH			1 1831	OH		SAMUEL FRENCH	27392
SMITH, CHARLES	1810	?NC			MO			1 C1830			NANCY GOLDEN	08150
SMITH, CHARLES LEONARD	1862	NC	073	1929	NC	073		1	NC	073	ELLEN FRANCES GORDON	60521
SMITH, CHARLES RICE	1801	VA		1874	AR		084	1 1822	VA		ELIZABETH LAW	60519
SMITH, CODDINGTON							005	1 C1800	?NC		SARAH JERNIGAN	60126
SMITH, DANIEL	1785	NC	046	1887	IL			1 C1805	NC	046	DORCAS MCDANIEL	27392
SMITH, DANIEL	1788	NC		1874	IN			1			NANCY SPAIN	60036
SMITH, DANIEL	1811	NC		1891	MO			1	?KY		MARY LILLY	60563
SMITH, DUNCAN	1788	NC	?082	1865	SC			1			ISABEL STEWART	12019
SMITH, EDWARD	C1740	VA		1792	VA		084	1 C1765	VA		SARAH RICE	60519

ANCESTOR INDEX	BIRTH	PL	CO	DEATH	PL	CO	LIVD	MARRIED	PL	CO	SPOUSE NAME	CODE
SMITH, ELIZABETH	1766	VA		1814	NC	084		1 1782	VA		REUBEN SMITH	60519
SMITH, FREDRICK	C1768	NC	073	C1863	NC	081		1			ELIZABETH LINEBERRY	60499
SMITH, GEORGE	1813	NC	046					1 1836	OH		MARTHA WRIGHT	27392
SMITH, GEORGE	C1785	NC	?067		TN			1 C1810	NC	?067	LUCY TAYLOR	60337
SMITH, GRADEN WILLIAM	1903	NC	081	1973	CA			1 2			LILLIAN CLOE	60499
SMITH, HENRY	C1745	PA		1811	NC	090	092	1 1767	NC	085	BARBARA HISON	60120
SMITH, HOLLOWAY	1805							1 1831	NC	096	TABITHA SAWYER	20335
SMITH, ISAAC		?VA		C1829	NC	103		1 2 1786			SARAH ONEILL ? PHEREBY	03125
SMITH, JACOB	1807	NC	013	1883	NC	055		1 1828	NC	049	REBECCA JUSTICE	20220
SMITH, JACOB	C1770	NC	092	1828	NC	092		1 C1796	NC	092	ELIZABETH HUTCHENS ?	60120
SMITH, JACOB L ?	C1804	NC			IL			1			LEVINIA SEWELL	60080
SMITH, JAMES	1770	NC	085	1838	NC	032		1 1792 2 1802	NC NC	085 085	ELLIS COLE EVE FEESOR	20229
SMITH, JAMES CICERO	C1833	NC	067					2	NC		MRS MELISSA ELIZABETH (SMITH) WHITE	60468
SMITH, JAMES, MAJ	C1735	NJ		1781	SC		085	2	NC	085	CLARA	20229
SMITH, JESSE	1751	NC		1826	SC			1 C1779			MARY BELLAMY	24285
SMITH, JOHN	1785	NC	070	1859	NC	070	027	1 1812	NC	070	THERESA/TREASY CROOM	12210
SMITH, JOHN				C1832			056	1				20210
SMITH, JOHN	C1787	NC	085	1831	NC	032		1	NC		MARTHA DOBSON	20229
SMITH, JOHN	1810	NC	046	1902	IA			1 1832	OH		CHARITY GILBERT	27392
SMITH, JOHN BUNYON	C1829	NC	?069		NC	?069		1	NC	?069	SARAH A	03315
SMITH, JOHN FARMER		NC	073					1 1821	NC	073	ELIZABETH GRIFFIN	60521
SMITH, JOHN LEWIS	1808	NC		1856				1			CYNTHIA BARR	60368
SMITH, JOHN MILTON	1826	NC	073	1920	NC	073		1 1850	NC	073	BETTIE ELIZABETH CURREY	60521
SMITH, JORDAN	1792	NC		1859	AL			1			JANE	60185
SMITH, JOSEPH		?VA		1785	NC	103		1			ANN	03125
SMITH, JOSEPH		?NC										08165
SMITH, JOSEPH	1730	MD		1814	NC	013		1 1764	?MD		REBECCA DATH	60110
SMITH, JOSEPH ARCHIE	1888	NC	072	1944	NC	070		1 1910	NC	028	CLEMENTINE/CLEMMIE WETHERINGTON	01012
SMITH, LARKIN	1808	NC	013	1897	GA			1 C1834	NC	061	LOUISA LONG	60110
SMITH, LEWIS	1763	PA			NC	049		1 1791	NC	086	MARY/POLLY WIKLE	20220
SMITH, MACK MCKINNIE	1853	NC	056	1893	NC	056		1 1884	NC	056	MARY THEODOSIA EDWARDS	03125
SMITH, MARGARET	1797	NC	086	1852				1 1820			JOHN MCKEE FAUCETT	08226
SMITH, MARTHA	1825	NC	065	C1865	TN			1 C1846	TN		MR PRESSLEY	60431
SMITH, MARTHA ANN	1860	NC		1900	SC			1	NC	082	NATHANIEL JAMES RUSS	60389
SMITH, MARY	1807	NC	046		OH			1 1831	OH		MICHAEL CHANEY	27392

ANCESTOR INDEX	BIRTH	PL	CO	DEATH	PL	CO	LIVD	MARRIED	PL	CO	SPOUSE NAME	CODE
SMITH, MARY CAROLINE		NC						1 1837	MS		JOHN WILLIAM GOING	08165
SMITH, MARY JANE	1802	NC		1875	NC	046		1			JAMES W HUGHES	11100
SMITH, MARY JANE/POLLY	C1800	NC	?005	1837	AL			1 1817	AL		JAMES MADISON BREWSTER	60126
SMITH, MELISSA ELIZABETH		NC						1			MR WHITE	60468
								2		NC	JAMES CICERO SMITH	
SMITH, MICAHEL	C1740	SCO		?VA			084	1			JUDITH RICE	60519
SMITH, MICAJAH KEGG/CAGE	C1750			1803	NC	086		1			ELIZABETH AGEE	08226
SMITH, NANCY					NC	086		1		NC	ABRAM WHITAKER	05070
SMITH, REUBEN	1761	VA		1831	VA		084	1 1782	VA		ELIZABETH SMITH	60519
SMITH, REUBEN	1749	PA		1835	NC	073						60521
SMITH, SALLIE		NC	020	1818	GA			1 1799	NC	020	WILLIAM CARMICHAEL SR	03065
SMITH, SAMUEL	1765	VA		1856	TX		013	1 1775	NC	013	MARY JARRETT	60110
SMITH, SARAH	1812	NC	092	1881	NC	106		1 1833	NC	092	THOMAS EVANS	60120
SMITH, STARK BLOUNT JR	1856	NC	010	1920	CA			1 1887	CA		MARTHA ADELEINE GRUPE	60069
SMITH, STARK BLOUNT, DR	1815	NC	010	1867	NC	010		1 1851	NC	010	JOANNA MAGDALENA DRIGGS	60069
SMITH, SUSAN	1811	NC	046		OH			1 1833	OH		WILLIAM HART	27392
SMITH, THOMAS							020					03065
SMITH, THOMAS	C1765	VA		C1825	GA		013	1			SALLIE	60405
SMITH, WILLIAM	C1806	NC						1 C1829	NC	013	ELIZABETH WHITAMORE	01054
								2 1875	KY		MARTHA SCOTT	
SMITH, WILLIAM					NC							05070
SMITH, WILLIAM					NC	?073		1			FIELDS	60499
SMITH, WILLIAM							073					60521
SMITH, WILLIAM BURNS	1856	NC	072	1916	NC	072		1 1877	NC	072	SALLIE ODUM/ODHAM	01012
SMITH, WILLIAM JR	1796	NC	084	1853	TN			1 1817	NC	084	NANCY HARRIS	60427
SMITH, WILLIAM LEONARD	1885	NC	073	1968	NC	073		1 1908			OLIVE PHELINA MILLER	60521
SMITH, WILLIAM O	1800	NC	065	C1855	TN			1 1822	NC	065	JANE MILLER	60431
								2 C1840	TN		LUCINDA	
SMITHWICK, EDMOND				C1774	NC	063						60594
SMYLIE/SMILEY, JAMES		SCO			NC	082	005	1			JANE WATSON	27697
SMYLIE/SMILEY, JAMES, REV	1780	NC	082	1853	MS		005	1			MARY COTTEN SMITH	27697
								2			SARAH ANN BISLAND	
								3			ANN HARRIET BATCHELOR	
SMYLIE/SMILEY, JANE		NC	082				005	1			JOHN WATSON	27697
SMYLIE/SMILEY, JEANNET	1773	NC		1847	MS		005					27697
SMYLIE/SMILEY, JOHN		NC	082				005	1			SUSAN SELLERS	27697
SMYLIE/SMILEY, MARY		NC	082				005	1			MATTHEW BOLLS	27697
SMYLIE/SMILEY, MATTHEW		NC	082				005	1 1807			REBECCA BROWN	27697
SMYLIE/SMILEY, NATHANIEL		NC	082	1839	MS		005	1			MARGARET SMITH	27697
SNIPES, THOMAS	C1780	NC	044	C1870	NC	064	?073	1 1806	NC	078	ELIZABETH HANKS	25087

ANCESTOR INDEX	BIRTH	PL	CO	DEATH	PL	CO	LIVD	MARRIED	PL	CO	SPOUSE NAME	CODE
SNOAD/SNODE, JOHN, COL				1743	NC	009		1 C1715	NC	009	ANN MARTIN	19130
SNODDY, AGNES/NANCY	1763	NC	085	1855	IN		054					20450
SNODDY, ELEANOR	1751			?MO			085	1 1772	NC	085	JAMES MORRISON	20450
SNODDY, ELIZABETH	1755			OH			085	1	?NC		MOSES MITCHEL	20450
SNODDY, FERGUS	1759	NC	?085	1785	SC		085					20450
SNODDY, JOHN	1758	NC	?085	1843	IN		054	1 C1778	NC		AGNES NIBLOCK	20450
								2 1796	KY		AGNES NEEL	
								3			MARY ANN	
SNODDY, MARGARET	1756			IN			085	1 1775	NC	085	JOSEPH MCCORKLE	20450
SNODDY, MARTHA SLOAN	1766	NC	085	1830	OH		054	1 1791	NC	?054	JOHN PURVIANCE	20450
SNODDY, MARY	1761	NC	?085	IN			054	1 1779	NC	085	SAMUEL MARTIN	20450
SNODDY, SAMUEL	1768	NC	085	?AR				1 1796	NC	085	MARY PURVIANCE	20450
SNODDY, SAMUEL	1727			1806	NC	054	085	1 C1748			ELIZABETH SLOAN	20450
SNODDY, SARAH	1753			?NC			085	1 1775	NC	085	ANDREW MITCHELL	20450
SNODDY, THOMAS	1772	NC	085	?AR				1 C1795	NC		SARAH PERKINS	20450
SNODDY, WILLIAM	1749			C1815	TN		085	1 1782	NC	085	MARGARET MCNEELY	20450
								2 1801	TN		ELIZABETH ORR	
SNYDER, FREDERICK	C1775	NC		1850	MO			1 C1796			ELIZABETH VANTRIESE	60027
SOLES, ISAIAH	C1805	NC	027		NC	027		1			TABITHA	24032
SOLES, JOSHUA	1832	NC	027	1898	NC	027		1 C1855				24032
								2 1859	NC	?027	ELENDER/ELEANOR BUFFKIN	
SOLES, LUPHENIA	1868	NC	027	1918	NC	027		1 1896	NC	027	MACK DANIEL/MCD FOWLER	24032
SOMMERVILLE/SUMMERVILLE, MARGARET		IRE			NC	085		1	?IR		JAMES SOMMERVILLE	04195
								2	PA		GEORGE DAVIDSON	
SOMMERVILLE/SUMMERVILLE, RHODA	1732	IRE		1831	TN		013	1 C1760	PA		HUMPHREY CUNNINGHAM	04195
SOUTHARD, MARY/POLLY	C1802	NC	078		NC	078		1 1823	NC	078	JABEZ BARRETT	60543
SOUTHARD, ROBERT/BOB								1 1801	NC	078	SARAH/SALLIE MILAM	60543
SOUTHERLAND, DANIEL	1749	NC	?070	1831	NC	035		1	NC	035	NEWKIRK	04135
SOUTHERLAND, PHILIP/PHIL		NC	035	C1837	NC	035		1	NC	035	RACHEL MALLARD	04135
SOUTHERLAND, ROBERT, II	1722	VA		1789	NC	035		1 1745	VA		JOYCE WOODSTOCK	04135
SOUTHERLAND, ROBERT, III	1747	VA		1835	NC	035		1 1777	NC	035	PATIENCE TOUILLE (TWILLEY)	04135
SOUTHERLAND, THOMAS	C1815	NC	?035		AL			1 C1846	?GA		MARGARET ANN	60074
SOUTHERLAND, WILLIAM BURTON	1797	NC	035	C1883	NC	035		1 C1816	NC	035	RHODA/RODA SOUTHERLAND	04135
SOUTHERN, JUDITH	1774	VA		1840	IN		092	1 1802	NC	090	JOHN L BURCH	60421
SOUTHERN, WILLIAM				1794	NC	090	092	1			MAGDALEN	60421
SOWELL, GEORGE					NC	051		1 C1801	?NC	?051	KESIA	19130
SOWELL, RACHEL	C1792			C1839	NC	051		1 1816	NC	051	JOHN BAKER	19130
SOWELL/SEWELL, ANN		NC		1840	NC	068		1 C1783			WILLIAM BARRETT	27758
SOWELL/SEWELL, ARCHIBALD MCKENZIE	1818	NC	068	1906	TX			1			MARY JANE MOORE	60229

ANCESTOR INDEX	BIRTH	PL	CO	DEATH	PL	CO	LIVD	MARRIED	PL	CO	SPOUSE NAME	CODE
SOWELL/SEWELL, ASA	1772	NC	029	1840	NC	068		1			KATHRYN MCKENZIE	60229
SOWELL/SEWELL, ISAAC		NC			NC	068		1			MARY QUIMBY	27758
SOWELL/SEWELL, ISAAC	1743	MA		C1785	NC			1			MARY QUINBY	60229
SPARKMAN, WILLIAM	1764	NC	009	1832	TN		051	1 1789	NC	051	ROSANNA WILLIAMS	60251
SPEIGHT, FRANCIS JR		VA		C1749	NC	024		1			KATHERN	19130
SPEIGHT, JONATHAN	C1784	NC			GA			1 C1804	NC		SARAH BARNES	01007
SPEIGHT, WILLIAM FRANCIS	1813	NC	045	1871	GA			1	GA		SALLIE/SARAH ANN MARIE YOUNG	01007
SPENCER, BENJAMIN		?PA			NC	?081		1	NC	?081	MARGARET/PEGGY COX	08095
SPENCER, BENJAMIN	1802	NC	081	1885	IN			1 1830	NC	081	HANNAH STALKER	08095
SPENCER, CALEB	1801	NC	014		GA			1 C1826	NC	?060	ELIZA M ASH	60524
SPENCER, CHRISTOPHER				C1795	NC	?053		1			JULIA MILLER	20335
SPENCER, ELIJAH	C1774	?NC	?067	1843	NC	?067		1			SARAH	06159
SPENCER, ISAAC	1772	NC	?081	1846	NC	081		1			MARY ELIZABETH HASKETT	08095
								2 1805	NC	081	MARY FARLOW	
SPENCER, ISRAEL	1816	NC	060	1880	MO			1 1838	MO		ELIZABETH/BESS	11010
								2 1847	MO		ELIZABETH MIRAM SPENCER	
SPENCER, MARGARET	1792	NC	081					1 ?1814			NATHAN FARLOW ?	08095
SPENCER, MIDGETT	1811			1855	NC	096		1 1833	NC	096	PRISCILLA CAHOON	20335
								2 1834	NC	096	LEVINA ANN MEEKINS	
SPENCER, NATHAN	1799	NC	053		NC	053	019	1			DORCAS WILLIAMS	20335
SPENCER, NATHAN				1815	NC	096	053	1 1790			MARY ARMSTRONG	20335
SPENCER, PELEAGE	1764	NC	053	1810	NC	053		1			MAHALIA GIBBS	20335
SPENCER, REBECCA	1797	NC	081					1			NATHAN DAVIS ?	08095
SPENCER, RICHARD				1799	NC	053		1 1778			MAMY JONES	20335
SPENCER, SALINA	C1824	NC	?067	C1885	TX			1 1841	NC	081	SPENCER CLAYBORN CALLICOATTE	06159
SPENCER, SIEBERT		NC	060	1823	MO			1			ANNA MARIE DIETZ	11010
SPENCER, THOMAS		NC	014	1849	MO			1 1812	NC	060	BETSY SENTER	11010
SPENCER, THOMAS				C1725	NC	030		1			SARAH	20335
SPENCER, WILLIAM	C1798	NC		1843	MO			1 C1818	NC		NANCY	60135
SPENGEL/SPENGLE, CATERINA/ CATHERINE	C1722				NC	081		1 1743	PA		DAVID/DEWALD FOUTS/PFAUTZ	23065
SPIVEY, AMOS M	1830	?NC	027	1905	AL			1 1848	?AL		PRISCILLA BLACKMON	60183
SPIVEY, CURTIS	C1794	?NC			AL		027	1			LUCY	60183
								2 C1854	?AL		CATHERINE MCLENDON	
SPIVEY, WILLIAM	C1765	?NC		C1845	AL		027					60183
SPLAWN, A GRAY	1834	NC	086	1907	NC	080		1 1860	NC	080	MARY ELIZABETH PONDER	60198
SPLAWN, WILLIAM S	1800	?NC		1884	NC	080		1			POLLY CAPSHAW	60198
								2 1850	NC	086	JANE WALDROP	
SPRINGER, GEORGE					NC	?089		1			SALLY BLOOM	24165
SPRINGFIELD, THOMAS		?VA		C1768	NC	044						14020

ANCESTOR INDEX	BIRTH	PL	CO	DEATH	PL	CO	LIVD	MARRIED	PL	CO	SPOUSE NAME	CODE
SPRUIELL/SPRUILL, BENJAMIN G	1824	NC	096					1			MARY C	25251
SPRUIELL/SPRUILL, JAMES A	C1800	NC	096	1895	TX			1 1823	NC	096	DIRECTOR LIVERMAN	25251
SPRUIELL/SPRUILL, ZEBULON A	1825	NC	096					1 1853	TX		MARGARET HARPER	25251
								2 1864	TX		MARY JANE RICE WEST	
SPRUILL, DEMPSEY	1779	NC	096	1842	NC	101		1 1799	NC	096	MARY DAVENPORT	02195
SPRUILL, HENRETTA	1807	NC	101	1875	NC	101		1 C1825	NC	101	JOHN DUNSTON	02195
								2	NC	101	JEREMIAH SWAIN	
SPRUILL, HEZEKIAH	1732			1804	NC	096		1			RHODA BAUM	20335
SQUIRES, JAMES JONES	1847	NC	073	1916	NC	073		1 1867	NC	073	SUSAN FRANCES PAUL	02256
SQUIRES, JAMES WILLIAM	1875	NC	073	1948	NC	073		1 1900	NC	073	LUCY JOBE	02256
SQUIRES, THOMAS	C1769			1865	NC	073		1 1802	NC	073	ELIZABETH GILL	02256
SQUIRES, THOMAS, II	1818	NC	073	1887	NC	073		1 1839	NC	073	SUSAN JONES	02256
STACEY, THOMAS	C1804	NC		C1866	TN			1 C1840	?TN		MARY A	07087
								2 1865			CANDACE SIMPSON	
STADLER, JOHN I	1792	NC	044	1860	NC	020		1 1812	NC	020	NANCY ARNOLD	60543
STADLER, ROBERT	C1760			C1791			044	1 C1780			MARY	60543
STADLER, ROBERT DICKY	1816	NC	020	1884	NC	020		1 1838	NC	020	LYDIA FRANCES ARNOLD	60543
								2 1862	NC	020	NANCY M BROWNING	
								3 1871	NC	020	MARY REID	
STADLER, SARAH DELILAH	1874	NC	020	1948	NC	020		1 1897	NC	020	WILLIAM DAVID BLALOCK	60543
STAFFORD, MARY	1717	NC	?028	1823	SC		079	1	NC		JOHN MAY	13264
STAFFORD, WILLIAM	C1662	VA		C1728	NC	030		1 C1683	VA		JANE BROWN	13264
STAFFORD, WILLIAM	C1689	VA		1765	NC	070	030	1 C1715	NC		ELIZABETH	13264
STALEY, SARAH	C1822	NC	046					1			JOHN MILLER	60480
STALLINGS JOB	C1750	NC	077		NC	037		1			MARY ALSTON	27322
STALLINGS MALACHI HUDSON	1803	NC	037	1881	LA			1 1850	LA		MATILDA ETTREDGE	27322
STALLINGS, LOCKHART	C1779	NC	?039					1 1828			JEMIMA PHILLIPS	60502
STAMEY, DANIEL	C1818	NC	?104					1 1839	NC	014	CATHERINE TAYLOR	25098
STAMEY, E C	1843	NC			GA			1			ELIZABETH	60163
STAMPER, SUSANNAH	1767	NC	085	1845	IN		006	1 1779	NC	104	JOHN PLEASANT BUNTON	60348
STANCIL, GODFREY				C1790	NC	?079		1			SARAH NOBLE/NOBLES	10010
STANCIL, NOBLE/NOBLES	C1771	?NC		C1845	NC	?079		1			NANCY HIGHSMITH	10010
STANDLEY, JAMES	1792	NC	104	C1874	MO		104	1 1818	NC	104	JANE TROTTER	25135
								2 1823	MO		MARY/POLLY TROTTER	
STANDLEY, JOHN	C1764	VA		C1850	MO		104	1	NC	104	REBECCA	25135
STANDRIDGE, JAMES	C1755	MD		1837	SC			1	NC		MARY WALLACE	60149
STANFIELD, VINCENT	1787	NC	092	C1849	AL			1			ANNA GOCHER/GOTCHER	60007
STANFIELD/STANDFIELD, EMILY ELIZABETH	1844	NC	078	1886	NC	061		1 1868	NC	061	JOAB CRISP	17135
STANFIELD/STANDFIELD, JOHN W	1789				NC	078		1 1810	NC	078	JANEY GREEN	17135
STANFIELD/STANDFIELD, WASHINGTON GREEN	1811	NC	078		NC	061		1 1838	NC		ARTMESIA LIPSCOMB	17135

184

ANCESTOR INDEX	BIRTH	PL	CO	DEATH	PL	CO	LIVD	MARRIED	PL	CO	SPOUSE NAME	CODE
STANLEY, ELIZABETH	1805			1873	NC	012		1 1829			LEWIS W WESCOTT	05070
STANLEY, ELIZABETH	1758			1832	NC	090		1			JOHN MASTEN	13120
STANLEY, JESSE	1769	NC						1 1787	NC		MARY STANLEY	25185
STANLEY, LANIE	1856	NC	073	1916	NC	073		1			JOHN CRABTREE	60131
STANLEY, VIRGINIA T	1858	NC	073	1931	NC	073		1			CHARLES F CRABTREE	60131
STANLEY, WILLIAM	1829	NC	?073	1903	NC	073		1			CAROLINE GOOCH	60131
STANLEY/STANALAND/STANLAND, PATRICK				C1775	NC	012		1			SUSANNAH	13052
STANLEY/STANALAND/STANLAND, SAMUEL A	C1757			1803	NC	012		1 C1783			RUTH HEWETT	13052
STANLEY/STANALAND/STANLAND, SAMUEL JR	C1795	NC	012					1 1806	NC	012	MARGARET BELL	13052
STANLEY/STANALAND/STANLAND, SAMUEL,III	C1817	NC	012	C1880				1 C1838			FRANCES ALICE	13052
STANSBURY, JOHN H	C1790	NC	104	C1848	NC	006		1 C1811	NC	104	ANN EARNEST	02295
STANSBURY, MARY M	1814	NC	006	C1904	VA		006	1 C1837	NC	006	DAVID COOK	02295
STANSBURY, MOSES	C1760	?MD		C1835	NC	?104	006	1 C1785	NC	104	SARAH	02295
STANSBURY, REBECCA	C1794	NC		C1874	KY			1 C1812			WILLIAM NIX	60146
STANSBURY, SAMUEL, II	C1727	MD		C1778	NC	020		1 1751	MD		MARY HARROD	60146
STANSBURY, SOLOMON	1755	MD		1842	KY		060	1 1791	NC	065	JANE/JAIN LEWING	60146
STANTON, SAMUEL	1737	?RI					046	1 1766	RI		SARAH STRETTON	60314
								2 1772			MARY MARSHALL	
STANTON, WILLIAM	1812	NC	?046	1896	IN			1 1835	NC	081	SARAH FARLOW	60314
								2 1844	NC	046	RACHEL LEONARD	
STARBUCK, REUBEN	1787	NC	046	1880	NC	046		1 1811	NC		MARY/POLLY BEESON	60140
STARBUCK, WILLIAM	1748	MA		1837	NC	046		1 1776	NC	046	JEAN/JANE TAYLOR	60574
STARNES/STARIN/STAHRIN, GRACE CAROLINE	1844	NC	013	1914	NC	013		1 C1868	NC	013	SIMS OWNBEY	20380
STARNES/STARIN/STAHRIN, JOHN				1781	NC	065						20380
STARNES/STARIN/STAHRIN, JOHN	1779			1855	NC	013	014	1 1802	NC	016	MARY ETTA HICE	20380
STARNES/STARIN/STAHRIN, THOMAS ALBERT	1818	NC	013	1897	NC	013		1 1842	NC	013	ELIZABETH MORGAN	20380
STARR, ADAM	1783	NC	046	1859	WI			1			MARY KICK	25126
STARR, JACOB	C1728	GER					046					25126
STARR, JACOB	C1752	?NC						1 1776	NC	046	ANNA MARIE WEITZEL	25126
STARR, JOHN	C1754	?NC			NC	?046		1 1776	NC	046	CATHERINE WEITZEL	25126
STARR, JOHN ADAM	C1750	?NC		C1819	NC	046		1 1773	NC	046	ANNA MARGARET WEITZEL	25126
STARR/STAR, FRANCES	C1809	NC			IN			1 1830	NC	085	IRA ELLIS	60381
STARR/STOEHR, JASPER				C1814	NC	085		1			CATHERINE	02170
STARR/STOEHR, JASPER	1772	?PA		1850	IL			1 1796	NC	092	ELLA ELSA WATKINS	02170

ANCESTOR INDEX	BIRTH	PL	CO	DEATH	PL	CO	LIVD	MARRIED	PL	CO	SPOUSE NAME	CODE
STARR/STOEHR, JOHN	1797	NC	085	1872	TX			1 1825	IL		SUSANNAH PARKER	02170
STATON/STAYTON, MOSES ALEXANDER	1799	NC		1836	MO			1			CATHERINE SMITH	60574
STATON/STAYTON, THOMAS	C1770	NC		1843	MO			1 C1788	NC		CATHERINE ALEXANDER	60574
STEELE, ANDREW	C1804	NC	?054	C1880	?AR			1 C1825	NC	?054	ELIZABETH WATTS	60485
STEELE, JACOB	C1820	NC	022	C1873	NC	022		1 1837	NC	081	EUNICE ALLDRIDGE	08355
STEELE, THOMAS	C1793	NC	022	C1855	NC	081						08355
STEELE, THOMAS	1757	PA		1838	NC	022		1	?PA		NANCY ANN PYLE	27417
STEELMAN, CHARLES	1786	NC	092	1855	NC	092		1 1807	NC	092	NANCY HOPPERS	20380
STEELMAN, GEORGE	C1753	DE		1800	NC	092		1 C1780			ELIZABETH	20380
STEELMAN, GEORGE	1812	NC	092	1893	NC	106		1 C1836	NC	092	NANCY CAROLINA WILLIAMS	20380
STEELMAN, MATTHIAS	C1723	DE		1793	NC	092		1 C1748			RUTH	20380
STEELMAN, SANFORD LEE	1838	NC	092	1895	NC	054		1 1860	NC	106	RUTH JANE WILLIAMS	20380
								2 1893	NC	054	MRS SUSAN (MACY) VESTAL	
STEELMAN/STEALMAN, CHARLES	C1760	DE		1845	NC	092	104	1 C1782	NC	092	MRS JANE (CRESON) CUNNINGHAM	08130
								2 1837	NC	092	MRS ELIZABETH DOUGLASS ?	
STEELMAN/STEALMAN, MARY/POLLY	1806	NC	092	1865	NC	006		1 1825	NC	092	THOMAS ATWOOD	08130
STEELMAN/STEALMAN, MATTHIAS	C1723	?DE		1793	NC	092		1 C1748	?DE		RUTH	08130
STEGALL, ELIZABETH/BETSY ANN	1834	NC	005	C1875	AR			1 1852	NC	097	WILLIAM ALVERSON HELMS	60532
STEGALL, MOSES	1735	WA		1835	NC	005						60532
STEGALL, MOSES	1810	NC	005		NC			1			FRANCES GRIFFIN	60532
STEGALL, THOMAS	1780	NC	005	1845	NC	005						60532
STEPHENS/STEVENS, HENRY				1814	NC	073		1 1787			JANE	13020
STEPHENS/STEVENS, MILLIE	1792	NC	073	1857	NC	?001		1 1812	NC	073	JAMES THOMAS	13020
STEPHENSON, DAVID	1749	NC	?011	1808	NC	099	029	1 C1775	NC	?029	CHARITY	60337
STEPP, REUBEN/RHEUBEN	C1805	NC			IN			1 C1826			SABRA WHITEHEAD	08073
STEPP/STAPP, JESSE M	C1811	NC					013	1			ADELINE A	60241
STEPP/STAPP, VESTER MITCHEL	1860	NC	013	1904	LA		061	1 1881	MS		MALINDA ABIGAIL CARNES	60241
								2			MITTIE	
STERRAT/STERRATT/STARRATT, BENJAMIN				C1778	NC	046						25195
STERRAT/STERRATT/STARRATT, JAMES		MD		C1804	NC	046		1 C1750			MARY/AGNES	25195
STEVENS, EDWARD	C1760	NC	056					1			UNA ANN	60513
STEWART, EDWARD	1767	NC	073				068	1 1787	NC	022	MARY MCPHERSON	25213
STEWART, GEORGE	1789	NC	022	1874	NC	068		1 1809	NC	068	CLARISSA DICKERSON	25213
STEWART, GEROGE	1814	NC	054	1887	TN			1 1836	TN		HARRIETT WOODARD	60112
STEWART, HAMBLEN/HAMILTON	1760	NC	092	1832	TN			1 C1780	NC	092		02414
STEWART, ISABEL	1795	NC	?082		SC			1			DUNCAN SMITH	12019
STEWART, JAMES	C1765			1812	NC	054		1 C1780				60112
STEWART, SAMUEL							073	1			JANE DICKEY	25213

ANCESTOR INDEX	BIRTH	PL	CO	DEATH	PL	CO	LIVD	MARRIED	PL	CO	SPOUSE NAME	CODE
STEWART, SPENCER	C1805	NC	?067	C1848	?TN			1 C1825	NC	?067	ELIZABETH HURLEY	60379
STEWART, THOMAS	C1780	NC	054	C1825	VA			1 C1800	NC	054	SARAH	60112
STEWART/STUART, CHARLES	C1740			1782	NC	022		1			ELIZABETH	08200
STEWART/STUART, HAPPY	C1764	NC	073	1824	NC	022		1	NC	022	JOSEPH FOUSHEE	08200
STEWART/STUART, JAMES				1773	NC	022		1			ANNE	08200
STICE, ANDREW JR	1766	NC	085	1818	IL			1 1789	NC	085	NANCY GREEN WILSON	27631
STICE, ANDREW SR		GER			NC	085		1	GER		KATRON COLLINS	27631
STICE, DAVID		NC	085					1	KY		SALLY MCCRACKER	27631
STICE, ESTHER	1779	NC	085	1855	IA			1 1804	KY		JAMES SIMMONS	27631
STICE, KATRON		NC	085		KY			1	NC	085	WILLIAM COLLINS	27631
STICE, PETER		PA						1	NC	085		27631
STILES, PHATHA/FAITHA	1788	NC	?013	1870	TN			1			JESSEE SAFLEY	60029
STILES, WILLIAM	C1760	NC			?TN		?013	1 C1783	NC		SUSAN REBECCA EDWARDS	60029
STILL, BOAZ/BOOZE	C1765	?VA		C1740	TN		086	1 C1788	NC	086	MARY LYDA	25149
STILLEY, JOHN	C1714	MD		C1796	NC	028	009	1 C1739	MD		GRACE FOUNTAIN	20415
STILLEY, JOHN	C1717	MD			?NC	?028	028	1 C1735	MD		GRACE FOUNTAIN	60589
STILLEY, STEPHEN	C1765	MD		1841	IL		009	1 1791	NC	028	ELIZABETH WHITFORD	20415
STILLEY, STEPHEN	C1765	MD					028	1 1791	NC	028	ELIZABETH WHITFORD	60589
STINSON, ALEXANDER	1776	NC	065	1853	IA			1 1800	NC	065	ELIZABETH BRADLEY	20095
STINSON, FREDERICK	C1800	NC		1847	IN			1 1827	IN		LYDIA EASTRIDGE	60333
								2 1839	IN		SARAH ANN WILSON	
STINSON, JOHN ANDREW					NC	065		1			MILLER	20095
STINSON, JOSHUA	C1760			1838	IN			1 1798	NC	085	ELIZABETH EASTBORNE	60333
STIREWALT, JACOB	1804	NC		1856	IL			1 1825	IN		JANE FLETCHER	60047
STOCKARD, JAMES ANDREW	1745	SCO		1818	TN		073	1			ELLEN TROUSDALE	27441
STOCKARD, JOHN RICHARD	1781	NC	073	1861	NC	001		1 1802			JANE STEWART	27441
								2 1810	NC	073	CATHERINE ALBRIGHT	
STOKES, ELENDER JANE	1795	NC			GA			1 1816	NC	035	HENRY HOUSTON	02145
STOKES, RICHARD C	1819	NC		1849	GA			1 1841	GA		NANCY ALTMAN	20425
STONE, JOSEPH		NC						1			ELIZABETH TEAGUE	11070
STONE, THOMAS	C1809	NC	084					1			AMANDA	11070
STORY, ROBERT				1789	GA			1	?NC		REBECCA	25145
								2			PRUDENCE	
STOUT, CHARLES	1742	PA		1822	NC	022		1 1767	NC	073	MARY NOBLETT	20435
STOUT, CHARLES	1742	PA		1822	NC	073		1 1767	NC	073	MARY NOBLITT	60558
STOUT, HANNAH	1788	NC	073	1844				1 1807	NC		SIMON MOON	60593
STOUT, MARY	1775	NC	073	1856	NC	073		1 1812	NC	022	JOHN STUART	60558
STOUT, PETER	1717	DE		1802	NC	022		1 1739	PA		MARGARET CYFERT	20435

187

ANCESTOR INDEX	BIRTH	PL	CO	DEATH	PL	CO	LIVD	MARRIED		PL	CO	SPOUSE NAME	CODE
STOWE, ABRAHAM	1762	VA		1841	NC	060		1	C1790	VA		JENNIE SIMMONS	04200
								2	C1795	NC	092	MARY HORIS/HARRIS	
								3	C1798	?VA		NETTIE TUCKER	
								4	1829	NC	065	MRS NANCY (HORSLEY) SUGGS	
STOWE, SALLIE/SARAH	1796	NC	092	1864	GA			1	C1818	NC	092	JOHN HECTOR RALLS	04200
STRADER, CONRAD		GER		C1809	NC	020							27542
STRADER, DAVID	C1775	NC	073	1826	NC	020		1				PRUDENCE	27542
STRADER, JOHANES CONRAD	C1729	?GR		1808	NC	020		1	C1751	?GR			60258
STRADER, WILLIAM CHRISTIAN	C1805	NC	020	C1895	NC	020		1	1827	NC	020	LUCINDA LOVELACE	27542
STRAHAN, MOSES JR	1794	NC		1834	MS			1	1814			LUCY CASSANDRA COTTINGHAM	10090
STRAHAN, MOSES SR	C1757	NC	070	1833	MS			1		NC		RACHEL HOWARD	10090
STRAWN, FIELDING	1804	NC		1866	AR			1	1826	AL		NANCY ANN THOMAS	60254
STRICKLAND, FREDERICK	C1736	NC	099	1825	TN			1				MARY GIBSON	60046
STRICKLAND, JOHN H		NC	?099		NC	?099		1		NC	?099	MARTHA HORTON	24139
STRICKLAND, KINDRED	1785	NC	099	1852	AL			1	1811	NC	099	TEMPY REAVES	27332
STRINGFELLOW, ELIZABETH							082	1				JESSE BALDWIN	60590
STRINGFELLOW, HENRY							?082						60590
STROP, EVE	C1818	NC			AL			1		NC		GEORGE WASHINGTON VAUGHAN	60039
STROUD, JOHN	1805	NC						1				DELILAH	60526
STROUD, WILLIAM	1831	NC						1				MARY E COATES	60526
STROUP, ADAM	1746	?MD		C1835	NC	060	094	1	C1770	?MD		CATHERINE/ELIZABETH	23065
STROUP, JACOB	C1723	?GR		1805	NC	060	094	1	C1745	?MD		CATHERINE/ELIZABETH REEL ?	23065
STROUP, JOSEPH	1776	NC	094	1856	NC	013	060	1	1798	NC	060	CATHERINE CREASMAN	23065
STROUP, SAMUEL ALEXANDER	1852	NC	013	1918	NC	013		1	1852	NC	013	ELLEN CORNELIA GARREN	23065
STROUP, SILAS	1816	NC	013	1896	NC	013		1	C1839	NC	013	SUSANNA/SUSAN HARPER	23065
STRUBLE/STRUBEL, BARBARA	1756	PA			KY		085	1	C1776	PA		JOHN HARPER	23065
STUART, ALEXANDER	1735	PA		C1768	NC			1	1759	VA		ELIZABETH PIKE	60558
STUART, CHARLES	1814	NC		1903	IA			1	1835	NC	022	RUTH HADLEY	60558
STUART, JOHN	1764	NC		1856	NC	022		1	1812	NC	022	MARY STOUT	60558
STUART, JOSEPH GURNEY	1845	NC		1922	IA			1	1872	IA		MARTHA HOSKINS	60558
STUCKEY, EDMOND	1747	VA		1831	SC		037	1	1769	?VA		NANCY ELIZABETH HOWELL ?	27303
								2				EDITH HOWELL	
								3				MRS REBECCA MCCATHERN	
STUDDARD, MAHALA	C1821	NC		C1855	IA			1	C1839			ANANIAS SIMPKINS	60200
STUDDARD, NANCY	1824	NC	090	1902	IA			1	1843			SAMUEL W BUFFINGTON	04080
								2	1854	IA		WESLEY HALL	
STUDDARD, RICHARD	C1800	NC	?090	C1841	IN			1	C1819	NC	?090		04080
STULTZ, ANNA	1819	NC	090	1897	IA			1	1831	IN		JAMES D HARTMAN	60364
STUTTS, JACOB				1796	NC	068	085	1				ELIZABETH	60234
STUTZMAN, DANIEL	C1795	NC	046	C1844	AR			1	1817	IN		CATHERINE ALLHANDS	02414
STUTZMAN, JOSEPH	C1775	NC	046	C1801	IN			1	C1794	NC	046	RACHEL CAIRNS/KARNS	02414

ANCESTOR INDEX	BIRTH	PL	CO	DEATH	PL	CO	LIVD	MARRIED	PL	CO	SPOUSE NAME	CODE
SUGG, AMY	C1766	NC	037	1818	NC	037		1 1775	NC	037	MICAJAH PETTAWAY	27441
SUGG, AQUILA				1791	NC	037		1 C1744	NC	037	LUCY READING	27441
								2			ELIZABETH MAUND	
SUGG, AQUILLA	1702	VA		1780	KY		037	1 1729	VA		ELIZABETH MAUND	13264
SUGG, AQUILLA	1768	VA		1845	NC	045		1 C1790	NC	034	NANCY HILL	13264
SUGG, AQUILLA	1706	VA		C1789	TN		037	1 C1734	VA		ELIZABETH MAUND	60032
								2		NC	037 MRS ABIGAIL (BONNER) JONES	
SUGG, AQUILLA, DR	1803	NC	045	1833	NC	045		1 C1829	NC	045	MARY SUGG	13264
SUGG, ELISABETH	1791	NC	099	C1855	NC	068	068	1 1817	NC	099	GEORGE HARWARD	14020
SUGG, GEORGE		ENG		1758	NC	009		1			JUDITH TYSON	27441
SUGG, JOHN	1732	VA		1790	NC	034	037	1 1755	NC		ELIZABETH MURPHREY	13264
SUGG, JOHN	1760	VA		C1814	NC	045		1 C1785	NC	034	MARTHA ALDRIDGE	13264
SUGG, MOSES	C1692	VA		C1784	NC	?099	?056					14020
SUGG, NOAH	C1745	NC	037	C1804	NC	037		1 1765	NC	037	MURPHREE HOWELL	27441
SUGG, WILLIAM	C1760	VA		C1820	NC	099		1 1780	NC	099	ELIZABETH SIMS	14020
SUGG/SUGGS, ELIZABETH	1794	NC	068	1893	TX			1 1815	NC	067	JOHN DUNCAN HARVEY	13175
SUGG/SUGGS, HARBERT/HARBARD				C1812	NC	067		1 1778			ZILPHIA WRIGHT	13175
SUGGS, EMILINE	C1830	NC	?029	C1861	NC	029		1			MR MARTIN	13090
								2 1851	NC	029	JAMES HENDERSON MATTHEWS	
SULLENS, JOHN				C1808	MO		046	1			JANE GILL	60422
SULLIVAN, CLEMENT/CLEMMA	C1776	NC	046	1861	TN			1 C1807	TN		ELIZABETH STEMBRIDGE	60404
SULLIVAN, FLETCHER	C1750	?MD		1817	TN		046	1 C1772	?VA		MARY ELLIOTT/ELLETT	60404
SULLIVAN, JOHN SR	C1720	?MD		C1796	NC	046		1 C1748	?MD			60404
SULLIVANT, WILLIAM	C1740	NC	047	C1825	TN							08065
SUMMA/SUMMY, FREDERICK	1767						060					60447
SUMMA/SUMMY, GEORGE	1805						060	1			JERUSHIA DAILY	60447
SUMMA/SUMMY, PETER							085					60447
SUMMERS, MANERING SR	C1770							1 1788	NC	092	SARAH MCCALLUM	60501
SUMMERS, ZACHARIAH	C1763	MD		1848	NC	054		1 1786	VA		SARAH DAWSON	60065
SUMMERS, ZEPORIAH				C1850				1 C1794	NC	020	CHRISTIAN STRADER	60258
SUMMIT, FRANCIS				C1810	NC	060						60260
SUMMIT, HENRY					IN			1 1815	NC	060	CATHARINE MAYERS/MYERS	60260
SUMNER, DEMPSEY	1712	VA		1779	NC	041		1			MARTHA BAKER	17147
SUMNER, ELIZABETH		NC	?024	1826	NC	041		1			JAMES BARNES	17147
SUMNER, JETHRO	1858	VA		1830	NC	041		1 C1780	VA		ELIZABETH TURNER	17147
SUMNER, JOHN VIVIAN		NC	041	1843	NC	041		1 1826	NC	041	ELIZABETH/BETSY BARNES	17147
SUMNER, MARGARET	1818	NC	013	1889	KY			1	NC	013	JOSIAH WILLIAMS	27318
SUMNER, MARTHA MONIMIA	1833	NC	041	1896				1 1857	NC	041	WILLIAM JOSEPH LAWRENCE	17147

ANCESTOR INDEX	BIRTH	PL	CO	DEATH	PL	CO	LIVD	MARRIED	PL	CO	SPOUSE NAME	CODE
SUMNER, SAMUEL				1765	NC	024		1			MARTHA/PATTY ALSTON	17147
SUMNER, SAMUEL		NC		1824	NC	013		1	NC			27318
SUMNER/SUMMER, ELIZABETH	1784			1848	MO			1	1800	NC	051 JOSEPH SUMNER	60248
SUMNER/SUMMER, JOSPEH	1773			1837	MO			1	1800	NC	051 ELIZABETH SUMNER	60248
SURLES, ROBERT	C1793	NC		1860				1	1816	NC	ELIZABETH BUSHEE	60263
SURLES, SAMUEL	1791	NC		1844	MO			1	1816		MASSA W SUDDETH	60263
SUTHERLAND, DANIEL				1792	NC	037		1	1777	NC	035 ANNE MCDOWELL	27441
SUTHERLAND, ELIZABETH	C1781			1840	NC	037		1	C1799	NC	037 ELISHA CROMWELL	27441
SUTHERLAND, JOHN				1810	NC	037		1			CLARY	60044
SUTHERLAND, JOHN	C1880	NC		1863				1			NANCY SHIVERS	60044
SUTTON, EDMUND/EDWARD	C1790	NC	086		GA			1	1825	NC	086 REBECCA GRIZZLE	60524
SUTTON, EPHRIAM	1769	NC	024	1819	NC	070		1	1797	SC	MRS MARTHA(MOORE)CORBY	20138
SUTTON, KISANN	C1823	NC		1906	IL			1		NC	JOHN TAYLOR	60409
SUTTON, SMITH	C1775							1	C1796	NC		60376
SUTTON, SOLOMON		NC	?009		NC	?079		1	C1765			MARY BLOUNT ?	06050
SUTTON, ZACHEUS/ZACHARIAH	1797	NC		1864	IN			1	C1817	VA	SUSANNAH APPLEGATE	60376
SWAFFORD, JAMES	C1740	?PA		C1810	NC	086	094	1	C1765	NC	?073 SARAH SEELY ?	25087
SWANN, AQUILLA				C1877	NC	064		1			SALLY	19183
SWANN, JOSEPH L	1844	NC	064	C1924	NC	064	093	1	C1880		EMMA J HIGGINS	19183
SWARTZLANDER, KATHERINE	1769	PA		1853	IN		?085	1	C1790		ABRAHAM ADAMS	60128
SWIFT, FLOWER	C1750	MD		1813	KY		081					60245
SWIFT, FLOWER	C1748	MD		1813	KY		081	1		VA	MARY BEDSAUL	60415
SWIFT, THOMAS	C1725	MD		C1802	NC	081	?073	1			MARTHA	60245
SWIFT, THOMAS SR	C1719	MD		C1806	NC	081		1	C1748		MARTHA LINDEN	60415
SWINDELL, JOSIAH				1806	NC	053		1			ESTHER	20335
SWINSON, AUSTIN/OSTEN	C1730	NC	?096	C1786	NC	035						02550
SWINSON, HENRY				C1850	NC	045		1			BERCHY	14030
SWINSON, JESSE	1759	NC	063	1834	NC	035		1	C1783	NC	035 NANCY ANN WINDERS	02550
SWINSON, JOHN	C1695			C1775	NC	079		1			ELSIE	02550
SWINSON, JOHN	C1730	NC	?096	C1800	NC	070		2	C1782	NC	035 SUSANNAH PARKER	02550
SWINSON, RICHARD				1716	NC	024		1			ELIZABETH	02550

T

| TABER/TABOR, JOHN | | ?VA | | | NC | 086 | 073 | 1 | | | ELIZABETH | 60400 |
| TABER/TABOR, MARY | 1768 | NC | ?073 | 1860 | TN | | 086 | 1 | 1784 | NC | 086 WILLIAM THOMPSON | 60400 |

ANCESTOR INDEX	BIRTH	PL CO	DEATH PL CO	LIVD	MARRIED PL CO	SPOUSE NAME	CODE
TABER/TABOUR, JOHN SR			C1806 NC 086		1	ELIZABETH SHARPE	60321
TABER/TABOUR, WILLIAM	1761	NC 073	1844 MS		1 1781 NC 086	SUSANNAH TUBB	60321
TABOR/TABER, ANDREW V	1824	NC 086	1890 MO		1 1842	RUHANEY COLLINS	60257
TABOR/TABER, ELI/ELY LEWIS	1793	NC ?086	C1847 MO		1 2	ELIZABETH HICKS JOHANNA HICKS	60257
TACKER/TUCKER, JOSHUA		NC 085	1848 TN		1 1803 NC 085	SUSSANAH KERNUT	27549
TACKER/TUCKER, SEABORN		MD	1806 NC 085		1 1762 MD	ELIZABETH HITCHCOCK	27549
TACKETT/TACKITT, BAYLIS COLE	C1806	NC 084	1881 IL		1 1827 KY	MILDRED TACKETT	60583
TACKETT/TACKITT, CHARLES C	C1815	NC 046	1900 KY		1 1833 KY	AMANDA RICE	60583
TACKETT/TACKITT, DAVID	C1790	NC	C1856 TN		1	SARAH THOMPSON	60583
TACKETT/TACKITT, GEORGE	C1780	NC	C1855 MS		1 C1805	ELIZABETH NICHOLSON	60583
TACKETT/TACKITT, GEORGE C	C1815	NC 046	C1881 KY		1 2	MARY ANN RICE ELIZABETH RICE	60583
TACKETT/TACKITT, PHILLIP	C1772	NC	C1855 AL		1 2	NANCY	60583
TACKETT/TACKITT, THOMAS	C1770	NC	C1855 KY		1 2	SARAH	60583
TACKETT/TACKITT, THOMAS	C1802	NC	C1875 IL				60583
TACKETT/TACKITT, THOMAS	C1809	NC	C1850 IN		1	AMELIA	60583
TACKETT/TACKITT, WILLIAM	C1772	NC	C1855 AR		1 2 1847 AR	SARAH HAWKINS	60583
TACKETT/TACKITT, WILLIAM	C1810	NC	MO		1	SALLIE	60583
TACKETT/TACKITT, WILLIAM, SR	1779	NC	1851 KY		1	AMY JOHNSON	60583
TAGGART, JAMES	1774	NC	1852 IN		1 1798 NC 016	RACHAEL PETERSON	60312
TALBERT/TOLBERT, ELIZABETH	C1806	NC ?067	C1860 ?TN				27257
TALKINGTON, STEVEN	1779	NC	1859 AR		1 1807 KY	SARAH ACOCK	60187
TANNER, MATHEW JR	1776	VA	1833 GA		1 2 1800 NC 020	ALSEY LANGLEY	60311
TAPLEY/TARPLEY, HOSEA	1691	?VA	NC 020		1 C1730 VA	SARAH GREEN	03020
TAPLEY/TARPLEY, HOSEA GREEN	1767	NC 044	1799 NC 020		1 1795	ELEANOR R MCFARLAND	03020
TAPLEY/TARPLEY, JOHN HOSEA	1735	VA	1770 NC 073		1 C1760 NC	LUCY PRYOR	03020
TAPLEY/TARPLEY, JOHN PRYOR	C1765	NC 044	GA				03020
TARBUTTON, HENRY	C1798	NC 082			1	SARAH	60104
TARLTON, BAXTER COLUMBUS	1891	NC 097	1975 NC 097		1	NANNIE NONNIE KIKER	60065
TARLTON, JOHN WILSON	1849	NC 097	1919 NC 097		1 1871 NC 097	SAPPHIRA CATHERON PURSER	60065
TART, NATHAN	C1730	?VA	1826 NC 010		1	MRS MARY EARLY	60029
TART, SARAH	1786	VA	1856 TN	087	1	ABRAHAM HAYNES	60029
TART, THOMAS	1761	VA	1850 NC 087	010			60029
TARVER, THOMAS	C1762	?NC ?071	C1835 NC 045		1 C1785	PHERIBY	13264
TARVER, WINIFRED	C1785	?NC	C1830 NC 045		1 C1800 NC 045	JAMES TAYLOR	13264

ANCESTOR INDEX	BIRTH	PL	CO	DEATH	PL	CO	LIVD	MARRIED	PL	CO	SPOUSE NAME	CODE
TATE, CATHERINE	1806	NC	073	1875	NC	?073		1 1826	NC	073	THOMAS GILL	02256
TATE, CELIA	1803	NC	073	1872	TN			1 1825	NC	073	THOMAS PETTIGREW	60324
TATE, CORNELIA ANN	C1827	NC	?073	C1890	TX			1 1851	TX		ELIHU JAMES KING BLAIR	60443
TATE, FRANCES/FANNY	C1773	VA		C1839	TN		086	1 C1790	NC	086	PETER WILLIS	60286
TATE, GEORGE	C1720			1774	NC	073		1			JINNET	02256
TATE, JAMES	1760			1838	NC	073		1 1785	NC	073	MARGARET NELSON	02256
TATE, JENET	C1768	NC	?073		NC	?073		1 1789	NC	073	JOHN NELSON	02256
TATE, JESSE	C1745	VA		1806	NC	086		1 C1767	VA		MARY	60286
TATE, THOMAS	C1796	NC	?073	C1875	TX			1	NC		MARY	60443
TATOM, ABNER								1 C1779	NC	044	MARY CURRIN	60464
TATOM, JOHN SR							044	1 1743	VA		ANN WRIGHT	60464
TATUM, SARAH H								1 1831	NC	046	JAMES E OGBURN	13120
TATUM, SIHON	C1775						038	1			PATSY	13120
TAYLOR, ABRAHAM	C1699			1751	NC	028		1			EDE	21035
TAYLOR, ABSALOM	C1786	NC		1856	AL		060	1 1810	NC	060	KATY CROUSE	15023
TAYLOR, ALEXANDER S	1811	NC		1869	TX			1			MARGARET HAYS DAVIS	27375
TAYLOR, ALICE	1844	NC	?019	1906	MO			1 1866	IL		WILLIAM LINDSAY	60409
TAYLOR, ANTHONY	1816	NC	006					1			PEARLINA SMITH	60418
TAYLOR, BENJAMIN	1780	VA		1853	NC	092		1 1803	VA		NANCY WILLIAMS	60393
TAYLOR, BENJAMIN	1816	NC	092	1888	UT			1			ANN JANE HIATT	60393
TAYLOR, BERRY	C1760	IRE					067	1	?IR			60337
TAYLOR, CLAYTON HINES	1810	NC	079	1888	NC	079		1 1842	NC	079	NANCY MANNING	60414
TAYLOR, DEMPSEY	C1740			1837	GA		?035	1 1783	NC	011	SALLY	27346
TAYLOR, DORCAS	C1772	?NC		C1845	TN		028	1	?NC		JAMES ARNOLD	27602
TAYLOR, GREEN	1794	NC	034	1860	NC	059		1 1819	NC	059	PENELOPE SIMMONS	21035
TAYLOR, HENRY	1803	NC	045	C1890	NC	045		1 1831	NC	103	MARTHA JONES	13264
TAYLOR, HENRY SKIPWITH	1815	NC	044	1876	TN			1 1846	TN		JANE ELIZA MAYO	16035
TAYLOR, HERBERT	C1785	NC		1839	FL			1 1814	GA		MARY HOLLAND	27346
								2 C1835	FL		HARRIET MCDANIEL	
TAYLOR, ISAAC	1744	NC	028	1823	NC	059		1 1779	NC	034	HENRIETTA HARDEE	21035
TAYLOR, JAMES	C1775	NC	034	1828	NC	045		1 C1800	NC	045	WINIFRED TARVER	13264
TAYLOR, JAMES LEE	1815	NC	065	1880	TX			1 1841	TN		ELIZABETH MARY PAINE	60518
TAYLOR, JAMES SR				C1819	TN		028	1	?NC		SARAH	27602
TAYLOR, JESSE	1845	NC	045	1916	NC	045		1 C1874	NC	045	MARY ANN GINN	13264
TAYLOR, JOHN	1808	NC	051	1881	NC	051		1 C1840	NC	051	ELIZABETH BRITT	60211
TAYLOR, JOHN	1823	NC	079	1878	IL			1	NC		KISANN SUTTON	60409
TAYLOR, JOHN	C1780	NC	079		NC	079		1 C1807	NC	?079	ANN MORNING WEAVER	60414
TAYLOR, JOHN	C1750	?NC			NC	079		1	?NC	?079	ALLIFAIR COLLINS	60414

ANCESTOR INDEX	BIRTH	PL	CO	DEATH	PL	CO	LIVD	MARRIED		PL	CO	SPOUSE NAME	CODE
TAYLOR, JOHN	1753			1800	NC	065		1	C1778	NC	065	MARGARET	60518
TAYLOR, JOHN	C1784	NC	065	1830	NC	065		1	1806	MC	065	MARY/POLLY NEELY	60518
TAYLOR, JOHN L	C1817	NC		1893	NC	056		1	C1837	CN	?056	BETSEY WILLIAMS	14030
TAYLOR, JOHN LARKINS	1805	NC	070	1858	FL								24213
TAYLOR, JOHN LARKINS	1805	NC	070	C1858	FL			1	1835	FL		REBECCA PALMER	27673
TAYLOR, JOSEPH	C1722			C1804	NC	059		1		NC	028		21035
TAYLOR, MADISON H	1839	NC	069		AL			1		AL		NANCY SULLIVAN	60260
TAYLOR, RICHARD	C1778	NC	070	1829	SC			1	1802	NC	070	ANN LARKINS	24213
TAYLOR, RICHARD BRYANT	1821	NC	059	1899	NC	059		1	1845	NC	059	MARGARET KORNEGAY	21035
								2	1863	NC	059	MRS ELIZABETH HARDY (BELL) HILL	
TAYLOR, RICHARD KOSCIUSKA	C1776	NC	070	1827	SC			1	1802	NC	070	ANN LARKINS	27673
TAYLOR, STANTON	1784	NC	034	1841	NC	059		1	1819	NC	059	NANCY BRUTON	21035
TAYLOR, TEGAL	1818	NC		1906	TN			1		TN		ELIZABETH COGDELL	60457
TAYLOR, THOMAS	C1780			1874	IN		?024	1				HANNAH NEWBY	25196
TAYLOR, THOMAS, JR	C1718	?NC		1772	NC	065		1	C1740	?NC		PENELOPE GOODWYN	60393
TAYLOR, THOMAS, SR	C1690	ENG		C1743	?NC			1	1714	?NC		ANN JONES ?	60393
TAYLOR, WILLIAM	1743	VA		1819	NC	103	034	1	C1765	?VA		MRS CELEYA EDWARDS	13264
								2		NC	?103	MARY EDWARDS	
								3		NC	059	MRS LYDIA (RASPBERRY) YOUNG	
TAYLOR, WILLIAM	C1750			1799	NC	070							24213
TAYLOR, WILLIAM		NC	070	1799	NC	070		1	C1773			SARAH	27673
TAYLOR, WILLIAM	1770	NC		C1845	TN			1		NC			60457
TAYLOR, WILLIAM B	C1797	NC		C1850	NC	045		1				NANCY BEST	14030
TAYLOR, WILLIAM VANNAH	1790	VA		1872	TN			1	1814	NC	044	FRANCES M HENDERSON	16035
TEAGUE, AARON							085						13105
TEAGUE, ABRAHAM	1793	NC	085		TX			1	1816	NC	085	CATHERINE PERMELIA BROWN	13105
TEAGUE, MOSES	C1739	VA		1793				1	1761	NC	085	ANN	13105
TELFORD, HUGH	1764	NC		1833	TN		073	1	C1785	NC			60587
								2	1808	TN		JANEY/JANE HARNEY	
								3	1824	TN		MRS SALLY BOWERS	
TELFORD, THOMAS	1786	NC	?073	1857	TN			1	1808	TN		ELIZABETH CHOWNING	60587
TEMPLE, BURWELL	1793	NC	099	1873	NC	099		1	1814	NC	099	HARRIOTT IVEY	11105
								2	1853	NC	056	MRS ELIZABETH/BETSY (WILLIAMSON) WHITLEY	
								3	1867	NC	099	MRS NANCY (WALTON) ROBERTSON	
TEMPLE, HENRY JR	1758	?VA		1820	NC	099		1	C1777	NC	?099	SARAH ROBERTSON	11105
								2	C1810	NC	?099	SARY	
TEMPLE, HENRY SR	C1732	?VA		1800	NC	099		1	C1753	?VA		ELIZABETH BARKER	11105
TEMPLE, JACKSON PETTIGREW	1863	NC	099	1945	NC	056		1	1899	NC	056	LOUISA JANE PARKER	11105
TEMPLE, JAMES PETTIGREW	1911	NC	056					1	1955	NC	070	MRS GRACE (TILLETT) WIGGINS	11105
TEMPLE, RUFUS FABIUS	1827	NC	099	1897	NC	099		1	1849	NC	059	MARY ELISHABA CROOM	11105

193

ANCESTOR INDEX	BIRTH	PL	CO	DEATH	PL	CO	LIVD	MARRIED	PL	CO	SPOUSE NAME	CODE
TEMPLETON, JOHN H	1812	NC	?054	1877	TN		?085	1 1837			AVIS WHITTY CASHION	60234
TEMPLETON, NANCY	C1810	NC	054		TN			1 C1832	NC	054	PALLIS GRIFFIN	60149
TEMPLETON, ROBERT							054	1 C1798			SARAH	60149
TEMPLETON, ROBERT		NC	?054	1816				1			SARAH	60234
TENNISON, MARY ANN ELIZA	1813	NC	013	C1875	AL			1 C1845	AL		JOHN D MILLER	27595
TENNISON, MATTHEW J	1820	NC	013					1 C1848	AL		MARY TURNER	27595
TENNISON, THOMAS	1817	NC	013					1 C1852	AL			27595
TERRY, MARY ANN	1828			1910	NC	038		1 1848	NC	090	TANDY MARSHALL	60456
TESH, JAMES MADISON	C1834	NC		1905	OK			1 C1853	?NC	?038	SUSAN JANE MARTIN	60428
TESH, JOHN C	C1798	NC						1			SUSANA	60428
THARP/THARPE/THORP/THORPE, WILLIAM	1757	?MD		1849	NC	054	046	1			RACHEL RICHARDS	04050
THIEME/TEEM, GEORGE WASHINGTON	1815	NC	014	1875	GA			1 1835	GA		ELIZABETH AVALIAE CANNUP/KNOPF	60013
THIEME/TEEM, JACOB	1730	GER		C1810	NC	016	085	1 1770	NC	065	SUSANNAH BEAVER/BIEBER	60013
THIEME/TEEM, PETTAR	1772	NC	065	1850	GA		085	1 1795	NC	016	BARBARA SCOTT	60013
THIGPEN, JAMES	1743	NC	037	1825	NC	037	079	1 1765	NC	037	LYDIA MAYO	02195
THIGPEN, JAMES L	1827	NC	037	1898	NC	037		1 1850	NC	037	MARTHA COBB	02195
THIGPEN, LEMUEL	1768	NC	037	C1841	NC	037	079	1 2 1815	NC NC	079 037	BETHIA MAYO ANNA CHERRY	02195
THOMAS, ANDREW JACKSON	1828	NC		1881	IN		085	1 1850	IN		MARGARET BECKNER	60202
THOMAS, BENJAMIN ANTIPAS	1820	NC					085	1 1844			SARAH STUART ?	60202
THOMAS, CORNELIA JANE HOLLOWAY	1813	NC	073	1899	IL			1 1836	NC	073	DAVID HORN	13020
THOMAS, DOVEY ELIZABETH	1825						085	1 1845	IN		SOLOMON PEARMAN/PIERMAN	60202
THOMAS, ELEANOR NARCISSUS	1814	NC		1897			085	1 1835	IN		BENJAMIN FRANKLIN SCALF	60202
THOMAS, ELKANAH P	1823			1905	IN		085	1			MARGARET ANN MCCONNELL	60202
THOMAS, GEORGE ARTERBURY	1819	NC	?013	1906	GA			1 1841	GA		SARA/SALLY FAIN	60261
THOMAS, GRIFFITH		?VA			NC	?073	073	1	?VA		CHARLOTTE HUFFMAN	13020
THOMAS, GRISHAM/GRISSOM	1783	VA		C1858	NC	068		1			SARAH OLIVER	24315
THOMAS, JACOB	1727	MD		1778	NC	085		1 1753	NC		MARGARET BREVARD	60342
THOMAS, JAMES	C1790	NC	073		NC	001		1 1812	NC	073	MILLIE STEPHENS	13020
THOMAS, JAMES F	1830	NC					085	1			CHARLOTTE/LOTTIE	60202
THOMAS, JANE R	1815	NC					085	1 1836	IN		ADAM CORMANY	60202
THOMAS, JOHN	C1792	SC		C1865	GA			1 C1815 2 1818	NC NC	?013 ?013	 MRS MARGARET (FAIN) WITZELL	60261
THOMAS, JOHN NEWTON	1827			1845			085					60202
THOMAS, KATHERINE MATILDA	1818	NC		1871	IN		085	1 1842	IN		LABAN R BURT	60202
THOMAS, MARGARET							085	1 1840	IN		ZIBA WINGET	60202
THOMAS, MARY	1801	NC		1871	TN			1 1821	TN		ALFRED MOUNT	60393
THOMAS, ROBERT ALBERT	1812	NC		1866	IN		085	1 1838	IN		MARGARET WALKER	60202

ANCESTOR INDEX	BIRTH	PL	CO	DEATH	PL	CO	LIVD	MARRIED	PL	CO	SPOUSE NAME	CODE
THOMAS, SAMUEL	1790	NC		1847	IN		085	1 1811	NC	054	MARGARET MCCLAIN MATHEWS	60202
THOMAS, SAMUEL SMUT	1821	NC	085	1896	IN			1 1847	IN		ELIZABETH BECKNER	60202
THOMAS, SARAH ANN	1833	NC		1909			085	1 1851			OSCAR DEWEY	60202
THOMAS, TILLMON/TILMON/TILLMAN	1804	NC	?068	1885	NC	068		1			HARRIET JUDD	24315
THOMAS, WILLIAM	1761	NC	085	1833	TN		054	1 1791	NC		ELIZABETH PURVIANCE	60342
THOMAS, WILLIAM	C1772	NC	?092	1797	NC	?092		1 C1800	NC		ELIZABETH	60393
THOMAS, WILLIAM O	1818	NC	?068	1885	NC	068		1			MARY CAMERON	24315
THOMASSON, ANDREW	1804	NC		C1867	NC	106		1 1826	NC	090	LEAH HAUSER	13120
THOMASSON, FLEMING SR	C1776	VA		1853	NC	090		1 1799	NC	020	SARAH GOMER	13120
THOMPSON ANN	C1768	NC	?092					1			DAVID OSBORNE	21095
THOMPSON ESTER G	C1770	NC	?092									21095
THOMPSON JOHN	C1745			1786	NC	092		1			MARY	21095
THOMPSON JOHN JR	C1780	NC	?092									21095
THOMPSON MARY	C1777	NC	?092					1			THOMAS SHERWOOD	21095
THOMPSON SYLVESTER	1766	NC	092	1826	OH		090	1 C1792			MARY SEWARD	21095
THOMPSON, AZARIAH					TN			1 1784	NC	073	CATHARINE ALLISON	02470
THOMPSON, DAVID				C1799	NC	086		1			ELENOR	60400
THOMPSON, DAVID	1784	NC	?086									60400
THOMPSON, ELISHA		NC						1			ELIZABETH	08240
THOMPSON, ELIZABETH	C1763						060	1	NC		WM GEO WASHINGTON BROWN	60200
THOMPSON, ELIZABETH	1789	NC	?086									60400
THOMPSON, ELIZABETH H	1821	NC	086	1883	NC	026		1 1837	NC	086	JOHN GREEN ESKRIDGE	05070
THOMPSON, HENRY	1787	MD		1862	MO		084	1 1807	NC	084	ELIZABETH LEE	60422
THOMPSON, ISAAC	C1800	NC		?MO				1 C1822	?VA		MARY ABIGAIL	60262
THOMPSON, JAMES	1773	NC	073	1848	TN			1 1800	TN		MARGARET BUCHANAN	02470
THOMPSON, JAMES	1783	NC		1868	VA			1			AGNES	08240
THOMPSON, JEHOIDAH	1793	NC	?086	1872	AR			1 C1817			MARGARET GREEN	60400
THOMPSON, JOHN	1771	NC	073	1843	NC	073						02470
THOMPSON, JOHN	1787	NC	?086									60400
THOMPSON, JOHN JR	1774	NC	022	1846	GA			1 1800			NANCY HAYGOOD	60110
THOMPSON, JOHN SR	C1725			C1814	NC	054	085	1 C1750				23065
THOMPSON, JOHN SR	1744	VA		C1811	NC	022		1 1770	NC	073	SUSANNAH LEA ANDREWS ?	60110
THOMPSON, JOHN, COL	C1750	?NC	?072	C1827	TN		073	1			GRIZELLA ALLISON	02470
THOMPSON, JOSEPH	C1737			1792	NC	073		1 C1768	?NC	?073	SARAH MCALLISTER	02470
THOMPSON, LAURENCE, CPT	C1710	?PA		C1800	TN		073	1			MARGARET LOGUE ?	02470
THOMPSON, MARGARET/PEGGY	C1760	?NC	?085		NC	?054		1 1784	NC	085	GEORGE CLAYTON	23065
THOMPSON, MARY, MRS								1 1788	NC	046	GEORGE KIRKMAN	21095

ANCESTOR INDEX	BIRTH	PL	CO	DEATH	PL	CO	LIVD	MARRIED	PL	CO	SPOUSE NAME	CODE
THOMPSON, RANDOLPH		VA		1818	TN		024	1 1802			ELIZABETH MEREDITH	27728
THOMPSON, SAMUEL	1814	NC		1848	TN			1	NC		MARY	25161
THOMPSON, SAMUEL	1750	PA		1837	NC	073		1 1785	NC	073	ELIZABETH DEBOW	60429
THOMPSON, SOLOMON	1799	NC	073	1868	NC	073		1 1828	NC	073	ELIZA PICKETT	60429
THOMPSON, THOMAS	C1716	?PA		C1795	NC	073		1			ANN LOGUE	02470
THOMPSON, THOMAS	1758	MD		1828	NC	084		1 1782	MD		PRISCILLA MACE	60422
THOMPSON, THOMAS				1796	NC	073		1	?PA		ANN LOGUE	60429
THOMPSON, THOMAS ARRINGTON	1810	NC	084	1898	MO			1 1834	TN		KERENHAPPUCH SELLERS	60422
THOMPSON, WILLIAM	1796	?NC		1888	GA			1 1818	NC	086	NANCY HENDERSON	01035
THOMPSON, WILLIAM	C1721	VA		C1772	NC	022		1 C1742	VA		HANNAH BELL	60110
THOMPSON, WILLIAM	C1760			1811	TN			1 1784	NC	086	MARY TABER	60321
THOMPSON, WILLIAM	C1760			1811	TN		086	1 1784	NC	086	MARY TABOR	60400
THOMPSON, WILLIAM	1791	NC	?086									60400
THOMPSON/THOMSON, ALFORD/ALFRED	C1815	NC	?103	1896	NC	105	069	1 1836 2 1879	NC NC	069 105	ELMINA R CROWELL MARTHA J EDMONDSON ?	03250
THOMPSON/THOMSON, EVERETTE		NC	?103	1830	NC	069		1			SARAH/SALLY NICHOLS ?	03250
THOMPSON/THOMSON, JOHN	1721	?NC		1784	NC	103	?024	1 1748			RACHEL PEACOCK ?	03250
THOMPSON/THOMSON, THOMAS	C1753	NC		C1830	NC	103		1			DEBORAH	03250
THORN/THORNE, CATHERINE	C1853	NC	069	C1888	NC	105		1			THOMAS RUFFIN LAMM	03250
THORN/THORNE, MARTIN R	C1825	NC		1862	VA		105	1 1845 2 1851	NC NC	069 069	ZINA LAMM MRS MARINDA/RENDA (SHARP?) THORN	03250
THORNBURGH, HENRY				1804	TN			1 1758	NC	046	RACHEL MOON	08265
THORNBURGH, SOPHIA	1781	NC	046	1862	IN			1 2 1827	TN IN		JOSEPH WILLIAMS OBED BARNARD	08265
THORNBURGH, WALTER					NC	046		1			MARGARET	08265
THRIFT, CYNTHIA ANNE	1841	NC	046	1905				1			JAMES IRA WILLS	08145
THRIFT, DAVID ANDERSON	1794	NC	073	1888	IA			1			LYDIA PARSONS	08145
THRIFT, ELI ELLISON	1831	NC	046	1918	CA			1			MARY GIVEN	08145
THRIFT, ISHAM				C1813	NC	?073		1	NC	?073	MARY STROWD	27417
THRIFT, JAMES DANIEL	1827	NC	046	1899				1			SARAH JANE BROWN	08145
THRIFT, MARY CAROLINA		NC		1904	OK			1			JOHN WHITE	08145
THRIFT, MARY E	1855	NC		1892				1			AARON MILLER	08145
THRIFT, PERRY	C1793	NC	?073	C1855	NC	022		1 C1815	NC	?073		27417
THRIFT, PINKNEY	1818	NC	?022	1886	MO			1 C1845 2 1881	NC MO	?022	SENEY/SINEY MRS ELIZABETH COLUMBIA (ANCEL) MABRY	27417
THRIFT, SUNLEY PARKER		NC						1			PEGGY JONES	08145
TILLETT, THOMAS	1762			1827	NC	030		1			DOROTHY/DOLLY BAUM	20335
TILLEY, ANNA	C1788	NC	092		MO			1 1807	KY		JAMES RICHARDSON	60514

ANCESTOR INDEX	BIRTH	PL	CO	DEATH	PL	CO	LIVD	MARRIED	PL	CO	SPOUSE NAME	CODE
TILLEY, HENRY		VA		C1790	NC	092		1			JEAN	60514
TILLEY, LAZARUS	C1768	NC	092	1914	KY			1 C1787	NC		ANN	60514
TINNEN, FRANCES	1769	NC	073	1845	NC	073		1 1786	NC	073	JOSEPH ARMSTRONG	27441
TINNEN/TINNIN/TENANT, JOHN		?PA			NC	073		1	?PA		MARY	60151
TINNIN, ROBERT				1796	NC	073		1 C1757	CN	?073	CATHERINE	20135
TINNIN, ROBERT	1763	NC	073	1834	NC	073		1 1799	NC	073	SARAH MASON	20135
TIPPET/TIPPETT, REBECCA	1807	?NC		1879	AR			1 1822			WILLIAM FORD	02414
TIPPETT, WILLIAM D	1833			1868	NC	001		1 1856	NC	056	ELIZA ANN HINTON	21115
TIPTON, THOMAS EDWARD	C1823	NC			TN			1 C1848	NC		SARAH	60390
								2 1858	TN		MINERVA MOORE	
TIREY, THOMAS	C1790	NC	?104		IN			1			MARY BEASLEY	60348
TODD, AUSTIN P		GA		1844	NC	053		1			MARY SAUNDERSON	20335
TODD, CAROLINE PRISCILLA	1820	TN		C1854	TN		?065	1 C1840	TN		JONATHAN HENRY HALL	60519
TODD, JAMES	C1803	NC	099	1878	NC	099		1			SARAH/SALLY	03250
TODD, MOSES		?NC		1816	NC	099	010	1	NC	?010	ANN/NANCY FILGO	03250
TODD, MOSES		NC	?010	1841	NC	099		1 1800	NC	099	ELIZABETH/BETSY MASSY	03250
TODD, SOPHIA W	1815	NC	099	1845	TN			1 1837	NC	099	MANN PATTERSON STEPHENSON	60337
TODD, WILLIAM		?VA		1769	NC	010		1			CATHARINE	03250
TOLAR, ROBERT	1804	NC	?011	1887	NC	011		1	NC	?011	FRANCES	60579
TOLER, CHARLES W	C1795	NC			IN			1 C1815			MARY	60567
TOLIVER, JOHN	C1760	NC					?085					60286
TOLIVER, NANCY	1785	NC		1869	TN			1 C1804	?NC		RUSSELL BREWER	60286
TOLLEY/TOLLY, DAVID	1837			1875	NC	107		1 1856	NC	107	SUSANNA WILSON	60154
TOLLEY/TOLLY, JOHN	C1810	NC		C1870	NC	066	107	1 C1834	NC	107	SUSANNA	60154
TOON, ANTHONY FENTRESS	1803			1853	NC	070	011	1			MARY COSTIN ?	12144
								2	NC	027	MRS. MARY (MCMILLAN) KELLY	
TORREY, BEATRICE	1757	SCO		1828	NC	083	029	1 C1770	?NC		MALCOLM PURCELL	27566
TORREY, JOHN	C1720	SCO			NC	?029	083	1 C1744	SCO		MARGARET	27566
TOWNSEND, A JAMES		NC		1848	MS							07078
TOWNSEND, ESTHER	1792	NC		1871	KY			1 1814	KY		JAMES MOSS	25229
TOWNSEND, HENRY	1773	NC		1839	KY							25229
TOWNSEND, HENRY	1770	NC	065	1834	KY			1			DEBORAH	25229
TOWNSEND, MARY ANN	1823	NC		1873	MS			1 1838	MS		HARVEY MILTON MERRITT	07078
TOWNSEND, SUSANNAH		NC						1 1821	KY		LEMUEL DENSON	25229
TRANSOU, PETER	1792	NC	090	1852	NC	038		1			REBECCA LEINBACH	60467
TRANTHAM, JOHN	1789	NC	085					1 1819			NANCY ELIZABETH CUNNINGHAM	60044
TRANTHAM, MARTIN	C1822	NC						1 1851	TN		MARY F MOYERS	60044
TRAYWICK, FRANCIS	C1734	VA		1819	GA		072	1 C1773			ANNA	60112

ANCESTOR INDEX	BIRTH	PL	CO	DEATH	PL	CO	LIVD	MARRIED	PL	CO	SPOUSE NAME	CODE
TRAYWICK, ROBERT	C1700	VA		C1769	NC	072	056	1 C1725	VA		MARGERY LUNSFORD ?	60112
TREADWELL, ADONIRAM	1700	CT		1782	NC	035		1		CT	BEULAH GREGORY	12090
TREADWELL, JOHN	C1735	?CT		1821	NC	087		1			SARAH HERRING ?	12090
TREADWELL, MIRIAM	C1761	NC	087	1836	AL			1		NC	087 GEORGE DEVANE	12090
TREADWELL, STEPHEN JR	1772	NC	067	1843	GA			1 1792	NC		JANE FISHER	12125
TRICE, EDWARD	C1737	VA		1800	NC	073		1		VA	TABITHA HARRISON	60110
TRICE, ELLEN	C1820	NC	073	C1883	NC	022		1 1849	NC		073 WILLIAM HORTON	60110
TRICE, PLEASANT	1802	NC	073	1875	NC	073		1 1842	NC		073 MARTHA JANE ATKINS	60110
TRIPLETT, LEWIS	C1794	NC	104					1 C1813	NC		104 BETSY CHURCH	60222
TRIPLETT, LUKE	1814	NC	104	1921	NC	102		1 C1834	NC		104 MARTHA/PATSY HAMPTON	60222
								2 1900	NC		102 ANNA HALL	
TRIPLETT, MAGGIE A	1856	NC	102	1899	OK			1 C1870	NC		?102 DAVID L SIMMONS	60222
TRIPLETT, THOMAS	C1765	VA					006	1 C1789	NC		?104 JANE FERGUSON	60222
TRIPP, ELI	1807	NC	?022	1864	TN		?073	1 C1829			IBBEY	25191
TRIPP, JOHN		?NC	?022	C1805	NC	022		1			?022 MARY	25191
TRIPP, JOHN		NC	?022				?073	1 C1805	NC			25191
TRIPP, JONATHAN	C1772	NC	?022				?073	1 C1795	NC		REBECCA	25191
TRIPP, MARY		NC	?022				?073	1			MR POWELL	25191
TRIPP, REUBEN		NC	?022				?073	1 C1795	NC			25191
TRIPP, WILLIAM		NC	?022				?073	1 C1818	NC			25191
TROSPER, ELIJAH	1773	KY		1834	MO		014	1			ABAGAIL	60339
TROSPER, ELIJAH LEONARD JR	1805	NC	014	1884	MO			1			MRS ELIZABETH ANN FOX	60339
TROSPER, NICHOLAS					NC	?014	014					60339
TROTTER, JANE	1800			1822	MO		104	1 1818	NC		104 JAMES STANDLEY	25135
TROTTER, MARY/POLLY	C1808			1883	MO		104	1 1823	MO		JAMES STANDLEY	25135
TROWELL, JAMES		NC	096		?SC							60252
TROWELL, JAMES	1761	NC	099	1850				1 1816			ALCEY MADDOX ?	60252
TROWELL, JOHN	1759	NC	077	1779	NC	077						60252
TROWELL, JOSEPH					NC	077		1 1683	NC		077 HONA BRIAN	60238
TROWELL, JOSEPH				C1735	NC	077		1			TABITHA	60238
TROWELL, JOSEPH				1735	NC	096	077	1 1683	NC		077 HONOR BRIAN	60252
								2			TABITHA	
TROWELL, JOSEPH		NC	096				?029					60252
TROWELL, SUSANNA	1685				NC	077						60238
TROWELL, SUSANNAH	1685	NC	077									60252
TROWELL, THOMAS		NC	077									60252
TROXLER, ADALINE	1803	NC	073	1874	MO			1 1824	NC		073 BRISCO M STONE WARREN	60145
TROXLER, BARNEY	C1753			1816	NC	073		1			ELIZABETH	60145

ANCESTOR INDEX	BIRTH	PL	CO	DEATH	PL	CO	LIVD	MARRIED	PL	CO	SPOUSE NAME	CODE
TROXLER, ELIZABETH	1775	NC	073					1 1799	NC	073	PETER HUFFMAN	27435
TROXLER, GEORGE H	C1775			1826	NC	073		1 C1802	NC	?073	MARGARET SHAW	60145
TRULOVE, LUCINDY					MO			1 1830	NC	092	WILLIAM MORRIS	60325
TRULOVE, SAMUEL					MO			1 1831	NC	092	ELIZABETH MORRIS	60325
TUCKER, ABBIT	1806	NC	046									21167
TUCKER, ANDERTON	1785	NC	046					1 1805	NC	046	STACY STORYE	21167
TUCKER, ANN				C1825	NC	069		1 C1790			JAMES S BATCHELOR	24250
TUCKER, CATHERINE	C1846	NC										60334
TUCKER, CHARITY	C1789			C1866	NC	069		1 1807			WRIGHT STEPHEN BATCHELOR	24250
TUCKER, DAVID, I	C1750			C1823	NC	054	085	1 C1780	NC	054	ESTHER/MARY ROBEY	02295
								2 C1800	NC	054	SALLY PHILLIPS	
TUCKER, DAVID, II	C1790	NC	054	C1876	VA		006	1 C1810	NC	054	POLLY	02295
TUCKER, DAVID, III	C1816	NC	054	C1904	NC	006		1 C1840	NC	006	MAHALA BLEVINS	02295
								2 1902	NC	006	MRS ROXIE (DARNELL) HART	
TUCKER, ELIZABETH A	C1848	NC										60334
TUCKER, JOHN	C1786	NC		C1850	?IL			1			ELIZABETH	60247
TUCKER, JOHN	C1803	NC						1 C1834	NC			60334
TUCKER, JOHN HAMPTON	1851	NC	106	1943	NC	092		1 1869	NC	106	MARY ANN BLAKELY	60334
TUCKER, LEAH	C1800	NC	046		?TN			1 1819	NC	046	WILLIAM INGLE	21167
TUCKER, LEVI	C1760	DE		1816	NC	046		1 C1782	?MD		MARGARET CAUSEY	21167
								2 1812			MARGARET THOMPSON	
TUCKER, LUKE	C1790	?NC	?035	C1870	NC	035		1 C1810			MARGARET PATTERSON	25254
TUCKER, MARGARET F	C1840	NC										60334
TUCKER, MARY M	C1849	NC										60334
TUCKER, NANCY	C1786	NC	046					1 C1807	?MD		CHARLES CAUSEY	21167
TUCKER, NANCY C	C1835	NC										60334
TUCKER, NATHAN	C1842	NC										60334
TUCKER, ROBERT D	C1838	NC										60334
TUCKER, SAMUEL	C1760	DE		1819	KY		046	1 1780			POLLY	21167
TUCKER, THOMAS	1816	?NC		1902	IL			1 1833	TN		ELIZABETH HUTSON	60105
TUCKER, WILLIAM C	C1844	NC										60334
TUCKER, ZADOCK	1793	NC	046	1875	NC	046		1 1818	NC	046	MARY TYRE	21167
TUGMAN, NANCY	C1807	NC		C1860	NC	?102		1 C1834	NC		BENJAMIN BROWN	60557
TUGMAN, WILLIAM	C1780	SC			NC	?006		1 C1805	NC		MARY HAWKINS	60557
TUMBLESON, ANN ELIZABETH	C1790	NC			IL		061	1 C1815	NC	?049	DAVID LAIRD	60323
TUNNELL, JOSEPH	1791			1843	NC	053		1			ESTHER GASKINS	20335
TUNSTALL, JOHN B	1792	VA		1862	NC	044		1 1823	VA		TABITHY GRIFFIN	06065
TUNSTALL, PATRICK ANDERSON	1832	VA		1881	NC	044		1 1859	NC	044	CELESTIA ANNA VAUGHEN	06065

ANCESTOR INDEX	BIRTH	PL	CO	DEATH	PL	CO	LIVD	MARRIED	PL	CO	SPOUSE NAME	CODE
TUNSTALL, VIRGINIA	1870	NC	044	1903	NC	044		1 1891	NC	044	WILLIAM RUFFIN BUCHANAN	06065
TURLINGTON, ELI SR	1829	NC	?056	1887	NC	056		1	NC	056	SARA WOODALL	03315
TURLINGTON, JIMMY	1857	NC	?056	1935	NC	?056		1	NC	056	SALLIE STEWART	03315
TURLINGTON, WILLIAM				C1795	NC	?063		1			MARY EASTWOOD	03315
TURLINGTON, WILLIS	1784	NC	063	1870	NC	056		1 1814	NC	029	SABRA CARTER	03315
TURNAGE, PENELOPE	C1773	NC	034		NC	?079		1 C1790	NC	034	BALAAM BELL	06050
								2 C1803	NC	079	JOSHUA DEANS ?	
TURNER, ANNA	C1785	VA		1839	AL		020	1 1805	VA		WILLIAM C BULL	60532
TURNER, FREDERICK	1762	NC		1829	TN			1 C1786	NC	028	MARY JONES	20080
TURNER, JOHN				C1795	NC	028						20080
TURNER, MARTIN	C1770	VA		1829	NC	020		1			MILDRED	60532
TURNER, THOMAS				1788	NC	100		1			MRS REBECCA TURNER	60594
TUSSEY, JOHN							085	1 C1790	NC	085	ELIZABETH HUNT	60027
TUSSEY, JONATHAN	1793	NC	085	1859	MO			1 1819	KY		MARY/POLLY DEWEESE	60027
TUTEN, CLAUDE E		?NC	009		NC	009		1			AMANDA TOLER	21175
TUTOR, MARSHALL ANDREW	1842	NC	099	1928	NC	099		1	NC	099	LAURA COTTEN	02450
TUTOR, OWEN	1820	NC	099					1			LUCINDA DAVIS	02450
TUTOR, SARA/SALLY DORA	1881	NC	099	1957	NC	048		1	NC	099	NATHAN IRA/A WESTER	02450
TUTTLE, BENJAMIN	C1790							1	NC		GATSEY FOX	60329
TUTTLE, JAMES	C1804				NC	090		1			NANCY	20448
TUTTLE, JOHN P	C1810				NC	?090		1			PHEBY	20448
TUTTLE, NOAH	1830	NC	079	1901	IA			1 1855	IA		BARBARA TEAS	60329
								2 1881	IA		MARGERY WILLIAMS	
TUTTLE, WILLIAM H	C1807	NC	?090	C1860	IN			1 1832	NC	090	CATHERINE REDDICK	25087
TWIFORD, WILLIAM TRUXTON	1805	NC	096					1 1841	NC	096	ANNIE OWENS	13120
TYNER/TYNOR, NICHOLAS	1749			1852			071	1			REBECCA	12008
TYSON, AARON JR	1825	NC	081	1864	?GA			1 1851	NC	068	ELIZA ANNE JOHNSON	60147
TYSON, AARON SR	1799	NC	?081	1852				1 1820			WINNIFRED NALL	60147
								2			MISS/MRS BURROUGHS	
								3 1837			MARY JANE	
TYSON, WILLIAM E	1853	NC	068	1928	AL			1 1872	AL		VIRGINIA CLAY DAVIS	60147
TYSOR, JULIA LACY	1877	NC	022	1965	VA			1 1897	NC	022	BENJAMIN JOSEPH BEALE	60172
TYSOR, LEONIDAS ALONZO	C1850	NC	?022	1926	VA			1 1876	NC	022	FANNIE HEATON MAUZY	60172

U

UNDERWOOD, JAMES	1752	NC	073	1884	OH			1	NC		MARGARET CAMPBELL	60194
UNDERWOOD, JOHN	C1780	NC	022		IN			1	NC	022	SALLY WATSON	60194

ANCESTOR INDEX	BIRTH	PL	CO	DEATH	PL	CO	LIVD	MARRIED	PL	CO	SPOUSE NAME	CODE
UNDERWOOD, JOHN					NC			1			CINTHIA BANDY	60463
UNDERWOOD, SAMUEL		PA		1774	NC	073		1 1738	PA		ANN TRAVILLER	60194
UNTHANK, JOSEPH		ENG						1			ANNA	60386
								2 1779	NC	046	MRS JUDITH (HORN?) THORNBURGH	
UNTHANK, JOSIAH	1780	NC	046					1 1801	NC	046	ANNIE BRITTAIN/BRITTON	60386
UNTHANK, REBECCA	1806	NC	046	1897	IN			1 1824	NC	046	JOHN HIATT	60386
UPTON, ADELAIDE L	1871	NC	018	1952	VA		030	1 1889	NC	018	MARK ROBERTS GREGORY	60307
UPTON, JOHN	C1770	NC	029	C1845	IL		022	1			ELEANOR BAXLEY	60270
								2			OZINA SHAW	
UPTON, JOHN	1839	NC	018	1892	NC	018		1 1867			CAROLINE JARVIS	60307
UPTON, JOSEPH	1803	NC	022	1861	IL			1 1830	IL		LORANNA MOORE	60270
UPTON, THOMAS	C1815			1848	NC	018		1			LUCY	60307
USSERY, MARY	1785	SC		C1865	TN		067	1 C1800	TN		SYLVANIUS FOWLER	06005
USSERY, WELCOME	1762	?NC					067	1	NC		LUCY GROCE	06005
USSERY, WILLIAM	C1727	VA					005	1	VA		SARAH BAYES	06005

V

ANCESTOR INDEX	BIRTH	PL	CO	DEATH	PL	CO	LIVD	MARRIED	PL	CO	SPOUSE NAME	CODE
VALENTINE, THOMAS T	C1786	NC	?069	1877	TN			2	?TN		MARY	60093
								3 1859	KY		LAVINIA UPCHURCH HENSON	
VAN HOOSER, ABRAHAM	C1756	NC		1834	IL			1			MARY WILLIAMS	27553
VAN HOY, ABRAHAM SR	1783			1860	MO			1 C1805	NC	090	VIRLINDA MARSHALL	27631
VAN HOY, JOHN SR		HOL		1798	NC	090		1	DE		ANN BUCKMASTER	27631
								2			JEMIMA	
VAN HOY, WILLIAM								1 1808	NC		SALLY JACKS	27631
VAN HOY, WILLIAM	C1810				NC	?089						60288
VAN HUSS, VALENTINE	1768	NC		1856	TN		085	1	VA		ABIGAIL WORLEY	06005
VANCE, MATTHEW	1764	SC		C1835	NC	014		1 C1790	SC		BARBARA MCVEY/MCVAY	23040
VANCE, TEMPERANCE	C1785			C1855	NC	107		1 C1805	NC	014	ARTHUR BUCHANAN	02470
VANCE, THOMAS	1800	SC		1851	NC	107		1 1828	NC	014	ELIZABETH BLALOCK	23040
VANDERPOOL, ABRAHAM	1766	NC	?085	C1833	?IN		006	1			PHOEBE ISAACS	60343
VANDERPOOL, ABRAHAM	1766	NC	?085	C1832	?IN			1 C1793	?NC	?104	PHOEBE ISAACS	60352
VANDERPOOL, ABRAHAM	1709	NY		C1778	NC	?104		1 C1734	?NJ		JANNETJE WIBLING	60352
								2 C1745	?VA		REBECCA	
VANDERPOOL, WILLIAM	1808	NC	006	1884	OK			1 1828	KY		MARY FUSON	60343
VANNOY, SAMUEL	1792	NC	104					1 1811			SALLY HOPPER	02252
VANNOY, TEMPERANCE/TEMPY	1789	NC	104					1 1808			DANIEL CAIN	02252
VANNOY, WILLIAM	1770	NC	104	1845	KY			1 1788			MARY	02252
VANOVER, NANCY		NC	006	1897	VA			1 1847	VA		WILLIAM KELLY KEEL	02470

ANCESTOR INDEX	BIRTH	PL	CO	DEATH	PL	CO	LIVD	MARRIED	PL	CO	SPOUSE NAME	CODE
VARBEL/WIRBLE, PHILIP		GER		C1778	NC	085		1 C1750	PA		DOROTHY GREENLIEF	27594
VARNER, JOHN ADAM	C1700	GER			NC	081		1			CATHARINE	60294
VAUGHAN, GEORGE WASHINGTON	C1803	NC		C1872	AL			1	?NC		EVE STROP	60039
VAUGHN, JESSE	1807	NC	090	1886	IN			1 1826	NC	090	OMARANNAH/MARANDA HALE	60237
								2 1850	IN		MRS HANNAH NEEDY	
								3 1877	IN		MRS FRANCES (PHELPS) HERRON	
VAUGHN, ZEBULON	C1764	NC		C1831	NC	090		1 1799	NC	090	REBECCA BASE	60237
								2 1817	NC	090	POLLY LISTER	
VENABLE/VENERABLE, MARY	1800	NC		1860	GA			1 1814	GA		WILLIAM OLIVER	60175
VESTAL, DAVID	1764	NC		1851	TN			1 1791	NC	092	MARY LONGINO	60251
VESTAL, JESSE	C1812	NC	022	1863	MO			1	NC			60570
								2	KY		MRS MARTHA/PATSY (DAVIS) KING	
VIARS, FANNIE	1780	NC	104	1847				1 1802	NC	104	BENJAMIN DARNELL	10154
VIARS, WILLIAM	1756	VA		1837	NC	104		1			ANNE SHEPHERD	10154
VILLINES, WILLIAM		?020						1 1825		078	MARY COCHRAN	60595
VINSON, JAMES	C1787	NC		1827	VA			1 1811	KY		RHODA SPERRY	60232
VINSON, NELLIE		NC						1			ALIE LEDFORD	60232
VINSON, THOMAS							071	1			ISABELLE	60331
VOGLEMAN/FOGLEMAN, GEORGE	C1705	GER		1785	NC	073		1 C1723	GER			60337
VOLK/FOLK/FOWLKES, ANDREAS SR	1722	GER		1790	NC	090	092	1	PA		ANNA MARGARETHA	60120
VOLK/FOLK/FOWLKES, ANDREW JR	C1765	PA		1815	NC	092	090	1 1788	NC	090	CATHARINE BOECKEL	60120
VOLK/FOLK/FOWLKES, HENRY	C1790	NC	092		NC	092		1 1813	NC	092	CEALY KING	60120
VOLK/FOLK/FOWLKES, REBECCA JANE	1848	NC	006	1922	VA		004	1 1865	NC	004	MARION BAZEL TAYLOR HAMM	60120
VOLK/FOLK/FOWLKES,WILLIAM ANDREW JACKSON	1815	NC	092	1896	NC	004	006	1 C1837	NC	104	MARY ANN LANE	60120
VONCANNON, JOHN	C1735	HOL		C1840	NC	014						03041

W

ANCESTOR INDEX	BIRTH	PL	CO	DEATH	PL	CO	LIVD	MARRIED	PL	CO	SPOUSE NAME	CODE
WACASTER, MICHAEL	1774	NC		C1872	AR			1			ELIZABETH	60132
WADDELL, ISABEL	C1754			1830	TN			1 1777	NC	085	WILLIAM MCKNIGHT	60443
WADDELL, WILLIAM							085					60443
WADDILL, CALVIN	C1816	NC		C1879	?NC	?005	005	1			MARY?	60584
WADDILL, FRANK	C1854	NC	?005	C1890	NC		097	1 1877	NC	005	JANE ELIZABETH DAVIS	60584
WADSWORTH, ADAM RINGSTAFF	1811			1880	NC	068		1			JENNIE GILCHRIST	22005
WADSWORTH, DELANEY/DELANA					?NC			1 1795	NC	028	JAMES BEESLEY	27600
WADSWORTH, JOHN WILLIAM	C1760	NC	029	1826	NC	068		1 C1785	NC		SARAH MCSWEEN	60040
WADSWORTH, MARTHA ADELAIDE	1863	NC	068	1936	NC	068		1 1881	NC	068	NEILL BLUE CAMERON	22005

ANCESTOR INDEX	BIRTH	PL	CO	DEATH	PL	CO	LIVD	MARRIED	PL	CO	SPOUSE NAME	CODE
WADSWORTH, NANCY	C1790	NC	068	C1847	GA			1 C1808	NC		DOUGALD MCKEITHAN	60040
WAGGONER, JOSEPH	1747	NC		1845	NC	090	092	1 C1772	NC	?090	DELPHUS/DELPHY	04195
WAGGONER, LEWIS	C1773	NC	?090	1830	NC	090		1 C1795	NC	090	ELIZABETH CROW ?	04195
WAGGONER, LEWIS								1 C1808	NC	090	LYDIA VASS ?	60456
WAGGONER, MILLY	1785			1840	NC	090		1 1802	NC	090	THOMAS MARSHALL	60456
WAGGONER, SAMUEL	1720	NC	?028	1805	NC	090	092	1 C1745				04195
WAGLEY/WAGLE/WEIGLE, ABRAHAM	1767	?PA		1843	TX		014	1			MARIA HENSON	03041
WAGLEY/WAGLE/WEIGLE, BARTLETT	1802	NC	014	1857	LA			1			MELINDA SCALLORN	03041
WAGLEY/WAGLE/WEIGLE, ELIZABETH	1767	NC	014									03041
WAGLEY/WAGLE/WEIGLE, JOHN	1798	NC	014	1868	AR			1			MARY ELIZA ALEXANDER	03041
WAGLEY/WAGLE/WEIGLE, JOSEPH	1804	NC	014	1878	TX			1			MARTHA STARKS	03041
WAGLEY/WAGLE/WEIGLE, MATILDA	1806	NC	014									03041
WAGLEY/WAGLE/WEIGLE, PHILLIP	1800	NC	014									03041
WAGONER, GEORGE	1796			1845	NC	046		1 1816	NC	?073	REBECCA WHITESELL	27542
WAGONER, GEORGE QUINCE	1831	NC		1912	NC	046		1 1854	NC	046	RACHEL KERNODLE	27542
								2 1896	NC	046	MARGARET SCOTTEN	
								3 1900	NC	046	NANCY HANNAH TROXLER	
WALKER, ABSALOM	1780	NC		1854	SC			1	SC		SUSANNAH JACKSON	60038
WALKER, ANNA M	1832	NC	046	1907	KS		081	1 1854			ELI STALEY MILLER	60480
WALKER, ANNE	1754	NC	085	1848	NC	049	014	1 C1781	NC	085	JOHN A BURNS/BURNES	23065
WALKER, ARON							100	1 1799	NC	099	NANCY PATTERSON	24012
WALKER, DAVID				C1778	NC	090		1 C1764			ANN SAVAGE ?	27686
WALKER, EDWARD	C1745	VA		C1799	NC			1 1776	VA		NANCY LARNED	60585
WALKER, JESSE	C1794	NC	086	1891	NC	086		1 1818	NC	086	MANIMIE WHITAKER	05070
WALKER, JOHN	1748	VA		1820	NC	086		1 1773	NC	046	URCILLA COVINGTON	05070
WALKER, JOHN	1761	?VA		1850	TN			1 C1795	NC	092	ELIZABETH JARVIS	27686
WALKER, JOHN ANDREW	1849	NC	104	1931	CO			1 1867	TN		MARTHA A SHARPE/SHUPE	27332
								2 1877	TN		WINA S WAGNER	
								3			POLLY	
WALKER, JOHN CALVIN							028					27548
WALKER, MAHLON CRAFFORD/CRAWFORD	1853	NC	028	1933	TX			1 1877	MO		ELIZA ANN HENSON	27548
WALKER, MARTHA ELLEN	C1833	NC			TN							60538
WALKER, MARY	C1740			C1798	NC	081	046	1	NC	?081	JAMES HUNTER	01040
WALKER, MOSES				1806	NC	078		1			ANNE	60050
WALKER, MOSES	C1728	NC	?010	1806	NC	078	020	1 C1752	?NC		NANCY/ANN	60494
WALKER, NANCY	C1781	NC	084	1837	TN		046	1 C1804	NC		WILLIAM WEATHERLY	60171
WALKER, RICHARD	1750	?VA		1831	TN		?104	1 1790	NC	014	ANSON SWEARNIGEN	27268
WALKER, SAMUEL	C1705	?PA		1783	NC	081						01040
WALKER, SAMUEL	C1775	NC		1858	NC	092		1 C1800	NC	092	HULDAH	12065

ANCESTOR INDEX	BIRTH	PL	CO	DEATH	PL	CO	LIVD	MARRIED	PL	CO	SPOUSE NAME	CODE
WALKER, SAMUEL	C1775	NC	?092	1858	NC	092		1			HULDA	14045
WALKER, SAMUEL	1789	NC		1865	MO			1			AGNES BRADFORD	60585
WALKER, SARAH ELIZABETH	1766				AL			1	1784	NC	092	EDMUND PACE	27686
WALKER, WINNEY								1	1822	NC	086	SIMMON BRADLEY	27268
WALL, HENRY	C1819	NC			IN		022	1	C1842	NC		JULIA	25159
WALL, ISSAC	C1794	NC	084					1	1818	NC	084	NANCY DUNCAN	05045
WALL, MARY	C1851	NC		C1890	AR		022	1			ROBERT A GILLIAM	25159
WALL, SAMUEL				1823	NC	081		1			MARY	17150
WALL, SOLOMAN	1782			1863	NC	081		1	1813	NC	081	MARY SAXTON	17150
WALL, WILLIAM MADISON	1821	NC	084	1869	UT			1	1840	IL		NANCY HAWS	05045
WALLACE, JOEL	1771	NC	065					1	C1794	TN		ESTHER HOUSTON	60395
								2	1828	AL		MRS REBECCA (WALL) SULLICK JONES	
WALLACE, JOHN C	1797	NC	016	1888	MO			1	1824			ELIZABETH TURNER ABERNATHY	20078
WALLACE, WILLIAM BLOUNT	1803	NC	?073	1888	GA			1	1825	NC	073	LAVINIA DESHONG	02170
WALLACE/WALLIS, THOMAS				1750	NC	024		1			ELIZABETH ROUNTREE ?	19130
WALSTON, HENRY		?NC		1849	GA		037	1		?NC	MARY	02170
WALSTON, PENINA	1810	NC		1876				1			THOMAS VAN SWEARINGEN	60381
WALTERS, JOHN	C1814	NC	083	C1902	NC	083		1		NC	083	LUCY J NANCE	60335
WALTERS, JOSEPH	C1840	NC	083	C1920	NC	083		1	C1869	NC	083	BETTIE SEALY	60335
WALTERS, LARKIN J	C1818	NC					054	1	C1841	NC		CASANDRA	60485
WALTERS, MASTON	C1882	NC	083	C1954	NC	083		1	C1904		083	CATTIE JOHNSON	60335
WALTERS, WILLIAM JR	C1781	NC	034	C1859	NC	083		1		NC	083	ABSELA PITTMAN	60335
WALTERS, WILLIAM SR	C1760			C1830	NC	083							60335
WALTON, ISAAC	1763	NC		1840	TN		024	1	C1783	NC	?010	CATHARINE PERRY	01006
								2	1825	TN		MRS ELIZABETH (WHITE) MANSKER	
WALTON, JESSIE	1732	VA			GA		092	1			MARY WALKER	60581
WALTON, MILDRED	C1760	?NC			TN			1		?NC	JOHN CRANE	60581
WALTON, REUBIN	1777	VA						1	1806	NC	078	ELIZABETH BRADSHEAR	03183
WALTON, WILLIAM				C1771	NC	024	010	1			RACHEL HUNTER	01006
WALTON, WILLIAM	C1775	?NC		1850				1			ELIZABETH CLEVELAND	60581
WARD, DAVID LINNEY				C1829	NC	085		1			LYDIA	08023
WARD, ELIZABETH							085	1			WILLIAM HADDOX	08023
WARD, ENOCH	1799	NC	083	1871	NC	083		1			EMILY RHODES	12144
WARD, ENOCH	1799			1876	NC	050		1	C1827			ISABELLA BANKS	27334
WARD, JAMES				C1743	NC	024		1			MARY	13175
WARD, JOHN	C1685	VA		1749	NC	096	010	1	C1705	NC	077	MRS ELIZABETH	24055
WARD, RACHEL								1	C1721	NC	024	JOSEPH MING	13175
WARD, TEMPE SARAH ANN	C1827	NC	?029	1890	CA			1	C1849	?TN	ANDREW WHITLEY ROGERS	60551

ANCESTOR INDEX	BIRTH	PL	CO	DEATH	PL	CO	LIVD	MARRIED	PL	CO	SPOUSE NAME	CODE
WARDEN, PETER	C1802	NC			IL			1 C1827			MILLY	60029
WARLICK, DANIEL		GER			NC	060	065	1			MARA BARBARA	25100
WARREN, BRISCO M STONE	1798	NC	073	1880	MO			1 1824	NC	073	ADALINE TROXLER	60145
WARREN, FREDERIC	1798	CT		1869	GA			1 1826	NC	005	MARY ANN MCREA	27313
WARREN, JACOB	C1755	?NC		1816	TN							04080
WARREN, JAMES MADISON	1786			1876	IN			1 1810	NC	081	ELEBTH CAVNESS	25196
WARREN, MARY ANN	1836	NC	073	1891	MO			1 1856	MO		GEORGE MICHAEL MALVIN	60145
WARREN, MARY/POLLY	C1790	NC						1 C1805 2 1830 3			THOMAS HOLMAN JESSE SPENCER EDWARDS	04080
WARREN, WILLIAM		?NC		C1885	NC	084	020	1			ANNY/ANNIE/AMY	60171
WARTERS, MARTHA	1845	NC	103	1925	NC	103	059	1 1864	NC	103	WILLIAM M GARRIS	07040
WARTERS, NEEDHAM	1802	NC	103	1857	NC	103	059	1 1838			PENELOPE HILL	07040
WASHBURN, GABRIEL	1752			1826	NC	086		1 1778			MRS PRISCILLA (MCSWAIN) JONES	05070
WASHBURN, JOHN	1780	NC	086	1857	NC	026		1	NC	086	MARY ANN MAGNESS	05070
WASHBURN, MOSES	1763	VA		1843	NC	107	014	1 1792	VA		AGATHA ETHERTON	25087
WASHBURN, PRISCILLA MAUNEY	1819	NC	086	1888	NC	026		1 1842	NC	026	ANDERSON CROWDER WILLIAMSON	05070
WASSON, ARCHIBALD	C1719	IRE		1785	NC	085		1 C1741 2 1769	?PA NC	085	ELIZABETH WOODS MRS ANN(KING)LANSDALE	60342
WATERS, ROBERT FRANKLIN	1856	NC	045	1909	AR		103	1 1878 2 1888	TN AR		NANCY E THOMPSON MRS MARGARET (ANDERSON) STAGGS	20007
WATERS, SIMON PETER	1828	NC	045	1907	AR		?059	1 1856 2 C1901	NC AR	103	NANCY JANE BRITT MRS MARTHA (SCOTT) CAMP/KENT	20007
WATFORD, WILLIAM	1755	NC	?010	1846	NC	010		1 1779 2 1816 3	NC NC NC	010 010 010	MRS PRESCILLA(OUTLAW)FRAZER MRS REBECCA OUTLAW ELIZABETH	60337
WATKINS, JOHN	C1749	MD		1822	TN		085	1 C1769 2 1787	MD NC	085	MARY BEALL MARY JONES	60249
WATKINS, JOHN				C1842	NC	100		1			MRS FANNY (LINDSAY) WATKINS	60594
WATKINS, JOHN B	C1773	MD		C1845	TN		085	1 1800	NC	085	SUSANNAH HUGHES	60249
WATKINS, PETER	C1755	NC	037	1824	KY			1 1789	NC	056	DELILAH GRICE	60109
WATKINS, STEPHEN	1790	NC	?035	1855	KY			1 1811	KY		POLLY/MARY HOLMES	60109
WATKINS, WILLIAM	C1710			1773	NC	079		1 C1740 2 C1770	NC NC	009 079	JANE DURDEN ? CHRISTIAN	13264
WATKINS, WILLIAM				1808	TN		085	1 1796	NC	085	SYLVIA WOOD	60249
WATLINGTON, FRANCES	1824	NC	020	C1890	NC	046		1 1854	NC	046	DAVID CHRISMON	60388
WATLINGTON, LEONIDAS L	1841	NC	?020	1920	NC	084		1 1867	NC	046	JANE HARIETT CHRISMON	60388
WATSON, CLAIBORN								1 1785	NC	092	NANCY HESTER	13120
WATSON, DAVID		SCO		C1822	NC	104		1	NC	104	HAMBY	60387
WATSON, DRURY	1800	NC	090					1 1824	NC	090	MARTHA HESTER	13120
WATSON, EPHRAIM				1821			056					60304
WATSON, JAMES	C1793	NC	099	C1859	NC	104		1 1822	NC	104	ELIZABETH DAVIS	60387

ANCESTOR INDEX	BIRTH	PL	CO	DEATH	PL	CO	LIVD	MARRIED	PL	CO	SPOUSE NAME	CODE
WATSON, JESSE FRANKLIN	1854	NC	104	1929	MO			1 1875	MO		JANE SMITH	60387
WATSON, LEWIS	1826	NC	104	1871	MO			1 1846	NC	104	CLARISSA FERGUSON	60387
WATSON, LITTELTON	C1793						056	1 C1820	?VA		ZELLA KEEN	60304
WATSON, ROBERT		VA		1823	NC	022		1			JANE	60194
WATSON, SALLY		VA			IN			1	NC	022	JOHN UNDERWOOD	60194
WATSON, SOLOMON	C1795			C1865			056					60250
WATSON, WILLIAM	C1815	NC	049		NC	023		1 1836	NC	061	LUCINDA MCDOWELL	60261
WATTERS, ELIZABETH MILDRED BROWN	1789			1845	NC	070		1 1810	NC	070	THOMAS JUNIUS DAVIS	27286
WATTERS, WILLIAM SR				1751	NC	070		1			SARAH	27286
WATTERS, WILLIAM, COL	1758	NC	070		NC	070		1			MARY IVIE MOORE	27286
WATTS, ABRAM		NC	?047									20073
WATTS, JOHN	1751	NC	?047		NC	063		1 1772			ELIZABETH	20073
								2 1810	NC	063	ELIZABETH KENNEDY	
WATTS, JOSEPH	C1808	NC		C1871	TN		023	1				24093
								2			NANCY	
WATTS, SAMUEL W S	1826	NC	063					1 1851	NC	063	HARRIET E CRAWFORD	20073
WATTS, WILLIAM	1781	NC	063	1859				1 1802	NC	063	NANCY	20073
								2 1845	NC	063	MARIA CRAWFORD	
								3 1854	NC	063	ANN ROBASON	
WAUSON, WILLIAM PINKNEY	1828	NC	?054	1901	TX			1 1853	AR		MINERVA OLIVE	60025
WEATHERFORD, JAMES PINKERTON	1830	NC			OK			1 1858	TN		SUSAN JANE WEATHERFORD	60554
WEATHERFORD, JOHN	1797	NC	?020	1866	TN			1			JUDITH RAINES	60554
WEATHERFORD, MARTHA		NC										60554
WEATHERFORD, WILLIAM T	1828	NC	020	1908	TN			1	TN		ADALADE HICKS	60554
WEATHERLY, ANDREW	1808	NC	?046	1887	AL			1 1834	AL		ASENATH NICKLES SIMS	60063
WEATHERLY, JAMES	1758			1793			046	1			SARAH MARTIN	60063
WEATHERLY, THOMAS	1734	?VA		1785			046	1			RACHAEL	60063
WEATHERLY, WILLIAM	1783	NC		1865	TN		046	1 C1815	NC	084	NANCY WALKER	60063
WEATHERS, JAMES	C1771	VA		C1863	NC	099		1 1804	NC	099	MARTHA/PATSEY JOYNER	20210
WEATHERS, MARY, MRS				C1805	NC	039						20210
WEATHERS, NANCY							065	1 1800	NC	065	MOSES BEATY	60503
WEATHERS, REBECCA	C1786	?NC			AL		065	1 C1803	NC	065	JAMES JACKSON	60503
WEATHERS, WILLIAM JR	1750	VA		C1782	NC	099		1			ELIZABETH	20210
WEATHERSBY, JOHN ROBERT	1853	NC	069	1929				1 1877			MARY ANN BUNN	04065
WEATHERSBY, WILLIAM STANLEY	1802			1899	NC	069		1 1850	NC	069	LUCINDA HALES	04065
WEATHINGTON, FRANCES MARION	C1805	NC			MO			1			SARAH HOLLIN	60416
WEAVER, BENJAMIN	C1750				NC	037		1			OLIVE	60414
WEBB, ABDIAS P	C1788				GA		022	1 C1808	NC	022	MARY FERRELL	60117
WEBB, EDMUND OLIVER	1809		022		GA							60117

ANCESTOR INDEX	BIRTH	PL	CO	DEATH	PL	CO	LIVD	MARRIED	PL	CO	SPOUSE NAME	CODE
WEBB, ELIZABETH AVERY	1811	NC	022					1 1833	GA		GEORGE W COE	60117
WEBB, JAMES	1791	NC		C1865	MS			1 C1814	AL		MARY FRANCES HARPER	60179
WEBB, MARY EDMONDSON	1782	NC	044	1837	KY			1 1801	NC	044	BAXTER DAVIS	60164
WEBB, ROBERT	1760			1843	NC	026		2			PEGGY ROACH	25100
WEBB, WILLIAM	1745	VA		1809	NC	044		1 1771	VA		FRANCES YOUNG	60164
WEBB, WILLIAM STANFORD	1817	NC	022									60117
WEBSTER, WILLIAM	C1745						081	1			GRACE	24073
WEISS/WISE, FREDERICK				1807	NC	060		1			BARBARA BECKLEY	25100
WEITZEL, ADAM	C1740	?PA		1822	NC	073		1			ANNA MARGARET BOON	25126
WEITZEL, HENRY	C1728	GER		C1798	NC	046		1			ANNA MARIA SOPHRONIA	25126
WEITZEL, JOHN	1750	?PA		1781	NC	046		1 1773	NC	046	ANNA MARIE TROG	25126
WEITZEL, PHILLIP	C1748	?PA		C1792	NC	046						25126
WELBORN, ALLEN GREEN	1824	NC	104					1			MARTHA M	06158
WELBORN, BOYDEN		NC	104									25121
WELBORN, JAMES DUDLEY	1803	NC	?085	18-1	MO			1 1823 2 1845	KY KY		MALINDA NEWMAN ZILPHA D NEWMAN	02135
WELBORN, JAMES HENRY	1811	NC	085	1899	MO			1 1836 2 1843	 IN		MARY R MOORE ELIZA JANE GAMBREL	17235
WELBORN, JAMES JR	1771	NC	085	1826	KY			1			ELIZABETH DUDLEY	02135
WELBORN, JAMES M		NC	104					1			NETTIE WELLS/WILES	25121
WELBORN, JAMES SR	1736	NC	?085	1811	KY			1			ISABEL TEAGUE	02135
WELBORN, JAMES W/M	C1817	NC	104					1			EMALINE	06158
WELBORN, JOHN O	C1828	NC	104	?1865				1 2 1860	NC NC	104 104	ADELINE/ADDIE GREEN MARY A SHORES/SHORS	06158
WELBORN, LAURA		NC	104					1			JOHNSON	25121
WELBORN, LEANDER	1844	NC	092	1917	SD			1 2 1880	 TN		MARTHA BROWN ALICE OWENS	25121
WELBORN, MAYBERRY	1795	VA		1878	NC	104		1 1815 2 1862	NC NC	104 104	ELIZABETH GREEN NANCY PRITCHETT	06158
WELBORN, MAYBERRY	1795	VA		1878	NC	104		1 1815 2 1862	NC NC	104 104	ELIZABETH GREEN NANCY PRITCHETT	25121
WELBORN, MELINE		NC	104									25121
WELBORN, MOSES	1783	NC	085	1851	IN			1 1807	NC	046	DEBORAH CHIPMAN	17235
WELBORN, PRUDENCE	1811			C1871	IL		085	1 C1828	NC	032	RUBEN KENNEDAY	60567
WELBORN, RANDEL	C1797	VA			NC	104						06158
WELBORN, SALLIE		NC	104					1			BARBER	25121
WELBORN, THOMAS	1735	NC	?010	1778	NC	?046		1 C1754	NC	?056	ESTHER	02135
WELBORN, TILDIA		NC	104									25121
WELBORN, WILLIAM	1733	NC	?070	1792	NC	?104		1	NC		HEPSIBAH STEARNS	02135
WELCH, JAMES D	1811	NC		1890	NC			1 1838			CAROLINE BULLOCH	60002

ANCESTOR INDEX	BIRTH	PL	CO	DEATH	PL	CO	LIVD	MARRIED	PL	CO	SPOUSE NAME	CODE
WELCH, JOHN		NC		1858	NC							60002
WELLMAN, JEREMIAH				1834	NC	085		1 1805	NC	085	MARY SAIN	02170
WELLS, HAYDON	C1744	VA		C1820	?AL		035	1 C1762			MARGARET	60576
WESCOTT, HENRY ARTHUR	1841	NC	012	1881	NC	012		1 1867	NC	070	CATHERINE M BEACH	05070
WESCOTT, LEWIS W	1809			1874	NC	012		1 1829			ELIZABETH STANLEY	05070
WESCOTT, MINNIE OLA KING	1869	NC	012	1947	NC	079		1 1886	NC	012	GEORGE HOLLAND PIVER	05070
WEST, DICEA EASTINGS	1801	NC	022	1887	NC	022		1 1818	NC	022	WESLEY MANN	08200
WEST, IGNATIUS	1750	NC	044	1831	NC	022		1 1777	NC	022	ELIZABETH MEACHAM	08200
WEST, JOHN	C1730	?NC		C1777	GA			1 C1753	NC		ELEANOR	27566
WEST, THOMAS	C1720			1808	NC	022	044	1			LUCY	08200
WESTBROOK, URIAH N	1826	NC		1892	NC			1			ELIZABETH DOUGHTRY	08219
WESTER, NATHAN IRA/A	1877	NC	048	1861	NC	048		1	NC	048	SARA DORA TUTOR	02450
WESTER, NORMA BLANCHE	1905	NC	048					1 1925	SC		ROYAL REAMS BROWN	02450
WESTER, SIDNEY JACKSON	1850	NC	048	1932	NC	048		1	NC	048	LOUISA JONES	02450
WESTMORELAND, MARTIN	1818			1873	NC	038		1 1845	NC	090	NANCY EMILY FULP	60456
WETHERINGTON, CLEMENTINE/CLEMMIE	1891	NC	028	1973	VA		072	1 1910	NC	028	JOSEPH ARCHIE SMITH	01012
WETHERINGTON, GASTON LENOIR	1858	NC	028	1927	NC	072		1 1882	NC	028	ANN/ANNIE DIXON WILLIS	01012
WHALEY, SAMUEL	C1820	?NC			?NC	?035		1 C1867	NC	?035	BETSY	24139
WHATLEY, ELISHA SR	C1769	NC	?100	1843	AL		073	1 C1794	GA		FERSEY GIBBS	60112
WHATLEY, SHIRLEY	C1700	VA		1783	NC	100	044	1 C1717	VA		REBECCA WHARTON	60112
WHEDBEE, RICHARD	1687			1746	NC	077		1 1709 2 C1729	NC	077	SARAH DURANT HANNAH REED ?	19230
WHEELER, ABSALOM	C1808	NC		1894	GA			1 1832	NC	104	ELIZABETH ELLER	60485
WHEELER, AMOS	C1779	MD			GA		006	1 C1800			SARAH	60485
WHEELER, BENJAMIN	C1790	NC	046					1 C1820	NC	046	AMY FRAZIER	06158
WHEELER, DAVID POTTER	1824	NC		1908	TX			1 1843	TN		HARRIET ELVIRA POPLIN	60204
WHEELER, ELIZABETH	C1811	NC	046					1 1831	NC	046	GEORGE B FRAZIER	06158
WHEELER, ELIZABETH	1829	NC	046	1914	NC	038		1 1853	NC	046	WILLIAM THOMAS MILLIS	60467
WHEELER, JESSIE		NC		1885	TN							60204
WHEELER, JOHN THOMAS		NC	?046					1			ELIZABETH LEDBETTER	60467
WHEELER, JOSEPH							?044					60029
WHEELER, MARY ANN	C1819	NC						1 1837	TN		JESSEE WASHINGTON GLIMP	60029
WHEELER, MILLY	C1782	NC			TN			1 1799	NC	044	GEORGE GLIMP	60029
WHEELER, NANCY	1802	NC	084	1887	IL			1 1828	VA		RUBEN BURCHAM	60022
WHEELER, RICHARD	C1775	NC	046	C1823	NC	046		1 C1800	NC	046	MARY	06158
WHEELER, SAMUEL	1815	NC			TN			1			LOUISA POPLIN	60204
WHEELEY, BENJAMIN				1829	NC	073		1			DOROTHY	60559
WHEELEY, JULIUS COLUMBIA FRANKLIN	1870	NC		1943	NC	078		1 1889	NC	078	EMILY THOMAS TRIM	60559

ANCESTOR INDEX	BIRTH	PL	CO	DEATH	PL	CO	LIVD	MARRIED	PL	CO	SPOUSE NAME	CODE
WHEELEY, OBADIAH B	C1841	NC		C1907	NC			1 1865	NC	078	MILDRED BRADSHER	60559
WHEELEY, WILLIAM/BILLIE	C1809	NC			NC			1 1834	NC	078	NANCY BLALOCK	60559
WHIDDON, LOTT	1797	NC		1880	GA			1 C1816			JUDITH DORMINEY	27756
WHIDDON, WILLIAM	C1760	NC		1818	GA			1			MARY DAVIS	27756
WHITAKER, ABRAM	1775	NC	?092	1867	NC	086		1	NC		NANCY SMITH	05070
WHITAKER, JOSHUA JR	1769	NC	085	1856	NC	013		1 1792	NC	085	NANCY CHILDERS	23065
WHITAKER, JOSHUA SR	1735	PA		1798	NC	085		1 1764	NC	085	MARY REED	23065
WHITAKER, MANIMIE	1801	NC	086	1877	NC	086		1 1818	NC	086	JESSE WALKER	05070
WHITAKER, MARGARET	1807	NC	013	1891	NC	013		1 1826	NC	013	DAVID GARREN	23065
WHITAKER, MIRIAM	1786	NC	085	1824	NC	013		1 C1804	NC	?013	LOT HARPER	23065
WHITAKER, PETER	1733	PA		1815	NC	013	085	1 1767	NC	085	MIRIAM F KENT	23065
WHITAKER, WILLIAM	1705	ENG		C1788	NC	085		1 1722	PA		ELIZABETH CARLETON	23065
WHITE, ABIGAIL	1833	NC	077	1897	IN			1 1868	IN		ROBERT COOK JOHNSON	10060
WHITE, ALICE HENRIETTA	1862	NC	064	1908	MS			1 1883	GA		LAURENCE STEWART WALL	60592
WHITE, DAVID				?NC	?081			1 1824	NC	081	RUTH BLAIR	60482
WHITE, GARDNER	C1788	NC		?NC	?064		014	1 1808	NC	099	SARAH BARLOW	60592
WHITE, GEORGE HENRY	1849	NC	022	1921	AR		099	1 1873	NC	099	ANNIE NICHOLS	20007
WHITE, GEORGE W	1830	NC	081	C1907	IA			1 1849	IN		MARY OWEN	60482
WHITE, HENRY	C1800	NC	010	1866	NC	010		1 C1825	NC	010	MARTHA	25226
WHITE, JACOB HILL JR	1814	NC	010	C1870				1	NC	010	E MILLIE HUGHES	12068
WHITE, JACOB SR	C1779	NC	010	C1835				1 1804	NC	010	ELIZABETH HOGGARD	12068
WHITE, JAMES SR		IRE					016					60093
WHITE, JAMES TAYLOR							014					60496
WHITE, JOABERT	C1805	NC	?060		GA			1 1829	NC	060	SALLY/SARAH MOWSER	60524
WHITE, JOEL	C1774			1845	IN			1	NC		SUSANNAH SEARS	60530
WHITE, JOHN		?NC			NC	077		1 1757	NC	077	LYDIA WINSLOW	10060
WHITE, JOHN JR	1770			1829	NC	022		1			HESTER BRANTLEY	20007
WHITE, JOHN SR		ENG		1799	NC	022	073	1			MARY	20007
WHITE, JOSEPH	1776	NC	073	C1860	MO			1 1811	?NC		MARGARET MABON/MEBANE	60142
								2 C1830	?TN		CATHERINE DAVIS	
WHITE, JOSEPH JOHN SR	1849	NC	010	1927	NC	010		1 1881	NC	010	ROSA GERTRUDE CAPEHART	12068
WHITE, JOSEPH W	C1830	NC	010	C1889	NC	010		1 1852	NC	010	MARTHA A	25226
WHITE, JOSHUA ASBURY	1811			1883	TN			1 1832	NC	044	PRUDENCE BUCHANAN	60234
								2 C1841			PRISCILLA BUCHANAN	
WHITE, JOSHUA SIMEON	C1830						038	1			CHARLOTTE E RIGHTS	20030
WHITE, LUKE SR	C1717	NC	024	C1769	NC	024						12068
WHITE, MEDIA	1785	NC		1855	TN		051	1	NC		MARY PENELOPE	60251

ANCESTOR INDEX	BIRTH	PL	CO	DEATH	PL	CO	LIVD	MARRIED	PL	CO	SPOUSE NAME	CODE
WHITE, REUBEN							014	1			MILLEY ALLEN	60496
WHITE, SAMUEL	1765	NC	077	1813	NC	077		1			ELIZABETH SYMONS	10060
WHITE, SHERWOOD	1810	NC	022	1899	NC	022		1			SUSANNAH BROOKS	20007
WHITE, THADDEUS	1800	NC	077	1865	IN			1	1826	NC	075 ELIZABETH BETSY PRITCHARD	10060
WHITE, WILLIAM				1818	NC	014		1			SOPHIA DAVENPORT	60496
WHITE, WILLIAM	C1828	NC		C1862			064	1	1856	NC	064 ZILPHA C MCKAY	60592
WHITEHEAD, JAMES	C1805	NC	047		NC	047		1	1825	NC	047 TEMPERANCE JONES	60594
WHITEHEAD, JOHN WILLOUGHBY	1826	NC	047					1			LOUVENIA WHITE	60594
WHITEHEAD, LITTLEBERRY JONES	1827	NC	047									60594
WHITEHEAD, SAMUEL BURKETT	1845	NC	047									60594
WHITEHURST, BATSON		?NC	?009		?NC	?079		1		?NC	?009 ELIZABETH	60414
WHITEHURST, RICHARD	C1755	?NC	?009		NC	079		1		NC	?079 POLLY MANNING	60414
WHITEHURST, SIMON	1755	VA		1848	FL		009	1			SCOTT	60384
WHITEHURST, SIMON		?VA			?NC	?009		1			ARGENT COX	60414
WHITEHURST, SUSANNAH	1786	NC	009				028	1	1805		JOHN WALL	60384
WHITENER/WEIDNER, ABEL ADOLPHUS	1826	NC	060	1906	NC	021		1	1848	NC	021 ELIZA GROSS	60534
WHITENER/WEIDNER, AVERY HILL	1862	NC	021	1942	NC	021		1	1889	NC	021 LAURA ELIZABETH WELCH	60534
WHITENER/WEIDNER, DANIEL	1750	NC	?005	1833	NC	060		1	1784	NC	060 MARY WILFONG	60534
WHITENER/WEIDNER, GEORGE	1801	NC	060	1880	NC	021		1	1824	NC	021 MARGARET DELLINGER	60534
WHITENER/WEIDNER, HENRY	1717	GER		1791	NC	060		1	C1745	PA	CATHERINE MUELL	60534
WHITESELL, REBECCA	1801	NC		C1892	NC	?001		1	1816	NC	073 GEORGE WAGONER	27542
WHITFORD, ELIZABETH		NC	?028	C1851	IL			1	1791	NC	028 STEPHEN STILLEY	20415
WHITFORD, MARTIN		NC	?028	C1803	TN			1		NC	?028 SARAH PUREFOY	20415
WHITFORD, MARTIN, REV	C1740						028					60589
WHITLEY, ARTHUR				1775	NC	037		1			SARAH	24250
WHITLEY, GEORGE	C1735				NC	067	?056					24165
WHITLEY, GEORGE				1763	NC	037						24250
WHITLEY, JOSIAH				C1831	NC	069		1			SARAH WHITLEY	24250
WHITLEY, JULIAN					NC	037		1			JACOB BARNES	15045
WHITLEY, SION W				1845	NC	069		1			CHERRY BATCHELOR	24250
WHITLEY, SOLOMON				1819	NC	069		1			NANCY	24250
WHITLEY, WILLIAM				?1751	NC	071		1			JULIAN	15045
WHITLOCK, JOHN NORMONT	C1771	NC	044	1850	IL			1			ABIGAIL	60004
WHITLOW, GRANVILLE H	C1782	NC	?044	1860	MO		044	1	1809	KY	NANCY BYRAM	60068
WHITLOW, HENRY	C1750	?VA		C1789			044	1	C1769	?VA	MARTHA RADFORD	60068
WHITLOW, JOHN	C1735	?VA		C1815	?KY		044	1	1755	VA	CATHERINE BARNET	60068
WHITLOW, JORDON	1760	VA			KY		044					60068

ANCESTOR INDEX	BIRTH	PL	CO	DEATH	PL	CO	LIVD	MARRIED		PL	CO	SPOUSE NAME	CODE
WHITLOW, NATHAN	C1736	?VA					044	1	1756	VA		DIANA HICKS	60068
WHITLOW, PLEASANT	C1765	?NC	?044	C1855	KY			1	1786	NC	044	TABITHA TUDOR	60068
WHITMAN, JAMES	C1785	NC		1847	NC	035		1	1810	NC	035	BARBARA HAUCHY	12019
WHITMIRE, CHRISTOPHER COLUMBUS	1851	NC	093	1907	NC	093		1				HANNAH GALLOWAY	60205
WHITMIRE, CHRISTOPHER, I	C1780	SC		1842	NC	093		1				ELIZABETH	60205
WHITMIRE, GENERAL GEORGE, I	1872	NC	093	1960	NC	065		1 2				SARAH ALICE JAMES PEARL VAUGHN	60205
WHITMIRE, GEORGE DEE GENERAL LEE	1903	SC		1964	NC	065		1				EULA LUCILLE RUTLEDGE	60205
WHITMIRE, GEORGE WASHINGTON	1830	NC	093	1877	NC	093		1				ELIZABETH GALLOWAY	60205
WHITMIRE, HENRY DEE	1838	NC	093	1920	NC	093							60205
WHITMIRE, JAMES MARION	C1837	NC	093	1913	NC	093		2				NANCEY YOUNG	60205
WHITMIRE, LAWRENCE G	1884	NC	093	1923	SC			1				ESTELLE MCABEE	60205
WHITMIRE, RICHARD	1805	NC	093	1891	NC	093		1				JUDITH JORDAN	60205
WHITMIRE, SALLIE MATILDA	1869	NC	093	1946	NC	093							60205
WHITMIRE, WILLIAM ALLEN, I	1900	SC		1974	NC	065		1 2	1928	VA		ANNIE MAE TIMS MRS MARY GLADYS (ANDERSON) WILLIAMS	60205
WHITMIRE, WILLIAM MANSEL	1877	NC	093	1958	NC	093		1				ANGIE MCCALL	60205
WHITSETT, MARGARET	C1760	NC		1844	TN			1	1782	NC	073	JOSEPH MCADAMS	60497
WHITSON, JAMES	1787	NC	?014	1841	AL								27569
WHITSON, THOMAS	1782	NC	?014		AL			1				ELIZABETH	27569
WHITSON, WILLIAM				C1806	NC	013		1				ANN	27569
WHITT, ELISHA	1854	NC						1				ADDIE GRAY	60537
WHITT, JOHN, II	1829	NC		1901				1				PHOEBE JOHNSON	60537
WHITT, MARGARET	1850	NC	022	1910	IN			1	C1874			ADOLPHUS MANN	60537
WHITTED, LEVI				1849				1	1795	NC	073	SARAH NEAL	60411
WHITTED, NANCY	C1796							1	C1812	NC	073	JOHN YOUNG	60411
WHITTED, WILLIAM SR	C1740			1814	NC	073		1	C1765				60411
WHITTENBURGH/WHITENBERGER, FREDERICK		?PA		1804	TN		014	1		NC		MARGARETTE	07018
WHITTENBURGH/WHITENBERGER, HENRY	C1707	GER		1766	NC	065		1	C1733	GER		MARIA MAGADALENA	07018
WHITTLE, NANCY	C1752			C1790	NC	081		1	C1770	NC	073	JOHN FUSHEE GARNER	60485
WHITWORTH, SAMUEL	1798	NC		1855	KY			1				ELIZABETH	60204
WHTALEY, MICHAEL SR	C1723	VA		1800	GA		044	1	C1741	VA		CATHERINE BIRD	60112
WICKLIFFE, ELIZABETH	1767	NC	028	1825	GA		057	1	1785	NC	028	NICHOLAS ADAMS BRAY	60519
WICKLIFFE, WILLIAM JR		NC	028	1775	NC	057	028	1				MARGARET WOOD ?	60519
WICKLIFFE, WILLIAM SR				1754	NC	028							60519
WIGGINS, JOHN	C1716			1786	NC	063	037	1 2				CATHERINE BAKER MRS ELIZABETH BLEVINS	60384
WIGGINS, JOHN	1767	NC	?047	1819	AL		037	1				FANNIE	60384

ANCESTOR INDEX	BIRTH	PL	CO	DEATH	PL	CO	LIVD	MARRIED	PL	CO	SPOUSE NAME	CODE
WIGGINS, THOMAS				1782	NC	063		1 1766			FRANCIS BROWN	60384
WIGGINS, WINNIFRED	C1743	NC	?037	1807	NC	024	?010	1 1763	NC	047	RICHARD HOSKINS	19230
WILES, NATHAN	C1826	NC						1 1847	NC	092	MARY JANE PATTERSON	60321
WILEY, ALEXANDER		?NC										60542
WILEY, MARY ANN	1813	NC	046	1863	IL			1 1834	NC	046	JESSE SHOEMAKER	60100
WILEY, SAMUEL	1793	NC	046	1823	NC	046		1 1815	NC	046	ELIZABETH MILLIS	12125
WILEY, TAYLOR	C1780	?NC						1 1810	GA		VERLINDER FENNY	60542
WILEY, THOMAS							046	1 C1810	NC	?046	MARY BIRNEY	60100
WILEY, THOMAS							073					60542
WILEY, WILLIAM	C1730	PA		1783	NC	046		1 2			ELIZABETH FERGUSON MARY	12125
WILEY, WILLIAM	C1785	?NC		C1835	GA			1 1804 2 1811	GA GA		ELIZABETH BINION NANCY YOUNGBLOOD	60542
WILEY, WILLIAM							073	1 C1772				60542
WILEY, WILLIAM JR	1760	NC	073	1838	IN			1 1787	NC	046	ANN SHANNON	12125
WILHELM, GEORGE LEWIS	1829	NC	085	1875	IL			1			CATHERINE HARTMAN	60511
WILHITE, BARBARA	C1785	NC						1			SAMUEL CATE	60501
WILKENS, ANNA THOMINA	1872	NC	009	1919	AL			1 1893	NC	009	WALTER SEATON DUNSTON	02195
WILKENS, GOTHE THOMEE	1850	SWE		1899	NC	009		1 1871	NC	009	HARRIET ROWENA HARVEY	02195
WILKERSON, JOHN YOUNG	1801			1865	NC	078		1 1821	NC	078	MARY WILEY JONES	60500
WILKERSON, MARGARET E	1826	NC		1904	AR			1 1843	NC	016	GEORGE M PLOTT	60182
WILKINS, JAMES W	C1800	NC		C1860	TN			1 C1820			CHAROLETTE	05065
WILKINSON, ANGUS	1797	NC	082	1835	MS		083	1			MIDDLETON	27697
WILKINSON, CATHERINE	1806	NC	082	1844	MS		083	1 1825	MS		JOHN MCDOUGALD	27697
WILKINSON, DANIEL MCFARLANE	1802	NC	082	1887	MS		083	1 1828	MS		MARY CAMPBELL SMYLIE	27697
WILKINSON, JOHN NEAL	1818	NC	083	1891	MS		082	1 1864	MS		SUSAN ELIZABETH GRIFFIN	27697
WILKINSON, JOSHUA	1756	NC		1818	NC	037		1 1780	NC		SARAH	16030
WILKINSON, MARY ANN	1785	NC	037	1862	NC	037		1 C1804	NC	037	LAMON DUNN	16030
WILKINSON, NANCY	1811	NC	082	1862	MS		083	1 1845	MS		JOHN A HUNTER	27697
WILKINSON, NEILL RAY	1809	NC	082	1892	MS			1 1837	MS		HULDA TREVILLION	27697
WILKINSON, PETER	C1764	?SC		1860	MS		083	1 C1794	NC	082	SARAH ANN MCNAIR	27697
WILLIAMS, ABSALOM				C1813	NC	083		1			SARAY	27404
WILLIAMS, ABSOLOM T		NC		1881	MO			1			POLLY ANN	13006
WILLIAMS, ADAM	C1784	NC		C1872	NC	056		1	NC	?035	AVY GOODSON	14030
WILLIAMS, BENJAMIN	1832	NC	019	1870	NC	053	019	1 1854	NC	053	RHODA H GIBBS	24210
WILLIAMS, BENJAMIN SR	C1767			1831	NC	019	?053					24210
WILLIAMS, BENNIAH	C1799	NC										60416
WILLIAMS, CAROLINA FISHER	1861	NC	012	1910	NC	012		1 1891	NC	012	SAMUEL MARION ROBBINS	02195

ANCESTOR INDEX	BIRTH	PL	CO	DEATH	PL	CO	LIVD	MARRIED	PL	CO	SPOUSE NAME	CODE
WILLIAMS, CHARITY	C1786	NC	022	1864	MS			1	NC	022	JOSEPH SPEARS BUCHANAN	60078
WILLIAMS, CHARLOTTA ANNIE/ANN	1824	NC	019	1903	NC	053	019	1 1846			JOSEPH FARROW	24210
WILLIAMS, CHRISTIAN	C1762	NC						1			ZACHARIAH HAMM	27404
WILLIAMS, DANIEL SOUTHERLAND	1847	NC	035	1928	TX			1 1875	TX		MARY FRANCES/FANNY KYLE	04135
WILLIAMS, DAVID SHADRACK	1801			C1876	NC	053		1			REBECCA SAWYER	20335
WILLIAMS, EDWARD				1783	NC			2 1772	?NC		ANN DIMMETT	27318
WILLIAMS, EDWARD JR		NC		C1815	NC	?013		1 1767	NC	?013	LEDDY WOOD	27318
WILLIAMS, ELICHA CHASE	1834	NC	019	1841	NC	?019	?053					24210
WILLIAMS, ELLIS I	1841	NC	092	1934	NC	106		1 1869	NC	106	ALSIE-ALCY WOOTEN	60569
WILLIAMS, FRANCIS KERR	1821	NC	092	1903	NC	106		1 C1840	NC	092	NANCY CAROLINE STEELMAN	20380
WILLIAMS, GAIL A	1921	NC	038					1 1949	NC	038	SHORE DAVID DAVIS	60546
WILLIAMS, GEORGE A	C1830	NC	073	1864	VA			1 1848	NC	099	MARY WOMBLE	27281
WILLIAMS, GRANDISON F	C1806	NC			MO			1			MARY ANN EVANS	13006
WILLIAMS, HENRY DALLAS	1865	NC	106	1953	NC	106		1 1893	NC	106	SARAH MARGARET WILLIAMS	60569
WILLIAMS, ISAAC	1785			1867	NC	106		1 1812	NC	092	DICY RIDINGS	20380
WILLIAMS, JACOB	1732	NC	?009	1781	NC	072		1			CHLOE WILDER	04135
WILLIAMS, JACOB DAWSON	1860	NC	?073	1926	NC	036		1 1883	NC	036	MARTHA ANICE RHODES/RHODS	27281
								2	NC	036	SUDIE GREEN	
WILLIAMS, JESSE	1795	NC	092	1878	NC	106		1			RUTH MARTIN	60569
WILLIAMS, JOHN	1775	NC		1848				1	NC	?013	MARY/POLLY ASHWORTH	27318
WILLIAMS, JOHN	1747	NC	011				092	1			ELIZABETH	60569
WILLIAMS, JOHN WILLIS	1797			1837	NC	019	?053	1 1822			DORCAS CREDLE	24210
WILLIAMS, JOHN WILLIS ?	1836	NC	019	1862	VA							24210
WILLIAMS, JOHN, MAJ	1736	VA		1795	NC	047		1 1767			MRS FRANCES (BUSTIN) SLATTER	12125
WILLIAMS, JONATHAN WILDER	1815	NC	035					1 C1837	NC	035	ELIZA JANE SOUTHERLAND	04135
								2 C1858	NC	035	DOROTHY ANN/DOLLY BROWN	
WILLIAMS, JOSHUA LACE	1811			1896	NC	106		1 1836			SARAH HUTCHINS	60546
WILLIAMS, JOSHUA WADE	1845	NC	092	1925	NC	106		1 1866	NC	106	SARAH DIXON/DICKSON	60546
WILLIAMS, JOSIAH	1817	NC	013	1860	TN			1	NC	?013	MARGARET SUMNER	27318
WILLIAMS, JULIUS RUFUS	1879	NC	106	1962	NC	106		1 1905	NC	106	LEECY NORMAN	60546
WILLIAMS, LAMUEL HARDISON	1838	NC	072	1899	NC	072		1 1876	NC	072	REBECCIA SCREWS	27374
WILLIAMS, LAURA F	C1841			C1878	NC	?053	?019	1 1854	NC	053	HESAKIAH BROWN	24210
WILLIAMS, MILBRE		NC	037	1848	TN		005	1 C1799			HEZEKIAH RORIE	19075
WILLIAMS, NATHAN		?NC										13006
WILLIAMS, NATHANIEL CHASE SR	1829	NC	019	1904	NC	053	019	1 1851	NC	053	EMALOUS GIBBS	24210
								2 1873	NC	053	MARGARET BROWN	
WILLIAMS, OWEN	1744	VA		1810	NC	?046	?090	1 1770	NC	022	KATHERINE CROFFORD	27429
								2 1799	NC	?090	SARAH WILLITS	
WILLIAMS, PAULINE	1883	NC	072	1922	NC	072		1 1907	NC	072	JERRY THOMAS SILANCE	27374

ANCESTOR INDEX	BIRTH	PL	CO	DEATH	PL	CO	LIVD	MARRIED		PL	CO	SPOUSE NAME	CODE
WILLIAMS, PHYSA REBECCA		NC			NC			1	1862	NC	106	JESSE MACKIE	60569
WILLIAMS, PLEASANT G	1823	NC	092	1905	NC	106		1	1839	NC	092	PHEBE HUTCHINS	60569
								2	1859	NC	106	RUTH REECE	
WILLIAMS, RILEY WILSON	1817	NC	081	1898	MO			1	1839	NC	020	LOVE CARTER	13006
WILLIAMS, ROBERT	1717	NC	?024	1763	SC								60477
WILLIAMS, RUTH JANE	1843	NC	092	1892	NC	054		1	1860	NC	106	SANFORD LEE STEELMAN	20380
WILLIAMS, SARAH MARGARET	1869	NC	106	1944	NC	106		1	1893	NC	106	HENRY DALLAS WILLIAMS	60569
WILLIAMS, STEPHEN DECATUR	1775	NC	035	?1862	NC	035		1	1802	NC	035	MARY/POLLY SOUTHERLAND	04135
WILLIAMS, THOMAS				1831	NC	092		1				SALLY/SARAH	20380
WILLIAMS, THOMAS	1772	NC	092	1857	NC	106		1	1793	NC	092	ELIZABETH HARDING	60569
WILLIAMS, THOMAS MASON	1829	?NC		1912	NC	012		1	1854	NC	012	SARAH ELIZABETH SWAIN	02195
WILLIAMS, TIMOTHY	1721	ENG					085	1				ELIZABETH	60569
WILLIAMS, WILLIAM	1719	?PA		C1770	NC	022		1	C1740	PA		MARGARET	27429
WILLIAMS, WILLIAM	C1770	NC		C1840	AL		035	1	1794		028	RACHEL NELSON	60015
WILLIAMS, WILLIAM BUXTON				1889	NC	100		1				ELIZA LOVETT	60030
WILLIAMS, WILLIAM LUSTER	1853	NC	013	1915	CA			1	1886	KY		HETTIE MAY BRYANT	27318
WILLIAMS, WILLIAM NATHANIEL/ NATHAN		NC	022					1	C1815			MARTHA DEROUTH	25206
WILLIAMS, WOLACE	C1823	NC	019	1831		019	?053						24210
WILLIAMSON, ANDERSON		NC	047	1803	NC	086		1				ELIZABETH HART	05070
WILLIAMSON, ANDERSON CROWDER	1818	NC	086	1895	NC	026		1	1842	NC	026	PRISCILLA MAUNEY WASHBURN	05070
								2	1888	NC	026	MAGGIE GROCE	
WILLIAMSON, ANTHONY	1792	NC	020	1878	TN			1	1818	NC	020	ELIZA KERR LEA	60375
WILLIAMSON, ARCHIBALD	1794	NC	086	1875	NC	026		1				NANCY CROWDER	05070
WILLIAMSON, GEORGE		?VA			NC	047							05070
WILLIAMSON, IVY	1843	NC	011	1918	FL			1	1863	FL		MARY ANN GREN	60224
WILLIAMSON, JAMES DAVID	1862	NC	065	1927	NC	065		1	C1897			MARY ISOBEL MASON	07115
WILLIAMSON, JOHN		NC	011										60224
WILLIAMSON, NATHAN				C1839	NC	020		1				SARAH SWIFT	60375
(WILLIS, ANN/ANNIE DIXON)	1863	NC	028	1936	NC	072		1	1882	NC	028	GASTON LENIOR WETHERINGTON)	(01012)
WILLIS, BENJAMIN	C1765	NC		C1835	NC	014	086	1	1793	NC	086	ANE GALIS/GATIS	60154
WILLIS, FRANCES/FANNY	C1797	SC		C1872	TN		086	1	C1817	?NC	?086	JESSE REYNOLDS	60286
WILLIS, JOSEPH	1805	?VA		1878	NC	090		1				JULIA CHENEY	60456
								2				LYDIA CHENEY	
WILLIS, MARSHALL	C1840	NC	028		NC	?028		1	C1860	NC	028	MARY ANN DIXON	01012
WILLIS, PETER	C1770	?VA		1850	TN		086	1					60286
								2	C1790	NC	086	FRANCES/FANNY TATE	
WILLIS, STEPHEN ZEBULON	1860	NC	107	1938	NC	013	066	1	1878	NC	107	HARRIET MARGARET TOLLEY	60154
WILLIS, THOMAS STEPHEN	1812	NC	086	1899	NC	066	107	1	C1833	NC	?107	KEZIAH GRINDSTAFF	60154

ANCESTOR INDEX	BIRTH	PL	CO	DEATH	PL	CO	LIVD	MARRIED		PL	CO	SPOUSE NAME	CODE
WILLIS, WILLIAM		VA		1782	NC	086							02470
WILLIS, WILLIAM M	1837	NC	107	1907	NC	066		1	C1859	NC	107	LUCINDA WILSON	60154
								2		NC	066	MRS NANCY L RADFORD	
WILLITS, HENRY	C1745			C1800	NC	090	085	1	C1768	NC	085	CHARITY	27429
WILSON, BENJAMIN	1774	NC	046	1856	IL			1	C1796			JANE WARNICK	60302
WILSON, CHARLES H	C1857	JAM		1915	VA		030	1	1880	NC	030	LOVEY ANNE HARRIS	60307
WILSON, CHARLES H	1894	NC	?031	1934	VA		030	1	1926	VA		MURIEL C GREGORY	60307
WILSON, DAVID	1742	NC	011	C1803	TN			1	C1775			JANE SHARPE ROWAN	60193
WILSON, DAVID CARROLL	1785	NC	065	C1855	TX			1	1804			JANE CARUTHERS	60193
								2				SARA DRIGGERS	
WILSON, GEORGE	1806	NC	013		TX			1		?IL		ELIZABETH MCCOY	25093
WILSON, JAMES SR				C1759	NC	024		1				ALIS	19130
WILSON, JAMES W	C1808	NC	014	1898	NC	107	066	1	C1830	NC	107	MAHALAH	60154
								2	C1869	NC	066	EMILY	
WILSON, JANE	C1770	PA			MO		060	1		NC	?060	ANDREW MILLER	60200
WILSON, JOHN				C1827	KY			2	1807	NC	044	CHARITY RAGLAND	06015
WILSON, JOHN	1755	PA		1849	SC		046						11100
WILSON, JOHN	C1801	ENG		1887	AL		087	1				HEPSIE DUDLEY	21115
								2				MRS MARY ANN (HUGHES) BUNN	
WILSON, JOHN ROPER	1787	NC	100	1865	AL		047	1	1805	NC	047	ELIZABETH/BETSY EZELL	25100
WILSON, JOSHUA	1759	VA		1844	AL		100	1	1783			MOLLY WILLIAMS	25100
								2	1786	NC	047	BARBARA ROPER	
WILSON, LUCINDA	1843	NC	107	1883	NC	066		1	1859	NC	107	WILLIAM M WILLIS	60154
WILSON, MARSHALL	C1800	NC	009		NC	009		1				EMILY PERKINS	24240
WILSON, MARY	1812	?NC						1		?IL		DR CHAS D NUCKOLLS	25093
WILSON, MARY JANE	1797	NC		1869	IL			1	1823			JAMES SANDERS	60302
WILSON, NANCY GREEN	1771	NC	085	1852	IL			1	1789	NC	085	ANDREW STICE	27631
WILSON, RACHEL	1809	NC	013					1		?IL		MARTIN MCCOY	25093
WILSON, ROBERT	C1729			C1806	NC	073		1				ANN	60130
WILSON, ROBERT FLETCHER	1847	NC	009	1918	NC	009		1	1865	NC	063	LOUISA GURGANUS	24240
								2	1900	NC	063	SUPHRONIA WILLIAMS	
WILSON, SALLY		NC	085										27631
WILSON, SAMUEL	C1750			C1798	NC	046							60302
WILSON, SETH PILKINTON	C1760	NC	009	C1825	NC	009		1	C1782	NC	063	MARY DUGGIN	24240
WILSON, SUSANNAH	1837	NC	107	1916	NC	013		1	1856	NC	107	DAVID TOLLEY	60154
WILSON, THOMAS	1785	NC	013	1830	IL			1	C1804	NC	013	ELIZABETH GARDNER	25093
WILSON, THOMAS		NC	085										27631
WILSON, THOMAS								1	1809	NC	073	HENRIETTA	60130
WILSON, THOMAS	1809	NC	013	1860	NC	107	066	1	C1829	NC	107	JUDITH ROBERSON/ROBESON	60154
WILSON, THOMAS	C1750	IRE					?060						60200

ANCESTOR INDEX	BIRTH	PL	CO	DEATH	PL	CO	LIVD	MARRIED	PL	CO	SPOUSE NAME	CODE
WILSON, WILLIAM	1746	SCO		1806	NC	085		1	NC		NANCY GREEN	27631
WILSON, WILLIAM		WAL		C1817	NC	013		1 C1896	?MD		CREANY THOMAS/THOMSON	60154
WILSON, WILLIAM	C1774	VA		C1862	NC	107	014	1 C1803	?NC	014		60154
WIMBERLEY, JAMES	1795	NC	010	1844	TN			1 C1822	TN		LOUISA B ACREE	20415
WIMBERLEY, JOHN, III	C1670	?NC		C1745	NC	010		1	NC	?010	ELIZABETH	20415
WIMBERLEY, LEVY JR	C1771	NC	010	C1846	TN			1	NC	?010	MARY	20415
WIMBERLEY, LEVY SR		NC	?010	C1819	KY			1	NC	?010	HANNAH	20415
WINDERS, WILLIAM H	1835	NC			?MS			1 1865	MS		SARAH E WILLIS	60003
WINDLEY, MARY ELIZA	1877	NC	009	1948	NC	009		1 C1895	NC	?009	HOWARD LUCAS BROOKS	11145
WINDLEY, SOLOMAN SAMPSON SATCHWELL	1849	NC	009	1905	NC	009		1 1871	NC	009	EDIE ELIZABETH WINDLEY	11145
WINGATE, EDWARD				C1734	NC	024						27562
WINGATE, EDWARD				1797	NC	077		1			SARAH CREECY	27562
WINGATE, JOHN RICHARD	1854	NC	077	1920	VA			2 1888	NC	024	CORNELIA ADREN DAIL	27562
WINGATE, JOSEPH	C1777	NC	077	1837	NC	077		1			KESIAH	27562
WINGATE, LEVI	C1810	NC	077	1881	NC	077		2 1853	NC	077	MARTHA M HARRELL	27562
WINGATE, WILLIAM				C1774	NC	077						27562
WINGATE, WRIGHT	1815	NC			?VA			1 C1840	?VA		ELIZABETH WITE/WYATT	08073
WINKLER, FRANCIS	1810	NC	?085		?TN			1 C1834	NC	?085		60519
WINKLER, JOHN	C1832	NC			IN							08073
WINKLER, JOHN LOGAN	1839	TN		1900	OK		?085	1 C1860			MARGARET PARKS	60519
								2 C1870				
								3 1884	TX		MRS JANE (WAINSCOTT) BROADSTREET RIPPATOE	
WINKLER, MATHAIS	C1774	NJ		C1847	NC	014		1 C1798	NC	014	CATHERINE	25098
WINSLOW, JOHN	C1690			1755	NC	077		1 1716	NC	077	ESTHER SNELLING	24260
WINSLOW, THOMAS	C1680			1745	NC	077		1 1704	NC	077	ELIZABETH CLEARE	24260
								2 1734	NC	077	MRS LEAH(PRITLOWE)SMITH	
WINSLOW, TIMOTHY	C1660			C1730	NC	077						24260
WINTER/WINTERS, SAMUEL	1797	?NC		1878	AL			1 C1818	TN		PHEEBE/PHOEBE	27311
WINTER/WINTERS, WILLIAM	C1770	NC					047	1 C1795	NC		MARY	27311
WINTERS, JAMES	1773	NC	?047	1848	TX		?022	1 1808	TN		RHODA CREEL BEAL	60234
WINTERS, ZACHARY					NC	014		1			TEMPERANCE	20448
WISE, HARNEY	C1798	NC	072	C1839				1	NC	072	PHOEBE NEWBOLD	60562
WISE, IRA	1824	NC	072	1876	IL			1 1847	IL		CATHERINE HOWERTON	60562
WISE, MATTHEW	C1775	NC	072	1808	NC	072		1 1797	NC	072	NANCY FREEMAN	60562
WISE, THOMAS	C1750	?VA		1807	NC	072		1			MARY	60562
WISEMAN, WILLIAM	C1787	NC	085	C1867	TN			1 1807	NC	085	SARAH MCBRIDE	25161
WISHON, ANDREW JACKSON	1833	NC		1912	NC	106		1 1855	NC	106	REBECCA DELANEY LAKEY	02357
WISHON, JULIA	1858	NC	106	1936	NC	088		1 1879	NC	106	EDWARD HOUSTON REECE	02357

ANCESTOR INDEX	BIRTH	PL	CO	DEATH	PL	CO	LIVD	MARRIED		PL	CO	SPOUSE NAME	CODE
WITT, ANNA MARGARET		?NC		C1848	IN			1			OH	DANIEL SHOEMAKER	60100
WITT, JANE			046		IN			1	C1788	NC		CONRAD SHOEMAKER	60100
WITT, MICHAEL								1		NC	046	SUSANNAH WIRICK	60100
WITT, ROSANNA	1786			1857	IL			1	C1799	NC		CHRISTIAN SHOEMAKER	60100
WOLFE, JAMES DOSTER	1810			1885	NC	?097		1				ADDIE CROWELL	11100
WOLFE, PHELARAH ELIZABETH	1854	NC	050	1916	TX			1	1871	TX		GEORGE H ARMSTRONG	60078
WOLFE, WILLIAM	C1792	?NC	?014	C1845	NC	013		1		NC	013	JANE	60078
WOLFE, WILLIAM WESLIE	1827	NC	013	1878	TX			1	1853	NC	050	MARGARET CORA MCMINN	60078
WOLIVER, JOSEPH JR	C1782	NC	065		VA		054	1	C1819			ELIZABETH	60564
								2	C1835	NC	104	ANN	
WOMACK, JOHN				C1764	NC	056		1				SARAH	08090
WOMACK, LUCY	C1763	?NC		1851	MO			1	1798	NC	078	WILIAM MCFARLAND	03020
WOMBLE, WILLIAM	C1838	NC	?099	C1914	NC	022		1	1866	NC	022	ELIZA HEARN	27543
								2	1880	NC	099	LUCETTA UPCHURCH	
WOMBLE/WOMBWELL, JACOB	C1794	NC	022	1875	NC	099	073	1	1819	NC	099	MARY LAWRENCE	27281
WOMBLE/WOMBWELL, MARY	C1830	NC	073	C1864	NC	073		1	1848	NC	099	GEORGE A WILLIAMS	27281
WOMBLE/WOMBWELL, THOMAS		VA		1807	NC	022		1	1793	VA		NANCY OUTLAND	27281
WOMMACK/WOMACK, ABNER	1764	VA		1844	KY			1	1787	NC	060	AGNES REID/REED	05045
WOMMACK/WOMACK, ABRAHAM	C1730	VA		1803	NC	060		1	C1764	VA		ELIZABETH	05045
WOOD, ISAAC	1792	NC		1874	KY			1	1817			ELIZABETH WARD	60109
WOOD, JAMES JR	1768	NC		1846	KY			1				AMY	60109
WOOD, JOHN	1782	NC		1861	NC	090		1	1807	NC	090	NANCY TILLEY	60566
WOOD, JOHN WILLIAM	1861	NC	090	1944	MT			1	1884	TN		MARY/MOLLY ELIZABETH BECKNER	60566
WOOD, WILLIAM H	1830	NC	090	1912	TN			1	1853	NC	090	EASTER/HISA AMOS	60566
WOOD/WOODS, BANNISTER							038	1				SALLIE	60467
WOOD/WOODS, CHARITY	C1730	NC	092	C1830	KY			1		NC	092	FRANCIS IGNATIUS COOMES	60075
WOOD/WOODS, DEMPSEY	1837	NC	010	C1834			073						60230
WOOD/WOODS, HARRIET JANE	1855	NC	073	1939	CA			1	1876	MO		MYRON WILLIAM SMITH	60305
WOOD/WOODS, HENDERSON	C1810	NC	073					1				SUSAN	60305
WOOD/WOODS, JAMES					NC	013		1				MARGARET	27318
WOOD/WOODS, JONATHAN		NC	028				?010	1				PENELOPE	20138
WOOD/WOODS, NANCY ANN	1745			1833	NC	013		1	C1762	NC	065	JOHN ASHWORTH	27318
WOOD/WOODS, NETTIE	1853	NC	038	1921	NC	038		1	1881	NC	038	WILLIAM GEORGE POTTS	60467
WOOD/WOODS, WILLIAM	C1740	NC	010				073						60230
WOOD/WOODS, WILLIAM	C1831	NC	073					1				JANE BROWN	60305
WOODARD JOSEPH	1819	NC	056		TN			1	1847	NC	056	ELVY ANN EDWARDS	60512
								2	1863	TN		MARTHA JANE SPIVY	
								3	1867	TN		MRS MARY ELIZABETH (OLDES) COWELL	

ANCESTOR INDEX	BIRTH	PL	CO	DEATH	PL	CO	LIVD	MARRIED	PL	CO	SPOUSE NAME	CODE
WOODARD, WARREN								1 1816	NC	056	SALLY HAMILTON	60512
WOODARD, WILLIAM	C1770			C1850	TN		?047	1 C1790	NC	?039	ELIZABETH	60112
WOODARD, WILLIAM	1790	NC	?039	C1870	TN			1 C1816	NC		MARY	60112
WOODBURN, THOMAS	C1743			C1822	NC	046		1 1772	NC	046	ANN FORBIS	05059
WOODELL, MARK	1796	NC		1874	NC	022		1			SARAH	27543
WOODFIN, DEMY/DENNA	1791	NC	013		NC			1	NC	013	JOSEPH DENNIS GASH	60143
WOODRUFF, JOHN T	C1815	NC	092		?NC	?092		1			ELISABETH CARTER	10010
WOODRUFF, MOSES		?NC	?092				092	1			CHARITY COCKERHAM	10010
WOODS, ANN	1753	PA		1793	NC	065		1 1770	PA		JAMES MONTGOMERY	25040
WOODS, ELLEN		?VA			NC			1			MISS/MRS CARTER	27583
WOODS, JOHN	C1720			1813	NC	073		1 C1750			ANN LOUEY/LOVEY MEBANE	60575
WOODS, JOSEPH								1 1812	NC	014	CHRISTINA SHELL	60454
WOODS, MATILDA	1792	NC	014	1869	MO			1 1813	NC	104	WILLIAM GIDEON/GIDDENS	60454
WOODS, WILLIAM	C1759	NC	073	1830	NC	073		1 1781	NC	073	ELEANOR/NELLIE LINDSEY	60575
WOODY, ELIZABETH							092	1			WATKINS	08190
WOODY, JAMES	C1752						092					08190
WOODY, JAMES	C1752	VA		C1850	KY		092					60290
WOODY, JOHN WESLEY	1786	NC	092	1866	GA		013	1 1818	NC	049	PRISCILLA TREADWAY	60290
WOODY, JONATHAN	1756	VA		C1850	IA		092	1 C1773	NC	092	MARY LOVEL	60290
								2 C1820	NC	013	MOLLY LOVINGOOD	
WOODY, JONATHAN R	1756	NC	092	C1855	IA		104	1			MARY/MOLLY LOVELL/LOVINGOOD	08190
WOODY, JULIANA	1814	NC	?073	1867	TX			1 1830	TN		ALFRED THOMPSON	25093
WOODY, MARY							092	1			JOHN DAVICE	08190
WOODY, NANCY							092	1			JOHN SLATTON/LATON	08190
WOODY, SARAH							092	1			ABNER NORRCE	08190
WOODY, TARLTON/TALTON	C1753						092	1			ELIZABETH LOGGINS	08190
WOODY, WILLIAM	C1724	ENG		C1795	SC		092	1 C1748	ENG		SARAH PERSEL	60290
WOODY, WILLIAM	C1750			C1845	NC	013	092	1 C1773	NC	092	ELIZABETH LOVEL	60290
WOODY, WILLIAM HENRY	C1804	NC	104				006	1			SARAH EDWARDS	08190
WOODY, WILLIAM JR	C1750						013	1			ELIZABETH LOVELL/LOVINGOOD	08190
WOODY, WILLIAM SR		ENG					092	1			SARAH PERCEL	08190
WOOLEY, ROBERT R		NC	067	1840	NC	067		1			MARTHA JANE CROWDER	27328
WOOLEY, WILLIAM				C1790	NC	067	005	1			ELIZABETH RAIFORD	27328
WOOLLARD, ISAAC		?NC	?009									60083
WOOLLARD, SAMUEL	C1770	?NC	?009	C1840	TN			1 1799	KY		MARY LAXTON	60083
WOOLLEY, WILLIAM RILEY	1811	NC						1 1829	TN		SARAH DOWNING	27375
WOOTEN, ALSIE/ALCY	1839	NC	092	1936	NC	106		1 1869	NC	106	ELLIS I WILLIAMS	60569
WOOTEN, JOHN, COL	C1737	NC	010		NC	079		1 C1759	NC	009	MARY JORDAN	13264

ANCESTOR INDEX	BIRTH	PL	CO	DEATH	PL	CO	LIVD	MARRIED	PL	CO	SPOUSE NAME	CODE
WOOTEN, SHADRACK	1739	NC	028	1812	NC	027						60318
WOOTEN, SHADRICK OLIVER	1807	NC	029	1851	TN			1 1827			ELIZABETH BLAKE	13175
WOOTEN, WILLIAM	C1700	VA		1792	NC	037	071	1 C1725	VA		ANN DEAN	13264
								2 C1755	NC	056	ANN BRYANT	
WOOTON, LEWIS	1800	NC	092	1850	IN			1 1819	NC	092	MARTHA PUCKETT	27429
WOOTON, RACHEL	C1770	NC	?015	1800	NC	092		1 C1790	NC	092	JAMES GUNSTON	27429
WOOTON, THOMAS SR	C1715	VA		1796	NC	092	044	1 C1735	VA		SUSANNAH	27429
WORLEY, ELIZABETH	C1720	NC						1	NC		THOMAS LEARY	60497
WORLEY, JOHN	C1690			1740	NC	096		1			ELIZABETH PERKINS	60497
WORSHAM, THOMAS B	C1838	NC		C1922	OK							60433
WORTHAM, JOHN	1804	NC		1867	TX			1 1827	TN		ELIZA M WALKER	60071
								2 1845	TX		CAREY ANN VAUGHAN	
WORTHINGTON, ROBERT	1801	NC		1858	AL			1 C1821	NC		HOLLAND	60298
WORTHINGTON, SUSAN MARIE	C1822	NC		C1892	AR			1 1841	AL		WILLIAM COWART	60298
								2 1857	AL		JESSE ROBSON	
WREN/WRENN, JOHN	1824	NC	032	1864	VA			1 1849	NC	032	DELILA/DELILAH JANE RICKARD	24315
WREN/WRENN, JOHN CARROLL	1792	?NC		1845	NC	032		1 1818	NC	085	MARY/MOLLY EDWARDS	24315
WRENN, JOSEPH T	C1821							1 1841	NC	046	MARY ANN BROOKS	24320
WRENN/WREN, PETER A	1845	NC	046	1892	AR			1 1872	TN		LAURA M THURMAN	03313
WRIGHT, AMOS	C1763	NC	073	1846	IN		085	1 C1782			ELIZABETH LOWE	60294
WRIGHT, ANTHONY	1779	NC		1857	?NC	?092		1 1802	NC		ISABELLA WELBERN	60113
WRIGHT, CHARITY	1799	NC		1882	IA			1 1817	IN		WILLIAM MAXWELL	60476
WRIGHT, ISAAC	1764	NC						1 C1783	NC		SUSANNAH PRIOR	60476
WRIGHT, JAMES	C1766	VA			SC			1	NC	092		60495
WRIGHT, JAMES THOMAS	1787	PA		1859	IN			1 1810	NC	090	RUHAMAH MCANALLY	60515
WRIGHT, JOHN	1784	NC		1864	KY			1			ELIZABETH GRIGSBY	02135
WRIGHT, JOHN	C1731	VA		1789	NC	092		1 C1753	VA		ANN WILLIAMS	60096
WRIGHT, JOHN	1716	PA			SC		073	1			RACHEL WELLS	60314
WRIGHT, JOHN	1716	PA		1790	NC	?073		1 C1737	VA		RACHEL WELLS	60476
WRIGHT, JOHN	C1727	VA		1789	NC	092		1 1758	VA		ANN WILLIAMS	60495
WRIGHT, JOHN	C1756	IRE		C1836	NC	090		1 C1780	PA		JANE	60515
WRIGHT, JOSEPH	1740	MD			NC			1 C1756	NC	?073	CHARITY	60476
WRIGHT, JOSHUA	1795	NC	081	1863	MO			1			MARY MORGAN	60294
WRIGHT, JOSIAH/JOSIAS				1825	IL		005	1 1778			APPHIA RANDLE	60206
WRIGHT, LEMUEL				C1796	NC	069	037	1 C1770	NC	?037	LUCREECY	60587
WRIGHT, LEMUEL	1771	NC	037	1839	TN		069	1	NC	069	CHARITY RICKS	60587
WRIGHT, LEMUEL/KIT	C1801	NC	069	C1885	TN			1 1825	TN		SARAH DRENNAN	60587
								2 1830	TN		MRS SUSAN (RICE) STULL	
								3 1843	TN		SARAH HICKMAN	

ANCESTOR INDEX	BIRTH	PL	CO	DEATH	PL	CO	LIVD	MARRIED	PL	CO	SPOUSE NAME	CODE
WRIGHT, LEWIS	1792	NC	069	1872	TN			1 1821	TN		TEMPERANCE EDDINS/EDDINGS	60587
WRIGHT, MORGAN	1800	?NC		1872	?KY			1 1822	KY		JANE ALLEN	03295
WRIGHT, NANCY	C1757	VA					092	1 1773	VA		LEWIS ELLIOTT	60495
WRIGHT, POLLY ANNA	1779	NC	005					1 C1797	NC	005	JOHN BROOKS	60206
								2				
WRIGHT, RICHARD	C1730			1784	NC	085	073	1			ANN	60294
WRIGHT, RICHARD JR	C1757	NC	085	C1833	NC	032	092	1 C1780	NC		MARY NANCY MORGAN	60354
								2 C1798	NC		CARY KITTRELL	
WRIGHT, RICHARD SR	C1730	VA		1784	NC	085	046	1 1757			ABIGAIL WIGERLY	03295
WRIGHT, RICHARD SR	C1730	VA		1784	NC	085		1 C1748	NC	085	MARY ELIZABETH JANE	60354
WRIGHT, SARAH/SALLY	C1781	NC	085	C1848	IN		092	1 C1796	NC	092	JOSIAH JOHNSON	60354
WRIGHT, THOMAS	1758	VA		1840	NC	092		1 1780	NC	092	MARY CLANTON	60096
WRIGHT, WILLIAM	1761	NC		C1842	IN			1 1789			MARTHA/BETSY MORGAN	03295
WRIGHT, WILLIAM	C1736	VA		1821	NC	068		1 C1760	NC	029	ELIZABETH FURR	13175
WRIGHT, ZYLPHIA	1761	NC	005	1831	NC	067		1 1778			HARBARD SUGG	13175
WYATT, JAMES		NC		1839	KY			1 C1799	NC		MARGARET SMITH	25199
WYATT, LORENZO DOW	C1819	NC		1902	AR			1 1849	KY		LUCINDA CAROLINE DUNAWAY	25199
WYNN/WYNNE, ROBERT HICKS	C1791	NC	039	1833				1 1814	NC	039	SUSAN BATTLE JEFFREYS	25215
WYNNE, THOMAS KNIBB				1794	NC	039		2	NC	039	NANCY HILL	25215
								3 1793	NC	047	POLLY EDWARDS	
WYRICK, MARY								1 1825	NC	046	WILLIAM OLIPHANT	60006

Y

ANCESTOR INDEX	BIRTH	PL	CO	DEATH	PL	CO	LIVD	MARRIED	PL	CO	SPOUSE NAME	CODE
YARBROUGH, JOSEPH	1821	NC		1897	TX			1 1847	NC	078	SARAH TAYLOR	60434
YATES, HILLIARD GARLAND	1832	NC	099	1922	TN			1 1861	TN		ARTHEA ELIZABETH HOWARD	60141
YATES, JAMES	1762			1844	TN			1 1784	NC	020	LYDIA ANN KILGORE	03070
YATES, JOHN	C1699			1779	NC	020		1 C1743			SARA	03070
YATES, JOHN	C1750							1 1779		020	JEMIMA ROPER	60083
YATES, JOHN	C1699			C1779	NC	020		2 C1748			SARAH	60083
YATES, JOSHUA	C1775	NC	?092	1849	TN			1 1795	KY		MARTHA STEWART	60041
								2 1844	TN		MRS SARAH J PYBAS	
YATES, MARY/POLLY	C1786	?NC	?020	C1844	TN			1 1804	NC	020	JAMES MCNEELEY	60083
YATES, STEPHEN	C1805	NC		C1870	TX			1 1828	GA		NANCY TOMLINSON	27549
YATES, THOMAS	1752	VA		1834	TN			1 1776	NC	020	REBECCA RAGSDALE	03070
YATES, WILLIAM	1744			1844	TN		020	1			AGNES PRICE	03070
								2			RACHEL CHILDRESS	
YATES, WILLIAM	1749	NC	?020	1844	TN			1	NC	020	AGNES PRICE	60083
YODER, PETER	1805	NC	060	C1870	MO			1 1832	NC	060	RACHEL HAWN	20078
								2 C1862	MO		MARTHA COVINGTON	

ANCESTOR INDEX	BIRTH	PL	CO	DEATH	PL	CO	LIVD	MARRIED	PL	CO	SPOUSE NAME	CODE
YORK, DORCAS	1780	NC	081	C1865	GA			1 1804	NC	081	ISAIAH BECK	60311
YORK, ELI	1771	NC	?073	1853	NC	081		1 1788	NC	081	SUSANNAH HARDEN	19170
YORK, HARDEN	C1792	NC	081	1837	IN			1 1817	NC	081	MARY/POLLY JONES	19170
YORK, HENRY	C1730	ENG		C1805	NC	?081		1 2 C1789	?NC NC	?073 081	 MARGARET LENDERMAN	19170
YORK, HIRAM		NC	081		?NC	?069		1 1823	NC	081	REBECCA	19170
YORK, JOSEPH	C1747			1809	MS		081	1 2 C1788	NC	081	 JEMIMA	60519
YORK, SEMORE				C1792	NC	081		1			SYLVANIA ALDRIDGE	60311
YORK, SUSAN MARY	C1813	AL		1857	MS		081	1 1835	AL		WILLIAM BURROW	60519
YORK, URIAH	C1789	NC	081	1835	AL			1 C1810	MS		REBECCA	60519
YOUNG, ARCHIBALD	C1750	NC	005	1834	TN			1 1769	NC	065	SARAH POWELL	60196
YOUNG, EDWARD				1791	NC	092		1			LUCY	60159
YOUNG, ELIZA	C1813	NC		1880	NC	?023		1 1828	NC	086	JOHN A HALL	08015
YOUNG, ELIZABETH	1771	NC	065		TN			1	NC	065	MR JUSTICE	60196
YOUNG, FRANCES		VA			NC	044		1 1771	VA		WILLIAM WEBB	60164
YOUNG, ISHAM				1837	?TN			1 1802 2 1802	NC NC	092 092	NANCY HARVEY NANCY HARVEY	60159
YOUNG, JACOB	C1764	NC	065	1836	IN		016	1 1792 2 C1831	KY KY		RACHEL GOODNIGHT CATHERINE	60344
YOUNG, JOHN	C1772	IRE		1852	NC	013	?014	1 C1795	NC	?014	ROSEANNAH HEMPHILL	04195
YOUNG, JOHN	C1780	NC		1822	NC	073		1 1812	NC	073	NANCY WHITTED	60411
YOUNG, JOHN	C1740			1806	NC	044						60411
YOUNG, JOHN				1781	NC	047		1			MRS SARAH (NORFLEET) YOUNG	60594
YOUNG, JOSEPH	C1760			1781	NC	073		1 C1779			MARGARET GALBREATH	60411
YOUNG, LEVI WHITTED	1813	NC	073	1853	TX			1 1837	NC	073	SARAH CLANEY	60411
YOUNG, NANCY SECTION	1804	NC	092	1881	KS			1 1827	TN		JOSEPH JOHN MOUNGER	60159
YOUNG, NAOMA	1856	NC	?107	1922	NC	066		1			FRANKLIN PIERCE SLAGLE	60439
YOUNG, PATTERSON				C1900	NC	?066		1			ELIZABETH HUGHES	60439
YOUNG, PENDLETON	1774	NC	065		TN							60196
YOUNG, ROBERT HARRISON	1851	NC	013	1912	NC	013		1 1873	NC	014	PAMELIA EMALINE GUDGER	04195
YOUNG, THOMAS	1806	NC	013	1852	NC	013		1 1831 2 1849	NC NC	013 013	ALIE EDMONSON SARAH JANE PATTON	04195
YOUNG, WILLIAM	C1735	ENG		1813	VA			1	NC	065	ELIZABETH STEGALE	60196
YOUNGBLOOD, SARAH	1784	NC	?056	1857	TX			1 1803	NC	056	JOHN AUSTIN	27346

2

Spouse Index

SPOUSE	ANCESTOR
ABERNATHY ELIZABETH TURNER	JOHN C WALLACE
ABERNATHY FRANCES R	JAMES F ABERNATHY
ABERNATHY MARY LITTLE	JOHN WASHINGTON ABRAMS
ABERNATHY SARAH	PETER CONRAD
ABERNATHY MRS RUTH (BARHAM)	JAMES PAINE
ABIGAIL MARY	ISAAC THOMPSON
ABIRD ANN	MURPHY KEMP
ACOCK FRANCES	WILLIAM COURSEY
ACOCK SARAH	STEVEN TALKINGTON
ACREE JOHN R	MARY BROWN
ACREE LOUISA B	JAMES WIMBERLEY
ADAMS ABRAHAM	KATHERINE SWARTZLANDER
ADAMS DANIEL	JEMIMA ADAMS
ADAMS DIANE	WILLIAM JOHNSON
ADAMS ELIZABETH	ARCHAELOUS CRAFT
ADAMS FANNY	WILLIAM SAUNDERS
ADAMS HANNAH	ELIJAH CHASTIAN
ADAMS MARY	FORTUNE DOBBS
ADAMS MARY	THOMAS BOWEN
ADAMS MARY/POLLY	TYREE ROBERTSON/ROBINSON
ADAMS NIMROD	NANCY JANE ? ETCHISON
ADAMS RACHEL	JOHN MOON
ADAMS SARAH	LODOWICK ADAMS DOBBS

SPOUSE	ANCESTOR
ADAMS WILLIAM ALBERT	VIRGINIA BRANN
ADCOCK EUNICE	JOSEPH PURGERSON, SR
ADER POLLY	ANDREW BURK/BURKE
AGEE ELIZABETH	MICAJAH KEGG/CAGE SMITH
AIKEN MRS MARY	DAVID FARLEY
ALBRIGHT CATHERINE	JOHN RICHARD STOCKARD
ALBRIGHT MARY	GEORGE VALENTINE CLAPP
ALBRITTON CLARA	WINSOR DIXON
ALDERMAN CHRISTIAN	REUBEN ROGERS/RODGERS
ALDERMAN ESTHER	WILLIAM COOPER ROGERS/RODGERS
ALDERMAN JEMIMA	WILLIAM COOPER ROGERS/RODGERS
ALDERSON ELIZABETH	JOEL MARTIN, SR
ALDERSON SARAH	JAMES ELLISON
ALDRIDGE AVA C	WILLIS EVERETT MURPHY/MURPHREY
ALDRIDGE ESTHER	RICHARD HILL
ALDRIDGE MARTHA	JOHN SUGG
ALDRIDGE MARY	JOHN MURPHREY/MURPHY
ALDRIDGE MARY JANE	BENNETTWILLIAM MURPHY/MURPHREY
ALDRIDGE SYLVANIA	SEMORE YORK
ALEXANDER ABIGAIL	FRANCIS BRADLEY
ALEXANDER ADOLPHUS W	ANN ADALINE DONALDSON
ALEXANDER AZARIAH	MARGARET MCCRACKEN
ALEXANDER CALPURNIA	WILLIAM SIMMONS
ALEXANDER CATHERINE	THOMAS STATON/STAYTON
ALEXANDER JAMES SAMPLE	ELIZABETH MCCRACKEN
ALEXANDER JANE	ABRAHAM ELLIOTT
ALEXANDER LAURA BLANCHE	CHARLES SHERIDAN HARTNESS
ALEXANDER MARY ELIZA	JOHN WAGLEY/WAGLE/WEIGLE
ALEXANDER NARCISSA	RANSOM GRAY
ALEXANDER NERO	LETITIA SIMMONS
ALEXANDER RUTH	JOHN W MCREE
ALEXANDER RUTH	JOSEPH CLARK
ALEXANDER SAMUEL	SARAH DENNIS
ALEXSON MARGARET	JAMES KING
ALGEE CYNTHIA LENORA	SETH HARRELL
ALLDRIDGE EUNICE	JACOB STEELE
ALLEN ANNE	EDWARD HALL
ALLEN ELIZA	WILLIAM EXUM
ALLEN ELIZA ADA	AMMA RIAH HEMINGWAY/HEMENWAY
ALLEN HENRY DAVIS	MARY/POLLY BARNES
ALLEN JANE	MORGAN WRIGHT
ALLEN JANEY J	JOHN RILEY BANKS
ALLEN LARVIS	LUCY FOSTER FELTS
ALLEN MILLEY	REUBEN WHITE
ALLEN	ELIZABETH RHODES
ALLEN NANCY URSULA	GIDEON JOHNSON
ALLEN NELLY	DRURY ALLEN
ALLEN PRISCILLA	WILLIAM FREEMAN SCOGGINS
ALLEN REBECCA	LEMUEL INGRAM
ALLEN SARAH ELIZABETH	JAMES MARION GARDNER
ALLEN URSULA	GIDEON JOHNSTON/JOHNSON
ALLEN MRS PHEBE (SCARLET)	ISAAC COX
ALLENDER LYDIA	STEPHEN BEECHER ADAMS
ALLHANDS CATHERINE	DANIEL STUTZMAN

SPOUSE	ANCESTOR
ALLISON CATHARINE	AZARIAH THOMPSON
ALLISON ELIZABETH ANN	OSBORNE GILES FOARD/FORD
ALLISON EPHRAM	JULIA ALLISON
ALLISON GRIZELLA	JOHN, THOMPSON, COL
ALLISON JULIA	EPHRAM ALLISON
ALLISON POLLY	ABSALOM HAWORTH
ALLISON SARAH ADDELINE	THOMAS BASERY SIMS/SYMS
ALLISON MRS ESTHER (NEILL)	JAMES DONALDSON
ALLMON HULDAH CLEMENTINE	CHARLES STANLEY CHAFFIN
ALLMON URIAS J	TEMPIE IVY
ALLOWAY-STRANGE NANCY	SOLOMON ISRAEL
ALLRED EASTER	THOMAS W BROWN
ALMA MINNIE	LEROY COLON HARVELL
ALSTON AMY	JOHN RICHARD BOBBITT
ALSTON MARTHA/PATTY	SAMUEL SUMNER
ALSTON MARY	JOB STALLINGS
ALTMAN NANCY	RICHARD C STOKES
AMANDA REBECCA	ARTHUR DAVIS
AMICK CATHERINE	DAVID CORTNER/COTNER
AMIS HANNAH	JAMES T SANFORD
AMIS WILLIAM	NANCY FUSSELL
AMOS EASTER/HISA	WILLIAM H WOOD
AMOS JOHN RUFUS	N FRANCIS BUFFORD
ANDERS/ANDREWS LAURA	HENRY C BANKS
ANDERSON CHARITY	THOMAS LAPSLEY/LAPSLIE, SR
ANDERSON CORNELIUS	ETTA MITTIE QUEEN
ANDERSON ELIZABETH	GEORGE ALLEN
ANDERSON ELIZABETH	ISAAC POPE
ANDERSON ELIZABETH THOMAS	FREDERICK HILSABECK
ANDERSON JAMES	NANCY IRVIN
ANDERSON MARY	ROBERT COURSEY
ANDERSON SUSANNA PARELLA	JOHN MCALPINE
ANDERSON TOBITHA	TIMOTHY PERKINS, JR
ANDERSON/AUSTIN ELIZABETH	GIDEON GREEN
ANDREW JANE	WILLIAM HOLLADAY
ANDREW/ANDREWS GEORGE WASHINGTON	AMANDA/MANDY MARTHA? KNIGHT
ANDREWS ALFRED GRAY	WINIFRED HYMAN
ANDREWS HILEY	LEVY RUSSELL
ANDREWS MARY ANN ELIZABETH	WILLIAM JONATHAN HARDISON
ANDREWS SUSAN	JOSEPH CADE/CALVIN NEWBERRY/NEWBURY
ANDREWS SUSAN	ROBERT BROWN
ANDREWS MANISIA GAINER MENETTA	FREDERICK WILLIAMS MAYO
ANGEL J/JOHN WILLIAM	MARY J BRAGG
ANGELL REBECCA	WILLIAM EVANS
ANTHONY BARBARA	CHARLES FULKS
ANTRIM SARAH	THOMAS BEALES/BEALS
APPLEGATE SUSANNAH	ZACHEUS/ZACHARIAH SUTTON
APPLEWHITE REBECCA	THOMAS MERRITT
ARCHIBALD WILLIAM	MARTHA MCCORKLE
ARICK/IRICK CATHARINE/KATE	RUKINS JELKS
ARKILL NANCY	JOB GOODWIN
ARMFIELD MRS MARY	JACOB BROWN
ARMSTRONG ANNE	JOHN BUTLER
ARMSTRONG GEORGE H	PHELARAH ELIZABETH WOLFE

SPOUSE	ANCESTOR
ARMSTRONG JOSEPH	FRANCES TINNEN
ARMSTRONG MARY	NATHAN SPENCER
ARMSTRONG PARTHENIA	JOHN W FAUCETT
ARMSTRONG ROBERT	NANCY GREEN/GREENE
ARNETT MAHALA	STEPHEN SCOTT
ARNEY/HARMON ELIZABETH	ADAM SETSER/SETZER
ARNOLD AMELIAN	JAMES GRAY
ARNOLD JAMES	DORCAS TAYLOR
ARNOLD LYDIA FRANCES	ROBERT DICKY STADLER
ARNOLD MARTHA JANE	ARCHIBALD MONROE HUNSUCKER
ARNOLD MARY/POLLY	MASTON RIPPY
ARNOLD NANCY	JOHN STADLER, I
ARNOLD THOMAS	POLLEY SEWELL
ARRINGTON ELBERT S	ELIZABETH GILLILAND
ARRINGTON JOHN D	MARTHA JOHANNA WILLIAMS DRAKE
ARRINGTON THOMAS	SEBITHA BELL
ARROWWOOD NANCY	THOMAS F AUSTIN
ARTHUR ELIZABETH	SILAS GASKINS
ASH ELIZA M	CALEB SPENCER
ASHE MARY	GEORGE MOORE
ASHE MARY SYBIL	JOHN OWEN MILLER
ASHE RICHARD JAMES	MARY PHEBE MITCHELL
ASHWORTH JOHN	NANCY ANN WOOD/WOODS
ASHWORTH MARY/POLLY	JOHN WILLIAMS
ASKEW ANNA	JOSIAH HARRELL
ASKEW SARAH ELIZABETH	GEORGE WASHINGTON CHARLTON
ASSUP JANE	JEHU DAVIS
ATHEARN PRINCE DEXTER	NANCY ELIZABETH HAYES
ATKINS ANNIE ELIZABETH	LAOMA LEE
ATKINS ELENOR	JOHN HIGSON
ATKINS ELIZABETH A	SAMUEL J KITTRELL
ATKINS JANE CULTON	JAMES HAMLETT/HAMBLET
ATKINS MARTHA JANE	PLEASANT TRICE
ATKINS MARY JANE	JAMES HAMLETT/HAMBLET
ATKINS NANCY	PLEASANT W KITTRELL
ATKINSON AVIE	MEAD/MEED GULLEY/GULLY
ATKINSON JANE	JAMES MADISON BLACK
ATKINSON NANCY	JOHN HECTOR RALLS
ATKINSON SAVARA/AVIE	MEAD GULLEY
ATWELL NANCY LOUISE	WILLIAM HARVEY RODGERS/ROGERS
ATWOOD JANE	JOHN JACKSON ROYAL/RIAL/ROIL
ATWOOD THOMAS	MARY/POLLY STEELMAN/STEALMAN
AUSTIN ELIZABETH	SQUIRE JAMES PENLEY/PENLY
AUSTIN JOHN	SARAH YOUNGBLOOD
AUTREY MARTHA	NEIL CULBREATH
AVENT SARAH	WILLIAM RAGLAND/RAGLIN
AVERY EDITH	EPHRAIM OXFORD BEASLEY
AVERY TABITHA	JOHN A FRYER
AVERY MRS LAURA ANN(SMITH)	JOSEPH ALLEN GASKINS
AWALT JOHN	CATHERINE LIMBAUGH
AWALT NANCY ANN	SOLOMAN LIMBAUGH
AXSON TAMSIE	JOHN, BLOODWORTH, MAJ
AXUM WILLIAM THOMAS	MARY FRANCES HELMS
AYCOCK SIMON	ELIZABETH BENNETT

SPOUSE	ANCESTOR
AYERS ANNE VIRGINIA	JAMES WILSON MILLER RUSSELL
BABB MARY	DANIEL FULLER
BABER MARY/POLLY	ADAM MARTIN
BAGGERLY EMILY ELIZABETH	JOHN MARTIN GAITHER
BAGGETT MIRIAM	JESSE LEE
BAGGETT MIRIAM	JESSE, LEE, SR
BAGLEY MILLEY	RHODUM GRIGG/GRIGGS
BAILEY KATIE	WILEY WEDLE LAMM
BAILEY MARY HELEN	THOMAS H MARKS
BAINS MARY	KING LUTEN/LUTON
BAIRD ANN	MURPHY KEMP
BAIRD LUCY	AMBROSE JONES
BAITY JOHN MORGAN	RACHEL EASTEP/ESTEP
BAITY WILLIAM	ANNA HADDOX
BAKER APSALY	TUNNEL/TURNER MURPHREY/MURPHY
BAKER CATHERINE	JOHN WIGGINS
BAKER ELIZA	LETHAN NORWOOD
BAKER ELIZABETH	CASPER CABLE
BAKER FLORA	WILLIAM PITT CAMERON
BAKER JOHN	RACHEL SOWELL
BAKER KATIE	THOMAS HARRINGTON
BAKER MARGARET	WILEY NICHOLS
BAKER MARTHA	DEMPSEY SUMNER
BAKER MARTHA/MATTIE JANE	MILTON WAKELAND COOPER
BAKER	NATHAN STANLEY CHAFFIN
BAKER NANCY ANN	HENRY ROBERSON
BAKER OLLY	AARON COX
BAKER PROVIDENCE	KING LUTEN/LUTON
BAKER WILLIAM	SUSAN ELIZABETH DEATON
BALCH ELIZABETH	JAMES ASHMORE
BALDRIDGE ALEXANDER	JANE RAMSEY
BALDRIDGE CPT JOHN	ISABELLA LUCKEY
BALDRIDGE JAMES L	NARCISSA HENDERSON
BALDWIN ANN	SAMUEL MILLIKAN, SR
BALDWIN CHARLOTTY	GEORGE DAVIS
BALDWIN DISEY	NATHAN JONES
BALDWIN ELIZABETH CHRISTILLA	JOHN W OWEN
BALDWIN JESSE	ELIZABETH STRINGFELLOW
BALDWIN PATIENCE	BENJAMIN THOMAS RUSH
BALDWIN SARAH	JOHN, PYLE, DR
BALDWIN SARAH	JOHN, PYLE, DR
BALDWIN SARAH	JOHN, PYLE, DR
BALDWIN STONEWALL JACKSON	ELIZABETH DRUSCILLA MEARES
BALL ELIZABETH	CHARLES JARVIS
BALL LEAKEY	SAMUEL BARRETT
BALL MRS MARY	LEVIN DUNCAN
BALL NANCY	JOHN ARMSTRONG
BALLARD MARY ANN	JEREMIAH BROWN
BALLENGER ANNIE LATNA	JOHN OATIS PLUMBLEE/PLUMLEY
BALLEW NANCY	WILLIAM MONTGOMERY
BANDY CINTHIA	JOHN UNDERWOOD
BANKS ISABELLA	ENOCH WARD

SPOUSE	ANCESTOR
BANKS JOSEPH T	REBECCA LYDAY/LYDA
BANKS MARGARET HILL	ADOLPHUS LAFAYETTE ORRELL
BANKS POLLY/MARY ANNA	JAMES JACKSON MASSEY
BANNER CYNTHIA	AUGUSTINE F C RANDLEMAN
BARBEE DELILAH	SANFORD JENKINS
BARBEE ELIZABETH	DAVID COBLE, JR
BARBEE ROSE	JAMES HARWARD/HARWOOD/HARROD
BARBER	SALLIE WELBORN
BARBOUR POLLY	CALVIN HENRY DILLARD
BARCLIFT MIRIAM	DE LA MARE, FRANCIS
BARCLIFT SAMUEL	MILLICENT COMMANDER
BARD MARY LOUISE	FRANCIS NATHANIEL BATTS
BARDIN WILLIAM	NANCY COOK
BAREFOOT LURANEY	ASA SCHWANNER/SWANNER
BAREFOOT MRS SALLY (EVANS)	WILEY/WILLIE HARRELL
BARENTT JEAN	WILLIAM MCMENAMY
BARKER AMY	CHARLES COX
BARKER DORTHY/DORCAS	ISAIAH S BECK, SR
BARKER ELIZABETH	HENRY TEMPLE, SR
BARKER GEORGE	SUSANNAH PERKINS
BARKER RUTHY	ISAIAH S BECK, JR
BARKLEY LOUISA M	MILAS S LOWRANCE
BARLOW LARKIN	SUSAN PENNELL
BARLOW	MICHAEL COUNCIL/COUNCILL
BARLOW SARAH	GARDNER WHITE
BARNARD MARY	JETHRO STARBUCK FOLGER
BARNARD OBED	SOPHIA THORNBURGH
BARNES DANIEL T	SUSANNA SIMS
BARNES EDITH	ALLEN JOHNSON, SR
BARNES ELIZABETH/BETSY	JOHN VIVIAN SUMNER
BARNES GERIAH	JOHN MULLIS
BARNES JACOB	JULIAN WHITLEY
BARNES JAMES	ELIZABETH SUMNER
BARNES JOSEPH	SELAH DELOACH
BARNES MARY/POLLY	HENRY DAVIS ALLEN
BARNES SARAH	JONATHAN SPEIGHT
BARNES ZELPHIA	JOSEPH FARMER
BARNET CATHERINE	JOHN WHITLOW
BARNETT MARTHA ANN/PATSY	BENJAMIN HARDIN/HARDEN/HARDING
BARNETT REBECCA	ISAIAH DEWEESE
BARNETT RIAL	MARY AUSTIN
BARNETT SARA JANE	STEVEN CASEY
BARNETT SARAH	JOHN DEAL
BARNETT SUSAN ADALINE	EDWIN SOLOMON BINNS, DR
BARNETT THOMAS	SARA CROSHA GRAVES
BARNHART JACOB	RHODA COX
BARNHILL LUCRETIA	NATHANIEL JACKSON LILLY
BARNHILL MARY LOUISE	ROBERT ALONZA BAILEY
BARR CATHARINE	JOHN MCCORKLE
BARR CYNTHIA	JOHN LEWIS SMITH
BARR JAMES	ELIZABETH MCCORKLE
BARRETT JABEZ	MARY/POLLY SOUTHARD
BARRETT LYDIA	IRVIN ALLEN
BARRETT MARY ELIZABETH	WILLIAM JESSE BLALOCK

227

SPOUSE	ANCESTOR
BARRETT SARAH A	WILLIAM A OAKLEY
BARRETT WILLIAM	ANN SOWELL/SEWELL
BARRETT WILLIAM RILEY	JANE C MUSE
BARRINGER MATHIAS	BARBARA RENDLEMAN
BARROW FANNY	JOHN LANIER
BARROW FRANCES	CRAWFORD DOBSON
BARROW NANCY	ALDERSON ELLISON HARVEY
BARROW RUTH	JEREMIAH BEAMAN
BARTEE DINAH	CASON GIBBS
BARTIE ELIZABETH	SAMUEL GREGORY MING
BARTON ISABELL	ABRAM CRABTREE
BARWICK MARTHA CAROLINE	GEORGEWASHINGTON COUNCIL/COUNCILL
BASE REBECCA	ZEBULON VAUGHN
BASS ANN	THOMAS JOHNSTON
BASS CHARLES D	PRICILLA RAY
BASS MARTHA JANE	LONNIE OLIVER HELMS
BASS SARAH	JOSEPH, BOON, III
BASSINGER JOHN	MARY ANN CHASTAIN
BATCHELOR ANN HARRIET	JAMES SMYLIE/SMILEY, REV
BATCHELOR CHERRY	SION W WHITLEY
BATCHELOR JAMES S	ANN TUCKER
BATCHELOR NATHAN WRIGHT	NANCY PERRY
BATCHELOR WRIGHT STEPHEN	CHARITY TUCKER
BATEMAN RUTH M	CALVIN JOSEPH MINTER BUCHANAN
BATES JOSEPHINE	CHARLES CHOAT HALL
BATSON THOMAS	ELIZABETH IVES
BATSON MRS NANCY E (BLADES) HOOD	THOMAS W BROWN
BATTS ANNIE JANE	AMOS M BROWN
BATTS CINTHIA ELIZA	WILLIAM GARDNER
BAUCOM ISHAM	ALEY PENNEY
BAUGAS SARAH	REUBEN ROUSSEAU
BAUM DOROTHY/DOLLY	THOMAS TILLETT
BAUM MARY MATILDA	JOHN DANIEL/DANIELS
BAUM RHODA	HEZEKIAH SPRUILL
BAUM ZILPHA	JAMES MASON
BAXLEY ELEANOR	JOHN UPTON
BAXTER ANN ELIZABETH	JAMES MADISON LAND
BAYES SARAH	WILLIAM USSERY
BAYLA/BAILEY PEGGY	VINCENT/VINSON KING
BAZEMORE PENELOPE	JESSE BAZEMORE, JR
BEACH CATHERINE M	HENRY ARTHUR WESCOTT
BEAL RHODA CREEL	JAMES WINTERS
BEAL SARAH	GILES BOWERS
BEALE BENJAMIN JOSEPH	JULIA LACY TYSOR
BEALL JANE	JOSEPH ALBEA
BEALL MARY	JOHN WATKINS
BEALS HANNAH	WILLIAM HOCKETT/HOGGATT
BEALS MARGARET	JAMES HORTON
BEALS MARY ANN	THOMAS HUNT
BEAM AARON	MARY SHULL
BEAM JOHN TEETER	REBECCA RANYOLDS
BEAM NANCY ANN/ANNA	JENKEY JENKINS
BEAM SUSAN AARON	ALBERT DIXON ESKRIDGE
BEAN ELIZABETH	WILLIAM BUTLER

SPOUSE	ANCESTOR
BEAN JOHN	ELIZABETH AWALT
BEAN MARY	ALEXANDER MCKEE
BEARD JANE	THOMAS H ORMSBY
BEARD MARY	JOHN GWYN
BEARD NEILL	ELIZABETH CARVER
BEARD REBECCA	JACOB LOWRANCE
BEARD WILLIAM B CARVER	MARY JANE MAY
BEASLEY ANN	JAMES MING
BEASLEY MARY	THOMAS TIREY
BEASLEY MARY OTEALIA	WILLIAM WALLACE CLEMENT
BEASLEY NANCY	ZACHARIAH HAM/HAMM
BEASLEY SOLOMON	CASSANDER ECLIN
BEASLEY MRS MARILDA (COLLINS)	EPHRAIM OXFORD BEASLEY
BEASON MARY ANN	GEORGE L PERRY
BEATY MOSES	NANCY WEATHERS
BEAVER/BIEBER SUSANNAH	JACOB THIEME/TEEM
BEAVERS ELIZABETH	JONATHAN HUTCHENS
BEAVERS JAMES	ELIZABETH FOOSHEE
BECHBILL MRS MARY ANN	HAMPTON QUEEN
BECK ANN	DANIEL HIGHSMITH
BECK ISAIAH	DORCAS YORK
BECK NANCY	JOSEPH KORNEGAY
BECK SUSANNAH	ROBERT PAINE
BECK/BECKE ANN	DANIEL HIGHSMITH
BECKLEY BARBARA	FREDERICK WEISS/WISE
BECKNER ELIZABETH	SAMUEL SMUT THOMAS
BECKNER MARGARET	ANDREW JACKSON THOMAS
BECKNER MARY/MOLLY ELIZABETH	JOHN WILLIAM WOOD
BECTON MARY ELEANOR	WILLIAM PETERSON MULLEN
BEDDINGFIELD MARTHA	WILLIAM WESLEY HILL
BEDSAUL MARY	FLOWER SWIFT
BEDWELL ALCEY	JOSEPH HOUSE
BEESLEY JAMES	DELANEY/DELANA WADSWORTH
BEESLY MARY J	WILLIAM DAWSON HUSON/HUSTON
BEESON ABSOLOM	MARY CLAMPITT
BEESON AMOS	DINAH CLAMPITT
BEESON HENRY HARRISON	OLIVE JANE BLAIR/BLEAR
BEESON MARY/POLLY	REUBEN STARBUCK
BEESON MIRIAM	JESSE DENNIS
BELL BALAAM	PENELOPE TURNAGE
BELL DAVID BARNES	MARGARET S PETTAWAY/PETWAY
BELL ELIZABETH	WILLIAM MCGILL
BELL ELIZABETH	JESSE JONES
BELL HANNAH	WILLIAM THOMPSON
BELL JOSEPH	MARY LAMB
BELL JOSHUA	PHEREBY NORFLEET
BELL LEVI	CHARLOTTE ADAMS
BELL MARGARET	STANLEY/STANALAND/STANLAND,SAMUEL JR
BELL MARY	JAMES COBB, JR
BELL MARY/POLLY	ROBERTS MCBRIDE
BELL REASON WRIGHT	MARY BRITT
BELL SEBITHA	THOMAS ARRINGTON
BELL SUSAN	MARTIN RUSH
BELL MRS MARY (LAMB)	MARK R GREGORY

SPOUSE	ANCESTOR
BELLAMY MARY	JESSE SMITH
BELVIN MARY A	JAMES WASHINGTON NORWOOD
BENNET/BENNETT SARAH/SALLIE	WILLIAM CRABTREE
BENNETT ELIZABETH	SIMON AYCOCK
BENNETT LUCY CLARISSA	ABEL EDWARDS
BENNETT MELISSA	HIRAM RAY/RHEA
BENOIT RACHAEL VIOLANTE	JAMES PRICE PICKETT
BENTLEY CLOE	JOHN HOLMES
BENTLEY MARY	CORNELIUS LEARY
BERGERON MARGARET	NILES BEAMAN
BERRY FANNY BUSH	WILLIS B PUGH/PEW
BERRY JAMES M	DORCAS JARVIS
BERRY -EMPHY (SIC)	MARY/POLLY MERCER
BERRY MRS ELIZABETH (LAUGHLIN)	BENJAMIN MCFARLIN, JR
BERTSCHIN CATHERINA	FREDERICK HILSABECK
BEST ARCENA VIRGINIA	MARCUS CICERO STEPHEN CHERRY
BEST LUCINDA	REUBEN MAYO
BEST MARGARET	BENNETT JOHN MURPHREY/MURPHY
BEST MARY	THOMAS PHILLIPS
BEST NANCY	WILLIAM B TAYLOR
BETHUNE MARY	STEPHEN J COBB
BETTIS ELINOR	EZEKIEL RUBOTTOM
BETTS CUMIE ELIZABETH	REDERICK BARTLEY AXUM
BIFFLE MARY	JACOB ELLER
BIGGS CLARA MORIAH	WILLIAM MACKEY
BIGGS DAVIS	ANNA MORRIS
BIGGS	FRANCIS LAWRENCE HAYNES
BILLS ALICE H	JAMES JONES
BINGHAM MARY	JAMES R PETTY
BINION ELIZABETH	WILLIAM WILEY
BINKLEY DANIEL	CAMMELIA RHOADES
BINKLY MARY	WILLIAM BAITY, SR
BIRD CATHERINE	MICHAEL WHTALEY, SR
BIRD CATHERINE	DAVID COBB
BIRD MRS RUTHA ANN (COBB)	MARCUS RYAN JOHNSON
BIRDWELL JOHN	MARY ALLEN
BIRMINGHAM SARAH	THOPILAS HOBGOOD/HOPGOOD
BIRNEY MARY	THOMAS WILEY
BISHOP ESTHER	BLOXUM JONES
BISHOP JOHN	SARAH BISHOP
BISHOP MARGARET ALICE	NASH CHEEK
BISHOP MARY	SAMUEL SELLARS, JR
BISHOP MRS SARAH COOPER	WILLIAM PHYSIOC
BISHOP SARAH	WILLIAM HALL
BISHOP MRS ASCENCION (MERRIT)	NICHOLAS GAMMON
BISLAND SARAH ANN	JAMES SMYLIE/SMILEY, REV
BLACK CHARLES	MARY GLENN
BLACK ELLENDER	ROBERT T BEDWELL
BLACK GEN GEORGE SEABORN	MARY ADELINE RALLS
BLACK MARTHA	JAMES BUCHANAN
BLACK MARY LOUELLA	J O A HARVELL
BLACK RACHAEL	AMBROSE COBB
BLACKBURN MARY	MOSES BRIDGES
BLACKBURN WILLIAM	CATHERINE POPLIN

SPOUSE	ANCESTOR
BLACKMAN BETHENEA	JOAB LEE
BLACKMAN MARY	DUNCAN NICHOLSON
BLACKMON PRISCILLA	AMOS M SPIVEY
BLACKNALL ELIZABETH	RICHARD HENRY COOKE
BLACKNALL ELIZABETH H	WILLIAM H JONES
BLACKWELDER MARGARET	MARTIN PHIFER, SR
BLACKWOOD ANNY	JOHN J FRONABERGER
BLAIR ELIHU JAMES KING	CORNELIA ANN TATE
BLAIR ELIZABETH	MOSES MCQUISTON
BLAIR OLIVE JANE	HENRY HARRISON BEESON
BLAIR RUTH	DAVID WHITE
BLAKE AARON	HAZELTINE ANN JOHNSTON
BLAKE DORCAS	WILLIAM HOOKS
BLAKE ELIZABETH	SHADRICK OLIVER WOOTEN
BLAKE MARGARET	PETER AMICK/EMMICH
BLAKE MARY	JOSHUA BARCLIFT/BARTLETT
BLAKE SARAH	JOHN OWEN
BLAKELEY FANNIE MILLER	ROBERT BROWN QUINN
BLAKELEY NANCEY	JACOB C LEE, SR
BLAKELEY THOMAS FRANKLYN	SARAH UNITY ROBERTS
BLAKELY MARY ANN	JOHN HAMPTON TUCKER
BLAKEMORE	JOHN HENRY LOPP/LAPP/LOOP, SR
BLALOCK ALFRED	HARRIET HARRISON
BLALOCK ELIZABETH	THOMAS VANCE
BLALOCK ELIZABETH/BETSY	ABRAHAM MOORE
BLALOCK EUPHRASIA ANGELINE	JAMES/JIM WHITE ARNOLD
BLALOCK FRANKLIN PIERCE	MARY JANE OAKLEY
BLALOCK NANCY	ROBERT BLALOCK
BLALOCK NANCY	WILLIAM/BILLIE WHEELEY
BLALOCK ROBERT	JUDITH/JUDY PEARCE
BLALOCK WILLIAM DAVID	SARAH DELILAH STADLER
BLANCHARD RACHEL	JESSE GARRETT
BLAND ARTHUR	POLLY A FELTS
BLAND ELIZABETH	ADAM GASKINS
BLAND SARAH T	SIMON SIKES BRINSON
BLANEY MARY JANE	THOMAS ELFE
BLANKENSHIP BETSY	GADSWELL PEARCE, JR
BLANTON CATHERINE	ELBERT S ARRINGTON
BLEAKLEY NANCY	JOHN H BADGER
BLEDSOE CAHTERINE	SIMPSON FORSYTH
BLEDSOE SARAH	WILLIAM HARDIN
BLEVINS JAMES	LYDIA SIZEMORE
BLEVINS MAHALA	DAVID TUCKER, III
BLEVINS MRS ELIZABETH	JOHN WIGGINS
BLEVINS WELLS	ELIZABETH PENNINGTON
BLOODWORTH THOMAS	TAMSIE PROCTER
BLOOM SALLY	GEORGE SPRINGER
BLOUNT ELIZABETH	EDMUND HOSKINS
BLOUNT LENNIE EULALIA	EBENEZER DUNSTON
BLOUNT MARY	WILLIAM BRYAN/BRYANT
BLOUNT SUSANNAH	JOHN BROOKS, JR
BLOUNT MRS LONA MATTIE (TINSLEY)	NEILL ANGUS RAY
BLUE CATHERINE	WILLIAM PITT CAMERON
BLUE DUNCAN	NANCY JACOBS

SPOUSE	ANCESTOR
BLUE ELIZABETH	SOLOMON BARLOW COUNCIL/COUNCILL
BLUE MRS MARY CAROLINE (MULLER)	WILLIAM HENRY MCMILLAN
BLUNK PURLINA	LOUIS TAYLOR FOX
BLUNT RUTH	THOMAS NORFLEET
BLYTHE ELIZABETH	ROBERT MCCORKLE
BLYTHE MARGARET	WILLIAM MCCORKLE
BOATRIGHT ELIZABETH	ORSBURN POWELL
BOATRIGHT REBECCA	SAMUEL RICHARD FORD
BODAT DOROTHY	WALTER JONES, REV
BODKIN SARAH	IVORY HAMBY
BOECKEL CATHARINE	ANDREW VOLK/FOLK/FOWLKES, JR
BOEHM MARIA CHRISTINA	JOHN JORG/GEOR HERDLEIN/HERTLEIN/HARTLINE
BOGUE WILLIAM	ELLENER/ELLENDER PERISHO/PARISHO
BOIL MRS ELIZABETH T	ISAAC ALFRED LEE
BOLES OLIVIA	RUFUS C FOWLER
BOLICK EUNICE ELEANOR	DENNIS WILLIAM MOOSE
BOLICK POLLY	ANDREW HOLLER
BOLLINGER NANCY	JACOB CABLE
BOLLINGER SALOME/SALMA	JACOB LEWIS CONRAD
BOLLMAN MARY OPAL	LONNIE ERNEST CASPER
BOLLS MATTHEW	MARY SMYLIE/SMILEY
BOND EMMALINE	LEWIS HENRY PHILLIPS
BOND HANCE	MARTHA ELIZABETH EELBECK
BOND HARRIETT DAVIS	RICHARD EPPES
BOND PENELOPE	BALISS HOUSE
BONDS ANNA	WILLIAM DAWSON HUSON/HUSTON
BONNER ABIGAIL	SIMON, CPT JONES
BONNER GARNET KATHLEEN	WILLIAM ANDERSON LITCHFIELD
BONNER	MARY FRANCES OLDHAM
BONNER SUSAN HEATH	THOMAS CLAYTON
BOOKOUT EASTER LETTIE	OSBOURN ROSS
BOOKOUT RACHEL	MOSES ROSS
BOON ANNA MARGARET	ADAM WEITZEL
BOON JOSEPH	SARAH BASS
BOON JOSEPH	MARY G GREEN
BOONE CATHERINE ROSANNA	JOHANN MARTIN COULTER
BOONE JUDITH DEANES	JOSEPH ALVIN DUPREE/DUPRE'
BOONE MARY/POLLY	JOHN COUCH
BOONE POLLY	THOMAS WRIGHT FROST
BOOTH CATHERINE	HENRY BAKER
BOOTH STEPHEN S	MINERVA J CATES
BORDEAUX ARMISTEAD H	SUSAN APPLEWHITE
BORDON REBECCA	JOSEPH BURCHAM
BOREN MOLLIE	RICHARD C A PIRKLE
BOSS CATHERINE	WILLIAM MORRIS, JR
BOSTICK ABSALOM	SUSANNAH DALTON
BOSTICK ABSALOM	NANCY DALTON
BOSWELL ELIZABETH	GEORGE W CHANDLER
BOURLAND ELIZA JANE	ANDERSON HALL
BOURLAND SALLIE	JOHN GILBERT
BOWEN AMELIA	LUKE PRIDGEN
BOWEN CHRISTINA CHANEY	CALVIN FREDERICK FULK
BOWERS MARTHE/PATSY	BENJAMIN MOORE
BOWERS MARY	JOHN GOODLOE

SPOUSE INDEX

SPOUSE		ANCESTOR
BROOKS	PRISCILLA	JOHN LEWIS
BROOKS	SUSANNAH	SHERWOOD WHITE
BROOKS	TIMEY/TINNA	VINCENT BRANN
BROOKS	MRS MAGGIE (BRANTLEY)	ENOCH PHILLIPS
BROOM	MRS ELIZABETH	ELLIS CLANTON
BROTHERS	ISRAEL	REBECCA EDWARDS
BROWER	ADALINE H	PETER SHAMBURGER
BROWN	ADDISON BARNETT	MARY CAROLINE/POLLY MCKEITHAN
BROWN	AGNES	ALEXANDER CRAIGHEAD, REV
BROWN	ALSEY	JOHN CASS MOYE
BROWN	ANDREW JACKSON	SARAH MILLER
BROWN	ANNAH	THOMAS WATTS HARRINGTON
BROWN	BENJAMIN	NANCY TUGMAN
BROWN	CATHERINE PERMELIA	ABRAHAM TEAGUE
BROWN	CECIL C	CORA LESTER DILLARD
BROWN	CORDELIA	NILUS HELMS
BROWN	DOROTHY ANN/DOLLY	JONATHAN WILDER WILLIAMS
BROWN	ELIZABETH	WRIGHTMAN/RIGHTMAN HILLIARD
BROWN	ELIZABETH	DRURY REEVES/REAVES, JR
BROWN	ELIZABETH	RIGHTMAN/WRIGHTMAN HILLIARD
BROWN	EMELINE DAVIS	MILLARD FILMORE OWEN
BROWN	EMILY JANE	JOSIAH TAYLOR KNIGHT
BROWN	FRANCIS	THOMAS WIGGINS
BROWN	HANNAH	HENRY PENNEY/PENNY
BROWN	HESAKIAH	LAURA F WILLIAMS
BROWN	JAMES	MARY JANE LOCK
BROWN	JANE	LEWIS DANIEL HICKS/HIX
BROWN	JANE	WILLIAM WOOD/WOODS
BROWN	JANE	WILLIAM STAFFORD
BROWN	JOEL	MARY SEAY
BROWN	KEZIAH	MATTHEW G BUFFALOE
BROWN	LUCY ANN	JOHN OWEN
BROWN	MARGARET	NATHANIEL CHASE WILLIAMS, SR
BROWN	MARTHA	LEANDER WELBORN
BROWN	MARY	ALEXANDER CALEZANCE MILLER
BROWN	MARY	JOHN R ACREE
BROWN	MARY	EZEKIEL HAISLEY
BROWN	MARY	ALFRED BLALOCK
BROWN	MARY ANN	WILLIS DIXON
BROWN	MARY CAROLINE	MARCUS BUTLER
BROWN	NANCY	GEORGE HENDRICKS
BROWN	NANCY ANN	JOHN HOPPES
BROWN	NANCY CLORINDA	WILLIAM HAYES
BROWN	NANCY JANE	HUGH KERR
BROWN	NANCY MARY	STEPHEN MARION HAIRGROVE
BROWN	NAOMI	SAMUEL MITCHELL CARRUTHERS
BROWN	PATIENCE	JOSHUA HADLEY
BROWN	PATIENCE	JOSHUA HADLEY
BROWN	POLLY	JESSE T FERGUSON
BROWN	REBECCA	MATTHEW SMYLIE/SMILEY
BROWN	REBECCA	DAVID HOLDER
BROWN	ROYAL REAMS	NORMA BLANCHE WESTER
BROWN	SARA	HENRY JACOBS
BROWN	SARAH	JOEL PERKERSON

235

SPOUSE	ANCESTOR
BROWN SARAH J	JOSEPH C CREEKMORE
BROWN SARAH JANE	JAMES DANIEL THRIFT
BROWN SOPHIA	SAMUEL CREASON/CRESON
BROWN SUSANNAH	ISHAM B FELTS
BROWN THOMAS	CHRISTIAN MAULE
BROWN WM GEO WASHINGTON	ELIZABETH THOMPSON
BROWN MRS ANN (SHEPPARD)	JAMES WALLACE COCKRUM
BROWN MRS ELIZABETH (HUNT)	WILLIAM CRABTREE
BROWNING MALINDA	ALLEN SCHOLES
BROWNING NANCY M	ROBERT DICKY STADLER
BRUCE REBECCA JANE	SAMUEL HUNTER, COL
BRUMBALOW ELIZABETH	EZEKIEL MORTON
BRUNER SOPHIA	NICHOLAS CREASON/CRESON
BRUTON NANCY	STANTON TAYLOR
BRYAN ELIZABETH	OLIVER HAMPTON
BRYAN ELIZABETH	HUGH, JR, PUGH
BRYAN ELLINDER	STANDLEY CHAFFIN
BRYAN MARY ANN	JESSE JOLLEY
BRYAN REBECCA	JOHN BOONE
BRYAN SAMUEL	ELIZABETH MCMAHAN
BRYANT AMANDA	JAMES F MACE
BRYANT ANN	WILLIAM WOOTEN
BRYANT FRANCES LOUISE	MICAJAH MANNING
BRYANT HARRIET LOUISE	FREDERICK JAMESHENRY PUGH BRYAN/BRYANT
BRYANT HETTIE MAY	WILLIAM LUSTER WILLIAMS
BRYANT MILLIE ADELAIDE	THOMAS B MCBEE
BRYANT MRS CATHERINE	JOSEPH BRYANT
BRYANT SUSANNAH	JOHN SETSER/SETZER, I
BRYANT/BRIANT ROSEY	JOHN KITTRELL
BRYSON RHODA	SHADRICK HYATT
BUCHANAN ARTHUR	TEMPERANCE VANCE
BUCHANAN BETTIE F	SAMUEL WAITE KNOTT
BUCHANAN ELIZABETH	EBENEZER NEWTON
BUCHANAN JOHN RUFFIN	NANCY A PITTARD
BUCHANAN JOSEPH MINTER	MARTHA H H BUCHANAN
BUCHANAN JOSEPH SPEARS	CHARITY WILLIAMS
BUCHANAN MARGARET	JAMES THOMPSON
BUCHANAN MARTHA G	THOMAS A MITCHELL
BUCHANAN MARTHA H H	JOSEPH MINTER BUCHANAN
BUCHANAN PRISCILLA	JOSHUA ASBURY WHITE
BUCHANAN PRUDENCE	JOSHUA ASBURY WHITE
BUCHANAN WILLIAM RUFFIN	VIRGINIA TUNSTALL
BUCHANAN ZULA	MILT ENGLISH
BUCKMASTER ANN	HOY, JOHN VAN SR
BUFFALOE WINEFRED JANE	JAMES TURNER BUFFALOE
BUFFINGTON SAMUEL W	NANCY STUDDARD
BUFFKIN BETHEL	MARY CROWSON
BUFFKIN ELENDER/ELEANOR	JOSHUA SOLES
BUFFORD N FRANCIS	JOHN RUFUS AMOS
BUIE REBECCA	DANIEL SHAW
BULL WILLIAM C	ANNA TURNER
BULLARD KATY	JOHN MORGAN
BULLOCH CAROLINE	JAMES D WELCH
BULLOCK ELIZABETH	THOMAS DUDLEY CLEMENT

SPOUSE INDEX

SPOUSE	ANCESTOR
BULLOCK PRISCILLA	RICHARD DONALDSON COOKE
BULLOCK SARAH	JOHN SIMS
BULLOCK SUSAN	WILLIAM THOMAS FARABOUGH
BULLOCK SUSANNAH	WILLIAM SIMS
BULLOCK MRS MARGARET (BRYANT)	JOHN LAWRENCE GRAHAM MANNING
BULLS NANCY J	EDWARD DEBNAM
BUMGARNER DELIAH	JOHN WESLEY KILBY
BUMGARNER MAUDE LOUVANNIE	VANBUREN ARVEY HOWARD
BUNCH ANNA	WILLIAM DEAL
BUNCH JUDY	JOHN MCDORMAN
BUNCH MAHALA AMY	SAMUEL SIMMONS
BUNCH MARY CAROLINE	CALEB KELLY
BUNCH MARY/POLLY	CHARLES HORTON
BUNN ELIZABETH	DAVID C MORGAN
BUNN MARY ANN	JOHN ROBERT WEATHERSBY
BUNN SALLY LYNN	SAMUEL LEE
BUNN MRS MARY ANN (HUGHES)	JOHN WILSON
BUNTON JOHN PLEASANT	SUSANNAH STAMPER
BUNTON KATIE	EDWARD M GIDEON/GIDDENS
BURCH CHARLES HILL	VELLA LEE HORTON
BURCH JOHN L	JUDITH SOUTHERN
BURCH WILLIAM HENRY	MARGARET BURROUGHS LONG
BURCHAM RUBEN	NANCY WHEELER
BURFOOT BATHSHEBA	PAUL PUGH/PEW
BURFORD FRANCES ELIZABETH	JACOB AARON BULL
BURGESS LYDIA	JAMES MERCER/MONROE BERRY
BURGESS MARY	ALFRED A SLEDGE
BURGESS SALLY	GEORGE MEDFORD
BURGIN BENJAMIN	LEAH MAN/MANN
BURGIN ELIZA	LAMBERT CLINGMAN CLAYTON, COL
BURGIN JOHN	ELIZABETH MAN/MANN
BURK ANDREW	POLLY ADER
BURLESON MARY CAROLINE	JOHN TURNER BLANKENSHIP
BURNETT ELIZABETH	ZACHEUS CORLEY/CAULEY/COLLEY
BURNETTE MARY/POLLY	OLIVER M/MARTIN CRUTCHFIELD
BURNS ELIZA JANE	BENJAMIN KEENER MILLSAPS
BURNS ELIZABETH	JAMES DAVID ROBERTS, JR
BURNS SARAH	JOHN LEATHERWOOD
BURNS/BURNES JOHN A	ANNE WALKER
BURRIS ALLEN	LUCY HINSON
BURRIS JANE	ALLEN L HIGHTOWER
BURRIS MARTIN	FRANCINA DENNY
BURROUGHS	AARON TYSON, SR
BURROW WILLIAM	SUSAN MARY YORK
BURT ELIZABETH	STEPHEN MARSHALL
BURT ELIZABETH	JAMES OLIVE
BURT HARDY	MARTHA LANE
BURT LABAN R	KATHERINE MATILDA THOMAS
BURT WILLIAM	MARTHA ELIZABETH EELBECK
BURTON A M	DEMPSEY SARGENT
BURTON ALLEN	SYLVIA REEVES
BURTON EMILY F	JAMES MILES KILLIAN GUINN
BURTON ESTHER	THOMAS RESPESS
BURTON JESSE	SALLY FRAZIER

237

SPOUSE INDEX

SPOUSE	ANCESTOR
BURTON NANCY KENAN	WILLIAM FREDERICK
BUSH SARAH	PLEASANT CHILDRESS
BUSHEE ELIZABETH	ROBERT SURLES
BUTLER ANITA LOUISE	ROBERT VERNON MOOSE
BUTLER JAMES AUGUSTUS	NANNIE MARTIN
BUTLER LUCRETIA	JAMES H MOORE
BUTLER LUCY	JEREMIAH ROWLAND
BUTLER MRS MARY ANN (BROWN)	LUNSFORD AYCOCK
BUTRAM JOSEPHINE	HENRY DYE
BUTT SARAH ELMINA	RICHARD C A PIRKLE
BUTTS SALLY	HENRY LOUDERMILK
BYFORD ANNA	JAMES SISSOM
BYNUM PRISCILLA D	JOHN HOLLIDAY DIXON, REV
BYRAM NANCY	GRANVILLE H WHITLOW
BYRD GEORGE W	MRS ELIZABETH BYRD
BYRD NANCY CAROLINE	WILLIAM ENSLEY MCCOURRY
BYRNE CAROLINE	KENNETH HAYNES
CABLE CASPAR	ELIZABETH BAKER
CABLE MILEY PEMIE	JACOB A MABERY
CAGLE NANCY	JEREMIAH ROWLAND
CAHO MARY ELIZABETH	JAMES CLAY ORMOND
CAHOON PRISCILLA	MIDGETT SPENCER
CAIN DANIEL	TEMPERANCE/TEMPY VANNOY
CAIN HANNAH	JOHN HEATH
CAIRNS/KARNS RACHEL	JOSEPH STUTZMAN
CAKE ANN	ANTHONY FILGO
CALDWELL JAMES F	BARBARA M MCCRACKEN
CALDWELL MARGARET LOUISE ISADORE	LEWIS TATE HOLLER
CALE JERSEY	HARDY COBB
CALLAWAY JOSHUA	ISABELLA GRAVES HENDERSON
CALLEN NANCY	LAIRD KIRKPATRICK
CALLICOATTE SPENCER CLAYBORN	SALINA SPENCER
CAMERON MARY	WILLIAM O THOMAS
CAMERON NEILL BLUE	MARTHA ADELAIDE WADSWORTH
CAMERON ROSA JANETTE	GEORGE WASHINGTON GARNER
CAMERON WILLIAM PITT	CATHERINE BLUE
CAMP SOPHIA	JOHN SHEPHERD FORD
CAMP/KENT MRS MARTHA (SCOTT)	SIMON PETER WATERS
CAMPBELL ARCHIBALD	REBECCA KIRK
CAMPBELL CATHERINE	NEIL MCMILLAN
CAMPBELL CATHERINE ANN	EDWIN JOHNSON PATE
CAMPBELL CATHERINE ANN	EDWIN JOHNSTONE PATE
CAMPBELL CATHERINE JEAN	WILLIAM HENRY MCMILLAN
CAMPBELL ELIZA	SIMON JOHNSON
CAMPBELL FLORA	JOHN CROOK LOVE
CAMPBELL JOHN	MARY EDWARDS
CAMPBELL JUDGE DAVID	ELIZABETH OUTLAW
CAMPBELL MARGARET	DUNCAN BLUE
CAMPBELL MARGARET	JAMES UNDERWOOD
CAMPBELL MARGARET	MOSES NEELY
CAMPBELL MARY ADALINE	JAMES WESLY SISK
CAMPBELL POLLY	EZEKIEL POLK

SPOUSE INDEX

SPOUSE	ANCESTOR
CAMPBELL SARAH	WILLIAM BALL
CAMPBELL MRS MARY (MCLEOD?)	JAMES HENDERSON MATTHEWS
CAMPFIELD CHARLES	REBECCA LYDAY/LYDA
CANNADAY RHODA	WILLIAM E SHARPLESS
CANNON CATHARINE	HARDEE JOHNSON
CANNON ELIZABETH	DARNEL GLOVER
CANNON LEWIS	SARAH PUGH
CANNON	HUGH PUGH, SR
CANNON NANCY	DAVID CLEMMER
CANNUP/KNOPF ELIZABETH AVALIAE	GEORGE WASHINGTON THIEME/TEEM
CANTER DELILAH LOUVENIA	DAVID J DENNY
CANTERBURY	NANCY ANNE FRANKLIN
CAPEHART ROSA GERTRUDE	JOSEPH JOHN WHITE, SR
CAPLE STERLING	MELISSA CATES
CAPPS DELILA	JARRELL KICKER
CAPPS SARAH	JOSEPH KUYKENDALL/KIRKENDALL
CAPSHAW POLLY	WILLIAM S SPLAWN
CARDEN MALINDA MISSOURI	GEORGE WASHINGTON BARCLAY
CARLETON ELIZABETH	WILLIAM WHITAKER
CARLISLE MRS MERCY	NEIL CAMERON
CARLOCK MARGARET/PEGGY	BENJAMIN MASSEY
CARLOCK/KERLOCK LYDIA	COLBERT SHERRILL
CARLTON LYDIA	WILLIAM MATHIS
CARLTON MARGARET SELINA	DRUARY MCGEE
CARMICHAEL JOHN WESLEY	SUSANNA CARMICHAEL
CARMICHAEL JOSEPH	ELIZABETH HOLDER
CARMICHAEL SOLOMON	SAYRE/SARAH/SALLY GRUBBS
CARMICHAEL SUSANNAH	JOHN WESLEY CARMICHAEL
CARMICHAEL WILLIAM	SALLIE SMITH
CARNAL ELIZABETH	DANIEL DEAN
CARNELLE/KERNALL MILDRED	DOUGLAS OLIVER
CARNES MALINDA ABIGAIL	VESTER MITCHEL STEPP/STAPP
CARNEY DELPHY	DANIEL SARGENT/SEARGENT/SARJENT
CARPENTER MARY	JOHN W MAY
CARPENTER SARAH ELIZABETH	PINKNEY ASBURY LOMAX
CARPENTER WILLIAM	ELIZABETH GIDEON/GIDDENS
CARR ELIZABETH	JOHN JOHNSTON
CARR WILLIAM	NANCY FOSSET
CARR/KERR ESTHER	ELIHU J MCCRACKEN
CARRAWAY SENERSHA	HANSEL HARDISON
CARRIGER CYNTHIA	SAMUEL BOONE
CARROL RACHEL	ISHAM ROYALL
CARROLL DELILAH	WILLIAM COX
CARROW ANN	HENRY HOOTEN MALLISON
CARROWAY MARY E	THOMAS RESPESS
CARRUTHERS MARY ANN	GEORGE WASHINGTON POTTER
CARRUTHERS WILLIAM	SARAH HARVEY
CARSON AGNES	JAMES DUFF
CARSON CATHERINE	ELIJAH CHASTIAN
CARSON PETER	RACHAEL COX
CARTER ANNE LAVINIA	FELIX HARRISON LEATHERWOOD
CARTER ANNIE E	NEILL ANGUS RAY
CARTER DR DAVID E	ADALINE PARKER
CARTER ELISABETH	JOHN T WOODRUFF

SPOUSE		ANCESTOR
CLANTON	SALLIE	HENRY ABERNATHY
CLANTON	SARAH	JOSEPH HENRY LEE
CLAPP	CATHARINE	JOHN HOBBS
CLAPP	MARIA	GEORGE CORTNER/COTNER
CLARK	ANTHONY	SARAH DUNLAP
CLARK	ANTHONY	MARY E OATES
CLARK	ELIZABETH SANDLIN	IRVIN ALLEN
CLARK	HANNAH	ROBERT CRAIGHEAD
CLARK	JESSE OSBORNE	IDA MELISSA ANN GASKINS
CLARK	JOHN	ELIZABETH ANDERSON
CLARK	JOSEPH	RUTH ALEXANDER
CLARK	LUCY	CALVIN RILEY REECE
CLARK	MARTHA A	JOHN MICHAEL PEARSON
CLARK	MARTHA JANE	ELIJAH GREEN KIMBRO/KIMBROUGH
CLARK	MARY	JOHN ALSTON
CLARK		ARTHUR HARRIS
CLARK	NANCY	NATHANIEL RUDD
CLARK	REBECCA	GEORGE CLANEY
CLARK	SARAH	GEORGE CROMARTIE
CLARK	SARAH	ANDREW MOORMAN
CLARK	SARAH	THOMAS MOORMAN
CLARK	SARAH/SALLY	JOHN HAWKINS GOODE
CLARK	THOMAS H	REBECCA RUDD
CLARK	WEEKS H	SUSAN GASKINS
CLARK	WESLEY ELBER	EMELINE HOLDER
CLARK	WILLIAM	REBEKAH HARMAN
CLARKE	TILGHMAN WARFIELD	JANE LEWIS
CLARY	NANCY WRIGHT	EBENEZER B FROST
CLAYTON	CHARITY	WILLIAM LEWIS
CLAYTON	EMELINE	HUMPHREY NORRIS COWDEN
CLAYTON	GEORGE	MARGARET/PEGGY THOMPSON
CLAYTON	LAMBERT CLINGMAN	ELIZA BURGIN/BURGAN
CLAYTON	LEAH MALINDA	JOSEPH ROBERT GARREN/GARN
CLAYTON	MARY	CHARLESWORTH BLOUNT
CLAYTON	MARY ALICE	THOMAS RITCHIE LISTER
CLAYTON	MARY LEAH	ZACHARIAH/ZACH OAKLEY
CLAYTON	SUSAN LOUISE	ALEXANDER LEWIS SHOAF
CLAYTON	THOMAS	LA MARE, SARY/SARAH DELAMAR/DE
CLEARE	ELIZABETH	THOMAS WINSLOW
CLEAVER	STEPHEN	ELEANOR R MCFARLAND
CLEBURN	MRS MARTHA	ELIJAH/ELI CANTRELL
CLEMENT	LUCY	WILLIAM HOLDER
CLEMENT	WILLIAM	JANE GOOCH
CLEMENTS	MARY	JEREMIAH G RESPESS
CLEMMENTS	MARGARETTE	PETER GOTT
CLEMSON/CLEMPSON	MAGARA	JOSEPH DAMERON KNIGHT
CLENNY	JAMES	ESTHER MCCRACKEN
CLEVELAND	BENJAMIN	MARY GRAVES
CLEVELAND	ELIZABETH	JAMES COFFEY
CLEVELAND	ELIZABETH	WILLIAM WALTON
CLEVELAND	MARY	BERNARD FRANKLIN
CLEVELAND	MARY GRAVES	ABEDNEGO/BEDNEY FRANKLIN
CLEVENGER	MRS NANCY	AARON SANDERS
CLIFFORD	JACOB	NANCY BOONE

SPOUSE	ANCESTOR
CLIFTON EDWIN	NANCY FOLK/FOLKS
CLIFTON JOHN	SARAH FARLOW/FORLAW
CLIFTON SARAH	DRURY ROBERTSON
CLINE MARY	ANDREAS/ANDREW KILLIAN/KILIAN
CLINE SARAH	SAMUEL LACKEY
CLODFELTER MARGARET	ADAM HARMAN/HARMON
CLONINGER MARY/MOLLIE	LEWIS CLEMMER
CLOPTON ELIZABETH	WILLIAM BALLARD
CLOUD POLLY	JOEL MILLS
COATES MARY E	WILLIAM STROUD
COATS FLORENCE	RUFUS PARRISH
COBB DAVID	CATHERINE BIRD
COBB ELLENER	EZEKIEL SANFORD
COBB ELLIE	WILLIAM MOORE
COBB FANNY	JAMES MAY, CAPT
COBB MARTHA	JAMES L THIGPEN
COBB MARY MATILDA	JACKSON C COX
COBB	GEORGE KERNODLE
COBB MRS JEMINA	PLEASANT CHANDLER
COBB PENELOPE	HENRY MASSENGILL
COBB SALENA	STERLING EDWARDS
COBB SELINA/SALINA	STERLING/STARLING EDWARDS
COBLE DAVID	PENNEY HOWARD
COBLE MARY	ELISHA BENNETT
COBURN CHLOE FRANCES	BENJAMIN HARVEY ROBERSON
COBURN/COGBURN MARTHA	ANDREW JACKSON BARNETT
COCHRAN JACOB	PATSY POOL
COCHRAN MARY	WILLIAM VILLINES
COCKERHAM CHARITY	MOSES WOODRUFF
COCKRUM RACHEL	MICHAEL HENDRICK MELTON
COE GEORGE W	ELIZABETH AVERY WEBB
COFFEE MARTHA/PATSY	ROBERT NORMAN
COGBURN MARTHA JANE	WILLIAM MONTGOMERY PYRON
COGDELL ELIZABETH	TEGAL TAYLOR
COGDILL	JOHN ARMSTRONG
COGDILL ROBERT	MALINDA DAVIS
COGDILL WILLIAM	NANCY DAVIS
COGWELL RHODY	SPELL MOUNGER/MONGER
COLBERT MARY EOSENTRICE	JAMES BLAIR/BLEAR
COLBREATH MARY	ISAAC PHARIS/FAIRIS/FARRISH
COLE ELIZABETH	JOHN FEEZOR
COLE ELIZABETH T	ISAAC B FELTS
COLE ELLIS	JAMES SMITH
COLE MARTHA	WILLIAM MOORE
COLE MARY E	MCCOMAS RHODES
COLE PHILIP	MARTHA CALDWELL
COLE RUEY	ALEXANDER EVELAN LOWRANCE
COLE SARAH	ANTHONY CHAMNESS
COLEE JULIUS LOUIS	MARY OLIPHANT
COLEMAN NANCY	YOUNG ALLEN
COLEMAN NANCY	GEORGE CHAMBERS
COLEY POLLY	ANDERSON KING
COLEY THOMAS	SIDDA PENNY
COLLIER LYDIA	THOMAS HARRINGTON

SPOUSE	ANCESTOR
COLLINS ALLIFAIR	JOHN TAYLOR
COLLINS CAHTERINE	AMBROSE JONES
COLLINS CHARLOTTE	NATHANIEL SKINNER
COLLINS KATRON	ANDREW STICE, SR
COLLINS MRS SARAH	GEORGE CUMMINGS/CUMMINS
COLLINS RUHAMEY	ANDREW V TABOR/TABER
COLLINS SARAH	HENRY ROBERSON, JR
COLLINS WILLIAM	KATRON STICE
COLLINS MRS SARA FRANCES (WALL)	JOHN OATIS PLUMBLEE/PLUMLEY
COLLY NANCY	LEWIS HALL
COLSON CHARITY	NATHANIEL/NATHAN DENSON
COLTRAIN MARTHA	SAMUEL MILLIKAN, JR
COMBS	ROBERT JENKINS
COMBS MRS CHARLOTTE (PLEDGER)	LEWIS MIDGETT
COMMANDER MILLICENT	SAMUEL BARCLIFT
COMMONS BELINDA	MICHAEL RAMSEY
COMPTON SALLIE ANNE	JAMES JEREMIAH BROOKS
CONDITT JOHN FIELDING	SARAH/SALLY CHEVES/CHEEVES
CONGER ABIGAIL	NATHANIEL/NATHAN GUERIN/GEURIN
CONGER ANGELINA	MARTIN VAN BUREN JOYCE
CONGER NANCY	JAMES F HAMILTON
CONNER ANN/NANCY	RICHARD HAMLETT/HAMBLET
CONNER EDWARD	SARAH GRISSIT/GRESSET
CONNER JESSIE M	RUSSELL ORAN HEATER
CONNER MILLS HENRY	ISTALENA LEIGH BOYCE
CONRAD JACOB LEWIS	SALOME/SALMA BOLLINGER
CONRAD MARY CLAIR	JOHANNAS/JOHN SHUFORD/SCHEUFFERT
CONRAD RUDOLPH	ANNA MARIA SCHELL
COOK ABAGAIL ELIZABETH	JOSEPH HAMILTON GREEN
COOK AMY	ABEDNEGO SANDERS
COOK BETTY NICHOLSON	DAVID GILES? BOWERS
COOK CHARLOTTE	DEMPSEY SARGENT
COOK DAVID	MARY M STANSBURY
COOK ELIZABETH	ZADOCK COOK
COOK MAGGIE	MALCOLM MCEACHIN
COOK MARGARET JANE	HENRY GREEN
COOK MARTHA	DAVID ROSSER
COOK MARY ANN	ZACHARIAH COLE
COOK MICHAEL	CATHERINE HUFFMAN
COOK NANCY	WILLIAM BARDIN
COOK NANCY	JAMES REAGAN
COOK NANCY RUCKER	JOHN S RUST
COOK PHEBE	JOHN SEAGRAVE
COOK RANSOM TURNER	ELIZABETH ANN DURHAM
COOK SARAH	JOSHUA HAWKINS
COOK SHEMUEL	NANCY ANN RUCKER
COOK SUSAN CATHERINE	JOHN W KING
COOKE CATHARINE	MARTIN SHOFNER
COOKE MARY/POLLEY	NATHANIEL EDWARDS
COOKE SARAH	JOHN DURANT
COOMES FRANCIS IGNATIUS	CHARITY WOOD/WOODS
COOPER DOROTHY	JAMES FARABOUGH
COOPER GEORGE	SARAH BISHOP
COOPER MALINDA	JOHN A FOOSHEE

SPOUSE	ANCESTOR
COOPER MILTON WAKELAND	MARTHA/MATTIE JANE BAKER
COOPER MRS SARAH	JOHN BISHOP
COOPER SARAH A	JESSIE COLVARD
COOPER WILLIAM	EMMALINE PENNEY
COOPER MRS ELIZABETH (JONES)	THOMAS GILL
CORBET	MOSES DUNCAN
CORBY MRS MARTHA(MOORE)	EPHRIAM SUTTON
CORDELL NANCY	W J BLACK
CORL BETSEY	ADAM COBBLE/CAUBLE/KABEL
CORLEW CELIA	JAMES JONES
CORLEW ELIZA JANE	ISRAEL FOGLEMAN
CORMANY ADAM	JANE R THOMAS
CORNELL MARY	WILLIAM BLOUNT COLEMAN
CORRELL DANIEL	NELLY/ELLEN PENCE
CORRELL HEZEKIAH ALEXANDER	CAROLINE REBECCA RUSSELL
CORSBIE ANN	JAMES JOB
CORTNER DAVID	CATHERINE AMICK/EMMICH
CORTNER JOHN MATTHEW	BARBARA LAU/LOW
COSBY ELIZABETH	JOSEPH MCADAMS
COSBY JAMES	MARGARET MCBRIDE
COTTEN LAURA	MARSHALL ANDREW TUTOR
COTTEN SARAH	HARRISON BOYCE
COTTEN MRS NANCY (JOHNSON)	HENRY NEWSOME
COTTER MRS LYDIA (DITTEMORE)	JAMES BECK
COTTINGHAM LUCY CASSANDRA	MOSES STRAHAN, JR
COTTON JEMIMA IRIS	NATHAN EDWARDS
COTTON MRS SARAH (CLAYBOURN)	ZADOCK SIMMONS
COUCH CHARLOTTE	STEPHEN ROOK/RUKE
COUCH SARAH	JAMES LEWIS
COUCH/CAPPS KATHERINE	ALFRED KUYKENDALL/KIRKENDALL
COULTER MARY MAGDALENE	JOHN FRY
COUMBE DORIS MATILDA	JAMES AUGUSTUS BUTLER
COUNCIL ELIZABETH ANN	BETHEL MEARES
COUNCIL SARAH	JOHN BROWNLOW
COURSEY ROBERT	MARY ANDERSON
COURSEY WILLIAM	FRANCES ACOCK
COVINGTON MARTHA	PETER YODER
COVINGTON URCILLA	JOHN WALKER
COWAN ANN FOSTER	OSBORNE GILES FOARD/FORD
COWART WILLIAM	SUSAN MARIE WORTHINGTON
COWELL RACHEL A	GIDEON OLDES
COWELL SARAH A	GIDEON OLDES
COWELL MRS MARY ELIZABETH (OLDES)	JOSEPH WOODARD
COX ALEXANDER	ELIZABETH ANN/LILIAN FLOWERS
COX ARGENT	SIMON WHITEHURST
COX ELIZABETH	GUILFORD MURPHY/MURPHREY
COX ELIZABETH	STRANGEMAN HUTCHINS
COX ELIZABETH	STRANGEMAN HUTCHENS
COX HANNAH	CHARLES COX
COX HANNAH	BENJAMIN MARSHBURN/MASHBURN
COX HANNAH	HUGH MOFFITT
COX HARRIET	RUFFIN HARWARD/HARWOOD/HARROD
COX LONE MAE	CURRIE REECE
COX MARGARET/PEGGY	BENJAMIN SPENCER

245

SPOUSE	ANCESTOR
COX MARTHA	JOSEPH ALLEN
COX MARY	CHARLES MOFFITT
COX MARY A	WILLIAM CURTIS HEATH, REV
COX POLLY	ROYAL POTTER
COX RACHAEL	PETER CARSON
COX REBECCA	BENJAMIN COX
COX RHODA	JACOB BARNHART
COX RUTH	SOLOMON COX
COX RUTH	WILLIAM COX
CRABB SUSAN	MOSES SEAGRAVE
CRABTREE CHARLES F	VIRGINIA T STANLEY
CRABTREE HANNAH	JAMES HASTINGS, SR
CRABTREE JOHN	LANIE STANLEY
CRAIG ISABEL	DAVID NELSON
CRAIG JEAN	WILLIAM NESMITH
CRAIG LUCY	ELIJAH JEFFERSON PIVER
CRAIG MARTHA	JOHN/JACK M PAUL
CRAIGHEAD JANE	WILLIAM MCREE
CRAIN FRIEND	ELIZABETH HOUSE/HAUS
CRANE JOHN	MILDRED WALTON
CRANFORD SARAH	HUGH GRIFFIN
CRAWFORD HARRIET E	SAMUEL W S WATTS
CRAWFORD MARIA	WILLIAM WATTS
CRAWFORD MARY	NEILL MCNAIR
CRAWFORD RODA	ISHAM MEDFORD
CRAWFORD SARAH	CALVIN CARRIGAN
CREASMAN CATHERINE	JOSEPH STROUP
CREASON/CRISSON NAOMI	JOSIAH MACE
CREDLE DORCAS	JOHN WILLIS WILLIAMS
CREECH JOHN	SARAH JANE CHANCY
CREECH JOHN BUNYON	POLLY DRIVER
CREECH JULIA COLUMBIA	DANIEL MORGAN HIGH
CREECY SARAH	EDWARD WINGATE
CREEL SUSANNAH	JOHN HAYNES, SR
CREUTZFUSSER MRS CATHARINA	JOHN ADAM SCHELHORN/SCHELLHORN/SCHOLLHORN
CREWS JAMES	POLLY FESSLER
CREWS MARY	JAMES MEREDITH
CREWS MILDRED	JOHN HESTER
CRIM FRANCIS	JOHN LINVILLE
CRISLIP COLUMBIA LUCEIVIA	CHARLES ROBERT HEATER
CRISP FANNIE	JONAS NELSON, JR
CRISP HIRAM	MYRA/MIRA DILLS
CRISP JOAB	EMILYELIZABETH STANFIELD/STANDFIELD
CRISP SUSAN/SUCKEY	JOHN SETSER/SETZER, II
CROCKER JULIA A	GEORGE WASHINGTON JOHNSON
CROFFORD KATHERINE	OWEN WILLIAMS
CROMWELL CINDERELLA	WILLIAM D PETTAWAY/PETWAY
CROMWELL ELISHA	ELIZABETH SUTHERLAND
CROOK LAURA	WILLIAM ROGERS/RODGERS
CROOM JULIA ANN	RANSOM GARRIS, SR
CROOM MARY ELISHABA	RUFUS FABIUS TEMPLE
CROOM THERESA/TREASY	JOHN SMITH
CROSS FRANCES	WILLIAM DOUGLAS DICKSON
CROSS MARGARETH	LEONARD FITE

SPOUSE	ANCESTOR
CROSS MRS ELEANOR	WILLIAM RUSSELL, SR
CROSS NANCY ANN	WILLIAM REX/RECKS
CROUSE KATY	ABSALOM TAYLOR
CROWDER MARTHA JANE	ROBERT R WOOLEY
CROWDER MILDRED	ELIJAH KIMBRO/KIMBROUGH
CROWDER NANCY	ARCHIBALD WILLIAMSON
CROWDER SARAH J	GEORGE W SELF
CROWELL ADDIE	JAMES DOSTER WOLFE
CROWELL ELKINA R	ALFORD/ALFRED THOMPSON/THOMSON
CROWELL NANCY	WILLIAM PYRON
CROWSON JACOB	ELIZABETH HILL
CROWSON MARY	BETHEL BUFFKIN
CRUM JACOB	ELIZABETH SEABOLT
CRUSER RACHEL	JAMES MCREE, REV
CRUSER RACHEL	JAMES MCREE
CRUTCHFIELD ELISHA JAMES	CLARISSA W FERGUSON
CRUTCHFIELD JOHN	JANE/JENNY WILLIAMS JELKS
CRUTCHFIELD MARTHA/PATSY	MATTHIAS M JOHNSON/JOHNSTON
CRYER FANNY	WILLOUGHBY LEE
CULBERTSON PHEBE	JOHN DORRIS
CULLEN ELIZABETH	DAVID MIMS/MIMMS
CUMMINGS/CUMMINS GEORGE	MARY MCQUISTON
CUMMINS REBECCA	NICHOLAS MORRIS
CUNNINGHAM ELIZABETH	ADAM BURNEY
CUNNINGHAM HUMPHREY	RHODA SOMMERVILLE/SUMMERVILLE
CUNNINGHAM MARY? MAGDALINE	AARON PATTON
CUNNINGHAM	ANN BUIE
CUNNINGHAM NANCY ELIZABETH	JOHN TRANTHAM
CUNNINGHAM SAMUEL	JANE CRESON/CRESSON
CUNNINGHAM MRS JANE (CRESON)	CHARLES STEELMAN/STEALMAN
CURREY BETTIE ELIZABETH	JOHN MILTON SMITH
CURRIE JEANETTE	ANGUS WILKERSON RAY
CURRIN MARY	ABNER TATOM
CURRIN MARY	RISDON KNOTT
CURRY CALVIN ALEXANDER	JANE ELIZABETH GREGORY
CURTIS BURCHET	HARTWELL KING
CURTIS REBECCA	MARMADUKE FRAZIER
CUTHBERTSON RUTH	JOHN MCCOLLUM
CUTHRELL FANNIE	JOHN C CHAUNCEY
CUZZINE ELIZABETH	THOMAS DILLS
CYFERT MARGARET	PETER STOUT
DAGG MARGARET JANE	WILLIAM PERRY DAVIS
DAIL CORNELIA ADREN	JOHN RICHARD WINGATE
DAIL WILLIAM A	NANCY P GOODWIN
DAILEY LYDIA V	WILLIAM OWEN CHAFFIN
DAILY JERUSHIA	GEORGE SUMMA/SUMMY
DALRYMPLE ANN	SION HARRINGTON
DALTON ELIZABETH	VALENTINE MARTIN
DALTON NANCY	ABSALOM BOSTICK, II
DALTON SUSANNAH	ABSALOM BOSTICK, III
DAMERON JUDITH	JOSEPH KNIGHT
DAMERON MARY ELIZABETH	GREEN JORDAN PETTIGREW

SPOUSE		ANCESTOR
DANIEL	ANN/NANCY	ABSALOM EILAND/ISLAND
DANIEL	ISAAC	NANCY PARKER
DANIEL	POLLY	MOSES CLUBB
DANIEL	MRS SALLY (SPENSER)	SAMUEL MIDGETT, III
DARBY	SYBELLA	ELIAS G COOK
DARDEN	ANN	WILLIAM ORMOND, SR
DARDEN	JULIA	WILLIAM HENLY
DARDEN	JULIA A	MARCELLUS J EDWARDS
DARDEN	MELISSA ANN CARR	WILLIAM ZENAS MORTON
DARDEN	NANCY	JOHN HOLLIDAY DIXON, REV
DARNALL	REV HENRY/HARRY	JANE GOODBREAD HENSON
DARNELL	BENJAMIN	FANNIE VIARS
DARTING	ISAAC	SARAH BOLIN/BOWLING
DATH	REBECCA	JOSEPH SMITH
DAVENPORT	ABSOLOM	ELIZABETH FRAZIER
DAVENPORT	MARY	DEMPSEY SPRUILL
DAVENPORT	NANCY	AMBROSE SHERRILL
DAVENPORT	SOPHIA	WILLIAM WHITE
DAVENPORT	TRAVIS	JANE FRAZIER
DAVEY	ELIZABETH	SAMUEL SELF
DAVICE	JOHN	MARY WOODY
DAVIDSON	ALEXANDER	MARY ELLIS
DAVIDSON	ALEXANDER	SARAH ELLIS
DAVIDSON	CATHERINE	ABRAHAM CRUSER MCREE
DAVIDSON	ELIZABETH	JAMES MCCRACKEN
DAVIDSON	GEORGE	SOMMERVILLE/SUMMERVILLE,MARGARET
DAVIDSON	JOHN	RACHAEL ELLIS
DAVIS	ANNA ELIZA	JOHN THOMAS MOORMAN
DAVIS	ANNIE	DAVID HARRIS CALLAHAN
DAVIS	ANNIE WATTERS	THOMAS CALIZANCE MILLER
DAVIS	ARTHUR	CELIA JASPER
DAVIS	BAXTER	MARY EDMONDSON WEBB
DAVIS	CATHERINE	JOSEPH WHITE
DAVIS	DENNIS H	SARAH/ADDIE GARDNER/GARNER
DAVIS	DENNIS H	AULINE GARDNER/GARNER
DAVIS	ELINORE	JOHN DOUTHIT, JR
DAVIS	ELIZABETH	DAVID FAUCETT/FAUSETT
DAVIS	ELIZABETH	JAMES WATSON
DAVIS	ELIZABETH HILLIARD	RICHARD W RESPESS
DAVIS	FLORENCE ELIZABETH	GEORGE WILSON HUDNELL
DAVIS	FREDERICK SOBIESKI	ELIZABETH MOORE QUINCE
DAVIS	HANNAH	JOHN ARMSTRONG
DAVIS	HANNAH	WILLIAM HOCKETT/HOGGATT
DAVIS	HARRIET	JUBILEE V ROGERS
DAVIS	JANE	NATHANIEL HILL, DR
DAVIS	JANE ELIZABETH	FRANK WADDILL
DAVIS	JERUSHA	WARREN KELLY SEELY
DAVIS	JOSEPH	CATHERINE FARMER
DAVIS	KISSIAH	JOHN ROBERTS
DAVIS	LEWIS	LUCY A LONGWORTH
DAVIS	LUCINDA	OWEN TUTOR
DAVIS	MARGARET	CHARLES BLAKLEY
DAVIS	MARGARET HAYS	ALEXANDER S TAYLOR
DAVIS	MARTHA ELLEN	WILLIAM LUTHER MORGAN

SPOUSE INDEX

SPOUSE	ANCESTOR
DAVIS MARY	WILLIAM MOFFITT
DAVIS MARY	JAMES MORGAN
DAVIS MARY	WILLIAM WHIDDON
DAVIS MARY ELLA	GEORGE WILSON HUDNELL
DAVIS MARY/MOLLIE	JAMES MORGAN, SR
DAVIS MARY/POLLY	LARKIN JOHNSTON/JOHNSON
DAVIS	ANDREW LYDA
DAVIS MRS SARAH	DANIEL MORROW
DAVIS NANCY	WILLIAM COGDILL, JR
DAVIS NANCY	EDMOND EDNEY
DAVIS NANCY	MAHLON MILLIKAN
DAVIS NANCY	EDWIN M SAULS
DAVIS RICHARD	ANNA L MOORE
DAVIS SARAH	THOMAS COX
DAVIS SARAH	ABSALOM HAWORTH
DAVIS SHORE DAVID	GAIL A WILLIAMS
DAVIS SOLOMON	ELIZABETH GIDEON/GIDDENS
DAVIS SOPHIA	THOMAS JONES ASHE
DAVIS SUSANNAH	DAVID DALTON
DAVIS THOMAS	BARBARY ARMSTRONG
DAVIS THOMAS	ZINA LEE
DAVIS THOMAS JUNIUS	ELIZABETH MILDRED BROWN WATTERS
DAVIS TOBITHA	TURNER SLEDGE
DAVIS VIRGINIA CLAY	WILLIAM E TYSON
DAVIS W BAXTER	AMELIA HOPKINS
DAVIS MRS HANNAH (TURNER)	PETER DAVIS
DAVIS MRS HARTWELL (HODGES)	JAMES DRAKE
DAW ABIGAIL	THOMAS BONNER
DAWSON HANNAH OLDHAM	LEWIS RATE BOND
DAWSON MARTHA/PATSY/MATTIE	JOHN HUSON/HUSTON
DAWSON MARY	LUDWELL GRIMES/GRYMES
DAWSON MARY	HUGH BLAIR
DAWSON SARAH	ZACHARIAH SUMMERS
DAWSON SARAH	AVINGTON MCELROY
DAY MARY JANE	LEVY H LITTLETON
DAY SARAH	SAMUEL BOONE
DEAN ANN	WILLIAM WOOTEN
DEAN ELIZABETH	RICHARD BOWMAN
DEAN JOHN	SUSANNAH BARTLESON
DEAN WILLIAM JASPER	ELIZABETH FRANCIS KNOTT
DEANES JUDITH PERRY	WILLIAM BOONE
DEANS NANCY W	ELISHA B HART
DEARMAN LILLIE MAGNOLIA	FLOYD MELTON SISK
DEARMIN JOHN BARNABAS	ELIZABETH GATES KELLAM
DEATHERAGE WILLIAM GALE	LETITIA SIMMONS
DEATON LEWIS	EMILY JANE FOWLER
DEBOW ELIZABETH	SAMUEL THOMPSON
DEBOW HANNAH	JOHN DOUGLAS/DOUGLASS
DEBOW JANE	ARCHIBALD MURPHEY
DEEN TEMPERANCE	JOHN GILMORE
DEES SALLY	EDGAR CORNELIUS KOONCE
DEGRAFFENREID MARY BAKER	GIDEON JOHNSTON/JOHNSON, JR
DELAMAR FRANCIS	MIRIAM BARCLIFT/BARTLETT
DELAMAR SARAH/SARY	THOMAS CLAYTON

SPOUSE	ANCESTOR
DELAMOUTHE BETHANY BAILEY	WILLIS MORGAN
DELLINGER MARGARET	GEORGE WHITENER/WEIDNER
DELOACH MARY	SOLOMON BRACEWELL/BRASWELL, SR
DELOACH SAMUEL	MARY BOYKIN
DELOACH SELAH	JOSEPH BARNES
DELPS MARY	WILLIAM CLEMSON
DEMPSEY JOSEPH	NANCY OLDHAM
DEMUTH ROSANNA	JOSEPH SHAMEL/SCHEMEL
DENBY MRS MARTHA	JOHN JOHNSTON
DENENT MARGARET	BENJAMIN PROCTOR HARRIS, SR
DENNING ELIZABETH	JOSEPH A LEE
DENNING LOUISA MARIA/ELIZA	ISAACWILLIAM HEMINGWAY/HEMENWAY
DENNIS ELIZABETH	HENRY MORGAN
DENNIS SARAH	SAMUEL ALEXANDER
DENNY ABRAHAM	MARY DIXON
DENNY ELIZABETH	WILLIAM BRAY
DENNY FRANCINA	MARTIN BURRIS
DENSON LEMUEL	SUSANNAH TOWNSEND
DENTON JOHN	JANE FRENCH
DEROUTH MARTHA	WILLIAM NATHANIEL/NATHAN WILLIAMS
DESHONG LAVINIA	WILLIAM BLOUNT WALLACE
DETHROW ELIZABETH T	VALENTINE CLEMMER
DEVANE ELIZABETH	ALEXANDER CROMARTIE
DEVANE GEORGE	MIRIAM TREADWELL
DEWEESE MARY/POLLY	JONATHAN TUSSEY
DEWEY OSCAR	SARAH ANN THOMAS
DEXTER THOMAS	NANCY JANE HILL
DEYTON ALLEY E	MALCOLM/MACK B/BERRY BYRD
DICK ELIZABETH	ANDREW LINDSAY
DICKENS MASON	ANDERSON KING
DICKERSON CLARISSA	GEORGE STEWART
DICKERSON OBEDIAH	RUTH DILLARD
DICKEY JANE	SAMUEL STEWART
DICKINSION JOHN	ANN NORRIS
DICKINSON REBECCA	JOEL NEWSOM
DICKSON ANN	JAMES ROBINSON
DICKSON ELIZABETH JANE	DONALD GRIFFITH
DIDEN ESTHER FREDDA	LEVI FAIRCHILD
DIDLAKE EDMUND H	SUSAN A LANE
DIETZ ANNA MARIE	SIEBERT SPENCER
DIGGS ANN	ANDREW MOORMAN
DILL JOSEPH	ELIZABETH (CROSKEY) DILLS, MRS
DILLARD CORA LESTER	CECIL C BROWN
DILLARD JANE	ANDREW HARRISON
DILLARD MRS PETTY	HEZEKIAH HARMAN
DILLIARD GILLY/ABIGAIL	REUBEN BARBEE
DILLON FRANK	NANCY AVELINE DEWEESE
DILLS ANN	PETER DILLS
DILLS MIRA/MYRA	HIRAM CRISP/CHRISP, JR
DILLS PETER	ANN DILLS
DIMMAUX KATHERINE	JOAB BROOKS, SR
DIMMETT ANN	EDWARD WILLIAMS
DIXON CLAREDA ANN	WILBURN LIMBAUGH
DIXON ELIZABETH	WILLIAM GOSS

250

SPOUSE	ANCESTOR
DIXON JANE	ELIJAH LEONARD MCARTHUR
DIXON JOHN	SUSANNAH LIPPS/LIPS
DIXON MARY ANN	MARSHALL WILLIS
DIXON MARY ELIZABETH	OLIVER MURPHY/MURPHREY
DIXON PHEBE	THOMAS RUBOTTOM
DIXON REBECCAH	WILLIAM MARSHILL
DIXON SARAH	GEORGE MARTIN
DIXON/DICKSON SARAH	JOSHUA WADE WILLIAMS
DOAK MARY	JAMES MATTHEWS
DOANE RUHAMA	WILLIAM CROMARTIE
DOBBINS MAHALA	PAUL FURR
DOBSON CATHERINE ANN	JAMES W GUINN
DOBSON MARTHA	JOHN SMITH
DODSON DENIAH	WHITMILL W LEIGH
DODSON JAMES	MARY ELIZABETH MILLIS
DODSON MARGARET	ALEXANDER BARKER
DOLLARHIDE JANE	ZIMRI BROWN
DONALDSON ELIZABETH	THOMAS MORTON
DONALDSON JANE	JOSEPH ALLISON
DONALDSON JOHN	SARAH BOONE
DONALDSON MARY	JAMES DUPREE/DUPRE'
DONELY MARTHA/PATSEY	MOSES HIATT
DORMAN POLLY	JOHN BLALOCK
DORMINEY JUDITH	LOTT WHIDDON
DORRELL SARAH	ELI HEARRELL
DORRIS SIMPSON L	NANCY J BEASLEY
DORSETT WILLIAM HEAD	CYNTHA CELINA PUNCH/PUNTCH
DORSETT WILLIAM HEAD	MARY E PUNCH/PUNTCH
DOSTER ELIZABETH	MOREN MOORE
DOUGHTRY ELIZABETH	URIAH N WESTBROOK
DOUGHTY ZILPAH	JOHN CHANCE
DOUGLAS MARY	PHILIP DAY
DOUGLAS/DOUGLASS DANIEL	RUTH MCCRACKEN
DOWELL CHARITY	ROBERT BRASHEARS/BRASSIEURS
DOWNEY MARGARET	WILLIAM RUSSELL, JR
DOWNEY NANCY	MATHIAS BERRY
DOWNING SARAH	WILLIAM RILEY WOOLLEY
DOZIER ELIZABETH RALSTON	WILLIAM CHESTER ABBEY
DRAKE BEADIE A	JAMES MADISON HONEYCUTT
DRAKE MARGARET LOUVINA	JOEL PATON SETSER/SETZER
DRAKE MARGET ISABEL	JOEL PATON SETSER/SETZER
DRAKE MARTHA JOHANNA WILLIAMS	JOHN D. ARRINGTON
DRAPER CYNTHIA	NORMAN SHAW
DRENNAN SARAH	LEMUEL/KIT WRIGHT
DREW ANN	BENJAMIN LANE
DRIGGERS SARA	DAVID CARROLL WILSON
DRIGGS JOANNA MAGDALENA	STARK BLOUNT, SMITH, DR
DRIGGS SHERMAN	MARY WOODMAN KIMBALL
DRIGGS MRS MARY WOODMAN (KIMBALL)	ELISHA, RHODES, COL
DRIVER POLLY	JOHN BUNYON CREECH
DRUM LEE O	MINNIE BELL LOWRANCE
DUCKWORTH SALLY	URIAH SHERRILL
DUDLEY ELIZABETH	JAMES WELBORN, JR
DUDLEY HEPSIE	JOHN WILSON

SPOUSE	ANCESTOR
DUDLEY JANE	JOSEPH GOOCH
DUGGER JAMES	MARGARET ROSS
DUGGIN MARY	SETH PILKINTON WILSON
DUKE EMILY C	JAMES N GREEN
DUKE EMILY C	JAMES N GREEN/GREENE
DUKE MARTHA	WILL RAGAN
DUKES MRS SARAH (THOMPSON)	THOMAS GILL
DUMAS MARY ELIZABETH	SOLOMON M BALLARD
DUNAGIN ISABELLA	JOSEPH MOSER
DUNAWAY LUCINDA CAROLINE	LORENZO DOW WYATT
DUNCAN ANDERSON FULLER	VIRGINIA ANN OVERTON
DUNCAN ELIZABETH	WILLIAM EMERSON
DUNCAN ELIZABETH	LEONARD FITE, JR
DUNCAN MOSES	UNITY SIMS
DUNCAN NANCY	ISSAC WALL
DUNCAN UNITY	LABON FOWLER
DUNCAN WILLIAM SEYMORE	ELIZABETH GRIFFIN JUSTICE
DUNLAP MARY	PLEASANT TROY KEY
DUNLAP SARAH	ANTHONY CLARK, JR
DUNN JULIA VIRGINIA	JAMES CLAY ORMOND
DUNN LAMON	MARY ANN WILKINSON
DUNN LAMON SESSIONS	GEORGIANNA VIRGINIA GATLIN
DUNN NANNA	DAVID SCARBOROUGH
DUNN REBECCA	JOSEPH SUMNER BATTLE, I
DUNN SALLIE	WINSOR DIXON
DUNN MRS DILLY (PARHAM)	STEPHEN CRUMP
DUNNAGAN HANNAH	WILLIAM MARSH
DUNSTON EBENEZER	JULIA ELIZABETH ROWE
DUNSTON JOHN	HENRETTA SPRUILL
DUNSTON KEZIAH	ELISHA SAWYER
DUNSTON WALTER SEATON	ANNA THOMINA WILKENS
DUPREE IDA ELIZABETH	NIMROD WYATT
DUPREE JOSEPH ALVIN	JUDITH DEANES BOONE
DUPREE REBECCA	STEPHEN EASON
DUPREE THOMAS	NANCY/ANN RENN/WREN/WRENN
DUPREE THOMAS BIRD	PENINA MAY
DUPREE THOMAS OHAGAN	ISABEL BOGART MORTON
DUPREE YSOBEL MORTON	JOHN STOCKARD LITCHFIELD
DUPREE MRS TABITHA (MORRIS)	JAMES DUPREE
DURANT ANN	WILLIAM BARCLIFT/BARTLETT
DURANT ELIZABETH	HARMON GASKINS
DURANT SARAH	RICHARD WHEDBEE
DURHAM ELIZABETH ANN	RANSOM TURNER COOK
DURHAM MARY L	ELLIS CLANTON
DURRETT CATHERINE	DOUGLAS OLIVER
DURRETT FRANCIS	ELIZABETH MOORE
DUSKIN RACHEL	JOSHUA COX
DYER DICY	JOSEPH GRAYSON
DYER MARY/POLLY	ALFRED NEEDHAM
DYER/DYAR BARBARA	ISAAC ANDERSON
DYER/DYAR ZIPPORAH	REUBEN ANDERSON
EAKIN ANN	GEORGE DAVIS

SPOUSE	ANCESTOR
EALY/ELEY ANN	JOHN JOHNSON
EARLY MARGARET	DENNIS MCCLENDON
EARLY MRS MARY	NATHAN TART
EARLY PENACE	ROBERT BROWN
EARNEST ANN	JOHN H STANSBURY
EARNHARDT/AARONHART MARIA ANN	JOHN GEORGE HERDLEIN/HERTLEIN/HARTLINE, JR
EASLEY SALLY	STEPHEN CRUMP
EASLEY SARAH	WILLIAM PINKERTON
EASLEY WILLIAM	SARAH NEATHERY
EASON JULIA ANN	FRANCIS HATTEN
EASON MAJOR STEPHEN	REBECCA DUPREE
EASON MARTHA JANE	JAMES ROSS MAY
EASON THERESA ANN	IVY BEAMAN
EASTBORNE ELIZABETH	JOSHUA STINSON
EASTEP MOSES	ELIZABETH JONES
EASTEP RACHEL	JOHN MORGAN BAITY
EASTRIDGE LYDIA	FREDERICK STINSON
EASTWOOD MARY	WILLIAM TURLINGTON
EATMAN ANNIE WRIGHT	D/DOCK K LAMM/LAMB
EAVES SARAH F	WILLIAM RANDOLPH DEBNAM
EBHECHT CATHERINE	PHILLIP CRAVER/GRABER/GREBER
EBORN MARY M	JOHN C CHAUNCEY
EDBETTER RICHARD ISAAC	ESTHER HARRIET JONES
EDDINGS MARY BRITE	RUBEN LEROY SISK
EDDINGS OBEDIENCE	EDOM MOON
EDDINS FRANCES	WILLIAM KILBY SR
EDDINS/EDDINGS TEMPERANCE	LEWIS WRIGHT
EDMONDSON CELIA	DIXON HARP
EDMONSON ALIE	THOMAS YOUNG
EDMONSON SARAH	AARON SANDERS
EDMUNDSON WILLIAM BURWELL	JULIA ANN PIPKIN
EDWARDS ABEL	LUCY CLARISSA BENNETT
EDWARDS BENJAMIN SHEPPARD	JEMIMA POWELL
EDWARDS DAVID	ELIZABETH MORRIS
EDWARDS ELIZABETH	HENRY DAWSON
EDWARDS ELIZABETH	RICHARD DABBS
EDWARDS ELIZABETH JANE	ARCHIBALD BROWN MCALPINE
EDWARDS ELVY ANN	JOSEPH WOODARD
EDWARDS JANE ELIZABETH	HARDY ORMOND
EDWARDS LINNIE	JOHN PROCTER
EDWARDS LUCINDA	JACOB FOUTS/PHOUTS
EDWARDS MARY	WILLIAM TAYLOR
EDWARDS MARY	JOHN CAMPBELL
EDWARDS MARY THEODOSIA	MACK MCKINNIE SMITH
EDWARDS MARY/MOLLY	JOHN CARROLL WREN/WRENN
EDWARDS	SALINE EDWARDS
EDWARDS	MARY/POLLY WARREN
EDWARDS MRS ANN MARIE	ALLEN GASKINS
EDWARDS MRS CELEYA	WILLIAM TAYLOR
EDWARDS NANCY	JOB PENDERGRAFT/PENDERGRASS
EDWARDS NANCY	LITTLEBERRY PARKS
EDWARDS POLLY	THOMAS KNIBB WYNNE
EDWARDS SARAH	WILLIAM HENRY WOODY
EDWARDS STERLING	SELINA/SALENA COBB

SPOUSE	ANCESTOR
EDWARDS SUSAN REBECCA	WILLIAM STILES
EILAND ELIZABETH	JESSE ALPHUS MITCHELL
ELAM MARY	HENRY LONDON
ELBANCK/EELBECK JOHN	ELIZABETH EELBECK, MRS
ELIZA MARTHA ANN	WILLIAM FELTON
ELLEDGE NANCY	NATHAN PHILIPS
ELLER ELIZABETH	ABSALOM WHEELER
ELLIOTT ABRAHAM	JANE ALEXANDER
ELLIOTT ELIZABETH	HUGH MAXWELL
ELLIOTT LEWIS	NANCY WRIGHT
ELLIOTT LUCINDA	RICHARD N HICKS
ELLIOTT MARTHA	ANDREW MCREE
ELLIOTT	JAMES HAMLETT/HAMBLET
ELLIOTT	JANE PARSONS
ELLIOTT ORPHA	JOHN MAYO
ELLIOTT/ELLETT MARY	FLETCHER SULLIVAN
ELLIS AMELIA FRANCIS	CHARLES STANLEY CHAFFIN
ELLIS HANNAH	JOHN HOSKINS
ELLIS HENRY GETER	CORNELIA FRANCES RAGAN
ELLIS IRA	FRANCES STARR/STAR
ELLIS LONNIE WASHINGTON	ZELMA GEROY MILLS
ELLIS LUCILE L	OSBORNE GILES FOARD/FORD
ELLIS MARY ELIZABETH	JAMES GILBERT
ELLIS MOSES	MARY MANGUM
ELLIS PAULINE	RUFUS MOZINGO, JR
ELLIS REBECCA	WILLIAM PHYSIOC
ELMORE ADA	JOHN HENRY LOPP/LAPP/LOOP, SR
ELMORE CICILIA	JOHN HAWORTH
ELMORE MARY	EDWARD RIPPY
ELMORE THOMAS	ANNA SANDERS
ELMORE VIRGINIA CECILIA	ROBERT JOHNSON
ELROD JANE	JESSE C HOLBROOK
ELROD SUSANNA	JOHN HUNTER OWEN
EMBRY NANCY	HENRY BUFFALOE
EMERICK JACOB	ELIZABETH FOOSHEE
EMERSON WILLIAM	ELIZABETH DUNCAN
ENGLAND MARY E	WILLIAM M, LT JOHNSTON
ENGLAND WILLIAM	MARY HADLEY
ENGLISH MARY	JACOB COCHRAN/COCKERHAM, SR
ENNIS HARRIET BROWN	JAMES BOMAN/BOWMAN HUDGINS
ERWIN ALEXANDER	SARAH ROBINSON
ERWIN JEAN	THOMAS DICK
ESKRIDGE ALBERT DIXON	SUSAN AARON BEAM
ESKRIDGE ELIZABETH	MATTHEW PRICE
ESKRIDGE JOHN GREEN	ELIZABETH H THOMPSON
ESKRIDGE RICHARD	ELIZABETH READ
ESKRIDGE RICHARD	ELIZABETH REYNOLDS
ESLINGER CATHERINE	GEORGE FRY
ESLINGER ELIZABETH	GEORGE HERMAN
ESTES RHODA	JOHN STEWART RUSSELL
ESTRIDGE SUSANNAH	JOHN CHEEK
ETCHINSON NANCY	NIMROD ADAMS
ETCHISON NANCY	NIMROD ADAMS, SR
ETHERTON AGATHA	MOSES WASHBURN

SPOUSE	ANCESTOR
ETTREDGE MATILDA	MALACHI HUDSON STALLINGS
EURE MRS ELIZABETH	SAMUEL POTTER
EVA CHRISTIANA	ANDREW ESLINGER/ESSLINGER
EVANS JAMES	ELIZABETH HARMAN
EVANS MARY ANN	GRANDISON F WILLIAMS
EVANS MILLY CHRISTENE	THOMAS DAVID HUTCHENS
EVANS NANCY	DAVID JAMES REGISTER
EVANS REBECCA	JOHN BROWNLOW
EVANS SAMUEL	ELIZABETH KENNEDY MCCULLAH
EVANS THOMAS	SARAH SMITH
EVERETT PENELOPE	JETHRO MURPHY/MURPHREY
EVERETT/EVRITT SARAH	OLIVER MORTON
EWELL OLIVIA PARTHENIA	EDWIN GORHAM HODGES
EWING WILLIAM E	JANE ELIZABETH MCCRACKEN
EXUM MARY	BARNABY MCKINNE, SR
EXUM SARAH	JOSIAH REYNOLDS
EZELL AMERICA ANN	JOHN CAUBLE/COBLE MILLER
EZELL ELIZABETH/BETSY	JOHN ROPER WILSON
FADDIS JEANY/JANE	WILLIAM HORN
FAIL/FAYLE ABIGAIL	ALEXANDER MCCRACKEN
FAIN MARTHA AUGELINE	JOHN W ROBERTSON/ROBINSON
FAIN SARA/SALLY	GEORGE ARTERBURY THOMAS
FAIR/FARE/FARR/FEHR DOROTHY	DAVID LINVILLE
FAIRCHILD PHOEBE	JAMES SEWELL
FAIRES ROBERT	SUSANNAH ORR
FAISON MARY	THOMAS HICKS
FANNIN MARTHA JANE	JESSE GRAHAM
FARLEY ANDREW	SARAH FARLEY
FARLEY MYRTLE MAE	OSCAR ALBERT BOYST
FARLOW MARY	ISAAC SPENCER
FARLOW SARAH	WILLIAM STANTON
FARLOW SARAH	JOHN CLIFTON
FARMER CATHERINE	JOSEPH DAVIS
FARMER ESTHER	JOSEPH GIBBS, JR
FARMER NANCY	AUSTIN SIMS
FARQUHAR MARY	GEORGE MAUZY
FARRAR REBECCA	AMBROSE E FOUSHEE
FARROW JOSEPH	CHARLOTTA ANNIE/ANN WILLIAMS
FARROW MARTHA	SYDNEY CATES
FARROW MARY	STEPHEN BROOKS
FARWELL ROSA ELENOR	FRANKLIN R BEATTY
FATHEREE	BENJAMIN H BUFFKIN
FAUCETT JOHN MCKEE	MARGARET SMITH
FAUCETT JOHN W	PARTHENIA ARMSTRONG
FAULK CAROLINE	JOHN BUTLER
FAULK JAMES	ELENDERPENELOPE SHEPHERD/SHEPPARD
FAUSETT RICHARD	MARY MCKEE
FAYLE/FAILE MARY	HENRY HOLLADAY
FEARS MRS JOICY (BOWDRE)	JOHN JOHNSON
FEE JOHN	PARTHENIA KELLON
FEENEY ORADELL	LEROY COLON HARVELL
FEENEY ORADELL	ROY C CARWELL

SPOUSE INDEX

SPOUSE	ANCESTOR
FEESOR EVE	JAMES SMITH
FEEZOR JOHN	ELIZABETH COLE
FELTNER MARY	RANCHER A BROWN
FELTON MARY	JOSHUA G JOLLIFF
FELTON WEALTHY	WILEY/WILLIE HARRELL
FENDER MARTHA	JOHN A SHAW
FENNY VERLINDER	TAYLOR WILEY
FERGUSON ANDREW	MARGARET ROSS
FERGUSON CLARISSA	LEWIS WATSON
FERGUSON ELIZABETH	WILLIAM WILEY
FERGUSON GEORGE	LYDIA HENDRICKS
FERGUSON JANE	THOMAS TRIPLETT
FERGUSON SAMUEL	SARAH PIERCE
FERRELL BENNETT	JULIA COLEMAN
FERRELL CLARY	JOHN, NORWOOD, CAPT
FERRELL ELIZABETH	JEREMIAH RHODES/ROHDS
FERRELL JUDITH	JOSHUA BEASLEY
FERRELL MARY	ABDIAS P WEBB
FERRELL MICKLEBERRY	NANCY COLEMAN
FERRIER ROSANNAH	FRANCIS ANDY/ANDERSON POINDEXTER
FERRILL MARY	JAMES DAVID ROBERTS, SR
FESSLER POLLY	JAMES CREWS
FEWOX EDITH	WILLIAM HARDY
FIELD LYDIA	RICHARD LEWIS
FIELDS	WILLIAM SMITH
FIELDS SAMUEL	CATHERINE DIXON
FILGO ANN/NANCY	MOSES TODD
FINCH MARY/POLLY	MARSHALL ROBARDS
FINCH RUTH ANN	PLEASANT CHANCE
FINLEY MARY ANN	JOHN PENNEY/PENNY
FINLEY MRS REBECCA	ISHAM MEDFORD
FINLEY SARAH ALICE	JOSEPH SANFORD
FINNEY ANNA	JOHN J LANNING
FIPPS MRS IZZIE(FOWLER)	MACK DANIEL/MCD FOWLER
FISCHER/FISCHERN ANNA MARIA	JACOB FAGGOT/FAGERT
FISCUS EVA MARIA	JACOB HILSABECK
FISH ANNE	LEWIS HENRY DUPREE
FISHER ANGELET	JOSEPH MAY
FISHER ELIZABETH	WILLIAM H HEWITT, JR
FISHER HENRY	MARGARET RENDLEMAN
FISHER JANE	STEPHEN TREADWELL, JR
FISHER SARAH/SALLY ANN	JAMES JAMES
FITCHETT HARRIET	JEREMIAH FIELD/FIELDS
FITE MARY	HENRY LYERLY/LAYRLE/LIERLY
FITZRANDOLPH EUNICE	GERSHOM HUNT
FLAMME ANGIE MARIE LA	LLOYD RANDOLPH COOPER
FLEETWOOD ELIZABETH/BETSY	GEORGE CRIDER
FLEETWOOD JUDITH	AARON FREEMAN
FLEMING MARTHA	MATTHEW JOUETT, II
FLEMING MRS MARTHA	PETER FLEMING
FLEMING MRS BETSY (FLEMING)	GEORGE FLEMING
FLETCHER ELIZABETH	ROBERT PLEASANTS
FLETCHER JANE	JACOB STIREWALT
FLETCHER SUSANNA	MOSES OVERTON

SPOUSE	ANCESTOR
FLETCHER SUSANNAH	BERNARD FRANKLIN
FLIN NANCY JANE	ANDREW CAIN
FLINCHAM ELIZA JANE	JOHN D MAYABB
FLOWER LUMEGA	JONATHAN STARKEY CLEMSON
FLOWERS ANN ELIZA	ALEXANDER COX
FLOYD PUGH	SARAH HEWITT
FLOYD SARAH	ISAAC MCELROY
FLYNN ELIZABETH	ISAIAH GUYMON
FLYNN ELIZABETH	ISAIAH GUYMON
FLYNN ERMA	GEORGE LOUIS POOLE
FOEMAN MARY	GEORGE WILSON HUDNELL
FOLGER JETHRO STARBUCK	MARY BARNARD
FOLKS JAMES	JENNY BRADFORD
FOLKS NANCY	EDWIN CLIFTON
FONTAINE FRANCES DE LA	JEMIMA JOHNSON/JOHNSTON
FOOTE BRIDGET	SIMON HADLEY, SR
FORBES MARTHA JANE	JAMES B RUSSELL
FORBIS ANN	THOMAS WOODBURN
FORD SAMUEL RICHARD	REBECCA BOATRIGHT
FORD WILLIAM	REBECCA TIPPET/TIPPETT
FOREHAND LUCYE/LOUVANNA	ENOCH/ENOS SCARBOROUGH
FOREHAND NANCY	JACOB BOYCE
FOREMAN FRANCES	MATHEW NORRIS
FORRESTER ELIZABETH E	JAMES T KIMBRELL
FORSHEE SUSAN	NATHAN FIKE
FORSYTH	JOHN KNOTT
FORTSON REBECCA OGILVIE	J RAYMOND BOYST
FORTUNE ROBERT GRIER	NELLIE SAFFORD BOYST
FOSCUE ELIZA	DANIEL S SANDERS
FOSSETT NANCY	WILLIAM CARR
FOSTER ANN	ROBERT DEBNAM
FOSTER ANNIE	ANGUS GARMAN KOONCE
FOSTER AVA O	AARON SAUNDERS
FOSTER ELEANOR CROWE	JEHU KIRKSEY
FOSTER HANNAH	GEORGE F HAMILTON
FOSTER PATSEY	JOHN BRANN
FOSTER SARAH	CARY FELTS
FOSTER MRS MARY JANE(CULBERTSON)	JAMES MILES KILLIAN GUINN
FOUNTAIN GRACE	JOHN STILLEY
FOUNTAIN GRACE	JOHN STILLEY
FOUSHEE AMBROSE E	REBECCA FARRAR
FOUSHEE CORNELIA FRANCES	ISAAC NEWTON MANN
FOUSHEE JOSEPH	HAPPY STEWART/STUART
FOUST ELIZABETH	JOSIAH FRAZIER
FOUTS HANNAH	JOHN GARREN/GARN
FOUTS JACOB	LUCINDA EDWARDS
FOUTS SUSAN	ISAAC MORGAN
FOUTS/PFAUTZ DAVID/DEWALD	CATERINA/CATHERINE SPENGEL/SPENGLE
FOUTS/PHOUTS JACOB	LUCINDA EDWARDS
FOWLER ELVIS	JUDA ROBINSON
FOWLER JOHN	MARY/MILLEY GLASS
FOWLER LABON	UNITY DUNCAN
FOWLER LEVINA	JAMES PACE, SR
FOWLER MACK DANIEL/MCD	LUPHENIA SOLES

SPOUSE	ANCESTOR
FOWLER MARY/POLLY	WILLIAM GRIFFIN
FOWLER ROSANNA	THOMAS MOORE
FOWLER SYLVANIUS	MARY USSERY
FOWLER WILLIAM	MARY JANE OATES/OATS
FOWLKES REBECCA JANE	MARION BAZEL TAYLOR HAM/HAMM
FOX CORA ALDINE	CHARLIE CLEVELAND OAKLEY
FOX GATSEY	BENJAMIN TUTTLE
FOX HAZEY V	HUGH CONLEY
FOX MARY	WILLIAM PALMER
FOX MARY ELLEN	LACY ALONZO NORWOOD MARSH
FOX MRS ELIZABETH ANN	ELIJAH LEONARD TROSPER, JR
FRAISER/FRASER SARAH	OBEDIAH MIZE
FRANCIS	WILLIAM MANSELL CRISP/CHRISP
FRANCK BARBARA	DANIEL W SHINE
FRANK BARBARA	JOHN CAHRLES GRIMES
FRANKLIN ABEDNEGO	MARY GRAVES CLEVELAND
FRANKLIN LUCY J	THOMAS H ORMSBY
FRANKLIN MARGUETTE	JOSEPH GREEN
FRANKS WILLIAM D	MARTHA/MATTIE CAROLINE HAYES
FRAZER MRS PRESCILLA(OUTLAW)	WILLIAM WATFORD
FRAZIER AMY	BENJAMIN WHEELER
FRAZIER ANN	BENONI BANNING
FRAZIER DANIEL	NANCY FRAZIER
FRAZIER GEORGE	JANE GRIMES
FRAZIER GEORGE B	ELIZABETH WHEELER
FRAZIER WILLIAM FRANKLIN	CAROLINE ELIZABETH JONES
FREDERICK MARY ANN	THOMAS JAMES MIDDLETON
FREDERICK WILLIAM	NANCY KENAN BURTON
FREEMAN AARON	JUDITH FLEETWOOD
FREEMAN AMILLICENT	JOSIAH PERRY
FREEMAN EMILY AUGUSTUS	THOMAS ROBBINS
FREEMAN HANNAH	THOMAS RHODES
FREEMAN MARY ELIZABETH	THOMAS RHODES
FREEMAN	JOSIAH PERRY
FREEMAN NANCY	MATTHEW WISE
FREEMAN NEEDHAM	MARTHA/POLLY MOORE
FRENCH SAMUEL	CATHERINE SMITH
FRIESLAND/FREESLAND CHRISTIANA	LOUIS/LEWIS/LUDWIG FISHER/FISCHER
FRISBEE/FRISBY MRS MARTHA (INGLE)	JOHN M PARHAM
FRIZZLE ALCINDA A	JOSIAH THERDON MURPHY/MURPHREY
FROST JOHN	REBECCA BOONE
FRY	JONATHAN MILLER
FULGHUM CHELLY	ALSEY BOYKIN
FULK CALVIN FREDERICK	CHRISTINA CHANEY BOWEN
FULK LYDIA	CALVIN FREDERICK FULK
FULK MARY/POLLY	PHILIP BOSS
FULK WILLIAM THOMAS	MARY ELIZABETH MILLIS
FULKS BARBARA	JOSEPH HOMESLEY
FULLENWIDER ELIZABETH	JACOB RENDLEMAN
FULLER JOHN R	MARY MALVENA JONES
FULLINGTON SALLY	WILLIAM HOGAN
FULLWOOD SARAH	LEVIN DUNCAN
FULP MARGENETH	NEWTON C DAWSON
FULP MICHAEL	PHEBE SCOTT

SPOUSE	ANCESTOR
FULP NANCY EMILY	MARTIN WESTMORELAND
FULTON ANN	THOMAS NEAL
FUNK MRS MARIAH JANE (LIEB)	MURPHY KEMP
FUNK MRS MARIAH JANE (LIEB)	MURPHY KEMP
FUR/FURRER MARY MAGDALENA	MARTIN CHRISTOPHER RANDLEMAN
FUR/FURRER MARY MAGDALENA	MARTINCHRISTOPHE RINTELMAN/RINGLEMAN
FURR ELIZABETH	WILLIAM WRIGHT
FUSON MARY	WILLIAM VANDERPOOL
FUSSELL MARY	JOHN RAINWATER
FUTRELL SUANNA	BURWELL CONNER
GABEL/GABLE SALOME	EBENEZER FAIRCHILD
GAINER BARSHEBA	WARREN DANIEL ANDREWS
GAINER DELSORA ELIZABETH	ICHABOD HARRIS LITTLE
GAINES MARGARET	JOHN PRYOR
GAITHER ELIZABETH	EBENEZER B FROST
GAITHER EMILY	JOHN ANDREW CHAFFIN
GALBREATH MARGARET	JOSEPH YOUNG
GALE HATTIE ESTELLE	WILLIAM THOMAS ORMOND
GALIS/GATIS ANE	BENJAMIN WILLIS
GALLAHER MARY	AMOS HARDIN/HARDEN/HARDING
GALLIHER ELIZABETH	JETHRO W MOUNGER/MONGER
GALLOWAY ELIZABETH	GEORGE WASHINGTON WHITMIRE
GALLOWAY HANNAH	CHRISTOPHER COLUMBUS WHITMIRE
GAMBILL FRANKY/FRANKIE	ALEXANDER JOHNSON
GAMBREL ELIZA JANE	JAMES HENRY WELBORN
GAMMON MARTHA ANN	WILLIAM R GAMMON
GARDENHIRE SARAH	WILLIAMSON MOUNGER/MONGER
GARDNER ASENATH	RICHARD MARION BEESON
GARDNER AULINE	DENNIS HARRIS DAVIS
GARDNER ELIZABETH	THOMAS WILSON
GARDNER EMMA ELIZA	CALVIN MOORE
GARDNER HANNAH	EVAN DAVIS
GARDNER LYDIA	TRISTRAM BARNARD
GARDNER SARAH	DENNIS HARRIS DAVIS
GARDNER SION WRIGHT	MARY W SCARBOROUGH
GARISON MAHALA	DANIEL BLACK ORRELL
GARMAN MARY MATILDA	JOHN MYERS
GARNER GEORGE WASHINGTON	ROSA JANETTE CAMERON
GARNER JOHN FUSHEE	NANCY WHITTLE
GARNER LEWIS OLIVER	ARRENIA RITTER
GARNER MOURNING	MURFREE DIXON
GARNER S ANNIE W	JAMES ALEXANDER JONES
GARNER VITIA CASSIE	DANIEL HARGETT BUCK
GARNER WILLIAM	SARAH GARNER
GARREN DAVID	MARGARET WHITAKER
GARREN ELLEN CORNELIA	SAMUEL ALEXANDER STROUP
GARREN JOHN	HANNAH FOUTS/PFAUTZ
GARRETSON MARTHA	BENJAMIN COX
GARRIS AMY	PRESTON FRANKLIN GARRIS
GARRIS PRESTON FRANKLIN	AMY GARRIS
GARRIS WILLIAM M	MARTHA WARTERS
GASH JOSEPH DENNIS	DEMY/DENNA WOODFIN

259

SPOUSE	ANCESTOR
GASKINS ESTHER	JOSEPH TUNNELL
GASKINS IDA MELISSA ANN	JESSE OSBORNE CLARK
GASKINS SUSAN	WEEKS H CLARK
GATES MICHAEL	CATHARINE GROVES
GATEWOOD SALLY	JESSE HAMLET
GATLEN SUSAN F	JAMES M MCCRACKEN
GATTON AMANDA A	JOHN E DRIVER
GAUNT ELIZABETH/BETTY	JACOB LOLLAR
GAUTREAUX ANNA PAULINE	BURRELL AYCOCK
GAVIN MARY RACHEL	JESSE CARROLL, SR
GEDDIE MARGARET CATHERINE	DANIEL MAXWELL
GENTRY NANCY	JOSEPH LASLEY
GENTRY WYATT	CLARA ELIZABETH BANKS
GEORGE HARDIN	ANGELINE MILLER
GEORGE	RICHARD HOLT
GEORGE REBECCA	BRUMBLY COKER, REV
GERARD FAE CAROL	WILLIAM THOMAS GILL
GERHARDT HENRY	EMILY JANE CARTER
GERHARDT JOHN C F	HARRIET COLSON CARTER
GIBBS EMALOUS	NATHANIEL CHASE WILLIAMS, SR
GIBBS FERSEY	ELISHA WHATLEY, SR
GIBBS MAHALIA	PELEAGE SPENCER
GIBBS MARY	HENRY ALBRIGHT
GIBBS PRISCILLA	JOHN CREDLE
GIBBS RHODA H	BENJAMIN WILLIAMS
GIBSON HANNAH	SAMUEL JACKSON
GIBSON JANE/JEAN	JOSEPHCOL HARDIN/HARDEN/HARDING
GIBSON MARTHA	HIRAM HARTNESS
GIBSON MARY	FREDERICK STRICKLAND
GIDEON/GIDDENS JAMES ISHAM	MARTHA/PATTY MILLS
GIDEON/GIDDENS WILLIAM	MATILDA WOODS
GIFFIN ISABELLA	JAMES MCCRARY
GILBERT CATHERINE	PHILIP BURNS
GILBERT CHARITY	JOHN SMITH
GILBERT JOHN	ELIZABETH RAY
GILBERT NANCY MARTIN	HIRAM HARDY HARGROVE
GILCHRIST JENNIE	ADAM RINGSTAFF WADSWORTH
GILES CLEO A	LEWIS O ROSS
GILKIE SARAH	JAMES RATLEDGE/RUTLEDGE, SR
GILL BETSY/ELIZABETH	MOSES NEAL
GILL ELIZABETH	THOMAS SQUIRES
GILL JANE	JOHN SULLENS
GILL THOMAS	CATHERINE TATE
GILL THOMAS	MARY JONES
GILLESPIE JANE	JAMES BROWN
GILLESPIE MARGARET	SAMUEL EUSEBIUS MCCORKLE
GILLIAM AGNES	BARTHOLOMEW KIMBALL
GILLIAM FRANCES/FRANKY	NATHANIEL MOORE
GILLIAM JAMES MASON	SOPHIA MOORE
GILLIAM PRISCILLA	JAMES HARRIS
GILLIAM ROBERT A	MARY WALL
GILLILAND ELIZABETH	ELBERT S. ARRINGTON
GILLILAND JOHN	DICIA INGLE
GILMORE SARAH JANE	EMANUEL RITCH

SPOUSE INDEX

SPOUSE	ANCESTOR
GINN MARY ANN	JESSE TAYLOR
GIROUD HENRIETTA	AQUILLA MILES
GIVEN MARY	ELI ELLISON THRIFT
GIVENS CELIA	JAMES POTTS
GIVENS MRS MARY(THOMPSON)	HENRY PENNEY/PENNY
GLASCOCK ELVIRA	NATHAN STANLEY CHAFFIN
GLASS MARY	DAVID PINKERTON
GLASS MARY/MILLEY	JOHN FOWLER
GLASSOCK FRANCIS/FANNIE	JONATHAN HAINS/HANES
GLENDENNING MARY	PHILIP HOCKETT/HOGGATT
GLENN MARY	CHARLES BLACK
GLIMP GEORGE	MILLY WHEELER
GLIMP JESSEE WASHINGTON	MARY ANN WHEELER
GLOSSUP WILLIAM	ORA LITTRELL
GOCHER/GOTCHER ANNA	VINCENT STANFIELD
GODFREY ELIZA M	ANDREW JACKSON KING
GODWIN MARTHA	JOHN COTTON
GODWIN PATSEY	MOODY PORTER
GOEPHERT MARIA	PETER SANER/SEHNERT
GOING JOHN WILLIAM	MARY CAROLINE SMITH
GOLDEN NANCY	CHARLES SMITH
GOLDSTON WINCY	ALEXANDER CRUMP
GOMER SARAH	FLEMING THOMASSON, SR
GOOCH CAROLINE	WILLIAM STANLEY
GOOCH JANE DUDLEY	WILLIAM CLEMENT
GOOCH MARTHA	JOSEPH B SHAW
GOODBREAD JANE	JOHN HENSON
GOODBREAD MARY	JESSIE H HENSON
GOODBREAD MARY/POLLY	JESSE HENSON
GOODBREAD SALLY	GEORGE WALTON BRADLEY
GOODBREAD SARAH	GEORGE WALTON BRADLEY
GOODE MARTHA JEFFERSON	ISAAC W NICHOLSON
GOODEN ANNA	WILLIAM BUTLER
GOODLOE JOHN	MARY BOWERS
GOODLOE	GIDEON JOHNSON
GOODLOE ROBERT GARRETT	MARY ANN HARPER
GOODMAN ELIZABETH	BENJAMIN ANDREW COLEMAN
GOODNIGHT RACHEL	JACOB YOUNG
GOODSON AVY	ADAM WILLIAMS
GOODWIN GEORGE WILLIAM	NANCY ELIZABETH HAYES
GOODWIN NANCY PENNY	WILLIAM ADISON DAIL
GOODWIN STEPHEN RICHARD	JUDITH ANN BOYCE
GOODWIN WILLIAM	ELIZABETH OWEN
GOODWYN PENELOPE	THOMAS TAYLOR, JR
GORDON ELIZA	MARMADUKE NORFLEET
GORDON ELLEN FRANCES	CHARLES LEONARD SMITH
GORDON FANNIE	FOSTER JARVIS, REV
GORDON POLLY	JOHN MEGGS
GORDON SALLY	JOHN ROUSSEAU
GORDON SARAH	THOMAS GUYMON
GORDON SARAH	THOMAS GUYMON
GORE DORCAS	DAVID REGISTER
GOSS MARY	HENRY BOSS
GOUGE POLLY	WILLIAM BLEVINS

SPOUSE		ANCESTOR
GOULEY	MARTHA	PATRICK HENRY MCBRIDE
GRADDY	SEREPTA	GEORGE WASHINGTON MOYE
GRADY	MARY	JAMES BROWN, JR
GRADY	MARY	THOMAS OWEN
GRAHAM	ELIZABETH LEE	SAMUEL BARRETT
GRAHAM	JANE	WILLIAM MCCORKLE
GRAHAM	JOHN	MARY, GRAHAM, MRS
GRAHAM	MALINDA	ROBERT DRURY SIMPSON
GRAHAM	MILDEN	JOHNATHAN HAIR
GRAHAM	MILLE	HIRAM RUSSELL
GRAHAM/GRIMES	JANE	ALVA ANDERSON LAM/LAMB
GRANT	ASA	AMELIA/MILLY LIMBAUGH
GRANT	NANCY	JOSEPH HOLDERFIELD
GRANT	POLLY	JESSE MORGAN
GRANT	RACHEL	JAMES SAMUEL MULLINS
GRAVES	ELIZABETH	THOMAS KIMBRO/KIMBROUGH
GRAVES	GANNON FRANKLIN	MARY ANN RANDOLPH JOHNSON
GRAVES	MARY	BENJAMIN CLEVELAND
GRAVES	SARA CROSHA	THOMAS BARNETT
GRAVITT	ABIGAIL	MOREN MOORE
GRAY	ADDIE	ELISHA WHITT
GRAY	MARY	JAMES GREEN
GRAY	SARAH	JOEL CLINTON COMMONS
GRAY	THOMAS	SARAH BEASLEY
GRAYBEAL	DAVID SMITH	TEXAS SLAGLE
GREEN	ADELINE/ADDIE	JOHN O WELBORN
GREEN	ELIZABETH	MAYBERRY WELBORN
GREEN	ELIZABETH	MAYBERRY WELBORN
GREEN	ELIZABETH	DANIEL SHINE
GREEN	ELIZABETH	NATHANIEL KING
GREEN	ELIZABETH M	JAMES LABON LITTLE
GREEN	FARNEFOLD	HANNAH KENT
GREEN	HENRY	MARGARET JANE COOK
GREEN	JAEL	JACOB MERCER
GREEN	JAMES N	EMILY C. DUKE
GREEN	JAMES N	EMILY C DUKE
GREEN	JAMES REDDICK	PRISCELLA E SESSOMS
GREEN	JANEY	JOHN W STANFIELD/STANDFIELD
GREEN	JESSE	CLARISSA JANE JOHNSON
GREEN	JOSEPH	ELIZABETH SHEARER
GREEN	LAVINA/NINA	JOHN HELMS
GREEN	MARGARET	JEHOIDAH THOMPSON
GREEN	MARTHA MABLE	ISHAM HARRIS, SR
GREEN	MARY CATHERINE	SAMUEL COLUMBUS HAYES, JR
GREEN	MARY G	JOSEPH BOON, IV
GREEN	MARY JANE	JAMES HAMPTON LITTLE
GREEN		JAMES DUKE
GREEN	MRS LORA	ELIAS G COOK
GREEN	NANCY	WILLIAM WILSON
GREEN	NANCY	LABON LITTLE
GREEN	POLLY	GEORGE MOTSINGER
GREEN	RAHCEL	WILLIAM BEALS/BALES
GREEN	SARAH	HOSEA TAPLEY/TARPLEY
GREEN	SARAH	JOHN BOBBITT

SPOUSE	ANCESTOR
GREEN SARAH/SALLY	RANSOM HAYES
GREEN SUDIE	JACOB DAWSON WILLIAMS
GREENE THOMAS C	SALLY J HOLLOMAN
GREENLEE DAVID	MARTHA/PATSEY MOUTRAY
GREENLIEF DOROTHY	PHILIP VARBEL/WIRBLE
GREER/GRIER JANNET	JOHN GRAY
GREGG HANNAH	JOHN MORRIS
GREGG MARGARET	BENJAMIN KIMSEY/KINZEY
GREGORY BEULAH	ADONIRAM TREADWELL
GREGORY MARK R	MARY LAMB
GREGORY MARK ROBERTS	ADELAIDE L UPTON
GREGORY MURIEL C	CHARLES H WILSON
GREN MARY ANN	IVY WILLIAMSON
GRICE DELILAH	PETER WATKINS
GRIFFIN DIANA	HENRY FAISON
GRIFFIN ELIZABETH	JOHN FARMER SMITH
GRIFFIN FRANCES	MOSES STEGALL
GRIFFIN MARTHA ANN	JAMES MAY HARRIS
GRIFFIN MARY/POLLY	WILLIAM A JOHNSON
GRIFFIN PALLIS	NANCY TEMPLETON
GRIFFIN SUSAN ELIZABETH	JOHN NEAL WILKINSON
GRIFFIN TABITHY	JOHN B TUNSTALL
GRIFFIN MRS HARRIET ALVIN(HOWARD)	JESSE E FRALEY
GRIFFITH SARAH	PAUL FURR
GRIGG MARY	AZARIAH HIATT
GRIGG MARY ANN	DAVID WILSON SHIVES
GRIGGS ELIZABETH	JOHN C GREEN/GREENE
GRIGGS SARAH	JARVIS GREEN/GREENE
GRIGSBY ALICE	BENJAMIN RUSH, JR
GRIGSBY ELIZABETH	JOHN WRIGHT
GRIGSBY	JOHN BROWNLOW
GRIMES CHRISTINA	MATHIAS SAPPENFIELD, III
GRIMES FRANCES	FRANCIS HATTON
GRIMES JOHN CHARLES	BARBARA FRANK
GRIMES THOMAS	CHLOE LEWELLING/LLEWELLING
GRIMES/GRYMES ELIZABETH JOHNSON	WILLIAM MOORE, REV
GRINDSTAFF KEZIAH	THOMAS STEPHEN WILLIS
GRISHAM WILLIE	MARY MALVENA JONES
GRISSIT SARAH	EDWARD CONNER
GRISSOM CYNTHIA	BARNEY EDWARD PARRISH
GRISSOM LYDIA	JOB PENNY
GRITES/CRITES MRS MARGARET (FULBRIGHT)	JOHN LINK
GRIZZLE REBECCA	EDMUND/EDWARD SUTTON
GROCE LUCY	WELCOME USSERY
GROCE MAGGIE	ANDERSON CROWDER WILLIAMSON
GROOMS JANE	RICHARD BARTLESON
GROOMS MAGGIE	JOHN S CLARK
GROOMS SARAH ELIZABETH	WILLIAM THOMAS CLARK
GROSS ELIZA	ABEL ADOLPHUS WHITENER/WEIDNER
GROSS NANCY CAROLINE	NATHAN HARRIS
GROVES CATHERINE	MICHAEL GATES
GRUBB CHARITY	RICHARD BEESON
GRUBBS SAYRE/SARAH/SALLY	SOLOMON CARMICHAEL

SPOUSE	ANCESTOR
GRUGGETT ALEXANDER GRIFFIN	SELIA/CELIA CAMELINE MORGAN
GRUPE MARTHA ADELEINE	STARK BLOUNT SMITH, JR
GUDGER PAMELIA EMALINE	ROBERT HARRISON YOUNG
GUGERTY OWEN "SQUIRE"	ISABELLA SHERRILL
GUICE RUTH	JOSEPH KUYKENDALL/KIRKENDALL
GULLEY/GULLY LEWIS	JANE ROWLAND/ROLAND
GULLICK ROXANNA JANE	WILLIAM P PLUMBLEE/PLUMLEY
GUNN STARLING	MARY ELIZABETH HOOPER
GUNN SUSANNAH	JAMES HENRY HARRIS
GUNSTON JAMES	RACHEL WOOTON
GUNTER DAN	ELIZABETH/BETTIE SIMMONS
GURGANUS LOUISA	ROBERT FLETCHER WILSON
GURGANUS MARY ANN	WARNER GORDON BAILEY, JR
GUTHRIE CENDERELLA P	GEORGE WILSON HUDNELL
GUY ANNE	EDWARD PEARSALL
GUYMON ISAIAH	ELIZABETH FLYNN/FLINN
GUYMON THOMAS	SARAH GORDON
GUYNUP WESLEY S	BERTHA KOONCE
GWALTNEY WILL	LUCINDA JANE LOWRANCE
GWINN MARIAN	FERNIE ARNOLD
GWYN BEDDY OAKES	ALEXANDER GUNN
HADDOX ANNA	WILLIAM BAITY, SR
HADDOX WILLIAM	ELIZABETH WARD
HADEN JENNET P/FANNIE	JAMES M KING
HADLEY HANNAH	JESSE JOHNSON/JOHNSTON
HADLEY MARGARET	JESSE REECE
HADLEY MARGARET	JOHN MARTIN
HADLEY RUTH	THOMAS LINDLEY
HADLEY RUTH	CHARLES STUART
HADLEY SIMON	BRIDGET FOOTE
HAGEN MRS MARTHA V WICKHAM	JOHN WESLEY SIMPSON
HAGER BARBARA	SAMUEL KILLIAN
HAGINS ADALINE	JOHN GIVENS
HAIR JOHNATHAN	ROBERT GRAHAM
HAIR JOHNATHAN	MILDEN GRAHAM
HAIR SARAH ANN	GIDEON S JACKSON
HALE EDA	CHARNALD HIGHTOWER
HALE JOHN	LOUISANA BADGER
HALE MARY A	ADAM HOUK
HALE OMARANNAH/MARANDA	JESSE VAUGHN
HALE/HAILS ROBERT	AILA/MAHALA HALL
HALES LUCINDA	WILLIAM STANLEY WEATHERSBY
HALL ALLEN	SABRA CULBREATH
HALL ANNA	LUKE TRIPLETT
HALL CHANEY	ABNER MULLINS
HALL CHARLOTTE	SMITH MCDONALD/MCDANIEL
HALL EDWARD	ANNE/ANNA ALLEN
HALL ELIZABETH	JAMES MCCORKLE
HALL ELIZABETH	SAMUEL ROSEBOROUGH
HALL ELIZABETH	JAMES MCCORKLE
HALL JAMES	PRUDENCE RODDY
HALL JANE	SAMUEL ROSEBOROUGH

SPOUSE INDEX

SPOUSE	ANCESTOR
HALL JOHN	MARY PYLE
HALL JOHN A	ELIZA YOUNG
HALL JOHN WESLEY	SUSAN REECE IVEY/IVIE
HALL JONATHAN HENRY	CAROLINE PRISCILLA TODD
HALL LEWIS	NANCY COLLY
HALL MARRY	LOFTUS PIPPIN
HALL MARTHA	MATTHEW JOHNSON/JOHNSTON
HALL MARTHA	DANIEL HAYMORE, JR
HALL MARY	JOHN W GIBBONS
HALL MARY ELIZABETH	ARCHIBALD NICHOLSON
HALL ROBERT	SARAH PYLE
HALL SARAH BENJAMIN	JOHN HIGSON
HALL SUSAN	JOHN CICERO KOONCE
HALL WESLEY	NANCY STUDDARD
HALL MRS RACHEL (MOORMAN)	JESSE DENNIS
HALSTEAD CHRISTENAH	JOHN WILLIAM FULLBRIGHT
HALTOM ANN ELIZA	THOMAS DAVE HARRIS
HALTOM JOEL	LUCINDA MORRIS
HAM ELIZA	WILLIAM HAM
HAM ELIZABETH	SOLOMON PERRY
HAM MILLY M	MARTIN CRAWFORD KEY
HAM MRS ELVIRA F	WASHINGTON MORRIS
HAM SMITHY	JOHN WILLIAM GARRIS
HAM TOBITHA/BITHY	SOLOMON PERRY
HAM ZACHARIAH	NANCY BEASLEY
HAMBY	DAVID WATSON
HAMILTON ELIZABETH CLORINDA	JOSEPH ELLER
HAMILTON MARY	ELIAS DEES
HAMILTON MARY	SOLOMON JONES
HAMILTON MARY A	JOHN C MCNEILL
HAMILTON NANCY ANN	NEWTON H AYCOCK
HAMILTON SALLY	WARREN WOODARD
HAMILTON SARAH	GEORGE W BUCHANAN
HAMM JAMES BASIL	MINNIE ALICE FOUTS/PHOUTS
HAMM MARION BAZEL TAYLOR	REBECCA JANE VOLK/FOLK/FOWLKES
HAMM ZACHARIAH	CHRISTIAN WILLIAMS
HAMMER MILTON	MARTHA IDUMA LOWRANCE
HAMMOND PENELOPE BONNER	WYRIOTT KEECH
HAMPTON EPHRAIM	LEMENDER HARRIS
HAMPTON JEDIDAH JANE	ABNER MULLINS, SR
HAMPTON MARTHA/PATSY	LUKE TRIPLETT
HAMPTON OLIVER	ELIZABETH BRYAN
HAMRICK SARAH	PERRY GREEN MAGNESS
HANBY FLORENCE	CHARLES DEEMS FOARD/FORD
HANCOCK ANN	ROBERT F PLEASANTS
HANCOCK MRS BERTHAMIA	NEIL CAMERON
HANCOCK REBECCAH ANN	DAVID J DENNY
HANCOCK SUSANNAH	WILLIAM MOON
HANCOCK MRS ELIZABETH (BROWN)	JAMES PAINE
HANDLEY KEZIA	BATT LEE
HANES/HAINES MARY	JONAS REYNOLDS/RENNULS, JR
HANKINS ROBERT W	SARAH S ALBRIGHT
HANKS ELIZABETH	THOMAS SNIPES
HANNA/HANNAH JOHN	SARAH MCCRACKEN, MRS

SPOUSE		ANCESTOR
HANNER	ISABELLE	CHRISTOPHER FIELD/FIELDS
HARBIN	JUDITH	BENJAMIN MARET/MERIT/MERRITT
HARDEE	HENRIETTA	ISAAC TAYLOR
HARDEE	MARY ANN	WYLIE THOMAS MOSELEY
HARDEMAN	MAJ BLACKSTONE	REBECCA JANE BRUCE HUNTER
HARDEN	SUSANNAH	ELI YORK
HARDIN	JEAN	MATHEW KUYKENDALL
HARDIN	MARGARET	ADAM KUYKENDALL
HARDIN	MARTHA	BENTON FIELD/FIELDS
HARDING	ELIZABETH	THOMAS WILLIAMS
HARDISON	CARNAVELLA	WILLIAM ZENAS MORTON
HARDY	SARA	LEMUEL LANIER
HARDY	WILLIAM	EDITH FEWOX/FOX
HARE	MARTHA ELIZABETH	LEWIS BOND
HARGROVE	MINNIE AGNES	VERNON SIDNEY BUFFALOE
HARKEY		ZACHARIUS/ZAMAH/ZACH LYERLY/LAYRLE/LIERLY
HARMAN	ZACHARIAH	REBEKAH PETTY
HARNEY	JANEY/JANE	HUGH TELFORD
HARPER	CICERO R	SARAH ELLEN MOORMAN
HARPER	HANNAH	ISAAC BROOKS
HARPER	HOLLON	TULLY MOSELEY
HARPER	JOHN	BARBARA STRUBLE/STRUBEL
HARPER	LOT	MIRIAM WHITAKER
HARPER	MARGARET	ZEBULON A SPRUIELL/SPRUILL
HARPER	MARTHA ELEANOR	WYLIE THOMAS MOSELEY
HARPER	MARY FRANCES	JAMES WEBB
HARPER	MARY JANE	OLIVER MURPHY/MURPHREY
HARPER	MILTILDA RICHARDSON	HIRAM RUSSELL
HARPER	MIRIAM	ROBERT LEE OWNBEY
HARPER	SUSANNA/SUSAN	SILAS STROUP
HARREL		NOAH FELTON
HARREL	PRISCILLA	GILBERT DYE
HARRELL	ANN	RICHARD FELTON, III
HARRELL	ANN	RICHARD FELTON, III
HARRELL	BARSHA EDNA	KINDRED HOLLOMAN
HARRELL	GEORGE NEVILLE	OPAL ELIZABETH HIGH
HARRELL	JOSIAH	ANNA ASKEW
HARRELL	MARTHA M	LEVI WINGATE
HARRINGTON	PHILEMON	FANNIE HARMAN
HARRIS	AARON	ANGELETTE FISHER MAY
HARRIS	CHARLES	CLARA ANN HIGH
HARRIS	ELIZABETH	CLIFTON BOWEN
HARRIS	EXPERIENCE	MARTIN RENDLEMAN
HARRIS	FANNIE	SAMUEL BAIRD
HARRIS	HIXIE	PINKNEY HALTOM
HARRIS	JAMES	PRISCILLA GILLIAM
HARRIS	JAMES HENRY	SUSANNAH GUNN
HARRIS	JOHN	SARAH HEADEN
HARRIS	JONATHAN SPIVEY	LOUISA DAVID FARROW
HARRIS	LEMENDER	EPHRAIM HAMPTON
HARRIS	LOLLIE MAUDE	WILLIAM MARSHALL BOYST
HARRIS	LOVEY ANNE	CHARLES H WILSON
HARRIS	MARTHA	NATHAN HARRELL SESSUMS
HARRIS	MARTHA/PATSY	REECE WILLIAM DAVIS

SPOUSE	ANCESTOR
HARRIS MARY	JOHN HUDGINS
HARRIS MARY/MOLLY	JOHN CHIPMAN
HARRIS MRS ELIZ	JOHN HARMAN
HARRIS MRS SUSAN WOOTEN	WILLIAM GARDNER
HARRIS NANCY	WILLIAM SMITH, JR
HARRIS OBEDIAH	REBEKAH JOHNSON
HARRIS PEGGY	WILLIAM B GRAHAM
HARRIS PHEBA	CASON GIBBS
HARRIS REBECCA	SAMUEL LITTLE
HARRIS RHODA ROSETTA	CHARLIE HALTOM
HARRIS SALLY	ELISHA B HART
HARRIS SUSANAH	LEONARD HIGDON
HARRIS SUSANNAH	JOHN GILLILAND
HARRISON CHARLES P	SUSAN BURTON PRICE
HARRISON ELIZA JANE	EDMUND REID HARRISON
HARRISON ELIZABETH	JOHN MURPHREY/MURPHY, CAPT
HARRISON HARRIET	ALFRED BLALOCK
HARRISON MARY	JOB/JOBE GREGORY
HARRISON NANCY	WARNER GORDON BAILEY
HARRISON SUSAN PAYNE	WILLIAM WOODSON KNIGHT
HARRISON TABITHA	EDWARD TRICE
HARRISON MRS CHRISTIAN (WILLIAMSON)	WILLIE W LAMM
HARROD MARY	SAMUEL STANSBURY, II
HART ELIZABETH	ANDERSON WILLIAMSON
HART MARY	JAMES ORMOND
HART SALLIE VANN	GROVER JACKSON NORWOOD, SR
HART WILLIAM	SUSAN SMITH
HART WILLIAM COLUMBUS	ANNIE BENNETT HILL
HART MRS ROXIE (DARNELL)	DAVID TUCKER, III
HARTEL ELIZABETH	MARTIN KELLER
HARTLINE HANNAH	PETER MILLER/MUELLER
HARTMAN CATHERINE	GEORGE LEWIS WILHELM
HARTMAN JAMES D	ANNA STULTZ
HARTMAN RENA	MARTIN HALEN MCCOURRY
HARTNESS MARION	MARY ANN JAMES
HARTSFIELD WILLIAM	MARY ELEANOR CARTER
HARVELL J O A	MARY LOUELLA BLACK
HARVEY ALDERSON ELLISON	CECELIA LANIER
HARVEY BURLETTA	WILLIAM JAMES HORN
HARVEY HARRIET ROWENA	GOTHE THOMEE WILKENS
HARVEY JOHN DUNCAN	ELIZABETH SUGG/SUGGS
HARVEY NANCY	ISHAM YOUNG
HARVEY NANCY	ISHAM YOUNG
HARVEY SARAH	WILLIAM CARRUTHERS
HARWARD GEORGE	ELISABETH SUGG
HARWARD JAMES	ROSE BARBEE
HARWARD/HARROD MALICHI	MARY HERNDON
HARWELL RHODA	JOEL RIVERS
HARWOOD ANNE	GEORGE DURANT
HASH HIRAM ALEXANDER	LEVA LOUDEMA OAKLEY
HASH JANE	BENJAMIN PHIPPS
HASKETT MARY ELIZABETH	ISAAC SPENCER
HASSELL SUSANNAH	PARKER QUINCE
HASTINGS ESTHER	THOMAS CATE

SPOUSE	ANCESTOR
HASTINGS MARGARET	LEWIS DAVIS
HASWELL MARY ANN	JAMES RICHARDS
HATCH ELIZABETH	DAVID HOLDER
HAUCHY BARBARA	JAMES WHITMAN
HAUN	ELIZABETH FLYNN/FLINN
HAUS/HOUSE CARATHINE	JOHN GEORGE DANIEL FREESLAND/FRIESLAND
HAUSER LEAH	ANDREW THOMASSON
HAWKINS ELLEANDER	BELL SIMMONS
HAWKINS JANE/JANIE	JOHN GOODE
HAWKINS MARY	JOHN DAVIS
HAWKINS MARY	WILLIAM TUGMAN
HAWKINS SARAH	WILLIAM TACKETT/TACKITT
HAWKINS TABITHA	ALLEN B JONES
HAWKS ELI	NANCY JANE BURCHETT/BORCHETT
HAWN RACHEL	PETER YODER
HAWORTH JOHN	CICILIA ELMORE
HAWORTH JOHN B	ELIZABETH BALLARD
HAWORTH RACHEL	ANTHONY CHAMNESS
HAWS NANCY	WILLIAM MADISON WALL
HAYES ANNA	JOHN OWEN
HAYES JANE	ROBERT ALGEE/ALGEA
HAYES RANSOM	SARAH/SALLY GREEN
HAYES SAMUEL COLUMBUS	MARY C GREEN
HAYES SAMUEL COLUMBUS	ELIZABETH HUGGINS
HAYES WILLIAM	NANCY CLORINDA BROWN
HAYGOOD NANCY	JOHN THOMPSON, JR
HAYMORE NANCY EMMALINE	WILLIAM NEUM HALL
HAYNES ABRAHAM	SARAH TART
HAYNES MARY G	KELLY BALDWIN
HAYNES TEMPIE ANN E	WILEY WEDLE LAMM
HAYS ARRA PERNICE	MOSES A MCCOLLUM
HAYS BETSY DELANY	JOHN PUGH
HAYS EDMOND	MARTHA FRAZIER
HAYS LUCINDA	JAMES H GIDEON/GIDDENS
HAYS MARTHA	ELIJAH GOSSETT/GOSSET
HAYS MRS MARY ANN	PATRICK HENRY MCBRIDE
HAYS/HAYES ELIZABETH	AUSTIN/ORSTON/GUSTON BEESLEY
HAYWOOD MRS HANNAH (GRAY)	JOSEPH GREEN
HAZEL RICHARD	ISABELLA SHERRILL
HAZLEWOOD REBECCA	JOSEPH HARPER
HEAD ELIZABETH	WILLIAM H. DIXON/DICKSON
HEADEN SARAH	JOHN HARRIS
HEARN ELIZA	WILLIAM WOMBLE
HEARNE WILLIAM	PRISCILLA GILLIAM
HEATH CHARITY JANE	WILLIAM FRANKLIN JONES
HEATH JOHN	LEVINA KILLEBREW
HEATHMAN ELIZABETH	WILLIAM MCBRIDE
HEDGEPETH RODA	BURRELL MOORE
HEFFNER CECELIA	GARFIELD WILLIAM PENLEY/PENLY
HEITMAN BESSIE LEIGH	CHARLES ALEXANDER KOONTZ
HELMS ALLEN	ANNA RICH
HELMS MARY FRANCES	WILLIAM THOMAS AXUM
HELMS WILLIAM ALVERSON	ELIZABETH/BETSY ANN STEGALL
HELTY PATIENCE	BENJAMIN RICKS

SPOUSE	ANCESTOR
HEMPHILL ROSEANNAH	JOHN YOUNG
HENDERSON ANNIE	WILLIAM BANKS
HENDERSON ELIZABETH	EDMUND FOSHEE
HENDERSON FRANCES M	WILLIAM VANNAH TAYLOR
HENDERSON ISABELLA GRAVES	JOSHUA CALLAWAY
HENDERSON JENNIE	JAMES ALEXANDER HARTNESS
HENDERSON NANCY	WILLIAM THOMPSON
HENDRICKS GEORGE	NANCY BROWN
HENDRICKS LYDIA	GEORGE FERGUSON
HENDRICKS TEMPIE/TEMPERANCE	WILLIAM OWEN CHAFFIN
HENLEY ANNE	RICHARD BULLOCK
HENLY WILLIAM	JULIA DARDEN
HENNIS ELIZABETH/BETTY	GEORGE WASHINGTON AMOS
HENRY WILLIAM	JANE RUSSELL
HENSLEY	THOMAS RAY/RHEA, SR
HENSLEY NANCY	LAZARUS GULLEY
HENSLEY PLEASANT	PAULINE METCALF/METCALFE
HENSON EDITH	SAMUEL ALLEN
HENSON ELIZA ANN	MAHLON CRAFFORD/CRAWFORD WALKER
HENSON JESSE	MARY/POLLY GOODBREAD
HENSON LAVINIA UPCHURCH	THOMAS T VALENTINE
HENSON MARIA	ABRAHAM WAGLEY/WAGLE/WEIGLE
HENSON	BARTLETT DILLS, SR
HENSON	ESTHER GREEN/GREENE
HENSON/HINSON CALVIN COLUMBUS	MARY MARGARITE MARKS
HERMAN FRANKLIN	ORPHAMAHALA ISENHOWER/EISENHAUER
HERMAN JOHN DANIEL	MARY/POLLY KILLIAN
HERNDON AQUILLA	MARY MOORE
HERNDON BENJAMIN	LYDIA MASSEY
HERNDON BETTEY	HILLAIRE ROUSSEAU
HERNDON CLAUDE NASH	ANNIE LEE MANN
HERNDON ELBERT	SUSAN MARGARET CHEEK
HERNDON ESTER	JOHN BARBEE
HERNDON REUBEN	NANCY JENKINS
HERNDON SIDNEY	FRANCES RODES/RHODES
HERRING	THOMAS LANIER
HERRING MOURNING	WILLIAM LEWIS
HERRING SARAH	ALEXANDER CARTER
HERRING THEANA	THOMAS LANIER
HERRINGTON LUCY	ELISHA PRICHARD
HERRON MARY SERRENA	JOHN BROOKINS GILLILAND
HERRON ROSA	ERNEST WILSON HELMS
HERRON MRS FRANCES (PHELPS)	JESSE VAUGHN
HESLEP CELIA	DANIEL GARNER
HESTER JOHN	MILDRED CREWS
HESTER JOHN	EMELINE LINVILLE
HESTER MARTHA	DRURY WATSON
HESTER NANCY	CLAIBORN WATSON
HEWETT RUTH	A STANLEY/STANALAND/STANLAND,SAMUEL
HEWITT SARAH	BENNETT PAGE
HEYDEN OLIVIA	WILLIAM DAVIDSON MCCRACKEN
HEYL JACOB	ELIZABETH BROOKS
HIATT ANN JANE	BENJAMIN TAYLOR
HIATT JOHN	REBECCA UNTHANK

SPOUSE	ANCESTOR
HIATT OTHNIEL	POLLY/MARY PEGG
HICE CALFERNA	SAMUEL BURTON FISHER
HICE MARY ETTA	JOHN STARNES/STARIN/STAHRIN
HICKERSON JOSEPH	NANCY ROUSSEAU
HICKMAN SARAH	LEMUEL/KIT WRIGHT
HICKS ADALADE	WILLIAM T WEATHERFORD
HICKS COL THOMAS	MARY FAISON
HICKS DIANA	NATHAN WHITLOW
HICKS ELIZABETH	ELI/ELY LEWIS TABOR/TABER
HICKS ELLEN	WILLIAM MARSH
HICKS JOHANNA	ELI/ELY LEWIS TABOR/TABER
HICKS LAURA TEMPIE	WILLIAM PENDER LOWE
HICKS NANCY	TILMAN CHANCE
HICKS PRISCILLA	SEAMORE DUNCAN
HICKS WILLIS	PHERIBY/FERRABEE BOOKER
HIGGINS BETSY	ROBERT PARKER
HIGGINS EMMA J	JOSEPH L SWANN
HIGH BUNBURY	CATHARINE HIGH
HIGH CATHARINE	BUNBURY HIGH
HIGH DANIEL MORGAN	JULIA COLUMBIA CREECH
HIGH HENRY SEYMORE	MARY LIZ OWEN
HIGHFILL CALLIE	IVY WESLEY LASLEY
HIGHSMITH NANCY	NOBLE/NOBLES STANCIL
HIGHSMITH SARAH	BENJAMIN ROGERS/RODGERS
HIGHSMITH/HYSMITH DANIEL	ANN BECK/BECKE
HIGHTOWER CANDACE	JESSE MCGAUGHY/MCGAHA
HILL AGNES	CHARLES HARRINGTON
HILL ANNIE BENNETT	WILLIAM COLUMBUS HART
HILL BRYANT	SUSAN MARIA SHAW
HILL ELIZABETH	JACOB CROWSON
HILL HANNAH LOUISE	MARMADUKE NORFLEET JEFFREYS
HILL JANE	PARKER QUINCE
HILL JEMIMA	WILLIAM HASTY
HILL JOHN	ELIZABETH/BETSY FELTS
HILL JUDITH	EDWARD BOYKIN, JR
HILL LANEY	EZEKIEL MURPHY/MURPHREY
HILL MARY	BENAJAH DIXON
HILL	SUSANNAH HILL, MRS
HILL NANCY	THOMAS KNIBB WYNNE
HILL NANCY	AQUILLA SUGG
HILL NANCY JANE	THOMAS DEXTER ARRINGTON
HILL PENELOPE	NEEDHAM WARTERS
HILL POLLY	AARON COX
HILL RACHEL	JOHN RUSS
HILL ROBERT	MARTHA MURPHREY/MURPHY
HILL SALEMMA	JOHN RUSS
HILL SALLY	ABNER HOLLOMAN
HILL TEMPERANCE	ELISHA PEEBLES/PEOPLES
HILL WHIT M	MARY M SHARP
HILL WILLIAM WESLEY	MARTHA BEDDINGFIELD
HILL MRS ELIZABETH HARDY (BELL)	RICHARD BRYANT TAYLOR
HILLIARD ELIZABETH	ARCHIBALD DAVIS
HILLIARD WILLIAM DANIEL	MARTHA A E MCELROY
HILLIARD WRIGHTMAN	CHLOE JONES

SPOUSE	ANCESTOR
HILLSMAN MARY	SAMUEL ELEY
HILSABECK JACOB	EVA MARIA FISCUS
HINDE FRANCES	BENNETT HILSMAN/HILLSMAN
HINES GEORGE WASHINGTON	MARTHA HILL
HINES MARTHA MELINDA	JOE BERRY GALLOWAY
HINES	WILLIAM RENN/WREN/WRENN
HINKLE REBECCA	JOHN FRANKLIN ADAMS
HINNANT PATIENCE	JOHN NEWSOM
HINSHAW ALMEDA	WILEY REECE
HINSHAW BENJAMIN	RUTH CARTER
HINSHAW ELIZABETH	BENJAMIN HINSHAW, SR
HINSHAW ELIZABETH	NICHOLAS CREEKMORE
HINSHAW MARGARET	JOSEPH CARTER
HINSHAW MARY	JOSEPH HADLEY
HINSON MALINDA	DAVID COBLE, JR
HINTON ELIZA ANN	WILLIAM D TIPPETT
HINTON MARY	WILLIS W NOWELL
HIPP MARY E	JAMES MURPHY
HISE BOBBIE JEAN	JACK DAVID ENGLISH
HISE SALLY	JOHN A LIMBAUGH
HISON BARBARA	HENRY SMITH
HITCHCOCK ELIZABETH	JOHN BEESON
HITCHCOCK ELIZABETH	SEABORN TACKER/TUCKER
HITCHCOCK RUTH	STEPHEN PERKINS
HIX SARAH	JAMES GREEN/GREENE
HOBBS DELILAH	WILLIAM DENNIS
HOBBS MARY ELIZABETH	WILLIAM BRITTON LEE
HOBDY MRS TALITHA (COTTON)	DEMPSEY POWELL
HOBSON JOHN R	EMILY LOWE
HODGE LOUISE	RUFUS PARRISH
HODGE RACHEL	SIMS OWNBEY
HODGES HARTWELL	THOMAS DAVIS
HODGES JAMES HENRY	MARTHA ANN LEWIS
HODGES JOHN	SALLIE PERRY
HODGES MRS MARTHA ANN (LEWIS)	WILLIAM JAMES RHODES
HODGIN REBECCA	WILLIAM DENNIS
HODGSON ROBERT	RACHEL MILLS
HODGSON ROBERT	RACHEL MILLS
HODGSON/HODGIN RACHEL EMMALINE	WILLIAM R REYNOLDS
HODGSON/HODGIN/HODSON GEORGE	DELILAH RULE
HODSON DAVID	ESTHER LAMB
HODSON RUTH	MOSES HOSKINS
HODSON/HODGIN SIMEON	SARAH OTWELL
HOFFMAN SALLY	PETER HARTMAN
HOGG JANE/JENNIE	LEWIS RING
HOGGARD ELIZABETH	JACOB WHITE, SR
HOGGARD PRISCILLA A (SESSUMS)	JAMES REDDICK GREEN/GREENE
HOGGATT ELIZABETH	MOSES HOSKINS
HOGGATT MRS MARY	GEORGE MOTSINGER
HOGSED/HOGSHEAD	JOSEPH MCGAUGHY/MCGAHA
HOLBROOK JOHN FRANKLIN	HAZELTINE ANN JOHNSTON
HOLCOMB MARY	JACOB RANDLEMAN
HOLCOMBE CATHERINE	JOSEPH PONDER
HOLCOMBE ELIZABETH	ROBERT PONDER

271

SPOUSE	ANCESTOR
HOLCOMBE WINNIE	JOHN PONDER
HOLDER ANNE ELIZABETH	JOSEPH LEINBACH
HOLDER CHARLES	MARIA MARGARETHE KRAUSE
HOLDER DAVID	REBECCA BROWN
HOLDER ELIZABETH	JOSEPH CARMICHAEL
HOLDER EMELINE	WESLEY ELBER CLARK
HOLDER HANNAH	MARK HARDEN
HOLDER MARGARET	HARDY FRAZIER
HOLIDAY MARY	JAMES KNOTT
HOLIDAY/HOLADAY SARAH	AARON MARIS
HOLLANBACK TERESA ELIZA	HENRY FISHEL, JR
HOLLAND ANNE	STEPHEN SENTER
HOLLAND JANE	WILLIAM BAIRD, SR
HOLLAND MARY	HERBERT TAYLOR
HOLLEN MARGARET	ELISHA COX
HOLLER NELLIE MAY	WALTER LOVETT MOOSE
HOLLIDAY HANNAH	ROBERT HART
HOLLIDAY SARAH	WILLIS DIXON
HOLLIFIELD EMZEY	ARTHUR MCFALLS
HOLLIN SARAH	FRANCES MARION WEATHINGTON
HOLLINGSHEAD ELEANOR	FRANCIS PALMER
HOLLOMAN KINDRED	BARSHA EDNA HARRELL
HOLLOMAN SALLY J	THOMAS CLINTON GREEN
HOLLOWAY FRANCES C	WILLIAM KING
HOLLOWAY PRISCILLA	THOMAS MCCRACKEN
HOLMAN RACHEL	HENRY JOHNSON
HOLMAN THOMAS	MARY/POLLY WARREN
HOLMES POLLY/MARY	STEPHEN WATKINS
HOLMES TUPSY CO [SIC]	WILLIAM HENRY ABERNATHY
HOLSHOUSER ELIZABETH	HERDLEIN/HERTLEIN/HARTLINE,SAMUEL
HOLSTON MARY	THOMAS BEDWELL
HOLT ELIZA ANGELINE	JOHN MCCRACKEN
HOLT FRANCES	NACY MEEKS
HOLT JOHN	ELIZABETH POGUE
HOLT MARTHA	JOHN SIDNEY JONES
HOLTON FANNIE H	SILAS GASKINS
HONEYCUTT SPICY	JAMES WILLIAM MYATT
HOOD LAURA ELLA	SAMUEL PETERSON ANDERSON
HOOK SARAH	JOHN RANDLEMAN
HOOKER ELIZABETH	JAMES JACKSON
HOOKER JAMES DIKERSON	VIRGINIA PARKER
HOOKS WARREN	ELISABETH ROBERTS
HOOPER MARY ELIZABETH/POLLY	STARLING GUNN
HOOPER REBECCA	WILLIAM DENNY
HOOTE MARY	JOHN LINEBARGER/LEINBERGER
HOOTEN MARY THOMAS	CHRISTOPHER A MALLISON
HOOTS PHISA ANN	THOMAS ALEXANDER SHERMER
HOPKINS AMELIA	W BAXTER DAVIS, SR
HOPKINS LUCINDA	JAMES P JOYCE
HOPKINS PRUDENCE	ZEBEDEE RUSSELL
HOPKINS SARAH	ISHAM MEDFORD
HOPPER SALLY	SAMUEL VANNOY
HOPPERS NANCY	CHARLES STEELMAN
HOPPES ADAMS	CATHERINE LINK

SPOUSE	ANCESTOR
HOPPES JOHN	NANCY ANN BROWN
HORD JANE	JOHN MIDDLETON FLEMING
HORD/HOARD MARY	JACOB JONES
HORIS/HARRIS MARY	ABRAHAM STOWE
HORN DAVID	CORNELIA JANE HOLLOWAY THOMAS
HORN MARY ANN	JOSEPH SUMNER BATTLE, I
HORN WILLIAM	JANE/JEANIE FADDIS/FADDES
HORNE KATE ROUTH	JAMES PHILIPS BATTLE
HORTON JEMINA	JAMES REDDICK RAMEY RUTLAND
HORTON MARTHA	JOHN H STRICKLAND
HORTON MARTHA GREY	CHARLES FRANKLIN DEBNAM
HORTON NARCISSA J	BARTHOLOMEW YATES DEBNAM
HORTON RACHEL	JOHN SCOTT
HORTON VELLA LEE	CHARLES HILL BURCH
HORTON WILLIAM	ELLEN TRICE
HORTON WILLIAM J	CATHERINE E DEBNAM
HOSKINS ANN	KING LUTEN/LUTON
HOSKINS MARTHA	JOSEPH GURNEY STUART
HOSKINS RICHARD	WINNIFRED WIGGINS
HOUCHINS NANCY	JAMES MCCRACKEN
HOUSE ANN	CONSTANT WILLIAMS HORTON
HOUSER JAMES A	HANNAH BROWN
HOUSER MRS HANNAH (MILLER)	JOHN SHAMEL/SCHEMEL
HOUSTON ESTHER	JOEL WALLACE
HOUSTON HENRY	ELENDER JANE STOKES
HOUSTON MARY	MARCUS T C KENNEDY
HOUSTON NANCY C	WILLIAM J OVERSTREET
HOUSTON SARAH	WILLIAM ELLIOTT MCREE
HOWARD ALVIN	ELIZABETH LOVELACE
HOWARD ARTHEA ELIZABETH	HILLIARD GARLAND YATES
HOWARD BARBARA EMMALINE	WILLIAM BRYANT CARTER
HOWARD EDRIE BROWN	HOYLE K KOONTZ
HOWARD ELIZABETH	ISSAC N JOHNSON
HOWARD PENNEY	DAVID COBLE, JR
HOWARD RACHEL	MOSES STRAHAN, SR
HOWARD SALLY/SALLIE	WILLIAM/BILLY BOONE
HOWARD SARAH	NIAL SCURLOCK
HOWARD SARAH	CHARLES JARVIS
HOWELL CATHERINE	EDWARD/NEDDIE BARKER
HOWELL EDITH	EDMOND STUCKEY
HOWELL JESSE	NANCY NICHOLSON
HOWELL LEAH	HENRY SAMUEL MCCLURE
HOWELL MARGARET	ISAAC JONES
HOWELL MARY EMMA/POLLY	MURPHY KEMP
HOWELL MARY/POLLY EMMA	MURPHY KEMP
HOWELL MURPHREE	NOAH SUGG
HOWELL RUTH	JOHN PHIPPS
HOWERTON BENJAMIN	PHOEBE NEWBOLD
HOWERTON CATHERINE	IRA WISE
HOY JOHN BOOKER	MARY GILBERT
HUBBELL MARY/POLLY	HENRY SANDERS SHOUSE
HUBER/HOOVER ELIZABETH	DAVID FOUTS/PHOUTS
HUCKABEE JOHN	EVE MCGREGOR
HUDDLESTON EFFIE	JOHN BULLOCK

SPOUSE	ANCESTOR
HUDSON JAMES	MARTHA MCSWAIN
HUDSON MARTHA	JONATHAN COWARD
HUFF MARY	ABRAHAM REECE
HUFFINE MARY	JACOB LINEBERRY
HUFFINES ELIZABETH/BETTIE	PETER APPLE
HUFFINES SUSAN	GEORGE KERNODLE
HUFFMAN CHARLOTTE	GRIFFITH THOMAS
HUFFMAN ELIZABETH	SOLOMON DIETZ, SR
HUFFMAN MARTHA CAROLINE	GILBERT HOLLER
HUFFMAN PETER	ELIZABETH TROXLER
HUFFMAN/HOFFMAN BARBARA	JOSEPH MAY
HUGGIN JANE	ELIJAH COX
HUGGINS ELIZABETH	SAMUEL COLUMBUS HAYES, SR
HUGHES CATHERINE	DAVID LEE, SR
HUGHES DARICUS	JOSEPH SCHOLES
HUGHES E MILLIE	JACOB HILL WHITE, JR
HUGHES ELIZABETH	PATTERSON YOUNG
HUGHES JAMES W	MARY JANE SMITH
HUGHES JOHN EDWARD	PHELOMA D EPPS
HUGHES LOUVICIA	WILLIAM ROBERTSON
HUGHES MARY/POLLY	WILLIAM POLK DOBSON
HUGHES SARAH	WILLIAM ADAMS
HUGHES SUSANNAH	JOHN B WATKINS
HULIN SARAH	JONATHAN HEATHMAN
HULL WILLIAM	JENNIE CRISP/CHRISP
HULLBROOKE ELIZABETH	JOSIAS SLOCUM
HUMPHREYS LOWRY	SIMON MOON
HUMPHRIES AMY	JAMES JONES
HUMPHRIES SUSANNAH	THOMAS HUSKEY
HUNNYCUTT SALLY	RUFUS PARRISH
HUNSUCKER ELIZABETH	GEORGE FREDERICK BOLLINGER
HUNSUCKER MARGARET/PEGGY	JOSEPH ISENHOWER/EISENHAUER
HUNT ELIZABETH	JOHN TUSSEY
HUNT MARGARET	JOHN BEALS/BALES
HUNT MARY MALINDA	JOHN HENRY MARTIN
HUNT MARY ROSA	ROLAND BRYANT/BRIANT
HUNT NETTIE LUCINDA	JULIUS HARRISON KENNEDY
HUNT SARAH/SALLY	EDWARD LEATHERWOOD
HUNT SUSANNAH	THOMAS RANKS
HUNTER ELIZABETH	JOHN MAY
HUNTER FEREBEE	JOSEPH LANE, III
HUNTER JAMES	MARGARET PHIPPS
HUNTER JAMES	MARY WALKER
HUNTER JOHN A	NANCY WILKINSON
HUNTER MARGARET	THOMAS OWEN
HUNTER RACHEL	WILLIAM WALTON
HUNTLEY SALLIE	PETER FINCANNON
HURLEY ELIZABETH	SPENCER STEWART
HURLEY ELLEN	ELI HAYS
HURT DICY A	BENJAMIN A PHILLIPS
HUSKE ELIZABETH	DANIEL CAIN
HUSON/HUSTON JOHN	MARTHA/PATSY/MATTIE DAWSON
HUSS JACOB VAN	JANE PIERCE
HUSSEY MARTHA	THOMAS KEY

SPOUSE	ANCESTOR
HUSTON WILLIAM	ELIZABETH MONTGOMERY
HUTCHENS THOMAS DAVID	MILLY CHRISTENE EVANS
HUTCHINS JOHN	JANE BRASSWELL
HUTCHINS OBEDIENCE	WILLIAM HARDING
HUTCHINS PHEBE	PLEASANT G WILLIAMS
HUTCHINS QUINTILLA	GEORGE C BRANDON
HUTCHINS SARAH	JOSHUA LACE WILLIAMS
HUTCHINS STRANGEMAN	ELIZABETH COX
HUTCHINS ZILPHIA	MILES SAWYER
HUTCHINSON MARY	DANIEL BLACK ORRELL
HUTCHINSON REBECCA	BENJAMIN DULANY/DULANEY, REV
HUTSON ELIZABETH	THOMAS TUCKER
HUTTO CINDERELLA	RICHARD HENDERSON
HYDER KATHRYN	ANDREW HAMPTON
HYMAN WINIFRED	ALFRED GRAY ANDREWS
ICE LOUISA JANE	ALVIS WASHINGTON HOLDER
IKARD SUSAN	PHILIP FRY
INGLE DICIA	JOHN GILLILAND
INGLE MARGARET	BENJAMIN HARRIS
INGLE WILLIAM	LEAH TUCKER
IPOCK JULIE	JOSEPH ALLEN GASKINS
IRVIN NANCY	JAMES ANDERSON
IRWIN ALLY	LARKIN SHEPHERD
ISAACK ELIZABETH	JOHN BLAIR
ISAACS PHOEBE	ABRAHAM VANDERPOOL
ISAACS PHOEBE	ABRAHAM VANDERPOOL
ISLEY MARY CATHERINE	JAMES EMSLEY JOBE
ISOM/ISHAM LUCY	ANGUS JOHNSON/JOHNSTON
ISRAEL ANNIE BELL	WILLIAM GARFIELD PENLEY/PENLY
ISRAEL DAVID R	JULIA C SLUDER
ISRAEL RALPH WEBB	HARRIET MELISSA PARHAM
IV JAMES THIGPEN	MARY PENELOPE/PENNY HILL
IVES ELIZABETH	THOMAS BATSON
IVES THOMAS	MARY/POLLY FINCH
IVEY EVALINA	GEORGEWASHINGTON HILLMAN/HILEMAN
IVEY HARRIOTT	BURWELL TEMPLE
IVEY MARY ANN	JAMES MOORE
IVEY MARY LELIA	JOHN HENRY EDDINGS
IVY HENRY	AGNES PEEBLES/PEOPLES
JACKS SALLY	HOY, WILLIAM VAN
JACKSON AGNES	DAVID D NUTT
JACKSON ANDREW	JEANNE/JANE SLOAN
JACKSON ANNE	WILLIAM, ARRINGTON, GEN
JACKSON CLARA ANN	SAMUEL HIGH
JACKSON ELIZABETH	WILLIAM HOLDER
JACKSON GIDEON S	SARAH ANN HAIR
JACKSON HELDA	JOSEPH PENNY
JACKSON ISAAC W	ELIZABETH NICHOLSON
JACKSON JAMES	REBECCA WEATHERS
JACKSON LIDDIA	ROWLAND MILAM

SPOUSE	ANCESTOR
JACKSON MARY	JAMES MILLIS
JACKSON MARY CATHERINE	WASHINGTON MORRIS
JACKSON MILLY	GEORGE D RITTER
JACKSON SAMUEL	HANNAH GIBSON
JACKSON SARAH	ALLEN GASKINS
JACKSON SUSANNAH	ABSALOM WALKER
JACKSON MRS MELLICENT (BROWN)	MARK R GREGORY
JACOB ANNE	JOHN GAITHER
JACOB RACHEL	BENJAMIN GAITHER
JACOBS ALFRED MAC	JANE ATWOOD
JACOBS SUSAN	JABIS BARRETT
JAMES ALICE	ROBERT MIDDLETON
JAMES ELIZABETH	JOHN PEARSALL
JAMES LUCRECY L	ABRAM PEAL BARNHILL
JAMES MARTHA PATSEY	ELISHA PARKER
JAMES MARY ANN	MARION HARTNESS
JAMES MARY F	SOLOMON D MARCUS
JAMES MARY JANE	DANIEL G LINEBERRY
JAMES SARAH ALICE	GENERAL GEORGE WHITMIRE, I
JANE CHARITY	DAVID M SHAW
JANE MARY	AARON TYSON, SR
JANE MARY ELIZABETH	RICHARD WRIGHT, SR
JARRATT MARY	BENJAMIN GIST
JARRATT WILLIAM DAVID	ANN AMANDA MCKINNEY
JARRETT MARY	SAMUEL SMITH
JARVICE SARAH	ROGER MASON, JR
JARVIS CAROLINE	JOHN UPTON
JARVIS DORCAS	JAMES MERCER/MONROE BERRY
JARVIS ELIZABETH	JOHN WALKER
JARVIS LEVI LEONADAS	RHODA FARROW
JARVIS MARY/POLLY	BENJAMIN MASON
JASPER	FRANCIS FONTAINE, JR
JEAN MRS MARTHA (MURDOCK)	ALEXANDER L NICHOLSON
JEFFREYS SUSAN BATTLE	ROBERT HICKS WYNN/WYNNE
JEFFRIES MARTHA	PLEASANT CHANDLER
JENKINS JENKEY	NANCY ANN/ANNA BEAM
JENKINS MARTHA	JESSE HARDEN
JENKINS MARTHA	THOMAS COX
JENKINS MRS MATILDA	JAMES P JOYCE
JENKINS NANCY	REUBEN HERNDON
JENKINS SANFORD	DELILAH BARBEE
JENKINS/DINKINS MARY	CHARLES CHOAT HALL
JENNINGS ALSON G	MARY PUGH
JENNINGS ANNA LETITIA/TISHA	JOHN NEEDHAM
JENNINGS ELIZABETH	HENRY FRANCE
JENNINGS LUCRETIA	HILLAIRE ROUSSEAU
JENNINGS MIRIAM	DAVID PRICHARD
JERNIGAN LOVY	LEMON HANDLEY LEE
JERNIGAN SARAH	CODDINGTON SMITH
JOB JAMES EMSLEY	MARY CATHERINE ISLEY
JOBE LEVI JONATHAN	CAROLINE GILL
JORE LUCY	JAMES WILLIAM SQUIRES
JOHN JANE	HARMON COX
JOHNS ELIZABETH	WILLIAM R ROSE

SPOUSE	ANCESTOR
JOHNS RICE S	MILBURY/MILBERRY REDFEARN/REDFERN
JOHNSON AMY	WILLIAM TACKETT/TACKITT, SR
JOHNSON ANN	MARTIN ALLEY GASH
JOHNSON CATHERINE	JOHNSON F PERKINS
JOHNSON CATTIE	MASTON WALTERS
JOHNSON CELIA	ELIAS G COOK
JOHNSON DELILAH	JAMES MADISON MATTHEWS
JOHNSON ELIZA ANNE	AARON TYSON, JR
JOHNSON ELIZABETH	ROBERT ROUSSEAU
JOHNSON FERBY	ALEXANDER PENNY
JOHNSON HARDEE	CATHERINE CANNON
JOHNSON ISABELL	GEORGE DOUGLAS
JOHNSON JANE ELIZABETH	DAVID SEYMORE DUNCAN
JOHNSON JOSIAH	SARAH/SALLY WRIGHT
JOHNSON LEWIS JAMES	SARAH ADELAIDE ROUSE
JOHNSON LT WILLIAM M	MARY E ENGLAND
JOHNSON LUCINDA ADELINE	STEPHEN MEGGS
JOHNSON MABEL CLARA	WILLIAM JULIAN RUSSELL
JOHNSON MATTHIAS M	MARTHA/PATSY CRUTCHFIELD
JOHNSON	LAURA WELBORN
JOHNSON MRS ELIZABETH	JAMES MCCORKLE
JOHNSON NANCY	EMANUEL EDMISSON
JOHNSON NANCY ANN	RICHARD LEDBETTER, III
JOHNSON NETTIE	GEORGE NEWTON MASSEY
JOHNSON PHOEBE	JOHN WHITT, II
JOHNSON POLLY	GEORGE KILLIAN/KILIAN
JOHNSON REBEKAH	OBEDIAH HARRIS
JOHNSON ROBERT COOK	ABIGAIL WHITE
JOHNSON RUTH MAUDE	WILLIAM JULIAN RUSSELL
JOHNSON SARAH	THOMAS JEFFERSON LISTER
JOHNSON SARAH	ROMULUS EDWARD LOWRANCE
JOHNSON SARAH	JOSEPH MORGAN
JOHNSON SARAH	LEONARD SAYLORS/SAILOR, JR
JOHNSON STEPHEN H	CATHERINE MCKAY MCMILLAN
JOHNSON SUSANNAH	JESSE LEE, JR
JOHNSON TOMASANN	JOSEPH GUTBRODT/GOODBREAD
JOHNSON/JOHNSTON CATHERINE	JOHN JOHNSON/JOHNSTON
JOHNSON/JOHNSTON JESSE	HANNAH HADLEY
JOHNSON/JOHNSTON ROBERT W	ANNA CHAMBERS
JOHNSON/JOHNSTON RUTH	WILLIAM CLAMPITT
JOHNSON/JOHNSTON TABITHA ALLEN	ROBERT BOOKER MAY
JOHNSTON GEORGE	ELIZABETH LINDSEY
JOHNSTON HANNAH	JEREMIAH PEARSALL
JOHNSTON HAZELTINE	JOHN FRANKLIN HOLBROOK
JOHNSTON JEMIMA	FRANCIS FONTAINE, III
JOHNSTON MARTHA	ELIAS W LAMM
JOHNSTON PENELOPE	GEORGE ANDERSON HOLT
JOHNSTON PENELOPE	GEORGE ANDERSON HOLT
JOHNSTON SAMANTHA-ELIZABETH	JOHN DUCKWORTH
JOHNSTON SARAH	JAMES MARSHBURN/MASHBURN
JOHNSTON WILLIE	WILL RYALS
JOHNSTONE DRUSILLA	BENJAMIN PATE
JOLLEY JESSE	MARY ANN BRYAN
JOLLEY REUBEN MANNING	SARAH REBECCA PIPPIN

SPOUSE	ANCESTOR
JOLLEY SARAH	WILLIAM TEMPLE COLE
JONES ABIGAIL	THOMAS, SHF BONNER
JONES ANN	WILLIAM HOUSTON, DR
JONES ANN	WILLIAM BELL
JONES ANN	ROBERT SANFORD
JONES ATLAS O	MARY FRANCIS CHEAIRS/CHEARS
JONES BETSY	MARY ELIZABETH BRANDON
JONES CASSANDRA MARTIN	JAMES GEORGE LEWIS
JONES CECILIA/SISLEY	JESSE F SHELTON
JONES CPT SIMON	ABIGAIL BONNER
JONES DAVID C	NEOMA BENNET
JONES EDITH	RICHARD KING
JONES ELIZABETH	MOSES EASTEP/ESTEP
JONES ELIZABETH	JOSEPH P GREEN
JONES ELIZABETH	JAMES WELBORN SHEPHERD
JONES ELIZABETH	SION PEARCE
JONES ELIZABETH	DARIUS MCCURDY
JONES ELIZABETH F	PINKNEY H RUSSELL
JONES EMILY A	WILLIAM C BROWN
JONES EMMA JEAN	REGINALD REAMS BROWN
JONES ESTHER HARRIET	RICHARD ISAAC LEDBETTER
JONES GRACIE	PERMINTER MORGAN
JONES HENRY	SARAH SHARP
JONES HENRY	MARY MCCRACKEN, MRS
JONES HONOUR	RICHARD ODOM
JONES IDA CORA	JOHN EDWARD COX
JONES JACOB	MARY HOARD/HORD
JONES JESSE	ELIZABETH BELL
JONES JOSIAH	CYNTHIA LUCILLE COPELAND
JONES JULIA ANN	SAMUEL CHANCY
JONES JULIE ANN	ADOLPHUS MCCRARY
JONES LOUISA	SIDNEY JACKSON WESTER
JONES LUCY	GEORGE GREEN/GREENE
JONES MAMIE	GEORGE WASHINGTON BARKER
JONES MAMY	RICHARD SPENCER
JONES MARTHA	HENRY TAYLOR
JONES MARY	JOHN WATKINS
JONES MARY	FREDERICK TURNER
JONES MARY	THOMAS GILL, SR
JONES MARY ANN	MASSEY M COPELAND
JONES MARY WILEY	JOHN YOUNG WILKERSON
JONES MARY/POLLY	HARDEN YORK
JONES NANCY ANN	JAMES BENJAMIN PALMER/PARMER
JONES NANCY BOAZ	DENNY,JOEL
JONES PEGGY	SUNLEY PARKER THRIFT
JONES REV CHARLES PINCKNEY	SARAH ANN MCLAUCHLIN
JONES RICHARD	ELIZABETH MARTIN
JONES SARAH/SALLY	ROBERT M DURHAM
JONES SUSAN	THOMAS SQUIRES, II
JONES SUSANNA	TULLY MOSELEY
JONES TACY	SHADRICK JONES MOORE
JONES TEMPERANCE	JAMES WHITEHEAD
JONES THOMAS	JANE PHIPPS
JONES VINKLER	EUNICE/UNITY ROGERS

SPOUSE INDEX

SPOUSE	ANCESTOR
JONES WILLIAM FRANKLIN	CHARITY JANE HEATH
JONES WILLIAM M	MARY ANN PRESSLEY
JONES MRS ABIGAIL (BONNER)	AQUILLA SUGG
JONES MRS EUNICE (ROGERS)	JOHN ROBERTS
JONES MRS PRISCILLA (MCSWAIN)	GABRIEL WASHBURN
JONES MRS REBECCA (WALL) SULLICK	JOEL WALLACE
JOPLIN LUCINDA	DANIEL NOLIN
JORDAN HARRIET WILLS	BURGESS SMITH
JORDAN JUDITH	RICHARD WHITMIRE
JORDAN MARY	JOHN WOOTEN, COL
JORDAN ROBERT CALHOUN	ELOISE BROOKS
JORDON NANCY	AARON NEAL
JOUETT MATTHEW	MARTHA FLEMING
JOYNER MARTHA/PATSEY	JAMES WEATHERS
JOYNER NANCY ANN	LEWIS RICKS
JOYNER NELSON	SUSANNAH JOYNER, MRS
JUDD HARRIET	TILLMON/TILMON/TILLMAN THOMAS
JULIAN LYDIA	WILLIAM FIELD/FIELDS
JULIAN LYDIA	WILLIAM FIELD
JUSTICE ELIZABETH GRIFFIN	WILLIAM SEYMORE DUNCAN
JUSTICE	ELIZABETH YOUNG
JUSTICE REBECCA	JACOB SMITH
KEARNEY CAROLINE C	ARCHIBALD DAVIS
KEECH MARY JANE	CHARLES JOHN LOCKYER
KEEL WILLIAM KELLY	NANCY VANOVER
KEELE SARAH	WILLIAM MAINER/MANER/MAYNER
KEEN ZELLA	LITTELTON WATSON
KEESE LUCY	BENJAMIN MARET/MERIT/MERRITT, JR
KEETOR OLIVE	CALEB CREEKMORE
KEILE SARAH	EDMOND CHAUNCEY
KELLAM ELIZABETH GATES	JOHN BARNABAS DEARMIN/DEARMON
KELLAM EMMA C	JOHN E DAVIS
KELLAM MRS NANCY (FORBES)	WILLIAM S ETHERIDGE
KELLER ALICE MATINA	JOHN WALTER KELLER
KELLERS MARY	JOHN MOORE
KELLON PARTHENIA	JOHN FEE
KELLY AMELIA	CHARLES BALDWIN
KELLY DRUSILLA FLOWERS	ANDREW JACKSON APPLEWHITE
KELLY MARY	GEORGE CROMARTIE
KELLY NANCY LUVATER	ROBERT THEODORE BOLICK
KELLY MRS MARY (MCMILLAN)	ANTHONY FENTRESS TOON
KELTON ELIZABETH R	WILLIAM DUNLAP CLARK
KEMP LUCINDA	WILLIAM JARVIS
KEMP SUSAN	SAMUEL ROEBUCK MCHUGH/MCCUE
KENDALL ELIZA ANN	STEPHEN CRUMP
KENDALL RUTH	JESSE HAISLEY
KENNEDAY RUBEN	PRUDENCE WELBORN
KENNEDY ELIZABETH	JOHN WATTS
KENNEDY MARY	JOHN BROOKS, JR
KENNEDY NANCY SERINA	JOHN KERR CALLEN
KENNEDY TEMPERANCE	RILAND KEY
KENNON ELIZABETH	JOHN JR, ALSTON, MAJOR

279

SPOUSE	ANCESTOR
KENT GEORGE	MARTHA/MATTIE CAROLINE HAYES
KENT MARY	HUGH CUNNINGHAM
KENT MIRIAM F	PETER WHITAKER
KERBY SUSANNAH	SAMUEL CLIFTON
KERNODLE RACHEL	GEORGE QUINCE WAGONER
KERNUT SUSSANAH	JOSHUA TACKER/TUCKER
KERR ELIZABETH	ALEXANDER CROMARTIE
KERR FRANKY	GEORGE BARKER
KETCHUM JUSTINA	ELIJAH REED
KEYS MAHALA	ADAM MOORE SELF
KIBLE NANCY	CHRISTOPHER FELTS
KICK MARY	ADAM STARR
KIDD BENJAMIN	RACHEL CREASMAN
KIKER NANNIE NONNIE	BAXTER COLUMBUS TARLTON
KILGORE LYDIA ANN	JAMES YATES
KILGORE THOMAS JR	PHEBE LEA
KILLEBREW ELIZA	NATHAN HARRELL SESSUMS
KILLEBREW LEVINA	JOHN HEATH
KILLIAN DANIEL WILKINSON	MARTHA ANN MCCLURE
KILLIAN MARY/POLLY	JOHN DANIEL HERMAN
KILPATRICK ANDREW	ELIZABETH MCCORKLE
KIMBLE JOHN	MARGARET LLOYD HOGAN
KIMBROUGH GRIZELLE	JOHN HINTON, COL
KIMMEY DIANA	ZEBULON CAUSEY
KINCAID ANNA	PHILIP CORLEW
KINCAID ANNA	PHILIP CORLEW
KINCAID ANNA	PHILIP CORLEW
KING ANDERSON	MASEN DICKENS
KING ANDREW JACKSON	ELIZA M GODFREY
KING CATHERINE	JOHN BYRD/BIRD
KING CEALY	HENRY VOLK/FOLK/FOWLKES
KING CLARA S	ROBERT ED MCCRACKEN
KING GILLY	JOHN JAMES KING
KING HARRIET SCOTT	ZACHARIAH HARMAN
KING JOHN JAMES	GILLY KING
KING MARTHA ANN	JOHN HOGAN
KING MARTHA BURCHET	THADDEUS WILLIAM FELTON
KING MARY	EDWARD BYRD/BIRD
KING MARY	JAMES LUTEN/LUTON
KING MARY ELLA	STEPHEN SILANCE
KING OLIVE	STEPHEN SILANCE
KING REBECCA	JAMES L SANFORD
KING VIOLET	FRANKLIN DOBSON
KING MRS MARTHA/PATSY (DAVIS)	JESSE VESTAL
KINKEY CATHARINE	WILLIAM COX
KIRBY ELIZABETH	JOHN INGRAM
KIRK MARY JANE	ABNER COBLE
KIRK REBECCA	ARCHIBALD CAMPBELL
KIRK SARAH	JOHN GRUBBS
KIRKLAND SARAH	JOSEPH ELLER
KIRKMAN EMILY JANE	THOMAS CAUSEY
KIRKMAN GEORGE	MARY THOMPSON, MRS
KIRKPATRICK LAIRD	NANCY CALLEN
KITCHEN/KINCHEN TALITHA	JESSE MCGEE

SPOUSE INDEX

SPOUSE	ANCESTOR
KITCHENS NANCY HINTON	JOHN F PERRY
KITTRELL CARY	RICHARD WRIGHT, JR
KLAFTER HARRIETT ZEIF	TIBOR/THEODORE KLAFTER
KLEIN MARY MAGDALENE	PETER MEISENHEIMER
KNIGHT JOSEPH DAMERON	MAGARA CLEMSON
KNIGHT JUDITH	SAMUEL CLEMENT
KNIGHT MARTHA	JOHN CAIN
KNIGHT RACHAEL	JAMES MEREDITH, JR
KNIGHT MRS REBECCA (JONES)	JAMES BRANN
KNOTT ELIZABETH	ATKINS NICHOLSON
KNOTT ELIZABETH FRANCIS	WILLIAM JASPER DEAN
KNOTT FIELDING R	MILDRED ANN KNOTT
KNOTT JOHN	CHARLOTTE DANIEL
KOENER ANNA CATERINA	NICHOLAS SCHRAMM
KOONCE EDGAR CORNELIUS	SALLY DEES
KOONTZ HOYLE K	EDRIE BROWN HOWARD
KORNEGAY MARGARET	RICHARD BRYANT TAYLOR
KRAUSE MARIA MARGRETHE	CHARLES HOLDER
KUYKENDALL LOUISE NAOMIE	FERNANDO HAYNES NORMAN
KYLE MARY FRANCES/FANNY	DANIEL SOUTHERLAND WILLIAMS
LACKEY MARY	CHARLES BURNEY
LACKEY MARY	HIMERICK/HYMERICK PERRY
LACY/LACEY LUCY	JOSEPH H MOUTRAY
LADD ELIZABETH	WILLIAM PATTERSON
LAFATER MARY MAE	JOSIAH H BUNN
LAFOON MARY	CORNELIUS KEITH
LAIRD DAVID	ANN ELIZABETH TUMBLESON
LAKE MARGARET	ADLEY NEAGLE
LAKEY REBECCA DELANEY	ANDREW JACKSON WISHON
LAMB ABNER	DINAH MCPHERSON
LAMB ALEXANDER	ABIGAIL EDWARDS
LAMB CATHERINE ELIZA	LEWIS CARROLL
LAMB ESTHER	DAVID HODGSON/HODSON
LAMB/LAM ALVA ANDERSON	JANE GRAHAM/GRIMES
LAMBERT THOMAS	NANCY PARTIN
LAMBETH MARGARET	DAVID D KENNEDY
LAMM THOMAS RUFFIN	CATHERINE THORN/THORNE
LAMM ZINA	MARTIN R THORN/THORNE
LAMON KATHRINE	JAMES CAMPBELL
LANCASTER SARIELDA	HUBBARD PARNELL
LANCASTER WENIFORD	JAMES CLARK
LAND THOMAS ANN	MARGARET ELLEN BRINSON
LANDERS MARY	HANS MICHAEL GOODNIGHT
LANDRUM NANCY	JESSE MCGEE
LANE AGNES	BENJAMIN KIMSEY/KIMZEY
LANE JOSEPH	PATIENCE MCKINNE
LANE MARTHA	HARDY BURT
LANE MARTHA/PATTY	JETHRO BATTLE
LANE MARY ANN	ANDREWJACKSON VOLK/FOLK/FOWLKES,WILLIAM
LANGHAM JANE	LAWSON GARNER
LANGLEY ALSEY	MATHEW TANNER, JR
LANGLEY MINDA L	WILLIAM BEDFORD HALL

SPOUSE INDEX

SPOUSE	ANCESTOR
LEDBETTER MARY	JOHN BRADLEY, SR
LEDBETTER MRS LYDIA(HOCKNEY)	JOHN WALL NORWOOD
LEDFORD ALIE	NELLIE VINSON
LEDFORD MARY/MOLLY	JOSEPH MYERS
LEE ABIGAIL	SOLOMON KING
LEE DORCAS WOOD	HARRIS KIMBRELL
LEE EDITH	PLEASANT L PARKER
LEE ELIZABETH	HENRY THOMPSON
LEE JOEL	MELISSA LINDSEY
LEE KEZIAH	WILLIS LOE
LEE LEAURIAH MAY	ALBERT WEST CLEMENT
LEE LIZZIE	JAMES GREGORY
LEE PATIENCE	WILLIAM W POPLIN
LEE PENELOPE	JOSEPH MARSHBURN/MASHBURN
LEE SARAH	HIRAM HARDY HARGROVE
LEE WILLIAM HENRY	FRANCES E HARRIS
LEE WILLIS	MARY LINDSEY
LEE WOODROW WILSON	CORNELIA DOCIA ELLIS
LEEPER ELISABETH	ROBERT PATRICK
LEGET MARGARET	ISAAC MCLEAN
LEGGETT ELIAZBETH	JESSE L SCHWANNER/SWANNER
LEGGETT MARY EMELINE	HARVEY BAKER ROBERSON
LEGRAND ANN	JOHN KIMBROUGH/KIMBRO
LEINBACH REBECCA	PETER TRANSOU
LEMMONS MARY	DANIEL BUIE
LEMOND JANE	JAMES ORR
LENDERMAN MARGARET	HENRY YORK
LENNON ANNA JANE	JOSHUA SINGLETARY
LEONARD ADA HYANTIAN	JESSE WRIGHT EDMUNDSON
LEONARD HANNAH	JOSEPH HEWETT
LEONARD MARGARET	ROBERT LINN
LEONARD RACHEL	WILLIAM STANTON
LEONARD MRS SOPHIA (NEELY)	EZEKIEL POLK
LEWING JANE/JAIN	SOLOMON STANSBURY
LEWIS CATHERINE S	THOMAS W BEAMAN
LEWIS FRANCES	ROBERT LEWIS
LEWIS GWEN	ABRAHAM MASSEY
LEWIS JANE MERIWETHER	SWEPSON SIMS
LEWIS JOHN	PRISCILLA BROOKS
LEWIS MRS MARY	CRESON/CRISSON/CREASON/CRISHON,ABRAHAM
LEWIS MRS MARY	ABRAHAM CRESON/CRESSON
LEWIS REBECCA A	THOMAS W BEAMAN
LEWIS RICHARD	LYDIA FIELD
LEWIS SARAH	WILLERFORD W LEWIS
LEWIS SUSANNAH	THOMAS BENGE, SR
LIDDELL MARY	WILLIS MCGEE
LIGHT ELLENDER	JOHN LOCKE
LIGHTFOOT BARTHOLOMEW	MARTHA/POLLY HARMAN
LILLINGTON CHRISTIAN	JAMES ALSTON
LILLY MARY	DANIEL SMITH
LIMBAUGH CATHERINE	JOHN AWALT
LIMBAUGH SOLOMAN	NANCY ANN AWALT
LINDEN MARTHA	THOMAS SWIFT, SR
LINDER CHARLOTTE	JOHN ORAND/ORRAN

SPOUSE	ANCESTOR
LINDEY ELIZABETH JANE	AXUM SANDERS
LINDLEY ELEANOR	GEORGE MARIS
LINDLEY RUTH	JOSHUA HADLEY
LINDSAY MARY ELIZA	WYATT FLETCHER BOWMAN
LINDSAY ROBERT	NANCY MCGEE
LINDSAY WILLIAM	ALICE TAYLOR
LINDSEY ATHANATIOUS	SARAH LLOYD/LOYD
LINDSEY EDWARD	RACHEL MURPHY
LINDSEY ELEANOR/NELLIE	WILLIAM WOODS
LINDSEY MARY	WILLIS LEE
LINDSEY MELISSA	JOEL LEE
LINEBERRY ELIZABETH	FREDRICK SMITH
LINEBERRY JACOB	MARY HUFFINE
LINTHICUM FRANCES	DANIEL SHERWOOD
LINVILLE JOHN	FRANCIS CRIM
LIPPS SUSANNAH	JOHN DIXON/DICKSON
LIPSCOMB ARTMESIA	WASHINGTONGREEN STANFIELD/STANDFIELD
LIPSCOMB THOMAS	POLLY SARGENT/SEARGENT/SARJENT
LISTER POLLY	ZEBULON VAUGHN
LISTER ROSA	LORENZA DOW MORROW
LITTLE ELIZABETH	GEORGE WILSON JONES
LITTLE ELIZABETH	JOHN BOONE, JR
LITTLE HARMON	MARY/POLLY SIMPSON
LITTLE JACOB	SARAH/SALLY E ADAMS
LITTLE JULIA ANN	CALEB GRIFFITH
LITTLE SAMUEL	ELIZABETH BOONE
LITTLE MRS HANNAH (HENSLEY)	WILLIAM H DIXON/DICKSON
LITTRELL ORA	WILLIAM GLOSSUP
LIVERMAN DIRECTOR	JAMES A SPRUIELL/SPRUILL
LIVINGSTON LUCINDA	RALPH MCGEE
LLEWELLYN CHLOE	THOMAS GRIMES
LLEWELYN GATSY ANN	SAMUEL CHERRY, II
LLOYD MARY	JOHN CLARKE
LLOYD MARY	JOHN HOGAN
LLOYD	JAMES MOORE
LLOYD SARAH	DANIEL HOGAN
LLOYD SARAH	ATHANATIOUS LINDSEY
LOCK MARY JANE	JAMES BROWN
LOCKE ELIZABETH	MARTIN PHIFER, JR
LOCKE MARY	JOHN CATHEY
LOCKE MATTHEW	GEORGE HOWARD
LOCKE MRS ELIZABETH	JOHN BRANDON
LOCKHART NANCY	CASON GIBBS
LOE WILLIS	KEZIAH LEE
LOFLIN ELIZA	ABSALOM JARRELL
LOGAN ISABELLA	RICHARD FORD
LOGGINS ELIZABETH	TARLTON/TALTON WOODY
LOGUE ANN	THOMAS THOMPSON
LOGUE ANN	THOMAS THOMPSON
LOMAX BERNICE GRACE	ANDREW FRANKLIN KILBY
LONDON EMELINE	SAMUEL PATTERSON
LONG LEAH	JOHN JONES
LONG LOUISA	LARKIN SMITH
LONG LOUISE	THOMAS LAMBERT, SR

SPOUSE	ANCESTOR
LONG MARGARET BURROUGHS	WILLIAM HENRY BURCH
LONG MRS ELIZABETH	FELIX MOTSINGER
LONG REBECCA	ROBERT POTTER
LONG SARAH	RICHARD LEARY
LONGINO ANNE	BEN HUNTER
LONGINO MARY	DAVID VESTAL
LONGMIRE STACEY ELIZABETH	WILLIAM GASH
LONGWORTH LUCY A	LEWIS DAVIS
LOPER LYDIA	JOHN POWERS
LOVE NANCY	RICHARD ARWINE/ERVIN
LOVE POLLY	JOSEPH HONEYCUTT
LOVE SARAH	DAVID COLEMAN
LOVEL ELIZABETH	WILLIAM WOODY
LOVEL MARY	JONATHAN WOODY
LOVELACE LUCINDA	WILLIAM CHRISTIAN STRADER
LOVELACE NANCY	ZADOCK LEACH
LOVELACE SARAH SELENE	THOMAS H MCGINN
LOVELADY REBECCA	JEREMIAH FRYER/FRYAR
LOVELL/LOVINGOOD ELIZABETH	WILLIAM WOODY, JR
LOVELL/LOVINGOOD MARY/MOLLY	JONATHAN R WOODY
LOVETT ELIZA	WILLIAM BUXTON WILLIAMS
LOVINGOOD MOLLY	JONATHAN WOODY
LOW BARBARA	JOHN MATTHEW CORTNER/COTNER
LOW PHILIP	SARAH CARROLL
LOWE ELIZABETH	WILLIAM DOBSON
LOWE ELIZABETH	AMOS WRIGHT
LOWE MARTHA	CHARLES HOBGOOD/HOPGOOD
LOWERY ELIZABETH	CHARLES MCKINNEY
LOWRANCE CATHERINE	JOHN PERKINS
LOWRANCE ISABELLA	WILLIAM SHERRILL
LOWRY ELIZABETH	EPPERSON FORSYTH
LUCKEY ISABELLA	JOHN BALDRIDGE
LUCKIE ANN	SAMUEL HILLIS
LUSTER MARGARET	JAMES BENNETT CONDITT/CONDICT
LUTEN ESTHER	ROBERT HICKS
LYDA MARY	BOAZ/BOOZE STILL
LYDAY REBECCA	JAMES WASLEY NORMAN
LYERLY DELILA	JOHN COBBLE/CAUBLE/KABEL
LYERLY ELIZABETH	JOHN COBBLE/CAUBLE/KABEL
LYERLY MALINDA	JOHN COBBLE/CAUBLE/KABEL
LYLES B	MRS JUDITH LYLES
LYONS SARAH	CHARLES WILSON CATES
LYTLE JEAN/REBECCA	JOHN MCCRACKEN
MABERY JACOB A	MILEY PEMIE CABLE
MABIE MRS MARY JANE (DYSON)	WILLIAM BAKER DAVENPORT
MABON/MEBANE MARGARET	JOSEPH WHITE
MABRY OLA SARAH	JOHN W BELL
MABRY MRS ELIZABETH COLUMBIA (ANCEL)	PINKNEY THRIFT
MACCANDLESS/MCCONNELL MARTHA ANN	HEZEKIAH JAMES BALCH, REV
MACE ANGEL	JOHN DORRIS
MACE PRISCILLA	THOMAS THOMPSON
MACKEY AMELIA	THOMAS B POLLARD

SPOUSE	ANCESTOR
MACKEY SARAH	ANDREW LYDA
MACKIE BENJAMIN	TENNESSEE REECE
MACKIE JESSE	PHYSA REBECCA WILLIAMS
MACKIE JOHN	NAOMI MOFFIT
MACKIE JOHN	NAOMI MOFFITT
MACKIE JOHN HENRY	NANCY ELIZABETH SIZEMORE
MACKIE REBECCA	JACOB HINSHAW
MACKIE REBECCA	JACOB HINSHAW
MACKIE ROBERT	ANNA MARTIN
MACKIE ROBERT	ANN/ANNA MARTIN
MACON ELIZABETH S	BARTHOLOMEW YATES DEBNAM
MACON PRICALLA M	THOMAS RICHARD DEBNAM
MACRHINE CATHERINE	CONRAD LONG
MACY PHOEBE	JOSEPH LEONARD
MADDEN BETSY	JOSEPH ALLISON
MADDEN ELIZABETH	PETER GLASSCOCK, JR
MADISON MARY	BIRD THOMAS LANIER
MADISON REBECCA	JOHN THOMAS JENNINGS
MAGADALENA MARIA	HENRY WHITTENBURGH/WHITENBERGER
MAGNESS MARY ANN	JOHN WASHBURN
MAGRUDER MARGARET	MANN SIMS
MAINS MRS MARY (MORRISON)	JAMES BECK
MALLARD RACHEL	PHILIP/PHIL SOUTHERLAND
MALLORY ELIZA	GEORGE WASHINGTON POTTER
MALLORY GEORGE S	ANN ADALINE DONALDSON
MALLOY BARBERY	JOHN MCPHAILL
MALONE LEAH	VICTOR MOREAU MURPHEY
MALVIN GEORGE MICHAEL	MARY ANN WARREN
MAN ELIZABETH/BETTY	JOHN BURGIN/BURGAN
MAN LEAH	BENJAMIN/BEN BURGIN/BURGAN
MANESS ELIZABETH	LEWIS OLIVER GARNER
MANGUM MARY	MOSES ELLIS
MANIFOLD ALICE	AARON BEALS/BALES
MANLEY ELIZABETH	SAMUEL KELTON
MANLOVE MARGARET	PEREZ CHIPMAN, JR
MANN ADOLPHUS	MARGARET WHITT
MANN ANNIE LEE	CLAUDE NASH HERNDON
MANN ISAAC NEWTON	CORNELIA FRANCES FOUSHEE
MANN MARTHA	THOMAS JONES
MANN	THOMAS NESBITT
MANN	WILLIAM SEYMOUR RUDD
MANN POLLY	LEWIS MIDGETT
MANN SARAH	SAMUEL MCCLEES
MANN WESLEY	DICEA EASTINGS WEST
MANNING FRANCES	HENRY JOLLEY
MANNING MARY	WILLIAM BRYAN/BRYANT
MANNING MINNIE	JOHN OSCAR MANNING
MANNING NANCY	CLAYTON HINES TAYLOR
MANNING POLLY	RICHARD WHITEHURST
MANNING SALLIE	JOHN/JACKIE BEST
MANSKER MRS ELIZABETH (WHITE)	ISAAC WALTON
MANUEL MARY	G WASHINGTON BURTON
MARGARETHA ANNA	ANDREAS VOLK/FOLK/FOWLKES, SR
MARIN RUTH	JOHN HIGH

SPOUSE INDEX

SPOUSE		ANCESTOR
MARIS	AARON	SARAH HOLLADAY
MARIS	GEORGE	ELEANOR/ELENDER LINDLEY
MARKS	ELIDA	CALVIN COLUMBUS HENSON/HINSON
MARKS	MARY MARGARITE	CALVIN COLUMBUS HENSON/HINSON
MARLIN	MARY	LEANDER GAITHER
MARSDEN	FRANCES ELIZABETH	STACY GILLIAM MAXWELL
MARSH	MAHALA/MAHALY	NEILL CARVER BEARD
MARSHALL	JANE/SUSAN	WILLIAM HENRY APPLEWHITE
MARSHALL	JANIE GERTRUDE	ARTHUR VERNON HUDGINS
MARSHALL	LUCILLE	HENRY GRADY BUCHANAN
MARSHALL	MARGARET ELLEN	ALLEN LITTLE
MARSHALL	MARY	THOMAS HINSHAW
MARSHALL	MARY	SAMUEL STANTON
MARSHALL	RUTH	JOSEPH HINSHAW
MARSHALL	SARAH	JOHN ROBARDS
MARSHALL	SUSAN	CARR DARDEN
MARSHALL	TANDY	MARY ANN TERRY
MARSHALL	THOMAS	MILLY WAGGONER
MARSHALL	VIRLINDA	HOY, ABRAHAM VAN SR
MARSHALL	WILLIAM A	LUCY ANN LIMBAUGH
MARSHBURN	JACOB JAMES	ANN JULIA POWELL
MARSHBURN	JAMES	SARAH JOHNSTON
MARSHBURN	JAMES MADISON	LOUISA POWELL
MARSHBURN	MRS LIZZIE CATHERINE (DAVIS)	JAMES WILLIAM PEARCE
MARSHILL	ANN	WILLIAM DAVIS
MARTIN	ADAM	MARY/POLLY BABER
MARTIN	ANN	ROBERT MACKIE/MACKEY/MACKAY
MARTIN	ANN	JOHN SNOAD/SNODE, COL
MARTIN	ANNA	ROBERT MACKIE
MARTIN	BARZILLA	JOHN GORDON
MARTIN	BENJAMIN F	SARAH ROUSSEAU
MARTIN	CAMILLA	HENRY E KNOTT
MARTIN	ELIZABETH	RICHARD JONES
MARTIN	ELIZABETH	THOMAS DILLS
MARTIN	HANNAH	JAMES JENNINGS
MARTIN	JANE/JEAN	ALEXANDER CRAIGHEAD, REV
MARTIN	JOHN R	RACHEL ROSS
MARTIN	MARTHA	JESSE D GARDNER
MARTIN		EMILINE SUGGS
MARTIN	NANCY	JOHN MCNEILL
MARTIN	NANCY E JANE	GEORGE WILLIAM KNIGHT
MARTIN	NANNIE	JAMES AUGUSTUS BUTLER
MARTIN	REBECCA	WILLIAM NEWSOME
MARTIN	REBECCA	THOMAS F HUGHES
MARTIN	RUTH	JESSE WILLIAMS
MARTIN	SAMUEL	MARY SNODDY
MARTIN	SARAH	JAMES WEATHERLY
MARTIN	SARAH	WHITNEY ROYALL
MARTIN	SARAH MEREDITH	HIRAM ROUSSEAU
MARTIN	SUSAN JANE	JAMES MADISON TESH
MARTIN	THOMAS SCOTT	ANN CLINGMAN POINDEXTER
MARTIN	MRS ELEANORE (GOODE)	DAVID DALTON
MARTIN	MRS EMILINE (SUGGS?)	JAMES HENDERSON MATTHEWS
MASON	ELEANOR/NELLY	ELIJAH BURCH

SPOUSE	ANCESTOR
MASON MARY ISOBEL	JAMES DAVID WILLIAMSON
MASON PERMELIA F	THOMAS POLLARD
MASON SARAH	ROBERT TINNIN
MASSENBURG LUCY	ARCHIBALD DAVIS
MASSEY ABRAHAM	GWEN LEWIS
MASSEY BENJAMIN	MARGARET/PEGGY CARLOCK
MASSEY CAROLINE	EDWARD R BARKER
MASSEY HANNAH	PLEASANT HARRIS
MASSEY JAMES JACKSON	POLLY/MARY ANNA BANKS
MASSEY LYDIA	BENJAMIN HERNDON
MASSEY MARY/POLLY	BENJAMIN RATLEDGE/RUTLEDGE
MASSEY NANCY	FRANCIS LAWRENCE HAYNES
MASSEY SARAH F	YANCEY M BRANN
MASSEY WARREN	NANCY MCDOUGALD
MASSY ELIZABETH/BETSY	MOSES TODD
MASSY/MASSEY HESTER	THOMAS CASSTEVENS
MASTEN ELIZABETH	RICHARD CLAMPITT
MASTEN JOHN	ELIZABETH STANLEY
MASTEN URSULA ANN	SIMON ELWOOD ALLEN
MASTERS HILLERY	MARY DAVIS/DAVIES
MATHEWS ISABELLA	RICHARD C CLAMPITT
MATHEWS JEMIMA	RICHARD CLAMPITT
MATHEWS MARGARET MCCLAIN	SAMUEL THOMAS
MATHEWS MARY	MARCUS RYAN JOHNSON
MATHIAS MARY BARBARA	MARTIN RUPPE
MATHIS CARLTON	MARY/POLLY SHELLEY
MATHIS WILLIAM	LYDIA CARLTON
MATSON FRANCES	NEIL CAMERON
MATTHEWS ABSALOM	ESTHER GREEN/GREENE
MATTHEWS ALSA/ALSEY	CHARITY PENNEY
MATTHEWS CHARLOTTE	ASHLEY MANNING
MATTHEWS ELIZABETH	WILLIAM MANNING
MATTHEWS JAMES HENDERSON	EMILINE MARTIN
MATTHEWS JAMES HENDERSON	EMILINE SUGGS
MATTICKS SARA ANNAPOLIS	JAMES BUCKNER BARRY
MAULDIN MARTHA	JERRY COOPER
MAULDIN NANCY	ANDREW HUGHES/HUSE
MAULE CHRISTIAN	THOMAS BROWN, I
MAUND ELIZABETH	AQUILLA SUGG
MAUND ELIZABETH	AQUILLA SUGG
MAUND ELIZABETH	AQUILA SUGG
MAUNEY ELIZABETH	BENJAMIN MAGNESS
MAUZY FANNIE HEATON	LEONIDAS ALONZO TYSOR
MAX LUCENIA	RANCHER A BROWN
MAXWELL ALEXANDER	SUSAN MCDANIEL/MCDONALD
MAXWELL HUGH	ELIZABETH ELLIOTT
MAXWELL JANET	JAMES DANIELJR GEDDIE/GFDDY/GADY
MAXWELL JOHN	ELIZABETH MCCLENDON
MAXWELL MURDOCK MCKINNON	ROBERTA PRISCILLA ROYALL
MAXWELL WILLIAM	CHARITY WRIGHT
MAY ANGELETTE FISHER	AARON HARRIS
MAY HEZEKIAH	JULIA ANN ANDREW
MAY JAMES ROSS	MARTHA JANE EASON
MAY JOHN	MARY STAFFORD

SPOUSE	ANCESTOR
MAY JOHN W	MARY CARPENTER
MAY JOSEPH	ANGELET FISHER
MAY MARY JANE	WILLIAM B CARVER BEARD
MAY NANCY	MOREAU ROSE
MAY NELLIE	MERRIMAN HARMAN
MAY PENINA	THOMAS BIRD DUPREE/DUPRE'
MAY SARAH W	THOMAS BIRD DUPREE/DUPRE'
MAY SUSANNAH	DUNCAN BOHANNON, II
MAYBERRY EVA ESTELLE	ROBERT YOUNG GILL
MAYBERRY LOUISA	JONES HENDERSON LOWRANCE
MAYE NANCY	JOHN ROBERT JORDAN
MAYERS/MYERS CATHARINE	HENRY SUMMIT
MAYNER/MAYNARD SARAH	EDWARD BRAY
MAYO AZELLA	WILLIAM JOSEPH LITTLE
MAYO BETHIA	LEMUEL THIGPEN
MAYO JANE ELIZA	HENRY SKIPWITH TAYLOR
MAYO LYDIA	JAMES THIGPEN
MCABEE ESTELLE	LAWRENCE G WHITMIRE
MCADAMS JOSEPH	MARGARET WHITSETT
MCADAMS JOSEPH	ELIZABETH COSBY
MCALEXANDER ANN CATHERINE	WILLIAM ELVIN BEARD
MCALLISTER SARAH	JOSEPH THOMPSON
MCANALLY RUHAMAH	JAMES THOMAS WRIGHT
MCARTHUR ELIJAH	JANE DIXON/DICKSON
MCARTHUR ELIJAH	JANE DIXON/DICKSON
MCBRIDE HANNAH	DANIEL PAFFORD
MCBRIDE LIDDIA	JAMES JARVIS
MCBRIDE MARGARET	JAMES COSBY
MCBRIDE RUTH	WILLIAM ROUSSEAU
MCBRIDE SALLIE	DANIEL HENDERSON
MCBRIDE SARAH	WILLIAM WISEMAN
MCBRIDE SARAH/SALLIE	DANIEL HENDERSON
MCBRIDE WILLIAM	ELIZABETH HEATHAMN
MCBRYDE CHRISTIAN	GILBERT MCMILLAN
MCCALL ANGIE	WILLIAM MANSEL WHITMIRE
MCCALLUM SARAH	MANERING SUMMERS, SR
MCCARTY ELIZABETH	SOLOMON PARKER
MCCATHERN MRS REBECCA	EDMOND STUCKEY
MCCAULEY ELIZA	WILLIAM G CRABTREE
MCCAY DANIEL S	RHODA JANE HILL
MCCLAMMY ELEANOR	ROBERT NIXON
MCCLAREN SARAH	WILLIAM JOHNSON
MCCLEARY ELEANOR	ROBERT MONTGOMERY
MCCLEARY ROBERT	ABIGAIL MCDOWELL
MCCLENDON ELIZABETH	JOHN MAXWELL
MCCLENNON MARY F	MARTIN ROWAN CHAFFIN
MCCLURE MARTHA ANN	DANIEL WILKINSON KILLIAN/KILIAN
MCCLURE SARAH J	ABEL/MAC BEATTY
MCCOLLUM JOHN	RUTH CUTHBERTSON
MCCOLLUM WILLIAM ISAAC	MARTHA ROGERS
MCCOMAS MRS HANNAH	THOMAS MILES
MCCOMMON ELIZABETH D	BYTHEN B BEARD
MCCONNELL MARGARET ANN	ELKANAH P THOMAS
MCCONNELL SARAH	JAMES ORR

SPOUSE INDEX

SPOUSE	ANCESTOR
MCCORKLE JOSEPH	MARGARET SNODDY
MCCORKLE MATTIE	ALEX/ALEXANDER ABERNATHY
MCCORNACK CHARLIE ROBERT	PEARL TERRY CRABTREE
MCCOURRY THOMAS	RUTH BYRD
MCCOURRY WILLIAM ENSLEY	NANCY CAROLINE BYRD
MCCOURRY ZEPHANIAH	JANE MCCOURRY, MRS
MCCOY ELIZABETH	GEORGE WILSON
MCCOY MARTIN	RACHEL WILSON
MCCRACKEN ELIHU J	ESTHER CARR/KERR
MCCRACKEN JAMES	JEAN/JANE MCCRACKEN, MRS
MCCRACKEN JAMES	ELIZABETH DAVIDSON
MCCRACKEN JAMES M	SUSAN F GATLEN
MCCRACKEN ROBERT	MARTHA A ROSS
MCCRACKEN WILLIAM DAVIDSON	MARY REBECCA RUSS
MCCRACKER SALLY	DAVID STICE
MCCRAW ELIZABETH	WILLIAM HUMPHRIES
MCCREA CHERRY ELIZABETH	WILSON HENDRICK
MCCRORY MARTHA EMILY	JOHN LEVI PERRY
MCCUBBIN JAMES	MARY COOK
MCCULLOCH SARAH	EVAN DOUTHIT
MCCUNE REBECCA	JOHN BIGGS
MCCURDY MARY SELLARS	LAIRD KIRKPATRICK
MCDANIEL DORCAS	DANIEL SMITH
MCDANIEL HARRIET	HERBERT TAYLOR
MCDANIEL JOHN	MARY BOONE
MCDANIEL MARY	JEFFREY BECK, JR
MCDANIEL MARY	JEFFREY BECK
MCDANIEL MARY/POLLY	MERRIDTH/MARADAY PRICE
MCDANIEL/MCDONALD SUSAN	ALEXANDER MAXWELL
MCDOUGALD JOHN	CATHERINE WILKINSON
MCDOWELL ABIGAIL	ROBERT MCCLEARY
MCDOWELL ANNE	DANIEL SUTHERLAND
MCDOWELL LUCINDA	WILLIAM WATSON
MCDOWELL NANCY	THOMAS BRADFORD
MCDUFFIE MARY	DAVID ROSSER
MCEWEN JAMES	JANE HALL
MCFARLAND ANNE	GEORGE CATHEY
MCFARLAND CATHRINE BUIE	JOHN MCNAIR
MCFARLAND ELEANOR R	HOSEA GREEN TAPLEY/TARPLEY
MCFARLAND WILLIAM	LUCY WOMACK
MCFARLIN BENJAMIN	ELIZABETH NELSON
MCFERRAN SUSAN ELIZABETH	MICHAEL FRANKLIN/JOSEPH M ELLER
MCGAUGHEY ELIZABETH	RICHARD HOLMES
MCGEE ANN/NANCY	ROBERT LINDSAY
MCGEE JOHN	HANNAH NEATHERY
MCGILL REBECCA	CHARLES H OATES/OATS
MCGLAMERY ELIZABETH	STANLEY CHAFFIN
MCGLAMERY/MCGLANMARIE SARAH	JOHN PURDUE HALE
MCGONIGLE BARBARA	JAMES SIMMONS
MCGRAW NANCY	JOSEPH MCADAMS
MCGREGOR EVE	JOHN HUCKABEE
MCHAFFIE HANEY EMELINE	WILLIAM PETTIS ROBARDS
MCIVER MARGARET	WILLIAM BUIE
MCIVER NANCY	DONALD MURDOCH MCSWEEN

290

SPOUSE	ANCESTOR
MCKAY ZILPHA C	WILLIAM WHITE
MCKEE MARY	RICHARD FAUCETT/FAUSETT
MCKEE MARY	RICHARD FAUSETT/FAUCETT
MCKEE MARY	LOTT M LEGUIN/LEGWIN
MCKEEL ELIZABETH	JOSEPH GAINER, JR
MCKEITHAN DOUGALD	WADSWORTH,NANCY
MCKELVEY JANE D	ROBERT CARR? MCCRACKEN
MCKELVEY WILLIAM	MARY ANN MCCRACKEN
MCKENNY REBECCA	JOHN MCGILL
MCKENZIE KATHRYN	ASA SOWELL/SEWELL
MCKIBBEN LINDORA TERESA	ROBERT JAHUE BELL
MCKIBBEN MARGARET	JOHN MATTHEWS
MCKIE/MACKIE MARY ANN	THOMAS HEMPHILL, CAPT
MCKILLIP/MCCALEB/MCCALEP MALINDA	JOHN HESTER, JR
MCKINLEY ANN	THOMAS MCGINN
MCKINLEY IRA	ANNIE BELL ISRAEL
MCKINNE PATIENCE	JOSEPH LANE, JR
MCKINNEY CHESTERFIELD	LUCINDA MEEK
MCKINNEY MARY	DAVID M CRAWFORD
MCKINNICK MARY/MARTHA	PETER, JR RECTOR
MCKINNIE SARAH	RICHARD BASS
MCKNIGHT CAROLINA	BENJAMIN GIST GRAHAM
MCKNIGHT MARGARET	JOHN PURVIANCE, SR
MCKNIGHT MOSES	ERIXENE MCEWEN ROSEBOROUGH
MCKNIGHT WILLIAM	ISABEL WADDELL
MCLAIN FANNEY	ELISAH HOBBS
MCLAUCHLIN SARAH ANN	CHARLES PINCKNEY JONES
MCLAUGHLIN LOVEDY	NEILL MCKEITHAN
MCLAUGHLIN MRS ANNA	CHARLES COMBS
MCLAURIN EFFIE	MALCOLM P MCNAIR
MCLEAN EFFIE	DANIEL DOUGLASS
MCLEAN FLORA	JOHN MCLEAN
MCLEAN JANET	JOHN S HARRINGTON
MCLEAN KATIE	ROBERT BULLARD
MCLEAN MARY	JOSEPH N MCLEAN
MCLENDON CATHERINE	CURTIS SPIVEY
MCLEOD ELIZABETH	TRAVIS JACKSON
MCLEOD MRS CHRISTIAN (MCINTOSH)	DANIEL MONROE MCKAY
MCLURE/MCCLURE JOHN	ANN MCCRACKEN
MCMAHAN ELIZABETH	SAMUEL BRYAN, SR
MCMILLAN CATHERINE MCKAY	STEPHENHOLLINGSWO JOHNSON/JOHNSTON
MCMILLAN DOUGALD	NANCY JACOBS
MCMILLAN	SUSAN CATES
MCMIN SALLIE L	JOHN FRANKLIN BALLARD
MCMINN MARGARET CORA	WILLIAM WESLIE WOLFE
MCMURRY/MCMURRAY EDWARD	SARAH, MCCRACKEN, MRS
MCMURTRY NANCY	HENRY B BAKER DOBSON
MCNABB ELVIRA	ABEL JACKSON LEATHERWOOD
MCNAIR SARAH ANN	PETER WILKINSON
MCNEELEY JAMES	MARY/POLLY YATES
MCNEELY MARGARET	WILLIAM SNODDY
MCNEELY MARY ELIZABETH	ALLEN DORMAN
MCNEIL MARTHA JANE	JOHN JACKSON KILBY
MCNEILL MARY ANN	ISHAM SANDERS

SPOUSE	ANCESTOR
MCNEW WILLIAM RILEY	HARRIET JANE ODELL
MCPETERS RACHEL ELIZEBETH	HIRAM NEWTON RAY/RHEA
MCPHAIL MARY	THOMAS MAXWELL
MCPHAILL CATHRIN ISABELLA	JAMES DANIEL GEDDIE/GEDDY/GADY
MCPHAILL MARY	THOMAS MAXWELL
MCPHERSON DINAH	ABNER LAMB
MCPHERSON MARY	EDWARD STEWART
MCQUARY MARGARET	THOMAS BOGLE MOOSE
MCQUEEN MARGARET	PHILIP MCRAE
MCQUISTON MARY	GEORGE CUMMINGS/CUMMINS
MCRAE CATHERINE	JOHN MCRAE
MCRAE CHRISTOPHER	JANET MCRAE
MCRAE ISABELLA	ALFRED JACKSON
MCRAE JANET	CHRISTOPHER MCRAE
MCRAE JOHN	CATHERINE MCRAE
MCRAE PHILIP	MARGARET MCQUEEN
MCREA MARY ANN	FREDERIC WARREN
MCREE RACHEL ELIZABETH	JOSEPH Y GUDGER
MCSWEEN SARAH	JOHN WILLIAM WADSWORTH
MCVEY/MCVAY BARBARA	MATTHEW VANCE
MCWILLIAMS LIDIA	DRURY DEEN
MEACHAM ELIZABETH	IGNATIUS WEST
MEACHAM WILLIAM	ELIZABETH CRUTCHFIELD
MEARES ELIZABETH DRUSCILLA	STONEWALL JACKSON BALDWIN
MEARES WILLIAM JAMES	DRUSILLA JANE PATE
MEASLEY DORAH	JOHN C CARTER
MEBANE ANN LOUEY/LOVEY	JOHN WOODS
MEBANE JENNET	WILLIAM ANDERSON
MEEK LUCINDA	CHESTERFIELD MCKINNEY
MEEKINS LEVINA ANN	MIDGETT SPENCER
MEISENHEIMER ELIZABETH	MELCHIOR FOGLEMAN
MELONEY/MALONEY MARY	ELI KIRK
MELTON MELONY	NICHOLAS NEWTON
MELTON MOURNING	WILLIAM PAFFORD
MENDENHALL MRS MARY	ISAAC BROWN
MENDENHALL SARAH	JEREMIAH KIMBROUGH
MERCER DOROTHY	NEILL BUIE
MERCER MARY/POLLY	-EMPHY (SIC) BERRY
MERCER TEMPIE ANN	WILLIAM HAYNES
MEREDITH ELIZABETH	RANDOLPH THOMPSON
MEREDITH JAMES	RACHAEL KNIGHT
MERRIAM NANCY	JESSIE COLVARD
MERRICK MRS ELIZABETH (JONES)	SAMUEL ASHE, GOV
MERRILL CHARITY	BOYD MCCRARY
MERRITT ELIZABETH	FIELDER DAVIS
MERRITT ELIZABETH/TAZZIE	ETHELDRED JELKS
MERRITT HARVEY MILTON	MARY ANN TOWNSEND
MERRITT MARGARET/PEGGY	JESSE CARROLL, JR
MERRITT MARY	LEMUELL DAVIS
MEWBORN EDITH	JOHN GRAY
MEYERS ANNIE	ERNEST WILSON HELMS
MEYERS NANCY	TOBIAS MOSER
MICKLER JANE	DUNCAN CURRY
MIDDLETON ANNA	ELIJAH CHASTIAN

SPOUSE		ANCESTOR
MIDDLETON		ANGUS WILKINSON
MIDGETT	EDWARD DANIEL	MARY/POLLY BASNIGHT
MIDGETT	ESTER	STEPHEN BARNETT
MIDGETT	MARY CAROLINE	SAMUEL WARRINGTON MASON
MIDYETT	THOMAS	BETHANY BANNISTER
MIKELS	SUSANNA	JOSEPH HUTCHENS
MILAM	SARAH/SALLIE	ROBERT/BOB SOUTHARD
MILLER	AARON	MARY E THRIFT
MILLER	ALEXANDER CALEZANCE	MARY BROWN
MILLER	ANDREW	JANE WILSON
MILLER	CEVILLA	JOHN MARTIN FRANCKE
MILLER	ELI STALEY	ANNA M WALKER
MILLER	ELIZABETH	ROBERT, CPT PAINE
MILLER	ELIZABETH	ROBERT PAINE
MILLER	EVE	JOSEPH CARTWRIGHT, SR
MILLER	GEORGE	MARGARET MCCULLOCH
MILLER	GEORGE WASHINGTON	ALEY HUBBARD
MILLER	JAMES	SARAH W SHINE
MILLER	JANE	WILLIAM O SMITH
MILLER	JOHN	SARAH STALEY
MILLER	JOHN D	MARY ANN ELIZA TENNISON
MILLER	JOHN OWEN	MARY SYBIL ASHE
MILLER	JULIA	CHRISTOPHER SPENCER
MILLER	LOVINA	ANDREW HOLLER, JR
MILLER	MARGARET	JAMES GAMMILL
MILLER	MARTIN	SOPHIA RINTELMAN/RINGLEMAN
MILLER	MARY	EDWARD HOUSTON
MILLER	MATILDA	WILLIAM PENLEY/PENLY
MILLER		JOHN ANDREW STINSON
MILLER	NANCY	ISHAM G GIDEON/GIDDENS
MILLER	OLIVE PHELINA	WILLIAM LEONARD SMITH
MILLER	PETER	HANNAH HARTLINE
MILLER	RACHEL	JOSEPH ORAND/ORRAN
MILLER	SARAH	ANDREW JACKSON BROWN
MILLER	THOMAS CALIZANCE	ANNIE WATTERS DAVIS
MILLIKAN	MARTHA	JAMES FRAIZER
MILLIKIN	HANNAH	ENOS BLAIR/BLEAR
MILLIS	ELIZABETH	SAMUEL WILEY
MILLIS	WILLIAM THOMAS	ELIZABETH WHEELER
MILLS	MARTHA/PATTY	JAMES ISHAM GIDEON/GIDDENS
MILLS	NANCY JANE	J/JOHN W C HARMON
MILLS	PHOEBE	ABRAHAM COOK
MILLS	PRISCILLA	MATTHEW/JOHN ? RUST
MILLS	PRISCILLA	MATTHEW RUST/RUSS
MILLS	RACHEL	PETER SIMMONS
MILLS	RACHEL	ROBERT HODGSON
MILLS	RACHEL	ROBERT HODGSON
MILLS	SARAH	WILLIAM COKER
MILLS	WILLIAM HENRY	CORINNA THEDOCIA JACKSON POPE
MILLS	ZELMA GEROY	LONNIE WASHINGTON ELLIS
MILLSAPS	THOMAS	SARAH FULLER
MILLWATER	MARY ELIZA	ROBERT PAINE
MILNER	JOHN	ELIZABETH GODWIN
MILNER	PITT	APSYLLAH HOLMES

SPOUSE		ANCESTOR
MIMS	LUCINDA	ISHAM/ISOM HICKS
MIMS		LITTLETON PEAVY
MING	JAMES	ANN BEASLEY
MING	JOSEPH	RACHEL WARD
MINGUS	CONRAD	MARY MAGDALAN BOVEY/POVEY
MINTER	ELIZABETH	ABNER BOHANNON
MINTER	NANCY	JULIUS RIDDLE
MISENHEIMER	CATHERINE	ZACHARIUS/ZAMAH/ZACH LYERLY/LAYRLE/LIERLY
MITCHEL	MOSES	ELIZABETH SNODDY
MITCHELL	ANDREW	SARAH SNODDY
MITCHELL	MARY PHOEBE	RICHARD JAMES ASHE
MITCHELL	SARAH	ANGUS GARMAN KOONCE
MITCHELL	SUSAN ARTIMISS	JAMES MADISON ANGEL
MITCHELL	THOMAS A	MARTHA G BUCHANAN
MIZELL	PATRICIA ELIZABETH	JAMES THOMAS GRIFFIN
MIZELL	SUSAN	ROBERT BULLARD
MOCK	DAVID	ELIZABETH OWEN
MOCK	PHILIP	MARY NEWSOME
MOFFIT	NAOMI	JOHN MACKIE
MOFFITT	HANNAH	JACOB COX
MOFFITT	NAOMI	JOHN MACKIE/MACKEY/MACKAY
MONGER	HENRY	ALSEY JONES
MONROE	LIZZIE VANCE	CHARLES HENRY BOYST
MONROE	MARGARET	JOHN 'MERCHANT' CAMERON
MONS	ELCIE	BIRD DEATHERAGE
MONTGOMERY	AGNES/NANCY	ALEXANDER MCCORKLE
MONTGOMERY	JAMES	ANN WOODS
MONTGOMERY	JANE	JOHN NELSON
MONTGOMERY	JANE	THOMAS BELL
MONTGOMERY	JANE	JOHN NELSON
MONTGOMERY	JOHN	SARAH MOORE
MONTGOMERY	MARTHA	JOHN MONTGOMERY
MONTGOMERY	NANCY ANNE	EDWIN INGRAM
MONTGOMERY	ROBERT	ELEANOR MCCLEARY
MONTGOMERY	MRS CATHERINE (SLOAN)	JOHN CLEVELAND
MOODY	ABIGAIL	JOHN LEONARD
MOON	JOHN	RACHEL ADAMS
MOON	RACHEL	HENRY THORNBURGH
MOON	SIMON	HANNAH STOUT
MOORE	ALLEY	HILLSMAN KING
MOORE	ANN	JOHN ANDERSON
MOORE	ANN	JOHN LENNON
MOORE	ANNA L	RICHARD DAVIS ASHE
MOORE	CATHERINE	MELCHEZEDIC SELF
MOORE	CECILIA/CALLIE ANN	AUSTIN/ORSTON/GUSTON BEESLEY
MOORE	CLARISSA	ELLIOTT DONNELL
MOORE	ELIZABETH	LEWIS BOBBITT
MOORE	ELIZABETH	RICHARD QUINCE
MOORE	ELIZABETH ELBA	JOHN FRANKLIN HOLBROOK
MOORE	JANE	THOMAS BELL
MOORE	JOHN L	MARY ELIZABETH HUDGINS
MOORE	LAURA ELIZABETH	WILLIAM HERRING SKINNER, JR
MOORE	LORANNA	JOSEPH UPTON
MOORE	LULA CATHERINE	ROBERT H MCCRACKEN

SPOUSE INDEX

SPOUSE		ANCESTOR
MOORE	LYDIA	CLIFTON JAMES
MOORE	MARGARET	WILLIAM HILL
MOORE	MARTHA JANE	FRANKLIN PIERCE BLALOCK
MOORE	MARY	SAMUEL CHERRY
MOORE	MARY	THOMAS DAVIS
MOORE	MARY	AQUILLA HERNDON
MOORE	MARY ANN	THOMAS B/BENTON LATTA
MOORE	MARY IVIE	WILLIAM, WATTERS, COL
MOORE	MARY JANE	ARCHIBALDMCKENZIE SOWELL/SEWELL
MOORE	MARY R	JAMES HENRY WELBORN
MOORE	MINERVA	THOMAS EDWARD TIPTON
MOORE	MIRIAM	JOHN NOLEN
MOORE		JOSEPH PERKINS
MOORE		JOHN MONTGOMERY
MOORE		MARY ORAND/ORRAN
MOORE	MRS MARY	THOMAS POWELL
MOORE	REV WILLIAM	ELIZABETH JOHNSON GRIMES/GRYMES
MOORE	SALLIE/TULEY	OBADIAH PEARCE
MOORE	SARAH	JOHN MONTGOMERY
MOORE	SOPHIA	JAMES MASON GILLIAM
MOORE	SUSANNAH	JOEL CROSS
MOORE	MRS LUCRETIA (BUTLER)	LEMUEL MOORE
MOORE	MRS SARAH ELIZABETH(HIGGINS)	LOUIS TAYLOR FOX
MOORMAN	MILLEY	JOHN SANDERS
MOOSE	FRANCES CAROLE	RICHARD ALEXANDER HARTNESS
MORAN	ELIZABETH	AMBROSE BULL
MORELAND	NANCY	THOMAS SIMPSON
MORGAN	DAVID	ELIZABETH BUNN
MORGAN	ELISABETH	ISAAC ELLIOTT
MORGAN	ELIZABETH	THOMASALBERT STARNES/STARIN/STAHRIN
MORGAN	JOHN	CATHARINE/KATY BULLARD
MORGAN	MARTHA/BETSY	WILLIAM WRIGHT
MORGAN	MARY	JOSHUA WRIGHT
MORGAN	MARY	JAMES PERISHO/PARISHO
MORGAN	MARY NANCY	RICHARD WRIGHT, JR
MORGAN		WILLIAM COVINGTON
MORGAN		REUBEN HARGROVE
MORGAN	MRS SARAH	SQUIRE BOONE
MORGAN	SALLY/SARAH	JOEL DOBBS
MORGAN	SARAH	COLBERT BLAIR
MORGAN	SARAH	COLBERT BLAIR/BLEAR
MORGAN	SUSANNAH	ASHER KERSEY
MORGAN	TALITHA	HENRY PARIS
MORGAN	THOMAS P	ELVA LASSITER
MORGAN	WILLIAM LUTHER	MARTHA ELLEN DAVIS
MORRIS	ANNA	DAVIS BIGGS
MORRIS	CELIA	HENRY CARTER
MORRIS	CLARY	WILLIAM DANIEL PLEASANTS
MORRIS	ELIZABETH	WILLIAM BALLARD
MORRIS	ELIZABETH	DAVID EDWARDS
MORRIS	ELIZABETH	DAVID EDWARDS
MORRIS	ELIZABETH	SAMUEL TRULOVE
MORRIS	FANNIE	KENNEDA SANDLIN
MORRIS	JOHN	HANNAH GREGG

295

SPOUSE	ANCESTOR
MORRIS LETTIE FOUST	WILLIAM JASPER SHELTON
MORRIS LUCINDA	JOEL HALTOM
MORRIS MARTHA/POLLY	STEPHEN LLOYD/LOYD
MORRIS MATTIE	DAVID SMITH GRAYBEAL
MORRIS NICHOLAS	REBECCA CUMMINS
MORRIS SUSANNAH	THOMAS ANGLE
MORRIS VOLENTINE	ELIZA MORRIS HALL
MORRIS WASHINGTON	MARY CATHERINE JACKSON
MORRIS WILLIAM	MARGARET SANDLIN
MORRIS WILLIAM	LUCINDY TRULOVE
MORRIS MRS ELIZABETH (CLOPTON)	WILLIAM BALLARD
MORRISETT MARY	SIMEON J FORBES
MORRISON CATHARINE	ALEXANDER MCCORKLE
MORRISON JAMES	ELEANOR SNODDY
MORRISON MARGARET	ROBERT MCCORKLE
MORTON ISABEL BOGART	THOMAS OHAGAN DUPREE/DUPRE'
MORTON JOSEPH/JOEY	MARGERAT/PEGGY HATLEY
MORTON MARY	HENRY ODUM/ODHAM
MORTON WILLIAM ZENAS	MELISSA ANN CARR DARDEN
MORTON WILLIAM ZENAS	CARNAVELLA HARDISON
MOSER REBECCA	DANIEL MOSER
MOSS JAMES	ESTHER TOWNSEND
MOSS JAMES BROWN	NANCY PERDUE/PURDUE
MOSS JAMES BROWN	NANCY W PERDUE
MOTSINGER EDNA	RILEY PEW/PUGH
MOTSINGER SUSANNAH	FRANCIS FLOYD
MOTZ CATHERINE	JOHANN WILLIAM HERMAN
MOULTON PATIENCE	JEREMIAH PEARSALL
MOUNGER JOSEPH JOHN	NANCY SECTION YOUNG
MOUNT ALFRED	MARY THOMAS
MOUTRAY JOSEPH H	LUCY LACY/LACEY
MOWSER SALLY/SARAH	JOABERT WHITE
MOYE JOHN CASS	ALSEY BROWN
MOYERS MARY F	MARTIN TRANTHAM
MOYLA/MOYLS MATTHEW	SUSAN F GATLEN
MOZINGO BENNIE HENRY	MARY VIVIAN CARTER
MUELL CATHERINE	HENRY WHITENER/WEIDNER
MULLINGTON ANN	JOSIAH LEWIS
MULLINS ADDIE MALINDA RUTHIE	WILLIAM BEDFORD HALL
MULLINS CATHERINE	MCCAMEY/M R MULLINS
MULLINS JAMES SAMUEL	RACHEL GRANT
MULLIS JOHN	MARTHA L JONES
MULLIS MRS GERIAH (BARNES)	WILLIAM GOFORTH
MUMFORD ELIZA	JAMES OWEN
MURPHEY ARCHIBALD	JANE DEBOW
MURPHREY ELIZABETH	JOHN SUGG
MURPHREY MARTHA	ROBERT HILL
MURPHREY TUNNEL/TURNER	APSALY BAKER
MURPHY MRS REBECCA	JOHN PINNELL
MURPHY RACHEL	EDWARD LINDSEY
MURPHY REBECCA	EZEKIEL KIGHT, SR
MURPHY SUSAN FRANCES	THOMAS JUNIUS DAVIS
MURRAY JANE	COLBERT BLAIR
MURRAY MARY DUGAN	JOHN M PLUMBLEE/PLUMLEY

SPOUSE	ANCESTOR
NEWMAN ELIZABETH GEORGE	AMBURS BARCLAY
NEWMAN MALINDA	JAMES DUDLEY WELBORN
NEWMAN SARAH	HENRY GOSSETT/GOSSET
NEWMAN ZILPHA D	JAMES DUDLEY WELBORN
NEWSOM WASHINGTON	ELIZABETH A PHILLIPS
NEWSOME ELIZABETH	JONAS MACE
NEWSOME MARY	PHILIP MOCK
NEWTON HELEN	THOMAS DULANY/DULANEY, III
NEWTON SARAH	ELIJAH JEFFERSON PIVER
NIBLOCK AGNES	JOHN SNODDY
NICHOLS ANNIE	GEORGE HENRY WHITE
NICHOLS MARTHA ANN	ALFRED WEBB RICH
NICHOLS WILEY	MARGARET BAKER
NICHOLS WILLIAM A	EMILY C DUKE
NICHOLS ZILPHIA	BYTHEL HAYNES
NICHOLSON CATHERINE	JOHN CLAMPITT
NICHOLSON DUNCAN	MARY BLACKMAN
NICHOLSON ELIZABETH	GEORGE TACKETT/TACKITT
NICHOLSON MARY/POLLY	ROBERT JELKS
NICHOLSON REBECCA	MATHIAS MASTEN CLAMPITT
NIX ELIZABETH	ARCHIBALD CARMICHAEL
NIX WILLIAM	REBECCA STANSBURY
NIXON MARY ANN	JAMES MIDDLETON, CAPT
NIXON ROBERT	ELEANOR MCCLAMMY
NOBLE JOHN	FRANCIS FLEMMING PAYNE
NOBLE MARY MAGDELON	JAMES BUCKNER BARRY
NOBLE/NOBLES SARAH	GODFREY STANCIL
NOBLETT MARY	CHARLES STOUT
NOBLITT MARY	CHARLES STOUT
NOE PETER	MARY CALDWELL
NOLAND STEPHEN	NANCY ELENER ADAMS
NOLEN JOHN	MIRIAM MOORE
NOLIN/NOLAND PASKENS	PATIENCE NOLAND, MRS
NOLTE/NULTY JUSTINIA AUGUSTA	PLEASANT M LEE
NORFLEET PHEREBY	JOSHUA BELL
NORMAN ANNIE	JOHN JONES, SR
NORMAN FERNANDO HAYNES	LOUISENAOMIE KUYKENDALL/KIRKENDALL
NORMAN JAMES WASLEY	REBECCA LYDAY/LYDA
NORMAN JEMIMA	WILLIAM ROWE
NORMAN JUANITA	CHARLIE THOMAS SIMS/SYMS
NORMAN LEECY	JULIUS RUFUS WILLIAMS
NORMAN NONNIE	JAMES WILLIAM ROGERS/RODGERS, SR
NORMAN POLLY	THOMAS M PITTARD
NORMAN WILLIAM P	SUSAN MARIA SHAW
NORMAN MRS NANCY (SETTLE)	ELIJAH LOMAX
NORMAN MRS SUSAN MARIA (SHAW)	BRYANT HILL
NORRCE ABNER	SARAH WOODY
NORRIS ANN	JOHN DICKINSON, JR
NORSWORTHY BESSIE ALMA	SIMEON LAWRENCE FORBES
NORTH MARIA SYBIL	ELISHA MITCHELL, PROF
NORTH SALLIE	FRANCIS FOARD/FORD
NORTON WINNEY/WINNIE	SAMUEL JOHNSON
NORWOOD GROVER JACKSON	SALLIE VANN HART
NORWOOD JACK	SOPHIA MOORE

SPOUSE	ANCESTOR
OTEY MRS MARY ANN ELIZA CHERRY	BENJAMIN D LANGFORD/LANGKFORD
OTTEY CHRISTOPHER	ELIZABETH GODFREY
OTTEY JOHN	ANN, OTTEY, MRS
OTWELL SARAH	SIMEON HODSON/HODGIN
OUTLAND NANCY	THOMAS WOMBLE/WOMBWELL
OUTLAW MARY ANNE	WILLIAM DICKSON PEARSALL
OUTLAW MILLICIENT	DAVID ASKEW
OUTLAW MRS REBECCA	WILLIAM WATFORD
OUTLAW PEGGY	WILLIAM GREEN/GREENE
OVERALL MARY/POLLY	WILLIAM M RAMSEY, JR
OVERTON NANCY	WILLIAM RILEY DAIL/DALE, SR
OVERTON VIRGINIA ANN	ANDERSON FULLER DUNCAN
OVERTON WILLIS	PINEY PEELE
OWEN ELIZABETH	STANLEY CHAFFIN
OWEN ISABELLA	JOSEPH GILL
OWEN JOHN W	ELIZABETH CHRISTILLA BALDWIN
OWEN JOSIAH	POLLY PHILLIPS
OWEN MARY	GEORGE W WHITE
OWEN MARY LIZ	HENRY SEYMORE HIGH
OWEN MILLARD FILMORE	EMELINE DAVIS BROWN
OWENS ALICE	LEANDER WELBORN
OWENS ANN ELIZABETH	SAMUEL GRADY KEEL
OWENS ANNIE	WILLIAM TRUXTON TWIFORD
OWENS ELIZABETH	NATHANIEL JUDD, SR
OWENS HARRIET W	ADLEY NEAGLE
OWENS MARY	JONATHAN HENRY HALL
OWINGS SANEY	STANDLEY CHAFFIN
OWNBEY SIMS	GRACECAROLINE STARNES/STARIN/STAHRIN
OZMENT THOMAS	ABIGAIL PARKER
PACE EDMUND	SARAH ELIZABETH WALKER
PADDOCK MARY C	CYRUS BARNARD
PAFFORD DANIEL	HANNAH MCBRIDE
PAFFORD WILLIAM	MOURNING MELTON
PAGE BENNETT	SARAH HEWITT
PAGE DANIEL BENNETT	ELIZABETH DORA REGISTER
PAGE JAMES	MARTHA LOUISA MCCRACKEN
PAIN CHARLOTTY	JOHN BALDWIN, JR
PAINE DANIEL	SYLVIA COMBS
PAINE ELIZABETH MARY	JAMES LEE TAYLOR
PAINE ZILPHIA	RICHARD GRAY
PAINTER ELIZABETH/BETTIE	MOSES LOWSON OAKLEY
PAISLEY ELEANOR	MICHAEL FINLEY
PALMER DOROTHY	ARCHIBALD LIPSCOMB
PALMER HELEN	LEWIS LEROY
PALMER REBECCA	JOHN LARKINS TAYLOR
PARHAM HARRIET MELISSA	RALPH WEBB ISRAEL
PARHAM POLLY	JETHRO BELVIN
PARIS ELLENDER	HENRY COBB, JR
PARKER CHARITY	JOHN CHESNUTT/CHESTNUTT
PARKER ELIZABETH	CHARLES CHESNUTT/CHESTNUTT
PARKER HANNAH	EDWARD GAITHER HYATT
PARKER LOUISA JANE	JACKSON PETTIGREW TEMPLE

SPOUSE	ANCESTOR
PARKER LYDIA	WILLIAM SHELTON
PARKER MARY	MICHAEL MURPHY/MURPHREY
PARKER MRS DIANA BRINN HARRIS	PETER PHYSIOC
PARKER NANCY	ISAAC DANIEL
PARKER PROTHANIA	LEVI BOOKOUT
PARKER SARAH	THOMAS OWEN
PARKER SOLOMON	ELIZABETH MCCARTY
PARKER SUSANNAH	JOHN STARR/STOEHR
PARKER SUSANNAH	JOHN SWINSON
PARKER VIRGINIA	JAMES DIKERSON HOOKER
PARKER ZILLA ANN	HENRY/JAMES HENRY OVERTON
PARKS BARBARA	MICHAEL CREASON/CRESON
PARKS ELLEN	HEZEKIAH/KIAH ALEXANDER CORRELL
PARKS HARRIETT	ABNER ROUSE
PARKS MARGARET	JOHN LOGAN WINKLER
PARNELL MARGARET LUCINDA	HENRY DYE
PARR BENJAMIN	MARTHA/PATSEY MCKINNEY
PARRISH FRANK	MARGARET PARRISH
PARRISH MARGARET	FRANK PARRISH
PARRISH SUSANNAH	JOHN BRISTOW
PARROTT ELIZABETH	LEMUEL HARDY
PARSONS CATHERINE	DR JOHN PARKER
PARSONS LYDIA	DAVID ANDERSON THRIFT
PARTIN NANCY	THOMAS LAMBERT, JR
PARTIN NANCY JANE	JAMES CHARLIE HORTON
PASCHAL ELIZABETH	DAVID MILTON POE, JR
PATE DRUSILLA JANE	WILLIAM JAMES MEARES
PATE MATILDA	ALEXANDER FOWLER
PATRICK ELIAS	SARAH HUNTINGTON
PATRICK ROBERT	ELISABETH LEEPER
PATRICK MRS CANDICE (TEMPLETON)	JESSE BAZEMORE
PATTERSON EUNICE	JOEL GRIGG/GRIGGS
PATTERSON JOSEPHINE	MALCOLM MCEACHIN
PATTERSON LUCINDA	WILLIAM M HENDRIX
PATTERSON MARGARET	LUKE TUCKER
PATTERSON MARK	DICEY RIDDLE
PATTERSON MARSILLA PARSADE	JAMES ROSS
PATTERSON MARTHA	ZACHARIAH MANN
PATTERSON MARTHA I	BENJAMIN D ROGERS, JR
PATTERSON MARY JANE	NATHAN WILES
PATTERSON NANCY	ARON WALKER
PATTERSON WILLIAM	ELIZABETH LADD
PATTERSON MRS MARIA P (TONDEE)	THOMAS ELKINS
PATTON AGNES	ROBERT RIGHT REA
PATTON CAROLINE	JOHN MCGAUGHY/MCGAHA
PATTON MATTHEW HOUSTON	MARGARET HOUSTON REA
PATTON NANCY	GEORGE PATTON
PATTON SARAH JANE	THOMAS YOUNG
PATTON SUSSANNAH	CHRISTOPHER CUNNINGHAM, SR
PATTY MARY JANE	JAMES ROBERT ABRAMS
PAUL JOHN	MARGARET PRATT
PAUL JOHN M	MARY/PEGGIE NELSON
PAUL REBECCA	ARCHIBALD MCLEAN
PAUL SUSAN FRANCES	JAMES JONES SQUIRES

SPOUSE	ANCESTOR
PAULK JACOB	CATHERINE HENDERSON
PEACE LUCY	LOUIS LEMAY
PEAL CYNTHIA	GIDEAN W BARNHILL
PEARCE JUDITH	ROBERT BLALOCK
PEARCE LUCRETIA	HENRY OLIVER
PEARCE MARY SUSAN	LOGAN BROOKS
PEARMAN/PIERMAN SOLOMON	DOVEY ELIZABETH THOMAS
PEARSALL DOROTHY	JAMES DICKSON
PEARSALL EDWARD	DOROTHY DAVIS
PEARSALL MRS CATHERINE (JAMES?)	THOMAS RUTLEDGE
PEARSON ELIZABETH	WYATTE FOARD/FORD
PEARSON MARIAM	ROBERT BOGUE
PEARSON RACHEL	ROBERT BOGUE
PEASE OPHELIA	WILLIS MONROE BARBEE
PEAVY JAMES H	NANNIE RAY MCARTHUR
PEDERSEN P J	NANCY ELIZABETH HAYES
PEEBLES CELIA	EDMOND BOWMAN
PEELE KITTY	WILLIS OVERTON
PEELE PINEY	WILLIS OVERTON
PEGG POLLY	OTHNIEL HIATT
PENCE ELIZA	JAMES HORACE ROUSSEAU
PENCE MELINDA	SOLOMON LOUDERMILK
PENCE NELLY/ELLEN	DANIEL CORRELL
PENDER JULIA	THOMAS GATLIN
PENDERGRASS MATILDA COGHILL	WILLIAM C BROWN
PENDERGRAST	JAMES HARRISON
PENDLETON MARY	THOMAS HARRISON
PENELOPE MARY	MEDIA WHITE
PENILINE CHARLES	ELIZABETH/BETSY LIMBAUGH
PENLAND CYNTHIA	HENRY GRINDSTAFF
PENLEY SQUIRE JAMES	ELIZABETH AUSTIN
PENLEY WILLIAM GARFIELD	ANNIE BELL ISRAEL
PENNELL WILLIAM	SUSAN PENNELL
PENNEY ALEY	ISHAM BAUCOM
PENNEY LYDIA	DAVID SAULS
PENNINGTON ELIZABETH	WELLS SIZEMORE
PENNINGTON JOANNA	DOUGLAS DICKSON
PENNINGTON MARY	JOHN GRAHAM/GRIMES
PENNINGTON MARY	JOHN GRAHAM/GRIMES
PENNINGTON POLLY	AAROD PERKINS
PENNINGTON REBECCA	JOHN/JACK PARSONS
PENNINGTON REBECCA	EDWARD/NEDDIE BARKER
PENRY JAMES	HANNAH BOONE
PEOPLES/PEEBLES AGNES	HENRY IVY/IVEY
PERCEL SARAH	WILLIAM WOODY, SR
PERKINS ANNE/ANNA	MICHAEL LINEBARGER
PERKINS BETHENIA	ABSALOM BOSTICK, I
PERKINS DEBORAH	LEONARD KEELING
PERKINS ELIZABETH	JOHN WORLEY
PERKINS ELIZABETH	WILLIAM HARDISON
PERKINS ELIZABETH/BETSEY	JACOB JR, SHERRILL
PERKINS EMILY	MARSHALL WILSON
PERKINS SARAH	THOMAS SNODDY
PERKINS MRS AGGATHA (MARR)	ROBERT PAINE

SPOUSE	ANCESTOR
PERKINSON MARY S	ELVIS GRISHAM
PERRY CATHARINE	ISAAC WALTON
PERRY CELIA	LEVEN STOKES CAFFEY
PERRY ELIZABETH	DEMPSEY POWELL
PERRY ELIZABETH	JESS/JESSE GREENE MANN
PERRY HANNAH	THOMAS CRUTCHFIELD
PERRY JOHN LEVI	MARTHA EMILY MCCRORY
PERRY PENELOPE	NATHAN SESSUMS
PERRY RICHARD	CATHERINE EASTARD
PERRY SALLIE	JOHN HODGES
PERSEL SARAH	WILLIAM WOODY
PERSON MARY	LEWIS BOBBITT, JR
PERSON REBECCA	JAMES SLEDGE
PETERS HANNAH	LEMUEL LANIER
PETERS POLLY	JAMES M COBB
PETERSON PRISCILLA	MATTHIAS BOLLINGER
PETERSON RACHAEL	JAMES TAGGART
PETERSON REBECCA SUTTON	JOHN BYRD/BIRD
PETTAWAY MICAJAH	AMY SUGG
PETTAWAY/PETWAY WILLIAM D	CINDERELLA CROMWELL
PETTIGREW THOMAS	CELIA TATE
PETTY HUBBARD	DOLLIE JANE DILLON
PETTY REBEKAH	ZACHARIAH HARMAN
PHARES MARTHA J	THOMAS GEDDIE/GEDDY/GADY
PHELPS HANNAH	JAMES PERISHO/PARISHO
PHELPS RACHEL	JAMES/DEMPSEY SARGENT
PHIFER MARGARET LOCKE	JAMES ERWIN
PHILBECK THOMAS F	ELIZA ALBERTHA KISER
PHILIPS LYDIA	JEFREY BECK
PHILIPS NATHAN	NANCY ELLEDGE
PHILLIPS ENOCH	MARY M POOLE
PHILLIPS JEMIMA	LOCKHART STALLINGS
PHILLIPS LYDIA	JEFFREY BECK, SR
PHILLIPS MARY	JOHN EDWARDS
PHILLIPS POLLY	JOSIAH OWEN
PHILLIPS RUTH	JOSEPH FORD
PHILLIPS SALLY	DAVID TUCKER, I
PHIPPS JANE	THOMAS JONES
PHIPPS MARGARET	JAMES HUNTER, JR
PHOUTS JOSEPH WILSON	MARTHA MALINDA SHEPHERD
PHOUTS MINNIE ALICE	JAMES BASIL HAM/HAMM
PHYSIOC WILLIAM	SARAH BISHOP
PICKETT ELIZA	SOLOMON THOMPSON
PICKETT JAMES PRICE	RACHAEL VIOLANTE BENOIT
PIERCE PRUDENCE	ANDREW JACKSON ? LAMBERT
PIERCE SARAH	SAMUEL FERGUSON
PIKE ELIZABETH	ALEXANDER STUART
PIKE JDG JACOB	ELIZABETH GIDEON/GIDDENS
PILAND SOPHIA	WILLIAM G RHODES
PILCHER ALVIS	MILDRED C PHILLIPS
PILCHER PHOEBE	JOHN RUPPE
PILCHER POLLY	MARTIN RUPPE
PINCHBACK CORA HELEN	JOSEPH JOHNSTON CHANDLER
PINKERTON DAVID	MARGARET PINKERTON

SPOUSE	ANCESTOR
PINKERTON MARGARET	DAVID PINKERTON
PINKERTON MARGARET	DAVID PINKERTON
PINNER MARGARET	SION/SIOMON B LEDBETTER
PIPKIN JULIA ANN	WILLIAM BURWELL EDMUNDSON
PIPKIN MARTHA	MALCOLM MCEACHIN
PIPPEN SARAH	REUBEN MANNING JOLLEY
PITMAN EDITH	JACK DAVID ENGLISH
PITTARD NANCY A	JOHN RUFFIN BUCHANAN
PITTMAN ABSELA	WILLIAM WALTERS, JR
PITTMAN SARAH	JAMES BULLARD
PITTMAN VIRGINIA	ROBERT BROWN
PITTS ELIZA J	CYRUS C HINSHAW
PITTS ELIZABETH	THOMAS KNIGHT
PITTS MRS HARRIET (SCOTT)	JOHN LOVE, JR
PIVER ELIJAH JEFFERSON	LUCY CRAIG
PIVER GEORGE HOLLAND	MINNIE OLA KING WESCOTT
PIVER PETER	REBECCA JANE DUDLEY ROGERS
PLANCET SALLY	CHRISTIAN SHOUSE
PLEDGE ELIZABETH	THOMAS POINDEXTER
PLOTT GEORGE M	MARGARET E WILKERSON
PLUMMER JOHN	RACHEL PATTERSON
POE ELIZABETH J	WILLIAM BREWER
POE EMILY	CALVIN K KING
POGUE ELIZABETH	JOHN HOLT
POHL FRANCES	JOHN ROLLINS
POINDEXTER ANNE	THOMAS EVANS
POINDEXTER ANNE CLINGMAN	THOMAS SCOTT MARTIN
POINDEXTER SUSAN ALSEY	ELLIS NORMAN
POINDEXTER TEMPLE	ELLIS NORMAN
POLK MARGARET	ROBERT C MCREE
POLK MARY EMELINE	AARON L LITTLE
POLLARD HILDA FRANCES	THOMAS FREEMAN ROBBINS
PONDER MARY ELIZABETH	A GRAY SPLAWN
POOL PATSY	JACOB COCHRAN/COCKERHAM, JR
POOL REBECCA	JOHN NEEDHAM
POOLE CATHERINE VAN	ZACHARIUS/ZAMAH/ZACH LYERLY/LAYRLE/LIERLY
POOLE MARY M	ENOCH PHILLIPS
POOLE	JOHN HUSON/HUSTON
POPE CORINNA THEDOCIA JACKSON	WILLIAM HENRY MILLS
POPE ELIZABETH A	JOHN WEATHERSBY EDGE
POPE ISAAC	ELIZABETH ANDERSON
POPE MRS ANN (MAYO)	LA MARE, FRANCIS DELAMAR/DE
POPLIN HARRIET ELVIRA	DAVID POTTER WHEELER
POPLIN LOUISA	SAMUEL WHEELER
POPLIN WILLIAM W	PATIENCE LEE
PORTER CPT ROBERT	JEAN MCCALL
PORTER ELIZA FRANCES	DOCTOR BASS
PORTER NANCY	JOHN OWNBEY
PORTER WILLIAM HENRY	GLADY ETHEL CLARK
PORTERFIELD ELEANOR	THOMAS OWEN
POTTER MARTHA JANE	EDWARD POLK CARTER
POTTER TEMPERANCE	BENJAMIN DARNELL
POTTS STEPHEN	MARGARET POTTS
POTTS WILLIAM GEORGE	NETTIE WOOD/WOODS

304

SPOUSE	ANCESTOR
POVEY/BOVEY MARY MAGDALENE	JACOB SETSER/SETZER
POWELL ANN JULIA	JACOB JAMES MARSHBURN/MASHBURN
POWELL BARBARA	ELIJAH WASHINGTON CONNER
POWELL CINITHA	WILLIAM GREEN/GREENE
POWELL ELIZABETH	SAMUEL MCREE
POWELL ISAAC	REBECCA M LANIER
POWELL JANE	JESSIE COYLE
POWELL JOSEPH DEMPSEY	CORINNA PRISCILLA LEMAY
POWELL JUDITH	WILLIAM SEAL/SEALS
POWELL LOUISA	JAMESMADISON MARSHBURN/MASHBURN
POWELL MARY	MILES BOBBITT
POWELL MARY	WILLIAM PYRON
POWELL MOSES	SUSANNAH JELKS
POWELL MR	MARY TRIPP
POWELL MRS SUSANNAH	JAMES DICKSON
POWELL SARAH	ARCHIBALD YOUNG
POWELL SARAHANN	ANDREW J JONES
POWELL SUSSANNA	JOHN BILLS
POWELL MRS NANCY (SINK)	JOSEPH DAMERON KNIGHT
POWERS FANNY	AUSTIN GRISHAM
POWERS SARAH	THOMAS ELKINS
POYNTER ELIZABETH BLAIR	HARRIS EPHRAIM
PRATHER AMELIA ELVIRA	LUCIUS QUINTUS CINCINNATIUS BUTLER
PRATT DINAH	RICHARD CLAMPITT
PRATT MARGARET	JOHN PAUL, SR
PRATT SUSANNA	EDWARD T HALEY/HAILEY
PRESSLEY ELIZABETH/MARY	TILLMAN HELMS, JR
PRESSLEY MARY ANN	WILLIAM M JONES
PRESSLEY	MARTHA SMITH
PRICE ABIGAIL	WILLIAM J BREWER
PRICE AGNES	WILLIAM YATES
PRICE AGNES	WILLIAM YATES
PRICE LINVILLE	MERI ETTA MCCLURE
PRICE NANCY	WILLIAM SIMPSON
PRICE SUSAN BURTON	CHARLES P HARRISON
PRICE MRS SUSANNA JANE (BEAL)	JAMES MCDOWELL DELLINGER
PRICHARD ELISHA	LUCY HERRINGTON
PRIDDY SARAH	JOHN SEAGRAVE
PRIDGEN SARA	BENJAMIN LANIER
PRINCE THOMASCINA	JOHN, EARLE, COL
PRIOR SUSANNAH	ISAAC WRIGHT
PRITCH SALLIE	SAMUEL MAYES
PRITCHARD ELIZABETH BETSY	THADDEUS WHITE
PRITCHETT BETTY	THOMAS HARVEY/HERVEY
PRITCHETT NANCY	MAYBERRY WELBORN
PRITCHETT NANCY	MAYBERRY WELBORN
PROBART WILLIAM	ELIZABETH LANE
PROCTER TAMSA	THOMAS, BLOODWORTH, MAJ
PROCTER TAMSIE	THOMAS BLOODWORTH
PROVOW JOHN	NANCY FREEMAN
PRUDENCE MARY	WILLIAM HAM/HAMM, SR
PRYOR LUCY	JOHN HOSEA TAPLEY/TARPLEY
PRYOR MATHEW	MARY NEELY
PUCKETT MARTHA	LEWIS WOOTON

SPOUSE	ANCESTOR
PUGH AMELIA	FREDERICK BRYAN/BRYANT
PUGH ELIZABETH	JOHN FRUIT
PUGH JESSE	REBECCA FRAZIER
PUGH MARTHA ANN	WILLIAM HINSON
PUGH MARY	JAMES LUTEN/LUTON
PUGH SARAH	LEWIS CANNON
PUGH WILLIS B	FANNY BUSH BERRY
PUGH MRS MARY ANN (HAMILTON)	JOHN BEST
PUGH/PEW PAUL	ABY BURGESS
PUNCH CYNTHA CELINA	WILLIAM HEAD DORSETT
PUNCH MARY E	WILLIAM HEAD DORSETT
PURCELL MALCOLM	BEATRICE TORREY
PUREFOY SARAH	MARTIN WHITFORD
PURGERSON JOSEPH	ETNA MOORE
PURSER SAPPHIRA CATHERON	JOHN WILSON TARLTON
PURVIANCE ELIZABETH	WILLIAM THOMAS
PURVIANCE JOHN	MARTHA SLOAN SNODDY
PURVIANCE MARGARET	WILLIAM POTTS
PURVIANCE MARY	SAMUEL SNODDY
PURVIANCE MRS MARTHA (KING)	WILLIAM MCCORKLE
PURVIS THEODORE BRADLEY	ELLEN ELAINE BEAL/BEALE
PUTNAM/PUTMAN PATSY	THOMAS GOSS, JR
PYBAS MRS SARAH J	JOSHUA YATES
PYLANT JOHN	EVE AWALT
PYLE MARY	JOHN HALL
PYLE NANCY ANN	THOMAS STEELE
PYLE SARAH	JOHN LINDLY/LINDLEY
PYLE SARAH	ROBERT HALL
PYLES SUSANNAH	DAVID JUSTICE
QUEEN ETTA M	CORNELIUS ANDERSON
QUEST MARY	SOLOMON LOUDERMILK
QUICK ELLA	HENRY GASTON CLARK
QUIMBY MARY	ISAAC SOWELL/SEWELL
QUIMBY MARY	ISAAC SOWELL/SEWELL
QUINCE ELIZABETH MOORE	FREDERICK SOBIESKI DAVIS
QUINCE JANE	JEHU DAVIS, III
QUINCE PARKER	JANE HILL
QUINCY MRS ADDIE (FINCH)	WILLIAM ADAIR QUINCY, JR
QUINCY MRS MARY (FLEMING)	WILLIAM ADAIR QUINCY
QUINN AMANDA	EDWARD ROSS RIPPY
QUINN ROBERT BROWN	FANNIE MILLER BLAKELEY
RADFORD MARTHA	HENRY WHITLOW
RADFORD MRS NANCY L	WILLIAM M WILLIS
RAGAN CORNELIA FRANCES	HENRY GETER ELLIS
RAGLAND ANN	THOMAS GRIFFIS/GRIFFITH
RAGLAND CHARITY	JOHN WILSON
RAGSDALE REBECCA	THOMAS YATES
RAIFORD BATHSEBA	LEVI OLIVER
RAIFORD CHARLOTTE	MCKINNIE OLIVER
RAIFORD CHARLOTTE	MCKINNEY OLIVER

306

SPOUSE	ANCESTOR
RAIFORD DRUSILLA	JOHN MASK, JR
RAIFORD ELIZABETH	WILLIAM WOOLEY
RAIFORD REDDEN	ELIZABETH OLIVER
RAINER/RAYNOR ANN/ANNIE	HOSEA G LANIER
RAINES JUDITH	JOHN WEATHERFORD
RAINS ANTHORY	NANCY GRIMES
RALLS JOHN HECTOR	SALLIE/SARAH STOWE
RALPH/ROLPHE	WILLIAM AMIS
RAMSAY ROBERT	AGNES/NANCY MCCORKLE
RAMSEY JANE	ALEXANDER BALDRIDGE
RAMSEY MARY S	LEMUEL R AMYETT
RAMSEY WILLIAM	MARIA BOYD
RAMSEY WILLIAM L	ELIZA NEVIN/NIVEN
RAND MRS ELIZABETH (HINTON)	THOMAS JAMES
RANDALL REBECCA	BANNESTER GRIGG/GRIGGS
RANDLE APPHIA	JOSIAH/JOSIAS WRIGHT
RANDLEMAN MARTIN CHRISTOPHER	MARIBAH LEMONS
RANDLEMAN MARY	JASON LEMONS
RANDLEMAN MICHAEL	JANE LEMONS
RANDOLPH LUCILLE G	CECIL DOUGLAS PICKETT
RANDOLPH MAHALA	DANIEL CONLEE/CONLEY
RANDOLPH POLLY	CHARLES SLAGLE
RANSOM RUTH	JOSEPH SARGENT/SEARGENT/SARJENT
RANYOLDS REBECCA	JOHN TEETER BEAM
RARY/RAIREY JANE	NATHANIEL REX/RECKS
RATCLIFF NANCY RUTHA	JAMES SAMUEL MULLINS
RATLEY CATHERINE ANN	ELI MALACHI DEES
RATTON	MOLLIE/MATTIE GREEN/GREENE
RAWLINGS MARY/POLLY	LAWSON HUFFMAN
RAY CYNTHIA	SAMUEL GRADY KEEL
RAY ELIZABETH	JOHN GILBERT
RAY NANCY	WILLIAM REX/RECKS
RAY PATRICK	POLLY/MARY LIMBAUGH
RAYNER MARY	ROGER MOORE
RAYROLDO LIA A	CHARLES STANLEY CHAFFIN
READ ELIZABETH	RICHARD ESKRIDGE
READE MILDRED HOWELL	ANDREW HARRISON
READING LUCY	AQUILA SUGG
READY ANN	BATCHELOR/BACHELOR/BACHLOTT,BENNETT
REAGOR ANTHONY WAYNE	RHODA BOONE
REAVES TEMPY	KINDRED STRICKLAND
REAVIS DELIA REAMS	ASA MARTIN PARHAM
REAVIS LUCY	LEWIS PARHAM
REAVIS MARY	HEARTWELL HYDE
REAVIS REBECCA	ROYAL POTTER
RECTOR A B	ELIZABETH SHOOK
RECTOR JANE	PETER GLASSCOCK, SR
RECTOR MARY	PETER GLASSCOCK, SR
REDD ANNE DANDRIDGE	SAMUEL DALTON
REDDICK CATHERINE	WILLIAM H TUTTLE
REDER SARAH C	HUGH RAY EYTCHESON
REDER SARAH C	HUGH RAY
REDFERN ELEANOR	MEREDITH BROGDON
REECE ABRAHAM	MARY HUFF/HOUGH

SPOUSE INDEX

SPOUSE	ANCESTOR
REECE ABRAHAM	MARY HOUGH
REECE CALVIN RILEY	LUCY C CLARK
REECE CATHARINE	JAMES DUKE
REECE EDWARD HOUSTON	JULIA WISHON
REECE JESSE	MARGARET HADLEY
REECE JOEL	NANCY GREENWOOD
REECE RUTH	PLEASANT G WILLIAMS
REECE TENNESSEE	BENJAMIN MACKIE
REECE WILEY	ALMEDA HINSHAW
REED CHARLOTTE	GENTRY COCKERHAM HODGES
REED ELIZABETH W	JOHN WRIGHT RANDLEMAN
REED H MORIAH/JOLLY	ELIAS PENNELL
REED HIRMA	SARAH/SALLY GIDEON/GIDDENS
REED MARY	JOSHUA WHITAKER, SR
REED ROBERT	MARGARET/PEGGY CARLOCK
REED SARAH	WILLIAM W MALLISON
REEL CATHERINE	JOHN RENDLEMAN, JR
REEL MARY	JOB PENDERGRAFT/PENDERGRASS
REEL	ADAM CREASMAN/CHRISTMAN
REES ELIZABETH	MATHEW NORRIS
REES/REESE FINETTA	REUBEN HOLMAN BOONE
REEVES ELIZABETH	SIMPSON CHANCE
REGISTER ELIZABETH DORA	DANIEL BENNETT PAGE
REID FRANCES/FANNY	JOHN OATES/OATS
REID MARY	ROBERT DICKY STADLER
REID/REED AGNES	ABNER WOMMACK/WOMACK
REINHEIMER PETER	ELIZABETH IRWIN/IRVIN
REITER MARGARETHA	JOHAN JACOB MEISENHEIMER
REITZEL MILLION	LYDIA C CRAVEN
REITZEL MRS PEGGY	PHILIP KIME
RENN NANCY/ANN	THOMAS DUPREE/DUPRE'
RENN MRS CATHERINE (GREGORY)	THOMAS HENRY HUDGINS
RESPASS MARY	HENRY SHAW
REVIS MARY	JESSE BRASSFIELD
REYNOLDS ELIZABETH	RICHARD ESKRIDGE
REYNOLDS GRACE	EDMOND BOWMAN
REYNOLDS HANNAH	WILLIAM HOCKETT/HOGGATT
REYNOLDS JANE	SOLOMON CARTER
REYNOLDS JESSE	FRANCES/FANNY WILLIS
REYNOLDS SOLOMAN	RACHEL FRAZIER
REYNOLDS WILLIAM R	RACHELEMMALINE HODGSON/HODGIN/HODSON
RHEW ANN	ROBERT DUKE
RHOADES CAMMELIA	DANIEL BINKLEY
RHOADES JUDITH	MARMADUKE NORFLEET
RHODES COL ELISHA	MARY WOODMAN KIMBALL
RHODES ELIZABETH	DANIEL MARSHBURN/MASHBURN
RHODES ELIZABETH	WILLIS W NOWELL
RHODES EMILY	ENOCH WARD
RHODES MRS AURY	MASSEY M COPELAND
RHODES WILLIAM JAMES	MARTHA ANN LEWIS
RHODES/RHODS MARTHA ANICE	JACOB DAWSON WILLIAMS
RHODES/ROHDS JEREMIAH	ELIZABETH FERRELL/FARRELL
RHYNE ELIZABETH	MARTIN SHUFORD/SCHEUFFERT
RICE AMANDA	CHARLES C TACKETT/TACKITT

SPOUSE	ANCESTOR
RICE ELIZABETH	GEORGE C TACKETT/TACKITT
RICE JUDITH	MICAHEL SMITH
RICE MARY ANN	GEORGE C TACKETT/TACKITT
RICE MARY ELIZABETH	ALEXANDER KERR
RICE SARA/SARAH ANN	ROBERT VANCE PENLEY/PENLY
RICE SARAH	EDWARD SMITH
RICE SARAH M	JAMES/JIM WHITE ARNOLD
RICH ANNA	ALLEN HELMS
RICH PHILOPENA	ISAAC ALBRIGHT
RICHARDS CANDICE ANN	WILLIAM HENRY ROBERTS
RICHARDS JAMES	MARY ANN HASWELL
RICHARDS RACHEL	THARP/THARPE/THORP/THORPE,WILLIAM
RICHARDS SARAH SIMMONS	ELIHUE MELTON
RICHARDS TERESA EUSEBIA	EMMOR GRAHAM
RICHARDSON CHRISTIAN	TOBIAS GODWIN
RICHARDSON EDITH	EDMUND ATCHISON/ETCHISON
RICHARDSON ELIZABETH BAILEY	JOHN VINCENT MAY
RICHARDSON GINSEY	ISAAC WHITEHEAD GUERIN/GEURIN
RICHARDSON JAMES	ANNA TILLEY
RICHARDSON JULIA BLANCHE	SAMUEL TILDEN ANDERSON
RICHARDSON OMA	AMBROS/AMBROSE BREWER/BRUER
RICHIE AMANDA CAROLINA	GEORGE CHRISTOPHER DEARMAN
RICKARD DELILA/DELILAH JANE	JOHN WREN/WRENN
RICKS CHARITY	LEMUEL WRIGHT
RICKS ELIZABETH	JAMES COLTRANE
RIDDLE DICEY	MARK PATTERSON
RIDDLE HENRY	NANCY RENNICK
RIDINGS DICY	ISAAC WILLIAMS
RIDINGS ELIZABETH	ALEXANDER SHERRILL
RIEHM ANNA CATHERINE	JOHANNES LEINBACH, JR
RIGGENS SUSANNAH	ERVIN HENDRICKS SIMS
RIGGS REBECCA L	THOMAS HENRY HUDGINS
RIGHTS CHARLOTTE E	JOSHUA SIMEON WHITE
RILEY JOHN	MARY REBECCA RUSS
RILEY MRS MARY REBECCA (RUSS)	WILLIAM DAVIDSON MCCRACKEN
RINGO HARBERT CORNELIUS	HULDAH ANN KNIGHT
RIPPY MARGARET	JOHN JACOB SHUFORD/SCHEUFFERT
RISON RICHARD	POLLY COBB
RITTER ARRENIA	LEWIS OLIVER GARNER
RITTER ELIZABETH	WILLIAM SILANCE
RITTER	JOHN F MARSHALL
RITTER WILLIAM DEDBERRY	MARGARET MYRICK
RIVERS A A	EFFIE M L RAY
RIVERS HANNAH	JOSHUA JEHU SCOTT
RIVES JULIA	LEANDER GAITHER
RIVES PRISCILLA	NIEL EZELL
ROACH JANE ELIZABETH	JOHN ROBERT PRESSLEY
ROACH PEGGY	ROBERT WEBB
ROACH SUSANNA	WILLIAM SPENCER MURPHY/MURPHREY
ROARK NANCY	WILLIAM GIPSON
ROBARDS MARSHALL	MARY/POLLY FINCH
ROBASON ANN	WILLIAM WATTS
ROBBINS BENJAMIN	RUTH PARKER
ROBBINS ELIZABETH	DAVID GARDNER/GARNER

SPOUSE	ANCESTOR
ROBBINS SAMUEL MARION	CAROLINA FISHER WILLIAMS
ROBBINS THOMAS	EMILY AUGUSTUS FREEMAN
ROBERSON MARY	JAMES HARDISON
ROBERSON/ROBESON JUDITH	THOMAS WILSON
ROBERTS ELISABETH	WARREN HOOKS
ROBERTS JOHN	EUNICE/UNITY ROGERS
ROBERTS JULIA	JAMES MONROE CARTER
ROBERTS MELVINY	FELIX GRUNDE CATES
ROBERTS NANCY	ABRAHAM SANDERS
ROBERTS PEGGY	JOB/JOBE GREGORY
ROBERTS SALLY ORGAIN	BENJAMIN MINCE CLIFTON
ROBERTSON ELIZABETH	ALEXANDER CLARK
ROBERTSON MARY	JOHN LINDSEY, SR
ROBERTSON MARY	RICHARD BEASON/BEESON
ROBERTSON NICHOLS	JANE HUNTER
ROBERTSON SARAH	HENRY TEMPLE, JR
ROBERTSON WILLIAM	LOUVICIA HUGHES
ROBERTSON MRS NANCY (WALTON)	BURWELL TEMPLE
ROBERTSON/ROBINSON JOHN W	MARY/POLLY ADAMS/ADDAMS
ROBESON JENNET	THOMAS NESMITH
ROBEY ESTHER/MARY	DAVID TUCKER, I
ROBINET CATHERINE	JOHN FOARD/FORD
ROBINS BETHIAH	JOHN NATION
ROBINS BITHIAH	JOHN NATION/NATIONS
ROBINS ELEANOR	JOSEPH NATION/NATIONS
ROBINSON CATHERINE	JAMES MOORE
ROBINSON ELEANOR	ABSALOM CARROLL
ROBINSON ELIZABETH	THOMAS HUNTER
ROBINSON ELIZABETH	JOSEPH W CREWS
ROBINSON JUDA	ELVIS FOWLER
ROBINSON SARAH ANN	ALEXANDER ERWIN
ROBISON MRS ANNA	EPHRAIM DELLINGER
ROBISON REBECCA ANN	DAVID MULLINS
ROBSON JESSE	SUSAN MARIE WORTHINGTON
RODDY PRUDENCE	JAMES HALL
RODGERS MARGARET	SHADRACK MATHIS
RODGERS/ROGERS MARGARET	SHADRACK MATHIS/MATHEWS
RODGERS/ROGERS RACHEL	ELIJAH LEE
RODY	GEORGE SHUFORD/SCHEUFFERT
ROGERS ANDREW WHITLEY	TEMPE SARAH ANN WARD
ROGERS COURTNEY	JESSE HARDEN
ROGERS IDA EMMA	WILLIAM THOMAS HARTON
ROGERS JOHN M	MARGARET CALDWELL
ROGERS MARGARET	JEFFERSON BARNETT
ROGERS MARTHE THWEATT	WILLIAM ISAAC MCCOLLUM
ROGERS MARY	SAMUEL CALDWELL
ROGERS RALPH	MRS JUDITH LYLES
ROGERS REBECCA	WILLIAM MCBRIDE
ROGERS REBECCA	PETER PIVER
ROGERS SARAH/POLLY	HILLAIRE ROUSSEAU
ROLLER ISAAC	MARIE SHELTON
ROLLINS MARY	DANIEL FOWLER
ROLLINS/ROLLINGS REBECCA	WILLIAM ROSS
ROMAN RACHEL	WILLIAM LAVENDER

SPOUSE	ANCESTOR
ROOK ELIZABETH	THOMAS SANDERS/SAUNDERS
ROPER BARBARA	JOSHUA WILSON
ROPER JEMIMA	JOHN YATES
RORIE HEZEKIAH	MILBRE WILLIAMS
ROSE MARTHA S	THOMAS HEADENGRAND BRAY
ROSE NANCY	COUNCIL JONES BEARD
ROSEBOROUGH ERIXENE MCEWEN	MOSES MCKNIGHT
ROSEBOROUGH SAMUEL	JANE HALL
ROSS JANE	ANDREW CATHEY
ROSS KATIE	LITTLETON YOUNG CAGLE
ROSS LEWIS O	CLEO A GILES
ROSS MARTHA A	ROBERT CARR? MCCRACKEN
ROSS RACHEL	JOHN R MARTIN
ROUSE ABNER	HARRIETT PARKS
ROUSE LANIE	WILLIAM HERRING SKINNER, JR
ROUSE SARAH ADELAIDE	LEWIS JAMES JOHNSON
ROUSSEAU WILLIAM	RUTH MCBRIDE
ROWAN JANE SHARPE	DAVID WILSON
ROWE CARRIE INEZ	JAMES CLARK MALLISON
ROWE JULIA ELIZABETH	EBENEZER DUNSTON
ROWE MARY CECILIA	SAMUEL TILDEN ANDERSON
ROWLAND JANE	LEWIS GULLEY/GULLY
ROWLAND MARY	JOSHUA HADLEY
ROWLAND/ROLLINS MARTHA	ELIJAH LEE
ROYAL JOHN JACKSON	JANE ATWOOD
ROYALL ISHAM	RACHEL CARROLL
ROYALL ROBERTA PRISCILLA	MURDOCK MCKINNON MAXWELL
ROYER SALLY	DANIEL PAFFORD
ROYSTER ELLA N	JOHN JOSIAH HUDGINS
RUBISON REASON	MARY ANN CHASTAIN
RUCKER NANCY ANN	SHEMUEL COOK
RUDD EMILY	LABON CATLETTE
RUDOLPH HANNAH	HENRY KIME
RUDOPH ELIZABETH	JOHN TEETER BEAM
RULE DELILAH	GEORGE HODGSON/HODGIN/HODSON
RUMBLEY LEVICY	EDWARD LINDSEY
RUSH SUSAN	WILLIAM GEORGE SANDERS
RUSS NATHANIEL JAMES	MARTHA ANN SMITH
RUSSELL CAROLINE REBECCA	HEZEKIAH/KIAH ALEXANDER CORRELL
RUSSELL JANE	WILLIAM HENRY
RUSSELL JOHN	ELIZABETH JANE FRAZIER
RUSSELL MARGARET	JOHN GORDON PEARCE
RUSSELL NANCY	JULIUS CONSTANTINE WILLI SCHYLER/SCHUYLER
RUSSELL PHEBE	JARED PERKINS
RUSSELL THOMAS	NANCY ANN FRAZIER
RUSSELL WILLIAM	MARGARET DOWNEY
RUST MATTHEW/JOHN?	PRISCILLA MILLS
RUTH JEAN	ROBERT MCQUISTON
RUTHERFORD HANNAH	JOHN STARKEY CLEMSON
RUTLEDGE EULA LUCILLE	GEORGE DEE GENERAL LEE WHITMIRE
SABISTON FANNIE	DANIEL HARGETT BUCK
SADLER MARTHA ROSE	JAMES RATLEDGE/RUTLEDGE, JR

SPOUSE	ANCESTOR
SAFLEY JESSEE	PHATHA/FAITHA STILES
SAILING/SALEN KATE	ISAAC HENRY
SAIN MARY	JEREMIAH WELLMAN
SANDEFUR MARY	ARTHUR ARRINGTON, JR
SANDERS ABRAHAM	NANCY ROBERTS
SANDERS ANN	THOMAS ELMORE
SANDERS FRANCES	JOHN M MCMINN
SANDERS FRANCES	JAMES POWELL
SANDERS JAMES	MARY JANE WILSON
SANDIFER PRISCILLA	SAMUEL HARPER
SANDUSKY KATHRYN AUGUSTA	JOHN HANBY FOARD/FORD
SANDY ELIZABETH	JOHN THOMAS BRYANT
SANFORD CORA VICTORIA	LUDOLPHUS GRAVES POOLE
SANFORD	JUDITH EMALINE DORSETT
SANFORD/STANFORD EZEKIEL	ELLENER COBB
SAPPINGTON MRS MARY ANN (ANDERSON)	JEREMIAH ROWLAND
SAPPNEFIELD MATHIAS	CHRISTINA GRIMES
SARGENT ELIZABETH	SIMON DOYLE
SARGENT ELIZABETH	SIMON W DOYLE
SARGENT POLLY	THOMAS LIPSCOMB
SARGENT RESIN T	ELIZABETH/BETSEY ANN ADAMS
SATER PRUDENCE	BENJAMIN HOWARD
SAUNDERS LUCY	DRURY PEEBLES
SAUNDERS REBECCA HARTT	HUGH ALLISON
SAUNDERS/SANDERS ELIZABETH	GEORGE WASHINGTON MCPEAK
SAUNDERSON MARY	AUSTIN P TODD
SAVAGE PHEREBEE	FRANCIS PUGH
SAWYER NANCY	HENRY FORD
SAWYER REBECCA	DAVID SHADRACK WILLIAMS
SAWYER TABITHA	HOLLOWAY SMITH
SAXTON MARY	SOLOMAN WALL
SAYERS MRS ELIZABETH	EPHRAIM PRICE
SCALF BENJAMIN FRANKLIN	ELEANOR NARCISSUS THOMAS
SCALLORN MELINDA	BARTLETT WAGLEY/WAGLE/WEIGLE
SCARBOROUGH ADDISON	JOSIE HOWELL
SCARBOROUGH DAVID	NANNA/NANNY DUNN
SCARBOROUGH MARY W	SION WRIGHT GARDNER/GARNER
SCARLET MARY	JOHN COX
SCATES NANCY MALISSA	JOHN BLACKWELL
SCHAFER CATHERINE	PETER SANER/SEHNERT
SCHEIBLE ELIZABETH	MICHAEL HOLT
SCHELL ANNA MARIA	RUDOLPH CONRAD
SCHOCKLEY/CHOCKLEY MARY/POLLY	DANIEL HAYMORE, SR
SCHOOLEY EDITH	ASHER KERSEY
SCHUFORD CATROUT	RUDOLPH CONRAD
SCOGGINS MATILDA	DAVID HOLDER
SCOTT AGNES	JOHN MATTHEWS
SCOTT BARBARA	PETTAR THIEME/TEEM
SCOTT ELIZABETH	WILLIAM HENRY HOOKS
SCOTT ELIZABETH PLEDGE	SAMUEL MARTIN
SCOTT JANE	ALEXANDER ALLEN
SCOTT JANE ARMISTEAD	ARCHIBALD DEBOW MURPHEY
SCOTT JANE/JENNY	JACOB CHESNUTT/CHESTNUTT
SCOTT MARTHA	WILLIAM SMITH

SPOUSE	ANCESTOR
SCOTT MARY	THOMAS PUGH
SCOTT MARY/POLLY	JOHN ARNOLD LITTLETON
SCOTT	SIMON WHITEHURST
SCOTT MRS JANNET	JOHN LOGUE
SCOTT SARAH	THOMAS NEATHERY
SCOTT SARAH	WILLIAM LITTLETON
SCOTT MRS MARY ANN (MARTIN)	WILLIAM DAWSON BLEDSOE
SCOTTEN MARGARET	GEORGE QUINCE WAGONER
SCREWS REBECCIA	LAMUEL HARDISON WILLIAMS
SCRUGGS NANCY	WILLIAM WASHINGTON HURST
SCURR ELIZABETH	JEREMIAH LAND
SCUTCHINS MARY	JAMES MERRITT
SEALY BETTIE	JOSEPH WALTERS
SEARLES JUDITH	THOMAS NICHOLAS PUREFOY
SEARS SUSANNAH	JOEL WHITE
SEATON PHOEBE	MASON CLEM
SEAY MARY	JOEL BROWN
SEAY SARAH ANN	THOMAS MINTON
SECHRIST ANNA	MATHIAS SAPPENFIELD, II
SEELEY MARY ELIZABETH	JOHN AUGUSTUS FREEMAN
SEELY SARAH MARY	NICHOLAS CHAPMAN
SELF ELIZABETH	CHARLES LONG
SELLARS CINDERELLA	JAMES LEE
SELLARS SAMUEL	ZILPHA SELLARS
SELLARS ZILPHA	SAMUEL SELLARS, SR
SELLERS KERENHAPPUCH	THOMAS ARRINGTON THOMPSON
SELLERS RHODA	JAMES FAULK
SELLERS SUSAN	JOHN SMYLIE/SMILEY
SELLERS/SELLARS WILLIAM T	JULIA W MCCRACKEN
SEMANS SUSANNAH	JACOB SHELSBERGER
SENTER BETSY	THOMAS SPENCER
SESSOMS PRISCELLA E	JAMES REDDICK GREEN
SESSUMS MRS PARTHENIA	JAMES W BRINKLEY
SETLIFF CHARLES	CANDICE CASPER
SETSER JOHN	SUSAN/SUCKEY CRISP
SETZER JACOB	MARY MAGDALAN BOVEY/POVEY
SEVACY JANE	ALFRED B MULLINS
SEWARD MARY	SYLVESTER THOMPSON
SEWELL HANNAH	BASLEY GRAVES MARCOM/MARKHAM
SEWELL LEVINIA	JACOB L ? SMITH
SEWELL POLLEY	THOMAS ARNOLD
SHADDY RACHEL	GEORGE FOGLEMAN
SHANNON ANN	WILLIAM WILEY, JR
SHARP JANE	GOODWIN KILLION
SHARP MARY	WILLIAM POLK
SHARP MARY M	WHIT M HILL
SHARPE ELIZABETH	JOHN TABER/TABOUR, SR
SHARPE/SHUPE MARTHA A	JOHN ANDREW WALKER
SHARPLESS RACHEL	BENJAMIN CHANCE
SHAW AMANDA	ROBERT PAINE
SHAW MARGARET	GEORGE H TROXLER
SHAW MARY	JOHN CURTIS, JR
SHAW NORMAN	CYNTHIA DRAPER
SHAW OZINA	JOHN UPTON

SPOUSE	ANCESTOR
SHAY SARAH	SAMUEL LEE
SHEARER ELIZABETH	JOSEPH GREEN
SHEARMAN LUCINDA R	MOSES C DEAN
SHEARON SARAH	SAMUEL CRUTCHFIELD
SHEFFIELD MARY	EDWARD ARMSTRONG
SHELL CHRISTINA	JOSEPH WOODS
SHELLEY ELIZABETH C	WILLIAM HILLIARD
SHELLEY MARY/POLLY	CARLTON MATHIS
SHELTON ELIZABETH	WILLIAM ARNOLD
SHELTON JESSE F	CECILIA/SISLEY JONES
SHELTON JOEL/JOSEPH	MARY/POLLY CHASTIAN
SHEPHARD ISABELLA JANE	BRANSON/BRENSON/BRANT BROWN
SHEPHARD/SHEPHERD WILLIAM	SARAH BROWN
SHEPHERD ANNE	WILLIAM VIARS
SHEPHERD CATHERINE	JACOB LONG
SHEPHERD DELPHIA	NATHANIEL J JUDD, JR
SHEPHERD JAMES WELBORN	ELIZABETH JONES
SHEPHERD MARTHA	JOHN EDWARDS FOUTS/PHOUTS
SHEPHERD MARTHA MALINDA	JOSEPH WILSON FOUTS/PHOUTS
SHEPHERD MILDRED	OBEDIAH MERRITT
SHEPPARD ELIZABETH	THEOPHILUS EDWARDS
SHEPPARD NELLIE	WILLIAM NORMAN
SHEPPARD MRS MARTHA (GLASGOW)	JOSEPH SCURLOCK
SHERMAN FRANCES	THOMAS GOSS, SR
SHERRIER MARY	ANDREW SHEETS
SHERRILL JACOB	ELIZABETH/BETSEY PERKINS
SHERRILL RACHEL	ABRAHAM MASSEY
SHERROD MARY/POLLY	THOMAS BEST
SHERWOOD ELEANOR	JEREMIAH FIELD/FIELDS
SHERWOOD THOMAS	MARY THOMPSON
SHIELDS MRS CATHERINE (WHITEHEAD)	THOMAS SHIELDS
SHINE DANIEL	BARBARA FRANCKE
SHINE SARAH WILLIAMS	JAMES MILLER
SHINN BETSY	ASA LEWIS
SHIPLEY JOSEPH	JANE MCCRACKEN
SHIPLEY ROBERT	MARY MCCRACKEN
SHIPMAN REBECCA	BENJAMIN KING
SHIRLEY SARAH	HENRY HOLTZCLAW
SHIVERS NANCY	JOHN SUTHERLAND
SHOEMAKER CHRISTIAN	ROSANNA WITT
SHOEMAKER CONRAD	JANE WITT
SHOEMAKER DANIEL	ANNA MARGARET WITT
SHOEMAKER JESSE	MARY ANN WILEY
SHOFNER MARGARET	PHILLIP BURROW
SHOOK ELIZABETH	A B RECTOR
SHOOPMAN ELIZABETH	WILLIAM BYRD
SHORE DELLA	JOB WORTH DAVIS
SHORE MARTHA	WILLIAM F RANDLEMAN
SHORES ABIRAM	ELIZABETH ROUSSEAU
SHORES DAVID	LUCY ROUSSEAU
SHORES LEVI	SARAH ROUSSEAU
SHORES NANCY	DAVID ROUSSEAU
SHORES/SHORS MARY A	JOHN O WELBORN
SHORT REBECCA	JEREMIAH BIRCHFIELD/BURCHFIELD

SPOUSE	ANCESTOR
SHORT MRS AGENES (RIGGAN)	RICHARD SHORT
SHOUSE CHRISTIAN	SALLY PLANCET
SHOWALTER MUIRAM	JAMES MADISON BURTON
SHRYER ZENAS M	LOUZINA MEREDITH
SHUFORD AMANDA OLA	LANDRUM BEATTY ROSS
SHULL ELIZABETH	WILLIAM F CANNON
SHUMATE WILLIS L	SARAH/SALLIE A FELTS
SIBELLA ELIZABETH	BENJAMIN SMITH
SIBLEY NANCY	STEPHEN DECATUR PETTY
SIGMON EASSIE	WILLIAM ABNER LOWRANCE
SILANCE JERRY THOMAS	PAULINE WILLIAMS
SILLS SARAH	RICHARD GAMMON
SILLS MRS CHARLOTTE (GRAY)	JOHN B SILLS
SIMMONS DAVID L	MAGGIE A TRIPLETT
SIMMONS DAVID WARD	HENRIETTA SANDERS
SIMMONS JAMES	ESTHER STICE
SIMMONS JENNIE	ABRAHAM STOWE
SIMMONS MATILDA	JACOB EBERHART, JR
SIMMONS PENELOPE	REDDING MCDONALD/MCDANIEL
SIMMONS PENELOPE	GREEN TAYLOR
SIMMONS PETER	RACHEL MILLS
SIMONTON MRS AMANDA (WILEY)	THOMAS JAMES MIDDLETON
SIMPKINS ANANIAS	MAHALA STUDDARD
SIMPSON ANN	THOMAS ELKINS
SIMPSON CANDACE	THOMAS STACEY
SIMPSON JAMES	NANCY HENSON
SIMPSON LETTIE	JOHN ADAMS
SIMPSON REBECCA	ABRAHAM LYDAY/LYDA
SIMPSON WILLIAM	NANCY PRICE
SIMS ASENATH NICKLES	ANDREW WEATHERLY
SIMS ELIZA	DAVID LOE
SIMS ELIZABETH	WILLIAM SUGG
SIMS JOANNA	JAMES OWNBEY
SIMS JOHN	SARAH BULLOCK
SIMS SWEPSON	JANE MERIWETHER LEWIS
SIMS UNITY	MOSES DUNCAN
SIMS WINNIFRED	HIRAM HARDY HARGROVE
SIMS/SYMS THOMAS BASERY	SARAH ADDELINE ALLISON
SINGLETON AVA	ALLEN BARNES/BARNS
SINGLETON ELIZABETH	JOSEPH A LEE
SINGLETON JOHN	FRANCES/POLLY LANGSTON
SIZEMORE MRS SALLY	ELIAS OSBORNE
SIZEMORE NANCY ELIZABETH	JOHN HENRY MACKIE/MACKEY/MACKAY
SIZEMORE POLLY	RANDALL HUBBARD
SKEEN ELIZABETH JANE	JAMES MARION GARDNER
SKILLINGTON ELIZABETH	STERLING SLEDGE
SKINNER ELIZABETH	MICAJAH PETTAWAY/PETWAY
SLAGLE FRANKLIN PIERCE	NAOMA YOUNG
SLAGLE IDA	DAVID SMITH GRAYBEAL
SLAGLE TEXAS	DAVID SMITH GRAYBEAL
SLATE JAMES SAMUEL	MARY ELIZABETH FOWLER
SLATE JOHN EDGAR	MARGARET BAKER
SLATTER MRS FRANCES (BUSTIN)	JOHN WILLIAMS, MAJ
SLATTON/LATON JOHN	NANCY WOODY

SPOUSE	ANCESTOR
SLAUGHTER FRANCIS	RICHARD DEAN
SLAUGHTER MARTHA CAROLINE	JOSHUA BOSLOCK, DR
SLEDGE ELIZA ANN PRISCILLA	THOMAS JEFFERSON LEMAY
SLOAN ANNE	JAMES ALEXANDER HARTNESS
SLOAN ELIZA	STEPHEN GIBBONS
SLOAN ELIZABETH	SAMUEL SNODDY
SLOAN HIRAM C	MARY C RAY
SLOAN JEAN	WILLIAM OATES/OATS
SLOSS SARAH	JONATHAN BLAIR
SLUDER JULIA C	DAVID ISRAEL
SMALL MARY	JAMES MCELROY
SMART ELIZABETH	DAVID BROOKS
SMART ENZA ELIZABETH	LANDRUM BEATTY ROSS
SHAW HENRY	MARY RESPASS
SMITH AGNES DUNN	AUGUSTUS W BRIDGES
SMITH ALEXANDER	KEZIAH LAMAR
SMITH ARAMINTA	JOSEPH DENSON
SMITH CATHERINE	MOSES ALEXANDER STATON/STAYTON
SMITH CATY	JEHU PEEBLES, JR
SMITH CLEMON	SUSAN PENNY
SMITH DANIEL	DORCAS MCDANIEL
SMITH DOROTHY	JAMES REDDICK RAMEY RUTLAND
SMITH DUNCAN	ISABEL STEWART
SMITH EDITH MARIE	JAMES ELMER ARNOLD
SMITH ELIZABETH	JOHN KITTRELL
SMITH ELIZABETH	HENRY CREASON/CRESON
SMITH ELIZABETH	REUBEN SMITH
SMITH ELIZABETH	ANDREW BASS
SMITH ELIZABETH	SOLOMON MILAM
SMITH HENRIETTA	WILLIAM R CARPENTER
SMITH JACOB	REBECCA JUSTICE
SMITH JAMES CICERO	MELISSA ELIZABETH SMITH
SMITH JANE	JESSE FRANKLIN WATSON
SMITH JANE	NEWTON RENSHAR EDNEY, JR
SMITH JOANNAH	DAVID BALDWIN
SMITH JOSEPH ARCHIE	CLEMENTINE/CLEMMIE WETHERINGTON
SMITH JUDITH C	PETER LIMBAUGH
SMITH LABEN	MILLY MORRIS
SMITH LEAH	BENJAMIN SANDERS/SAUNDERS
SMITH LUCINDA	IRA BELISLE
SMITH MALINDA	KELLY SIMMONS
SMITH MARGARET	NATHANIEL SMYLIE/SMILEY
SMITH MARGARET	JAMES WYATT
SMITH MARTHA ANN	NATHANIEL JAMES RUSS
SMITH MARTHA EMALINE	WILLIAM ABNER BENNETT
SMITH MARTHA WILLIAM	THOMAS HEADENGRAND BRAY
SMITH MARY	PARKS, MAJOR
SMITH MARY	MALCOLM MCALPINE
SMITH MARY	SAMUEL GRAY
SMITH MARY ANN	THOMAS HEADENGRAND BRAY
SMITH MARY CAROLINE	JOHN WILLIAM GOING
SMITH MARY COTTEN	JAMES SMYLIE/SMILEY, REV
SMITH MARY W	JESSE HOWARD
SMITH MARY/POLLY	THOMAS REID

SPOUSE	ANCESTOR
SMITH MICAJAH KEGG/CAGE	ELIZABETH AGEE
SMITH MRS ANN	FRANCIS BYTHEL HAYNES
SMITH MYRON WILLIAM	HARRIET JANE WOOD/WOODS
SMITH NANCY	ABRAM WHITAKER
SMITH NANCY	LARKIN BROOKS
SMITH NANCY A	HIRAM RAY DICKSON
SMITH NELLIE OGILVIE	JAMES BRUCE ORRELL
SMITH PEARLINA	ANTHONY TAYLOR
SMITH PENELOPE	ALEXANDER OUTLAW, COL
SMITH PHOEBE	JACOB MATTHEWS
SMITH PRUDENCE CATHERINE GARNER	THOMAS DUNNAGAN MARSH
SMITH RACHEL	DANIEL MCNEILL
SMITH RACHEL	JESSE BRASSFIELD
SMITH REBECCA ANN	ALLEN HELMS
SMITH REUBEN	ELIZABETH SMITH
SMITH SALLY	HARDY SANDERS
SMITH SARAH	THOMAS EVANS
SMITH SARAH ANN	JONATHAN SMITH BOSTICK
SMITH SARAH JANE	DUNCAN CURRY
SMITH SOPHIA	JAMES MONROE BOONE
SMITH SUSAN	WEEKS CLARK
SMITH WASHINGTON	MARY SELF
SMITH WILLIAM BURNS	SALLIE ODUM/ODHAM
SMITH WILLIAM O	JANE MILLER
SMITH MRS LEAH(PRITLOWE)	THOMAS WINSLOW
SMITH/SCHMIDT MARY	GEORGE MOUSER
SMITHERMAN MRS GAIL ADELINE (WILLIAMS)	SHORE DAVID DAVIS
SMITHWICK JOHN	HANNAH KENT
SMITHWICK MARY	JAMES HARDISON
SMITHWICK MRS HANNAH (KENT)	FARNEFOLD GREEN
SMYLIE MARY CAMPBELL	DANIEL MCFARLANE WILKINSON
SNAP MARGARET	JOHN/SAMUEL RENDLEMAN
SNAP MARGARET	JOHANNES RINTELMAN/RINGLEMAN
SNEAD NANCY	DANIEL GOOCH
SNELLING ESTHER	JOHN WINSLOW
SNETHEN HANNAH	WILLIAM LEWIS
SNODDY MARGARET	JOSEPH MCCORKLE
SNODEN SARAH	JOSHUA BARCLIFT/BARTLETT
SNOW ELIZABETH	MOREN MOORE
SNYDER ROXANNA	THOMAS WILLIAM ALLISON
SNYDER MRS SALLIE (PENROD)	ZACHARIUS/ZAMAH/ZACH LYERLY/LAYRLE/LIERLY
SOLES JOSHUA	ELENDER/ELEANOR BUFFKIN
SOLES LUPHENIA	MACK DANIEL/MCD FOWLER
SOLLEY SARAH	DAVID PRICHARD
SOMMERVILLE JAMES	SOMMERVILLE/SUMMERVILLE,MARGARET
SOPHRONIA ANNA MARIA	HENRY WEITZEL
SORRELL ANALIZER	WILLIAM H DILLARD
SOUDER CATHERINE	PHILLIP GUTBRODT/GOODBREAD, JR
SOUTHARD MARY/POLLY	JABIS BARRETT
SOUTHARD	SAMUEL DENNY
SOUTHARD ROBERT/BOB	SARAH/SALLIE MILAM
SOUTHERLAND ELIZA JANE	JONATHAN WILDER WILLIAMS
SOUTHERLAND MARY/POLLY	STEPHEN DECATUR WILLIAMS
SOUTHERLAND RHODA/RODA	WILLIAM BURTON SOUTHERLAND

SPOUSE INDEX

SPOUSE	ANCESTOR
SOWELL ANN	WILLIAM BARRETT
SPAIN NANCY	DANIEL SMITH
SPARKS ANNIE	DAVID PINKERTON
SPARKS JANE	DAVID J ENGLISH
SPARKS JESSE M	SARAH HOWELL
SPARKS THOMAS M	MARY ANN COOK
SPARROW MRS REBECKER (MIDGETT)	JEREMIAH MEEKINS
SPECK EVA	MICHAEL AWALT
SPEIDEL ANNA	PHILIP BOSS
SPENCE ELIZA	LORENZO DOW ORRELL
SPENCER ELIZABETH	RICHARD SAUNDERSON/SANDERSON
SPENCER ELIZABETH MIRAM	ISRAEL SPENCER
SPENCER JANE	HENRY GIBBS
SPENCER JESSE	MARY/POLLY WARREN
SPENCER MARY	SIMON HADLEY, JR
SPENCER SALINA	SPENCER CLAYBORN CALLICOATTE
SPENCER SARAH JANE	NIMROD ADAMS, JR
SPENCER SIEBERT	ANNA MARIE DIETZ
SPENGEL CATHERINE	DAVID/THEOBALD FOUTS/PFAUTZ
SPENGEL CATRINA	DEWALD FOUTS/PHOUTS
SPERRY LOIS	JOSEPH PERKINS
SPERRY MIRIAM	TIMOTHY PERKINS
SPERRY RHODA	JAMES VINSON
SPIER MARY	JAMES COKER
SPILLMAN ELIZA JANE	JOHN T PHILLIPS
SPIVY MARTHA JANE	JOSEPH WOODARD
SPLAWN MARGARET ELIZABETH	RANSOM P PONDER
SPOON	DANIEL APPLE
SPOON	FANNY BROWN
SPRATT/SPROT MARTHA	ARCHIBALD MCNEAL
SPRUIELL/SPRUILL JAMES A	DIRECTOR LIVERMAN
SPRUILL CAROLINE	JOSEPH ALLEN GASKINS
SPRUILL DEMPSEY	MARY DAVENPORT
SPRUILL HENRETTA	JOHN DUNSTON
SPRUILL LOIS	JOHN MIDGETT
SPRUILL ROSANAH	THOMAS LEIGH
SPURGEON MRS SARAH (MOTSINGER)	ELI LORANCE/LOWRANCE
SQUIRES JAMES JONES	SUSAN FRANCES PAUL
SQUIRES JAMES WILLIAM	LUCY JOBE
SQUIRES THOMAS	ELIZABETH GILL
SQUIRES THOMAS	SUSAN JONES
SR MARTIN PHIFER	MARGARET BLACKWELDER
STACKHOUSE SARAH JANE	NEDDY EDWARDS
STACY WILLIAM RUSSELL	MARY ELLEN BARNETT
STADLER ROBERT DICKY	MARY REID
STADLER SARAH DELILAH	WILLIAM DAVID BLALOCK
STADLER SUSANNAH PARKER	LUKE ARNOLD
STAFFORD MARY	JOHN MAY
STAFFORD MARY	MAY HOLCOMBE
STAGGS MRS MARGARET (ANDERSON)	ROBERT FRANKLIN WATERS
STALCOP RACHEL	ISAAC BRACKEN
STALCUP NANCY	JOHN HENRY CARMICHAEL
STALEY SARAH	JOHN MILLER
STALEY SARAH	DAVID FOX

318

SPOUSE	ANCESTOR
STALKER HANNAH	BENJAMIN SPENCER
STAMEY ELIZA	W GRANVILLE KELLER
STAMPER JOANNAH	GORDON PERKINS
STANALAND SAMUEL A	MARGARET BELL
STANDLEY ANNA	SIMON LINDLY/LINDLEY
STANDLEY JAMES	MARY/POLLY TROTTER
STANDLEY JAMES	JANE TROTTER
STANDLEY	JOHN CARROLL
STANDRIDGE JUNIUS HILLYER	MARY TALITHA HOOPER
STANFIELD EMILY ELIZABETH	JOAB CRISP/CHRISP
STANFIELD MARTHA BANKS	JAMES BOMAN/BOWMAN HUDGINS
STANFIELD WASHINGTON GREEN	ARTHESIA LIPSCOMB
STANLEY ALICE	JOHN HUTCHENS
STANLEY ELIZABETH	LEWIS W WESCOTT
STANLEY ELIZABETH	JOHN MASTEN
STANLEY ELIZABETH	CADWALLADER PITTS
STANLEY MARJORY	JOHN FRAZIER
STANLEY MARY	JESSE STANLEY
STANLEY UNITY	JESSE DENNIS
STANLEY VIRGINIA T	CHARLIE CRABTREE
STANSBURY JOHN H	ANN EARNEST
STANSBURY MARY M	DAVID COOK
STANSBURY REBECCA	WILLIAM NIX
STANSBURY SOLOMON	JANE/JENNET LEWIN
STARBUCK ABIGAIL	JOHN SIMMONS
STARBUCK EUNICE	ADAM SMITH
STARKEY ELIZABETH	MICHAEL DELP
STARKS MARTHA	JOSEPH WAGLEY/WAGLE/WEIGLE
STARLING VANDALIA	LEWIS DUPREE, COL
STARNES GRACE CAROLINE	SIMS OWNBEY
STARNES THOMAS ALBERT	ELIZABETH MORGAN
STARR ELIZABETH	HENRY JOHNSTON/JOHNSON, JR
STARR HANNAH	THOMAS NEELY
STARR SALOMA/SALLY	ESAU JOHNSTON/JOHNSON
STARR/STAR FRANCES	IRA ELLIS
STATON LOVEY	HENRY ANDERSON
STEARNS HEPSIBAH	WILLIAM WELBORN
STEELE HANNAH	DAVID LEACH
STEELE LEONA IRENE	ISAAC HAMPTON LOWRANCE
STEELE NANCY	SAMUEL HALL
STEELMAN CHARLES	JANE CRESON/CRESSON
STEELMAN MARY/POLLY	THOMAS ATWOOD
STEELMAN NANCY CAROLINE	FRANCIS KERR WILLIAMS
STEELMAN SANFORD LEE	RUTH JANE WILLIAMS
STEGALE ELIZABETH	WILLIAM YOUNG
STEGALL ELIZABETH/BETSY ANN	WILLIAM ALVERSON HELMS
STEMBRIDGE ELIZABETH	CLEMENT/CLEMMA SULLIVAN
STEPHEN ANN	THOMAS HARRINGTON
STEPHENS EDWARD L	ANN MCCRACKEN
STEPHENS MARTHA E	CHESLEY MEREDITH ADAMS
STEPHENS MILLIE	JAMES THOMAS
STEPHENSON JONATHAN	NANCY KELLUM
STEPHENSON JUDITH	JOEL CONNER
STEPHENSON MANN PATTERSON	SOPHIA W TODD

SPOUSE	ANCESTOR
STEPP LUCY	JOHN EDWARD NITE
STERNS CATHERINE	CHARLES WILLIAM POLK
STEVENS CAROLINE	BENJAMIN JESSE SKINNER
STEVENS HARRIET	JAMES H JOHNSON
STEVENS MRS NANCY ANN (HAMLET)	FRANCIS FOARD/FORD
STEVENSON WILLIAM MORTIMORE	ANN ADALINE DONALDSON
STEWART ANNA	CHARLES HAMMOND
STEWART DICEY	THOMAS WYNNE PLEASANTS
STEWART HAPPY	JOSEPH FOUSHEE
STEWART ISABEL	DUNCAN SMITH
STEWART JANE	TEMPLE BLAKELY
STEWART JANE	JOHN RICHARD STOCKARD
STEWART MARTHA	JOSHUA YATES
STEWART MARTHA CHRISTENE	JAMES FRED HAM/HAMM
STEWART MARY	BENJAMIN HAYGOOD
STEWART	WILLIAM CROMARTIE
STEWART	RUTH PARSONS
STEWART SALLIE	JIMMY TURLINGTON
STEWART SUSANNA	ALEXANDER CARTER
STICE ANDREW	NANCY GREEN WILSON
STICE DAVID	SARAH MCCRACKEN
STIERWALT MARGARET	JOHN THOMAS BRYANT
STILES PHATHA/FAITHA	JESSEE SAFLEY
STILES WILLIAM	SUSAN REBECCA EDWARDS
STILL BOAZ/BOOZE	MARY LYDA
STILL THOMAS ALLEN	ESTHER BARNHART
STILLEY JOHN	GRACE FOUNTAIN
STILLEY RACHEL	JOHN PIERCE IPOCK
STILLEY STEPHEN	ELIZABETH WHITFORD
STILWELL NANCY ANN	DANIEL COULTER
STINSON ALEXANDER	ELIZABETH BRADLEY
STINSON HARRIET REBECCA	JAMES ALEXANDER CLARK
STIREWALT JOHN	ELIZABETH RENDLEMAN
STOCKARD ELIZABETH	ROBERT ALGEE/ALGEA
STOCKARD JANE STEWART	JACOB LONG
STOCKARD JOHN R	CATHERINE ALBRIGHT
STOCKINGER CHRISTINA	RUDOLPH CONRAD
STOCKTON DAVIS	ELIZABETH BERTRAM
STOKES ELENDER JANE	HENRY HOUSTON
STOKES REBECCA	JAMES MCELROY
STOKES SARAH	THOMAS CAFFEY
STONE AMELIA/EMELIA	JESSE MOORE
STONE ELIZA	DANIEL PAFFORD
STONE ELIZABETH	AZARIAH DENNY
STONE SUSAN	VINCENT RUST/RUSS
STONEMAN NANCY	LEVI BURCHAM
STORYE STACY	ANDERTON TUCKER
STOUGH LEAH	ELI B HONEYCUTT
STOUGHTON JANE	ABNER COBLE
STOUT HANNAH	SIMON MOON
STOUT MARY	JOHN STUART
STOUT RACHEL	JOHN ALLEN
STOVER EMMILINE	THOMAS M KIMSEY/KIMZEY
STOVER MARY	ABSALOM HAWORTH

320

SPOUSE	ANCESTOR
STOWE ABRAHAM	MARY HORN
STOWE SALLIE/SARAH	JOHN HECTOR RALLS
STRADER CHRISTIAN	ZEPORIAH SUMMERS
STRADER ZEPORIAH	ELI FORD
STRAIN ELIZABETH	HARDY HARRINGTON
STRASENBURGH GORDON RANDALL	GLADY ETHEL CLARK
STRAWMAT ELEANOR ANN	CHARLES GARNER
STREET TEMPERANCE	RICHARD ELIJAH SHELTON
STRETTON SARAH	SAMUEL STANTON
STRICKLAND KINDRED	TEMPY REAVES
STRICKLAND RACHEL	JOSEPH MCADAMS
STRINGFELLOW ELIZABETH	JESSE BALDWIN
STRODE MARTHA	MORGAN BRYAN
STROP EVE	GEORGE WASHINGTON VAUGHAN
STROUD ICIE ANN	HANNIBAL CRITTENDEN ROBINSON
STROUD PHOEBE	ISAAC BEESON
STROUD TABITHA/ABI	THOMAS HOGAN
STROUP JOSEPH	CATHERINE CREASMAN/CHRISTMAN
STROW SARAH	SPENCER BIRD/BURD/BYRD
STROWD MARY	ISHAM THRIFT
STRUBLE BARBARA	JOHN HARPER
STRUTTON SALLEY	WILLIAM MILLS
STUART JOHN	MARY STOUT
STUCKEY EDMOND	EDITH HOWELL
STULL MRS SUSAN (RICE)	LEMUEL/KIT WRIGHT
STULTS CATHERINE	JONATHAN COLLIER
STURGILL FRANCES	TIMOTHY PERKINS
SUDDETH MASSA W	SAMUEL SURLES
SUGG AMY	MICAJAH PETTAWAY/PETWAY
SUGG AQUILLA	ABIGAIL BONNER
SUGG AQUILLA	NANCY HILL
SUGG ELIZABETH	GEORGE HARWARD/HARWOOD/HARROD
SUGG ELIZABETH	JOHN DUNCAN HARVEY
SUGG HARBARD	ZYLPHIA WRIGHT
SUGG JOHN	ELIZABETH MURPHREY/MURPHY
SUGG KISSIAH	WILLIAM MACE, II
SUGG MARY	AQUILLA SUGG, DR
SUGG MARY	WILLIS DIXON
SUGG QULLIA	LOUVANNER GARDNER/GARNER
SUGG WILLIAM	ELIZABETH SIMS/SIMMS
SUGGS MRS NANCY (HORSLEY)	ABRAHAM STOWE
SULLINS NOAH	MILLY M BYERS
SULLINS TRAIN	MERI ETTA MCCLURE
SULLIVAN NANCY	MADISON H TAYLOR
SULLIVAN SUSANNAH	ROBERT BULL
SULLIVANT NANCY	WILLIAM HARVEY/HERVEY
SUMMERS DONNA MARIE	JOHN HANBY FOARD/FORD, JR
SUMMERS JOHN	NANCY MYERS
SUMMERS MINNIE	WILLIAM HENRY GILL
SUMMERS NANCY M	HENRY W DEARMAN
SUMMERS SALLY	ABNER ROSE
SUMMERVILLE RHODA	HUMPHREY CUNNINGHAM
SUMNER ELIZABETH	JAMES BARNES
SUMNER ELIZABETH	ELISHA BATTLE

SPOUSE	ANCESTOR
SUMNER ELIZABETH	JOSPEH SUMNER/SUMMER
SUMNER JOSEPH	ELIZABETH SUMNER/SUMMER
SUMNER MARGARET	JOSIAH WILLIAMS
SUMNER SAMUEL	MARTHA/PATTIE ALSTON
SUTHERLAND ELIZABETH	ELISHA CROMWELL
SUTHERLAND PHILEMON	JANE ANN FEWELL
SUTTLE ELIZABETH	JAMES MORROW
SUTTON HELEN	JOHN MILLER
SUTTON KISANN	JOHN TAYLOR
SUTTON MARY	LEMUEL HARDY, JR
SWAIN JEREMIAH	HENRETTA SPRUILL
SWAIN SARAH ELIZABETH	THOMAS MASON WILLIAMS
SWANN ELIZABETH	JOHN BAPTISTA ASHE
SWANN EVA W	WILLIAM SHERMAN GILES
SWANNER HENRY	ELIZABETH WORLEY LEARY
SWANNER JESSE L	ELIZABETH LEGGETT
SWANNER THOMAS	DEBE LEGGETT
SWARTZLANDER KATHERINE	ABRAHAM ADAMS
SWEARINGEN THOMAS VAN	PENINA WALSTON
SWEARNIGEN ANSON	RICHARD WALKER
SWEPSON SARAH	LEONARD HENLEY SIMS
SWERINGEN ROSIANNA	JOHN BURCHAM, SR
SWIFT SARAH	NATHAN WILLIAMSON
SWINDAL OWEN	ELIZA JANE CAMPBELL
SWINGLE MARY MAGDALEN	WILLIAM BAKER DAVENPORT
SWINGLE SARAH	ALFRED DAVENPORT
SWOFFORD ENOCH	MARY/POLLY FRAZIER
SYKES MARTHA ANN	HENRY TARPLEY BOYCE
SYMMES ELIZABETH	BENJAMIN MAULDIN
SYMONS ELIZABETH	SAMUEL WHITE
TABER MARY	WILLIAM THOMPSON
TABOR ARRENA	JOHN KINSEY MILLER
TABOR MARY	WILLIAM THOMPSON
TACKETT MILDRED	BAYLIS COLE TACKETT/TACKITT
TALBERT ELIZABETH	ABRAHAM/ABRAM MILES
TALBERT SUSANNAH	ASHER KERSEY
TALLEY NOCHOLAS	JANE ELIZABETH CLAMPITT
TANKERSLY TABITHA	PHILIP G G BURFORD
TANNER ELIZABETH	ISAIAH S BECK, JR
TAPLEY HOSEA GREEN	ELEANOR R MCFARLAND
TAPLEY JOHN HOSEA	LUCY PRYOR
TARPLEY CATHARINE ETHLANA	ISAAC BATTS
TART PATSEY	ASA OVERTON
TART SARAH	ABRAHAM HAYNES
TARTER SUSAN VIRGINIA	WILLIAM MARSH
TARVER WINIFRED	JAMES TAYLOR
TATE CATHERINE	THOMAS GILL, II
TATE CELIA	THOMAS PETTIGREW
TATE FRANCES/FANNY	PETER WILLIS
TATE JAMES	MARGARET NELSON
TATE JENET	JOHN NELSON
TATE SUSAN L	JACOB L SHERRILL

322

SPOUSE	ANCESTOR
TATUM NANCY	SAMUEL BRIDGES
TATUM SARAH H	JAMES E OGBURN
TAYLOR CATHERINE	DANIEL STAMEY
TAYLOR DORCAS	JAMES ARNOLD
TAYLOR ELIZABETH	GEORGE N KELLER
TAYLOR HENRY	MARTHA JONES
TAYLOR JAMES	WINIFRED TARVER
TAYLOR JEAN/JANE	WILLIAM STARBUCK
TAYLOR JEREMIAH M	MARY GILBERT
TAYLOR JESSE	MARY ANN GINN
TAYLOR JOHN	MARY/POLLY NEELY
TAYLOR JOHN	KISANN SUTTON
TAYLOR JUDITH	SOLOMON BURRIS
TAYLOR LUCINDA ADALINE	FRANKLIN DEMARCUS HAYMORE
TAYLOR LUCY	GEORGE SMITH
TAYLOR MALINDA	ENOCH HAM/HAMM
TAYLOR MARGARET ANN MORNING	JOHN LAWRENCE GRAHAM MANNING
TAYLOR MARGARET/PEGGY	HENRY LOUDERMILK
TAYLOR MARY	WILLIAM MATTHEWS
TAYLOR MARY	THOMAS PUCKETT, SR
TAYLOR NANCY	MIRTILLO/MERTILLA KNIGHT
TAYLOR PATIENCE	JOHN HARRIS
TAYLOR PATIENCE	JOHN HARRIS
TAYLOR SARAH	JOSEPH YARBROUGH
TAYLOR SARAH	VINCENT CHANCE
TAYLOR SINAH	MICHAEL FINLEY
TAYLOR WILLIAM	FRANCES GASSAWAY
TEAGUE ABRAHAM	CATHERINE PERMELIA BROWN
TEAGUE ELIZABETH	JOSEPH STONE
TEAGUE ISABEL	JAMES WELBORN, SR
TEAGUE NANCY	JACOB LEROY MCGEE/MCGHEE
TEAS BARBARA	NOAH TUTTLE
TEMPLES MARY ANN	JAMES M KING
TENNISON REUBEN	NANCY SCOTT
TERRELL ABIGAIL	WILLIAM RUSH
TERRELL ABIGAIL	WILLIAM RUSH
TERRELL RUTH	ISAAC BROOKS
TESH JAMES MADISON	SUSAN JANE MARTIN
THATCHER MARY	GEORGE HODGSON
THIGPEN JAMES	MARTHA COBB
THIGPEN JAMES	LYDIA GREY MAYO
THIGPEN LEMUEL	ANNA CHERRY
THIGPEN MRS MARY (PARKER)	EATON COBB
THILBY ELIZABETH	BENJAMIN GRAYSON
THOGMARTIN WILLIAM	ORA LITTRELL
THOMAS CORNELIA JANE HOLLOWAY	DAVID T F HORN
THOMAS ELIZABETH	JEREMIAH BROOKS
THOMAS GRIFFITH	CHARLOTTE HUFFMAN
THOMAS JAMES	MILLIE STEPHENS/STEVENS
THOMAS KATHLEEN	LLOYD RANDOLPH COOPER
THOMAS MARTHA	JOHN HARRIS/HARRISS
THOMAS MARY ELIZABETH	CALVIN DOMAS KEY
THOMAS	JOHN HEATH
THOMAS NANCY ANN	FIELDING STRAWN

SPOUSE INDEX

SPOUSE	ANCESTOR
THOMAS POLLY/MARY	THOMAS HIGHTOWER
THOMAS SAMUEL	MARGARET MCCLAIN MATHEWS
THOMAS SARAH	JOHN MOORMAN
THOMAS TEMPERANCE	ELIJAH, PRICE, COL
THOMAS/THOMSON CREANY	WILLIAM WILSON
THOMASSON FLEMING	SARAH GOMER
THOMPSON ALFRED	JULIANA WOODY
THOMPSON BERTHA	WILLIAM ABNER LOWRANCE
THOMPSON CONSTANCE	ALMOND L BELVIN
THOMPSON ELIZABETH	WILLIAM GEORGE WASHINGTON BROWN
THOMPSON ELIZABETH H	JOHN GREEN ESKRIDGE
THOMPSON GRACE	DANIEL BROWN
THOMPSON HENRY	ELIZABETH LEE
THOMPSON JOHN	NANCY HAYGOOD
THOMPSON JOSEPH	SARAH MCALLISTER
THOMPSON MARGARET	LEVI TUCKER
THOMPSON MARGARET/PEGGY	GEORGE CLAYTON, JR
THOMPSON MARY	JESSE LEWIS
THOMPSON MARY	THOMAS HADLEY
THOMPSON NANCY E	ROBERT FRANKLIN WATERS
THOMPSON PETER	MARY POTTS
THOMPSON ROBERT/ROY FRANKLIN	RENA MAY ARRINGTON
THOMPSON SARAH	DAVID TACKETT/TACKITT
THOMPSON SOLOMON	ELIZA PICKETT
THOMPSON SUSAN ELIZABETH	JOHN MILLER LITCHFIELD
THOMPSON THOMAS ARRINGTON	KERENHAPPUCK SELLERS
THOMPSON THOMAS M	REBECCA JANE DUDLEY ROGERS
THOMPSON WILLIAM	MARY TABER/TABOR
THOMPSON WILLIAM	HANNAH BELL
THOMPSON/THOMSON ALFORD/ALFRED	ELMINA R CROWELL
THOMPSON/THOMSON ELMINA	WOODSON EATMAN
THORN/THORNE BERRY H	MARINDA/RENDA SHARP/SHARPE
THORN/THORNE CATHERINE	THOMAS RUFFIN LAMM/LAMB
THORN/THORNE MARTIN R	MARINDA/RENDA SHARP/SHARPE
THORN/THORNE NANCY ANN	THOMAS RUFFIN LAMM/LAMB
THORN? MRS MARINDA/RENDA (SHARP?)	MARTIN R THORN/THORNE
THORNBURGH HENRY	RACHEL MOON
THORNBURGH MRS JUDITH (HORN?)	JOSEPH UNTHANK
THORNTON CATHERINE	ELISHA SAWYER
THORNTON DOZIER	LUCY HILL
THORNTON SARAH/SALLIE	ISAC ROSS SHINN
THREET SARAH	JOHN POE
THURMAN LAURA M	PETER A WRENN/WREN
THWEAP/THWEATT MARTHA	JOHN ROGERS
TILLETT ELIZABETH	SIMEON BURGESS
TILLETT SARAH	WILLIAM S ETHERIDGE
TILLEY NANCY	JOHN WOOD
TIMBERLAKE RUTH	JOSEPH G PLEASANTS
TIMS ANNIE MAE	WILLIAM ALLEN WHITMIRE, I
TINNEN FRANCES	JOSEPH ARMSTRONG
TINNIN CATHERINE	THOAMS MCCRACKEN
TIPPETT JOHN	NANCY AVELINE DEWEESE
TIPPETT REBECCA	WILLIAM FORD
TIPPETT SUKE	JACOB FERRIBO/FARABOUGH

SPOUSE	ANCESTOR
TIPPIT GERTRUDE	JOHN THOMAS JENNINGS
TIPPS MR	BARBARA AWALT
TIPPS POLLY	PETER LIMBAUGH
TIPPS SARAH	MICHAEL AWALT
TIPPS SARAH	MICHAEL AWALT
TIPTON KATE	JOHN TURNER BLANKENSHIP
TIPTON LUCINDA	ABEDNIGO BENJAMIN HYATT
TIREY SUSANNAH	JOHN MILLER
TIREY THOMAS	MARY BEASLEY
TOBIAS MARY	MALACHI BROGDON
TODD CAROLINA PRISCILLA	JONATHAN HENRY HALL
TODD MARY	JESSE STATON ANDERSON
TODD MARY	JOHN CRAVER/GRABER/GREBER
TODD MARY	THOMAS MCGINN
TODD MOSES	BETSEY/ELIZABETH MASSEY/MASSY
TODD MRS MARGARET (TUCKER)	JESSE STATON ANDERSON
TOLBERT ELIZABETH	SPENCER MORGAN
TOLBERT/TALBOTT JANE	JOHN CAVE
TOLER AMANDA	CLAUDE E TUTEN
TOLIVER NANCY	RUSSELL BREWER
TOLLEY DAVID	SUSANNAH WILSON
TOLLEY HARRIET MARGARET	STEPHEN ZEBULON WILLIS
TOMLIN/TOMLINSON MARY/POLLY	INGRAM ALAN GILL
TOMLIN/TOMLINSON MOLLIE/MARY	THOMAS GILL
TOMLINSON ELIZABETH	JOHN BLAIR/BLEAR
TOMLINSON LOUISA	SOLOMON LAMM
TOMLINSON NANCY	STEPHEN YATES
TOMPKINS MARY	JOSEPH SEWELL
TOMS MRS MELINDA JANE (WEBB)	JACOB RHYNE SHUFORD/SCHFUFFERT
TORREY BEATRICE	MALCOLM PURCELL
TOTTEN SARAH REBECCA	HENRY MOLER, SR
TOUILLE/TWILLEY PATIENCE	ROBERT SOUTHERLAND, III
TOWNLEY MARY	JOHN REDFERN/REDFERN
TRADEWELL SARAH H	SIMON FARMER
TRAMMELL MINERVA JANE	NOAH WEBSTER BOONE
TRANSOU JAMES W	MARY A ROUSSEAU
TRANSOU JANE	SYLVANUS DAVID DAVIS
TRAVILLER ANN	SAMUEL UNDERWOOD
TRAVIS ELIZABETH	JOHN ALEXANDER
TRAVIS MRS SUSANNAH	LA MARE, FRANCIS DELAMAR/DE
TRAWICK FRANCES ANNA	ENOCH EILAND/ISLAND
TRAYLOR PASCHAL	MILLIE ANGLE
TRAYWICK MARTHA	BATCHELOR/BACHELOR/BACHLOTT,BENNETT
TREADWAY PRISCILLA	JOHN WESLEY WOODY
TRENTHAM MARY ELVIRA	ANDREW JACKSON BRADLEY
TREUTLEN ANN	MASSEY M COPELAND
TREVILLION HULDA	NEILL RAY WILKINSON
TRICE ELLEN/ELLENDER	WILLIAM HORTON
TRICE NANCY	SOLOMON G BARBEE
TRICKEY MRS MARGARET	DAVID PINKERTON
TRICKEY MRS MARGARET	DAVID PINKERTON
TRIM EMILY THOMAS	JULIUS COLUMBIAFRANKLIN WHEELEY
TRIPLETT LEWIS	BETSY CHURCH
TRIPLETT LUKE	MARTHA/PATSY HAMPTON

SPOUSE	ANCESTOR
TRIPLETT THOMAS	JANE FERGUSON
TRIPLETT VERLINDA	RICHARD FERGUSON
TRIPP CAROLINE	VALENTINE HARRIS
TROG ANNA MARIE	JOHN WEITZEL
TROTTER JANE	JAMES STANDLEY
TROTTER MARY/POLLY	JAMES STANDLEY
TROUSDALE ALEXANDER	NANCY EMILY ALLEN
TROUSDALE ELLEN	JAMES ANDREW STOCKARD
TROUSDALE MARY	JACOB SEWELL
TROUT MARY	BARNABAS BAXLEY
TROXLER ADALINE	BRISCO M STONE WARREN
TROXLER ELIZABETH	PETER HUFFMAN, JR
TROXLER NANCY HANNAH	GEORGE QUINCE WAGONER
TRULOVE LUCINDY	WILLIAM MORRIS, JR
TRULOVE SAMUEL	ELIZABETH MORRIS
TRUSS FANNY	KINCHEN GAMBLE
TRYON SELDON	PATIENCE E BIZZELL
TUBB SUSANNAH	WILLIAM TABER/TABOUR
TUCKER ELIZABETH	CALEB KNOTT
TUCKER FRANCES	WILLIAM PRUITT/PREWIT
TUCKER JOHN HAMPTON	MARY ANN BLAKELY
TUCKER MARY ANN	JESSE STATON ANDERSON
TUCKER MIRIAM GIBSON	BURKHEAD NEWTON MANN
TUCKER NETTIE	ABRAHAM STOWE
TUCKER NORRIS AMBROSE	MARGARET ALICE MCCOURRY
TUDOR TABITHA	PLEASANT WHITLOW
TUGMAN NANCY	BENJAMIN BROWN
TUGMAN WILLIAM	MARY HAWKINS
TUMBLESON ANN	DAVID LAIRD
TUNNELL MAHETTABLE	WILLIAM N BROOKS
TUNSTALL VIRGINIA	WILLIAM RUFFIN BUCHANAN
TURNBOUGH GRACE EMMELINE	JOHN CHARLES BROWN
TURNER ANNA	WILLIAM C BULL
TURNER ELIZABETH	JETHRO SUMNER
TURNER FREDERICK	MARY/POLLY JONES
TURNER JARRE	ISAAC CALLAHAN
TURNER MARGARET EVELINE	JAMES WILBURN KELLER
TURNER MARTHA	WILLIAM M BOBBITT
TURNER MARY	WEST HARRIS, SR
TURNER MARY	MATTHEW J TENNISON
TURNER	JARRELL KICKER
TURNER MRS REBECCA	THOMAS TURNER
TURNER NANCY	JESSE HARRELL
TURNER NANCY	JESSE E FRALEY
TURNER POLLY	SOLOMON PAINE
TURTLE MARY	DAVID PINKERTON
TURTLE/TUTTLE MARY	DAVID PINKERTON
TUSSEY JOHN	ELIZABETH HUNT
TUTOR SARA DORA	NATHAN IRA/A WESTER
TUTTLE BENJAMIN	GATSEY FOX
TUTTLE ELIZABETH	IVY WESLEY LASLEY
TUTTLE MARY	JOHN GORDON
TWIFORD BENJAMIN	ELIZA ANNE GRAY
TYNER SARAR CRAWFORD	FRANCIS COOK EDWARDS

SPOUSE	ANCESTOR
TYNER/TINER LUCY	JAMES BOONE
TYRE MARY	ZADOCK TUCKER
TYSON AARON	ELIZA ANNE JOHNSON
TYSON JUDITH	GEORGE SUGG
TYSON SIBERAH	JOSEPH GILBERT
TYSOR JULIA LACY	BENJAMIN JOSEPH BEAL/BEALE
TYSOR LEONIDAS ALONZO	FANNIE HEATON MAUZY
ULSH WILLIAM HOWARD	ADDIE IRENE GARNER
UNDERWOOD JAMES	MARGARET CAMPBELL
UNDERWOOD JOHN	SALLY WATSON
UNDERWOOD	FILLITHA/TALLITHA JELKS
UNDERWOOD OLIVE	ISAAC COX
UNTHANK REBECCA	JOHN HIATT
UPCHURCH LUCETTA	WILLIAM WOMBLE
UPCHURCH MARTHA M	KISER ALFORD
UPTEGROVE ELIZABETH C	EDMUND S KERBY
UPTON ADELAIDE	MARK ROBERTS GREGORY
UPTON JOHN	CAROLINE JARVIS
USSERY WELCOME	LUCY GROCE
VADEN REBECCA	JAMES BENNETT CONDITT/CONDICT
VALENTINE NANCY	DAVID LEE, JR
VALENTINE SOPHIA	JAMES DRAKE
VANCE HANNAH	JOHN LOWERY
VANCE MALINDA	HARVEY ALEXANDER MACE
VANCE TEMPERANCE	ARTHUR BUCHANAN
VANDERPOOL ABRAHAM	PHOEBE ISAACS
VANHOOK MARY/POLLY	ALEXANDER ROSE, JR
VANHOOK MRS MARY/POLLY	ALEXANDER ROSE, JR
VANHOY WILLIAM	ROSEY COBLE
VANNOY TEMPERANCE/TEMPY	DANIEL CAIN
VANOVER NANCY	WILLIAM KELLY KEEL
VANTRIESE ELIZABETH	FREDERICK SNYDER
VANZANT ELIZABETH	ABRAHAM KUYKENDALL/KIRKENDALL
VANZANT JOEL	SARAH E/SALLY LIMBAUGH
VARNER CATHERINE	MICHAEL FOUTS
VAUGH LUCY DE	ELIAS BRANCH
VAUGHAN CAREY ANN	JOHN WORTHAM
VAUGHAN GEORGE WASHINGTON	EVE STROP
VAUGHEN CELESTIA ANNA	PATRICK ANDERSON TUNSTALL
VAUGHN JESSE	OMARANNAH/MARANDA HALE
VAUGHN PEARL	GENERAL GEORGE WHITMIRE, I
VAUGHT SARAH/SALLY	FRANCIS COLEY
VEACH LURANAH	GREENBERRY GAITHER
VEAL SEABORN J	FLORIA RAY
VEASEY FRANCINA	WILLIAM MCCLELAN
VEAZEY JOHN	JANE RABUN
VENABLE/VENERABLE MARY	WILLIAM OLIVER
VENTERS SAPHRONIA	FURNIFOLD GASKINS
VESTAL RACHEL	FRANCIS BULLOCK
VESTAL MRS ELIZABETH (FOGLEMAN)	JOHN/JACK JOHNSON

327

SPOUSE	ANCESTOR
VESTAL MRS SUSAN (MACY)	SANFORD LEE STEELMAN
VIARS WILLIAM	ANNE SHEPHERD
VICKREY CHARLOTTE	PETER FIELD/FIELDS
VICKREY JERETER	JOSEPH NATION
VIERS/VIARS FANNIE	BENJAMIN DARNELL
VINSON GEORGANNA	RANSOM GARRIS, JR
VINSON ISABELLE	ROBERT DUKE/DUKES
VIVION LUCY PEMBERTON	NOAH SIMMONS
VOLUNTINE WINEFRED	WILLIAM BUFFALOE
WADDAIL ALICE	PETER F DEBNAM
WADDELL ISABEL	WILLIAM MCKNIGHT
WADE ELEANOR	ARCHELAUS COFFEY
WADSWORTH JOHN	ELIZABETH CARPENTER
WADSWORTH JOHN WILLIAM	SARAH MCSWEEN
WADSWORTH MARTHA ADELAIDE	NEILL BLUE CAMERON
WADSWORTH NANCY	DOUGALD MCKEITHAN
WADSWORTH WILLIAM	CATHERINE MCSWAIN
WAGGONER MILLY	THOMAS MARSHALL
WAGGONER NANCY JANE	JOHN A SHAW
WAGGONER MRS SARAH (BOONE)	ISAAC COX
WAGNER WINA S	JOHN ANDREW WALKER
WAGNON LELLA ARVILLA	ISAAC LINDSAY ABERNATHY
WAGONER GEORGE	REBECCA WHITESELL
WAINWRIGHT KENNON HARPER	NARCISSA ANN COOKE
WAINWRIGHT MARGUERITE	RICHARD GRANDE CATES
WAITES ANNY	MOREN MOORE
WAKEFIELD MARTHA	GEORGE HIATT
WALCHER ELIZABETH	DANIEL VALENTINE HARKEY
WALDROP JANE	WILLIAM S SPLAWN
WALK BARBARA	WILLIAM FRANK
WALKER ANNA BARBARY	JAMES MOORE/MOOR/MORE
WALKER ANNA BARBARY	JAMES MOORE
WALKER ANNA M	ELI STALEY MILLER
WALKER ANNE	JOHN A BURNS/BURNES
WALKER CASSAN HARRIET	JOSEPH MARION HARTNESS
WALKER CATY	WILLIAM ORR
WALKER DAVID BURNET	LOVIE CLEMENTINE ARWINE/ERVIN
WALKER ELIZA M	JOHN WORTHAM
WALKER JAMES	SUSAN ELIZABETH DEATON
WALKER JENNY	GEORGE FULP/FULPS
WALKER JESSE	MANIMIE WHITAKER
WALKER JOHN	ELIZABETH JARVIS/GERVES
WALKER JOHN	URCILLA COVINGTON
WALKER LEVINIA	JESSE BUNN
WALKER MARGARET	ROBERT ALBERT THOMAS
WALKER MARTHA	ROBERT DONALDSON
WALKER MARTHA	ROBERT DONALDSON
WALKER MARY	JESSIE WALTON
WALKER MARY	JOHN NEATHERY
WALKER MARY	JAMES HUNTER
WALKER MARY E	DAVID M CRAWFORD
WALKER NANCY	WILLIAM WEATHERLY

SPOUSE		ANCESTOR
WALKER	NANCY	BENJAMIN MAGNESS
WALKER	PATIENCE	BENONI LEE
WALKER	POLLY	ELIAS PENNELL
WALKER	SARAH	JAMES MERCER/MONROE BERRY
WALKER	WILLIAM	SARAH MCBRIDE
WALL	ANN	BENJAMIN FEWELL
WALL	GEORGIA ANN	JAMES BENNETT CONDITT/CONDICT
WALL	JINCY	JOSHUA HIGHTOWER
WALL	JOHN	SUSANNAH WHITEHURST
WALL	KITTY	DAVID PACE
WALL	LAURENCE STEWART	ALICE HENRIETTA WHITE
WALL	LYDIA	BENNETT CREECH
WALL	MARY	ROBERT A GILLIAM
WALL	NANCY	JOHN LOVE, JR
WALL/WALLS	MATILDA	JESSE WILLIAM CRAIN
WALLACE	AGNESS	EDMUND ANDREWS
WALLACE	MARY	JAMES STANDRIDGE
WALLICE/WALLACE	MARY	WILLIAM JELKS
WALLICE/WALLACE	SARAH	DIXON/DICKSON JELKS
WALTON	CAROLINE	KING LUTEN/LUTON
WALTON	ELIZABETH	ROBERT GILBREATH
WALTON	ELIZABETH	GEORGE LEDBETTER, CAPT
WALTON	MILDRED	JOHN CRAIN/CRANE
WARD	ELIZABETH	ISAAC WOOD
WARD	ELIZABETH	JAMES FOY
WARD	ELIZABETH	JAMES FOY
WARD	ELIZABETH	JOHN NOBLE/NOBLES
WARD	ELIZABETH	WILLIAM HADDOX
WARD	GEORGIA	RUFUS MOZINGO, SR
WARD	NANCY	DEMPSEY PERKERSON
WARD	NANCY	DANIEL BRYANT CARTER
WARD	PHOEBE	PHILLIP SHULL
WARD	RACHEL	JOSEPH MING
WARD	REBECCA	GREEN AUSTIN
WARD	RUTH	WILLIAM GRIFFIN/GRIFFIETH
WARD	SARAH	THOMAS REDMOND FARABOUGH
WARLICK	EVE CHRISTINA/CATHERINE	JOHN MARTIN SHUFORD/SCHEUFFERT
WARNICK	JANE	BENJAMIN WILSON
WARR	WILLIAM HENRY	FANNIE EZELL
WARREN	BRISCO M STONE	ADALINE TROXLER
WARREN	FREDERIC	MARY ANN MCREA
WARREN	LILLIE LEE	JOHN THOMAS PHILLIPS
WARREN	MARY ANN	JOHN GORDON PEARCE
WARREN	MARY/POLLY	THOMAS HOLMAN
WARREN	RUTH	EZEKIEL CLAMPITT
WARREN	SARAH	MATTHEW RABUN
WARREN	SUSANNAH	WILLIAM TERRELL BROOKS
WARTERS	MARTHA	WILLIAM M GARRIS
WASHBURN	JOHN	MARY ANN MAGNESS
WASHBURN	PRISCILLA MAUNEY	ANDERSON CROWDER WILLIAMSON
WASSON	MARY JANE	JOHN PURVIANCE
WASSON	RUTH	JOHN MCCRARY
WATERS	SIMON PETER	NANCY JANE BRITT
WATKINS	ANNIE	WILLIAM ORMOND, JR

SPOUSE	ANCESTOR
WATKINS ELLA ELSA	JASPER STARR/STOEHR
WATKINS MARY	JOSEPH DENSON
WATKINS	ELIZABETH WOODY
WATKINS PETER	DELILAH GRICE
WATKINS RACHEL	JAMES JONES
WATKINS RESE	MILLIE ANGLE
WATKINS MRS FANNY (LINDSAY)	JOHN WATKINS
WATLINGTON FRANCES	DAVID CHRISMON
WATSON DORCAS	JOHN HIGSON
WATSON JANE	JAMES SMYLIE/SMILEY
WATSON JEREMIAH	CATHERINE DIXON
WATSON JOHN	JANE SMYLIE/SMILEY
WATSON JOHN CURREY	SARAH WATSON HALL
WATSON LEWIS	CLARISSA FERGUSON
WATSON LITTLETON	ZELLA KEEN
WATSON LUCINDA	GEORGE PALMER
WATSON SALLY	JOHN UNDERWOOD
WATSON SOPHIA CARY	JOHN WEST LITCHFIELD, REV
WATSON WILLIAM	LUCINDA MCDOWELL
WATSON MRS SUSAN ANN (HARRIS)	REDDING STARKE BRINKLEY
WATSON MRS SUSAN ANN (HARRIS)	REDDING STARKE BRINKLEY
WATTERS ELIZABETH MILDRED BROWN	THOMAS JUNIUS DAVIS
WATTS ELIZABETH	ANDREW STEELE
WATTS ELIZABETH	SION HARRINGTON
WATTS MARGARET	DANIEL KILLIAN/KILIAN
WATTS	BATCHELOR/BACHELOR/BACHLOTT,BENNETT
WEATHERFORD SUSAN JANE	JAMES PINKERTON WEATHERFORD
WEATHERLY WILLIAM	NANCY WALKER
WEATHERS TELITHA	ALFRED POOL SMITH
WEATHERSBY THEODOCIA/SOPHIA	ALLEN EDGE
WEATHINGTON FRANCES MARION	SARAH HOLLIN
WEAVER ANN MORNING	JOHN TAYLOR
WEAVER ELISU	NANCY K JONES
WEAVER	CATHERINE AWALT
WEBB ELIZABETH	THOMAS DENNIS
WEBB MARY EDMONDSON	BAXTER DAVIS, JR
WEBB REUBEN	SOPHIA AWALT
WEBB WILLIAM	FRANCES YOUNG
WEBB WINIFRED	JOSHUA BEASLEY
WEEDON ELIZABETH	WILLIAM ISAAC COLVERT/CALVERT
WEEKS ELIZABETH	ARCHELAUS HAMMOND
WEHRLE MARY	DANEIL HUFF/HOUGH
WEISS ATHELENDA	ABRAHAM LYDAY/LYDA
WEITZEL ANNA MARGARET	JOHN ADAM STARR
WEITZEL ANNA MARIE	JACOB STARR
WEITZEL CATHERINE	JOHN STARR
WELBERN ISABELLA	ANTHONY WRIGHT
WELBORN MOSES	DEBORAH CHIPMAN
WELCH JOHN	MARY GILBERT
WELCH LAURA ELIZABETH	AVERY HILL WHITENER/WEIDNER
WELCH MARY	MESHACH COUCH
WELDER SOPHIA CATHERINE	JACOB ALBRIGHT
WELLER MARGARET ANN	DANIEL VALENTINE HARKEY
WELLMAN MARGARET	MARTIN SANER/SEHNERT

SPOUSE		ANCESTOR
WELLS	ELIZABETH	JACOB JOHNSON/JOHNSTON, SR
WELLS	MRS MARY ANN	BENJAMIN MINCE CLIFTON
WELLS	NANCY	JACOB PROCTORJR ? JOHNSON/JOHNSTON
WELLS	NANCY	JOSIAH MORRISON
WELLS	RACHEL	JOHN WRIGHT
WELLS	RACHEL	JOHN WRIGHT
WELLS/WILES	NETTIE	JAMES M WELBORN
WESCOTT	HENRY ARTHUR	CATHERINE M BEACH
WESCOTT	LEWIS W	ELIZABETH STANLEY
WESCOTT	MINNIE OLA KING	GEORGE HOLLAND PIVER
WEST	DICEA EASTINGS	WESLEY MANN
WEST	ELI	DELAIAH/LILA BARNES
WEST	FRANCES/FANNY	JOHN HAILE/HAIL/HALE
WEST	IGNATIUS	ELIZABETH MEACHAM
WEST	MARY	JOHN WILLIAM BULLARD
WEST	MARY JANE RICE	ZEBULON A SPRUIELL/SPRUILL
WEST	NANCY	SPENSER HALTOM
WEST	PATRICIA OVERSTREET	SAMUEL LEE
WEST	PATSY	WILLIAM DUNCAN
WESTER	NATHAN IRA/A	SARA/SALLY DORA TUTOR
WESTER	NORMA BLANCHE	ROYAL REAMS BROWN
WESTMORELAND	MARTIN	NANCY EMILY FULP
WETHERINGTON	CLEMENTINE/CLEMMIE	JOSEPH ARCHIE SMITH
WETHERINGTON	GASTON LENIOR	ANN/ANNIE DIXON WILLIS
WHALEY	SARAH	JESSE LANIER
WHARTON	REBECCA	SHIRLEY WHATLEY
WHATLEY	LYDIA	BRYANT EILAND/ISLAND
WHEELBARGER	SARAH	JOHN MOLER
WHEELER	MARY ELIZABETH	WILLIAM THOMAS MILLIS
WHEELER	MILLY	GEORGE GLIMP
WHEELER	SALLIE	MATTHEW COUNCIL/COUNCILL
WHEELER	SARAH	THOMAS BEATTY, JR
WHEELER	ZILPHIA	SAMUEL BURTON
WHITAKER	ABRAM	NANCY SMITH
WHITAKER	JOSHUA	NANCY CHILDERS/CHILDRESS
WHITAKER	JOSHUA	MARY REED/REID
WHITAKER	MANIMIE	JESSE WALKER
WHITAKER	MARGARET	DAVID GARREN/GARN
WHITAKER	MARK	CATHERINE BOONE
WHITAKER	MIRIAM	LOTT HARPER
WHITAKER	PETER	MIRIAM F KENT
WHITAKER	WILLIAM	ELIZABETH CARLETON/CARLTON
WHITAKER	MRS LEAH CRAWLEY(LENOIR)	JOHN WALL NORWOOD
WHITAMORE	ELIZABETH	WILLIAM SMITH
WHITBY	MRS MARTHA ANN (HERBERT)	TEAGLE WALTER CUTHRELL
WHITE	AMANDA E	JOSEPH DEANS
WHITE	ANNA ELIZABETH	BENAJAH/BENNAJAH HIATT
WHITE	BETTIE	WOODSON EATMAN
WHITE	BETTY	THOMAS BANKS
WHITE	DOLLY	ABSALOM BOSTICK, II
WHITE	FRANCES	WILLIAM GEORGE SANDERS
WHITE	GEORGE HENRY	ANNIE AUGUSTUS NICHOLS
WHITE	ISAAC	ANNE REED
WHITE	JANE	WILLIAM MILLIKAN

SPOUSE INDEX

SPOUSE	ANCESTOR
WHITE JOEL	SUSANNA SEARS
WHITE JOHN	MARY CAROLINA THRIFT
WHITE LOUISA JANE BARNETT	JOEL PATON SETSER/SETZER
WHITE LOUVENIA	JOHN WILLOUGHBY WHITEHEAD
WHITE LUCINDA	JAMES M LUTHER
WHITE MARGARET	ROBERT CARUTHERS
WHITE MARY	JOSEPH M CARTWRIGHT, JR
WHITE	MELISSA ELIZABETH SMITH
WHITE SHERWOOD	SUSANNAH WARREN BROOKS
WHITE WILLIAM	ELIZABETH BOONE
WHITE WILLIAM	ZILPHA C MCKAY
WHITE MRS MARY JANE (HENDON)	GEORGE CROMARTIE
WHITE MRS MELISSA ELIZABETH (SMITH)	JAMES CICERO SMITH
WHITEHEAD ARIAMINTA	CHRISTIAN MILLER
WHITEHEAD MARY	MICAJAH HEMINGWAY/HEMENWAY
WHITEHEAD MARY	BENJAMIN DENSON
WHITEHEAD SABRA	REUBEN/RHEUBEN STEPP
WHITEHURST MARGARET	MICAJAH MANNING
WHITEHURST PRISCILLA	JAMES BRYAN/BRYANT
WHITEMAN BARBARA	DAVID CORTNER/COTNER
WHITESELL CATHERINE	HENRY JOHNSTON/JOHNSON, SR
WHITESELL REBECCA	GEORGE WAGONER
WHITFIELD JEMINA HEYWARD	ROBERT MIDDLETON
WHITFIELD MARY	JOHN DICKSON PEARSALL
WHITFIELD SARAH	JOSEPH GREEN
WHITFORD ELIZABETH	STEPHEN STILLEY
WHITFORD ELIZABETH	STEPHEN STILLEY
WHITFORD MARTIN	SARAH/MARY PUREFOY
WHITINGTON PEGGY	ALLEN JOHNSON, SR
WHITLEY JULIAN	JACOB BARNES
WHITLEY MARY	BIGGERS JACKSON
WHITLEY RHODA	JOHN HENDERSON
WHITLEY SARAH	JOSIAH WHITLEY
WHITLEY MRS ELIZABETH/BETSY (WILLIAMSON)	BURWELL TEMPLE
WHITLOCK ELIZABETH ADELINE	LUCIUS QUINTUS CINCINNATIUS BUTLER
WHITMIRE CHRISTOPHER COLUMBUS	HANNAH GALLOWAY
WHITNEY ELIZABETH	ISHAM ROYALL
WHITSETT KEZIAH	ALLEN MCDONALD
WHITSETT MARGARET	JOSEPH MCADAMS
WHITT ESTHER	JONATHAN JOB
WHITT MARGARET	JOSEPH ADOLPHUS MANN
WHITTED JANE	SAMUEL BURTON FISHER
WHITTED NANCY	JOHN YOUNG
WHITTEN JOHN	MARY REAGAN
WHITTEN SILAS REAGAN	ELEANOR KEE EARLE
WHITTIER BARBARA	JOHN PATTERSON
WIBLING JANNETJE	ABRAHAM VANDERPOOL
WICKLIFFE ELIZABETH	NICHOLAS ADAMS BRAY
WIGERLY ABIGAIL	RICHARD WRIGHT, SR
WIGFIELD ARTHUR	JENNIE CRISP/CHRISP
WIGGINS	ELIZABETH JELKS
WIGGINS MRS GRACE (TILLETT)	JAMES PETTIGREW TEMPLE
WIKLE MARY/POLLY	LEWIS SMITH

SPOUSE		ANCESTOR
WILBURN	PRUDENCE	RUBEN KENNEDAY
WILCOXSON	MARTHA	JOHN WESLEY KILBY
WILDER	AMITTEE	JASON GREGORY
WILDER	CHLOE	JACOB WILLIAMS
WILES	WILLIAM LARKIN	RACHEL CLARISSA HARRIS
WILEY	JANE	WILLIAM M SECREST
WILEY	MARY	THOMAS LANGLEY
WILEY	MARY ANN	JESSE G SHOEMAKER
WILEY	MARY MILLIS	ROBERT GRAY
WILFONG	MARY	DANIEL WHITENER/WEIDNER
WILHELM	SOPHIA	DAVID WILSON SHIVES
WILHOIT	JAMES BUCHANAN	SARAH JANE BARNES
WILKERSON	MARGARET	GEORGE PLOTT
WILKERSON	SUSAN M	GEORGE WASHINGTON POOLE
WILKINS	CECILE	WILLIE EVERETTE OAKLEY
WILKINS	JAMES ALEXANDER	MARTHA O ESTES
WILKINS	MARY STEPNEY	JACOB HOLT
WILKINS	MATILDA	LEMUEL INGRAM
WILKINSON	ELIZABETH	JAMES W RILEY
WILKINSON		BARNABY GODWIN
WILKINSON	PETER	SARAH ANN MCNAIR
WILLIAMS	ABEL	MARGARET/PEGGY CARLOCK
WILLIAMS	ADELINE	JAMES A DEBNAM
WILLIAMS	ANN	JOHN WRIGHT
WILLIAMS	ANN	JOHN WRIGHT
WILLIAMS	BEDY TAYLOR	JOHN GREEN
WILLIAMS	BEDY/OBEDIENCE TAYLOR	JOHN GREEN
WILLIAMS	BETSEY	LUKE LAMB
WILLIAMS	BETSEY	JOHN L TAYLOR
WILLIAMS	CAROLINA FISHER	SAMUEL MARION ROBBINS
WILLIAMS	CELET/CELETA	CHARLES MCCALL
WILLIAMS	CHARITY	WILLIAM HIATT
WILLIAMS	CHARITY	JOSEPH SPEARS BUCHANAN
WILLIAMS	CHARLOTTA ANN/ANNIE	JOSEPH FARROW
WILLIAMS	CHRISTIAN	ZACHARIAH HAM/HAMM
WILLIAMS	CLARISSA	JOHN SHINE
WILLIAMS	DORCAS	NATHAN SPENCER
WILLIAMS	ELIZABETH	THOMAS HICKS
WILLIAMS	ELLIS I	ALSIE/ALCY WOOTEN
WILLIAMS	EULA ALCY	WILLIAMLUTHER MACKIE/MACKEY/MACKAY
WILLIAMS	FRANCES	JOHN HODGES DRAKE, DR
WILLIAMS	GEORGE A	MARY WOMBLE/WOMBWELL
WILLIAMS	GEORGE HODGES	MARY ANN MASON
WILLIAMS	HANNAH	HAMPTON QUEEN
WILLIAMS	HENRIETTA	MATHEW PYOR, JR
WILLIAMS	HENRY DALLAS	SARAH MARGARET WILLIAMS
WILLIAMS	JACOB DAWSON	MARTHA ANICE RODES/RHODES
WILLIAMS	JESSE	RUTH MARTIN
WILLIAMS	JOHN	MARY/POLLY ASHWORTH
WILLIAMS	JOHN WILLIS	DORCAS CREDLE
WILLIAMS	JOSEPH	SOPHIA THORNBURGH
WILLIAMS	JOSIAH	MARGARET SUMNER
WILLIAMS	JULIUS RUFUS	LEECY NORMAN

SPOUSE		ANCESTOR
WILLIAMS	LEVISA	ISAAC BEESON
WILLIAMS	MARGARET	JESSE ARNETT
WILLIAMS	MARGARET	ANTHONY CHAMNESS
WILLIAMS	MARGERY	NOAH TUTTLE
WILLIAMS	MARTHA	EPHRAIM PRICE
WILLIAMS	MARTHA SARAH	JOSEPH NELSON
WILLIAMS	MARY	WILLIAM JELKS
WILLIAMS	MARY	HOOSER, ABRAHAM VAN
WILLIAMS	MARY ALEXANDER	JAMES PAINE
WILLIAMS	MARY ANN	WILLIAM ARRINGTON, GEN
WILLIAMS	MARY POLLY	JOHN WESLEY SIMPSON
WILLIAMS	MARY/POLLY	MATHEW PYOR, JR
WILLIAMS	MOLLY	JOSHUA WILSON
WILLIAMS	NANCY	BENJAMIN TAYLOR
WILLIAMS	NANCY CAROLINA	GEORGE STEELMAN
WILLIAMS	PAULINE	JERRY THOMAS SILANCE
WILLIAMS	PHYSA R	JESSE MACKIE/MACKEY/MACKAY
WILLIAMS	PLEASANT G	RUTH REECE
WILLIAMS	RICHARD	ELIZABETH MORRIS
WILLIAMS	RILEY WILSON	LOVE CARTER
WILLIAMS	ROSANNA	WILLIAM SPARKMAN
WILLIAMS	ROXANNA	MARCUS RYAN JOHNSON
WILLIAMS	RUTH JANE	SANFORD LEE STEELMAN
WILLIAMS	SARAH MARGARET	HENRY DALLAS WILLIAMS
WILLIAMS	SUPHRONIA	ROBERT FLETCHER WILSON
WILLIAMS	TEMPERANCE	WILLIAM LEWIS HINTON
WILLIAMS	THOMAS	ELIZABETH HARDING
WILLIAMS	URRISA/EUNICE	WILLIAM MONTGOMERY PYRON
WILLIAMS	WILLIAM	RACHEL NELSON
WILLIAMS	MRS MARY GLADYS (ANDERSON)	WILLIAM ALLEN WHITMIRE, I
WILLIAMSON	ANDERSON CROWDER	PRISCILLA MAUNEY WASHBURN
WILLIAMSON	ARCHIBALD	NANCY CROWDER
WILLIAMSON	ISAAC	ELEANOR KEY
WILLIAMSON	MARY	DUNCAN GREEN CAMPBELL
WILLIARD	SOLOMON	HANNAH CLAMPITT
WILLIS	ANN/ANNIE DIXON	GASTON LENOIR WETHERINGTON
WILLIS	BETTIE	ABEL OLIVE
WILLIS	ELIZABETH	JAMES BUCHANAN
WILLIS	FRANCES/FANNY	JESSE REYNOLDS/RUNNELS
WILLIS	PETER	FRANCES/FANNY TATE
WILLIS	SARAH E	WILLIAM H WINDERS
WILLIS	WILLIAM M	LUCINDA WILSON
WILLITS	SARAH	OWEN WILLIAMS
WILLOUGHBY	POLLY	NATHANIEL W PRIDGEON
WILLS	JAMES IRA	CYNTHIA ANNE THRIFT
WILLSON	ROSANNAH	JOHN MCALLISTER
WILSON	ABIGAIL	DAVID MILTON POE, SR
WILSON	ALEXANDER	NANCY FUSSELL
WILSON	BETSY	ROBERT BOOKER MAY
WILSON	CANDACE	NATHAN MILLS
WILSON	CHARLES H	MURIEL C GREGORY
WILSON	CHARLES H	LOVEY ANN HARRIS
WILSON	ELIZABETH	HENRY RUPPE
WILSON	ELIZEBETH	HENRY RAY/RHEA

SPOUSE		ANCESTOR
WILSON	ELVIRA	WILLIAM HERRING SKINNER, SR
WILSON	GENNET	JOHN HOLMES
WILSON	HULDAH	JACOB SHERRILL
WILSON	JANE	ANDREW MILLER
WILSON	JOHN	CHARITY RAGLAND
WILSON	JOHN	SARAH BOONE
WILSON	JOSEPH J	ELIZA PARHAM
WILSON	LUCINDA	WILLIAM M WILLIS
WILSON	MARY	THOMAS CARDWELL
WILSON	MARY	WILLIAM BLALOCK/BLAYLOCK
WILSON	MARY	BENJAMIN BOONE
WILSON	MARY/MARIA	EZEKIEL POLK
WILSON	MEHITABLE	WILLIAM OWEN CHAFFIN
WILSON	MYRTLE LOIS	CHARLES W RAY/RHEA
WILSON	NANCY GREEN	ANDREW STICE, JR
WILSON	RACHAEL	MARK COOK
WILSON	RACHEL	HENRY COBB
WILSON	SARAH	THOMAS GORDON
WILSON	SARAH ANN	FREDERICK STINSON
WILSON	SOPHIA ANN	THOMAS JEFFERSON HOOPER
WILSON	SUSANNA	DAVID TOLLEY/TOLLY
WILSON	THOMAS	EASTER COBB
WILSON	WILLIAM	CHARLOTTE HUCKABEE
WILSON	MRS ANNA C (BINGHAM)	JOHN SAMUEL LACKEY
WIMBERLY	ELIZABETH	FREDERICK P CULLEN
WIMBLEY	MARY	THOMAS CAUSEY
WINDERS	NANCY ANN	JESSE SWINSON
WINDLEY	EDIE ELIZABETH	SOLOMAN SAMPSONSATCHWELL WINDLEY
WINDLEY	MARY ELIZA	HOWARD LUCAS BROOKS
WINGATE	EDWARD	SARAH CREECY
WINGATE	JOHN RICHARD	CORNELIA ADREN DAIL
WINGATE	LEVI	MARTHA M HARRELL
WINGET	ZIBA	MARGARET THOMAS
WINKLER	SARAH	SOLOMON KELLER
WINSLOW	LYDIA	JOHN WHITE
WINSTON	CATHERINE	EZEKIEL PENNY
WINTERS	DELPHIA JANE	CHRISTOPHER DUNBAR GILES
WIRICK	SUSANNAH	MICHAEL WITT
WISE	CLARA	PHILIP COULTER
WISE	HARNEY	PHOEBE NEWBOLD
WISE	LOVEY	JAMES BENJAMIN PALMER/PARMER
WISE	MARY	NEEDHAM OLIVER
WISE	MARY	NEEDHAM OLIVER
WISE	MATTHEW	NANCY FREEMAN
WISE/WEISS	BARBARA	THOMAS RHYNE/REIN
WISEMAN	ELIZABETH	HEZEKIAH OWEN
WISHON	JULIA	EDWARD HOUSTON REECE
WISON	PAMELA	MARCUS T C KENNEDY
WITE/WYATT	ELIZABETH	WRIGHT WINGATE
WITHERSPOON	SARAH	WILLIAM ROUSSEAU
WITT	CHARITY	DUNCAN CARMICHAEL
WITT	CHARITY	DUNCAN/DUNKIN CARMICHAEL
WITT	JANE	CONRAD SHOEMAKER, JR
WITTY	MARY	JAMES BRITTAIN

SPOUSE	ANCESTOR
WITZELL MRS MARGARET (FAIN)	JOHN THOMAS
WOLF JOHNATHAN	SARAH MULLINS
WOLFE SARAH E	PLEASANT ISRAEL
WOLFE WILLIAM WESLIE	MARGARET CORA MCMINN
WOMACK ELIZABETH	BENJAMIN STEPHEN COLEMAN
WOMACK ISABELLA	WILLIAM N HAWS
WOMACK JOHN	LUCY PRYOR
WOMACK LUCY	WILLIAM BLALOCK
WOMACK MARY	SAMUEL MCREE
WOMACK MARY	WILLIAM ROWLAND/ROLAND
WOMACK	JOHN HARMAN
WOMBLE JACOB	MARY LAWRENCE
WOMBLE MARY	GEORGE A WILLIAMS
WOMBLE THOMAS	NANCY OUTLAND
WOOD CENA	JOHN WILSON BOONE
WOOD JOHN CAMPBELL	MRS FRANCES E DENSON
WOOD LEDDY	EDWARD WILLIAMS, JR
WOOD LYDIA ELVA	DANIEL WEBSTER HODGIN
WOOD NANCY ANN	JOHN ASHWORTH
WOOD SARA JOHN	WILLIS MONROE BARBEE
WOOD SYLVIA	WILLIAM WATKINS
WOOD WILLIAM	POLLY RUPPE
WOOD WILLIAM H	EASTER/HISHA AMOS
WOOD/WOODS ANN/ANNA	WILLIAM GAUNT/GUANT
WOODALL SARA	ELI TURLINGTON, SR
WOODARD HARRIETT	GEROGE STEWART
WOODELL CELINA	ZACHARIAH MANN
WOODFIN DEMY/DENNA	JOSEPH DENNIS GASH
WOODRUFF JOHN T	ELISABETH CARTER
WOODS ANN	JAMES MONTGOMERY
WOODS ELIZABETH	ARCHIBALD WASSON
WOODS MARTHA/PATSY	JOSEPH; ALLISON, GEN
WOODS MATILDA	WILLIAM GIDEON/GIDDENS
WOODS NETTIE	WILLIAM GEORGE POTTS
WOODS WILLIAM	JANE BROWN
WOODS MRS REBECCA (BERRY)	JOHN EARLE, COL
WOODSTOCK COMFORT	GEORGE MALLARD
WOODSTOCK JOYCE	ROBERT SOUTHERLAND, II
WOODWARD MARY	JOHN GRIGG/GIRGGS
WOODWARD/WOODARD THOMAS	LYDIA LANGSTON
WOODY NELLIE	JAMES COGDILL
WOODY SUSANNAH	GEORGE ROBERSON/ROBESON
WOODY WILLIAM	SARAH PARCEL/PERCEL
WOODY WILLIAM HENRY	SARAH POLLY ? EDWARDS
WOOLARD ELLEN	MOSES ALLIGOOD
WOOLLEY ELIZABETH	JOHN ALBERT DONNELL
WOOTEN ALSIE-ALCY	ELLIS WILLIAMS, I
WOOTEN MARY	JAMES JOHNSON
WOOTEN MRS ESTHER (ALDRIDGE)	ISAAC KORNEGAY
WOOTON LEWIS	MARTHA/PATTY PUCKETT
WOOTON RACHEL	JAMES GUNSTON
WORLEY ABIGAIL	HUSS, VALENTINE VAN
WORLEY ELIZABETH	THOMAS LEARY
WORLEY MARGARET	JESSE CREECH

SPOUSE	ANCESTOR
WORTH MATILDA	LATHAM FOLGER
WORTHY MARY	NEILL CAMERON
WREN/WRENN JOHN	DELILA/DELILAH JANE RICKARD
WREN/WRENN JOHN CARROLL	MARY/MOLLY EDWARDS
WRENN MARY/POLLY	GREEN WALKER BUNN
WRIGHT ANN	JOHN TATOM, SR
WRIGHT CHARITY	WILLIAM MAXWELL
WRIGHT LEMUEL	CHARITY RICKS
WRIGHT LYDIA	HEZEKIAH/LONG'KIAH BURGESS
WRIGHT MARTHA	GEORGE SMITH
WRIGHT MARY	JOHAN FRIE-DERICH HER RINTELMAN/RINGLEMAN
WRIGHT MARY	JUSTUS/JUSTICE REYNOLDS
WRIGHT MARY	JOHN FREDERICK HERMAN RANDLEMAN
WRIGHT MARY M	ELTHA C A PARKS
WRIGHT NANCY	HOLLAND MCGEE
WRIGHT RACHEL	WILLIAM HOWREN
WRIGHT SARAH/SALLY	JOSIAH JOHNSON
WRIGHT SELINA	WILLIAM CRAVER/GRABER/GREBER
WRIGHT THIRZIA	SOLOMON REYNOLDS
WRIGHT WILLIAM	MARTHA/BETSY MORGAN
WRIGHT WINNIFRED	ALFRED JOHNSON/JOHNSTON
WRIGHT ZILPHIA	HARBERT/HARBARD SUGG/SUGGS
WYATT ELIZABETH	JAMES OATES/OATS
WYMAN MARY/POLLY	PHILIP BOSS
WYNN ELIZABETH	JACOB EBERHART, JR
WYNN RACHEL	ELKANAH DAVENPORT
WYNNE EVALINA BELMONT	RICHARD FREEAR
WYRICK MARY	WILLIAM OLIPHANT
YARBOROUGH MARTHA	JAMES HUTCHENS
YATES MARY/POLLY	JAMES MCNEELEY
YATES NANCY	ABSALOM JARRELL
YEOMANS LOUISA	JOHN BELLENFANT/BALLANFANT
YORK DORCAS	ISAIAH S BECK, SR
YORK ELI	SUSANNAH HARDEN
YORK HARDEN	MARY/POLLY JONES
YORK LOUISA	WILLIAM GREEN DURHAM
YORK SARAH	MARK HARDEN, JR
YORK SUSAN	WILLIAM BURROW
YOUNG AVE	SAMUEL MARCOM/MARKHAM
YOUNG CLARA	GREEN JORDAN PETTIGREW
YOUNG ELIZA	JOHN A HALL
YOUNG FRANCES	WILLIAM WEBB
YOUNG GEORGE BROWN	CHARITY BARDIN
YOUNG ISABELLA	ANDREW JACKSON BROWN
YOUNG ISHAM	NANCY HARVEY
YOUNG JOHN	ROSEANNAH HEMPHILL
YOUNG JOHN	NANCY WHITTED
YOUNG JOHN A	MARGARET INEZ HUNSUCKER
YOUNG JOSEPH	LUCY PERKINS
YOUNG MARTHA/PATSY	WILLIAM GUDGER
YOUNG MARY ELLEN	GEORGE MAUZY
YOUNG NANCEY	JAMES MARION WHITMIRE

SPOUSE	ANCESTOR
YOUNG NAOMA	FRANKLIN PIERCE SLAGLE
YOUNG SALLIE/SARAH ANN MARIE	WILLIAM FRANCIS SPEIGHT
YOUNG SARAH MARGARET	JOHN CICERO KOONCE
YOUNG SUSANNAH	WILLIAM GILL
YOUNG MRS LYDIA (RASPBERRY)	WILLIAM TAYLOR
YOUNG MRS SARAH (NORFLEET)	JOHN YOUNG
YOUNGBLOOD NANCY	WILLIAM WILEY
YOUNGBLOOD SARAH	JOHN AUSTIN
YOUNGER CORA BELLE	JOHN FILLMORE HUGHES
YOUNGER MARY/POLLY	JOSEPH GILBERT
YOUNGMAN SUSANNAH	CONRAD SHOEMAKER, SR
YOW BETSY	LEWIS GARNER
ZEBULIN EDITH	JOHN HENRY LOPP/LAPP/LOOP, SR
ZIKE JOSEPH	EMELINE LINVILLE
ZIKE MRS EMELINE (LINVILLE)	JOHN HESTER, JR

SPOUSE INDEX: DOUBTFUL NAMES
MAIDEN NAMES
DOUBLE SURNAMES

SPOUSE	ANCESTOR
ABERNATHY, MARGARET	THOMAS BEATTY, SR
ABERNATHY, NANCY	ENOS MORGAN
ALDERMAN, THERESA	ALLEN BEACH
ALDRIDGE, ESTHER (MRS WOOTEN)	ISAAC KORNEGAY
ALLEN, ELIZABETH	EZEKIAL B CURRIE
ANCEL, ELIZABETH COLUMBIA (MRS MABRY)	PINKNEY THRIFT
ANDERSON, MARGARET (MRS STAGGS)	ROBERT FRANKLIN WATERS
ANDERSON, MARY ANN (MRS SAPPINGTON)	JEREMIAH ROWLAND
ANDERSON, MARY GLADYS (MRS WILLIAMS)	WILLIAM ALLEN WHITMIRE, I
ANDREWS, SUSANNAH LEA	JOHN THOMPSON, SR
BARHAM, RUTH (MRS ABERNATHY)	JAMES PAINE
BARNES, GERIAH (MRS MULLIS)	WILLIAM GOFORTH
BARNES, JOSEPH	DELAIAH/LILA BARNES
BEAL, SUSANNA JANE (MRS PRICE)	JAMES MCDOWELL DELLINGER
BELL, ELIZABETH HARDY (MRS HILL)	RICHARD BRYANT TAYLOR
BERRY, REBECCA (MRS WOODS)	JOHN EARL, COL
BINGHAM, ANNA C (MRS WILSON	JOHN SAMUEL LACKEY
BIRD, MOLLIE	JAMES ARMSTRONG
BLADES, NANCY E (MRS HOOD)	THOMAS W BROWN
BLOUNT, MARY	SOLOMON SUTTON
BOHANNAN, MARY	JOSEPH BARBEE
BOHANNON /BUCHANAN, JOHN	ELEANOR MCCRACKEN
BONNER, ABIGAIL (MRS JONES)	AQUILLA SUGG

338

SPOUSE	ANCESTOR
BOOKOUT, MARMADUKE	RACHEL MOON
BOONE, SARAH (MRS WAGGONER)	ISAAC COX
BOWDRE, JOICY (MRS FEARS)	JOHN JOHNSON
BRADLEY, ELIZABETH	JAMES MOON
BRADLEY, MILLY	LITTLEBERY BELISLE
BRANTLEY, MAGGIE (MRS BROOKS)	ENOCH PHILLIPS
BRIGHT, ANN (MRS NELSON)	THOMAS GASKINS
BROWN, ANN	JOSEPH MOON
BROWN, ELIZABETH (MRS HANCOCK)	JAMES PAINE
BROWN, MARY ANN (MRS BUTLER)	LUNSFORD AYCOCK
BROWN, MELLICENT (MRS. JACKSON	MARK R GREGORY
BROWN, RACHEL	WILLIAM ALLRED
BRYAN, MARGARET	JAMES MCDANIEL/MCDONALD
BRYANT, MARGARET (MRS BULLOCK)	JOHN LAWRENCE GRAHAM MANNING
BUNCH, NANCY	ISAAC PHILLIPS
BURGESS, ABY (MRS NEEDHAM)	PAUL PUGH/PEW
BURNEY, ELIZABETH	WILLIAM OLIPHANT
BUSTIN, FRANCES (MRS SLATTER)	JOHN WILLIAMS, MAJ
BUTTER, LUCRETIA (MRS MOORE)	LEMUEL MOORE
CAIN, NANCY	GRAY BARBEE
CAMPBELL?CROOM, ELIZABETH/BETSY	WILLLIAM MAXWELL
CANNADY, MARGARET	JAMES BECK
CASS, ELIZABETH	ABRAM/ABRAHAM COOK
CHERRY, MARY ANN ELIZABETH (MRS OTEY)	BENJAMIN D LANGFORD/LANKFORD
CLAYBOURN, SARAH (MRS COTTON)	ZADOCK SIMMONS
CLOPTON, ELIZABETH (MRS MORRIS)	WILLIAM BALLARD
COBB, RUTHA ANN (MRS BIRD)	MARCUS RYAN JOHNSON
COLLIER	ELIZABETH (LANE) PROBERT
COLLINS, MARILDA (MRS BEASLEY)	EPHRAIM OXFORD BEASLEY
CONRAD, SARAH	NATHANIEL KETNER
COTTON, TALITHA (MRS HOBDY)	DEMSEY POWELL
COSTIN, MARY	ANTHONY FENTRESS TOON
COX, MARY	STEPHEN LEE
CRESON, JANE (MRS CUNNINGHAM)	CHARLES STEELMAN/STEALMAN
CROOM?CAMPBELL, ELIZABETH/BETSY	WILLIAM MAXWELL
CROW, ELIZABETH	LEWIS WAGGONER
CULBERTSON, MARY JANE (MRS FOSTER)	JAMES MILES KILLIAN GUINN
DARNELL, ROXIE (MRS HART)	DAVID TUCKER, III
DAVIS, LIZZIE CATHERINE (MRS MASHBURN)	JAMES WILLIAM PEARCE
DAVIS, MARTHA/PATSY (MRS KING)	JESSE VESTAL
DAVIS, NATHAN	REBECCA SPENCER
DAYVAULT, LYDIA	DANIEL SEFIRD/SEFFERT
DEANS, JOSHUA	PENELOPE TURNAGE
DE LA FONTAINE, FRANCES	JEMINA JOHNSON/JOHNSTON
DILLEMORE, LYDIA (MRS COTTER)	JAMES BECK
DOCTON, RACHEL	ABNER EASON
DOUGLASS, MRS ELIZABETH	CHARLES STEELMAN/STEALMAN
DUKE, NANCY	ROBERT PLEASANTS
DURDEN, JANE	WILLIAM WATKINS
DYSON, MARY JANE (MRS MABIE)	WILLIAM BAKER DAVENPORT
EASTRING/EASTARD, CATHERINE	RICHARD PERRY
EDMONDSON, MARTHA J	ALFORD/ALFRED THOMPSON/THOMSON
EVANS, SALLY (MRS BAREFOOT)	WILEY/WILLIE HARRELL

SPOUSE	ANCESTOR
FAIN, MARGARET (MRS WITZELL)	JOHN THOMAS
FARLOW, NATHAN	MARGARET SPENCER
FARMER, MARY	JOHN MOON
FEARN, MARY	JOSEPH BARBEE
FINCH, ADDIE (MRS QUINCY)	WILLIAM ADAIR QUINCY, JR
FITZGERALD, TEMPERANCE LOUISE (MRS BRADSHAW)	HIRAM DICKSON
FLEMING, BETSY (MRS FLEMING)	ROBERT PLEASANTS
FLEMING, MARY (MRS QUINCY)	WILLIAM ADAIR QUINCY
FOGLEMAN, ELIZABETH (MRS VESTAL)	JOHN/JACK JOHNSON
FORBES, NANCY (MRS KELLAM)	WILLIAM S ETHERIDGE
FORT, THAMER	WILLIAM GRAY MCDANIEL/MCDONALD, JR
FOWLER, IZZIE (MRS FIPPS)	MAC DANIEL/MCD FOWLER
FOWLER, MARY	JOSHUA PRUITT/PREWIT
FRISBY, DILLIAD/GILLIAD RESTER	FIDELIO SLUDER
FULBRIGHT, MARGARET (MRS GRITES/CRITES)	JOHN LINK
GIBBS, SUSANNAH	JEFFREY BECK, SR
GIBSON, SUSANNAH	DAVID LAY
GLASGOW, MARTHA (MRS SHEPPARD)	JOSEPH SCURLOCK
GODFREY, REBECCA	MORRIS COBB
GOODE, ELEANORE (MRS MARTIN)	DAVID DALTON
GRAY, AGNES	JAMES MCDANIEL/MCDONALD, I
GRAY, CHARLOTTE (MRS SILLS)	JOHN B SILLS
GRAY, HANNAH (MRS HAYWOOD)	JOSEPH GREEN
GREGORY, CATHERINE (MRS RENN)	THOMAS HENRY HUDGINS
GREEN, AMY	WILLIAM CARAWAN
GREEN, FANNIE	JOHN DECATUR BARRY
GRESHAM, LOUVENIA	WILLIAM FORREST/FORRESTER
HAMILTON, MARY ANN (MRS PUGH)	JOHN BEST
HAMLET, NANCY ANN (MRS STEVENS)	FRANCES FOARD/FORD
HARDIN, MARY	JAMES PAINE, COL
HARRIS, SUSAN ANN (MRS WATSON)	REDDING STARKE BRINKLEY
HARRISON, SARAH ANNE	JONATHAN SINGLETARY
HAWKINS, RACHEL	JOHN MARTIN
HENDERSON, MRS SARA A (NORDVIG)	BENJAMIN DARNELL, JR
HENSLEY, HANNAH (MRS LITTLE)	WILLIAM H DIXON/DICKSON
HERBERT, MARTHA ANN (MRS WHITBY)	TEAGLE WALTER CUTHRELL
HERNDON, MARY JANE (MRS WHITE)	GEORGE CROMARTIE
HERRING, SARAH	JOHN TREADWELL
HIGGINS, SARAH ELIZABETH (MRS MOORE)	LOUIS TAYLOR FOX
HIGNITS, RACHEL	EDWARD MILLIS
HINTON, ELIZABETH (MRS RAND)	THOMAS JAMES
HOCKNEY, LYDIA (MRS LEDBETTER)	JOHN WALL NORWOOD
HODGES, CAROLINE	SOLOMON BEASLEY
HODGES, HARTWELL (MRS DAVIS)	JAMES DRAKE
HOLSTEIN, BARBARA	ROLAND MANN
HOOD, MRS NANCY E (BLADES)	THOMAS W BROWN
HOPKINS, MARTHA	SAMUEL BARNHILL, JR
HORN?, JUDITH (MRS THORNBURGH)	JOSEPH UNTHANK
HORSLEY, NANCY (MRS SUGGS)	ABRAHAM STOWE
HOWARD, HARRIET ALVIN (MRS GRIFFIN)	JESSE E FRALEY
HOWARD, SARAH	MIAL SCURLOCK
HOWELL, NANCY ELIZABETH	EDMOND STUCKEY
HUGHES, MARY ANN (MRS BUNN)	JOHN WILSON
HUMPHREY, ANN	WILLIAM MACE

SPOUSE	ANCESTOR
HUMPHREY, MARY	JAMES BARNES
HUNT, ELIZABETH (MRS BROWN)	WILLIAM CRABTREE
HUTCHENS, ELIZABETH	JACOB SMITH
INGLE, MARTHA (MRS FRISBEE/FRISBY)	JOHN M PARHAM
JAMES?, CATHERINE (MRS PEARSALL)	THOMAS RULLEDGE
JEFFERSON, SUSANNAH	WILEY PEARCE
JENNINGS, MARY	JAMES PRICHARD
JESSUP, MARY ANN	GEORGE DARDEN, CAPT
JOHNSON, ELIZABETH RACHEL JOHNSON	JOHN SCARBOROUGH/SCARBROUGH, SR
JOHNSON, NANCY (MRS COTTEN)	HENRY NEWSOME
JONES, ANN	THOMAS TAYLOR, SR
JONES, ELIZABETH (MRS COOPER)	THOMAS GILL
JONES, ELIZABETH (MRS MERRICK)	SAMUEL ASHE, GOV
JONES, ESTHER SUSAN	WILLIAM L MAY
JONES, REBECCA (MRS KNIGHT)	JAMES BRANN
KENT, HANNAH (MRS SMITHWICK)	FARNEFOLD GREEN
KIMBALL, MARY WOODMAN (MRS DRIGGS)	ELISHA RHODES, COL
KING, ANN (MRS LANSDALE)	ARCHIBALD WASSON
KNIGHT, AMANDA/MANDY	GEORGE WASHINGTON ANDREW/ANDREWS
LA FLAMME, ANGIE MARIE	LLOYD RANDOLPH COOPER
LAMB, MARY (MRS BELL)	MARK R GREGORY
LASSITER, CHRISTIAN	NATHAN CULLEN
LAUGHLIN, ELIZABETH (MRS BERRY)	BENJAMIN MCFARLIN, JR
LEDBETTER, MARY (MRS BRADLEY)	JOHN GULBRODT/GOODBREAD
LEE, MARTHA A	EDMUND S KERBY
LEIB, MARIAH JANE (MRS FUNK)	MURPHY KEMP
LENOIR, LEAH CRAWLEY (MRS WHITAKER)	JOHN WALL NORWOOD
LEWIS, MARTHA ANN (MRS HODGES)	WILLIAM JAMES RHODES
LINDSAY, FANNY (MRS WATKINS)	JOHN WATKINS
LINSVILLE, EMELINE (MRS ZIKE)	JOHN HESTER, JR
LLEWELLYN, AMY	ABRAHAM LITTLE
LOGUE, MARGARET	LAURENCE THOMPSON, CAPT.
LUNSFORD, MARGERY	ROBERT TRAYWICK
LYONS, MARANER (MRS LEATHERS)	ADOLPHUS ERVIN COLE
MACY, SUSAN (MRS VESTAL)	SANFORD LEE STEELMAN
MADDOX, ALCEY	JAMES TROWELL
MARR, AGATHA (MRS PERKINS)	ROBERT PAINE
MARTIN, MARY ANN (MRS SCOTT)	WILLIAM DAWSON BLEDSOE
MASON, SUSANNAH	JAMES CAMPBELL
MASSEY, WINEY	STEPHEN SENTER
MASTIN, MARY	DRURY DEEN
MAYO, ANN (MRS POPE)	FRANCES DELAMAR/DE LA MAR
MCCARTY, MARY AGATHA (MRS LARKIN)	RICHARD KOSCIUSKA TAYLOR
MCINTOSH, CHRISTIAN (MRS MCLEOD)	DANIEL MONROE MCKAY
MCLEOD, CHRISTIAN	DANIEL DOUGLASS
MCLEOD?, MARY (MRS CAMPBELL)	JAMES HENDERSON MATTHEWS
MCMILLAN, MARY (MRS KELLY)	ANTHONY FENTRESS TOON
MCSWAIN, PRISCILLA (MRS JONES)	GABRIEL WASHBURN
MERCHANT, RACHEL	JONATHAN DEWEESE
MERRIT, ASCENCION (MRS BISHOP)	NICHOLAS GAMMON
MIDGETT, REBECKER (MRS SPARROW)	JEREMIAH MEEKINS

SPOUSE	ANCESTOR
MIDYETT, MARY	BURNS B SMITH
MILLER, AMY	NATHAN SAULS
MILLER, HANNAH (MRS HOUSER)	JOHN SHAMEL/SCHEMEL
MOORE, MARTHA (MRS CORBY)	EPHRAIM SUTTON
MOORMAN, RACHEL (MRS HALL)	JOHN WILLIAM FULLBRIGHT
MORGAN, SEALY	NATHAN MILLS
MORRIS, SARAH A	JOSHUA JONES
MORRIS, TABITHA (MRS DUPREE)	JAMES DUPREE
MORRISON, MARY (MRS MAINS)	JAMES BECK
MORSE, ELIZABETH	THOMAS CRAFT
MOSER, CATHERINE	FREDERICK FULK
MOTSINGER, SARAH (MRS SPURGEON)	ELI LORANCE/LOWRANCE
MULLER, MARY CAROLINE (MRS BLUE)	WILLIAM HENRY MCMILLAN
MURDOCK, MARTHA (MRS JEAN)	ALEXANDER L NICHOLSON
MURPHY, SARAH	ALEXANDER CHESNUTT?CHESTNUTT
NEELY, SOPHIA (MRS LEONARD)	EZEKIEL POLK
NEILL, ESTHER (MRS ALLISON)	JAMES DONALDSON
MICHOLS, SARAH/SALLY	EVERETTE THOMPSON/THOMSON
NORDVIG, SARAH A (MRS LARSON)	BENJAMIN DARNELL, JR
NORFLEET, SARAH (MRS YOUNG)	JOHN YOUNG
ODOM, RICHARD	HONOUR JONES
OLDES, MARY ELIZABETH (MRS COWELL)	JOSEPH WOODARD
ONEAL, DORCAS	JOHN JARVIS, CAPT
ONEILL, SARAH	ISAAC SMITH
OUTLAW, PRESCILLA (MRS FRAZER)	WILLIAM WATFORD
PARHAM, DILLY (MRS DUNN)	STEPHEN CRUMP
PARKER, MARY (MRS THIGPEN)	EATON COBB
PEACOCK, RACHEL	JOHN THOMPSON/THOMSON
PENROD, SALLIE (MRS SNYDER)	ZACHARIUS/ZAMAH/ZACH, LYERLY/LYRLE/LIERLY
PENNY, CHARITY	ALSA/ALSEY MATTHEWS
PETILLO, JANE (MRS LANIER	FRANCIS POINDEXTER
PHELPS, FRANCES (MRS HERRON)	JESSE VAUGHN
PLEDGER, CHARLOTTE (MRS COMBS)	LEWIS MIDGETT
POWELL, MARGARET	ROBERT NEATHERY
PRITLOWE, LEAH (MRS SMITH)	THOMAS WINSLOW
PURVIANCE, MARTHA (MRS KING)	WILLIAM MC CORKLE
RAMSEY, ELIZABETH	WILLIAM KELTON
RASPBERRY, LYDIA (MRS YOUNG)	WILLIAM TAYLOR
RAY, ISABELLA	THOMAS CHRISTOPHER
RAY, SALLY	JOHN BELLENFANT/BALLANFANT
READING, LUCRETIA	WILLIAM MURPHY/MURPHREY
REED, HANNAH	RICHARD WHEDBEE
REEL, CATHERINE/ELIZABETH	JACOB STROUP
RENFROW, PRISCILLA	WILLIS MURPHY/MURPHREY
RHEA, JANE	GEORGE ALEXANDER
RICE, SUSAN (MRS STULL)	LEMUEL/KIT WRIGHT
RIGGAN, AGNES (MRS SHORT)	RICHARD SHORT
RIPPATOE, MRS JANE (MRS WAINSCOTT)	JOHN LOGAN WINKLER
RIVES, SUSAN	MATTHEW CREWS
ROBINSON, PRUDENCE	WILEY MATTHEW MULLINS
ROGERS, EUNICE (MRS JONES)	JOHN ROBERTS

SPOUSE	ANCESTOR
ROSE, LURANY/LANEY	NATHAN LAMM/LAMB
ROUNTREE, ELIZABETH	THOMAS WALLACE/WALLIS
RUSS, MARY REBECCA (MRS RILEY)	WILLIAM DAVIDSON MCCRACKEN
SAVAGE, ANN	DAVID WALKER
SAVAGE, LUCY	JOHN JARVIS/GERVES
SCARLET, PHEBE (MRS ALLEN)	ISAAC COX
SCOTT, HARRIET (MRS PITTS)	JOHN LOVE, JR
SCOTT, MARTHA (MRS CAMP/KENT)	SIMON PETER WATERS
SEELY, SARAH	JAMES SWAFFORD
SESSUMS, PRISCILLA A (MRS HOGGARD)	JAMES REDDICK GREEN/GREENE
SETTLE, NANCY (MRS NORMAN)	ELIJAH LOMAX
SHARP?, MARINDA/RENDA (MRS THORN)	MARTIN R THORN/THORNE
SHAW, SUSAN MARIA (MRS NORMAN)	BRYANT HILL
SHEIFFLER, MARY	SIMON SHULL
SHEPPARD, ANN (MRS BROWN)	JAMES WALLACE COCKRUM
SHERROD, MANISIA GAINER MANETTA ANDREWS	FREDERICK WILLIAMS MAYO
SIMPSON, CATHERINE	ARCHIBALD MCELROY
SIMPSON, SUSAN	LEVY PARKS
SINK, NANCY (MRS POWELL)	JOSEPH DAMERON KNIGHT
SLOAN, CATHERINE (MRS MONTGOMERY)	JOHN CLEVELAND
SMITH, ELIZABETH	JOHN MORGAN
SMITH, LAURA ANN (MRS AVERY)	JOSEPH ALLEN GASKINS
SMITH, MELISSA ELIZABETH (MRS WHITE)	JAMES CICERO SMITH
SPECK, CATHERINE	GEORGE AWALT
SPENSER, SALLY (MRS DANIEL)	SAMUEL MIDGETT, III
STANFORD, SALLY	JOSHUA CREECH, SR.
STEPHENS, MARY	JOHN CRUMP
STUART, CATHERINE	JOHN BURTON
STUART, SARAH	BENJAMIN ANTIPAS THOMAS
STUTTS, ELIZABETH	LEONARD FURR
SUGGS?, EMILINE (MRS MARTIN)	JAMES HENDERSON MATTHEWS
TEMPLETON, CANDICE (MRS PATRICK)	JESSE BAZEMORE
THAMES, DICEY	WILLIAM GRAY MCDANIEL/MCDONALD, SR
THARP/THORP, WILLIAM	AMELIA/MILLY HEATH
THOMAS, MARY	THOMAS JAMES
THOMPSON, LAWRENCE	MARGARET LOGUE
THOMPSON, MARY (MRS GIVENS)	HENRY PENNEY/PENNY
THOMPSON, SARAH (MRS DUKES)	THOMAS GILL
THOMPSON, THOMAS	ANN LOGUE
TILLETT, GRACE (MRS WIGGINS)	JAMES PETTIGREW TEMPLE
TINSLEY, LONA MALLIE (MRS BLOUNT)	NEILL ANGUS RAY
TONDEE, MARIA P (MRS PATTERSON)	THOMAS ELKINS
TUCKER, MARGARET (MRS TODD)	JESSE STATON ANDERSON
TURNER, HANNAH (MRS DAVIS)	PETER DAVIS
VAN HUSS, JACOB	JANE PIERCE
VASS, LYDIA	LEWIS WAGGONER
WAGONER, MARY BARBARY	JOHN APPLE
WAINSCOTT, JANE (MRS BROADSTREET	JOHN LOGAN WINKLER
WALL, NANCY A	JOHN KILBY
WALL, REBECCA (MRS JONES)	JOEL WALLACE
WALL, SARA FRANCES (MRS COLLINS)	JOHN OATIS PLUMBLEE/PLUMLEY

SPOUSE	ANCESTOR
WALTON, NANCY (MRS ROBERTSON)	BURWELL TEMPLE
WEBB, MELINDA JANE (MRS TOMS)	JACOB RHYME SHUFORD/SHEUFFERT
WEST, MARY	ARTHUR ARRINGTON
WHIDDEN, MARTHA/PATSY	JOHN L MOORE
WHITE, ELIZABETH (MRS MANSKER)	ISAAC WALTON
WHITEHEAD, CATHERINE (MRS SHIELDS)	THOM SHIELDS
WICKER, JEMIMA	GIDEON CREWS
WILEY, AMANDA	THOMAS JAMES MIDDLETON
WILLIAMS, GAIL ADELINE (MRS SMITHERMAN)	SHORE DAVID DAVIS
WILLIAMSON, CHRISTIAN (MRS HARRISON)	WILLIE W LAMM
WILLIAMSON, ELIZABETH/BETSY (MRS WHITLEY)	BURWELL TEMPLE
WOOD, MARGARET	WILLIAM WICKLIFFE, JR
WRIGHT, MIRA	GEORGE W MACE
WYNNE, ELVIRA	WILLIAM PLEASANTS

3

Contributor Index

ALPHABETICAL LIST OF CON-
TRIBUTORS. FOR ADDRESSES,
LOOK FOR THE CONTRIBUTOR'S
CODE NUMBER IN ITS CORRECT
NUMERICAL SEQUENCE IN THE
LIST WHICH BEGINS ON PAGE
354.

Name	Number	Name	Number	Name	Number
BALLARD HAZEL F	60257	BLIETZ RUTH H	60070	BURGEMEYER MRS BARBARA C	27734
BARCLIFT PRESTON W	60310	BLIVEN JUNE KIGHT	27760	BUSH MARY PYRON	60144
BAREKMAN MISS JUNE B	02065	BLOMQUIST ANN	60438	BUTTS MRS ROBIN HARRIS	02540
BARKER RALPH E	60541	BOBBITT JOHN W	02280	BYRD THOMAS M	02550
BARLEY MRS CHAS. A.	27546	BOHLER HERBERT C	60439	CAMPBELL DOROTHY M	60145
BARNES JACQUELYN D.	25159	BOHNERT VIOLET M	02295	CAMPBELL MARTHA K	03015
BARNETT EDWARD B	60258	BONNER MRS CARL Y	27549	CAMPBELL MRS LEON E	03020
BARNETT MRS JOHN RUCKMAN	27270	BOONE HOWELL	27586	CANNADY MRS JOHN W	03035
BATTS MRS ROBERT A	02135	BOOTH SUE PEARCE	60391	CANNON MRS CHARLIE R JR	03041
BAUER MRS LOUISE S	02145	BOSLET MARY ETTA	25195	CANTERBURY RUTH	25223
BAXTER LORRAINE	60107	BOTTOM ODETTE	60108	CAREY MRS ROBERT J	60262
BEATTIE JOSEPHINE	02168	BOULTON MRS DON C	60109	CARLSON MRS J WALTER	60111
BEATY MRS CARL E	25112	BOYKIN J ROBERT III	02343	CARMICHAEL MRS ERMA V	03065
BECK JOHN V	60259	BOYKIN L C	27554	CARPENTER MRS JAMES A	03070
BECK MR DONALD E	60311	BOYST DOROTHEA BELL	60544	CARROLL R FRANCIS	60112
BEEMAN RAY	60535	BRACHMAN MRS ROBERT	60062	CARTER LAVELLE	27420
BEENE MRS WARREN L	02170	BRANCH MRS WILLIAM G	02355	CARUSO MARY JANE BURKETT	60392
BEESON MISS AILENE	02175	BRASWELL JOYCE R	02357	CAST MRS VIC C.	25133
BEHNKEN MRS JOHN	02180	BREHM MRS H B	60440	CAUGHEY DR DALE W JR	03125
BELISLE HUBERT L	27260	BRENENSTALL DOLORES	60312	CHANCE HILDA	60009
BELL AMOS V	60236	BRETT MISS CHARLOTTE M	25040	CHANEY MRS HENRY G	60263
BELLAMY MRS ROBERT M	02195	BRIGGS MRS BEN R	60191	CHAPMAN GLADYS E	60338
BELLKNAP CLARENCE T	60235	BROOKS ANN E	60441	CHAUNCEY MRS ESTHER MCFARLANE	27573
BENGE JOHN JR	60336	BROOKS ROY	02412	CIESLIK SALLY	60313
BENTLEY RICHARD C	27413	BROTHERS MRS W R	02414	CLANTON MRS JAMES O	03155
BERRY ANNA MAE	60260	BROWN ANNE TAYLOR	60211	CLARK GEORGE D	60443
BISCHOFF VIVIAN VAUGHN	60237	BROWN EVELYN P	60101	CLARK JAMES W	60113
BISHOP ANNA MAE WILEY	60542	BROWN MRS BARBARA J	60212	CLARK WANDA L	60339
BISHOP ELIZA H	60071	BROWN MRS GLADYS	02435	CLEMMER MAVIS STREET	60063
BLACKSHEAR MRS NORA WHITENER	60534	BROWN MRS J P	60016	CLERICO MRS KENNETH J	25162
BLAKE IRENE W	60143	BROWN REGINALD R	02450	CLINKSCALES MRS W T JR	03183
BLAKENEY MRS BETTY	02252	BRUCE MRS PAUL O	60261	CLUBB JAMES WILLIAM	60340
BLALOCK JOHN HOYT	60102	BRYAN MRS G WERBER	60238	COFFEY MARVIN D	60264
BLALOCK VIRGINIA	60437	BRYANT CLEO ORLAN	60442	COLE CHARLES M JR	60146
BLALOCK W. ERNEST	02256	BUCHANAN JOEL R	02470	COLEMAN CLAIRE TYSON	60147
BLAND CAROLYN C	60592	BUCK MRS RUBY B	27537	COLEMAN RONALD D	60393
BLANKENSHIP BARBARA	60390	BUFFALOE MRS HAZEL H	27302	COLLINS MRS HARRY G	27269
BLANKS JAMES R	60337	BULAND MRS JOE A JR	02478	COLVERT MRS CARROLL	60545
BLAYLOCK J BURCH	60543	BUNTON DAVIS T	60213	COMBS MR & MRS EDWIN L	03210
BLECHA MRS GLADYS DUDLEY	60210	BURCH KATHLEEN SMITH	60110	CONANT ANNE D	03213

CONNER MRS DON	60266	DAVIDSON RUTH C	60269	EFURD MRS MORRIS	60215
CONNER MRS KATHY R	60265	DAVIS GAIL W	60546	ELLER MRS ROGER F	05035
COOK MICHAEL	60192	DAVIS MRS BRYAN L	60100	ELLIS MISS GAYLE	05045
COOPER MILTON B	60267	DAVIS MRS N D	25178	ELSTON MRS CAROLE	27596
CORBUS PATRICIA A	60394	DAVIS MRS WILLIAM L	04050	ELVEY HAZEL OUSLEY	60194
CORNELIUS KATHLEEN	60395	DAVIS MRS WILLIAM R	60344	EMERSON CRAIG C	05059
CORRELL ANNE R	03250	DAVIS TIMOTHY ANDREW	60020	EMERSON DR K C	05065
COULTER MRS W J	60444	DAWSON MRS NETTIE HIGHTOWER	04053	ENGELMANN CORINNE	60349
COWART MARGARET M	60046	DAY MISS W VERNON	60015	ENGLISH JACK LEE	60315
COX FREDA R	27761	DEAN DORIS E	60214	ERWIN E D	60533
COX MR ELDON E	03270	DEAN MRS BETTY L	60547	ESKRIDGE MRS POE W JR	05070
COX, WILLIAM J. JR.	25167	DEBNAM MR & MRS WILBUR T	04065	ETCHISON MRS LESTER	60271
COYNE MRS HAZEL	27339	DEGLER MARYLEA SOUERS	60270	EVANS DR BETTY D	60097
CRABBS HARRIETT	60445	DELAHUNT MARY LOU	04080	FABER GORDON L	60316
CRABTREE GEORGE W	60170	DEMARCUS FRED E	04085	FALKENBERRY MRS ROSWELL L	60117
CRAIG MRS C W	60148	DENNIS MARY WRIGHT	60314	FALLER MRS WARREN L	06005
CRAIG MRS WILLIAM E	27286	DEURING MRS DOLORES B	04103	FANT MRS ALBERT E JR	06015
CRAIN MRS ELIZABETH	60341	DEVAULT MARY RUTH	60345	FEE GEORGE W	25097
CRAVENS MRS JACK	60114	DIBLAKE MRS R I	60150	FENTRESS MRS JOHN S	06050
CRAVER MR SAMUEL C	03295	DIGGS JAMES C	60346	FERGUSON MRS DAVID B	60060
CRAWFORD HILDY	60268	DIXON MRS CLAIRE M	60061	FILINGERI JUDY B	06065
CRAWFORD MRS. THOMAS M.	27382	DIXSON MRS CHARLES	60450	FINLEY PAULINE	60096
CREASON GARY L	03313	DODD ELLA FRANCES	04135	FINLEY REX B	06070
CREECH CHARLES W	03315	DOKE MRS ELSIE	27348	FIORI MRS CHARLES	60451
CREEKMORE ROBERT R	60115	DONNELL MARION PROCTOR	60193	FISHER LUCY E	06075
CREWS FREDA FERGUSON	60446	DORRIS MR CLETUS L	04155	FLANAGAN MRS CLARA H R	60576
CRITCHFIELD MARY C	60447	DOSS MRS WARREN A	60347	FLEMING MRS LOIS	60350
CROKER RODGER N	60149	DRIGGS HARRY S	60069	FLETCHER MRS G B	06080
CROTHERS MRS LUELLA M	25199	DUFF MRS RAMONA	60239	FLOURNOY MISS MADGE E	60059
CRUISE MRS T J	03328	DUNCAN ALICE C	60099	FLOWERS MRS BILL	06085
CURRY CALVIN H	60396	DUNCAN JOSEPH M	04195	FLYNT DOROTHY CAIN	60398
CURRY THOMAS F JR	27532	DUPUIS NANCY TAYLOR	60548	FOARD MR JOHN H JR	06090
CUSHMAN MRS JAMES A	60342	DUSEK MRS BRENDA NORWOOD	25235	FOLLETTE DIXIE	06100
DAFFT P R	60397	DUSENDSCHON LEE	60348	FOREMAN MRS CARSON	25127
DAIL JEAN	25171	DUVAL MRS J B	04200	FOUTS MARY E	06145
DAMIANO MARION H	60343	DYE SHIRLEY SCOTT	27568	FOWLER DELBERT MARCOM	27593
DARLING G D	60448	DYKES MRS H ASHLIN	60116	FOWLER MR AND MRS DAVID	60549
DARWIN DERO A JR	60171	EADES DORIS L	60098	FOWLER RICHARD G	60399
DASEN FAYE MITCHELL	27543	EDNEY BERNICE WARD	27334	FOWLKES MRS JOHN R	25158
DAVENPORT JOAN M	60449	EDWARDS JEWELL W	60240	FOX MRS DENNIS	60031

Name	No.
FRAME MARY S	60550
FRAZIER JOSEPH R	06158
FREE MRS B C	06159
FREEMAN INEZ	60400
FRICKE JULIE R	60551
FRITCHMAN BARBARA	60000
FRYE LILLIAN HARRIS	60195
FULP RICHARD V	06195
GAHAN THELMA PURVIS	60172
GAINES MARTHA NEAL	60452
GAINES PAT	07015
GAITHER JAMES M & PEGGY W	07017
GAMBLE MRS LEO E	07018
GAMMON DAVID	60594
GARMON MRS SHIRLEY BLACKWELL	60272
GARRETT JASAMYN SANDERS	60453
GARRIS PRESTON F	07040
GATES MRS DENZIL E	60351
GENTRY MRS R C	27583
GEORGE SUSAN J	60401
GERMANY MRS JOHN R	07078
GHIGLERI SIRLEEN	60095
GIDLEY JOYCE WARR	60317
GILL FAE G	60118
GILMER MRS G. W.	25129
GILMORE HASKELL D	60552
GODSEY MRS BRENDA	07087
GOLIGHTLY FAY L	60196
GOODBREAD JAMES P TALIAFERRO	60402
GOODDING ROBERT A	60022
GOODPASTURE MRS BURL E	60032
GORMLEY MYRA D VANDERPOOL	60352
GOSSUM MRS F M JR	07095
GOURLEY MRS WINIFRED M	60197
GRACEY MRS MARTHA JANE	60454
GRAF EVELYN ESTER	60455
GRAHAM MRS JOHN W JR	07115
GRAVELLE MARY G	25229
GRAY MISS RUTH	60151
GRAY MRS GERTRUDE E	60004
GREEN MRS M LEONARD	60532
GREEN VIRGINIA S	60198
GREGORY BELINDA	60318
GREGORY MRS PEGGY H	60152
GRIFFEY JOY HILLIARD	60010
GRIFFIN WILMA	25238
GRIFFIS VERNA ATHEY	60119
GRIFFITH ANNA LAURA	60273
GRIFFITH DAN WESLEY	07168
GRIMES WILLIAM S	60033
GRISHAM ETHEL M	25241
GROSS MRS LANIS	60216
GRUBBS ELIZABETH A	60456
GUZAK BETTY J ARNOLD	60013
HABELMAN CAROLYN	60030
HACKNEY MRS C R	07187
HACKSMA MRS J M	60531
HAINLINE LYMAN S	08010
HALL EILEEN	08015
HALL MADGE L	60173
HAMM THOMAS D	60120
HAMPTON MRS CHARLES H	08023
HAND ROBERTA ANNETTE	60319
HANE MRS CLARA M	60094
HANSLER MYRNA L	27291
HARDEN LOIS	60553
HARDEN WILLIAM COUNCIL JR	60320
HARDISON MISS SULA H	08040
HARKEY KENNETH MICHAEL	60217
HARNESS MRS JAMES	08053
HARPER THELMA L	60353
HARRELL OWEN D	27562
HARRINGTON MRS HUGH	60093
HARRIS GLORIA HENDRICKS	60554
HARRIS KAREN	60555
HARRIS SYLVIA JOHNSON	60457
HARRISON MRS J H	60241
HART JEAN M	60458
HARTNESS CAROLE M	60153
HARVEY BROWN SR	08065
HARVEY MARY BUTLER	08070
HARVEY MRS MATTIE BALDWIN	60403
HASH HIRAM J	08073
HAUN MRS WEYNETTE PARKS	08090
HAWORTH MRS CHESTER C	08095
HAWORTH MRS EARL E	60274
HAYES MARJORIE M	60218
HAYNES DOROTHY A	60459
HEATH MRS MAX B	60596
HEDDINS MRS EARL	08120
HEIDORN PATRICIA ANN	08130
HEINEK MRS MARGARET	60154
HELMHOLZ MRS MARJORIE B	60460
HEMMINGWAY RUTH KEELING	60058
HENDERSON LILLIAN FAY	08145
HENDERSON MRS M E	08150
HENDRICKS MRS B W	60174
HENDRIX BOYD T JR	60005
HENDRIX GE LEE CORLEY	08165
HENSON MRS G W	08185
HENSON MRS RUTH GOOD	08190
HERNDON DR C NASH	08200
HERRING MRS MARJORIE H	25141
HIATT MS MARTY	60219
HICKS HOWARD J	60321
HIGGINS VICTORIA B	08219
HILL MRS LEILA W	08226
HILL MRS LOUIS C	60404
HILSABECK CARTER LAVELLE	60354
HINTON DAVID	60275
HINTON MRS MAE P	60155
HOBBS DORCAS M	08240
HODGIN ARTHUR D	08265
HOFFPAUIR PAT VINSON	60322
HOGAN CAPT CLEO	08275
HOGUE MISS EMMA L	60121
HOLLENBECK RETHA DABBS	60242
HOLMAN MRS BERKELEY N	60556
HOLMES CLAUDIA	60276
HOLMES DOROTHY HURST	60461

HOLT MAXINE	60243	JOHNSON EDDIS	10060	KIRKLAND MRS JOHN H JR	11100
HONEA THOLBERT MILTON	60462	JOHNSON HARIADENE	60468	KIRKLAND MRS MARGARET B	60123
HONKAMP HELEN ALLEN	60277	JOHNSON JOHNNIE M	60220	KIRKPATRICK EUNICE T	11105
HOOTEN MRS RAYMOND	25145	JOHNSON MRS ROSS B	27560	KIRKPATRICK MRS RUBY F	60283
HORKAN MRS G A	60057	JOHNSON MRS SIDNEY P	10090	KIRKSEY MARY BESS	60043
HORTON MRS WILMA WILLIAMS	27281	JOHNSON MRS SUE H	60280	KLAUS MRS PATRICIA A	60284
HOWARD MRS EUGENIA W	60175	JOHNSON MRS THOMAS M	60156	KLINE RUTHELA DEAL	60055
HOWENSTEIN MARY	60463	JOHNSTON MRS JOSEPH E	27728	KLYVER EFFIE S	60490
HOYLE MRS MIKE L	60464	JOLLEY JAMES B	10120	KNIGHT ANNE F	60360
HUCKS MRS SAMUEL E	08355	JONES LEMUEL C	60157	KNIGHT KENNETH B	60469
HUFFMAN RICHARD H	27435	JONES MRS IRENE DOBSON	60406	KNIPPERS MRS D HAROLD	60086
HUGHES MRS LINDSEY W	60355	JORDAN VIVIAN HILL	60090	KNOTT MRS ROBERT	60561
HUGHES SHELBY N	27477	JOSSERAND JANETTE	60158	KOCH MRS PHYLIS MARTYN	60124
HUGHS CARLETON N	60405	JOWDY FRANCES R	27378	KOONTZ MRS LU J	11145
HUGHSTON MRS RICHARD L	60034	JOYCE MRS FRANK M	10154	KORTAN LORETTA L	25121
HUMPHREY MRS H E	25226	JOYNER MRS V R	10153	KRELL RUTH N ROSS	60411
HUNSUCKER MRS CHARLES R	60045	JUDD DAN	60281	LACKEY PINKNEY L	12005
HUNT MARJORIE	60056	JULIAN WILMA	60089	LAIRD LUCILLE	60323
HUNTER BILLIE GENE HORNER	60278	JUNKINS VIRGINIA CLAYTON	60357	LAMBERT ROGER D	60528
HUNTER MRS JANET A	60092	JURGENS MRS LENA C	60407	LAMPTON MRS WILLIAM A	12008
HUNTZINGER EVERETT LEROY	60530	JURGENSEN RUTH	60087	LANCASTER MRS BETTY NEEDHAM	60324
HURTT RUTH M	60356	KARISNY RUTH E	11010	LANDY LOUISE G	12015
HUSTON LAWRENCE W	60465	KAUTZ GLORIA MAY	60358	LANE MRS CLARA B	12019
IRVIN DOROTHY D	27758	KAY JEAN	60221	LANE MRS DANIEL M	25251
ISBILL OVETA M	09030	KEATING NORMA S	60559	LANG HENRIETTA H	60176
IVEY SANDRA	60557	KEITH DARRELL S	27745	LARIS MRS ELIZABETH	60470
JACKSON DELWOOD S	10010	KEITH MARY LEE KEMP	60408	LARROUX BEVERLY CHASTAIN	27335
JACKSON MRS MARY E H	25204	KELLER ELIZABETH P	25098	LATHAM LADONNA H	27599
JACKSON SYLVIA	60068	KEMPF JUDITH M	60409	LATTA LUCILE	60471
JACOBSON LUCY MILLER	27488	KENDALL MRS PHYLLIS	60159	LAUER MRS EDNA	60054
JEFFRIES MRS BECKY MCGAHA	60091	KENNEDY MRS GUINNDOLYN F	60359	LAUGHLIN ELIZABETH	25149
JENKINS BETTE HANLON	60006	KEY BETTY	60088	LAWRENCE BARBARA	60562
JENKINS MRS LEONA	60466	KEY LANCE E	27476	LAWS DR KEITH R	60085
JENNINGS LAURA OLMSTED	60558	KILDUFF MRS RODNEY	27375	LAWSON MRS DORIS	60053
JIMENEZ VIRGINIA	60122	KIMBRO MRS WILEY	11070	LEACH MARY L	25093
JOHNS VERLAN R	60279	KING BETTY W	60560	LEARY HELEN F M	12040
JOHNSON DARLA MORGAN	60467	KING LEOLA ANN	60529	LEDBETTER MARVIN A	12050
JOHNSON DR DAVID P	60044	KING MAY RINGO	60026	LEE CORNELIA ELLIS	12075
JOHNSON DR LOUIS JR	60017	KING MRS R A	60410	LEE HOWARD B	12065
JOHNSON DR ROBERT H JR	10085	KINSELL DORIS BRINKLEY	60282	LEE JOSEPH B	12068

Name	No.	Name	No.	Name	No.
LEGUIN MARY BELLE	27366	MAXFIELD ANNA BELLE CAMPBELL	60129	MERCER JOE M	60199
LEHNERT LENA	25143	MAXWELL L W	13095	MEREDITH ELIZABETH	60200
LEMMON OWEN K	60472	MAXWELL LOIS S	60042	MERRITT JENNIE SMITH	60287
LENNON GEORGE BRADLEY SR	12090	MAXWELL MRS MAURICE J	60476	MIDDLETON MRS RUTH E.	25161
LEPINE KATE	12100	MAYBERRY MRS GRACE FRANK	60001	MILLER ANDREW W	27697
LEUTWYLER CLARA MAE	60361	MAYES MRS BETTY	60130	MILLER JANET M	60569
LEVERTON MRS WILSON	27280	MAYFIELD STEPHEN	13105	MILLER MRS GEORGE	27602
LEVIN PAT JUSTICE	60412	MAYNE WINFIELD SWIFT	60415	MILLER MRS JOYCE	60525
LIMBAUGH J T	25191	MCBRYDE MARY B	60082	MILLER MRS JOYCE	27533
LINES JACK	60125	MCCALL ELIZABETH A	60477	MILLER MRS LOWELL	60480
LINN MRS STAHLE JR	12125	MCCARTHY LYNETTE	14019	MILLER NANCY N	27682
LIPSCOMB D J	60126	MCCARTY MRS JUSTIN P	14020	MILLER PHYLLIS V	60481
LITCHFIELD MRS JOHN S	12140	MCCLELLAND MR & MRS CLIFTON A	14030	MING WILLIAM L	13175
LITTLE ANN C W	12144	MCCLENNY MRS F B	60285	MITCHELL MRS L R	60021
LLOYD GLENDA GARDNER	60362	MCCORNACK MR JOHN C	60131	MOBERLY ETHEL	60570
LOESCHER DOROTHY DORSETT	60084	MCCRACKEN EVELYNE	27301	MOHN JANICE	60160
LONERGAN MONICA M	60363	MCCRACKEN JOHN R	14050	MONTAG LEONA	60288
LOVE MRS CLARENCE	60127	MCCRACKEN MRS JEAN LEE	14045	MOORE AMOS L JR	60051
LUCAS DORIS ANN BUTLER	27475	MCCROSKEY GEORGE ALFRED	60244	MOORE LUCY	60416
LUCAS MARY ELLEN	60413	MCDONALD DELORES HAWKINS	60478	MOORE MRS SAM J JR	27276
LYDA CAROLYN H	60473	MCDONALD HUBBARD W JR	60568	MOORE SYLVIA G	60417
LYNCH MRS WILLIAM R	12210	MCDOWELL BOBBIE DUNCAN	60041	MOOTY HELENE	60482
MABEE BETTY L	13006	MCGINN HARRY B	27380	MORGAN MRS JACKIE	60571
MACKENZIE ANNE PRICE	27740	MCHUGH M L	60023	MORRIS JOSEPH F	60325
MACKEY MRS BEVERLEE A	60563	MCKAY EILEEN MUND	25198	MORRIS LTC(RET) & MRS C E	60024
MADDOX E P	60564	MCKINNIE ZERA GREEN	14105	MORROW MRS HENRY SLOAN	60178
MALONE GLADYS HORN	13020	MCNEELY DEANNA	25185	MORTON BERNICE	60050
MANN ALICE CHAMBERS	60565	MCNEW MRS JUNE COKER	60479	MORTON WILLIAM TROUP	60572
MANNING MS. LOUISE J.	60414	MCREE LARRY	27406	MOSER PAMELA	60289
MARCUS TREVA JO	60222	MCREYNOLDS RICHARD L	60527	MOSER PAUL	60573
MARLOWE JAMES I	13052	MCSWAIN MRS A S JR	60286	MOSLEY MRS ALLENE	60224
MARSH GEORGE E	60052	MD BERNARD MATHIS MALLOY,	60083	MOUSER MRS BEN	60132
MARSHALL BETTY L	60566	MD GUY S CLARK,	27313	MOYER MRS PHILIP L	60225
MARSHALL FLORENCE HOUGHTON	60128	MD RUTH E DINKINS	04115	MUENCH RUTHE C	60049
MARSHALL MRS GERALDINE	60474	MEAD MRS E L	60223	MULLEN MRS EARL	60483
MARTIN HOWARD W	27773	MEADER DOROTHY	60364	MUNSON DOROTHY	60484
MASTERS BERNIETA HARNESS	60567	MEDFORD ISOM E	27548	MURPHY WILLIAM L JR	13264
MATTHEWS DR & MRS WILLIAM P	13090	MEEKINS DAVID & JANE	13120	MURRAY SUZANNE	60011
MATTINGLY MRS WILLIAM T SR	60475	MEGGS MR J E	60526	NACCARATO JOYCE M	60418
MAULDIN MRS JOHN TYLER	60008	MEHRKAM MRS WOODROW B	60177	NAFF MRS H M	15005

NAZOR MRS MARY LOUISE	60081	PAUL PATRICIA BRINKLEY	60227	PRIOR LUCILE	60575
NEATHERY MRS MILTON W	27268	PAULK MRS J E	17080	PRUITT A B	17220
NEITZEL MRS ROBERT S	60419	PAYNE MARJORY	25135	PUGH MRS JAMES F	17235
NELMS HARRY A	15023	PAYTON ALBERTA R	27495	PULLEY MRS C BRYSON	17240
NELMS JUNE	60080	PEARSALL STEPHEN C	17085	PURCELL COL. & MRS W R	27566
NELSON THELMA M	60290	PEASE JANET K	60294	QUALLS MRS DEE	60368
NEUFORTH KAREN P	60524	PECKHAM WILLIE MAY	60328	QUEEN MISS MARJORIE E	18010
NICHOLS PAUL L	60291	PENDERGRAFT ALLEN	17090	RAGUZIN SUE NITE	60491
NICHOLSON JEAN H	60486	PENLEY MRS MICHAEL W	17100	RAINWATER H IVAN	60492
NICHOLSON JOHN H	60040	PENNINGTON MRS PAUL	17105	RALEY MRS LORRAINE L	19017
NIEDERMAIER MRS LOUISE P	15045	PENNY MORRIS	60489	RAMBO MARGARET S.	25144
NOVAK LUCILE V	15098	PERKINS DONALD D	60079	RAMSEY LEE KEMP	60164
O'TOOLE MRS DONALD G	27775	PERO LOU	60014	RAMSEY YETIVE D	27699
OAKLEY WILLIE EVERETTE	60420	PERRY MRS BAXTER	17129	RAY JUDSON W	60133
ODOM MRS STEVE	60365	PETTY MRS JAMES SIBLEY	60162	RAY THOMAS BROADFIELD	60048
OGBURN JANE CARTER	27292	PEVEY MRS FRANCES LAMKIN	60295	REA ANN W	60179
ORMOND MRS JUNE T	16030	PHILLIP RUTH	17135	REA HAZEL	19040
ORR MRS JOHN E	60366	PHILLIPS G HOWARD	17140	REDFERN ROSALIND	60012
ORRELL ROBERT S	60326	PHILLIPS KATHERINE	27306	REDMOND ROBERT L	60331
ORRICK MRS L S	16035	PHILLIPS MRS JANE	60593	REED MARGARET KILLGORE	60421
ORTON MRS JUNE POWELL	60292	PHILLIPS VIRGINIA HARDING	17147	REENER LYNN BOYD	27553
OSENBAUGH ELIZABETH M	60487	PICKARD JAMES W	17150	REESE JUNE O	60039
OSF SISTER MARY FRANCIS CATES	03120	PICKETT LUCILLE G R	27467	REGA MRS JULIA M	60165
OVERBECK MRS CHARLES	25206	PIERCE JOHN G	60329	REINHEIMER RITA	60493
OVERBY MRS JAMES R	60293	PINNELL COL SAMUEL W	17165	REX JOYCE A	60067
OVERTON ALTON L	60226	PLEASANTS WILLIAM K	25215	REYNOLDS MISS KATHERINE	19075
PACE MISS MABEL B	17005	PLUMBLEE MRS ELIZABETH C	17170	RICH MRS LINVIL G	60494
PAGE WILLIAM E III	17025	POLK BETTY JANE	60296	RICHMOND W A	19095
PAINE MRS. THOMAS FITE JR.	07027	POOLE MRS JOHNNIE W	25213	RIEGLER ETHEL M	60246
PAINTER MRS DIXIE	60327	POOLE MRS JOYCE PERKERSON	60522	RIORDAN ALICE F	60369
PALMER DR JOHN T	60201	POOLE WILLIAM C	60163	RITCHIE MRS V IRVIN	60495
PALMER ROGER E	25253	POOR MARIE	17185	ROARK PRESTON	25242
PALMER RUTH H.	60367	PORTER BETTY J	60574	ROBBINS GEORGE S	60180
PARKER DORIS	17046	PORTER MRS JANINE	17187	ROBERTS HELEN	60007
PARR LARRY W	17070	POTTS FRANK A	17195	ROBERTS MRS DOROTHY P	25254
PASKETT ERIS R.	25156	PRAMBERG NOREEN	17213	ROBERTS MRS MARY L	60422
PATRICK S J	60161	PRATT BETH PERISHO	60330	ROBERTS SALLY R	19115
PATTERSON BONNIE GARDNER	60488	PRICE MRS ROBERT R	60245	ROBERTSON HAYWOOD L	19130
PATTERSON SHERRY L	60523	PRIDDY MRS MAXINE E	27402	ROBINSON MARY D	60297
PATTON MRS WILLIAM F	17075	PRIDGEN ANGELA S	60521	ROBINSON MR ANGUS P	60423

RODRIGUEZ MRS B M	60002	SEGULIA FRANCES F	60076	STALLINGS GINGER WINTERS	27311
ROGERS GLENN NORMAN	27714	SEIBERT RONALD J	27531	STALLINGS MR RALPH	60502
ROGERS JANE	27365	SEITZ BEATRICE WEST	20095	STEELMAN RUTH A	20380
ROSACRANS MRS RICHARD	60370	SEXTON RUTH	60499	STEPHENSON VIRGINIA	60519
ROSE BEN LACY	19177	SHAMBURGER MILDRED MCKNIGHT	60427	STEWART D B	60075
ROSE HELEN YORK	19170	SHARPLESS EDITH GARNER	60520	STEWART MARY COLEMAN	25168
ROSEBOROUGH JOAN	60182	SHAW MRS DIXIE HOOPER	20105	STILLEY MR VAN A	20415
ROSS GERALDINE C	19183	SHAW RALPH W AND BONNIE J	25134	STINSON ROY M	60333
ROSS MRS GRADY	25100	SHAW RUTH MAXEY	60135	STOKES A J	20425
ROWE CAROLYN L	60591	SHELTON MRS S	20125	STORM LT COL MARY L USAF (RET)	60047
ROYCE NANCY C	60496	SHEPHERD MRS HAROLD	20135	STOUT MR & MRS GARLAND P	20435
RUBOTTOM THOMAS WILLIAM	60424	SHERMAN ANNA S	20138	STRATHANN SIBYL D.	25174
RUDD VELMA A	19227	SHIVES MRS IRENE M	60299	STRIEBECK MRS L E	27322
RUDOLPH ROSEDELL ARMSTRONG	60078	SHULTZ MRS W M	60373	STROHECKER J W	60375
RUGELEY MRS H H	19230	SILANCE LEON E	27374	STROPLE JOE	60581
RUSSELL MARTHA SWANNER	60497	SIMMONS PAULINE	27555	STUART MRS THOMAS I	20448
RUSSELL MRS RICHARD W	60425	SINGLETARY NORMAN EDWARD	60579	STUMPP LILLIAN J	60582
RUSSELL THOMAS L	60134	SITTLER MRS EDWARD C	60300	STUPEK CHARLOTTE COULTAS	60184
RYAN VETA A	60181	SMITH CARL R	60036	STUTESMAN JOHN HALE	20450
SAKARIS KAY WATERS	20007	SMITH CAROL P	60500	SUDDETH BOBBIE J	27438
SALVATORE MRS MARCIA KOEGEL	60202	SMITH CONNIE C	60580	SUTTON RAYMOND E	60376
SANDERS ANN SAULS	60577	SMITH JERRY RAY	60332	SWANSON WINIFRED L	60503
SANDERS MRS R M SR	20030	SMITH MARJORIE E	60374	SWEET MRS LESTER Y	60504
SAPANAS JANET MORGAN	25257	SMITH MISS KARON MAC	20229	SWOFFORD DOYLE P	25087
SATHRE MRS ANN	60498	SMITH MRS CHARLES A	20210	TACKITT JAMES WILLIAM	60583
SAUPE MRS ALLEN	20060	SMITH MRS DONALD E	25115	TALLEY SHIRLEY	25117
SCHARREL ETHEL CLEMENTS	60371	SMITH MRS H A	20220	TARLTON MARGARET	60065
SCHMIDT DORCAS W	20073	SMITH MURRIEL L	20245	TAYLOR MARGARET	60518
SCHNEIDER MRS NELLIE	60247	SOLARI MARILYN R	60136	TAYLOR MARY T	60505
SCHOLES MED HOOPER JR	60066	SOFER BETTY	60301	TAYLOR OWEN PHILLIPS	60230
SCHRAMM MRS W W	20078	SOUTHGATE CLAUDINE	60137	TAYLOR ROBERT E	25196
SCHUCK HELEN HUFF	60426	SOWELL MRS LEON B	60229	TAYLOR WILLIAM FREDERICK	21035
SCHWEIKART MS. MERVA E	27392	SPAFFORD MRS G D	27700	TESH MRS KENNETH L	60428
SCHWEIZER CHARLES B	60298	SPAKE VIRGINIA HOLT	20330	THOMPSON EUGENE C JR	60231
SCOTT EDITH	60077	SPEAROW JOYCE	25108	THOMPSON GEORGIA	60302
SCOTT MARY DULANY	60372	SPENCER PAULA	20333	THOMPSON HAROLD LEE	21095
SCOTT MILDRED M	60228	SPENCER R S JR	20335	THOMPSON JAMES L	60429
SEAGRAVE RONALD ROY	60578	SPIVEY THOMAS K	60183	THOMPSON MR & MRS A G JR	21080
SEAHOLM MISS ERNEST MAE	20080	SPONSLER KATHLYEEN M	60501	THOMPSON MRS LESBA L	60138
SEDGLEY MRS M W	20085	SPORE HELEN E	20350	THOMPSON MRS SAMUEL L	60139

THRASHER BILLIE SLOCUM	60074	WALTERS JUDITH ALLISON	60027	WILLIAMS AUDREY L	27318
THRIFT LETTIE B	27417	WALTERS MICHAEL EARL	60335	WILLIAMS ELLEN AMIDON	24210
TILLITSON DONALD K	60064	WARD SHIRLEY	60187	WILLIAMS HELLEN T	24213
TIPPETT MRS. CARSEY L.	21115	WARD WALLACE T	24055	WILLIAMS MRS DAVID J	60306
TOAZ MILDRED	60073	WARE MRS NELDA ANDERSON	60381	WILLIAMS NONA REED	60588
TODD MRS EVELYN	60185	WATIES MRS T A JR	60233	WILLS ROBERTA J	60385
TRAMMELL MRS L N	60186	WATKINS FRANK E	60249	WILSON CHARLES H	60307
TRICKETT MRS ANNE	01006	WATKINS MRS JOHN T	24073	WILSON EDITH L	24243
TRYON MRS J L	21165	WATSON BOBBY L	60250	WILSON MRS CHARLES L JR	24240
TUCKER CAROLYN JUNE	60430	WATSON MARY JULIA	60304	WILSON MRS DIXIE L	60589
TUCKER P. RUFFIN	21167	WATSON MRS CLAIR	60586	WILSON MRS SALLIE L.	01007
TUCKER SAM E	60334	WATSON R E	60251	WINDERS SHIRLEY RHODES	60003
TURNER DORA MAE	60072	WATSON RUTH TROWELL	60252	WINDHAM MRS J ROBERT	24250
TURNER PAUL	21173	WATT MRS. LORAINE	27631	WINSLOW MR RAYMOND A	24260
TUTEN MRS OLIVE P	21175	WATTS MRS JOSEPH	24093	WISNER MRS VENA B	60432
TYNDALL MRS T BRUCE	27328	WEAVER LEONA L	60509	WISS MRS NORMAN F JR	27441
ULSH HOWARD	22005	WEBB BILLEE SNEAD	27657	WOMACK HELEN RING	60516
UPTON ELOISE BARBEE	60377	WEBER JOHN H SR	25126	WOOD MRS MARGARETTE E	27600
UTZINGER PAULINE R	60378	WEINMAN ANNE MCREE	60166	WOOD WANDAH REA	60206
VANNATTA C L	23015	WENDELL BETTY J	60305	WOODARD E W	60512
VASSOS MRS CAROLYN	60379	WERTZ EDITH MOON	60382	WOODARD MRS JANET H	24285
VERNATTI MRS W J JR	23040	WESLEY IRMA HARDESTY	60510	WOODIE HELON P	60513
VICTOR MARLLYS	60303	WEST MARGARET	60383	WOODROW MRS KATHLEEN L	60188
VINSON WILLIAM JARRELL	60232	WEST MARGRET JENNINGS	60253	WOODS E P	60514
VOCHKO MRS ETHEL S.	23065	WHALEY MRS MARY K	24139	WOOTON MR RICHARD C	27429
VOIGTLANDER ELIZABETH VON	23070	WHEBY MRS MARION R	60037	WORSHAM JAMES N	60433
VOLLHEIM MARGE GOTT	60506	WHEELER ELLEN JAYNE MARIS	60203	WORTS SUE MILLER	27595
WADDLE LAURA	60584	WHEELER J H	60204	WRENN ELLEN A	24320
WADE MRS ROBERT V	27715	WHEELER MRS. JANELL	60485	WRENN MRS BARBARA T	24315
WADE OPHELIA	60507	WHITE HAZEL M	24153	WRIGHT CORDELIA B	60386
WALKER DOROTHY HILLMAN	60431	WHITE MRS ELSIE KOHL	60587	WRIGHT DAVID W	60515
WALKER FRANCES TEMPLETON	60234	WHITLEY EDITH C	24165	WRIGHT MIRIAM WALKER	27686
WALKER LOVONNE SANDERS	27332	WHITMIRE CINDY E	60205	YARBROUGH DAN	60434
WALKER MRS FRANK H	24012	WHITTEN JOYCE HAMBLETON	60029	YATES BETTY A	60254
WALKER MRS JAMES H	60508	WIGGINS LARRY	60384	YATES HOWARD D	60141
WALKER MRS JANE	60585	WIGHTMAN MRS DORRIS	60167	YORK BARBARA LEE	60025
WALKER MRS NADINE	60380	WILCOX MRS LOUISE	60168	YOST MILDRED SHOUSE	25027
WALKER MRS STEVE	27594	WILEY LAWANDA CARTER	60517	YOUNG MRS RUTH WATSON	60387
WALKER WILLIAM LEE	60038	WILHELM OLIVE	60511	YOUNG SOULE JOHNSON	60590
WALL MRS EDMOND O	24032	WILHITE KENNETH T	60035	ZEBOSKI MRS VIRGINIA C	60207
WALSH MRS EDMOND J	60248	WILKINS MRS GLENN A	60140	ZUTAUT MAGDALINE	60019

01006
MRS ANNE TRICKETT
5809 FOREST LANE
DALLAS TX 75230

01007
MRS SALLIE L WILSON
ROUTE 1 BOX 858
LITHIA FL 33547

01011
IRMA ADAMS
1815 RIVERMONT #6
LYNCHBURG VA 24503

01012
MRS MILTON E ADAMS
5309 HELENE DR
CHARLESTON SC 29405

01035
MRS CHARLES C ALEXANDER
903 MYERS AVE
COLUMBIA TN 38401

01040
VEARL G ALGER
2151 OAKLAND RD SP 123
SAN JOSE CA 95131

01054
MRS DOROTHY HALE AMIS
8730 FERNCLIFF AVE NE
BAINBRIDGE ISLAND WA 98110

01065
MRS LOUISE J ANDREW
18 VIOLET LANE
SOMERS POINT NJ 08244

02065
MISS JUNE B BAREKMAN
GENEALOGICAL SERVICES & PUB
CHICAGO IL 60641

02135
MRS ROBERT A BATTS
1707 AUDOBON DR
MURRAY KY 42071

02145
MRS LOUISE S BAUER
31 VILLAGE IN THE WOODS
SOUTHERN PINES NC 28387

02168
JOSEPHINE BEATTIE
31 LUCINDA LANE
MIDDLETOWN CT 06457

02170
MRS WARREN L BEENE
2610 HUCKLEBERRY LN
PASADENA TX 77502

02175
MISS AILENE BEESON
4303 TALLWOOD DRIVE
GREENSBORO NC 27410

02180
MRS JOHN BEHNKEN
12 S MADISON LA
NEWPORT NEWS VA 23606

02195
MRS ROBERT M BELLAMY
P O BOX 381
WASHINGTON NC 27889

02252
MRS BETTY BLAKENEY
WEST 1224 RIVERSIDE #1007
SPOKANE WA 99201

02256
W. ERNEST BLALOCK
205 WILLOW LAKE RD
GREENSBORO NC 27405

02280
JOHN W BOBBITT
2502 EYE ST NW
WASHINGTON DC 20037

02295
VIOLET M BOHNERT
42 W CLEARVIEW DR
SHREWSBURY PA 17361

02343
J ROBERT BOYKIN III
200 W GREEN ST
WILSON NC 27893

02355
MRS WILLIAM G BRANCH
1919 CAROLYN AVE
DENHAM SPRINGS LA 70726

02357
JOYCE R BRASWELL
P O BOX 53
LAURINBURG NC 28352

02412
ROY BROOKS
BOX 661
FOREST CITY NC 28043

02414
MRS W R BROTHERS
1843 N ST PAUL
WICHITA KS 67203

02435
MRS GLADYS BROWN
P O BOX 182
FRANKLINTON NC 27525

02450
REGINALD R BROWN
P O BOX 25808
RALEIGH NC 27611

02470
JOEL R BUCHANAN
114 BERWICK DR
OAK RIDGE TN 37830

02478
MRS JOE A BULAND JR
1100 E TERESA
SAPULPA OK 74066

02540
MRS ROBIN HARRIS BUTTS
RTE 2 BOX 120
ST JOSEPH LA 71366

02550
THOMAS M BYRD
903 WASHINGTON ST
CARY NC 27511

03015
MARTHA K CAMPBELL
2585 EDGEWOOD AVE
ALLIANCE OH 44601

03020
MRS LEON E CAMPBELL
3369 LOCKMOOR LANE
DALLAS TX 75220

03035
MRS JOHN W CANNADY
287 GHOLSON AVE
HENDERSON NC 27536

03041
MRS CHARLIE R CANNON JR
4779 ADAMS RD
DUNWOODY GA 30338

03065
MRS ERMA V CARMICHAEL
12418 E ST ANDREW DR
SUN CITY AZ 85351

03070
MRS JAMES A CARPENTER
2101 NASHVILLE RD
BOWLING GREEN KY 42101

03120
SISTER MARY FRANCIS CATES OSF
SAINT FRANCIS CONVENT
MISHAWAKA IN 46544

03125
DR DALE W CAUGHEY JR
1923 ASHBROOK DR
WILMINGTON NC 28403

03155
MRS JAMES O CLANTON
618 JOHN GLENN DR
GARLAND TX 75040

03183
MRS W T CLINKSCALES JR
860 VALLEY MEADE DR
MARIETTA GA 30067

03210
MR & MRS EDWIN L COMBS
417 OLDE POINT ROAD
HAMPSTEAD NC 28443

03213
ANNE D CONANT
305 FAIRFAX
BROWNSVILLE TX 78520

03250
ANNE R CORRELL
355 FAIRFAX DR
WINSTON SALEM NC 27104

03270
MR ELDON E COX
4233 S W 62ND CT
MIAMI FL 33155

03295
MR SAMUEL C CRAVER
231 WHITE LICK RD
MOORESVILLE IN 46158

03313
GARY L CREASON
P O BOX 1496
LENOIR NC 28645

03315
CHARLES W CREECH
RT 1 BOX 196
ZEBULON NC 27597

03328
MRS T J CRUISE
13902 PERTHSHIRE
HOUSTON TX 77079

04050
MRS WILLIAM L DAVIS
1015 N WASHINGTON STREET
RUTHERFORDTON NC 28139

04053
MRS NETTIE HIGHTOWER DAWSON
15 S WASHINGTON ST
EMPORIA KS 66800

04065
MR & MRS WILBUR T DEBNAM
P O BOX 336
ZEBULON NC 27597

04080
MARY LOU DELAHUNT
RR 2 BOX 60
AVON IL 61415

04085
FRED E DEMARCUS
2834 LEISURE WOODS LANE
DECATUR GA 30034

04103
MRS DOLORES B DEURING
1602 BRENTWOOD WAY
SIMPSONVILLE SC 29681

04115
RUTH E DINKINS MD
OLD MEDLIN RD
MEDINA TN 38355

04135
ELLA FRANCES DODD
BOX 217
LOVELADY TX 75851

04155
MR CLETUS L DORRIS
4407 LIMEWOOD
WINTER HAVEN FL 33880

04195
JOSEPH M DUNCAN
960 THE SIXTEENTH FAIRWAY
DUNWOODY GA 30338

04200
MRS J B DUVAL
503 SYCAMORE ST
DECATUR GA 30030

05035
MRS ROGER F ELLER
405 VERNON TERRACE
RALEIGH NC 27609

05045
MISS GAYLE ELLIS
1439 E STRATFORD AVE
SALT LAKE CITY UT 84106

05059
CRAIG C EMERSON
15138 GEORGIA RD
WOODBRIDGE VA 22191

05065
DR K C EMERSON
560 BOULDER DR
SANIBEL FL 33957

05070
MRS POE W ESKRIDGE JR
2069 QUEEN ST
WINSTON SALEM NC 27103

06005
MRS WARREN L FALLER
901 W STOREY
MIDLAND TX 79701

06015
MRS ALBERT E FANT JR
104 BAYOU CIRCLE
GULFPORT MS 39501

06050
MRS JOHN S FENTRESS
3519 SHEPHERD ST
CHEVY CHASE MD 20815

06065
JUDY B FILINGERI
APT 162
DALLAS TX 75234

06070
REX B FINLEY
3126 GRAIL ST
WICHITA KS 67211

06075
LUCY E FISHER
9801 MALLARD CREEK RD
CHARLOTTE NC 28213

06080
MRS G B FLETCHER
41 DECATUR ST
PORTSMOUTH VA 23702

06085
MRS BILL FLOWERS
214 WATERWORKS ST
DALTON GA 30720

06090
MR JOHN H FOARD JR
P O BOX 487
KANNAPOLIS NC 28081

06100
DIXIE FOLLETTE
RT 6 BOX 497
SALISBURY NC 28144

06145
MARY E FOUTS
2504 BROOKLAWN AVE
PEKIN IL 61554

06158
JOSEPH R FRAZIER
20120 LORAIN RD APT 102
FAIRVIEW PK OH 44126

06159
MRS B C FREE
1208 W FAIRVIEW ST
ALVIN TX 77511

06195
RICHARD V FULP
6260 E MERCER WAY
MERCER ISLAND WA 98040

07015
PAT GAINES
RTE 1 BOX 318 A
MISSION TX 78572

07017
JAMES M & PEGGY W GAITHER
RTE 5 BOX 105
HICKORY NC 28601

07018
MRS LEO E GAMBLE
333 KANSAS STREET
SPRINGFIELD CO 81073

07027
MRS. THOMAS FITE PAINE JR.
3 REDBUD DR.
NASHVILLE TN 37215

07040
PRESTON F GARRIS
RT 4 BOX 243
LA GRANGE NC 28551

07078
MRS JOHN R GERMANY
13602 GLEN ERICA
HOUSTON TX 77069

07087
MRS BRENDA GODSEY
RT 11 BOX 605
FLORENCE AL 35630

07095
MRS F M GOSSUM JR
201 COURT DRIVE
FULTON KY 42041

07115
MRS JOHN W GRAHAM JR
3458 MANCHESTER DR
CHARLOTTE NC 28210

07168
DAN WESLEY GRIFFITH
1609 KAREN LANE
IOWA PARK TX 76367

07187
MRS C R HACKNEY
BOX 1198
HUNTSVILLE TX 77340

08010
LYMAN S HAINLINE
410 E SUMMIT
MACOMB IL 61455

08015
EILEEN HALL
1720 S PARK AVE
MELBOURNE FL 32901

08023
MRS CHARLES H HAMPTON
815 TRAILING HEART RD
ROSWELL NM 88201

08040
MISS SULA H HARDISON
ROUTE 3
COLUMBIA TN 38401

08053
MRS JAMES HARNESS
312 GREENLEAF ST
LONGVIEW TX 75605

08065
BROWN HARVEY SR
1667 VALLEY RD
CLARKSVILLE TN 37040

08070
MARY BUTLER HARVEY
1600 WESTBROOK AVE #613
RICHMOND VA 23227

08073
HIRAM J HASH
8890 MORGANTOWN RD
INDIANAPOLIS IN 46217

08090
MRS WEYNETTE PARKS HAUN
243 ARGONNE DR
DURHAM NC 27704

08095
MRS CHESTER C HAWORTH
803 KINGSTON CT
HIGH POINT NC 27260

08120
MRS EARL HEDDINS
1409 S MONROE
SAN ANGELO TX 76901

08130
PATRICIA ANN HEIDORN
505 E VAN BUREN
JANESVILLE WI 53545

08145
LILLIAN FAY HENDERSON
128 1/2 DAVIS ST
WYANDOTTE MI 48192

08150
MRS M E HENDERSON
BOX 177
MOORELAND OK 73852

08165
GE LEE CORLEY HENDRIX
3 ACORN CT
GREENVILLE SC 29609

08185
MRS G W HENSON
213 OAKDALE
PASADENA TX 77506

08190
MRS RUTH GOOD HENSON
59 SO 38TH ST
MESA AZ 85206

08200
DR C NASH HERNDON
1600 LYNWOOD AVE
WINSTON SALEM NC 27104

08219
VICTORIA B HIGGINS
1760 SECOND AVE, APT 5 S
NEW YORK NY 10028

08226
MRS LEILA W HILL
6130 S IVY ST
ENGLEWOOD CO 80111

08240
DORCAS M HOBBS
P O BOX 752
PIKEVILLE KY 41501

08265
ARTHUR D HODGIN
2601 NORTHWEST A ST
RICHMOND IN 47374

08275
CAPT CLEO HOGAN
P O BOX 2132
ASHEVILLE NC 28802

08355
MRS SAMUEL E HUCKS
2386 MAPLEWOOD AVE
WINSTON SALEM NC 27103

09030
OVETA M ISBILL
1518 HICKORY LANE
BETTENDORF IA 52722

10010
DELWOOD S JACKSON
1738 CEDAR AVE
CINCINNATI OH 45224

10060
EDDIS JOHNSON
840 E COLUMBUS STREET
MARTINSVILLE IN 46151

10085
DR ROBERT H JOHNSON JR
3410 WALTON WAY
AUGUSTA GA 30909

10090
MRS SIDNEY P JOHNSON
BOX 68
WEST MS 39192

10120
JAMES B JOLLEY
C/O ENTERPRISE RESEARCH CENTER
ENTERPRISE AL 36331

10153
MRS V R JOYNER
2358 PARENTAL HOME ROAD
JACKSONVILLE FL 32216

10154
MRS FRANK M JOYCE
264 RIGGS DR
CLEMSON SC 29631

11010
RUTH E KARISNY
P O BOX 153
BALL LA 71405

11070
MRS WILEY KIMBRO
303 CRUME AVE
CLINTON KY 42031

11100
MRS JOHN H KIRKLAND JR
145 RUTLEDGE RD
GREENWOOD SC 29646

11105
EUNICE T KIRKPATRICK
17-B VALLEY TERRACE APTS
DURHAM NC 27707

11145
MRS LU J KOONTZ
P O BOX 125
NEW LONDON NC 28127

12005
PINKNEY L LACKEY
517 VIEWMONT NE
LENOIR NC 28645

12008
MRS WILLIAM A LAMPTON
BOX 467
TYLERTOWN MS 39667

12015
LOUISE G LANDY
1427 SOUTH MADISON
SAN ANGELO TX 76901

12019
MRS CLARA B LANE
RT 1 BOX 7-B
BLUFFTON SC 29910

12040
HELEN F M LEARY
1305 CAMILLE CT
RALEIGH NC 27609

12050
MARVIN A LEDBETTER
254 ROYAL PINE DR
ARDEN NC 28704

12065
HOWARD B LEE
29120 FIRTHRIDGE RD
RANCHO PALOS VERDES CA 90274

12068
JOSEPH R LEE
APT 102-H
WASHINGTON DC 20008

12075
CORNELIA ELLIS LEE
1866 N GRAHAM ST
MEMPHIS TN 38108

12090
GEORGE BRADLEY LENNON SR
R.R. 2
NEVIS MN 56467

12100
KATE LEPINE
4502 COVENTRY RD
FAYETTEVILLE NC 28304

12125
MRS STAHLE LINN JR
P O BOX 1948
SALISBURY NC 28144

12140
MRS JOHN S LITCHFIELD
RT 2 BOX 155
WASHINGTON NC 27889

12144
ANN C W LITTLE
2800 SANDIA DR,
RALEIGH NC 27607

12210
MRS WILLIAM R LYNCH
234 WILLOW BEND
HUNTSVILLE TX 77340

13006
BETTY L MABEE
4545 YERBA SANTA DR
SAN DIEGO CA 92115

13020
GLADYS HORN MALONE
2924 LINDEN LEA
IRVING TX 75061

13052
JAMES I MARLOWE
8011 HILLCREST DRIVE
MANASSAS VA 22110

13090
DR & MRS WILLIAM P MATTHEWS
303 SHADOW VALLEY ROAD
HIGH POINT NC 27260

13095
L W MAXWELL
411 WHITEHALL CIRCLE
PARIS TN 38242

13105
STEPHEN MAYFIELD
695 CAROLLO AVE
SLIDELL LA 70458

13120
DAVID & JANE MEEKINS
139 WEST ANDREWS AVE
HENDERSON NC 27536

13175
WILLIAM L MING
371 BROUGHTON
WACO TX 76710

13264
WILLIAM L MURPHY JR
P. O. BOX 26482
RALEIGH NC 27611

14019
LYNETTE MCCARTHY
306 S GROVE
NORMAL IL 61761

14020
MRS JUSTIN P MCCARTY
2222 N PADRE ISLAND DR
CORPUS CHRISTI TX 78408

14030
MR & MRS CLIFTON A MCCLELLAND
1112 JAMES ST
WHITEVILLE NC 28472

14045
MRS JEAN LEE MCCRACKEN
11002 428TH AVE SE
NORTH BEND WA 98045

14050
JOHN R MCCRACKEN
2410 ANIHINIHI ST
PEARL CITY HI 96782

14105
ZERA GREEN MCKINNIE
1508 ELIZABETH ST
WEST MONROE LA 71291

15005
MRS H M NAFF
610 JEFFERSON ST
TALLULAH LA 71282

15023
HARRY A NELMS
322 VISTA TRAIL
CONCORD TN 37720

15045
MRS LOUISE P NIEDERMAIER
3922 S BUCKNER BLVD
DALLAS TX 75227

15098
LUCILE V NOVAK
26 RAYMOND ST
NASHUA NH 03060

16030
MRS JUNE T ORMOND
2606 N L ST
MIDLAND TX 79701

16035
MRS L S ORRICK
3629 WEDGWAY
FORT WORTH TX 76133

17005
MISS MABEL B PACE
6-H ASHLEY HOUSE LOCKWOOD DR
CHARLESTON SC 29401

17025
WILLIAM E PAGE III
P O BOX 602
SEBRING FL 33870

17046
DORIS PARKER
913 WEST 5TH
PAWHUSKA OK 74056

17070
LARRY W PARR
1211 BEECH HAVEN RD
ATLANTA GA 30324

17075
MRS WILLIAM F PATTON
315 EAST CRAWFORD
PARIS IL 61944

17080
MRS J E PAULK
4139 WINDMERE PLACE
SARASOTA FL 33531

17085
STEPHEN C PEARSALL
7704 SURACI CT #101
ANNANDALE VA 22003

17090
ALLEN PENDERGRAFT
RR 5-10A
SEDONA AZ 86336

17100
MRS MICHAEL W PENLEY
17102 PACIFIC COAST HWY #202
HUNTINGTON BEACH CA 92649

17105
MRS PAUL PENNINGTON
38042 RIVER DRIVE
LEBANON OR 97355

17129
MRS BAXTER PERRY
RTE 2 BOX 136
BUCHANAN TN 38222

17135
RUTH PHILLIP
605 BENTON AVE
MISSOULA MT 59801

17140
G HOWARD PHILLIPS
3700 DARBYSHIRE DR
COLUMBUS OH 43220

17147
VIRGINIA HARDING PHILLIPS
511 N WILLOW AVE
FAYETTEVILLE AK 72701

17150
JAMES W PICKARD
P O BOX 578
RANDLEMAN NC 27317

17165
COL SAMUEL W PINNELL
USAA BLDG
FAIRFAX VA 22031

17170
MRS ELIZABETH C PLUMBLEE
RT 3 BOX 259
BURLINGTON NC 27215

17185
MARIE POOR
RR 1 BOX 28
KENNEY IL 61749

17187
MRS JANINE PORTER
1209 FERNWOOD CT
COEUR D'ALENE ID 83814

17195
FRANK A POTTS
12777 MASON MANOR DR
ST LOUIS MO 63141

17213
NOREEN PRAMBERG
59 WASHINGTON ST
NEWBURYPORT MA 01950

17220
A B PRUITT
25 HEATHERWOOD APTS
GREENVILLE SC 29607

17235
MRS JAMES F PUGH
ROUTE 3 BOX 74A
CHECOTAH OK 74426

17240
MRS C BRYSON PULLEY
RT 1 ISLE OPINES
WATERLOO SC 29384

18010
MISS MARJORIE E QUEEN
2343 CHAMBERS LAKE DRIVE
LACEY WA 98503

19017
MRS LORRAINE L RALEY
4760 SPRINGFIELD DR
ATLANTA GA 30338

19040
HAZEL REA
STAR ROUTE BOX 194
BUFFALO MO 65622

19075
MISS KATHERINE REYNOLDS
1605 BANKS
HOUSTON TX 77006

19095
W A RICHMOND
P O BOX 202
MORGAN CITY LA 70380

19115
SALLY R ROBERTS
2712 W BERWYN RD
MUNCIE IN 47304

19130
HAYWOOD L ROBERTSON
CHESAPEAKE HOUSE APT 1107
VIRGINIA BEACH VA 23455

19170
HELEN YORK ROSE
320 NO SIXTH
SEMINOLE OK 74868

19177
BEN LACY ROSE
1221 RENNIE AVE
RICHMOND VA 23227

19183
GERALDINE C ROSS
7981 BEAVER LAKE DR
SAN DIEGO CA 92119

19227
VELMA A RUDD
BOX 388
DEL RIO TX 78840

19230
MRS H H RUGELEY
2202 W 10TH STREET
AUSTIN TX 78703

20007
KAY WATERS SAKARIS
7227 WOODLAND WEST DR
HOUSTON TX 77040

20030
MRS R M SANDERS SR
RT 1 BOX 551-A
WILMINGTON NC 28405

20060
MRS ALLEN SAUPE
RTE 2 BOX 183
MOORES HILL IN 47032

20073
DORCAS W SCHMIDT
318 BRUNSWICK ST
SOUTHPORT NC 28461

20078
MRS W W SCHRAMM
850 ELM TREE LANE
ST LOUIS MO 63122

20080
MISS ERNEST MAE SEAHOLM
107 BRIGHTWOOD APT F
SAN ANTONIO TX 78209

20085
MRS M W SEDGLEY
552 JAN DR
FAIRHOPE AL 36532

20095
BEATRICE WEST SEITZ
214 W VAN BUREN ST
JANESVILLE WI 53545

20105
MRS DIXIE HOOPER SHAW
3532 W LA STATE DRIVE
KENNER LA 70062

20125
MRS S SHELTON
1303 E 79
KANSAS CITY MO 64131

20135
MRS HAROLD SHEPHERD
2103 SEVEN GABLES HWY
CAPITOLA CA 95010

20138
ANNA S SHERMAN
312 DE VANE ST
FAYETTEVILLE NC 28305

20210
MRS CHARLES A SMITH
9322 CREEL CREEK DR
DALLAS TX 75228

20220
MRS H A SMITH
1223 WAKE FOREST RD
RALEIGH NC 27604

20229
MISS KARON MAC SMITH
ROUTE 1 BOX 190
NIXON TX 78140

20245
MURRIEL L SMITH
328 SO MAPLE
MT PROSPECT IL 60056

20330
VIRGINIA HOLT SPAKE
210 S ROWAN AVE
SPENCER NC 28159

20333
PAULA SPENCER
3461 N EDISON ST
ARLINGTON VA 22207

20335
R S SPENCER JR
P O BOX 159
ENGELHARD NC 27824

20350
HELEN E SPORE
ROUTE 1 BOX19
KILDARE OK 74642

20380
RUTH A STEELMAN
4303 TALLWOOD DRIVE
GREENSBORO NC 27410

20415
MR VAN A STILLEY
718 9TH STREET SE
WASHINGTON DC 20003

20425
A J STOKES
P O BOX 1
NAHUNTA GA 31553

20435
MR & MRS GARLAND P STOUT
1209 HILL STREET
GREENSBORO NC 27408

20448
MRS THOMAS I STUART
270 W COMMERCIAL AVE
LOWELL IN 46356

20450
JOHN HALE STUTESMAN
305 SPRUCE STREET
SAN FRANCISTO CA 94118

21035
WILLIAM FREDERICK TAYLOR
BOX 147
HOOKERTON NC 28538

21080
MR & MRS A G THOMPSON JR
ROUTE 1 BOX 233
BURLINGTON NC 27215

21095
HAROLD LEE THOMPSON
7685 SO JAY RD
WEST MILTON OH 45383

21115
MRS. CARSEY L. TIPPETT
P O BOX 488
ZEBULON NC 27597

21165
MRS J L TRYON
4421 RIDGECREST CIR #167
AMARILLO TX 79109

21167
P. RUFFIN TUCKER
2521 COMMONWEALTH AVE
CHARLOTTE NC 28205

21173
PAUL TURNER
317 DRUID LANE
TULLAHOMA TN 37388

21175
MRS OLIVE P TUTEN
RT 1 BOX 64F
BOYDTON VA 23917

22005
HOWARD ULSH
4 MAGNOLIA RD
CHARLESTON SC 29407

23015
C L VANNATTA
6901-D ROSWELL RD
SANDY SPRINGS GA 30328

23040
MRS W J VERNATTI JR
ROUTE 4 BOX 233
REEDS SPRINGS MO 65737

more

23065
MRS ETHEL S. VOCHKO
30322 BENECIA AVE.
LAGUNA NIGUEL CA 92677

23070
ELIZABETH VON VOIGTLANDER
2013 PAULINE COURT
ANN ARBOR MI 48103

24012
MRS FRANK H WALKER
ROUTE 1 BOX 274
EDEN NC 27288

24032
MRS EDMOND O WALL
P O BOX 225
WHITEVILLE NC 28472

24055
WALLACE T WARD
600 OAKLEY PL
ALEXANDRIA VA 22303

24073
MRS JOHN T WATKINS
111 COLLEGE DR
HAMMOND LA 70401

24093
MRS JOSEPH WATTS
P O BOX 311
WILLOWS CA 95988

24139
MRS MARY K WHALEY
103 LAWSHE CIRCLE
GARNER NC 27529

24153
HAZEL M WHITE
910 PENNSYLVANIA AVE APT 702
KANSAS CITY MO 64105

24165
EDITH C WHITLEY
1909-G N CENTENNIAL ST
HIGH POINT NC 27260

24210
ELLEN AMIDON WILLIAMS
RT 1 BOX 63
SWAN QUARTER NC 27885

24213
HELLEN T WILLIAMS
300 WEST FIFTH ST
SOUTH BETHANY DE 19930

24240
MRS CHARLES L WILSON JR
403 S. MAIN STREET
ROBERSONVILLE NC 27871

24243
EDITH L WILSON
SUNRISE ACRES RT 1 LOT 12
FLETCHER NC 28732

24250
MRS J ROBERT WINDHAM
P O BOX 14741
ALBUQUERQUE NM 87191

24260
MR RAYMOND A WINSLOW
P O BOX 652
HERTFORD NC 27944

24285
MRS JANET H WOODARD
15 HUNTERS FOREST DR
CHARLESTON SC 29407

24315
MRS BARBARA T WRENN
401 SO DOGWOOD AVENUE
SILER CITY NC 27344

24320
ELLEN A WRENN
P O BOX 3
HAMPTON VA 23669

25027
MILDRED SHOUSE YOST
35 N JOHN ST
BLOOMFIELD IN 47424

25040
MISS CHARLOTTE M BRETT
218 EAST 4TH ST, APT 4A
SPENCER IA 51301

25087
DOYLE P SWOFFORD
208 LOWDEN HUNT DR
HAMPTON VA 23666

25093
MARY L LEACH
4614 LAKE PARK DR
WICHITA FALLS TX 76302

25097
GEORGE W FEE
403 NO CEDAR ST
MISHAWAKA IN 46544

25098
ELIZABETH P KELLER
922 HAWTHORNE DR NE
LENOIR NC 28645

25100
MRS GRADY ROSS
2138 SHERWOOD AVE
CHARLOTTE NC 28207

25108
JOYCE SPEAROW
4682 GALLUP AVE
CLEVELAND OH 44127

25112
MRS CARL E BEATY
2508 NEW HAMPSHIRE
JOPLIN MO 64801

25115
MRS DONALD E SMITH
2023 E SINTO
SPOKANE WA 99202

25117
SHIRLEY TALLEY
1023 14TH ST BOX 1
OROVILLE CA 95965

25121
LORETTA L KORTAN
1069 CIRCLE DR
BROOKINGS SD 57006

25126
JOHN H WEBER SR
3512 W LAKEFIELD APT 3 WEST
MILWAUKEE WI 53215

25127
MRS CARSON FOREMAN ✓
RT 1
WALTONVILLE IL 62894

25129
MRS G. W. GILMER
409 CHURCH ST
MT PLEASANT SC 29464

25133
MRS VIC C. CAST
139 SPRINGDALE LAKE ESTATES
BELTON MO 64012

25134
RALPH W AND BONNIE J SHAW
1967 S LONE PINE
SPRINGFIELD MO 65804

25135
MARJORY PAYNE
355 BEDFORD CENTER RD
BEDFORD HILLS NY 10507

25141
MRS MARJORIE H HERRING
12016 MIDLAKE DR
DALLAS TX 75218

25143
LENA LEHNERT
RT 3 BOX 49
MOSES LAKE WN 98837

25144
MARGARET S. RAMBO
7 LAKESIDE KNOLLS
HILLSBORO IL 62049

25145
MRS RAYMOND HOOTEN
920 KEITH DR
PERRY OH 31069

25149
ELIZABETH LAUGHLIN
2916 SOUTH EAST STREET
KIRKSVILLE MO 63501

25156
ERIS R. PASKETT
83 E 2ND SOUTH
TOOELE UT 84074

25158
MRS JOHN R FOWLKES
2119 S WARD
CARUTHERSVILLE MO 63830

25159
JACQUELYN D. BARNES
675 NE INNES LA
BEND OR 97701

25161
MRS RUTH E. MIDDLETON
6154 MEADOW LANE CIRCLE
KANSAS CITY MO 64118

25162
MRS KENNETH J CLERICO
2034 S W HIGH ST
TOPEKA KS 66604

25167
WILLIAM J. COX, JR.
1522 DROXFORD LANE
HOUSTON TX 77008

25168
MARY COLEMAN STEWART
P O BOX 382
CAMDEN AL 36726

25171
JEAN DAIL
3105 53RD AVE E
BRADENTON FL 33508

25174
SIBYL D. STRATMANN
915 WEST ASH ST
SALINA KA 67401

25178
MRS N D DAVIS
616 WRIGHTS MILL RD
AUBURN AL 36830

25185
DEANNA MCNEELY
1413 SCOTTSDALE
CHAMPAIGN IL 61820

25191
J T LIMBAUGH
BLDG 406, BOX 481
FORT MYER VA 22211

25195
MARY ETTA BOSLET
P O BOX 2392
RIVERSIDE CA 92516

25196
ROBERT E TAYLOR
130 E FOURTH ST
GREENVILLE OH 45331

25198
EILEEN MUND MCKAY
7550 SW 141 ST
MIAMI FL 33158

25199
MRS LUELLA M CROTHERS
1518 GREENBROOK LANE
FLINT MI 48507

25204
MRS MARY E H JACKSON
BOX 726
CANADIAN TX 79014

25206
MRS CHARLES OVERBECK
421 LAKESHORE DR
FAYETTEVILLE NC 28305

25213
MRS JOHNNIE W POOLE
P O BOX 587
RAMSEUR NC 27316

25215
WILLIAM K PLEASANTS
502 ROLLINS AVE
HAMLET NC 28345

25223
RUTH CANTERBURY
431 N CROWN POINT
ADA OK 74820

25226
MRS H E HUMPHREY
5758 MELODY ST
FT WORTH TX 76134

25229
MARY G GRAVELLE
42 IRVING LANE
ORINDA CA 94563

25235
MRS BRENDA NORWOOD DUSEK
4 HARMIN RR 3
COLLINSVILLE IL 62234

25238
WILMA GRIFFIN
RT 1 BOX 12
SNOW CAMP NC 27349

25241
ETHEL M GRISHAM
1033 BERKLEY AVE
PUEBLO CO 81004

25242
PRESTON ROARK
RR 8 BOX 173
MANCHESTER KY 40962

25251
MRS DANIEL M LANE
1504 GUILFORD LA
OKLAHOMA CITY OK 73120

25253
ROGER E PALMER
3752 DEL MAR DR
WOODBRIDGE VA 22193

25254
MRS DOROTHY P ROBERTS
9733 CHEROKEE RD
RICHMOND VA 23235

25257
JANET MORGAN SAPANAS
11 WILLIAMS
FT LEON WD MO 65473

27260
HUBERT L BELISLE
12117 SE 29 ST
CHOCTAW OK 73020

27268
MRS MILTON W NEATHERY
450 FOREST RD
ATHENS GA 30605

27269
MRS HARRY G COLLINS
1465 PANORAMA DR
BIRMINGHAM AL 35216

27270
MRS JOHN RUCKMAN BARNETT
106 MCTIGHE DR
BELLAIRE TX 77401

27276
MRS SAM J MOORE JR
RT 2 BOX 436
WALLER TX 77484

27280
MRS WILSON LEVERTON
54 B PINE LAKE DR
WHISPERING PINES NC 28389

27281
MRS WILMA WILLIAMS HORTON
700 PEBBLEBROOK DR
RALEIGH NC 27609

27286
MRS WILLIAM E CRAIG
901 S SANTA FE
SALINA KS 67401

27291
MYRNA L HANSLER
2004 W WALL
MIDLAND TX 79701

27292
JANE CARTER OGBURN
312 FINLEY ST
N WILKESBORO NC 28659

27301
EVELYNE MCCRACKEN
211 VINE
GREENVILLE IL 62246

27302
MRS HAZEL H BUFFALOE
8200 KROMER ST
AUSTIN TX 78758

27303
MRS ELOISE T ALLISON
P O BOX 564
RINGOLD LA 71068

27306
KATHERINE PHILLIPS
1712 KENILWORTH AVE #7
CHARLOTTE NC 28203

27311
GINGER WINTERS STALLINGS
112 CAMBRIDGE CIRCLE
LAFAYETTE LA 70503

27313
GUY S CLARK, MD
2419 CASTILLO ST
-- -----

27318
AUDREY L WILLIAMS
P. O. BOX 2691
MONTEREY CA 93940

27322
MRS L E STRIEBECK
1924 NOBLE AVE
SPRINGFIELD IL 62704

27328
MRS T BRUCE TYNDALL
4704 WAVERLY LANE
JACKSONVILLE FL 32210

27332
LOVONNE SANDERS WALKER
ROUTE 3 BOX 74
TECUMSEH OK 74873

27334
BERNICE WARD EDNEY
409 E HIGH ST
LEXINGTON KY 40508

27335
BEVERLY CHASTAIN LARROUX
RT 1 BOX 114
LOCUST GROVE OK 74352

27339
MRS HAZEL COYNE
5601 BETHEL PIKE APR 535
MUNCIE IN 47302

27346
LOREN D AUSTIN
1424-26 SOUTH TERRACE RD
TEMPE AZ 85281

27348
MRS ELSIE DOKE
804 SWAN ST
SPRINGFIELD MO 65807

27356
MRS HAMILTON ALBAUGH JR
144 FOREST DRIVE
SHORT HILLS NJ 07078

27365
JANE ROGERS
401 N EVERETT ST
KENNETT MO 63857

27366
MARY BELLE LEGUIN
1112 CADDO
ARKADELPHIA AR 71923

27374
LEON E SILANCE
RT 3 BOX 433
JACKSONVILLE NC 28540

27375
MRS RODNEY KILDUFF
822 DONAGHEY
CONWAY AR 72032

27378
FRANCES R JOWDY
P O BOX 909
WASHINGTON NC 27889

27380
HARRY B MCGINN
RT 3 BOX 344
GREENWOOD SC 29646

27382
MRS. THOMAS M. CRAWFORD
625 S BELTLINE BLVD
COLUMBIA SC 29205

27392
MS. MERVA E SCHWEIKART
2612 SO WAYNE ST
ARLINGTON VA 22206

27402
MRS MAXINE E PRIDDY
1508 W MCALESTER
SULPHUR OK 73086

27404
MRS DOROTHY H AVERY
STAR ROUTE BOX 108
CLAVERACK NY 12513

27406
LARRY MCREE
194 GREENWOOD DRIVE
MADISON AL 35758

27413
RICHARD C BENTLEY
6541 JAFFE CT #12
SAN DIEGO CA 92119

27417
LETTIE B THRIFT
BOX 81
ONAWA IA 51040

27420
LAVELLE CARTER
814 W AVALON RT 1
KUNA ID 83634

27429
MR RICHARD C WOOTON
3517A SOUTH STAFFORD
ARLINGTON VA 22206

27435
RICHARD H HUFFMAN
307 NORTHVIEW DR
RICHARDSON TX 75080

27438
BOBBIE J SUDDETH
P O BOX 205
CHINA GROVE NC 28023

27441
MRS NORMAN F WISS JR
12 CHESTNUT PL
SHORT HILLS NJ 07078

27467
LUCILLE G R PICKETT
204 E PINE ST
WINNSBORO TX 75494

27475
DORIS ANN BUTLER LUCAS
10146 W AVE I
LANCASTER CA 93534

27476
LANCE E KEY
S.R. 28, MONTE ROAD
EAGLE RIVER AK 99577

27477
SHELBY N HUGHES
404 STATE ST
WILLIAMSTON NC 27892

27488
LUCY MILLER JACOBSON
6410 NIXON
LAKEWOOD CA 90713

27495
ALBERTA R PAYTON
573 E PROVIDENCIA AVE
BURBANK CA 91501

27531
RONALD J SEIBERT
1432 ARTHUR AVE
LAKEWOOD OH 44107

27532
THOMAS F CURRY JR
4200 HARGILL DR
ORLANDO FL 32806

27533
MRS JOYCE MILLER
307 CENTER ST
HOLLY MI 48442

27537
MRS RUBY B BUCK
307 N 30TH ST
WILMINGTON NC 28405

27542
CHARLES D APPLE
ROUTE 7 BOX 392-A
REIDSVILLE NC 27320

27543
FAYE MITCHELL DASEN
6901 BUFFALO RD BOX 200
RALEIGH NC 27604

27546
MRS CHAS. A. BARLEY
327 S LAFAYETTE
BREMERTON WA 98312

27548
ISOM E MEDFORD
BOX 2826
HUNTSVILLE TX 77340

27549
MRS CARL Y BONNER
330 N STEWARD
FAIRFIELD TX 75840

27553
LYNN BOYD REENER
609 W BUCHANAN
LITCHFIELD IL 62056

27554
L C BOYKIN
RT 1 BOX 127
CAMDEN SC 29020

27555
PAULINE SIMMONS
RT 2
POMONA MO 65789

27560
MRS ROSS B JOHNSON
240 QUAY ST
LAKEWOOD CO 80226

27562
OWEN D HARRELL
5425 INVERCHAPEL RD
SPRINGFIELD VA 22151

27566
COL. & MRS W R PURCELL
720 AUMOND RD
AUGUSTA GA 30909

27568
SHIRLEY SCOTT DYE
2114 AVENUE R
HUNTSVILLE TX 77340

27569
JO ANNE ALLENBAUGH
21742 GRACE AVE
CARSON CA 90745

27573
MRS ESTHER MCFARLANE CHAUNCEY
5940 BRINDA AVE
NORFOLK VA 23502

27583
MRS R C GENTRY
1604 ELM ST
DENVER CO 80220

27586
HOWELL BOONE
BOONES FARM RD
MOCKSVILLE NC 27028

27593
DELBERT MARCOM FOWLER
5708 WILLOW LANE
DALLAS TX 75230

27594
MRS STEVE WALKER
1409 9TH ST NW
MIAMI OK 74354

27595
SUE MILLER WORTS
2111 ASH AVE
LAS VEGAS NV 89101

27596
MRS CAROLE ELSTON
BOX 172
DONNELLSON IA 52625

27599
LADONNA H LATHAM
ROUTE 2 BOX 255
CLINTON KY 42031

27600
MRS MARGARETTE E WOOD
9332 DUNLOGGIN RD
ELLICOTT CITY MD 21043

27602
MRS GEORGE MILLER
RR 2 BOX 198 E10
FAIRVIEW TN 37062

27631
MRS. LORAINE WATT
P O BOX 61
GODFREY IL 62035

27657
BILLEE SNEAD WEBB
651 SHERWOOD WAY NE
CORVALLIS OR 97330

27673
MRS GEORGE T ACOSTA
528 LAWTON AVE
JACKSONVILLE FL 32208

27682
NANCY N MILLER
P O BOX 331
BRANDON FL 33511

27686
MIRIAM WALKER WRIGHT
931 MESSINA DR
PUNTA GORDA FL 33950

27697
ANDREW W MILLER
2256 GLENWOOD CIRCLE
COLORADO SPRINGS CO 80909

27699
YETIVE D RAMSEY
501 SAN JACINTO
LA PORTE TX 77571

27700
MRS G D SPAFFORD
810 SHADY LANE
BELLEVILLE KS 66935

27714
GLENN NORMAN ROGERS
RT 1 BOX 87
CAMERON NC 28326

27715
MRS ROBERT V WADE
2791 ENGLEWOOD DR NE
NORTH CANTON OH 44721

27728
MRS JOSEPH E JOHNSTON
4325 CLAY AVE
FT WORTH TX 76109

27734
MRS BARBARA C BURGEMEYER
1150 CULPEPPER CIRCLE
CHARLESTON SC 29407

27740
ANNE PRICE MACKENZIE
2007 SUNSHINE SQ
LONGVIEW TX 75601

27745
DARRELL S KEITH
616 LONGVIEW STREET
CARROLLTON GA 30117

27756
HELEN ALTMAN
5701 LOUISE LANE
AUSTIN TX 78731

27758
DOROTHY D IRVIN
RR 1 BOX 607
SAHUARITA AZ 85629

27760
JUNE KIGHT BLIVEN
5842 PADDON CIR
SAN JOSE CA 95123

27761
FREDA R COX
717 CEDAR DR
KNOXVILLE TX 37912

27773
HOWARD W MARTIN
2120 GRANT
EL PASO TX 79930

27775
MRS DONALD G O'TOOLE
32720 MCCONNEL CT
WARREN MI 48092

60000
BARBARA FRITCHMAN
811 MILLER ST
WINSTON SALEM NC 27103

60001
MRS GRACE FRANK MAYBERRY
210 MCELWEE ST
N WILKESBORO NC 28659

60002
MRS B M RODRIGUEZ
515 GIUFFRIAS
METAIRIE LA 70001

60003
SHIRLEY RHODES WINDERS
106 DOVER DR
LAFAYETTE LA 70503

60004
MRS GERTRUDE E GRAY
17833 6TH AVE SW
SEATTLE WA 98166

60005
BOYD T HENDRIX JR
3076 KINNAMON RD
WINSTON SALEM NC 27104

60006
BETTE HANLON JENKINS
RT 2 BOX 173
GUTHRIE CENTER IA 50115

60007
HELEN ROBERTS
16 PARKVIEW DR
TUSCALOOSA AL 35401

60008
MRS JOHN TYLER MAULDIN
2804 ANDREWS DR NW
ATLANTA GA 30305

60009
HILDA CHANCE
61 WEATHERVANE RD
ASTON PA 19014

60010
JOY HILLIARD GRIFFEY
ROUTE 4 BOX 212
CLARKSVILLE TN 37040

60011
SUZANNE MURRAY
2130 P ST NW #625
WASHINGTON DC 20037

60012
ROSALIND REDFERN
BOX 1747
MIDLAND TX 79702

60013
BETTY J ARNOLD GUZAK
3895 EMBARCADERO DR
DRAYTON PLAINS MI 48020

60014
LOU PERO
1006 DELAWARE
BEND OR 97701

60015
MISS W VERNON DAY
3000 13TH AVE SOUTH APT 1
BIRMINGHAM AL 35205

60016
MRS J P BROWN
409 N 17TH
MANHATTAN KS 66502

60017
DR LOUIS JOHNSON JR
729 WOODLAWN DR
COOKEVILLE TN 38501

60018
J DAVID BAKER
333 NORTH GREEN ST
TUPELO MS 38801

60019
MAGDALINE ZUTAUT
6109 SPRING LAKE DR
HUNTSVILLE AL 35811

60020
TIMOTHY ANDREW DAVIS
1604 S 4TH AVE
YAKIMA WA 98902

60021
MRS L R MITCHELL
70 GRASSLAND DRIVE
JACKSON TN 38301

60022
ROBERT A GOODDING
15611 EDENVALE
FRIENDSWOOD TX 77546

60023
M L MCHUGH
202 RAVENEL ST
COLUMBIA SC 29205

60024
LTC(RET) & MRS C E MORRIS
1253 SE 15TH ST
OCALA FL 32670

60025
BARBARA LEE YORK
505 MERRILL
HOUSTON TX 77009

60026
MAY RINGO KING
312 IVANHOE
EUGENE OR 97404

60027
JUDITH ALLISON WALTERS
P O BOX 129
BOTHELL WA 98011

60028
EMILY ANTHONY
P O BOX 28
SAUTEE GA 30571

60029
JOYCE HAMBLETON WHITTEN
134 W CLYDESDALE ST
MT MORRIS MI 48458

60030
CAROLYN HABELMAN
RT 3 BOX 253
BLACK RIVER FALLS WI 54615

60031
MRS DENNIS FOX
BOX 171
YALE IA 50277

60032
MRS BURL E GOODPASTURE
2307 TERRACE AVE
VICTORIA TX 77901

60033
WILLIAM S GRIMES
410 ISLAND VIEW
ALPENA MI 49707

60034
MRS RICHARD L HUGHSTON
605 W BROADWAY
MIDLAND TX 79701

60035
KENNETH T WILHITE
402 BEN AVE
LILBURN GA 30247

60036
CARL R SMITH
1455 COBB BLVD
KANKAKEE IL 60901

60037
MRS MARION R WHEBY
681 UPTON RD NW
ATLANTA GA 30318

60038
WILLIAM LEE WALKER
196 S OLIVER ST
ELBERTON GA 30635

60039
JUNE O REESE
2012 11TH ST
TUSCALOOSA AL 35401

60040
JOHN H NICHOLSON
6340 RIVER OVERBROOK DR NW
ATLANTA GA 30328

60041
BOBBIE DUNCAN MCDOWELL
RT 4 BOX 179A
RIPLEY MS 38663

60042
LOIS S MAXWELL
604 SHERWOOD CIR
FAIRFIELD AL 35064

60043
MARY BESS KIRKSEY
1112 F THORNWOOD DR
BIRMINGHAM AL 35209

60044
DR DAVID P JOHNSON
DRAWER CG
UNIVERSITY AL 35486

60045
MRS CHARLES R HUNSUCKER
RT 5 BOX 594
COVINGTON GA 30209

60046
MARGARET M COWART
7801 TEA GARDEN RD SE
HUNTSVILLE AL 35802

60047
LT COL MARY L STORM USAF (RET)
21 COTTONTAIL LANE
SULLIVAN IL 61951

60048
THOMAS BROADFIELD RAY
4800 VILLAGE CREEK DR
ATLANTA GA 30338

60049
RUTHE C MUENCH
3011 SAN MIGUEL
TAMPA FL 33609

60050
BERNICE MORTON
113 CEDAR LANE
TROUTDALE OR 97060

60051
AMOS L MOORE JR
RT 1, BOX 462A
MACCLESFIELD NC 27852

60052
GEORGE E MARSH
1614 ANDOVER COURT
OKLAHOMA CITY OK 73120

60053
MRS DORIS LAWSON
301 NORTH 10TH ST
INDIANOLA IA 50125

60054
MRS EDNA LAUER
RT 2 BOX 13
LONE WOLF OK 73655

60055
RUTHELA DEAL KLINE
6408 GALAXIE DR
OKLAHOMA CITY OK 73132

60056
MARJORIE HUNT
709 MAYO
CARLINVILLE IL 62626

60057
MRS G A HORKAN
P O BOX 682
MOULTRIE GA 31768

60058
RUTH KEELING HEMMINGWAY
114 MARTINIQUE
TAMPA FL 33606

60059
MISS MADGE E FLOURNOY
2300 5TH AVE N, BOX 106
BIRMINGHAM AL 35203

60060
MRS DAVID B FERGUSON
3000 DRAKESTONE
OKLAHOMA CITY OK 73120

60061
MRS CLAIRE M DIXON
120 OAKRIDGE DR
WARNER ROBINS GA 31093

60062
MRS ROBERT BRACHMAN
1000 E RAVINE LANE
MILWAUKEE WI 53217

60063
MAVIS STREET CLEMMER
RT 1 BOX 151
RIPLEY MS 38663

60064
DONALD K TILLITSON
STAR ROUTE, BOX 584
LUCERNE VALLEY CA 92356

60065
MARGARET TARLTON
RT 3 BOX 165
CHINA GROVE NC 28023

60066
MED HOOPER SCHOLES JR
38 RAMBLEWOOD TRAIL
LAWRENCEVILLE GA 30245

60067
JOYCE A REX
8812 NE 4TH
MIDWEST CITY OK 73110

60068
SYLVIA JACKSON
2612 S W 65
OKLAHOMA CITY OK 73159

60069
HARRY S DRIGGS
1164 E CALVERT ST
SOUTH BEND IN 46613

60070
RUTH H BLIETZ
494 AMHERST AVE
DES PLAINES IL 60016

60071
ELIZA H BISHOP
629 N FOURTH ST
CROCKETT TX 75835

60072
DORA MAE TURNER
P O BOX 53
CHANDLER HEIGHTS AZ 85227

60073
MILDRED TOAZ
BOX 179
KIOWA OK 74553

60074
BILLIE SLOCUM THRASHER
P O BOX 958
BRANDON FL 33511

60075
D B STEWART
5204 WHITESBURG DR S
HUNTSVILLE AL 35802

60076
FRANCES F SEGULIA
P O BOX 45
TORNILLO TX 79853

60077
EDITH SCOTT
881 S TENTH ST
SALINA KS 67401

60078
ROSEDELL ARMSTRONG RUDOLPH
2800 STERLING
OKLAHOMA CITY OK 73127

60079
DONALD D PERKINS
4280 N OCEAN BLVD 27C
FT LAUDERDALE FL 33308

60080
JUNE NELMS
P O BOX 71
YUKON OK 73099

60081
MRS MARY LOUISE NAZOR
5937 POPLAR PIKE EXT APT 13
MEMPHIS TN 38138

60082
MARY B MCBRYDE
2515 DITTMER RD
OKLAHOMA CITY OK 73127

60083
BERNARD MATHIS MALLOY, MD
2520 L STREET NW
WASHINGTON DC 20037

60084
DOROTHY DORSETT LOESCHER
2520 E CRESTVIEW DR
APPLETON WI 54911

60085
DR KEITH R LAWS
3226 FAIRFIELD RD
OLYMPIA WA 98501

60086
MRS D HAROLD KNIPPERS
P O BOX 192
BETHANY OK 73008

60087
RUTH JURGENSEN
434 N W 19 STREET
OKLAHOMA CITY OK 73103

60088
BETTY KEY
99 N AUBURNDALE ST
MEMPHIS TN 38104

60089
WILMA JULIAN
516 SW 57TH ST
OKLAHOMA CITY OK 73109

60090
VIVIAN HILL JORDAN
1530 HAWTHORNE ST
HOUSTON TX 77006

60091
MRS BECKY MCGAHA JEFFRIES
2512 BELLAIRE DR
MOORE OK 73160

60092
MRS JANET A HUNTER
2704 N W 42
OKLAHOMA CITY OK 73112

60093
MRS HUGH HARRINGTON
608 MELODY LANE
JONESBORO AR 72401

60094
MRS CLARA M HANE
425 S HAYES
ENID OK 73701

60095
SIRLEEN GHIGLERI
P O BOX 571
APTOS CA 95003

60096
PAULINE FINLEY
644 SW 2ND ST
MOORE OK 73160

60097
DR BETTY D EVANS
P O BOX 1429
ARDMORE OK 73401

60098
DORIS L EADES
ROUTE 2 BOX 114
CATAWBA NC 28609

60099
ALICE C DUNCAN
1212 HYLTON HGTS
MANHATTAN KS 66502

60100
MRS BRYAN L DAVIS
169 CANTERBURY RD
BLACKBURN VIC AUSTRALIA

60101
EVELYN P BROWN
11 40 NW 36
OKLAHOMA CITY OK 73118

60102
JOHN HOYT BLALOCK
1039 STRAP HINGE TRAIL
STONE MOUNTAIN GA 30083

60103
CLISTA LEE ANDERSON
821 NW 66 ST
OKLAHOMA CITY OK 73116

60104
JOYCE ALLISON
12 SE 77 TERR
OKLAHOMA CITY OK 73149

60105
BETTY L ADCOCK
10 SUNSET DR, RR 1
CLINTON IL 61727

60106
A B ANGLE
APT 403; 18304 GULF BLVD
REDINGTON SHORES FL 33708

60107
LORRAINE BAXTER
2937 NW 11TH
OKLAHOMA CITY OK 73107

60108
ODETTE BOTTOM
BOX 2
ABBOTT TX 76621

60109
MRS DON C BOULTON
1701 N E 63RD ST
OKLAHOMA CITY OK 73111

60110
KATHLEEN SMITH BURCH
1468 RAGLEY HALL RD NE
ATLANTA GA 30319

60111
MRS J WALTER CARLSON
RT 4 BOX 141-A
YAKIMA WA 98908

60112
R FRANCIS CARROLL
803 N CRAIG
VICTORIA TX 77901

60113
JAMES W CLARK
1317 BEECHWOOD DR
DEL CITY OK 73115

60114
MRS JACK CRAVENS
4643 GILBERT RD
MEMPHIS TN 38116

60115
ROBERT R CREEKMORE
P O BOX 71
OLD FORT NC 28762

60116
MRS H ASHLIN DYKES
391 COLLIER RD NW
ATLANTA GA 30309

60117
MRS ROSWELL L FALKENBERRY
436 LAPSLEY ST
SELMA AL 36701

60118
FAE G GILL
312 W BELL ST
STATESVILLE NC 28677

60119
VERNA ATHEY GRIFFIS
RT 1 BOX 386
ARCADIA FL 33821

60120
THOMAS D HAMM
3200 LONGVIEW AVE, #18
BLOOMINGTON IN 47401

60121
MISS EMMA L HOGUE
APT 14
PORTLAND OR 97225

60122
VIRGINIA JIMENEZ
2804 TEXOMA DR
OKLA CITY OK 73119

60123
MRS MARGARET B KIRKLAND
1205 N GREGSON ST
DURHAM NC 27701

60124
MRS PHYLIS MARTYN KOCH
4312 SE FLAVEL
PORTLAND OR 97206

60125
JACK LINES
924 SO 16TH AVE
YAKIMA WA 98902

60126
D J LIPSCOMB
1996 BENSON AVE
SMYRNA GA 30080

60127
MRS CLARENCE LOVE
4129 N W 58TH
OKLAHOMA CITY OK 73112

60128
FLORENCE HOUGHTON MARSHALL
930 NORMAL RD NI
DEKALB IL 60115

60129
ANNA BELLE CAMPBELL MAXFIELD
1420 EAST 32ND ST
KEARNEY NB 68847

60130
MRS BETTY MAYES
RT 2 BOX 131-A
HILLSBOROUGH NC 27278

60131
MR JOHN C MCCORNACK
5302 N ARROW DR
PEORIA IL 61614

60132
MRS BEN MOUSER
P O BOX 378
SPADE TX 79369

60133
JUDSON W RAY
501 W ALABAMA AVE
ANADARKO OK 73005

60134
THOMAS L RUSSELL
P O BOX 886
HUNTSVILLE AL 35804

60135
RUTH MAXEY SHAW
RT 4 BOX 34
HARRAH OK 73045

60136
MARILYN R SOLARI
1872 JANETTE LANE
ANAHEIM CA 92802

60137
CLAUDINE SOUTHGATE
5885 DRYDEN RD
WEST PALM BEACH FL 33406

60138
MRS LESBA L THOMPSON
1745 MEREDITH LANE, BELLEAIR
CLEARWATER FL 33516

60139
MRS SAMUEL L THOMPSON
RT 2 BOX 186
CHESNEE SC 29323

60140
MRS GLENN A WILKINS
504 N BUXTON APT 7
INDIANOLA IA 50125

60141
HOWARD D YATES
79 RIDGEWOOD RD
JACKSON TN 38301

60142
MRS JAMES A ANDERSON JR
P O BOX 25013
HOUSTON TX 77005

60143
IRENE W BLAKE
3209 NW 37TH ST
OKLAHOMA CITY OK 73112

60144
MARY PYRON BUSH
1349 CIRCLEWOOD
WACO TX 76710

60145
DOROTHY M CAMPBELL
2752 NW 22
OKLAHOMA CITY OK 73107

60146
CHARLES M COLE JR
20919 PARK BRUSH CT
KATY TX 77450

60147
CLAIRE TYSON COLEMAN
708 BRIARCLIFF RD
WARNER ROBINS GA 31093

60148
MRS C W CRAIG
1708 DOUGLAS
MIDLAND TX 79701

60149
RODGER N CROKER
904 EAST WALLACE
LLANO TX 78643

60150
MRS R I DIDLAKE
2608 N WARREN AVE
OKLAHOMA CITY OK 73107

60151
MISS RUTH GRAY
506 SOUTH JACKSON
SAN ANGELO TX 76901

60152
MRS PEGGY H GREGORY
7130 EVANS
HOUSTON TX 77061

60153
CAROLE M HARTNESS
ROUTE 1 BOX 388
STATESVILLE NC 28677

60154
MRS MARGARET HEINEK
RT 3
NEW CARLISLE IN 46552

60155
MRS MAE P HINTON
630 LINDEN ST
CHICO CA 95926

60156
MRS THOMAS M JOHNSON
719 STORY WOOD DR
HOUSTON TX 77024

60157
LEMUEL C JONES
831 NORTH 18TH ST
WACO TX 76707

60158
JANETTE JOSSERAND
704 MANOR CIRCLE
MCALLEN TX 78501

60159
MRS PHYLLIS KENDALL
P O BOX 667
CROCKETT TX 75835

60160
JANICE MOHN
16662 EDISON ST NE
ANOKA MN 55303

60161
S J PATRICK
RR 2
IOWA FALLS IA 50126

60162
MRS JAMES SIBLEY PETTY
1016 N W 41ST
OKLAHOMA CITY OK 73118

60163
WILLIAM C POOLE
RT 1 BOX 194
JASPER GA 30143

60164
LEE KEMP RAMSEY
110 ALLISON DR
DALLAS GA 30132

60165
MRS JULIA M REGA
P O BOX 3882
PORT ARTHUR TX 77640

60166
ANNE MCREE WEINMAN
606 SHORT ST
HARTSELLE AL 35640

60167
MRS DORRIS WIGHTMAN
2108 ROBIN HOOD RD
ALBANY GA 31707

60168
MRS LOUISE WILCOX
1301 S RENO ST
EL RENO OK 73036

60169
AURORA MAY SUTHERLAND ALBONICO
1125 SHADYOAK PLACE
SANTA ROSA CA 95404

60170
GEORGE W CRABTREE
1016 ASH DR
ROGERS AR 72756

60171
DERO A DARWIN JR
405 N DIXIE AVE
COOKEVILLE TN 38501

60172
THELMA PURVIS GAHAN
9800 CHESTERTON PL
OKLAHOMA CITY OK 73120

60173
MADGE L HALL
10000 MILLER CIR, APT 209
OKLAHOMA CITY OK 73132

60174
MRS B W HENDRICKS
210 CHERRY ST
COCHRAN GA 31014

60175
MRS EUGENIA W HOWARD
4196 SENTINEL POST RD NW
ATLANTA GA 30327

60176
HENRIETTA H LANG
314 ELIZABETH RD
SAN ANTONIO TX 78209

60177
MRS WOODROW B MEHRKAM
1070 GARDENIA DR
HOUSTON TX 77018

60178
MRS HENRY SLOAN MORROW
301 JANEWAY AVE
GREENWOOD SC 29646

60179
ANN W REA
C/O HAZEL REA
BUFFALO MO 65622

60180
GEORGE S ROBBINS
97 BURNS ST
MARINETTE WI 54143

60181
VETA A RYAN
712 ELMWOOD DR
EDMOND OK 73034

60182
JOAN ROSEBOROUGH
1217 S W 5TH ST
GRAND PRAIRIE TX 75051

60183
THOMAS K SPIVEY
P O BOX 1000
KOUNTZE TX 77625

60184
CHARLOTTE COULTAS STUPEK
457 A MANZANITA AVE
SANTA CRUZ CA 95062

60185
MRS EVELYN TODD
31212 BRAE BURN #3
HAYWARD CA 94544

60186
MRS L N TRAMMELL
565 E WESLEY RD NE
ATLANTA GA 30305

60187
SHIRLEY WARD
316 W GEORGIA
ANADARKO OK 73005

60188
MRS KATHLEEN L WOODROW
3100 S W 41ST ST
OKLAHOMA CITY OK 73119

60189
LELLA & ISAAC ABERNATHY
3717 NABHOLTZ LN
MESQUITE TX 75150

60190
MRS GLORIA BUTLER ANGEL
1190 ARBOR VISTA DR NE
ATLANTA GA 30329

60191
MRS BEN R BRIGGS
4711 WATAUGA RD
DALLAS TX 75209

60192
MICHAEL COOK
1411 ETHIER RD #C
RENTON WA 98055

60193
MARION PROCTOR DONNELL
#15 OAKLAWN PARK
MIDLAND TX 79701

60194
HAZEL OUSLEY ELVEY
415 LA FONDA AVE
SANTA CRUZ CA 95065

60195
LILLIAN HARRIS FRYE
BOX 91 105 W EDWARDS
PAYSON IL 62360

60196
FAY L GOLIGHTLY
3830 CHILDRESS
HOUSTON TX 77005

60197
MRS WINIFRED M GOURLEY
687 E HUNTER ST
DOUGLAS GA 31533

60198
VIRGINIA S GREEN
7538 ARMAND CIR
TAMPA FL 33614

60199
JOE M MERCER
1535 OAKHORNE
HARBOR CITY CA 90710

60200
ELIZABETH MEREDITH
1720 S GESSNER
HOUSTON TX 77063

60201
DR JOHN T PALMER
878 WILDWOOD TRAIL
SANTA ROSA CA 95405

60202
MRS MARCIA KOEGEL SALVATORE
2937 LEASA COURT NE
MARIETTA GA 30066

60203
ELLEN JAYNE MARIS WHEELER
2324 NW 45 ST
OKLAHOMA CITY OK 73112

60204
J H WHEELER
508 13TH ST
LEVELLAND TX 79336

60205
CINDY E WHITMIRE
5830 CEDARS EAST #6
CHARLOTTE NC 28212

60206
WANDAH REA WOOD
2122 E JOHNS
DECATUR IL 62521

60207
MRS VIRGINIA C ZEBOSKI
4538 JUNO WAY
SACRAMENTO CA 95825

60208
D L BRANN BAILEY
P O BOX 946
RAYMONDVILLE TX 78580

60209
MRS V E BAILEY
RT 2 BOX 350D-1
COLUMBIA SC 29210

60210
MRS GLADYS DUDLEY BLECHA
1111 S GRAY ST
STILLWATER OK 74074

60211
ANNE TAYLOR BROWN
9111-G DERBYSHIRE RD
RICHMOND VA 23229

60212
MRS BARBARA J BROWN
6583 S DOWNING ST
LITTLETON CO 80121

60213
DAVIS T BUNTON
613 S COMMERCE AVE
RUSSELLVILLE AR 72801

60214
DORIS E DEAN
1637 TRUCKEE WAY
WOODLAND CA 95695

60215
MRS MORRIS EFURD
620 W CASS
GILMER TX 75644

60216
MRS LANIS GROSS
P O BOX 3211
SAN ANGELO TX 76902

60217
KENNETH MICHAEL HARKEY
640 CAMELLIA TERRACE CT N
NEPTUNE BEACH FL 32233

60218
MARJORIE M HAYES
350 FARALLONE
TACOMA WA 98466

60219
MS MARTY HIATT
21 62ND PLACE #7
LONG BEACH CA 90803

60220
JOHNNIE M JOHNSON
405 DAVIS DR
ATHENS TX 75751

60221
JEAN KAY
RR 1
PAYSON IL 62360

60222
TREVA JO MARCUS
121 EDGEHILL WAY
SAN FRANCISCO CA 94127

60223
MRS E L MEAD
P O BOX 177
NICE CA 95464

60224
MRS ALLENE MOSLEY
3317 VICTORIA PARK RD
JACKSONVILLE FL 32216

60225
MRS PHILIP L MOYER
170 MCKNIGHT DR
LAGUNA BEACH CA 92651

60226
ALTON L OVERTON
1538 MAXWELL ST
COLORADO SPRINS CO 80906

60227
PATRICIA BRINKLEY PAUL
2359 OAK ST #2
JACKSONVILLE FL 32204

60228
MILDRED M SCOTT
3067 LAUGHTER RD S
HERNANDO MS 38632

60229
MRS LEON B SOWELL
1207 BELVN
SAN MARCOS TX 78666

60230
OWEN PHILLIPS TAYLOR
501 W 124TH AVE
TAMPA FL 33612

60231
EUGENE C THOMPSON JR
110 E 56TH ST
SAVANNAH GA 31405

60232
WILLIAM JARRELL VINSON
512 BILTMORE AVE
LYNCHBURG VA 24502

60233
MRS T A WATIES JR
2903 TRENHOLM RD
COLUMBIA SC 29204

60234
FRANCES TEMPLETON WALKER
1304 LAWSON AVE
MIDLAND TX 79701

60235
CLARENCE T BELLKNAP
215 QUEENSBURY #3
HUNTSVILLE AL 35802

60236
AMOS V BELL
144 E 72ND
TACOMA WA 98404

60237
VIVIAN VAUGHN BISCHOFF
5516 CARLSON DR
SACRAMENTO CA 95819

60238
MRS G WERBER BRYAN
103 TUCSON DR
SUMTER SC 29150

60239
MRS RAMONA DUFF
7640 KENSINGTON DR
CITRUS HEIGHTS CA 95610

60240
JEWELL W EDWARDS
7420 WESTGATE DR
CITRUS HEIGHTS CA 95610

60241
MRS J H HARRISON
2030 WINROCK #507
HOUSTON TX 77057

60242
RETHA DABBS HOLLENBECK
1440 SKOKIE RD 89L
SEAL BEACH CA 90740

60243
MAXINE HOLT
205 DAVIS ST
TULLALAH LA 71282

60244
GEORGE ALFRED MCCROSKEY
2271 SHADE AVE
FLORENCE AL 35630

60245
MRS ROBERT R PRICE
601 HARTWOOD AVE
STILLWATER OK 74074

60246
ETHEL M RIEGLER
2230 W LAYTON AVE APT 312
MILWAUKEE WS 53221

60247
MRS NELLIE SCHNEIDER
56 SOUTH 3RD ST E
SALT LAKE CITY UT 84111

60248
MRS EDMOND J WALSH
218 CAPE WAY
GENEVA IL 60134

60249
FRANK E WATKINS
1332 EL CORRAL LANE
LAKE SAN MARCOS CA 92069

60250
BOBBY L WATSON
P O BOX 6952
GREENVILLE SC 29606

60251
R E WATSON
6023 CHRISHIN DR
COLUMBUS GA 31904

60252
RUTH TROWELL WATSON
ROUTE 2
GREENVILLE SC 29607

60253
MARGRET JENNINGS WEST
1705 QUAKER
EUGENE OR 97402

60254
BETTY A YATES
3812 CIMMARON
MIDLAND TX 79703

60255
RICHARD F ALBRIGHT
2359 E DUNN RD
MERCED CA 95340

60256
PEGGY ATKINSON
212 AGATE WAY
BROOMFIELD CO 80020

60257
HAZEL F BALLARD
314 W FIRST ST
MOUNTAIN HOME AR 72653

60258
EDWARD B BARNETT
RT 1 BOX 404
NAGS HEAD NC 27959

60259
JOHN V BECK
906D MAXWELL TERRACE
BLOOMINGTON IN 47401

60260
ANNA MAE BERRY
1199 COOLEY RD
LIVE OAK CA 95953

60261
MRS PAUL O BRUCE
4544 CRESANT LANE
DOUGLASVILLE GA 30135

60262
MRS ROBERT J CAREY
4610 RICHEY RD
YAKIMA WA 98908

60263
MRS HENRY G CHANEY
811 N 7TH
ST MARYS KS 66536

60264
MARVIN D COFFEY
1018 CLAY ST
ASHLAND OR 97520

60265
MRS KATHY R CONNER
608 S HOWARD CIRCLE
TARBORO NC 27886

60266
MRS DON CONNER
RR 1 BOX 29
GRAINOLA OK 74652

60267
MILTON B COOPER
3501 AVONDALE CIRCLE
CARLSBAD CA 92008

60268
HILDY CRAWFORD
3101 S FAIRVIEW #143
SANTA ANA CA 92704

60269
RUTH C DAVIDSON
3452 ELM AVE #106
LONG BEACH CA 90807

60270
MARYLEA SOUERS DEGLER
ROUTE 1
MATTOON IL 61938

60271
MRS LESTER ETCHISON
1915 SOUTH K ST
ELWOOD IN 46036

60272
MRS SHIRLEY BLACKWELL GARMON
4314 WINFIELD DR
CHARLOTTE NC 28205

60273
ANNA LAURA GRIFFITH
RT 1 BOX 306
MAYFIELD KY 42066

60274
MRS EARL E HAWORTH
4301 W PEARL
PASCO WA 99301

60275
DAVID HINTON
BOX 848
CLARKSVILLE TN 37040

60276
CLAUDIA HOLMES
C/O FULLER
CHARLEMONT MA 01339

60277
HELEN ALLEN HONKAMP
8805 4TH AVE SO
BIRMINGHAM AL 35206

60278
BILLIE GENE HORNER HUNTER
1604 S W 69TH
OKLAHOMA CITY OK 73159

60279
VERLAN R JOHNS
2004 FREMONT AVE
ST PAUL MN 55119

60280
MRS SUE H JOHNSON
6201 WILLERS WAY
HOUSTON TX 77057

60281
DAN JUDD
1609 6TH AVE NW
AUSTIN MN 55912

60282
DORIS BRINKLEY KINSELL
1110 S ALHAMBRA CIR
CORAL GABLES FL 33146

60283
MRS RUBY F KIRKPATRICK
217 N DUNBAR AVE
WAUKESHA WI 53186

60284
MRS PATRICIA A KLAUS
1508 GARROW CIRCLE
HAMPTON VA 23663

60285
MRS F B MCCLENNY
805 NORTH 2ND ST
BELLAIRE TX 77401

60286
MRS A S MCSWAIN JR
4600 KENNY LANE
WACO TX 76710

60287
JENNIE SMITH MERRITT
30 SARATOGA ST
SUMTER SC 29150

60288
LEONA MONTAG
RR 1 BOX 193
NORA SPRINGS IA 50458

60289
PAMELA MOSER
1212 GREENBRIAR CT
NORMAN OK 73069

60290
THELMA M NELSON
10803 BUTTE DR SW
TACOMA WA 98498

60291
PAUL L NICHOLS
1475 YOUNTVILLE CRS RD
NAPA CA 94558

60292
MRS JUNE POWELL ORTON
7505 MIKE COURT
N RICHLAND HILLS TX 76118

60293
MRS JAMES R OVERBY
608 TRADEWIND CIRCLE
NEWPORT NEWS VA 23602

60294
JANET K PEASE
10310 W 62ND PL #102
ARVADA CO 80004

60295
MRS FRANCES LAMKIN PEVEY
ROUTE 1 BOX 17 BB
CAT SPRING TX 78933

60296
BETTY JANE POLK
RT 1 BOX 1925
DAVIS CA 95616

60297
MARY D ROBINSON
5747 E 5TH PL
TULSA OK 74112

60298
CHARLES B SCHWEIZER
2 LAKEWOOD DR
EDWARDSVILLE IL 62025

60299
MRS IRENE M SHIVES
310 S W HUGHES
DES MOINES IA 50315

60300
MRS EDWARD C SITTLER
4118 S 40TH WEST AVE
TULSA OK 74107

60301
BETTY SOPER
P O BOX 627
PLATTE CITY MO 64079

60302
GEORGIA THOMPSON
1240 SEMOR DR
DECATUR IL 62521

60303
MARLLYS VICTOR
1902 CLAIRMONT AVE
CAMBRIDGE OH 43725

60304
MARY JULIA WATSON
ROUTE 1, BOX 385
TEMPLE TX 76501

60305
BETTY J WENDELL
6190 ATWOOD AVE
LAS VEGAS NV 89108

60306
MRS DAVID J WILLIAMS
2801 S W 172ND ST
SEATTLE WA 98166

60307
CHARLES H WILSON
2922 REPLICA COURT
PORTSMOUTH VA 23703

60308
HUGH DORSEY AMOS
145 W BELMONT DR
CALHOUN GA 30701

60309
NORMA CHAFFIN BAKER
4500 NEELY
MIDLAND TX 79703

60310
PRESTON W BARCLIFT
RT 7 BOX 305
FLORENCE AL 35630

60311
MR DONALD E BECK
5704 RIDGEWAY AVE
ROCKVILLE MD 20851

60312
DOLORES BRENENSTALL
6050 JANSEN DR
SACRAMENTO CA 95824

60313
SALLY CIESLIK
368 WILLOW TREE LANE
ROCHESTER MI 48063

60314
MARY WRIGHT DENNIS
RR 1
MODOC IN 47358

60315
JACK LEE ENGLISH
1827 S JOHNSON FERRY RD NE
ATLANTA GA 30319

60316
GORDON L FABER
3930 69TH ST
URBANDALE IA 50322

60317
JOYCE WARR GIDLEY
6664 LAWNDALE AVE #3
HOUSTON TX 77023

60318
BELINDA GREGORY
706 N JEFFERSON
WORTHINGTON IN 47471

60319
ROBERTA ANNETTE HAND
P O BOX 576
CANADIAN TX 79014

60320
WILLIAM COUNCIL HARDEN JR
5101 15TH ST
TAMPA FL 33610

60321
HOWARD J HICKS
BOX 325 RT 2
HEISKELL TN 37754

60322
PAT VINSON HOFFPAUIR
P O BOX 1083
JENNINGS LA 70546

60323
LUCILLE LAIRD
WALTONVILLE IL 62894
WALTONVILLE IL 62894

60324
MRS BETTY NEEDHAM LANCASTER
3904 BYERS
FORT WORTH TX 76107

60325
JOSEPH F MORRIS
12074 MCKELVEY RD
MARYLAND HEIGHTS MO 63043

60326
ROBERT S ORRELL
1234 SUWANNEE RD
DAYTONA BEACH FL 32014

60327
MRS DIXIE PAINTER
4305 PASEO DR
ST JOSEPH MO 64503

60328
WILLIE MAY PECKHAM
4031 GLENDALE AVE NE
SALEM OR 97305

60329
JOHN G PIERCE
RR 3 BOX 283
CHARITON IA 50049

60330
BETH PERISHO PRATT
WILLIAMSTOWN MO 63473
WILLIAMSTOWN MO 63473

60331
ROBERT L REDMOND
539 EAST 60TH ST
SAVANNAH GA 31405

60332
JERRY RAY SMITH
ROUTE 1
KEOTA OK 74941

60333
ROY M STINSON
1230 42ND PLACE APT 5
W DES MOINES IA 50265

60334
SAM E TUCKER
23522 BLACKBURN RD
BEDFORD OH 44146

60335
MICHAEL EARL WALTERS
ROUTE 1 BOX 22-B
SHANNON NC 28386

60336
JOHN BENGE JR
38 N BROADWAY
DES PLAINES IL 60016

60337
JAMES R BLANKS
304 HEIGHTS AVE
TULLAHOMA TN 37388

60338
GLADYS E CHAPMAN
4501 FRANKLIN AVE
DES MOINES IA 50310

60339
WANDA L CLARK
1304 EAST MIAMI
MCALESTER OK 74501

60340
JAMES WILLIAM CLUBB
6120 NORTH OLIVER
WICHITA KS 67220

60341
MRS ELIZABETH CRAIN
124 SITTER ST
PLEASANT HILL MO 64080

60342
MRS JAMES A CUSHMAN
4904 WEDGEVIEW DR
HURST TX 76053

60343
MARION H DAMIANO
1243 SYCAMORE ST
TURLOCK CA 95380

60344
MRS WILLIAM R DAVIS
710 SECOND ST
CORONADO CA 92118

60345
MARY RUTH DEVAULT
135 N BROADWAY
MCKENZIE TN 38201

60346
JAMES C DIGGS
ROUTE 3 BOX 123
GLOUCESTER VA 23061

60347
MRS WARREN A DOSS
930 GLENWOOD TER
ANNISTON AL 36201

60348
LEE DUSENDSCHON
4850 LEONE DR
INDIANAPOLIS IN 46226

60349
CORINNE ENGELMANN
2502 SOMBROSA PL BOX 155
CARLSBAD CA 92008

60350
MRS LOIS FLEMING
414 BALTIMORE ST
WATERLOO IA 50701

60351
MRS DENZIL E GATES
3607 BELLA VISTA DR
MIDWEST CITY OK 73110

60352
MYRA D VANDERPOOL GORMLEY
8402 57TH ST WEST
TACOMA WA 98467

60353
THELMA L HARPER
3318 MACKLAND AVE NE
ALBUQUERQUE NM 87106

60354
CARTER LAVELLE HILSABECK
1606 ELMHURST DR
AUSTIN TX 78741

60355
MRS LINDSEY W HUGHES
1641 S MILLWOOD
WICHITA KS 67213

60356
RUTH M HURTT
6715 SHALLOWFORD
LEWISVILLE NC 27023

60357
VIRGINIA CLAYTON JUNKINS
204 ALBERTA DR
NEWPORT NEWS VA 23602

60358
GLORIA MAY KAUTZ
BOX 425
CULBERTSON NE 69024

60359
MRS GUINNDOLYN F KENNEDY
P O BOX 98
CENTREVILLE AL 35042

60360
ANNE F KNIGHT
5812 SOUTHCREST RD
BIRMINGHAM AL 35213

60361
CLARA MAE LEUTWYLER
707 ORLAND BLVD
AUSTIN TX 78745

60362
GLENDA GARDNER LLOYD
9519 TREMONT COURT
ORANGEVALE CA 95662

60363
MONICA M LONERGAN
1901 12TH ST SW
AUSTIN MN 55912

60364
DOROTHY MEADER
PERU IA 50222
PERU IA 50222

60365
MRS STEVE ODOM
4314 HARVARD
MIDLAND TX 79703

60366
MRS JOHN E ORR
2620 48TH
LUBBOCK TX 79413

60367
RUTH H. PALMER
P. O. BOX 25
KITTY HAWK NC 27949

60368
MRS DEE QUALLS
113 FALLS DR
EULESS TX 76039

60369
ALICE F RIORDAN
5301 NW 70TH ST N
KANSAS CITY MO 64151

60370
MRS RICHARD ROSACRANS
P O BOX 324
MOXEE CITY WA 98936

60371
ETHEL CLEMENTS SCHARREL
2734 POLK ST
HOLLYWOOD FL 33020

60372
MARY DULANY SCOTT
P O BOX 866
TOMBALL TX 77375

60373
MRS W M SHULTZ
318 WHITAKER RD
LUTZ FL 33549

60374
MARJORIE E SMITH
ROUTE 1
ST PAUL KS 66771

60375
J W STROHECKER
521 DELAWARE
OAK RIDGE TN 37830

60376
RAYMOND E SUTTON
P O BOX 1718
LAS VEGAS NV 89101

60377
ELOISE BARBEE UPTON
2634 PARKVIEW DR
SAN ANGELO TX 76901

60378
PAULINE R UTZINGER
1404 8 1/2 AVE SE
ROCHESTER MN 55901

60379
MRS CAROLYN VASSOS
364 JONATHAN COURT
NEWPORT NEWS VA 23602

60380
MRS NADINE WALKER
405 N VAN BUREN
LITCHFIELD IL 62056

60381
MRS NELDA ANDERSON WARE
56 EDGELEA DR
CLINTON IL 61727

60382
EDITH MOON WERTZ
3133 CLAIREMONT DR #4
SAN DIEGO CA 92117

60383
MARGARET WEST
ROUTE 1 BOX 449
LEBANON TN 37087

60384
LARRY WIGGINS
470 NE 18TH AVE #107
HOMESTEAD FL 33033

60385
ROBERTA J WILLS
40 N HILL TERRACE
MANSFIELD PA 16933

60386
CORDELIA B WRIGHT
RT 1 BOX 256
SPICELAND IN 47385

60387
MRS RUTH WATSON YOUNG
16869 MEADOW PARK DR
SUN CITY AZ 85351

60388
GOLDEN V ADAMS JR
961 WEST 100 SOUTH
PROVO UT 84601

60389
MRS EDNA EARL BALDWIN
5515 DASHWOOD APT 78
HOUSTON TX 77081

60390
BARBARA BLANKENSHIP
9125 WOODPARK LANE APT D
KNOXVILLE TN 37923

60391
SUE PEARCE BOOTH
2306 HORER AVE
ZION IL 60099

60392
MARY JANE BURKETT CARUSO
5154 LOCH LOMOND DR
HOUSTON TX 77096

60393
RONALD D COLEMAN
3775 THOUSAND OAKS CIRCLE
SALT LAKE CITY UT 84117

60394
PATRICIA A CORBUS
4550 HIGEL AVE
SARASOTA FL 33581

60395
KATHLEEN CORNELIUS
1008 BOWMAN
BORGER TX 79007

60396
CALVIN H CURRY
1313 HODGES DR
TALLAHASSEE FL 32308

60397
P R DAFFT
2557 BRANDYWINE DR
DALLAS TX 75234

60398
DOROTHY CAIN FLYNT
2270 OVERTON RD
AUGUSTA GA 30904

60399
RICHARD G FOWLER
1309 AVONDALE
NORMAN OK 73069

60400
INEZ FREEMAN
3628 HOLIDAY COURT NE
ALBUQUERQUE NM 87111

60401
SUSAN J GEORGE
7919 W WELDON
PHOENIX AZ 85033

60402
JAMES P TALIAFERRO GOODBREAD
RT 1 BOX 285
CLEVELAND OK 74020

60403
MRS MATTIE BALDWIN HARVEY
3260 S W 17TH ST
MIAMI FL 33145

60404
MRS LOUIS C HILL
P O BOX 199
GONZALES TX 78629

60405
CARLETON N HUGHS
1022 BRIAR RIDGE
HOUSTON TX 77057

60406
MRS IRENE DOBSON JONES
317 W 5TH ST
BOONE IA 50036

60407
MRS LENA C JURGENS
3216 E 8TH ST
DES MOINES IA 50316

60408
MARY LEE KEMP KEITH
1619 CAMARO DR
CARROLLTON TX 75006

60409
JUDITH M KEMPF
RURAL ROUTE
DAWSON IA 50066

60410
MRS R A KING
2220 POLLARD
TYLER TX 75701

60411
RUTH N ROSS KRELL
222 LANGTON
SAN ANTONIO TX 78216

60412
PAT JUSTICE LEVIN
1034 LAMPETER RD
LANCASTER PA 17602

60413
MARY ELLEN LUCAS
423 3RD ST NE
WASECA MN 56093

60414
MS. LOUISE J. MANNING
1389 QUARI ST, APT 106
AURORA CO 80011

60415
WINFIELD SWIFT MAYNE
P. O. BOX 605
OKOBOJI IA 51355

60416
LUCY MOORE
328 MILWAUKEE
EXCELSIOR SPRINGS MO 64024

60417
SYLVIA G MOORE
501 EAST 7TH ST
MCCOOK NE 69001

60418
JOYCE M NACCARATO
1366 GREENFIELD AVE
SALT LAKE CITY UT 84121

60419
MRS ROBERT S NEITZEL
110 JOFFRION ST
MARKSVILLE LA 71351

60420
WILLIE EVERETTE OAKLEY
402 REAMS AVE
ROXBORO NC 27573

60421
MARGARET KILLGORE REED
4430 TONAWANDA
HOUSTON TX 77035

60422
MRS MARY L ROBERTS
1345 IDYLBERRY RD
SAN RAFAEL CA 94903

60423
MR ANGUS P ROBINSON
13812 S EDBROOKE AVE
RIVERDALE IL 60627

60424
THOMAS WILLIAM RUBOTTOM
3012 PITTSBURG
HOUSTON TX 77005

60425
MRS RICHARD W RUSSELL
6325 JUNEAU RD
FT WORTH TX 76116

60426
HELEN HUFF SCHUCK
1430 FOUNTAIN VIEW #336
HOUSTON TX 77057

60427
MILDRED MCKNIGHT SHAMBURGER
ROUTE 1 BOX 625
TYLER TX 75708

60428
MRS KENNETH L TESH
STAR RT 1715 RD 5.2 NW
QUINCY WA 98848

60429
JAMES L THOMPSON
501 BARRINGTON RD
SIGNAL MOUNTAIN TN 37377

60430
CAROLYN JUNE TUCKER
4883 ROSWELL RD NE APT N-3
ATLANTA GA 30342

60431
DOROTHY HILLMAN WALKER
#8 RALEIGH
CONROE TX 77302

60432
MRS VENA B WISNER
1017 COLLEGE ST
MILTON-FREEWATER OR 97862

60433
JAMES N WORSHAM
41 DONATA LANE
STAMFORD CT 06905

60434
DAN YARBROUGH
510 JULIA ST
JACKSONVILLE FL 32202

60435
GARRY ADAMS
BOX 422
DAVENPORT WA 99122

60436
JAMES ELMER ARNOLD
RFD #1
YANCEYVILLE NC 27379

60437
VIRGINIA BLALOCK
11707 HAZEN RD
HOUSTON TX 77072

60438
ANN BLOMQUIST
427 E RICHMOND ST
ORLANDO FL 32806

60439
HERBERT C BOHLER
RD 8 GARDEN PLACE
FLEMINGTON NJ 08822

60440
MRS H B BREHM
BOX 1023
PRATT KS 67124

60441
ANN E BROOKS
117 S WESTMORELAND
DALLAS TX 75211

60442
CLEO ORLAN BRYANT
4011 W 95TH ST TERR
OVERLAND PARK KS 66207

60443
GEORGE D CLARK
3647 UNDERWOOD
HOUSTON TX 77025

60444
MRS W J COULTER
ROUTE 4 BOX 153
KENSINGTON GA 30707

60445
HARRIETT CRABBS
RR
PROLE IA 50229

60446
FREDA FERGUSON CREWS
#110 1310 N COLLEGE ST
GONZALES TX 78629

60447
MARY C CRITCHFIELD
1901 N 2ND APT #111
MCALLEN TX 78501

60448
G D DARLING
P O BOX 865
COSTA MESA CA 92627

60449
JOAN M DAVENPORT
3728 ALBEMARLE ST NW
WASHINGTON DC 20016

60450
MRS CHARLES DIXSON
P O BOX 5
LUCAS IA 50151

60451
MRS CHARLES FIORI
1516 HILLSIDE
RENO NV 89503

60452
MARTHA NEAL GAINES
1305 CHARLESTON
GARLAND TX 75041

60453
JASANYN SANDERS GARRETT
703 MEADOW LANE
HAYTI MO 63851

60454
MRS MARTHA JANE GRACEY
1231 CASTLEROCK AVE
WENATCHEE WA 98801

60455
EVELYN ESTER GRAF
10700 EAST 84TH TERRACE
RAYTOWN MO 64138

60456
ELIZABETH A GRUBBS
1518 OLD HOLLOW RD
WINSTON SALEM NC 27105

60457
SYLVIA JOHNSON HARRIS
829 ONEAL LANE
HENDERSON TN 38340

60458
JEAN M HART
6177 PROPHECY PLACE
COLUMBIA MD 21045

60459
DOROTHY A HAYNES
7701 N E 55TH ST
KANSAS CITY MO 64119

60460
MRS MARJORIE B HELMHOLZ
1925 N LINDEN CIRCLE
TUCSON AZ 85715

60461
DOROTHY HURST HOLMES
5530-G HOLLY ST
HOUSTON TX 77081

60462
THOLBERT MILTON HONEA
105 VALLEY OAKS DR
SANTA ROSA CA 95405

✓60463
MARY HOWENSTEIN
5 S RICHLAND ST
FREEBURG IL 62243
Underwood

60464
MRS MIKE L HOYLE
P O BOX M
MATADOR TX 79244

60465
LAWRENCE W HUSTON
256 WELLINGTON CRESCENT
MOUNT CLEMENS MI 48043

60466
MRS LEONA JENKINS
1301-W MAIN AVE
CLINTON IA 52732

60467
DARLA MORGAN JOHNSON
3815 ROBIN HOOD RD
WINSTON SALEM NC 27106

60468
HARIADENE JOHNSON
1711 N EDGEWOOD ST
ARLINGTON VA 22201

60469
KENNETH B KNIGHT
1444 OLD TOWN RD
WINSTON SALEM NC 27106

60470
MRS ELIZABETH LARIS
CHANGE OF ADDRESS:
1040 C Cold Stream Circle
Emmaus, PA 18049

60471
LUCILE LATTA
109 E 6TH ST
LOGAN IA 51546

60472
OWEN K LEMMON
8540 PARKER RD
INDEPENDENCE OR 97351

60473
CAROLYN H LYDA
6255 DAYTON PIKE BOX 4
HIXSON TN 37343

60474
MRS GERALDINE MARSHALL
2700 LINDA DR
ENNIS TX 75119

60475
MRS WILLIAM T MATTINGLY SR
RT 1 BOX 206
MARION KY 42064

60476
MRS MAURICE J MAXWELL
1227 FAIRMOUNT AVE
COUNCIL BLUFFS IA 51501

60477
ELIZABETH A MCCALL
964 ALAMEDA LA
SARASOTA FL 33580

60478
DELORES HAWKINS MCDONALD
5624 URBANVIEW
FT WORTH TX 76114

60479
MRS JUNE COKER MCNEW
851 BROOKFIELD PARKWAY
AUGUSTA GA 30907

60480
MRS LOWELL MILLER
1102 NE 10TH ST
BENTONVILLE AR 72712

60481
PHYLLIS V MILLER
6945 HUBBARD DR
HUBER HEIGHTS OH 45424

60482
HELENE MOOTY
RT 2 BOX 8 SHADY GROVE FARM
GRUNDY CENTER IA 50638

60483
MRS EARL MULLEN
2108 E MEADOWBROOK RD
JACKSON MS 39211

60484
DOROTHY MUNSON
850 AARON B-103
PORT CHARLOTTE FL 33952

60485
MRS. JANELL WHEELER
P. O. BOX 336
SKELLYTOWN TX 79080

60486
JEAN H NICHOLSON
1621 ALACA PLACE
TUSCALOOSA AL 35401

60487
ELIZABETH M OSENBAUGH
ROUTE 1
LUCAS IA 50151

60488
BONNIE GARDNER PATTERSON
2249 N W 54TH ST
OKLAHOMA CITY OK 73112

60489
MORRIS PENNY
2507 GREEN MOUNTAIN RD SE
HUNTSVILLE AL 35803

60490
EFFIE S KLYVER
30 EARLY DR
PORTSMOUTH VA 23701

60491
SUE NITE RAGUZIN
5008 BRIARBROOK
DICKINSON TX 77539

60492
H IVAN RAINWATER
2805 LIBERTY PLACE
BOWIE MD 20715

60493
RITA REINHEIMER
409 S 3RD AVE W
NEWTON IA 50208

60494
MRS LINVIL G RICH
BOX 1185
CLEMSON SC 29631

60495
MRS V IRVIN RITCHIE
13360 S E OATFIELD RD
MILWAUKIE OR 97222

60496
NANCY C ROYCE
3406 ASH DR
DICKINSON TX 77539

60497
MARTHA SWANNER RUSSELL
1604 RICHLAND DR
RICHARDSON TX 75081

60498
MRS ANN SATHRE
1103 OBSERVATORY DR
ORLANDO FL 32808

60499
RUTH SEXTON
1103 TABOR ST
HIGH POINT NC 27262

60500
CAROL P SMITH
6722 IRONGATE
BAHAMA NC 27503

60501
KATHLYEEN M SPONSLER
213 COLLINS
HUMESTON IA 50123

60502
MR RALPH STALLINGS
2410 NW 23RD ST
OKLAHOMA CITY OK 73107

60503
WINIFRED L SWANSON
3014 HARDIES LANE
SANTA ROSA CA 95401

60504
MRS LESTER Y SWEET
P. O. BOX 926
MURPHYS CA 95247

60505
MARY T TAYLOR
5173 JOMAR DR
CONCORD CA 94521

60506
MARGE GOTT VOLLHEIM
4151 E PLATT
FRESNO CA 93702

60507
OPHELIA WADE
ROUTE 1 BOX 66
BRAGG CITY MO 63827

60508
MRS JAMES H WALKER
3102 PRINCETON
MIDLAND TX 79701

60509
LEONA L WEAVER
1943 DAWSEY APT 1
TALLAHASSEE FL 32303

60510
IRMA HARDESTY WESLEY
1414 LILAC RD
CHARLOTTE NC 28209

60511
OLIVE WILHELM
4321 MADISON
KANSAS CITY MO 64111

60512
E W WOODARD
3515 WASHINGTON
PASADENA TX 77503

60513
HELON P WOODIE
RT 1
LAUREL SPRINGS NC 28644

60514
E P WOODS
P O BOX 1546
OROVILLE CA 95965

60515
DAVID W WRIGHT
4097 MIDDLE RIDGE RD
PERRY OH 44081

60516
HELEN RING WOMACK
3461 MANANA DR
DALLAS TX 75220

60517
LAWANDA CARTER WILEY
P O BOX 152
EFFINGHAM IL 62401

60518
MARGARET TAYLOR
2515 RIATA LANE
HOUSTON TX 77043

60519
VIRGINIA STEPHENSON
1505 AUTUMN RD
PONCA CITY OK 74601

60520
EDITH GARNER SHARPLESS
9103 CHANUTE DR
BETHESDA MD 20814

60521
ANGELA S PRIDGEN
3112 CAROVEL COURT
RALEIGH NC 27612

60522
MRS JOYCE PERKERSON POOLE
3304 SUGAR MILL RD
AUGUSTA GA 30907

60523
SHERRY L PATTERSON
1003 N BEDFORD
TUCSON AZ 85710

60524
KAREN P NEUFORTH
ROUTE 4 BOX 74A
GREAT BEND KS 67530

60525
MRS JOYCE MILLER
ROUTE 2
CLARION IA 50525

60526
MR J E MEGGS
2700 SW 16TH AVE APT 246
AMARILLO TX 79102

60527
RICHARD L MCREYNOLDS
1901 ARNOLD
TOPEKA KS 66604

60528
ROGER D LAMBERT
205 HARTER DR
SUMMERVILLE SC 29483

60529
LEOLA ANN KING
5904 HOWARD DR
MECHANICSVILLE VA 23111

60530
EVERETT LEROY HUNTZINGER
P O BOX 152
MARKLEVILLE IN 46056

60531
MRS J M HACKSMA
1815 GRANT RD
WENATCHEE WA 98801

60532
MRS M LEONARD GREEN
10502 BOB WHITE DR
HOUSTON TX 77096

60533
E D ERWIN
ROUTE 2
CALHOUN GA 30701

60534
MRS NORA WHITENER BLACKSHEAR
1237 PEACHTREE BATTLE AVE NW
ATLANTA GA 30327

60535
RAY BEEMAN
1246 GOODMAN
MEMPHIS TN 38111

60536
ARDITH BELL BAILEY
ROUTE 3 BOX 29
GUTHRIE CENTER IA 50115

60537
LEATRICE ALLEN
809 HARMON
DANVILLE IL 61832

60538
MRS VELMA BRADY ALTON
4227 N BALTIMORE CT
KANSAS CITY MO 64116

60539
ALBERT LOVENCY AYCOCK
1721 BONITA LANE
CARLSBAD CA 92008

60540
MRS ELLEN BAAL
RR 2 BOX 340
SHERRILL IA 52073

60541
RALPH E BARKER
301 N 6TH ST
PONCA CITY OK 74601

60542
ANNA MAE WILEY BISHOP
1760 WEXFORD DR
VIDOR TX 77662

60543
J BURCH BLAYLOCK
P O BOX 147
YANCEYVILLE NC 27379

60544
DOROTHEA BELL BOYST
1801 WEST BEND CT
CLEMMONS NC 27012

60545
MRS CARROLL COLVERT
10616 ROYAL CHAPEL DR
DALLAS TX 75229

60546
GAIL W DAVIS
35 EDITH AVE
WINSTON SALEM NC 27106

60547
MRS BETTY L DEAN
P O BOX 942
WESLACO TX 78596

60548
NANCY TAYLOR DUPUIS
5 IRVING LANE
ORINDA CA 94563

60549
MR AND MRS DAVID FOWLER
3100 SOUTHWEST 31ST ST
TOPEKA KS 66614

60550
MARY S FRAME
LAYDON MANOR APT 2-4
HOOPESTON IL 60942

60551
JULIE R FRICKE
54 TYRINGHAM RD
ROCHESTER NY 14617

60552
HASKELL D GILMORE
7717 N W 28 TERRACE
BETHANY OK 73008

60553
LOIS HARDEN
7600-129 SE #40
RENTON WA 98055

60554
GLORIA HENDRICKS HARRIS
12841 ADENMOOR AVE
DOWNEY CA 90242

60555
KAREN HARRIS
740 BRIERCLIFF LN
LAKE OSWEGO OR 97034

60556
MRS BERKELEY N HOLMAN
1801 LAVACA ST 9L
AUSTIN TX 78701

60557
SANDRA IVEY
2410 HANNON STREET
WEST HYATTESVILLE MD 20783

60558
LAURA OLMSTED JENNINGS
1009 GEORGE ST
SHARON PA 16146

60559
NORMA S KEATING
4653 AVE RIO DEL ORO
YORBA LINDA CA 92686

60560
BETTY W KING
1161 NOGALES ST
LAFAYETTE CA 94549

60561
MRS ROBERT KNOTT
2604 NORTH L STREET
MIDLAND TX 79701

60562
BARBARA LAWRENCE
801 LANCASHIRE UNIT 5
EDWARDSVILLE IL 62025

60563
MRS BEVERLEE A MACKEY
3420 CHICAGO BLVD
FLINT MI 48503

60564
E P MADDOX
1 QUEENSBORO CIRCLE
JOHNSON CITY TN 37601

60565
ALICE CHAMBERS MANN
11312 LINKS COURT
RESTON VA 22090

60566
BETTY L MARSHALL
BOX 476
CHESTER MT 59522

60567
BERNIETA HARNESS MASTERS
P O BOX 404
BONITA CA 92002

60568
HUBBARD W MCDONALD JR
RT 1 BOX 256-B
CLIO SC 29525

60569
JANET M MILLER
1515 WOODS RD APT 202
WINSTON SALEM NC 27106

60570
ETHEL MOBERLY
35 A WETZEL CIRCLE
CLINTON MO 64735

60571
MRS JACKIE MORGAN
2306 INDIAN TRAIL
AUSTIN TX 78703

60572
WILLIAM TROUP MORTON
2723 HENRY ST
AUGUSTA GA 30909

60573
PAUL MOSER
433 S MAIN AVE
SPRINGFIELD MO 65806

60574
BETTY J PORTER
7302 ONYX DR SW
TACOMA WA 98498

60575
LUCILE PRIOR
262 PRIOR LANE
ATHERTON CA 94025

60576
MRS CLARA H R FLANAGAN
215 YOUNG AVE
HENDERSON NC 27536

60577
ANN SAULS SANDERS
1307 S POPE ST
BENTON IL 62812

60578
RONALD ROY SEAGRAVE
165-I WEBSTER RD RT 16
DOUGLAS MA 01516

60579
NORMAN EDWARD SINGLETARY
1617 CAMPBELL AVE
ORLANDO FL 32806

60580
CONNIE C SMITH
RT 7 BOX 110
ABILENE TX 79605

60581
JOE STROPLE
5336 BARRETT AVE
EL CERRITO CA 94530

60582
LILLIAN J STUMPP
1819 E 12TH ST
IDAHO FALLS ID 83401

60583
JAMES WILLIAM TACKITT
1830 JOHNSON DR
CONCORD CA 94520

60584
LAURA WADDLE
RT 5 BOX 113-E4
LEXINGTON TN 38351

60585
MRS JANE WALKER
57 OCEAN VIEW DR
PITTSBURG CA 94565

60586
MRS CLAIR WATSON
RT 1 BOX 207
WILLIAMSPORT IN 47993

60587
MRS ELSIE KOHL WHITE
2820 SAN MEDINA
DALLAS TX 75228

60588
NONA REED WILLIAMS
4160 DUNHAVEN RD
DALLAS TX 75220

60589
MRS DIXIE L WILSON
RR 1 BOX 135
CARBONDALE KS 66414

60590
SOULE JOHNSON YOUNG
17611 CALICO DR
SUN CITY AZ 85373

60591
CAROLYN L ROWE
RT 1 BOX 99
OTTERBEIN IN 47970

60592
CAROLYN C BLAND
PO BOX 637
SOUTHERN PINES NC 28387

60593
MRS JANE PHILLIPS
1518 W WATERVIEW
PORTLAND TX 78374

60594
DAVID GAMMON
119 BROOKS AVE
RALEIGH NC 27607

60595
SUSAN DURRETT AMBUHL
460 KOPPLOW
SAN ANTONIO TX 78221

60596
MRS MAX B HEATH
2206 ROLLING RD
GREENSBORO NC 27403

60596

GREENSBORO NC 27403

4

Supplement

COUNTY NAME	DATE FORMED	PARENT COUNTY/COUNTIES	DESCENDANT COUNTY/COUNTIES
Alamance	1849	Orange	none
Albemarle	1664	(a County Palatime*)	
Alexander	1847	Caldwell, Iredell, Wilkes	none
Alleghany	1859	Ashe	none
Anson	1750	Bladen	1753 Rowan; 1762 Mecklenburg; 1779 Montgomery, Richmond; 1842 Union
Ashe	1799	Wilkes	1849 Watauga; 1859 Alleghany
Avery	1911	Caldwell, Mitchell Watauga	none
Bath	1696	(a County Palatine*)	
Beaufort	1712	original precinct of Bath	1760 Pitt; 1872 Pamlico
Bertie	1722	Chowan	1729 Tyrrell; 1741 Edgecombe, Northhampton; 1759 Hertford
Bladen	1734	New Hanover	1749 Anson; 1754 Cumberland; 1764 Brunswick; 1787 Robeson; 1808 Columbus
Brunswick	1764	New Hanover, Bladen	1808 Columbus
Buncombe	1791	Burke, Rutherford	1808 Haywood; 1833 Yancey; 1838 Henderson; 1851 Madison

* The Counties Palatine were established by the Lords Proprietors of Carolina as intermediate levels of justice between the precinct courts and the Governor and Council. The Counties Palatine were not counties in the current sense of the word, and the kinds of records that are usually the most useful for genealogical research were kept by the precincts until 1739 when the Counties Palatine were formally abolished and the precincts were elevated to county status.

COUNTY NAME	DATE FORMED	PARENT COUNTY/COUNTIES	DESCENDANT COUNTY/COUNTIES
Burke	1777	Rowan	1791 Buncombe; 1833 Yancey; 1841 Caldwell; 1842 McDowell; 1861 Mitchell
Bute	1764	Granville	1779 disestablished (divided into Warren and Franklin)
Cabarrus	1792	Mecklenburg	none
Caldwell	1841	Burke, Wilkes	1847 Alexander; 1849 Watauga; 1861 Mitchell; 1911 Avery
Camden	1777	Pasquotank	none
Carteret	1722	Craven	none
Caswell	1777	Orange	1791 Person
Catawba	1842	Lincoln	none
Chatham	1771	Orange	1907 Lee
Cherokee	1839	Macon	1861 Clay; 1872 Graham
Chowan	1668	original precinct of Albemarle	1722 Bertie; 1729 Tyrrell; 1759 Hertford; 1779 Gates
Clay	1861	Cherokee	none
Cleveland	1841	Lincoln, Rutherford	none
Columbus	1808	Bladen, Brunswick	none
Craven	1705	original precinct of Bath	1722 Carteret; 1729 New Hanover; 1746 Johnston; 1779 Jones; 1872 Pamlico
Cumberland	1754	Bladen	1771 Wake; 1785 Moore; 1855 Harnett; 1911 Hoke
Currituck	1668	original precinct of Albemarle	1729 Tyrrell; 1870 Dare
Dare	1870	Currituck, Tyrrell, Hyde	none
Davidson	1822	Rowan	none
Davie	1836	Rowan	none
Dobbs	1759	Johnston	1791 disestablished (divided into Lenoir and Glasgow)
Duplin	1750	New Hanover	1784 Sampson
Durham	1881	Orange, Wake	none
Edgecombe	1741	Bertie	1746 Granville; 1758 Halifax; 1777 Nash; 1855 Wilson
Forsyth	1849	Stokes	none
Franklin	1779	Bute	1881 Vance
Gaston	1846	Lincoln	none
Gates	1779	Chowan, Hertford, Perquimans	none
Glasgow	1791	Dobbs	1799 name changed to Greene
Graham	1872	Cherokee	none
Granville	1746	Edgecombe	1752 Orange; 1764 Bute; 1881 Vance
Greene	1799	formerly Glasgow County	none
Guilford	1771	Orange, Rowan	1779 Randolph; 1785 Rockingham
Halifax	1758	Edgecombe	1774 Martin
Harnett	1855	Cumberland	none
Haywood	1808	Buncombe	1828 Macon; 1851 Jackson
Henderson	1838	Buncombe	1855 Polk; 1861 Transylvania
Hertford	1759	Bertie, Chowan, Northhampton	1779 Gates
Hoke	1911	Cumberland, Robeson	none
Hyde	1712	original precinct of Bath	1870 Dare
Iredell	1788	Rowan	1847 Alexander
Jackson	1851	Haywood, Macon	1861 Transylvania; 1871 Swain
Johnston	1746	Craven	1752 Orange; 1759 Dobbs; 1771 Wake; 1855 Wilson

COUNTY NAME	DATE FORMED	PARENT COUNTY/COUNTIES	DESCENDANT COUNTY/COUNTIES
Jones	1779	Craven	none
Lee	1907	Moore, Chatham	none
Lenoir	1791	Dobbs	none
Lincoln	1779	Tryon	1841 Cleveland; 1842 Catawba; 1846 Gaston
Macon	1828	Haywood	1839 Cherokee; 1851 Jackson; 1871 Swain
Madison	1851	Buncombe, Yancey	none
Martin	1774	Halifax, Tyrrell	none
McDowell	1842	Rutherford, Burke	1842 Mitchell
Mecklenburg	1762	Anson	1768 Tryon; 1792 Cabarrus; 1842 Union
Mitchell	1861	Yancey, Watauga, Caldwell, Burke, McDowell	1911 Avery
Montgomery	1779	Anson	1841 Stanly
Moore	1784	Cumberland	1907 Lee
Nash	1777	Edgecombe	1855 Wilson
New Hanover	1729	Craven	1734 Bladen, Onslow; 1750 Duplin; 1764 Brunswick; 1875 Pender
Northampton	1741	Bertie	1759 Hertford
Onslow	1734	New Hanover	none
Orange	1752	Bladen, Granville, Johnston	1771 Chatham, Guilford, Wake; 1777 Caswell; 1849 Alamance; 1881 Durham
Pamlico	1872	Beaufort, Craven	none
Pasquotank	1668	original precinct of Albemarle	1729 Tyrrell; 1777 Camden
Pender	1875	New Hanover	none
Perquimans	1668	original precinct of Albemarle	1779 Gates
Person	1791	Caswell	none
Pitt	1760	Beaufort	none
Polk	1855	Henderson, Rutherford	none
Randolph	1779	Guilford	none
Richmond	1779	Anson	1899 Scotland
Robeson	1787	Bladen	1911 Hoke
Rockingham	1785	Guilford	none
Rowan	1753	Anson	1771 Guilford, Surry; 1777 Burke; 1788 Iredell; 1836 Davie; 1822 Davidson
Rutherford	1779	Tryon	1791 Buncombe; 1841 Cleveland; 1842 McDowell; 1855 Polk
Sampson	1784	Duplin	none
Scotland	1899	Richmond	none
Stanly	1841	Montgomery	none
Stokes	1789	Surry	1849 Forsyth
Surry	1771	Rowan	1777 Wilkes; 1789 Stokes; 1850 Yadkin
Swain	1871	Jackson, Macon	none
Transylvania	1861	Henderson, Jackson	none
Tryon	1768	Mecklenburg	1779 disestablished (divided into Lincoln and Rutherford)
Tyrrell	1729	Bertie, Chowan, Currituck, Pasquotank	1774 Martin; 1799 Washington; 1870 Dare
Union	1842	Anson, Mecklenburg	none
Vance	1881	Granville, Franklin, Warren	none
Wake	1771	Cumberland, Johnston, Orange	1881 Durham
Warren	1779	Bute	1881 Vance
Washington	1799	Tyrrell	none

COUNTY NAME	DATE FORMED	PARENT COUNTY/COUNTIES	DESCENDANT COUNTY/COUNTIES
Watauga	1849	Ashe, Caldwell, Wilkes, Yancey	1861 Mitchell; 1911 Avery
Wayne	1779	Dobbs	1855 Wilson
Wilkes	1777	Surry	1799 Ashe; 1841 Caldwell; 1847 Alexander; 1849 Watauga
Wilson	1855	Edgecombe, Nash, Johnston, Wayne	none
Yadkin	1850	Surry	none
Yancey	1833	Burke, Buncombe	1849 Watauga; 1851 Madison; 1861 Mitchell

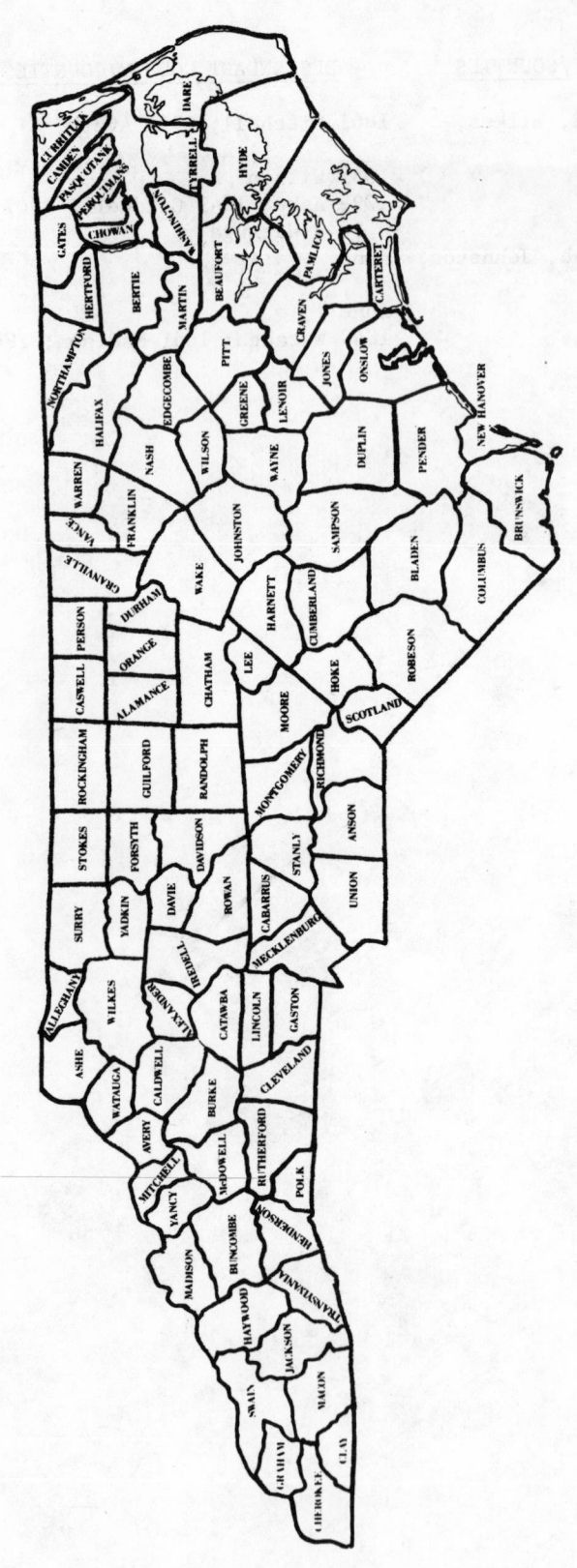

THE NORTH CAROLINA COUNTIES

378